Addressing Global Health Goals With AI-Enhanced Medical Tourism

Viana Hassan
https://orcid.org/0000-0002-7372-5059

European Tourism and Events Training Academy, Malta & American University of Malta, Malta

Vikas Sharma
https://orcid.org/0009-0009-3174-5965

Swami Vivekanand Subharti University, India

IGI Global
Scientific Publishing
Publishing Tomorrow's Research Today

Vice President of Editorial Melissa Wagner
Director of Acquisitions Mikaela Felty
Director of Book Development Jocelynn Hessler
Production Manager Mike Brehm
Cover Design Jose Rosado

Published in the United States of America by
IGI Global Scientific Publishing
701 East Chocolate Avenue
Hershey, PA, 17033, USA
Tel: 717-533-8845 | Fax: 717-533-7115
Website: https://www.igi-global.com E-mail: cust@igi-global.com

Library of Congress Cataloging-in-Publication Data

LCCN: 2026006198 (CIP Data Pending)
ISBN13: 9798337389448
Isbn13Softcover: 9798337389455
EISBN13: 9798337389462
British Cataloguing in Publication Data
A Cataloguing in Publication record for this book is available from the British Library.

Table of Contents

Detailed Table of Contents

The rapid integration of artificial intelligence (AI) into healthcare is reshaping medical tourism by transforming efficiency, value creation, and the sustainability of global health systems. This chapter examines the economic implications of AI adoption in cross-border healthcare, focusing on its role in optimizing clinical decision-making, patient flow management, pricing, and resource allocation. AI-enabled tools enhance operational efficiency and patient experience while generating new sources of economic value for healthcare providers, intermediaries, and destination countries. At the same time, the expansion of AI-driven medical tourism raises critical concerns regarding health system sustainability, equity, data governance, and regulatory alignment. By adopting an economo-technical perspective, the study highlights both the opportunities and the structural trade-offs associated with AI deployment, particularly the risk of reinforcing dual-track healthcare systems and exacerbating inequalities between domestic and international patients.

This chapter examines the role of artificial intelligence in transforming the medical tourism sector within the broader context of sustainability and digital healthcare innovation. The purpose of this chapter is to analyze how AI-driven technologies contribute to improving operational efficiency, enhancing patient accessibility, and supporting sustainable healthcare service delivery in international medical travel. The chapter explores the integration of technologies such as telemedicine systems and AI-based logistics optimization in healthcare infrastructures that serve

Preface

INTRODUCTION

The subject of this book centers on the growing relationship between artificial intelligence (AI) and medical tourism as an emerging pathway for improving healthcare delivery on a global scale. Medical tourism has developed into an important international phenomenon in which individuals travel across national borders to obtain medical treatment, rehabilitation services, wellness therapies, or specialized surgical procedures that may be more affordable, accessible, or advanced than those available in their home countries. At the same time, artificial intelligence has become one of the most transformative innovations in modern healthcare, introducing advanced capabilities such as predictive analytics, intelligent diagnostics, robotic-assisted procedures, virtual consultations, personalized treatment planning, and automated patient management systems. The integration of these two domains has created a new interdisciplinary field in which digital intelligence can enhance the safety, efficiency, transparency, and patient-centeredness of cross-border healthcare services. Rather than viewing medical tourism simply as a commercial healthcare activity, this book positions AI-enhanced medical tourism as a strategic model capable of supporting broader international health objectives through smarter and more connected healthcare systems.

Beyond operational improvements, the subject matter also addresses the broader implications of AI-enhanced medical tourism for global health systems and policy. The increasing use of AI in international healthcare raises important questions regarding ethics, accountability, patient privacy, data governance, and social equity. While AI has the potential to improve healthcare accessibility and reduce costs, it may also create new inequalities if advanced technologies are concentrated only in wealthier institutions or countries. Similarly, the cross-border movement of sensitive health data introduces concerns about cybersecurity and regulatory coordination between nations. This book therefore examines AI-enhanced medical tourism not only as a technological development but also as a complex social and policy issue that requires responsible governance. By combining perspectives from healthcare innovation, tourism management, digital transformation, economics, and global public health, the volume provides a comprehensive overview of a rapidly evolving field that is becoming increasingly relevant to the future of international healthcare.

A DESCRIPTION OF WHERE TOPIC FITS IN THE WORLD TODAY

In the contemporary world, the topic of AI-enhanced medical tourism occupies a highly significant position at the intersection of healthcare innovation, international mobility, and global public health transformation. Healthcare systems across many countries are currently facing unprecedented pressure due to rapidly aging populations, the increasing prevalence of chronic diseases, rising treatment costs, shortages of healthcare professionals, and unequal access to specialized medical services. At the same time, globalization has made international travel easier, faster, and more affordable, allowing patients to seek healthcare beyond the boundaries of their own countries. As a result, medical tourism has evolved from a limited niche industry into a major global sector that connects healthcare institutions, technology providers, governments, and patients within a rapidly expanding international network. Within this changing environment, artificial intelligence has emerged as a powerful tool capable of reshaping how medical tourism operates by improving clinical accuracy, increasing operational efficiency, and enhancing patient experience across borders. Consequently, this topic fits directly into some of the most important healthcare and economic discussions taking place in the world today.

The relevance of this subject is particularly visible in the growing digital transformation of healthcare systems worldwide. Hospitals, clinics, and healthcare organizations are increasingly adopting AI-powered tools to support disease diagnosis, medical imaging, robotic surgery, personalized medicine, predictive analytics, and administrative automation. These technologies are no longer experimental concepts but are becoming integrated into routine healthcare delivery in both developed and emerging economies. When these same innovations are applied to medical tourism, they create opportunities for international patients to receive safer, more coordinated, and more personalized care. AI can help patients compare healthcare providers internationally, predict treatment outcomes, estimate medical expenses, reduce language barriers through automated translation systems, and ensure continuity of care after returning home. In this way, AI-enhanced medical tourism reflects the broader movement toward digitally connected healthcare ecosystems that are becoming increasingly common in the modern world. The topic therefore fits within the global shift from traditional healthcare systems toward intelligent, patient-centered, and data-driven healthcare delivery models.

This topic also fits within current global efforts to improve healthcare accessibility and achieve international health development goals. Organizations such as the United Nations and the World Health Organization continue to emphasize the importance of universal health coverage, equitable access to care, and improved health outcomes as central priorities for sustainable development. Many countries still struggle to provide timely and affordable specialized healthcare to all citizens, particularly in low- and middle-income regions where healthcare infrastructure remains limited. AI-enhanced medical tourism offers one possible solution by enabling patients to access quality treatment in other countries while using intelligent systems to make the process more transparent and manageable. Virtual consultations, AI-assisted diagnostics, and digital follow-up platforms can reduce geographic barriers that once limited healthcare access. Because of this, the topic aligns closely with international discussions about how technology can support more inclusive healthcare systems and contribute to global health goals in a practical and measurable way.

Ultimately, the topic fits into the world today because it reflects the convergence of multiple global trends: digital transformation, globalization, sustainability, patient empowerment, and health equity. It represents a new model of healthcare in which technology not only improves clinical performance but also expands the possibilities of how and where healthcare can be delivered. AI-enhanced medical tourism is therefore not simply a specialized academic topic; it is part of a larger transformation that is redefining healthcare systems worldwide. Its growing importance in research, policy, and practice makes it a timely and necessary subject for scholarly examination, particularly at a time when the world is searching for innovative solutions to increasingly complex health challenges.

A DESCRIPTION OF THE TARGET AUDIENCE

The target audience for Addressing Global Health Goals With AI-Enhanced Medical Tourism is intentionally broad because the subject itself lies at the intersection of multiple disciplines, professional sectors, and policy environments. First, this book is designed for academic researchers and scholars working in areas such as healthcare management, medical tourism, public health, digital health innovation, hospitality management, and international business. Researchers who are examining the future of healthcare delivery will find the volume particularly valuable because it brings together diverse theoretical perspectives and empirical insights into how artificial intelligence can influence international patient mobility. Scholars in tourism and hospitality studies can also benefit from the book's exploration of patient experience, trust, service quality, and sustainability, while public health researchers may find its discussion of health equity, governance, and global healthcare access especially relevant. By combining technological, economic, ethical, and operational perspectives, the book offers a comprehensive scholarly resource that can support future research and curriculum development in higher education.

A second important audience includes graduate and doctoral students who are studying emerging healthcare systems and international service industries. Students enrolled in master's and PhD programs in healthcare administration, tourism management, hospital administration, health informatics, digital transformation, and policy studies increasingly require interdisciplinary learning materials that reflect the realities of modern healthcare. This book provides those learners with both conceptual frameworks and contemporary case-based discussions that can help them understand how AI is changing the structure of medical tourism worldwide. Because the volume addresses real-world applications as well as theoretical models, it can serve as a reference text for coursework, literature reviews, seminar discussions, and dissertation research. Students preparing for careers in healthcare leadership or health policy will also benefit from understanding how technology-driven patient mobility is becoming a significant component of future healthcare systems.

The book is equally relevant for healthcare administrators, hospital executives, and clinical managers who are directly involved in managing international patient services. Hospitals and specialty clinics that serve foreign patients are increasingly adopting digital systems to improve patient coordination, diagnostic accuracy, and operational efficiency. Decision-makers within these institutions need a deeper understanding of how AI can be implemented responsibly while maintaining quality care and patient trust. This volume offers practical insights into areas such as intelligent diagnostics, virtual consultation systems, resource optimization, and cross-border continuity of care, making it useful for leaders seeking to improve organizational performance. Healthcare managers can use the book to better understand how AI may strengthen competitiveness in the international healthcare market while also addressing concerns related to ethics, data protection, and institutional accountability.

Overall, the target audience for this book includes anyone who seeks a deeper understanding of how artificial intelligence is transforming international healthcare delivery. Its interdisciplinary approach ensures that it can serve both academic and professional readers, offering a meaningful contribution to those working at the intersection of healthcare, technology, tourism, and global policy. Because AI-enhanced medical tourism is rapidly becoming a significant part of the modern healthcare landscape, the insights presented in this volume are relevant to a wide range of stakeholders who are shaping the future of healthcare worldwide.

DESCRIPTION OF THE IMPORTANCE OF EACH CHAPTER SUBMISSION

Chapter 1: The Economics of Artificial Intelligence in Medical Tourism—Efficiency, Value Creation, and Global Health Sustainability

This chapter is important because it investigates the economic implications of AI adoption in medical tourism. It explains how artificial intelligence can improve efficiency, optimize pricing, enhance patient flow management, and create value for healthcare providers and destination countries. The chapter contributes by connecting digital transformation with broader issues of sustainability and healthcare economics. It also raises important questions about inequality and the risk of creating dual healthcare systems, making it an essential contribution to understanding the financial dimensions of AI-enhanced healthcare mobility.

Chapter 2: The Economics of AI—Medical Tourism within Sustainability Transformation

This chapter is important because it focuses specifically on how AI contributes to sustainable transformation within the medical tourism industry. It examines the relationship between digital innovation, healthcare accessibility, and environmental and economic sustainability. By analyzing AI-driven logistics, telemedicine, and operational efficiency, the chapter shows how technology can improve service delivery while supporting long-term healthcare resilience. Its contribution lies in linking medical tourism to sustainability objectives that are increasingly important in global health policy.

Chapter 3: Improving Global Patient Access through AI-Enhanced Medical Tourism Implications for Global Health Outcomes

This chapter is important because it directly addresses how AI-enhanced medical tourism can improve healthcare accessibility worldwide. It explains how technologies such as predictive analytics, telemedicine, and intelligent diagnostics can reduce barriers related to geography, information, and cost. The chapter contributes to the book by showing how digital healthcare mobility can support health equity and better health outcomes. It strongly reinforces the book's central theme of connecting medical tourism to global health improvement.

Chapter 4: Impact of Artificial Intelligence on Medical Tourism: An Indian Perspective

This chapter is significant because it offers a country-specific analysis of how AI is influencing medical tourism in India. It highlights India's growing role as a global healthcare destination and examines how intelligent systems can improve service quality and international competitiveness. The chapter contributes practical insight into how a major medical tourism destination is adapting to technological change. Its regional focus makes the discussion more grounded and applicable.

Chapter 5: AI-Driven Medical Tourism Governance: Economic Efficiency, Equity, and Accountability in Cross-Border Healthcare

This chapter is highly important because it addresses one of the most critical issues in AI-enhanced medical tourism: governance. It examines how efficiency gains must be balanced with fairness, accountability, and ethical responsibility. By proposing a structured governance framework, the chapter provides practical guidance for policymakers and healthcare institutions. Its contribution is essential for responsible implementation.

Chapter 6: Case Studies and Emerging Best Practices in AI-Powered Medical Tourism

This chapter is important because it presents real-world examples of how AI is being applied in medical tourism. It allows readers to see how theory translates into practice across healthcare systems. By identifying emerging best practices, the chapter offers practical lessons for stakeholders. It bridges academic knowledge with professional application.

Chapter 7: AI-Enabled Diagnostics, Treatment Planning, and Clinical Decision

This chapter is important because it focuses on the clinical core of AI-enhanced healthcare. It explains how AI supports pathology, biomarker analysis, and precision medicine in cross-border care. Its contribution lies in showing how intelligent systems can directly improve patient outcomes. This strengthens the scientific rigor of the volume.

Chapter 8: AI-Enhanced Medical Tourism as a Catalyst for Achieving Global health Goals- A Qualitative Exploration

This chapter is important because it provides qualitative insights from healthcare professionals and policymakers. It explores perceptions of how AI-based medical tourism can support global healthcare goals. The chapter contributes a human-centered understanding of innovation. It complements the quantitative studies in the volume.

Chapter 9: AI Enhanced Medical Tourism for Achieving Sustainable Development Goal 3: Advancing Affordable, Accessible, and Quality Healthcare

This chapter is important because it explicitly links AI-enhanced medical tourism with Sustainable Development Goal 3. It proposes a framework connecting technology to affordability, accessibility, and healthcare quality. Its contribution is valuable for policymakers and researchers seeking measurable impact. It aligns the book closely with international development priorities.

Chapter 10: Neural Pathways of Care: AI-Infused Medical Tourism in the Architecture of Global Health Systems

This chapter is significant because it introduces a new conceptual model for understanding interconnected digital healthcare systems. It explains how AI can create integrated care networks that improve continuity across borders. Its contribution lies in advancing theoretical understanding of global health systems. The chapter offers innovative conceptual value.

Chapter 11: Virtual and Intelligent Medical Tourism Systems: Enhancing Patient Experience

This chapter is important because it examines how AI and VR improve patient engagement and trust. It demonstrates how immersive digital systems can strengthen healthcare decision-making and satisfaction. The chapter contributes by focusing on patient-centered innovation. It highlights future possibilities in healthcare delivery.

Chapter 12: Integrating Artificial Intelligence with Ayurveda-Based Medical Tourism in Uttarakhand for Achieving Global Wellness Targets

This final chapter is important because it combines advanced digital innovation with Ayurveda-based healthcare in Uttarakhand. It demonstrates how traditional wellness systems can be enhanced through AI. The chapter contributes a distinctive interdisciplinary perspective. It provides a meaningful conclusion by connecting innovation with holistic global wellness.

A CONCLUSION OF HOW BOOK IMPACTS THE FIELD AND CONTRIBUTES TO THE SUBJECT MATTER:

In conclusion, Addressing Global Health Goals With AI-Enhanced Medical Tourism makes a meaningful and timely contribution to the growing body of knowledge at the intersection of healthcare innovation, international patient mobility, and global health development. The book advances the field by moving beyond traditional discussions of medical tourism as a purely economic or service-based activity and repositioning it as a strategic component of future healthcare systems. Through its multidisciplinary approach, the volume demonstrates that artificial intelligence is not simply a technological addition to existing medical tourism practices, but a transformative force capable of redefining how healthcare is delivered, experienced, and managed across national borders. By integrating perspectives from healthcare management, digital transformation, economics, sustainability, ethics, and public policy, the book creates a broader understanding of how intelligent systems can support more effective and patient-centered global healthcare. For researchers, the book provides a foundation for future studies by identifying emerging themes and unanswered questions that require further investigation. For practitioners, it offers practical insight into how AI can be applied to improve patient experience, operational performance, and healthcare accessibility. For policymakers, it presents evidence that can inform decisions about regulation, governance, and strategic planning. By serving these multiple audiences, the book extends its influence beyond academic discourse and into real-world healthcare development. This broad relevance increases the book's long-term value as both a scholarly resource and a professional reference.

Ultimately, Addressing Global Health Goals With AI-Enhanced Medical Tourism contributes to the subject matter by presenting a forward-looking vision of healthcare in which technological intelligence and international care delivery work together to address some of the most pressing health challenges of the modern era. It demonstrates that AI-enhanced medical tourism has the potential to become more than a specialized sector within healthcare; it can become a meaningful instrument for improving global well-being, expanding access to treatment, and supporting sustainable healthcare systems. By critically examining both the opportunities and the challenges of this transformation, the book makes a significant contribution to understanding how innovation can shape the future of healthcare worldwide.

Acknowledgment

The completion of *Addressing Global Health Goals With AI-Enhanced Medical Tourism* has been made possible through the support, collaboration, and dedication of many individuals and institutions whose contributions deserve sincere recognition. As editors of this volume, we wish to express our deepest gratitude to all those who have assisted in transforming this important scholarly project into a meaningful academic contribution.

First and foremost, we would like to thank all the chapter authors who contributed their expertise, time, and scholarly commitment to this volume. Each contributor brought a unique perspective to the subject of artificial intelligence and medical tourism, enriching the book with diverse insights from healthcare management, digital innovation, public health, sustainability, economics, and policy studies. Their willingness to share original research, critical analysis, and practical experience has greatly strengthened the intellectual quality of this work. Without their dedication and academic professionalism, this book would not have been possible. We also extend our sincere appreciation to the reviewers and academic colleagues who provided valuable feedback during the development of this manuscript. Their thoughtful comments, constructive suggestions, and critical observations helped improve the clarity, depth, and academic rigor of the chapters. The peer review process played an essential role in ensuring that the content of this book meets the standards expected of an international scholarly publication. We are grateful for their time, expertise, and commitment to advancing knowledge in this emerging field.

Special thanks are due to the publishing team whose guidance and professional support helped shape this project from its earliest stages to final completion. Their assistance throughout the editorial process, including proposal development, manuscript coordination, formatting, and communication, was invaluable. The encouragement and patience shown during the preparation of this volume helped us navigate the challenges of managing a multidisciplinary international publication. Their contribution has been instrumental in bringing this book to readers worldwide.

We would also like to acknowledge the institutions and organizations that supported the editors and contributors throughout this project. The academic environments provided by our respective universities and professional institutions created the foundation for meaningful research and interdisciplinary collaboration. We are especially thankful to European Tourism and Events Training Academy, American University of Malta, and Swami Vivekanand Subharti University for encouraging research that bridges healthcare, tourism, and technological innovation. Institutional support has played an important role in enabling this work to move forward. We also wish to recognize the healthcare professionals, researchers, policymakers, and practitioners around the world whose work continues to inspire the study of AI-enhanced medical tourism. Their efforts in improving patient care, healthcare accessibility, and innovation in international medical services have provided the real-world context that makes this topic both timely and relevant. Their commitment to improving global healthcare systems serves as the broader motivation behind this volume. Finally, we offer our heartfelt gratitude to our families, friends, and colleagues for their patience, understanding, and encouragement throughout the preparation of this book. Academic work often requires long periods of concentration, collaboration, and perseverance, and their support has been deeply appreciated. Their encouragement provided the strength needed to complete a project of this scale.

It is our sincere hope that this volume will contribute to ongoing discussions about the future of healthcare and inspire further research into how artificial intelligence can be used responsibly to improve medical tourism and global health outcomes. To everyone who contributed to this work in ways both large and small, we offer our deepest thanks and appreciation.

Introduction

The healthcare industry is entering a period of unprecedented transformation in which technological advancement is redefining the ways medical services are delivered, experienced, and managed across the world. Among the most influential developments in this transformation is the rapid integration of artificial intelligence (AI) into healthcare systems, where intelligent technologies are improving diagnostic accuracy, enhancing treatment planning, streamlining hospital operations, and supporting more personalized patient care. At the same time, medical tourism has become an increasingly important component of the global healthcare economy, allowing patients to travel across borders in search of affordable, timely, and specialized medical services. The convergence of these two powerful forces has created a new frontier in international healthcare—one that holds the potential to reshape the future of global health delivery.

Addressing Global Health Goals With AI-Enhanced Medical Tourism arrives at a particularly important moment in this global transition. Around the world, healthcare systems continue to face significant challenges, including rising costs, uneven access to care, workforce shortages, aging populations, and growing patient expectations. In many regions, traditional healthcare delivery models are struggling to meet these demands efficiently. AI offers a compelling opportunity to address these pressures by making healthcare more predictive, more precise, and more responsive. When integrated into medical tourism, AI can help create a more connected and intelligent system of care that extends beyond national boundaries and supports patients throughout the entire healthcare journey.

One of the most valuable aspects of this volume is its recognition that AI-enhanced medical tourism should not be viewed solely as a technological innovation or an economic opportunity. Rather, the editors and contributors present it as a strategic approach that can contribute to broader global health objectives. The chapters in this book demonstrate how intelligent technologies can improve healthcare accessibility, strengthen continuity of care, increase patient trust, and optimize clinical outcomes for individuals seeking treatment internationally. More importantly, the book places these developments within the larger context of global health policy and sustainable healthcare, emphasizing the importance of responsible innovation in a rapidly changing healthcare environment. This volume also deserves recognition for its multidisciplinary perspective. The subject of AI-enhanced medical tourism cannot be fully understood through a single academic lens. It requires the integration of healthcare science, technology management, economics, ethics, tourism studies, and public policy. The contributors to this book represent a diverse range of expertise and geographic perspectives, enabling a richer and more comprehensive exploration of the subject. Their collective work reflects the complexity of modern healthcare systems and highlights the importance of collaboration across disciplines in shaping future healthcare solutions.

A particularly strong contribution of this book is its balance between optimism and critical analysis. While the potential benefits of AI in medical tourism are substantial, the volume does not ignore the challenges associated with technological adoption. Questions surrounding patient privacy, data security, accountability, algorithmic bias, and healthcare inequality are thoughtfully examined throughout the chapters. This balanced approach enhances the scholarly value of the book and ensures that readers gain a realistic understanding of both the opportunities and the responsibilities that accompany digital transformation in international healthcare.

The relevance of this book extends to a wide audience. Researchers will find it an important contribution to emerging scholarship on healthcare innovation and international patient mobility. Healthcare administrators and hospital leaders will discover practical insights into improving service delivery and patient experience through digital tools. Policymakers will benefit from the discussion of governance and regulatory implications. Students will gain a valuable understanding of one of the most dynamic developments in modern healthcare. By serving these multiple audiences, the book establishes itself as both an academic resource and a practical guide for future healthcare leadership. Another notable strength of the volume is its global orientation. The healthcare challenges facing nations today are increasingly interconnected, and no country can address them in isolation. AI-enhanced medical tourism reflects a broader movement toward international cooperation in healthcare, where technology can help bridge geographical limitations and create more inclusive systems of care. By examining case studies, regional experiences, and policy frameworks from multiple countries, this book contributes to a deeper understanding of how healthcare innovation can support global well-being in diverse social and economic contexts.

Perhaps the most important message of this volume is that the future of healthcare will depend not only on technological advancement, but also on how that technology is applied to serve humanity. Artificial intelligence has the capacity to transform healthcare systems, but its true value lies in its ability to improve lives.

By connecting AI with the human-centered goals of medical tourism, this book reminds readers that innovation should ultimately be measured by its contribution to patient well-being, accessibility, and equity. This perspective gives the book both academic significance and social importance. In presenting this volume, the editors have provided a timely and thoughtful contribution to an area of growing international relevance. The book challenges readers to think critically about the future of healthcare and offers meaningful insights into how AI can support more sustainable and effective medical tourism systems. It is a welcome addition to the literature and a valuable resource for anyone seeking to understand how technology can be harnessed to address the evolving needs of global health in the twenty-first century.

Chapter 1
The Economics of Artificial Intelligence in Medical Tourism:
Efficiency, Value Creation, and Global Health Sustainability

Constantinos Challoumis
http://orcid.org/0000-0002-7436-0506
National and Kapodistrian University of Athens, Greece & Philips University, Cyprus

ABSTRACT

The rapid integration of artificial intelligence (AI) into healthcare is reshaping medical tourism by transforming efficiency, value creation, and the sustainability of global health systems. This chapter examines the economic implications of AI adoption in cross-border healthcare, focusing on its role in optimizing clinical decision-making, patient flow management, pricing, and resource allocation. AI-enabled tools enhance operational efficiency and patient experience while generating new sources of economic value for healthcare providers, intermediaries, and destination countries. At the same time, the expansion of AI-driven medical tourism raises critical concerns regarding health system sustainability, equity, data governance, and regulatory alignment. By adopting an economo-technical perspective, the study highlights both the opportunities and the structural trade-offs associated with AI deployment, particularly the risk of reinforcing dual-track healthcare systems and exacerbating inequalities between domestic and international patients.

DOI: 10.4018/979-8-3373-8944-8.ch001

1. INTRODUCTION

Medical tourism manifests as the cross-border movement of patients to avail themselves of healthcare services. The emergence of Artificial Intelligence (AI) technologies has added a new layer of complexity to economic theory within the medical tourism space, suggesting the ability to increase cross-border patient traffic through lower costs and reduced risks. At the same time, AI has the potential to reduce operating costs, thereby creating new market segments that relax constraints on price-elasticity of demand. By expanding the feasible set of medical tourism exchanges, AI introduces new trade-offs and opportunities for the various economic actors involved.An initial exploration of the economics surrounding medical tourism when supplemented with AI inputs reveals three classes of higher-order relationships: improvements in efficiency within the medical facilities and service providers themselves; the creation of value-adding services that modify the way medical services are produced and marketed to patients; and the advent of fundamentally new medical risks associated with the movement of patients outside their country of residence. Theory suggests that these three dimensions combine to create opportunities for AI to play a role in making medical tourism more efficient, more strongly aligned with value-creation and medically justified price-setting, and safer from a public health perspective. These attributes combined to suggest that AI could play a useful role in making medical tourism more sustainable, from the perspective of both public-sector health authorities and the AI technology providers themselves.Artificial intelligence (AI) broadly refers to "computers and other machines that are capable of performing tasks considered to require intelligence". The scope encompasses any process executing a specific set of operations but particularly addresses machine learning, which takes advantage of large datasets to improve performance without user intervention. Several AI technologies could enhance medical tourism, especially in hospitals. The costs associated with imaging, scheduling and data analysis are sizable in absolute terms and relative to the prices charged to the patient. Hospitals address these problems with specialized high-cost equipment and staff while lacking the scale to optimize their usage(Alowais et al., 2023; Bekbolatova et al., 2024; Esmaeilzadeh, 2024; Hassan and Bellos, 2022; Jiao et al., 2023; Krishnan et al., 2023; Kuwaiti et al., 2023; Reshadi and Chehragh, 2025; Secinaro et al., 2021; Varnosfaderani and Forouzanfar, 2024; Wolff et al., 2020; Zhang et al., 2025; Zuhair et al., 2024). AI can enhance health-care provision by improving clinical decision-support tools for non-specialized personnel in lower-cost facilities. Moreover, AI-assisted pathways may reduce operational inefficiencies of health services in general, and more so in the case of international medical centers where patients expect to receive care within shorter time frames, regardless of the applicable queuing theory.Health economics provides the framework to synthesize the economic rationale behind the role of AI in the medical-tourism sector. Indeed, AI may improve the quality and cost of health-care services through greater efficiency, thereby enabling increased capital flows to health tourism and other economic sectors. Cost, productivity and outcome—though intertwined concepts—are distinct features of health services, and only the latter two appear to be accounted in the AI discussions. Enhancing productivity is seen as a key condition for value creation. Notwithstanding, value concepts that consider AI-enabled health-care services complementary to nearby, less elaborate—though generally more affordable—facilities remain absent. The incorporation of AI may overcome the price discrimination frequently associated with such differentiated supply.The definition of artificial intelligence (AI) is broad, encompassing a range of tools and technologies that simulate human intelligence and perform cognitive tasks such as learning and problem solving. In the context of medical tourism, the scope narrows substantially to focus on applications in diagnostic, operational, and patient-facing domains. Evidence from these areas establishes that AI-enabled health systems can achieve substantial gains in efficiency, quality, and equity. This rationale is particularly relevant in markets for cross-border care, which trade travel-related risk for price, speed, convenience, and clinical outcome.The Economic of Artificial Intelligence Overview outlines the economic principles relevant to the field. Rephrasing Adam Smith's definition of economics, it is the study of that which is valuable to people. Measurement boundaries are defined, and opening and closing linkages explained. Acknowledging that "what may not be a cost to one is a cost to another," the discussion emphasizes opportunity cost—particularly travel time and expense, travel-related health risk, risk of differential outcomes across patient groups, and the capacity on the receiving side to absorb the incoming demand—and how this might account for major risks associable and micro.

The previous section established a definition of Artificial Intelligence in Medical Tourism and delineated the measurement boundaries for the economics of cross-border care. International healthcare pathways possess special economic characteristics that are interdependent with the economics of medical tourism; hence, further exposition is warranted. Cross-border care incurs the usual opportunity costs inherent in any economic activity; however, specific conditions pertaining to demand and market structure within the health service sector also apply. In addition to these opportunity costs, medical tourism exhibits scale effects, specifically, increasing returns to scale. These combined concepts offer insight into the rationale for cross-border movement of patients—underlying factors such as comparative advantage and trade also complete the economic reasoning underpinning the growing volume of international healthcare.Although the international transfer of patients, their travel-related health risks, and the accessibility and equity of cross-border healthcare services are important considerations, it is the global health system sigma—the capacity of the world to deliver healthcare as a social good—that remains paramount (El Arab and

Al Moosa, 2025; Ciecierski-Holmes et al., 2022; Khanna et al., 2022; Lam, 2025; Rady, 2024; Sharma et al., 2023; Tarasenko, 2025; Vithlani et al., 2023; Wahl et al., 2018). The idea that positive or negative externalities can influence overall healthcare quality across borders is an intuitive one, but setting the logic out more explicitly adds clarity to the discussion. Although neither safety nor access should be sacrificed in pursuit of improved cross-border health outcomes, their pursuit must be tempered by the relevance of global health.

This study is an attempt at understanding the economic impacts of artificial intelligence on the medical tourism industry based on the discussions prior. It specifically seeks to find answers to these research questions: (1) What effects does the use of artificial intelligence have on operational efficiency, cost structures, and service quality in providers of medical tourism? (2) How much can AI-driven technologies add to value creation and new pricing dynamics in cross-border healthcare markets? (3) What are the economic risks and institutional challenges that come with integrating AI into international healthcare services related to sustainability, equity, and global health outcomes? These questions will steer an analysis toward understanding the economic mechanisms through which AI reshapes medical tourism by looking at operational optimization, value creation, and policy implications within global healthcare systems.

2. BACKGROUND

Efficiency gains through AI in medical tourism stem from enabling operational optimization in facilities, as well as support for clinical triage, resource allocation, and patient scheduling. In the first category–indirectly influencing the cross-border nature of care–successful implementation of AI-supported solutions can enhance throughput, reduce waiting times, facilitate cost-effective staff deployment, and closely align capacity with demand. In the second category, AI technology reduces clinical errors, shortens response times, and helps to match patient requirements with resource availability and readiness. Consequently, capacity and speed effects can be brought into play to enhance the overall desirability of international patient care.The support of several hospitals by a central AI operation can lead to gains in throughput or reduced waiting times that will enhance the attractiveness for cross-border patients. AI-assisted systems for clinical triage, patient scheduling, and resource allocation–including for surgical rooms–should ensure the right patient is at the right place at the right time. The service of predictive queuing theory states that with identical distributional characteristics repressive waiting has no effect; and in outpatient diagnostic or surgical intervention with a determined time consumption of the procedure the elimination of waiting does not influence the quality of service.

AI applications to support patient-generated clinical data or teleconsultations with follow-up advice can help identify conditions for which a visit is essential, can help detect redundancy in examination ordering by allowing knowledge-sharing, can identify controls needing to be consolidated or can identify patients requiring intervention(Abràmoff et al., 2022; Aykın et al., 2023; Hamid, 2024; Hossain et al., 2025; McCoy et al., 2025; Rossi et al., 2021; Rudd and Igbrude, 2023; Schwalbe and Wahl, 2020; Shaik, 2025; Tokareva, 2025). These solutions have the potential to enhance early detection and shorten response times, thus improving prognosis levels and associated successful care rates for patients originating from risk-oriented populations.

2.1. Operational Optimization in Healthcare Facilities

Artificial intelligence can provide efficiency gains in medical tourism through operational optimization in healthcare facilities. AI technologies help improve operations by increasing throughput, reducing patient wait times, and enabling better staffing decisions. With improved patient flow, the capacity for treating patients can be increased, which can lower the cost per patient. By enabling better service utilization, AI technologies can also reduce wait times. These factors together lead to cost savings and a higher satisfaction level as regarded by the patients.Countries and regions offering services to foreign patients are increasingly utilizing artificial intelligence to optimize patient flow in their institutions. International healthcare centers are investing in AI technologies to increase their capacity while decreasing the risk for patients traveling for care. AI-enabled dynamic scheduling will allow the scheduling of inbound patients while minimizing the waiting time for surgeries. At the pre-admission stage, AI-assisted patient allocations will ensure that arrival queues at the admission stage are kept at manageable levels. AI-based predictive analytics will be used in staffing decisions at any level, allowing scheduling with maximum efficiency(Alnasser, 2023; Da Silva, 2024; Durham and Blondell, 2017; Hendrix et al., 2021; Reddy, 2024; Shang et al., 2024; Ullagaddi, 2025; Voets et al., 2021). The latter scheduling will also incorporate seasonal trends in utilization, determining staffing requirements accordingly.

2.2. Case Studies of AI Applications in Global Hospitals

Artificial intelligence (AI) technologies have already been adopted by several prominent hospitals around the world, demonstrating their impact on healthcare efficiency and clinical decision-making. One high-profile example is Memorial Sloan Kettering Cancer Center (MSKCC) in the United States, which partnered with International Business Machines (IBM) Watson Health to develop the Watson for Oncology system that supports oncologists when selecting treatment options. This AI system analyzes large datasets of clinical guidelines, medical literature, and patient records in order to recommend evidence-based therapies for cancer care. Studies examining this implementation show high levels of agreement between AI-generated treatment recommendations and decisions made by multidisciplinary medical teams, illustrating the potential of AI in clinical decision-support systems. Another important collaboration is between Moorfields Eye Hospital (MEH) in the United Kingdom and Google DeepMind (GDM). Together they developed a deep-learning system capable of diagnosing a wide range of retinal diseases using optical coherence tomography (OCT) scans. The AI system can identify more than fifty different eye conditions and provide referral recommendations with accuracy comparable to experienced ophthalmologists. This case demonstrates how artificial intelligence can significantly enhance diagnostic accuracy while reducing the time required to detect serious eye conditions, thereby improving patient outcomes and increasing hospital efficiency.

Artificial intelligence is also extensively used in radiology departments of major hospitals. For example, Mount Sinai Health System (MSHS) in New York has implemented AI-powered imaging analysis tools that assist radiologists in detecting abnormalities in computed tomography (CT) and magnetic resonance imaging (MRI) scans. These systems prioritize urgent cases by automatically identifying critical conditions such as intracranial hemorrhage or pulmonary embolism. By accelerating diagnostic workflows and reducing reporting delays, AI-assisted radiology platforms improve the overall efficiency of hospital operations and contribute to better clinical outcomes for patients.

Institutions such as the Mayo Clinic (MC) in the United States have adopted artificial intelligence for predictive analytics and early disease detection. AI algorithms analyze large volumes of electronic health records (EHRs) and diagnostic data to identify patterns associated with disease progression and treatment responses. These tools enable clinicians to anticipate complications, personalize treatment strategies, and allocate hospital resources more effectively. Such applications demonstrate how AI technologies can transform healthcare delivery by integrating predictive analytics with clinical decision-making processes.

AI systems assist in patient triage and scheduling as well as the allocation of physical resources needed to provide care. When a health service provider is able to optimally manage its resources, queuing time can be reduced. Queues form whenever demand for a commodity exceeds the immediate supply available. Queuing theory deals with the mathematical description and depiction of queues which enable solutions for optimal resource allocation in order to minimize queue lengths or waiting times. The application of queuing theory ranges from retailing and agriculture to telecommunications and traffic engineering. It has had a substantial impact on service industries, where the time spent by customers in a queue is often an important factor in their level of satisfaction. AI introduces novel algorithms and uses machine learning to improve these algorithms. These packages therefore permit a provider to offer lower prices and get a larger part of the market, which commonly results in a longer queue. A longer queue would incite a higher administration expense and a consideration by management to reduce a queue. In addition to the previously indicated application in managing operating rooms, models are being developed to optimally allocate nursing technicians outside the actual operation theatre(Ahmed, 2025; Alquayt et al., 2025; Arefin and Zannat, 2025; Frischhut and Levaggi, 2024; Goktas and Grzybowski, 2025; Liu et al., 2025; Manickam et al., 2022; Poalelungi et al., 2023; Sachdeva and Jain, 2025; Victor, 2025). Actual patient treatment does not happen all the time; patients also need to be transported and prepared. These supportive steps can take time, and it is important to study the optimal allocation of these nurses on duty that supervise patient flow in the entire operative process.

2.3. Imaging, Diagnostics, and Predictive Analytics

Imaging, diagnostics, and predictive analytics have witnessed remarkable progress due to AI advancements, making many clinical decisions faster and more reliable. In these areas, recent AI developments are often data-driven and machine-learning-based. The data for training comes from the installation of dedicated and often focused systems that manage a specific task, in some cases supported by large public or private organizations capable of establishing data banks, such as the United States National Institute of Health (NIH) or Google. These organizations provide datasets from a large number of images annotated by specialized radiologists whose information allows algorithms to learn features that make the main procedures, such as breast tumor diagnosis, work almost at the same level of specialists, and in some cases even surpass them.Although the degree of performance and usefulness of these systems tends to be described from a more clinical perspective, with the level of true positive and false negative as the most used parameters, the main contribution to medical tourism is their capacity to accelerate and decrease the cost of the final decision when they are used as an assistant decision support system, when the artificial intelligence system provides the score of probability for many classes, and the specialist uses this score just as a help in the path for the final diagnosis, and not as the diagnosis coming from the machine. The increase of these systems in the medical centers used for international treatment is capable of diminishing the typical delay that occurs when biopsies create resource constraints in the diagnosis path, permitting the execution of elective international procedures with less risk associated with the diagnosis(Andritsos and Tang, 2013; Elhaddad and Hamam, 2024; Hadley et al., 2020; Kastrup et al., 2024; Krittanawong and Kaplin, 2021;

Oso et al., 2025; Ouanes and Farhah, 2024; Pagallo et al., 2023; Perna et al., 2022; Yun and Zhang, 2025).

2.4. Value Creation and Pricing Dynamics

Cost reduction and quality improvement jointly determine the price of healthcare services, with demand elasticity reflecting the willingness to pay for quality. Relative demand elasticities indicate the scope for price discrimination in segmented markets. AI assists in the development and marketing of bundled services with common outcomes and mitigates risks associated with craftsmanship by revealing potential hidden errors. These insights facilitate outcomes-based pricing and risk-sharing arrangements between providers and payers. Adoption of such arrangements generates negative feedback, leading to continued or increased investment in the production process. Cross-border economic relations enable exploitation of price elasticity differentials among international partners.AI lowers the cost of operating a medical facility by accelerating the clinical care pathway and enhancing the quality of outputs(Challoumis, 2023a). Measurable indicators for these dimensions include Length of Stay (LOS) in hospital, post-discharge complications, readmission rates, and patient satisfaction levels. The price-consuming relationship considers the service market as a Black Box; cost reduction, attitudes toward service quality, and price elasticity of demand exert a direct effect on service pricing(Brenna and Spandonaro, 2015; Durham and Blondell, 2014; Fajkis-Zajączkowska et al., 2025; García-Vidal et al., 2019; Gou et al., 2024; Hosny and Aerts, 2019; Khalifa and Albadawy, 2024; Kumar et al., 2023; Perna et al., 2022; Roppelt et al., 2023; Silcox et al., 2024). The combination of lower prices together with the maintenance of quality enhances the demand for products and potential revenue.

2.5. Cost Reduction and Quality Enhancement

Evidence of improved quality in AI-assisted care is still accumulating, but several performance indicators should respond positively to implementation. Length of stay (LOS), readmission rates, complication rates, and patient satisfaction are often used to benchmark service-level quality. AI-driven enhancements in clinical decision support, diagnostics, and imaging accuracy, as outlined previously, have the potential to reduce complications and the need for secondary procedures, positively influencing both LOS and readmission rates. The shift from in-person consultations to virtual health check-ups, complementing perioperative care, not only reduces travel-related health risks but has also been associated with positive patient feedback(Kadirov et al., 2025; Klingelhöfer et al., 2025; Tornimbene et al., 2025).

2.6. Value Capture, Bundled Services, and Outcomes-Based Pricing

Improved cost and quality dynamics enables a myriad of market mechanisms with implications on value capture, including bundled services, outcomes-based pricing, price discrimination, and access. Strategies that align price with cost elasticity in mass, emergent, and elective segments enhances capture. AI analytics can further enable service recovery, minimizing the risk of monitoring performance.A prominent property of medical methods is that the probability of a patient experiencing a hospital-acquired disease is positively correlated with LOS, with the patient's defence mechanisms being compromised for an extended period of time. Therefore, a hospital trying to limit the expected negative impact would benefit from possible reduction of LOS.

2.7. Market Segmentation and Demand Elasticity

Cross-border medical care for elective and non-urgent conditions exhibits a degree of demand price elasticity. Luxury segments demonstrate responsiveness to price changes. Synthesis of supply-demand insights highlights the accessibility impact of AI-driven cost reductions. Segment-specific care quality variations warrant analysis, addressing funding, maintenance, or expertise factors. Travel-related health and safety risks must also be examined, as heightened demand influxes or demographic factors may compromise care quality.Cost reductions and quality enhancements enable adoption of price discrimination strategies, catering to both sensitive and inelastic demand. Expanding access for lower-income groups remains a priority, with comprehensive AI applications mitigating inequities(Alnasser, 2023; Da Silva, 2024; Durham and Blondell, 2017; Hendrix et al., 2021; Reddy, 2024; Shang et al., 2024; Ullagaddi, 2025; Victor, 2025; Voets et al., 2021). Consideration of travel-related factors influencing addressable market size is essential. Health tourism infrastructure upgrades should be synchronous with rising demand to minimize risk exposure during the process.

3. ANALYSIS

Standards and regulations play an important role in both the effectiveness of a healthcare system and the specific applications of AI in medicine. They should be carefully developed to minimize the time needed to assess the safety and effectiveness of healthcare services and products and to enable access to international markets for novel healthcare solutions that improve health outcomes, reduce costs, or increase efficiency. Thus, a regulatory environment supportive of healthy competition through technology and quality, providing the information necessary for patients, and stimulating innovation is desirable. The use of AI in medical tourism should also consider aspects related to (i) development of international standards to ensure data protection; (ii) establishment of appropriate reimbursement models that support the adoption of AI; and (iii) inclusion of the ethical and legal implications associated with the introduction of AI-based solutions.There is a need for international standards to ensure the privacy and protection of medical information, facilitate the accreditation of AI developers and providers in different countries, and support companies that wish to enter new markets. AI algorithms must be reliable, secure, continuous and easy to use, and their complexity should be minimized. In addition, regulations should prioritize the establishment of a civil framework that allocates responsibilities and guarantees consumers. A reimbursement model that supports the introduction of processes and tools that facilitate the continuous assessment of AI solutions can be decisive for the adoption of AI solutions (El Arab and Al Moosa, 2025; Aykın et al., 2023; Ciecierski-Holmes et al., 2022; Khanna et al., 2022; Lam, 2025; Schwalbe and Wahl, 2020; Shaik, 2025; Sharma et al., 2023; Tarasenko, 2025). The mapping of services in which AI can have a positive impact on LOS, complaints, readmission, costs, patient experience and quality of life, and that for which patients would be willing to pay additional amounts can guide the selection of priority areas.

3.1. Analysis and Change to Standardization and Regulatory Environment

International standards for health care management and outcomes measurement have a direct bearing on data requirements and hence the desirability of AI-supported prediction, diagnostics and risk evaluation in a medical tourism setting. Importantly, there are many potential standards (STDs) in government recommendations and the private sector, including initiatives such as the Joint Commission International standardization framework(the Joint Commission International standardization initiative is one example). Governments also have an interest in minimizing the cost of cross-border transfer of patients; a high level of standardization makes it easier for the professional group supplying these services to manage risk. Consequently, action from the regulatory authorities to harmonize international standards in these areas could act to bring about an increased demand from the travel market(Challoumis, 2025a, 2025b). Cross-national differences in laboratory practices and standards-in-pathology are another example of an area where standardization would facilitate the use of foreign pathology/diagnostic services.Governments should also explore the possibility of regulation through mutual recognition of standards in their respective countries; setting up a smooth regulatory framework is crucial. Regulatory issues surrounding international trade in services may need to be clarified further; currently, there is insufficient attention on this vital area. The regulation must fulfil the basic supply separability condition (the service must not have to be physically provided in the country) for trade to occur(Abràmoff et al., 2022; Aykın et al., 2023; Hamid, 2024; Hossain et al., 2025; McCoy et al., 2025; Rudd and Igbrude, 2023; Schwalbe and Wahl, 2020; Shaik, 2025; Tokareva, 2025).

3.2. Reimbursement Models and Incentives

AI adoption in medical tourism requires appropriate reimbursement models with incentives for providers to integrate AI-enabled systems in diagnostics, operations, and patient management of international medical pathways. Substantial efficiency gains reduce costs and release resources that can be used for quality improvements. Innovations during hospitalization also facilitate bundled service, outcomes-based pricing, and shared risk arrangements between producers and payers. Market segmentation in cross-border care broadens potential demand. A comprehensive analysis of both supply-side and demand-side factors is essential to assess the total effect on AI-enabled tourism.Governments, policy makers, and the private sector have the opportunity to develop a hospital sector where demand exceeds supply, thus creating the conditions for favorable international collaboration and investment(Alnasser, 2023; Da Silva, 2024; Durham and Blondell, 2017; Hendrix et al., 2021; Reddy, 2024; Rossi et al., 2021; Shang et al., 2024; Ullagaddi, 2025; Victor, 2025; Voets et al., 2021).

3.3. Ethical and Legal Dimensions

Policies to protect privacy provide information to patients about the intended use and potential risks of any data provided for its use and establish criteria and conditions for the processing and commercialization of personal data by different types of actors are essential. However, they should be flexible enough to cover a wide range of uses of these data that might emerge with the rapid advance of AI technology tailored for healthcare. Ensuring privacy protection and anticipating its breaches when possible are fundamental options for the development of AI in a Health Tourism context.Ensuring that enhanced efficiency in the health system as a whole implies real and sustainable gains is fundamental as the increase in Health Tourism generates indirect costs in the local population that is rarely computed or factored into the decision to pursue such options(Ahmed, 2025; Alquayt et al., 2025; Da Silva, 2024; Durham and Blondell, 2017; Goktas and Grzybowski, 2025;

Liu et al., 2025; Manickam et al., 2022; Poalelungi et al., 2023; Sachdeva and Jain, 2025; Victor, 2025).

3.4. Case Studies and Empirical Evidence

AI-Enabled Healthcare Service Providers Examples Artificial intelligence solutions have been integrated into clinical and operational workflows at several global healthcare institutions. Some examples are: IBM Watson Health has been deployed in hospitals in the United States, South Korea, and India to assist with oncology decision-making by reading medical literature and patient records to help physicians choose the best cancer treatments for their patients. Google DeepMind Health is another system that has found widespread adoption. It has worked with organizations like Moorfields Eye Hospital in the United Kingdom to build deep-learning models for diagnosing retinal diseases that have performance comparable to leading ophthalmologists. Aidoc, an AI radiology platform, is used by hospitals across the United States and Europe to help radiologists detect critically urgent conditions such as intracranial hemorrhage from CT scans in real time. In China, Ping An Good Doctor uses AI-based diagnostic assistance integrated with its telemedicine service offering support to hospitals managing large patient volumes through automated triage and clinical decision-support tools. Another example would be Siemens Healthineers whose AI-enabled imaging platforms are being used in hospitals around the world to improve diagnostic accuracy, reduce scanning time, and increase workflow efficiency. These are examples of how hospital operations can be transformed today by AI-enabled healthcare technologies through improved diagnostic accuracy and reduced delays in treatment; thus strengthening the economic and operational foundations of medical tourism as well as cross-border healthcare services.

3.5. AI-Driven Diagnostics in Surgical Clinics

An international surgical clinic reports successful adoption of AI in its diagnostic services and triage processes. Deep-learning algorithms analyze CT images of lung cancer lesions, enabling faster diagnosis(Ahmed, 2025; Alnasser, 2023; Da Silva, 2024; Durham and Blondell, 2017; Hendrix et al., 2021; Reddy, 2024; Shang et al., 2024; Ullagaddi, 2025; Victor, 2025; Voets et al., 2021).

3.6. Operational AI in International Medical Centers

AI technologies are transforming virtually every aspect of how healthcare activities are planned and executed, and hospitals and clinics that look after international patients are no exception. From the moment patients begin their care journey, Artificial

Intelligence systems can help hospitals help them by streamlining operations, reducing waiting times for diagnosis and treatment, and lowering overall costs. In addition to improving operational efficiency, investment in AI also supports expansions in clinical service offerings that create a more attractive, competitive value proposition and lead to improvements in service quality that drive patient satisfaction.In major medical centers, deploying operational AI involves optimizing the management of healthcare activities as they progress through hospitals. This includes optimizing patient flow within hospitals to minimize waiting time between different stages of care and ensuring sufficient spare capacity at critical points in the process to reduce patient risk(Alquayt et al., 2025; Arefin and Zannat, 2025; Frischhut and Levaggi, 2024; Goktas and Grzybowski, 2025; Liu et al., 2025; Manickam et al., 2022; Oso et al., 2025; Ouanes and Farhah, 2024; Poalelungi et al., 2023). Costing is another key element in optimizing operations, and AI-driven cost reduction enables lower pricing that supports market positioning in tourism for healthcare.

3.7. Methodological Approaches for Economic Evaluation

Cost-effectiveness analysis (CEA) and budget impact modeling provide the primary foundations for economic evaluation. Cost-effectiveness analysis determines the relative cost per unit of health gain (e.g. Disability-Adjusted Life Years [DALY]) from an AI-driven change against a relevant comparator. Budget impact modeling estimates the financial cost of adopting AI technology from the perspective of a specific decision-maker. The economic framework also embraces real options analysis to capture the value of parallel investment decisions in fields such as staffing, facilities, logistics and travel insurance. Uncertainty in the long-term stability of the global COVID-19 pandemic accentuates the importance of considering scenario planning approaches to Capital Expenditure (CAPEX) and Operating Expenditure(OPEX) decisions in the medical tourism sector. Data on the total and incremental costs and effects of adopting AI technologies in medical tourism must be assembled predominantly through a combination of expert opinion and literature review. Validating the accuracy of these estimates represents a key challenge since continuous improvement guidelines necessitate the iterative—rather than one-shot—estimation cycle customary in applied health economic research. In particular, the principal influences on travel-related health risks and travel-related contagion severity for the population of interest require special attention(Ahmed, 2025; Alnasser, 2023; Da Silva, 2024; Durham and Blondell, 2017; Reddy, 2024; Sachdeva and Jain, 2025; Ullagaddi, 2025; Victor, 2025).

3.8. Cost-Effectiveness Analysis and Budget Impact

Economic evaluation methods must be appropriate to the intervention and accompanying uncertainty. Cost-effectiveness analysis is common in health technology assessment, particularly for drugs and devices. However, many AI-enabled improvements are process- rather than product-driven and focus on enabling cost savings. In these cases, Budget Impact Analysis (BIA)is typically more relevant. Cost-effectiveness analysis is applied in cases where the new technology is not already in widespread use to ascertain whether the incremental health benefits justified the costs, while budget impact analysis is appropriate for further expansions when the health benefits can be explicitly quantified. Shortage of AI-ready skills is a possible brake on implementation. A shortage of skilled clinical staff in specific regions could limit the realistic implementation of diagnosis-support AI; although evident locally, such shortages are typically accommodated in medical tourism because of the cross-border patient flows. It is therefore important to map the specific qualifications needed for a given model of implementation and assess the local available headcount for the required specialty.Real options and scenario-planning methods are often useful for modelling economic decisions in a cross-border context, allowing for exploration and cautious decision-making in the face of great uncertainty. They are less often applied when the cross-border aspects concern the demand rather than the supply side; for example, the effects of a deterioration in regional geopolitical stability on the uptake of shoreline medical services, but a number of modelling attempts exist(Alquayt et al., 2025; Arefin and Zannat, 2025; Frischhut and Levaggi, 2024; Hadley et al., 2020; Kastrup et al., 2024; Liu et al., 2025; Manickam et al., 2022; Ouanes and Farhah, 2024; Poalelungi et al., 2023).

3.9. Data Sources and Measurement Challenges

Data sources for estimating the economic impact of artificial intelligence (AI) in medical tourism operate in a sparse-information environment where a mixture of primary and secondary data provide the best available basis for robust analysis. A range of external sources validate specific measures required for cost-effectiveness assessment during the appraising stage of investment, budget-impact modelling, and cross-border care as a whole. All require careful evaluation of sectoral context, feature underexplored industry dimensions, or are being produced and assessed in response to identified knowledge gaps.Nevertheless, concrete outcome measures can be identified for both micro- and meso-level AI applications. The clinical performance of AI-driven diagnostics in surgical clinics, for example, is supported in 18 with an internal validation cohort of at least 40 patients and peer-reviewed outcome data downloaded from PubMed, Scopus, or Europe PMC. Supporting evidence also offers open-access efficiency metrics, including patients served per annum and complete editing time per image. At the operational scale, the international medical center in Singapore and its AI capabilities serve as a validated practical example, enabling assessment of effects on patient flow and cost. Finally, the industry report by McKinsey 1 provides quantitative information on patient characteristics, waiting times, utilization rates, and satisfaction scores, covering AI-assisted triage, scheduling, resource allocation, and diagnostic models that span direct-to-patient, operational, and data-analytical application domains. Other avenues exist for cross-checking the results(Brenna and Spandonaro, 2015; Durham and Blondell, 2014; Fajkis-Zajączkowska et al., 2025; García-Vidal et al., 2019; Hosny and Aerts, 2019; Klingelhöfer et al., 2025; Roppelt et al., 2023; Tornimbene et al., 2025).

3.10. Policy Recommendations for Sustainable Practice

Investment priorities and risk management strategies should assist AI adoption across the medical tourism ecosystem. AI-based applications may warrant initial attention for improving partner facilities' operational efficiency: shortening wait times, boosting patient turnover, optimizing staffing levels, and decreasing costs through medical knowledge synthesis and utilization. Risks of AI adoption—and especially dependence—should be monitored regularly and mitigated through diversification of health data and technology sources. Practical partnerships should be established with hardware producers or cloud service providers to ensure that technology supply remains diversified, physical service quality is maintained, and simultaneous downtime of systems becomes unlikely(Andritsos and Tang, 2013; Elhaddad and Hamam, 2024; Hadley et al., 2020; Kastrup et al., 2024; Krittanawong and Kaplin, 2021; Oso et al., 2025; Ouanes and Farhah, 2024; Pagallo et al., 2023; Yun and Zhang, 2025).

3.11. Collaboration Frameworks and Knowledge Transfer

Strengthening collaboration frameworks that promote knowledge transfer among national and international stakeholders enhances training capacity, creates synergies, and breaks the information silos inherent in a rapidly evolving landscape. Efforts to standardize internal operational and external patient-facing AI applications should also consider the operational integration and interoperability of applications across multiple care delivery pathways originating from different countries and regions and terminating in different regulatory environments. Development engagements that support the establishment of non-competitive regional hubs for advanced services and skills creation, incubation, product validation, and testing lower risk for all partners and generate substantial benefits through technology sharing and deployment.

Specialization by region, combined with a regional networked delivery and testing approach, will heighten the efficient use of human capital resources of all types. Addressing operational decision-making through AI tools offers substantial near-term and quantifiable benefits(Challoumis, 2024a; Challoumis and Eriotis, 2025). Travel, destination, and procedure-specific operational AI requires limited skill-measurement factors, is easily transferable, and generates significant gains through the application of queuing and distribution equivalence principles(Abràmoff et al., 2022; Hamid, 2024; Hendrix et al., 2021; Hossain et al., 2025; McCoy et al., 2025; Reddy, 2024; Rossi et al., 2021; Shang et al., 2024; Tokareva, 2025; Ullagaddi, 2025; Voets et al., 2021).Comprehensive monitoring, evaluation, and improvement mechanisms strengthen stakeholder confidence. AI investment in the international medical tourism industry should enhance efficiency, value creation, and sustainability. Objective data and analyses must confirm this, closing the costs–benefits gap. Realization of the theoretical economic benefits of AI adoption in medical tourism depends on dedicated and impartial industry monitoring(Challoumis, 2023b, 2024b).

4. LIMITATIONS

While this study contributes valuable insights, it is important to highlight some limitations. First, the analysis is mostly conceptual and based on literature rather than large-scale empirical datasets. Although this study synthesizes economic theory, healthcare management insights, and emerging evidence from artificial intelligence applications, quantitative data on the economic impact of AI in medical tourism markets are not available. Future research using panel data or hospital-level operational datasets may provide stronger empirical support for the mechanisms described here.

Second, because technological development in artificial intelligence happens so quickly, there is some uncertainty about how long the solutions now being used in healthcare systems will continue to work well and stay stable over time. The majority of AI-enabled medical tools are still at the early adoption stage; their economic performance may alter as technologies advance, regulatory frameworks evolve further and healthcare institutions continue adapting their operational models. Therefore results from this study should be viewed through the lens of a constantly changing technological environment.

Third, this study mainly discusses the economic and operational impacts of AI in medical tourism by focusing on aspects like efficiency gains, value creation, and market dynamics. It does not go into detail about other important dimensions such as patient behavioral responses or cultural factors influencing healthcare mobility or political/institutional differences between healthcare systems that can significantly affect real-world outcomes for AI-enabled medical tourism. These areas should be further explored through interdisciplinary research.

Differences between countries in regulatory frameworks, healthcare infrastructure, and technological readiness might affect how generalizable the conclusions presented in this study are. The economic effects of AI integration into medical tourism will depend on the level of digital maturity, institutional capacity, and policy environments within a country. For this reason, the conceptual framework presented here should be viewed as a basis for further empirical studies that investigate regional variations in AI adoption and dynamics within healthcare markets.

5. FUTURE RESEARCH DIRECTIONS

Future research on the economics of artificial intelligence in medical tourism can advance along several complementary dimensions. First, there is a clear need for robust empirical evaluation of efficiency gains attributable to AI adoption. While current studies often rely on case-based or descriptive evidence, future work should employ panel data, quasi-experimental designs, or natural experiments to quantify cost reductions, productivity improvements, and waiting-time minimization across hospitals, clinics, and destination countries. Such approaches would allow researchers to distinguish short-term operational gains from long-term structural efficiency effects in cross-border healthcare markets.

A second promising direction concerns value creation and distribution among stakeholders. Research should examine how AI-generated value is allocated between patients, providers, intermediaries (such as medical tourism facilitators and platforms), and host-country health systems. This includes investigating pricing dynamics, surplus extraction, and the potential for AI to either reduce or exacerbate informational asymmetries between international patients and healthcare providers. Comparative studies across regions with different levels of digital maturity would be particularly valuable.

Third, future studies should focus on the interaction between AI-driven medical tourism and domestic health system sustainability. While AI may attract high-value foreign patients and generate fiscal inflows, it may also risk crowding out local populations or reallocating scarce medical resources. Research is needed to model these trade-offs, assessing whether AI-enhanced medical tourism strengthens public health financing, human capital retention, and infrastructure investment, or whether it contributes to internal inequalities and dual-track healthcare systems.Another critical avenue lies in global health equity and ethical economics. Scholars should explore how AI can be designed and governed to support inclusive access, transparency, and patient safety in cross-border care. This includes examining algorithmic bias in triage, diagnosis, and patient selection, as well as the economic implications of unequal data availability between developed and developing medical tourism destinations. Integrating ethical AI frameworks with welfare economics could provide a more holistic assessment of social outcomes.Finally, future research should address regulatory, institutional, and macroeconomic spillovers. This includes analyzing how data protection regimes, cross-border liability rules, and AI governance frameworks influence investment incentives and international competitiveness in medical tourism. At the macro level, research could explore how AI-driven medical tourism affects balance of payments, health-sector specialization, and long-term development trajectories in host countries, particularly in emerging economies positioning healthcare as a strategic export sector.Together, these research directions can move the literature beyond descriptive accounts toward a coherent economic theory of AI-enabled medical tourism, grounded in efficiency analysis, value creation, and global health sustainability.

6. CONCLUSION

AI technologies are likely to improve efficiency in medical tourism – a system of health-care delivery in which patients are engaged in an informed, voluntary choice to cross international borders for an elective procedure – by reducing travel-related risk and/or costs, improving quality and/or safety, or expanding the range of available services. AI fulfills this important role because it can reduce costs, increase quality, and enhance the predictive capabilities of local and long-distance care systems in ways documented in the health-economics literature (see, Figure 1, based onPython 3.13).However, the prospect of improved efficiency alone does not guarantee a positive business case for AI adoption; value creation matters, too. Valuation frameworks that capture the essence of these concepts in the medical-tourism context are therefore required. Economic principles of opportunity cost, economies of scale, and comparative advantage provide the foundation; once articulated, the efficient allocation of resources in a cross-border context reveals the incentives and trade-offs among key players in an international medical-tourism system. Such an analysis contributes to sustainability in global health by mapping the social costs, safety risks, and health-care outcomes of travel for an elective procedure.

At the same time, using AI in medical tourism brings up important economic, institutional, and ethical issues. Problems related to sharing data across borders, keeping patients' information private, agreeing on regulations, and training the workforce are major challenges that must be tackled to ensure the sustainable development of AI-enabled healthcare systems. Without proper governance frameworks and international standards, the benefits of adopting AI might not be evenly shared and could even make inequalities in access to healthcare between different countries and populations worse.From a larger viewpoint related to economics, bringing AI into medical tourism affects how sustainable global health systems are. Improvements driven by AI in efficiency and quality may bring more international patients; encourage investment in healthcare infrastructure; and enhance the role of healthcare as an export service for many countries. But policymakers need to weigh these benefits against potential downsides carefully: pressure on domestic healthcare capacity; unequal allocation of medical resources; and ethical concerns about algorithmic decision-making.In sum, this paper adds to the growing body of work on the economics of artificial intelligence in healthcare by offering a conceptual framework that connects the adoption of AI with efficiency gains, mechanisms for creating value, and sustainability in global health. By integrating economic theory with perspectives from healthcare operations and international patient mobility, it has shown how AI can be a transformative force within the medical tourism ecosystem. Future studies need to further investigate empirical evidence regarding the economic impacts brought about through the adoption of AI, how value is distributed among different stakeholders and what policy frameworks are required for enabling AI-enabled medical tourism to develop in a way that is socially beneficial as well as economically sustainable.

REFERENCES

Abràmoff, M., Roehrenbeck, C., Trujillo, S., Goldstein, J., Graves, A., Repka, M., & Silva, E.III. (2022). A reimbursement framework for artificial intelligence in healthcare. *NPJ Digital Medicine*, *5*(1), 89. Advance online publication. DOI: 10.1038/s41746-022-00621-w

Ahmed, S. I. (2025). *The role of artificial intelligence applications in marketing health tourism in Egypt*. International Journal of Tourism and Hospitality Studies., DOI: 10.21608/ijthsx.2024.325337.1122

Alnasser, B. (2023). The economic impact of artificial intelligence on healthcare: A literature review. *E-Health Telecommunication Systems and Networks*, *12*(3), 27–41. DOI: 10.4236/etsn.2023.123003

Alowais, S., Alghamdi, S., Alsuhebany, N., Alqahtani, T., Alshaya, A., Almohareb, S., Aldairem, A., Alrashed, M., Bin Saleh, K., Badreldin, H., Al Yami, M., Al Harbi, S., & Albekairy, A. (2023). Revolutionizing healthcare: The role of artificial intelligence in clinical practice. *BMC Medical Education*, *23*(1), 428. Advance online publication. DOI: 10.1186/s12909-023-04698-z

Alquayt, A., Aljuhani, O., Alharthi, A., Alqahtani, R., Khan, A., Al-Jedai, A., Almoeen, A., Alshennawi, M., Badreldin, H., Aljouie, A., Alnasser, L., Alshehri, A., Alzahrani, M., Alhaidal, H., Alhajaji, R., Alotaibi, S., Redhwan, E., Alharthi, F., Alghamdi, B., & Al Sulaiman, K. (2025). AI-driven healthcare innovations for enhancing clinical services during mass gatherings (Hajj): Task force insights and future directions. *BMC Health Services Research*, *25*(1), 456. Advance online publication. DOI: 10.1186/s12913-025-13045-5

Andritsos, D., & Tang, C. (2013). The impact of cross-border patient movement on the delivery of healthcare services. *International Journal of Production Economics*, *145*(2), 702–712. DOI: 10.1016/j.ijpe.2013.05.025

Arefin, S., & Zannat, N. T.Global Health Institute Research Team United states. (2025). Securing AI in global health research: A framework for cross-border data collaboration. *Clinical Medicine and Health Research Journal*, *5*(2), 1187–1193. Advance online publication. DOI: 10.18535/cmhrj.v5i02.457

Aykın, Ö., Uluhan, F., Gümüş, İ., Çabuk, Ş., Bozbayir, U., Duran, V., Özbay, C., Özbay, B., Gündoğmuş, Ş. E., Şengül, M. T., & Övey, I. (2023). *Artificial intelligence and telemedicine applications in health tourism marketing*. Eurasian Journal of Health Technology Assessment., DOI: 10.52148/ehta.1396111

Bekbolatova, M., Mayer, J., Ong, C., & Toma, M. (2024). Transformative potential of AI in healthcare: Definitions, applications, and navigating the ethical landscape and public perspectives. *Healthcare (Basel)*, *12*(2), 125. Advance online publication. DOI: 10.3390/healthcare12020125

Brenna, E., & Spandonaro, F. (2015). Regional incentives and patient cross-border mobility: Evidence from the Italian experience. *International Journal of Health Policy and Management*, *4*(6), 363–372. DOI: 10.15171/ijhpm.2015.65

Challoumis, C. (2023a). Risk on the tax system of the E.U. from 2016 to 2022. *Economics*, *11*(1), 55–72. DOI: 10.2478/eoik-2023-0058

Challoumis, C. (2023b). From savings to escape and enforcement savings. *Cógito (Salvador)*, *XV*(4), 206–216. https://cogito.ucdc.ro/COGITO_DECEMBER_2023.pdf

Challoumis, C. (2024a). The index of the cycle of money: The case of Switzerland. *Journal of Risk and Financial Management*, *17*(4), 135. Advance online publication. DOI: 10.3390/jrfm17040135

Challoumis, C. (2024b). From economics to economic engineering (The cycle of money): The case of Romania. *Cógito (Salvador)*, *XVII*(2), 161–170. https://cogito.ucdc.ro/issues/COGITO%20no.2_27062024%20_BT.pdf

Challoumis, C. (2025a). The inflation according to the cycle of money (C.M.). *Economic Alternatives*, *2025*(2), 324–353. DOI: 10.37075/EA.2025.2.03

Challoumis, C. (2025b). The impact factor of tangibles and intangibles of controlled transactions on economic performance. *Economic Alternatives*, *31*(1), 64–76. DOI: 10.37075/EA.2025.1.04

Challoumis, C., & Eriotis, N. (2025). The impact of artificial intelligence on the Greek economy. *Journal of Open Innovation*, *11*(1), 100578. Advance online publication. DOI: 10.1016/j.joitmc.2025.100578

Ciecierski-Holmes, T., Singh, R., Axt, M., Brenner, S., & Barteit, S. (2022). Artificial intelligence for strengthening healthcare systems in low- and middle-income countries: A systematic scoping review. *NPJ Digital Medicine*, *5*(1), 100. Advance online publication. DOI: 10.1038/s41746-022-00700-y

Da Silva, R. G. L. (2024). The advancement of artificial intelligence in biomedical research and health innovation: Challenges and opportunities in emerging economies. *Globalization and Health*, *20*(1), 49. Advance online publication. DOI: 10.1186/s12992-024-01049-5

Durham, J., & Blondell, S. (2014). Research protocol: A realist synthesis of cross-border patient mobility from low-income and middle-income countries. *BMJ Open*, *4*(11), e006514. Advance online publication. DOI: 10.1136/bmjopen-2014-006514

Durham, J., & Blondell, S. (2017). A realist synthesis of cross-border patient movement from low and middle income countries to similar or higher income countries. *Globalization and Health*, *13*(1), 68. Advance online publication. DOI: 10.1186/s12992-017-0287-8

El Arab, R. A., & Al Moosa, O. A. (2025). Systematic review of cost effectiveness and budget impact of artificial intelligence in healthcare. *NPJ Digital Medicine*, *8*(1), 89. Advance online publication. DOI: 10.1038/s41746-025-01722-y

Elhaddad, M., & Hamam, S. (2024). AI-driven clinical decision support systems: An ongoing pursuit of potential. *Cureus*, *16*(8), e57728. Advance online publication. DOI: 10.7759/cureus.57728

Esmaeilzadeh, P. (2024). Challenges and strategies for wide-scale artificial intelligence (AI) deployment in healthcare practices: A perspective for healthcare organizations. *Artificial Intelligence in Medicine*, *151*, 102861. Advance online publication. DOI: 10.1016/j.artmed.2024.102861

Fajkis-Zajączkowska, N., Zawada, A., Bojko, M., & Kolasa, K. (2025). Comprehensive analysis of frameworks for evaluating artificial intelligence solutions in healthcare: A descriptive review. Computers in Biology and Medicine, 196(Pt B). *Computers in Biology and Medicine*, *110750*, 110750. Advance online publication. DOI: 10.1016/j.compbiomed.2025.110750

Frischhut, M., & Levaggi, R. (2024). With a little help from my (neighbouring) friends. "Border region patient mobility" in the European Union: A policy analysis. *Health Policy (Amsterdam)*, *146*, 105114. Advance online publication. DOI: 10.1016/j.healthpol.2024.105114

García-Vidal, C., Sanjuán, G., Puerta-Alcalde, P., Moreno-García, E., & Soriano, Á. (2019). Artificial intelligence to support clinical decision-making processes. *EBioMedicine*, *46*, 27–29. DOI: 10.1016/j.ebiom.2019.07.019

Goktas, P., & Grzybowski, A. (2025). Shaping the future of healthcare: Ethical clinical challenges and pathways to trustworthy AI. *Journal of Clinical Medicine*, *14*(5), 1605. Advance online publication. DOI: 10.3390/jcm14051605

Gou, F., Liu, J., Xiao, C., & Wu, J. (2024). Research on artificial-intelligence-assisted medicine: A survey on medical artificial intelligence. *Diagnostics (Basel)*, *14*(14), 1472. Advance online publication. DOI: 10.3390/diagnostics14141472

Hadley, T., Pettit, R., Malik, T., Khoei, A., & Salihu, H. (2020). Artificial intelligence in global health—A framework and strategy for adoption and sustainability. *International Journal of MCH and AIDS*, *9*(1), 121–127. DOI: 10.21106/ijma.296

Hamid, M. M. A. (2024). *The impact of applying artificial intelligence in developing medical tourism in Egypt*. International Journal of Tourism and Hospitality Studies., DOI: 10.21608/ijthsx.2024.288682.1094

Hassan, V., & Bellos, G. (2022). COVID-19: Reshaping medical tourism through artificial intelligence (AI) and robotics. *Athens Journal of Tourism*, *9*(2), 87–104. DOI: 10.30958/ajt.9-2-2

Hendrix, N., Veenstra, D., Cheng, M., Anderson, N., & Verguet, S. (2021). Assessing the economic value of clinical artificial intelligence: Challenges and opportunities. *Value in Health : The Journal of the International Society for Pharmacoeconomics and Outcomes Research*, *25*(3), 331–339. DOI: 10.1016/j.jval.2021.08.015

Hosny, A., & Aerts, H. (2019). Artificial intelligence for global health. *Science*, *366*(6468), 955–956. DOI: 10.1126/science.aay5189

Hossain, M. A., Arafat, M. S., Desai, K., Akter, S., & Asha, A. I. (2025). The economic impact of AI-driven remote patient monitoring: A business intelligence perspective on healthcare cost optimization. *International Interdisciplinary Business Economics Advancement Journal*, *6*(5), 39–67. Advance online publication. DOI: 10.55640/business/volume06issue05-03

Jiao, W., Zhang, X., & D'Souza, F. (2023). The economic value and clinical impact of artificial intelligence in healthcare: A scoping literature review. *IEEE Access : Practical Innovations, Open Solutions*, *11*, 123445–123457. DOI: 10.1109/ACCESS.2023.3327905

Kadirov, A., Maksimov, A., & Okhotnikov, I. (2025). Digital technologies as a driver of cross-border trade (on the example of the global telemedicine market). *Russian Journal of Management*, *13*(1), 211–232. DOI: 10.29039/2500-1469-2025-13-1-211-232

Kastrup, N., Holst-Kristensen, A., & Valentin, J. (2024). Landscape and challenges in economic evaluations of artificial intelligence in healthcare: A systematic review of methodology. *BMC Digital Health*, *2*(1), 88. Advance online publication. DOI: 10.1186/s44247-024-00088-7

Khalifa, M., & Albadawy, M. (2024). AI in diagnostic imaging: Revolutionising accuracy and efficiency. *Computer Methods and Programs in Biomedicine Update*, *5*, 100146. Advance online publication. DOI: 10.1016/j.cmpbup.2024.100146

Khanna, N., Maindarkar, M., Fernandes, J., Paul, S., Bhagawati, M., Ahluwalia, P., Ruzsa, Z., Sharma, A., Kolluri, R., Singh, I., Laird, J., Fatemi, M., Alizad, A., Saba, L., Agarwal, V., Sharma, A., Teji, J., Al-Maini, M., Rathore, V., & Suri, J. (2022). Economics of artificial intelligence in healthcare: Diagnosis vs. treatment. *Healthcare (Basel), 10*(12), 2493. Advance online publication. DOI: 10.3390/healthcare10122493

Klingelhöfer, D., Braun, M., Dröge, J., Groneberg, D., & Brüggmann, D. (2025). Research on artificial intelligence, machine and deep learning in medicine: Global characteristics, readiness, and equity. *Globalization and Health, 21*(1), 28. Advance online publication. DOI: 10.1186/s12992-025-01128-1

Krishnan, G., Singh, S., Pathania, M., Gosavi, S., Abhishek, S., Parchani, A., & Dhar, M. (2023). Artificial intelligence in clinical medicine: Catalyzing a sustainable global healthcare paradigm. *Frontiers in Artificial Intelligence, 6*, 1227091. Advance online publication. DOI: 10.3389/frai.2023.1227091

Krittanawong, C., & Kaplin, S. (2021). Artificial intelligence in global health. *European Heart Journal, 42*(23), 2322–2324. DOI: 10.1093/eurheartj/ehab036

Kumar, P., Sharma, S., & Dutot, V. (2023). Artificial intelligence (AI)-enabled CRM capability in healthcare: The impact on service innovation. *International Journal of Information Management, 69*, 102598. Advance online publication. DOI: 10.1016/j.ijinfomgt.2022.102598

Kuwaiti, A. A., Nazer, K., Al-Reedy, A., Al-Shehri, S., Al-Muhanna, A., Subbarayalu, A., Al Muhanna, D., & Al-Muhanna, F. (2023). A review of the role of artificial intelligence in healthcare. *Journal of Personalized Medicine, 13*(6), 951. Advance online publication. DOI: 10.3390/jpm13060951

Lam, M. L.-L. (2025). Increasing adoptive capacities of innovative health technologies in the global health care system. *Darnios Aplinkos Vystymas, 22*(1), 143–151. Advance online publication. DOI: 10.52320/dav.v22i1.381

Liu, J., Mao, S., Lu, L., Jing, Y., Yang, X., Xu, H., & Ren, Y. (2025). The impact of digital economy on the supply chain resilience of cross-border healthcare e-commerce. *Frontiers in Public Health, 13*, 1570338. Advance online publication. DOI: 10.3389/fpubh.2025.1570338

Manickam, P., Mariappan, S. A., Murugesan, S., Hansda, S., Kaushik, A., Shinde, R., & Thipperudraswamy, S. (2022). Artificial intelligence (AI) and internet of medical things (IoMT) assisted biomedical systems for intelligent healthcare. *Biosensors (Basel), 12*(8), 562. Advance online publication. DOI: 10.3390/bios12080562

McCoy, L., Bihorac, A., Celi, L., Elmore, M., Kewalramani, D., Kwaga, T., Martinez-Martin, N., Prôa, R., Schamroth, J., Shaffer, J., Youssef, A., & Fiske, A. (2025). Building health systems capable of leveraging AI: Applying Paul Farmer's 5S framework for equitable global health. *BMC Global and Public Health, 3*(1), 58. Advance online publication. DOI: 10.1186/s44263-025-00158-6

Oso, O. B., Alli, O. I., Babarinde, A. O., & Ibeh, A. I. (2025). Navigating cross-border healthcare investments: A risk-opportunity model for emerging markets. *Engineering and Technology Journal, 10*(2). Advance online publication. DOI: 10.47191/etj/v10i02.10

Ouanes, K., & Farhah, N. (2024). Effectiveness of artificial intelligence (AI) in clinical decision support systems and care delivery. *Journal of Medical Systems, 48*(1), 98. Advance online publication. DOI: 10.1007/s10916-024-02098-4

Pagallo, U., O'Sullivan, S., Nevejans, N., Holzinger, A., Friebe, M., Jeanquartier, F., Jean-Quartier, C., & Miernik, A. (2023). The underuse of AI in the health sector: Opportunity costs, success stories, risks and recommendations. *Health and Technology, 14*(1), 1–14. DOI: 10.1007/s12553-023-00806-7

Perna, R., Cruz-Martinez, G., & Fuentes, F. J. M. (2022). Patient mobility within national borders. Drivers and politics of cross-border healthcare agreements in the Spanish decentralized system. *Health Policy (Amsterdam), 126*(11), 1187–1193. DOI: 10.1016/j.healthpol.2022.09.009

Poalelungi, D. G., Musat, C., Fulga, A., Neagu, M., Neagu, A.-I., Piraianu, A., & Fulga, I. (2023). Advancing patient care: How artificial intelligence is transforming healthcare. *Journal of Personalized Medicine, 13*(8), 1214. Advance online publication. DOI: 10.3390/jpm13081214

Rady, H. A. W. A. (2024). *The role of artificial intelligence to enhance health tourism applications in Egyptian tourist destinations. Minia Journal of Tourism and Hospitality Research.* MJTHR., DOI: 10.21608/mjthr.2024.281385.1150

Reddy, S. (2024). Generative AI in healthcare: An implementation science informed translational path on application, integration and governance. *Implementation Science : IS, 19*(1), 57. Advance online publication. DOI: 10.1186/s13012-024-01357-9

Reshadi, M. S., & Chehragh, A. M. (2025). A review of medical tourism entrepreneurship and marketing at regional and global levels and a quick glance into the applications of artificial intelligence in medical tourism. *AI & Society, 40*(5), 4011–4027. DOI: 10.1007/s00146-024-02178-6

Roppelt, J., Kanbach, D., & Kraus, S. (2023). Artificial intelligence in healthcare institutions: A systematic literature review on influencing factors. *Technology in Society*, *75*, 102443. Advance online publication. DOI: 10.1016/j.techsoc.2023.102443

Rossi, G., Feldberg, B., Krois, J., & Schwendicke, F. (2021). Evaluation of the clinical, technical, and financial aspects of cost-effectiveness analysis of artificial intelligence in medicine: Scoping review and framework of analysis. *JMIR Medical Informatics*, *10*(5), e33703. Advance online publication. DOI: 10.2196/33703

Rudd, J., & Igbrude, C. (2023). A global perspective on data powering responsible AI solutions in health applications. *AI and Ethics*. Advance online publication. DOI: 10.1007/s43681-023-00302-8

Sachdeva, C., & Jain, P. (2025). AI-driven innovations in healthcare administration: Streamlining processes for improved operational efficiency. *International Journal of Multidisciplinary Research*, *7*(3), 37788. Advance online publication. DOI: 10.36948/ijfmr.2025.v07i03.37788

Schwalbe, N., & Wahl, B. (2020). Artificial intelligence and the future of global health. *Lancet*, *395*(10236), 1579–1586. DOI: 10.1016/S0140-6736(20)30226-9

Secinaro, S., Calandra, D., Secinaro, A., Muthurangu, V., & Biancone, P. (2021). The role of artificial intelligence in healthcare: A structured literature review. *BMC Medical Informatics and Decision Making*, *21*(1), 125. Advance online publication. DOI: 10.1186/s12911-021-01488-9

Shaik, N. (2025). Artificial intelligence in healthcare economics: Transforming cost efficiency, member experience, and preventative care. *European Journal of Computer Science and Information Technology*, *13*(9), 104–114. DOI: 10.37745/ejcsit.2013/vol13n9104114

Shang, Z., Chauhan, V., Devi, K., & Patil, S. (2024). Artificial intelligence, the digital surgeon: Unravelling its emerging footprint in healthcare – The narrative review. *Journal of Multidisciplinary Healthcare*, *17*, 4011–4022. DOI: 10.2147/JMDH.S482757

Sharma, S., Chauhan, Y., & Tyagi, R. (2023). Artificial intelligence based applications in medical tourism. In 2023 14th International Conference on Computing Communication and Networking Technologies (ICCCNT) (pp. 1–6). IEEE. DOI: 10.1109/ICCCNT56998.2023.10308020

Silcox, C., Zimlichmann, E., Huber, K., Rowen, N., Saunders, R., McClellan, M., Kahn, C.III, Salzberg, C., & Bates, D. (2024). The potential for artificial intelligence to transform healthcare: Perspectives from international health leaders. *NPJ Digital Medicine*, *7*(1), 97. Advance online publication. DOI: 10.1038/s41746-024-01097-6

Tarasenko, E. (2025). Technological transformation of medical tourism in Russia as an important segment of the service sector economy. *AlterEconomics*, *22*(2), 320–339. Advance online publication. DOI: 10.31063/AlterEconomics/2025.22-2.8

Tokareva, O. (2025). Conceptual model for assessing the economic efficiency of AI solutions in healthcare. *Economics and Management*, *6*(6), 804–815. DOI: 10.35854/1998-1627-2025-6-804-815

Tornimbene, B., Rioja, Z. B. L., Brownstein, J., Dunn, A., Faye, S., Kong, J., Malou, N., Nordon, C., Rader, B., & Morgan, O. (2025). Harnessing the power of artificial intelligence for disease-surveillance purposes. *BMC Proceedings*, *19*(S4, Suppl 3), 20. Advance online publication. DOI: 10.1186/s12919-025-00320-w

Ullagaddi, P. (2025). Cross-regional analysis of global AI healthcare regulation. *Journal of Computer and Communications*, *13*(5), 35–52. DOI: 10.4236/jcc.2025.135005

Varnosfaderani, S. M., & Forouzanfar, M. (2024). The role of AI in hospitals and clinics: Transforming healthcare in the 21st century. *Bioengineering (Basel, Switzerland)*, *11*(4), 337. Advance online publication. DOI: 10.3390/bioengineering11040337

Victor, A. (2025). Artificial intelligence in global health: An unfair future for health in Sub-Saharan Africa? *Health Affairs Scholar*, *3*(3), qxaf023. Advance online publication. DOI: 10.1093/haschl/qxaf023

Vithlani, J., Hawksworth, C., Elvidge, J., Ayiku, L., & Dawoud, D. (2023). Economic evaluations of artificial intelligence-based healthcare interventions: A systematic literature review of best practices in their conduct and reporting. *Frontiers in Pharmacology*, *14*, 1220950. Advance online publication. DOI: 10.3389/fphar.2023.1220950

Voets, M., Veltman, J., Slump, C., Siesling, S., & Koffijberg, H. (2021). Systematic review of health economic evaluations focused on artificial intelligence in healthcare: The tortoise and the cheetah. *Value in Health : The Journal of the International Society for Pharmacoeconomics and Outcomes Research*, *25*(3), 340–349. DOI: 10.1016/j.jval.2021.11.1362

Wahl, B., Cossy-Gantner, A., Germann, S., & Schwalbe, N. (2018). Artificial intelligence (AI) and global health: How can AI contribute to health in resource-poor settings? *BMJ Global Health*, *3*(4), e000798. Advance online publication. DOI: 10.1136/bmjgh-2018-000798

Wolff, J., Pauling, J., Keck, A., & Baumbach, J. (2020). The economic impact of artificial intelligence in health care: Systematic review. *Journal of Medical Internet Research, 22*(2), e16866. Advance online publication. DOI: 10.2196/16866

Yun, T., & Zhang, L. (2025). International partnerships in AI-driven healthcare: Opportunities and challenges for advancing the UN sustainable development goals—A perspective. *Healthcare (Basel), 13*(16), 2053. Advance online publication. DOI: 10.3390/healthcare13162053

Zhang, J., Xiang, S., & Li, L. (2025). Economic implications of artificial intelligence-driven recommended systems in healthcare: A focus on neurological disorders. *Frontiers in Public Health, 13*, 1588270. Advance online publication. DOI: 10.3389/fpubh.2025.1588270

Zuhair, V., Babar, A., Ali, R., Oduoye, M., Noor, Z., Chris, K., Okon, I., & Rehman, L. U. (2024). Exploring the impact of artificial intelligence on global health and enhancing healthcare in developing nations. *Journal of Primary Care & Community Health, 15*, 21501319241245847. Advance online publication. DOI: 10.1177/21501319241245847

ADDITIONAL READINGS

Challoumis, C., Eriotis, N., & Dimitrios, V. (2025a). The Role of Pressure Groups in Greek Economic Structure. *WORLD (Oakland, Calif.), 6*(4), 150. https://doi.org/https://doi.org/10.3390/world6040150. DOI: 10.3390/world6040150

Challoumis, C., Eriotis, N., & Vasiliou, D. (2025b). Social Movements' Impact on the Greek Economy During the Financial Crisis. *Economies (Basel), 13*(9), 269. https://doi.org/https://doi.org/10.3390/economies13090269. DOI: 10.3390/economies13090269

Challoumis, C., Eriotis, N., & Vasiliou, D. 2026. HISTORICAL ASPECTS OF THE ECONOMIC FOUNDATIONS OF CONTEMPORARY ENVIRONMENTAL LAW. Veredas Do Direito 23, 1–35. https://doi.org/https://doi.org/10.18623/rvd.v23.n1.4143

Kreft, S. F., & Sobel, R. S. (2005). Public policy, entrepreneurship, and economic freedom. *The Cato Journal.*

Scholvin, S., & Malamud, A. 2020. Is Brazil a Geoeconomic Node? Geography, Public Policy, and the Failure of Economic Integration in South America. Brazilian Polit. Sci. Rev. 14. https://doi.org/DOI: 10.1590/1981-3821202000020004

Suslov, V. I., & Basareva, V. G. (2020). ECONOMIC DEVELOPMENT AND PUBLIC POLICY: SCANDINAVIA AND SIBERIA. *Interexpo GEO-Siberia, 3*(1), 209–218. Advance online publication. DOI: 10.33764/2618-981X-2020-3-1-209-218

Swanstrom, T., Dreier, P., & Mollenkopf, J. (2002). Economic Inequality and Public Policy: The Power of Place. *City & Community, 1*(4), 349–372. Advance online publication. DOI: 10.1111/1540-6040.00030

The East Asian miracle: economic growth and public policy, 1994. . Choice Rev. Online 32. DOI: 10.5860/CHOICE.32-1052

Tzovas, C. (2007). Some economic determinants of the depreciation policy decisions of firms operating in Greece. *Glob. Bus. Econ. Rev., 9*(4), 418–428. DOI: 10.1504/GBER.2007.015103

Ud Din, M., Mangla, I. U., & Jamil, M. (2016). Public Policy, Innovation and Economic Growth: An Economic and Technological Perspective on Pakistan's Telecom Industry. *LAHORE J. Econ., 21*(Special Edition), 369–391. Advance online publication. DOI: 10.35536/lje.2016.v21.isp.a16

KEY TERMS AND DEFINITIONS

AI-Enabled Medical Tourism: A subset of medical tourism in which artificial intelligence technologies are integrated into clinical, administrative, or marketing processes to enhance patient experience, improve outcomes, and optimize cross-border healthcare delivery.

Algorithmic Bias: Systematic errors in AI systems arising from biased data or model design, which may lead to unequal treatment, misdiagnosis, or exclusion of certain patient groups in medical tourism decision-making and care pathways.

Artificial Intelligence (AI): The use of computational systems capable of performing tasks that typically require human intelligence—such as learning, reasoning, pattern recognition, and decision-making—applied in healthcare to support diagnosis, treatment planning, patient management, and operational efficiency.

Cross-Border Healthcare Regulation: The set of national and international legal rules governing the provision of healthcare services across borders, including licensing, liability, reimbursement, and patient rights in AI-supported medical tourism.

Data Governance: The legal, technical, and organizational frameworks that regulate how health data are collected, processed, shared, and protected, particularly in cross-border contexts involving sensitive personal and medical information.

Digital Health Platforms: Online or cloud-based systems that integrate AI tools to facilitate patient information exchange, remote consultations, appointment coordination, pricing transparency, and post-treatment follow-up in medical tourism markets.

Economic Spillovers: Indirect economic effects generated by AI-driven medical tourism, such as job creation, technology transfer, infrastructure development, and impacts on related sectors like hospitality, insurance, and transportation.

Efficiency in Healthcare: The degree to which healthcare resources—such as labor, capital, technology, and time—are utilized to achieve the maximum possible health outcomes at the lowest feasible cost, particularly through automation and data-driven decision-making.

Global Health Sustainability: A broader concept referring to the long-term ability of global health systems to deliver equitable, safe, and efficient healthcare across countries, supported by responsible technology use, cross-border cooperation, and ethical governance.

Health Equity: The principle that all individuals should have fair and just access to healthcare services and outcomes, regardless of nationality, income, or social status, and that AI adoption should not exacerbate existing inequalities.

Health System Sustainability: The capacity of a healthcare system to maintain quality, accessibility, and financial viability over time, while balancing domestic healthcare needs with the demands of international patients and technological innovation.

Medical Tourism: The practice of individuals traveling across national borders to obtain medical, surgical, or wellness services, motivated by factors such as cost differentials, quality of care, availability of advanced treatments, or reduced waiting times.

Value Creation: The process by which AI adoption generates economic, clinical, and experiential benefits for stakeholders, including improved patient outcomes, cost savings, service personalization, and enhanced competitiveness of healthcare providers and destinations.

Chapter 2
The Economics of AI:
Medical Tourism Within Sustainability Transformation

Constantinos Challoumis
http://orcid.org/0000-0002-7436-0506
National and Kapodistrian University of Athens, Greece & Philips University, Cyprus

ABSTRACT

This chapter examines the role of artificial intelligence in transforming the medical tourism sector within the broader context of sustainability and digital healthcare innovation. The purpose of this chapter is to analyze how AI-driven technologies contribute to improving operational efficiency, enhancing patient accessibility, and supporting sustainable healthcare service delivery in international medical travel. The chapter explores the integration of technologies such as telemedicine systems and AI-based logistics optimization in healthcare infrastructures that serve global patients. Through a conceptual analytical framework and visualization tools, including heatmap analysis, this chapter evaluates the multidimensional relationships between technological innovation and key performance dimensions of medical tourism systems. The findings suggest that artificial intelligence can significantly enhance economic performance and expand access to healthcare services while simultaneously supporting sustainability objectives through improved resource management and efficiency.

1. INTRODUCTION

An overarching aim is to examine how the economics of AI enhancement in the Medical Tourism (MT) sector interacts with the goal of sustainable development.

DOI: 10.4018/979-8-3373-8944-8.ch002

The analysis centers on three trade-offs of AI-enhanced MT, connecting supply-side economic factors, patient access to MT services, and the sustainability of AI-enhanced Medical Tourism Services. The analysis seeks to answer the following research questions: 1. To what extent can the capital and operating cost savings of diffusing AI services in MT alleviate economic pressure? 2. Will the price elasticity of demand for MT services enable increased patient flows without increasing carbon emissions? 3. What role does quality assurance play in the supply-side functioning of the AI-enhanced MT economy? These questions aim to establish the presence or absence of core theoretical links between AI-enhanced medical tourism development and the determinants of sustainable development on economic, environmental, and social grounds.AI-Enhanced Medical Tourism as a Key Term refers to the intersection of digital healthcare technologies supported by Artificial Intelligence (AI) and the provision of tourism as a services product(Alnasser, 2023; Aykın et al., 2023; Goktas & Grzybowski, 2025; Gou et al., 2024; Hassan & Bellos, 2022; Hendrix et al., 2022; Shang et al., 2024; Sharma et al., 2023; Vithlani et al., 2023; Jing Zhang et al., 2025; Zuhair et al., 2024). The concept of AI-Enhanced Medical Tourism converges with the definition of Medical Tourism—"the sector of the tourism industry, in which individuals travel across international borders for the purpose of medical care; where the care is already planned and organized, and the main purpose of the trip is to obtain medical care" and increases the breadth of Medical Tourism with the business expansion of digital services in healthcare. The AI-enhanced delivery of care services supports patients by reducing waiting times, optimizing treatment/operation/surgery procedures, and ensuring a speedy postoperative path. The drivers of AI-enhanced Medical Tourism and the synergy between AI-enhanced Medical Tourism and sustainability transformation rest on the interconnected concepts of Economic Growth, Quality of Life, and Environmental Sustainability(Arab & Moosa, 2025; Basirat et al., 2025; Ciecierski-Holmes et al., 2022; Esmaeilzadeh, 2024; Hossain et al., 2025; Jiao et al., 2023; Jorshary et al., 2025; Khanna et al., 2022; Krishnan et al., 2023; Rady, 2024; Reddy, 2024; Reshadi & Chehragh, 2025; Rodić et al., 2025; Rossi et al., 2022; Tarasenko, 2025; Voets et al., 2022; Wolff et al., 2020).The chapter is more focused on an academic audience, as well as on policymakers, consisting of scholars, students, and stakeholders in the healthcare and tourism industries. Although the discussion can be helpful for practitioners such as managers in hospitals, providers of tourism services, and other relevant parties, the discussion continues to be mainly conceptual and theoretical without much practical advice. In order to make it easier for other audiences to understand what the discussion is all about, some clarity and organization should be introduced into it.

2. BACKGROUND

2.1 Theoretical Foundations: AI, Medical Tourism, and Sustainability

The background for this chapter is designed to establish a clear conceptual basis for discussing the interrelationship between artificial intelligence (AI), medical tourism, and sustainable transformation. The applications of AI in the healthcare sector can be mainly traced back to gains in efficiency, decision support systems, telemedicine, and optimal use of clinical and logistic processes. In contrast, medical tourism is mainly motivated by disparities between countries regarding cost, quality, and availability of health services. Finally, sustainable transformation adds yet another perspective by considering ecological footprint, resource utilization, and balanced access to medical treatment.In relation to literature in the field of AI application in healthcare, there has been an emphasis on the potential of AI technology to bring about savings in operational expenditure, an increase in diagnostic accuracy, and ultimately better patient outcomes due to data-based decisions and processes. On the other hand, research in the field of economic effects of medical tourism focuses on aspects like pricing, quality assurance, and cost of travel as major factors influencing medical tourism. It has been observed that demand for medical tourism is highly elastic with respect to price. Even though these areas of investigation are highly developed individually, they are usually considered separately, thus hindering the process of analyzing the cumulative influence of these strands. In the context of the thematic review of the scholarly work on the issue under discussion, three distinct themes of analysis become apparent. Thus, first of all, increased efficiency due to the utilization of artificial intelligence in the sphere may contribute to reduced costs and improved performance of health care services, resulting in better competitiveness among foreign medical systems. Secondly, the economic factors behind medical tourism include the issues of price elasticity, income effects, and the quality of health care available in different countries. Thirdly, the sustainability-related concerns pertain to the relationship between mobility, the environment, and access to services.

The present chapter aims to fill this gap by proposing a coherent analytical framework that will tie the use of AI technologies to cost structures, demand dynamics, and the potential outcomes in terms of sustainability. In this respect, it explores the possible effect that the cost savings generated by the use of AI technologies might have on the elasticity of prices and, subsequently, on cross-border patient traffic in relation to sustainable goals in environmental and social terms. Through the combination of all three dimensions mentioned above, this chapter intends to contribute to the broader understanding of the economic impact of AI within global healthcare sectors. The literature review included in this chapter consists of theoretical, empirical, and normative scholarly papers that relate to the topic of interest. Specifically, the chosen articles combine recent peer-reviewed studies together with foundational papers that set out key definitions and approaches used in this area. Instead of referring to the relevant sources cumulatively, they are used to build further arguments in the chapter.This strategy improves the clarity of the analysis and helps to ensure that the literature review has a direct bearing on the research questions and structure of the analysis. With a tighter focus and clearer structure, the literature review sets a stronger analytical framework for the study. Through the elimination of redundancy, clarification of distinctions, and focusing on synthesis rather than listing, the chapter takes on greater relevance in the scholarly literature. (Albahri et al., 2023; Bang-Ning et al., 2025; Das, 2024; Feng et al., 2022; Işık et al., 2025; Karadayi-Usta, 2024; Richie, 2022; Siddik et al., 2025; Tripathi & Shalki, 2023; Ueda et al., 2024; S. Wang & Zhang, 2024; Jie Zhang & Zhang, 2023).

2.1. AI-Driven Efficiency in Healthcare Services

AI enhances healthcare services through decision-support algorithms, telemedicine, logistics optimization, and automated clinical pathways. It boosts productivity and quality by minimizing costs and delays while maximizing available staff. However, productivity gains may be offset by higher service quality expectations. Algorithmic decision-support systems, such as IBM Watson, enable the processing of vast medical databases(López-Naranjo et al., 2025). These facilitate diagnosis, prognosis, and treatment within specialist areas, with potential for more precise treatment selection and prognosis in equally resourced regions. Increased precision in travel decisions responds to patients' lower willingness to pay for expected-quality deviations and amplifies the impact of travel-time differences. At an aggregated level, cross-border patient flows are expected to respond to cost differences. Higher-quality care, particularly via better surgical impetus and postoperative follow-up, permits greater reliance on local services at reduced quality.Telemedicine enhances the adoption of elective procedures by lowering adjunct care travel time and cost. The treatment chain can also be expedited by AI-driven optimization of logistical flows and scheduling of care by offering pre-emptive surgery through clinical pathways. The overall impact of improvements in quality and availability, together with more competitive pricing, must ultimately be performance- and specialty-specific, as in other areas of production(Alharbi et al., 2025; Andrianto et al., 2025; Koçak et al., 2025; Kupi, 2025; Lundström & Lindvall, 2023; Mahmood et al., 2024; Majid et al., 2023; Moyano-Fernández et al., 2024; Overgaard et al., 2023; Quinn et al., 2021; Ranjbar et al., 2024; Siyao, 2024).

2.2 Medical Tourism as an Economic Phenomenon

Medical Tourism is a market-driven wave of cross-border healthcare that relies on comparative cost advantages and pricing factors to access necessary care. A number of determinants combine to shape such decisions, with quality, ease of access, and acceptable risk levels featured prominently. The supply chain involved has certain characteristics. First, services to non-residents represent only a portion of an area's total healthcare offering, and as such may be relatively limited in geographical breadth or sophistication. Second, capacity is subject to borders, and transport costs are real, though these are not always significant. Third, patient cross-border flows are usually one-way, though a departure from home base may be for one procedure and return immediately afterwards, or those residents abroad may visit the origin jurisdiction for minor procedures or follow-up care. Such flows complement, and do not replace, domestic healthcare provisioning.Efficiency-based cost structures determine comparative advantage, and cost covers capital expenditure, staff salaries and support, materials, etc., and therefore only those destinations with lower quality-adjusted costs can attract non-residents(BADULESCU & BADULESCU, 2014; Daykhes et al., 2020; Madappa, 2015; Sultana et al., 2014; R. Wang & Geng, 2024). A shift in exchange rates will naturally affect the relative costs of these services, whilst a change in any factor affecting the cost of production for tourists care is likely to change tourist flows. Price elasticity considerations – together with the composition of demand driven by income, cost of travel, and care requirements – affect potential demand and, hence, destinations' capacity to respond. The quality of care available has an undeniable bearing upon the volume of tourists seeking health services, and although medical tourism is usually considered low risk, it may nonetheless be subject to mortality or Moroccan risk.(Arab et al., 2025; Balsalobre-Lorente et al., 2023; Bhushan & Misra, 2025; Bosmans et al., 2021; Claessens et al., 2022; Crigger et al., 2022; Erdős et al., 2025; Erwin & Paputungan, 2025; Nasarian et al., 2024; Roski et al., 2021; Strika et al., 2024; Wang et al., 2024).

2.3 Sustainability Transformation in Healthcare and Tourism

Sustainability transformation refers to a multi-dimensional process towards improved environmental quality, reduced resource use, and enhanced equity, inclusiveness, and well-being. In the healthcare and tourism industries, this necessitates decarbonization, reduction of pollution, and technology upgradation, combined with widening access to healthcare services and development of local resources. Modalities range from public and private supply-side development assistance, user and tourism taxes, and multilateral development bank support to regulations controlling trade in cross-border labour services.Economic theory stimulates consumer interest both in the sustainability of these sectors and in the budgetary implications of travel decisions. As governments and multilateral institutions respond to sustainability concerns, travel expenditure becomes a more salient component of overall consumption, with the demand for foreign travel and non-resident expenditure highly sensitive to relative prices and tourism authorities encouraging security, quality, and sustainability in tourism travel. Information technology, along with evolving telepresence technology, has prompted the growth of hospitality and destination economics and has introduced new possibilities for virtual travel that complement and compete with real travel(Bartels et al., 2022; Chang, 2025; Cristian & Tileagă, 2024; Dang et al., 2020; Elkhwesky et al., 2022; García-Gómez et al., 2025; Gaur et al., 2023; Gordon et al., 2024; M. Li et al., 2021; Mercolli et al., 2024; Nishant et al., 2020; Schuitmaker et al., 2025; Song & Chen, 2025; Vishwakarma et al., 2023).

2.4 Market Dynamics and Economic Impacts

Demand-side processes have a deterministic role in influencing the economic feasibility of AI adoption in medical tourism—the attractiveness of this investment to suppliers—because health capital costs are a small share of total costs. The capital requirement is thus driven primarily by support functions requiring high capital outlays, such as telepresence for triaging and routine follow-up; scheduling of transfusions, bed allocation, and ward nursing; lifecycle demand forecasting; and supporting supply chain activities. Hence, combined demand-side and cost-benefit aspects need to be assessed to define the attractiveness of introducing AI in medical tourism. Cross-border services can also be viewed as a separate export market offering both price-elastic demand and service-exchange-rate effects that influence the relative prices of care in receiving countries.The travel-demand equations will allow quantification of these effects: shifts in the demand curve, their degree of price sensitivity, and their implications for economic accessibility. The economic dimension needs to be explored in its entirety: functional price sensitivity of participating countries, travel behavior, and their ability to compensate for potential price changes. Are these prices sensitive in the logical direction? How far do they move following a price-elastic demand shift? What overall differences in price-elasticity behavior can be assessed? A detailed investigation is warranted on ownership and quality aspects of the country-specific service-quality package. For example, is medical tourism a government-supported activity? Quality controls from the demand side (patient safety, experience, satisfaction) can be outlined, as can accreditation and verification systems. Data sources will include government agencies, specialized consulting companies, and international organizations, with supply aspects (for example, verification) sourced mainly from inputs by specialized multinationals(Aquino et al., 2022; Damoah et al., 2021; De Micco et al., 2025; Doo et al., 2024; Ghasemi et al., 2021; Louati et al., 2024; Shin et al., 2025; Yogeshappa et al., 2024).

2.5 Cost-Benefit Analyses of AI Adoption in Medical Tourism

Cost-benefit analyses of AI adoption in medical tourism services quantify implications for capital and operating costs, cost avoidance, and welfare. Implementation requires capital investment, including initial hardware and algorithm development, plus ongoing infrastructure and personnel costs. Operating costs include training set assembly, data preparation for classification and control, and routine verification of decisions, particularly for sensitive telepresence services. A well-structured training set facilitates algorithmic learning for subsequent operations.Algorithmic decision-support services are assumed to be 10 per cent more productive and cost 10 per cent less than human equivalents, with telemedicine and telepresence offering additional cost savings. Use of AI for scheduling, logistics, and clinical-pathway coordination is estimated to reduce overall costs by 4 per cent. Given the volume of medical tourism, the precautionary principle suggests that total operating savings of 1–2 per cent should be a target for successful AI integration. Based on estimated capital investment in AI technology across the medical industry, the implied annualized operating cost for algorithmic decision support amounts to US$274 billion for the medical travel sector. If successful, these services could yield present-value savings of US$87 billion.Cost savings, resulting in an effective decline in service price, alter travel decisions through a reduced-price elasticity of demand. With medical tourism services having lower income elasticity than other travel services, shifts toward cheaper source locations also affect travel time(Dávid & Dadkhah, 2023; Fiske et al., 2025; Das, 2022; Khinvasara et al., 2024; Y.-H. Li et al., 2024; Ramteke et al., 2024; Richie et al., 2025; Thapliyal et al., 2025; Von Gerich et al., 2025; Zhang et al., 2024).

2.6 Demand Shifts, Price Elasticity, and Access

Based on the estimated cost-benefit analyses of using generative AI for service provision as well as for capital-intensive operations with limited labor inputs, demand for cross-border healthcare services can be expected to increase, ceteris paribus. The price elasticity of demand for medical tourism is around −1.2 (in absolute value). This means that a 5% increase in price would reduce demand for healthcare services abroad by about 6%, inducing a 5% decrease in travel by foreign patients seeking healthcare services. Such differentials affect all other travelers adversely as well, given the substitution in demand between travel and accommodation by foreign patients and all other travelers.The demand sensitivity to price changes also raises equity concerns. A high price elasticity implies that a large share of demand comes from individuals and households for whom travel represents a discretionary expenditure. As price minimizes travel for healthcare services abroad, a higher price level affects travel for non-health-related reasons less; this hinders access for lower-income groups and regions that depend on these patients for health-related tourism(BADULESCU & BADULESCU, 2014; Daykhes et al., 2020; Madappa, 2015; Sultana et al., 2014; R. Wang & Geng, 2024). In other words, too sharp an increase in prices for cross-border health care could leave low- and middle-income populations with fewer options for accessing health services.(Beladi et al., 2017; Foley et al., 2019; Hua et al., 2023; Onyango, 2025; Quttainah et al., 2025; Sezgin, 2023; Shehzad et al., 2024; Stogiannos et al., 2023; Van Wynsberghe, 2021; Wang et al., 2024).

2.7 Supply-Side Considerations: Quality, Accreditation, and Oversight

The credibility of medical-surgical services and reassurance about the correctness of complicated healthcare decisions are necessary for patients in all countries, even more if they cross a border to seek care. Consequently, the absence of proper oversight or randomly obtained information could damage the supply of AI-informed healthcare in Medical Tourism. Patients must trust that providers meet a minimum standard.Setting standards for quality and safety in cross-border healthcare has proven to be crucial for stimulating demand. Internationally recognized accreditation enhances the quality profile of service providers, especially for countries that are less well known among buyers. Moreover, the risky characterization of Medical Tourism means that regulation must encompass not only quality but also subtle factors that affect AI use and consequent health outcomes. These include the security of the medical infrastructure – data and facilities – necessary to implement new technologies safely, the recognition of the hospital by the foreign patient (through an international accreditation), the level of protection involving the loss of data, and the possibility that a second surgery might be needed, with consequences for the value chain. Information regarding any of these elements must be conveyed to stakeholders – such as tariffs associated with data loss – to maintain the consistency of services.Hence, oversight must guarantee not only standard adherence but also fraud prevention. Risk strategies – determining what could go wrong in a care pathway or in a specific operation, quantifying its impact and probability – could minimize financial losses.

3. ANALYSIS

Furthermore, the extent of the research could be made even stronger by adding some other aspects that may not be developed fully enough at the moment. For example, the chapter should make its methodological framework clearer, especially when considering all the connections between such variables as cost savings, demand, and sustainability. Although there is a discussion on some of the connections mentioned, there are no explanations regarding how these connections were established and especially those that have been depicted using the heatmap.Additionally, some important aspects of international health care still need further investigation. They concern the results of treatment, continuity after treatment, and the dangers of fragmented health care across national boundaries. More attention must be paid to the institutional and legal frameworks of each state because they determine how possible and safe it is to use artificial intelligence in international health care. This will allow the chapter to assess implementation difficulties. In terms of economics, there should be more research about business models and their costs.Although cost-benefit analyses have been made, more in-depth analyses on investment requirements, the return on investment, and feasibility in general for different healthcare systems are needed to make a better case. The different roles played by various stakeholders like hospitals, insurance companies, regulatory agencies, and the patients themselves should also be better defined, as each one will have their own incentives and constraints within the system. Finally, the issue of equity must be developed further. Medical tourism involving advanced artificial intelligence could widen the gap between those who are rich and educated and can afford to benefit from it and those left behind in the destination countries, with some of the resources possibly being redirected away from locals. Environmental concerns must also be elaborated in terms of the full environmental impact of increased emissions related to air travel, electricity use by digital facilities, supply chain considerations, and possible rebound effects.

3.1 Policy and Regulatory Frameworks

Expected research findings will clarify healthcare governance requirements for AI-enhanced medical tourism. Analysis of cross-border care regulations will identify areas for harmonization, concession, and patient rights protection. Examination of data governance will specify necessary standards for effective AI safety without stifling innovation. Finally, appraisal of incentive frameworks will yield pointers for driving transformation along sustainable lines.Cross-Border Healthcare Regulations: Efficacious harmonization of healthcare regulations across market jurisdictions, facilitating cross-border care, remains a major policy challenge. In regulated markets, safeguards ensure that medical procedures for local residents meet sufficient quality and safety standards. For the medical tourism trade to function safely and effectively, harmonized scrutiny, oversight, and post-operative care through a widely accepted regulatory framework appears desirable. An examination of the central requirements in such a proposal for market participants ought to include: licensing and accreditation of service providers; patient and consumer rights; insurance, liability, and recourse for malpractice; follow-up care; and surveillance for quality, safety, and efficacy.Data Governance, Privacy, and AI Safety: The immense computing power of AI presents considerable opportunities and risks. Databases, while allowing machine learning to yield superior pregnancy or survival outcome metrics compared to systems without such learning, should also enable ever-increasing AI algorithms with improved functionality. Also, greater convergence in AI capabilities could be considered a double-edged sword as it partners with single AI developers. Therefore, while use-training, input-output, and development partnerships ought to be encouraged, at the same time, appropriate data standards covering privacy, consent, security, and accountability throughout the AI ecosystem demand formulation. These would serve the vital purpose of minimizing the probability of disastrous harm or damage during the AI development cycle while ensuring maximum advancement velocity.Incentives for Sustainable Investment: available evidence suggests the possibility of comparatively lower-cost, climate-neutral care pathways, if not actual pathways, adopting a significantly reduced carbon footprint. In principle, economy-wide price, subsidy, disincentive, regulatory, and procurement instruments can help steer investment in desired decarbonization directions(Challoumis, 2025a; Challoumis et al., 2025). Therefore, it is useful to assess these from a healthcare perspective and prescription. Sustainable investment subsidies or fiscal incentives could be explored for health-related investment in strategically-priority sectors; carbon-emission taxes for harmful sectors like fossil fuels; and a public-private partnership model for climate-risk and infrastructure-heavy development, such as green hydrogen production(Jacob, 2024).

3.2 Cross-Border Healthcare Regulations

While AI has the potential to improve accessibility to healthcare services, appropriate regulation is necessary to ensure safe and reliable services. The primary issues include the legal status of foreign patients, the qualification of institutions and medical professionals, and the assurance of patients' right to make informed decisions. A supportive regulatory environment can also enhance participation and ensure that cross-border tariffs reflect cost-based supply.Incentives for Sustainable Investment. The promotion of AI-enhanced cross-border healthcare can enable a shift of demand from regions with high-carbon energy to regions with clean energy. Such adjustment should be facilitated by harmonizing sustainability standards, data governance for cloud computing, and investment promotion. Without appropriate encouragement, private markets are unlikely to deliver a socially optimal volume of sustainable investment. Pricing policy should thus encourage investments that are consistent with climate and environmental goals. Green public procurement, lending and subsidy policies, and the regulation of development banks can support investment for sustainability without compromising equity or development. Public finance can additionally help by mobilizing private funds into sustainable, contributing to a green financial system(Al-Talabani et al., 2019; Alshamsi, 2024; Charow et al., 2021; Fan et al., 2023; Figueiredo et al., 2024; García-Madurga & Grilló-Méndez, 2023; Terranova et al., 2024; Turner, 2011; C.-J. Wu et al., 2021).

3.3 Data Governance, Privacy, and AI Safety

Validation, verification, and safety of AI technologies typically fall outside the standard business responsibility frameworks. Evolving technologies bring new privacy, security, and safety risks that must be understood and addressed through expanded governance and the development of norms for accountable and responsible use. Given the massive explosion of medical information and the intense focus on patient-centered alternatives, AI technologies will likely require legal, privacy, and oversight controls that establish public trust while enabling algorithmic performance. Adapting laws governing the collection, storage, sharing, and selling of sensitive personal information will be critical for preventing reckless decision-making from harming sensitive personal data. Allocating resources for carefully calibrated federal support and technical partnerships to strengthen cybersecurity and ensure data privacy is essential for enabling data flows while safeguarding patient interests. Businesses involved in medical tourism, particularly those marketing abroad, need to comply with all aspects of data privacy laws in both jurisdictions. Conversely, patients must understand their rights with respect to data privacy, so they can navigate potential pitfalls when obtaining cross-border care.Data governance must not only safeguard the privacy of personal information but also provide standards for individual accountability and corporate responsibility in the development and application of AI. Data use involves serious ethical considerations for informing decisions that exploit sensitive personal information, necessitating the incorporation of individual privacy preferences into all aspects of data handling. Public trust in the privacy of shared data depends on establishing transparency around the policies and practices of all players in the data ecosystem. A compliance model for certifying adherence to appropriate principles and practices can provide the assurance patients require when sharing sensitive information needed to maximize the value of AI.(Alaflak et al., 2025; Alsahafi et al., 2023; Burki et al., 2024; Khan et al., 2025; Labkoff et al., 2024; Reuben et al., 2024; Samala et al., 2020; Tsekouropoulos et al., 2023).

3.4 Incentives for Sustainable Investment

Governments can catalyze accelerated adoption of AI applications across medical tourism services by creating supporting investment incentives, with expected benefits for developing and emerging economies. These include one-time capital subsidies to offset up-front implementation costs; recurring operating subsidies to compensate for slow user-acquisition rates, followed by gradual net-savings declines; tax measures to incentivize private investment at scale; public procurement rules directing sustained support to suppliers meeting or exceeding sustainability thresholds; and public-private partnerships that harness synergies in technology transfer, talent, or customer acquisition.Sustainable investment incentives are particularly important in medical tourism, where health and tourism authorities from low-cost developing countries are keen to attract AI-enabled medical tourism services. Capturing such opportunities requires close collaboration across the medical and travel sectors in both host and source countries. Investment incentives should thus be sensitively managed to ensure that the benefits of AI adoption accrue to the economies and communities incurring the associated costs(Beckers et al., 2021; Champendal et al., 2025; Chowdhary & Majumdar, 2025; Hryciw et al., 2023; Larson et al., 2025; Suanpang & Pothipassa, 2024).

3.5 Technology Diffusion, Innovation, and Competitiveness

A wide range of airports, hotels, tourist operations, clinics, hospitals, and related enterprises must work as a unit to achieve a goal that is much more challenging than running any one enterprise by itself. Even more challenge lies in making AI work over the entire range of specialties involved in providing cross-border healthcare—surgery (often multiple specialties), anesthesia, radiology, laboratory medicine, pathology, rehabilitation, etc. The complexities of the surgery itself might be manageable except for failures in one or more of the supporting specialties, and the systems for integrating AI with those subspecialties may not succeed more than 5%-10% of the time. Attention to these failure modes will be an important part of tracking technology diffusion in AI-enhanced medical tourism.Achieving AI-enhanced medical tourism demand in regions not already providing it likely requires exposure of medical professionals from those regions to doctors at established medical tourism centers. Such exposure can lead to internships and study visits in both directions. With success going both ways, mutual trust may be so high that patients at the less expensive center will choose to be treated there even for very complex procedures, simply based on price. After initial success with such trade, the addition of second-order travel for patients responding to requests of doctors practicing in the other direction will become a strong logical network. After the

AI-enhanced systems are in place or not too long afterward, the stability of both the region pair and the trade network will benefit from the technical standardization of AI-enhanced medical tourism(Burki et al., 2024; Charow et al., 2021; Figueiredo et al., 2024; García-Madurga & Grilló-Méndez, 2023; Reuben et al., 2024; Terranova et al., 2024; Tsekouropoulos et al., 2023; Turner, 2011).

3.6 AI Applications Across Specialties in Medical Tourism

The healthcare services industry has yet to experience the same kind of transformation-driven economy that other sectors have. Imitation-based learning is limited, and capital, technology, or effort cannot simply be purchased in order to replicate other regional or country successful businesses. Capital necessity is high with long durations between investment and delivery of returns. Risks exist not only because systems are heavily maintained by people but must also remain safe and healthy for other human beings(Challoumis, 2024; Challoumis & Eriotis, 2025). Current costs to users have long relative durations due to higher total costs with lower relative disposable income, especially in developing countries. AI applications could be put in place quickly and at a low level of cost for quality, supporting economic healthcare systems from healthcare services to tourism locally and internationally. Considering these fundamental points, companies starting to utilize AI applications across medical specialties are of high importance for regional economies, travel suppliers, and tourist attractions as they set worldwide trends and are usually the first adopters of innovations. A large number and variety of key leading-edge effects on these companies have profound effects on future medical and healthcare service offerings, supporting real adoption costs, quality, and risks of use. A review of the literature on AI in Healthcare generally is a good introduction to AI use in Medical Tourism. However, such reviews rarely highlight special pathways that have or could influence medical tourism in the near future and have had or can have successful non-destructive failures. This provides a succinct overview of current and future AI cases across specialties that have or might have a direct impact on Medical Tourism(Cristian & Tileagă, 2024; Elkhwesky et al., 2022; García-Gómez et al., 2025; Gaur et al., 2023; Gordon et al., 2024; M. Li et al., 2021; Schuitmaker et al., 2025).

3.7 Workforce Implications and Training

AI-enhanced medical tourism changes skill needs and creates new opportunities for workers. Skills demands shift in patient-facing roles such as triage and telemedicine, and in technical jobs supporting data-handling, diagnostics, and image analysis. An emerging demand for training in AI-assisted working environments requires upskilling and recredentialing.Teleportation might remain a technology for science fiction, but the demand for relocation over long distances is being diminished through AI-assisted remote communication combined with highly developed service organizations. The reduction of travel distance reduces travel time, a crucial factor for medical tourism. This is particularly relevant within areas of greater regional concentration in the provision of specialized medical services, given the higher technology-related service share and relative resistance to local competition(Challoumis, 2025c, 2025b). Based on the AI developments and challenges in medical service delivery, travel-related skills, and the workplace infrastructure related to travel decision-making, economy-related passenger transport as an industry service, and the associated changes in the national and regional economy require particular attention. Some of these developments face a marked dichotomy between the transport benefits and service provision capability, and the overall AI-supported labor relocation capabilities.(Arab et al., 2025; Balsalobre-Lorente et al., 2023; Bhushan & Misra, 2025; Bosmans et al., 2021; Claessens et al., 2022; Crigger et al., 2022; Erwin & Paputungan, 2025; Nasarian et al., 2024; Strika et al., 2024).

3.8 Environmental and Social Dimensions

AI can introduce new patterns of demand for medical service provision across borders. However, greater openness and increased traffic can also raise concerns about environmental costs, inequities in access, and patent-centric care. Addressing these issues is essential to ensure alignment with the principles of sustainability. Proposed indicators evaluate the economic, environmental, and social dimensions of AI-enabled demand in medical tourism, while three categories of analysis focus on the environmental footprint of AI-assisted service delivery, the social dimensions of cross-border care, and questions of patient safety and ethics.The economic literature on AI-enabled demand for cross-border healthcare is limited. Evidence on price responsiveness remains scarce, yet some degree of elasticity is a common assumption in demand models for tourism, external labour, and other services. Price reductions, shifts in real exchange rates, and transport cost changes have also been found to influence the geographical distribution of medical tourism, albeit not always significantly(BADULESCU & BADULESCU, 2014; Daykhes et al., 2020; Madappa, 2015; Sultana et al., 2014; R. Wang & Geng, 2024). With these considerations in mind, the analysis investigates expected changes in demand for cross-border healthcare services from AI adoption, drawing on the factors highlighted by the literature on tourism demand.

3.9 Ethical Considerations and Patient-Centricity

As with other digital services, ethical issues associated with the deployment of AI technologies in healthcare are being voiced. Of particular concern are the potential for AI to infringe upon patient autonomy, engender bias, and render processes opaque. Such issues are not unique to healthcare per se but take on added complexity when considering patient-centered staging across healthcare and tourism and an increasingly cross-border framework. Services enabled through the AI "cultural stack"—the full lifecycle of shaping data to deploying decisions—follow processes that require blending data with reasoning, know-how, and community values(El Arab & Al Moosa, 2025). Releasing AI applications into tourism and healthcare risks disturbing both individual and social values and carries broader considerations regarding the future interaction of service work with automated decision-making. Central to any ethical discussion in healthcare is the principle of consent. Barriers to communication between the patient and the decision-maker can impede genuine consent. Two forms of consent integration, technologically-augmented or technology-driven, can distort the nature of the active dialogue. Failure to meaningfully merge the two is inherent in areas such as radiological assessments that regularly form part of remote-involved procedures. Non-transparent prediction and interpretation processes render testing for bias impossible, yet have consequences that are left entirely with the travelling patient. Public trust hinges on transparency and communicability. The scope of the analysis can be further strengthened by incorporating additional dimensions that are currently underdeveloped. In particular, the chapter would benefit from a clearer articulation of the methodological foundations underpinning the empirical and conceptual claims. While relationships between variables such as cost reduction, demand, and sustainability are presented, the derivation of these relationships—especially those illustrated through the heatmap—requires further clarification. A more explicit explanation of the analytical approach, including how influence levels, cost implications, and sustainability effects are assessed, would enhance the transparency and robustness of the conclusions.Furthermore, there are a number of critical dimensions of international health care that have not been thoroughly addressed. Among these are patient results, post-treatment health care continuity, and potential dangers linked to fragmented treatment chains. Governance and liability issues, along with legal differences among countries involved, need closer attention, since these factors influence greatly the feasibility and safety of AI-enabled medical tourism. Lack of such considerations hinders our evaluation of possible problems in implementing this approach.Finally, when considering the economic aspects, this chapter lacks some insights into business cases for AI-enabled medical tourism and the costs incurred in its development. It is true that economic aspects, including cost-benefit analysis, have been mentioned, but still, a deeper consideration of investment needs, return on investment, and economic feasibility is needed here. Moreover, the involvement and actions of various players, such as hospitals, insurers, and patients, should be distinguished more clearly.Issues related to equity should also be developed further. The increased adoption of medical tourism enabled by AI can lead to inequalities since such a trend will benefit only wealthier and technologically savvy individuals, while it might have adverse impacts on the local population living in countries of destination. Such an approach would result in a more balanced discussion of the problem. Lastly, there is a need to address the issue of the environment by developing a holistic approach that covers the impacts of increased transportation emissions, energy consumption of technology, supply chain management problems, and rebound effects.

3.10 Limitations and Analytical Challenges

The chapter focuses on a timely and relevant issue, but suffers from flaws that undermine its quality and impact. Some of the major arguments about cost savings, elasticity of demand, and sustainability lack a sufficient methodological foundation, while the overall methodology used by the author remains ambiguous. The literature reviewed by the author is quite extensive, yet it does not include a systematic review of findings and tends to cover such concepts as efficiency and trust repeatedly without developing their meaning further. Patient safety, legal responsibility, differences in regulation, equality, and the environmental impact are among the issues that could be considered more carefully.

DISCUSSION

The structure of the chapter is logically organized; nevertheless, its development could be made more effective by making sure the argument becomes cumulative and consistent. There are several cases where background information and analysis overlap in nature, and analysis is more descriptive than explanatory. For this reason, the chapter will be organized according to a process of transition that includes concept, analytical framework, and implications. The focus of this strategy will involve ensuring that each part is well linked to the research questions while at the same time minimizing redundancy. It will thus become easier to develop discussion in a way that shows the role that AI plays in influencing medical tourism and its related impacts.The chapter does a good job of recognizing and addressing numerous issues, challenges, and trends that arise due to the implementation of artificial intelligence technology in medical tourism and the international healthcare system. Such topics as efficiency improvement, cost dynamics, patient mobility across borders, quality assurance, data governance, ethical issues, changes in the workforce, and sustainability are addressed quite adequately, which implies the author's deep awareness of the modern reality. All these issues are strongly relevant to the topic of the book and illustrate the role of the technology in question for healthcare and tourism. Nevertheless, despite the fact that the topics are considered and explained well enough, the relationships between various variables are described mainly in conceptual terms. The links between the use of the technology and cost savings, demand increase, and even the sustainability of the results achieved can hardly be demonstrated empirically, although it is possible to say that they seem to make sense. Moreover, the separation between current reality and future perspectives could be improved.Some of the arguments have been presented in a forward-looking way without making the proper distinction between the present status and the future trends.

The heatmap depicted in Figure 1 shows the relative influence of artificial intelligence applications on key operational and sustainability factors in the medical tourism ecosystem. The visualization, as depicted in the figure, seeks to explore the interaction between various operational factors, such as cost reduction mechanisms, the accessibility of telemedicine, logistics optimization, quality assurance, patient flow, and environmental impact, and the four primary dimensions of the healthcare tourism system, which include economic impact, operational efficiency, patient accessibility, and sustainability(El Arab et al., 2025). The relative influence of the variables, as depicted in the visualization, can be determined by the color intensity of each cell, with the darker the color, the higher the influence. Several key trends are depicted in the visualization. For instance, the influence of cost reduction and logistics optimization, which are AI-based, on the economic impact and operational efficiency of the system appears to be significant.These findings are indicative of the impact of artificial intelligence on improving resource allocation and scheduling processes, as well as reducing administrative and operational costs within healthcare systems serving international patients. At the same time, there is a strong correlation between telemedicine access and patient accessibility, which is indicative of the importance of digital health technologies in improving cross-border healthcare accessibility and communication between patients and healthcare providers before and after receiving treatment. Another interesting dimension is sustainability. The environmental impact factor has shown the strongest correlation with sustainability outcomes, which is indicative of the importance of artificial intelligence-driven optimization technologies in improving resource allocation and reducing waste and environmental impacts within healthcare systems serving medical tourists. This is more important today, as healthcare systems are looking to optimize their operational efficiency and sustainability, and environmental outcomes.The heatmap is a multidimensional representation of how artificial intelligence technologies impact the performance of medical tourism systems. From the visualization of the heatmap, it is evident that artificial intelligence technologies do not impact any of the dimensions of medical tourism in isolation; instead, it impacts all of its dimensions at once. These dimensions include its economic performance, its efficiency in delivering healthcare services, its sustainability, and its accessibility in terms of healthcare services. Therefore, artificial intelligence technologies can be seen as having a systemic impact on the overall transformation of the medical tourism industry.

Figure 1. Heatmap of Artificial Intelligence Applications and Their Impact on Medical Tourism Sustainability Dimensions (author's scheme)

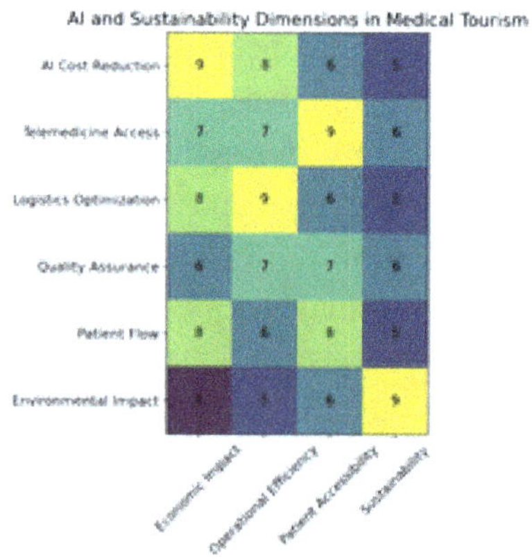

Though this chapter has been able to effectively show the key role of artificial intelligence in terms of improving efficiency, cutting costs, and increasing demand, there is more focus on the advantages of adopting AI rather than the risks and challenges that come with this adoption. These include concerns such as patient safety when it comes to bordering treatment, maintaining consistency with regard to treatments, making sure that AI decisions are accountable, and other such related factors. For a better balanced and robust evaluation, there is a need for more attention to be focused on the high-impact issues that will have direct implications on the feasibility and sustainability of artificial intelligence-enabled medical tourism. Some of these issues include governance models, regulatory oversight, liability considerations, measures for consumer protection, and the difficulties of implementation in various healthcare environments. Moreover, the trade-offs related to sustainability issues need to be further explored to avoid bias in the evaluation.Furthermore, the chapter would gain from an analysis of the unintended effects of telemedicine, including the possibilities of increasing inequality, diverting resources from local communities, and the dependence on technology solutions in the highly complex world of health care. In doing so, the chapter should limit the focus to fewer topics, which would then be analyzed in more depth. This will certainly increase the credibility of the chapter by creating a proper balance between the opportunities and limitations associated with telemedicine.

Evaluation Frameworks and Metrics

Indicators for assessing Economic Performance: productivity gains, cost savings, employment and investment impacts; for Health Outcomes: clinical effectiveness, safety, and experience; for long-term effects on Healthcare Systems: resilience, spare capacity, and aggregate costs.The economic dimension of sustainability encompasses conventional cost-benefit analysis but extends beyond purely monetary benefits to encompass productivity improvements and associated effects on employment. Reduced wait times for patients can be thought of as a welfare-enhancing benefit, albeit with potentially regressive implications: the ability of North-to-South medical tourism patients to travel for care is likely to be highly price-elastic, which means it could be harder for lower-income patients in affluent economies to afford such treatment.The ideal evaluation metrics for this dimension of economic sustainability would consider indicators such as additional productivity for healthcare delivery attributed to the adoption of AI and skills-differentiated quality and price elasticities that make travel for medical care affordable for affluent-country residents. In such a valuation framework, capital and operating costs and savings from adopting the AI-enhanced use case must be calculated. In cases with negative costs, positive welfare impacts would provide motivation for subsidizing their realization (Feng et al., 2022; Işık et al., 2025; Karadayi-Usta, 2024; Koçak et al., 2025; Majid et al., 2023; Moyano-Fernández et al., 2024; Overgaard et al., 2023; Quinn et al., 2021; Ranjbar et al., 2024; Siddik et al., 2025; Siyao, 2024).

3.11 Sustainable Economic Performance Indicators

An integrated sustainability transformation encompassing the economy, the environment, and society examines the trade-offs and synergies that underlie sustainability policies. Economic performance is informed by the theory of medical tourism and its AI-enabled efficiency improvements.AI technology has the potential to streamline process efficiency by reducing internal operating costs, thus lowering the prices of healthcare services and stimulating demand from both local and international patients. Price elasticities of demand from patients in different countries reflect cross-currency comparisons of costs and travel times. These shifts in demand, in turn, affect economic performance indicators, such as productivity growth in AI-enhanced healthcare services(Challoumis, 2023, 2025a).

4. CONCLUSIONS

The prospect of an AI-enhanced medical tourism market presents an opportunity to transform the global healthcare ecosystem. AI adoption to AI-Empowered Medical Tourism has the potential to impact healthcare system costs. Policies can stimulate productivity improvement and governance mechanisms can address technology risks. These elements collectively determine whether a large-scale and equitable global market in cross-border healthcare services can develop. Empirical analysis quantifies capital and operating costs, demand structure, and welfare. Key considerations include sunlight services, quality, and available expertise.

The proposed analysis links market dynamics to macroeconomic effects in settings with abundant AI-optimized Medical Services. Primary and secondary research identifies price elasticity of demand; input structure, capital outlay, and operating cost of AI-enhanced care; and standard economic drivers of travel demand. Cost-benefit evaluation quantifies the effect of AI adoption on healthcare-system productivity. Results reveal the relevance of capital cost, impact on equity, and quality risk in shaping AI adoption decisions in medical tourism.

REFERENCES

Al-Talabani, H., Kilic, H., Ozturen, A., & Qasim, S. O. (2019). Advancing medical tourism in the United Arab Emirates: Toward a sustainable health care system. *Sustainability (Basel), 11*(1), 230. Advance online publication. DOI: 10.3390/su11010230

Alaflak, A., Sharma, N., & Gawshinde, S. (2025). The impact of social media branding and AI on promoting green tourism in emerging economies like Egypt. Journal of Hospitality and Tourism Insights. Advance online publication. https://doi.org/DOI: 10.1108/JHTI-08-2024-0886

Albahri, A. S., Duhaim, A. M., Fadhel, M. A., Alnoor, A., Baqer, N. S., Alzubaidi, L., Albahri, O. S., Alamoodi, A. H., Bai, J., Salhi, A., Santamaría, J., Ouyang, C., Gupta, A., Gu, Y., & Deveci, M. (2023). A systematic review of trustworthy and explainable artificial intelligence in healthcare: Assessment of quality, bias risk, and data fusion. *Information Fusion, 96*, 156–191. DOI: 10.1016/j.inffus.2023.03.008

Alharbi, A., Elshamly, A., Shawky, N., & Mahgoub, I. (2025). Unlocking sustainable performance in SMEs: The interplay of green AI management, pro-environmental behaviour in the tourism and hospitality sector: UK. *Journal of Posthumanism, 5*(4). Advance online publication. DOI: 10.63332/joph.v5i4.1053

Alnasser, B. (2023). The economic impact of artificial intelligence on healthcare: A literature review. *E-Health Telecommunication Systems and Networks, 12*(3), 27–41. DOI: 10.4236/etsn.2023.123003

Alsahafi, R., Alzahrani, A., & Mehmood, R. (2023). Smarter sustainable tourism: Data-driven multi-perspective parameter discovery for autonomous design and operations. *Sustainability (Basel), 15*(5), 4166. Advance online publication. DOI: 10.3390/su15054166

Alshamsi, A. (2024). A review of the United Arab Emirates healthcare systems on medical tourism and accreditation. *Frontiers in Health Services, 4*, 1329252. Advance online publication. DOI: 10.3389/frhs.2024.1329252

Andrianto, T., Tangit, T. M., & Minh, N. C. (2025). Adoption of artificial intelligence (AI) technology in enhancing tourist experience: A conceptual model. Journal of Tourism. *Hospitality and Travel Management, 3*(1), 302. Advance online publication. DOI: 10.58229/jthtm.v3i1.302

Aquino, Y. S. J., Rogers, W., Braunack-Mayer, A., Frazer, H., Win, K., Houssami, N., Degeling, C., Semsarian, C., & Carter, S. (2022). Utopia versus dystopia: Professional perspectives on the impact of healthcare artificial intelligence on clinical roles and skills. *International Journal of Medical Informatics, 169*, 104903. Advance online publication. DOI: 10.1016/j.ijmedinf.2022.104903

Aykın, Ö., Uluhan, F., Gümüş, İ., Çabuk, Ş., Bozbayir, U., Duran, V., Özbay, C., Özbay, B., Gündoğmuş, Ş. E., Şengül, M. T., & Övey, I. (2023). *Artificial intelligence and telemedicine applications in health tourism marketing*. Eurasian Journal of Health Technology Assessment., DOI: 10.52148/ehta.1396111

Badulescu, D., & Badulescu, A. (2014). Medical tourism: Between entrepreneurship opportunities and bioethics boundaries: Narrative review article. *Iranian Journal of Public Health, 43*(4), 406–415. https://www.ncbi.nlm.nih.gov/pmc/articles/PMC4433721/

Balsalobre-Lorente, D., Abbas, J., He, C., Pilař, L., & Shah, S. A. R. (2023). Tourism, urbanization, and natural resources rents matter for environmental sustainability: The leading role of AI and ICT on sustainable development goals in the digital era. *Resources Policy, 82*, 103445. Advance online publication. DOI: 10.1016/j.resourpol.2023.103445

Bang-Ning, H., Jitanugoon, S., & Puntha, P. (2025). AI-powered sustainable tourism: Unlocking circular economies and overcoming resistance to change. *Business Strategy and the Environment, 34*(5), 5781–5802. Advance online publication. DOI: 10.1002/bse.4276

Bartels, R., Dudink, J., Haitjema, S., Oberski, D., & Veen, A. (2022). A perspective on a quality management system for AI/ML-based clinical decision support in hospital care. *Frontiers in Digital Health, 4*, 942588. Advance online publication. DOI: 10.3389/fdgth.2022.942588

Basirat, S., Raoufi, S., Bazmandeh, D., Khamoushi, S., & Entezami, M. (2025). Ranking of AI-based criteria in health tourism using fuzzy SWARA method. *Computer and Decision Making: An International Journal, 2*, 530–545. Advance online publication. DOI: 10.59543/comdem.v2i.13795

Beckers, R., Kwade, Z., Zanca, F., & Medica, P. (2021). The EU medical device regulation: Implications for artificial intelligence-based medical device software in medical physics. *Physica Medica : PM : An International Journal Devoted to the Applications of Physics to Medicine and Biology : Official Journal of the Italian Association of Biomedical Physics (AIFB), 83*, 1–8. DOI: 10.1016/j.ejmp.2021.02.011

Beladi, H., Chao, C.-C., Ee, M. S., & Hollas, D. (2017). Does medical tourism promote economic growth? A cross-country analysis. *Journal of Travel Research, 58*(1), 121–135. DOI: 10.1177/0047287517735909

Bhushan, A., & Misra, P. (2025). Unlocking the potential: Multimodal AI in biotechnology and digital medicine—Economic impact and ethical challenges. *NPJ Digital Medicine, 8*(1), 619. Advance online publication. DOI: 10.1038/s41746-025-01992-6

Bosmans, H., Zanca, F., & Gelaude, F. (2021). Procurement, commissioning, and QA of AI based solutions: An MPE's perspective on introducing AI in clinical practice. *Physica Medica : PM : An International Journal Devoted to the Applications of Physics to Medicine and Biology : Official Journal of the Italian Association of Biomedical Physics (AIFB), 83*, 257–263. DOI: 10.1016/j.ejmp.2021.04.006

Burki, A. K., Mafaz, M. N. A., Ahmad, Z., Zulfaka, A., & Isa, M. Y. B. (2024). Artificial intelligence and environmental sustainability: Insights from PLS-SEM on resource efficiency and carbon emission reduction. OPSearch. *American Journal of Operations Research, 3*(10), 277–288. Advance online publication. DOI: 10.58811/opsearch.v3i10.141

Challoumis, C. (2023). Risk on the tax system of the E.U. from 2016 to 2022. *Economics, 11*(2), 55–72. DOI: 10.2478/eoik-2023-0058

Challoumis, C. (2024). Impact factor of liability using the Sensitivity Method. In Bayrakdar, S., & Chodnicka-Jaworska, P. (Eds.), *Current dynamics in business and economics: Theoretical approaches and empirical discoveries* (pp. 77–86). Peter Lang., DOI: 10.3726/b22541

Challoumis, C. (2025a). Economocracy: Global economic governance. *Economies (Basel), 13*(8), 230. Advance online publication. DOI: 10.3390/economies13080230

Challoumis, C. (2025b). The impact factor of tangibles and intangibles of controlled transactions on economic performance. *Economic Alternatives, 31*(1), 64–76. DOI: 10.37075/EA.2025.1.04

Challoumis, C. (2025c). The inflation according to the cycle of money (C.M.). *Economic Alternatives, 2025*(2), 324–353. DOI: 10.37075/EA.2025.2.03

Challoumis, C., & Eriotis, N. (2025). The impact of artificial intelligence on the Greek economy. *Journal of Open Innovation, 11*(3), 1–13. DOI: 10.1016/j.joitmc.2025.100578

Challoumis, C., Eriotis, N., & Vasiliou, D. (2025). Social movements' impact on the Greek economy during the financial crisis. *Economies (Basel), 13*(9), 269. Advance online publication. DOI: 10.3390/economies13090269

Champendal, M., Lokaj, B., De Gevigney, V. D., Brulé, G., Zaghir, J., Boiko, P., Lovis, C., Müller, H., Schmid, J., & Ribeiro, R. T. (2025). Exploring environmental sustainability of artificial intelligence in radiology: A scoping review. *European Journal of Radiology*, *194*, 112558. Advance online publication. DOI: 10.1016/j.ejrad.2025.112558

Chang, I.-Y. (2025). Using AI tools to promote sustainable tourism practices: Opportunities and ethical consideration in the post-pandemic era. *Proceedings of Forum Manajemen Indonesia's International Conferences*. https://doi.org/DOI: 10.47747/fmiic.vi2.2976

Charow, R., Jeyakumar, T., Younus, S., Dolatabadi, E., Salhia, M., Al-Mouaswas, D., Anderson, M., Balakumar, S., Clare, M., Dhalla, A., Gillan, C., Haghzare, S., Jackson, E., Lalani, N., Mattson, J., Peteanu, W., Tripp, T., Waldorf, J., Tavares, W., & Wiljer, D. (2021). Artificial intelligence education programs for health care professionals: Scoping review. *JMIR Medical Education*, *7*(2), e31043. Advance online publication. DOI: 10.2196/31043

Chowdhary, S. P., & Majumdar, K. (2025). Health tourism catalyst for growth in developing nations. *Journal of Public Affairs*, *25*(3), e70060. Advance online publication. DOI: 10.1002/pa.70060

Ciecierski-Holmes, T., Singh, R., Axt, M., Brenner, S., & Barteit, S. (2022). Artificial intelligence for strengthening healthcare systems in low- and middle-income countries: A systematic scoping review. *NPJ Digital Medicine*, *5*(1), 100. Advance online publication. DOI: 10.1038/s41746-022-00700-y

Claessens, M., Oria, C., Brouwer, C., Ziemer, B., Scholey, J., Lin, H., Witztum, A., Morin, O., Naqa, I., Van Elmpt, W., & Verellen, D. (2022). Quality assurance for AI-based applications in radiation therapy. *Seminars in Radiation Oncology*, *32*(4), 421–431. DOI: 10.1016/j.semradonc.2022.06.011

Crigger, E., Reinbold, K., Hanson, C., Kao, A., Blake, K., & Irons, M. (2022). Trustworthy augmented intelligence in health care. *Journal of Medical Systems*, *46*(2), 12. Advance online publication. DOI: 10.1007/s10916-021-01790-z

Cristian, M., & Tileagă, C. (2024). Challenges and perspectives of AI in sustainable tourism. *Management of Sustainable Development*, *16*(1), 14–26. Advance online publication. DOI: 10.54989/msd-2024-0012

Damoah, I. B., Ayakwah, A., & Tingbani, I. (2021). Artificial intelligence (AI)-enhanced medical drones in the healthcare supply chain (HSC) for sustainability development: A case study. *Journal of Cleaner Production*, *322*, 129598. Advance online publication. DOI: 10.1016/j.jclepro.2021.129598

Dang, H.-S., Nguyen, T.-M.-T., Wang, C.-N., Day, J. D., & Dang, T. M. T. (2020). Grey system theory in the study of medical tourism industry and its economic impact. *International Journal of Environmental Research and Public Health, 17*(3), 961. Advance online publication. DOI: 10.3390/ijerph17030961

Das, D. C. (2022). From AI in Healthcare to Spirituality in Tourism: A Cross-Sectoral Review of Emerging Practices. *Business and Social Sciences, 1*(1), 1–8.

Das, S. (2024). Application of AI technology for the development of destination tourism towards an intelligent information system. *Economic Affairs, 69*(3). Advance online publication. DOI: 10.46852/0424-2513.3.2024.31

Dávid, L., & Dadkhah, M. (2023). Artificial intelligence in the tourism sector: Its sustainability and innovation potential. Equilibrium. *Quarterly Journal of Economics and Economic Policy, 18*(2), 473–497. DOI: 10.24136/eq.2023.019

Daykhes, A. N., Jakovljevic, M., Reshetnikov, V. A., & Kozlov, V. V. (2020). Promises and hurdles of medical tourism development in the Russian Federation. *International Journal of Environmental Research and Public Health, 17*(12), 4589. Advance online publication. DOI: 10.3390/ijerph17124589

De Micco, F., Di Palma, G., Ferorelli, D., De Benedictis, A., Tomassini, L., Tambone, V., Cingolani, M., & Scendoni, R. (2025). Artificial intelligence in healthcare: Transforming patient safety with intelligent systems—A systematic review. *Frontiers in Medicine, 11*, 1522554. Advance online publication. DOI: 10.3389/fmed.2024.1522554

Doo, F., Vosshenrich, J., Cook, T., Moy, L., Almeida, E., Woolen, S., Gichoya, J., Heye, T., & Hanneman, K. (2024). Environmental sustainability and AI in radiology: A double-edged sword. *Radiology, 310*(2), e232030. Advance online publication. DOI: 10.1148/radiol.232030

El Arab, R. A., & Al Moosa, O. A. (2025). Systematic review of cost effectiveness and budget impact of artificial intelligence in healthcare. *NPJ Digital Medicine, 8*(1), 548. Advance online publication. DOI: 10.1038/s41746-025-01722-y

El Arab, R. A., & Al Moosa, O. A. (2025). Systematic review of cost effectiveness and budget impact of artificial intelligence in healthcare. *NPJ Digital Medicine, 8*(1), 548. Advance online publication. DOI: 10.1038/s41746-025-01722-y

El Arab, R. A., Al Moosa, O. A., & Sagbakken, M. (2025). Economic, ethical, and regulatory dimensions of artificial intelligence in healthcare: An integrative review. *Frontiers in Public Health, 13*, 1617138. Advance online publication. DOI: 10.3389/fpubh.2025.1617138

El Arab, R. A., Al Moosa, O. A., Sagbakken, M., Ghannam, A., Abuadas, F. H., Somerville, J., & Al Mutair, A. (2025). Integrative review of artificial intelligence applications in nursing: Education, clinical practice, workload management, and professional perceptions. *Frontiers in Public Health, 13*, 1619378. Advance online publication. DOI: 10.3389/fpubh.2025.1619378

Elkhwesky, Z., El Manzani, Y., & Salem, I. E. (2022). Driving hospitality and tourism to foster sustainable innovation: A systematic review of COVID-19-related studies and practical implications in the digital era. *Tourism and Hospitality Research*. Advance online publication. DOI: 10.1177/14673584221126792

Erdős, F., Thinakaran, R., Firuza, B., & Koloszár, L. (2025). The rise of AI in tourism - A systematic literature review. *Geo Journal of Tourism and Geosites, 60*(2 supplement), 1254–1265. Advance online publication. DOI: 10.30892/gtg.602spl22-1498

Erwin, E., & Paputungan, I. (2025). Bibliometric analysis of innovation and sustainability in health tourism. *Indonesian Journal of Innovation Studies, 26*(2). Advance online publication. DOI: 10.21070/ijins.v26i2.1312

Esmaeilzadeh, P. (2024). Challenges and strategies for wide-scale artificial intelligence (AI) deployment in healthcare practices: A perspective for healthcare organizations. *Artificial Intelligence in Medicine, 151*, 102861. Advance online publication. DOI: 10.1016/j.artmed.2024.102861

Fan, Z., Yan, Z., & Wen, S. (2023). Deep learning and artificial intelligence in sustainability: A review of SDGs, renewable energy, and environmental health. *Sustainability (Basel), 15*(18), 13493. Advance online publication. DOI: 10.3390/su151813493

Feng, J., Phillips, R., Malenica, I., Bishara, A., Hubbard, A., Celi, L., & Pirracchio, R. (2022). Clinical artificial intelligence quality improvement: Towards continual monitoring and updating of AI algorithms in healthcare. *NPJ Digital Medicine, 5*(1), 106. Advance online publication. DOI: 10.1038/s41746-022-00611-y

Figueiredo, N., Abrantes, J. L., & Costa, S. (2024). Mapping the sustainable development in health tourism: A systematic literature review. *Sustainability (Basel), 16*(5), 1901. Advance online publication. DOI: 10.3390/su16051901

Fiske, A., Radhuber, I., Willem, T., Buyx, A., Celi, L., & McLennan, S. (2025). Climate change and health: The next challenge of ethical AI. *The Lancet. Global Health, 13*(7), e1314–e1320. Advance online publication. DOI: 10.1016/S2214-109X(25)00124-X

Foley, B. M., Haglin, J. M., Tanzer, J. R., & Eltorai, A. E. (2019). Patient care without borders: A systematic review of medical and surgical tourism. *Journal of Travel Medicine*, *26*(6), taz049. Advance online publication. DOI: 10.1093/jtm/taz049

García-Gómez, J., Blanes-Selva, V., Álvarez-Romero, C., De Bartolomé Cenzano, J. C., Mesquita, F. P., Pazos, A., & Doñate-Martínez, A. (2025). Mitigating patient harm risks: A proposal of requirements for AI in healthcare. *Artificial Intelligence in Medicine*, *167*, 103168. Advance online publication. DOI: 10.1016/j.artmed.2025.103168

García-Madurga, M. Á., & Grilló-Méndez, A. J. (2023). Artificial intelligence in the tourism industry: An overview of reviews. *Administrative Sciences*, *13*(8), 172. Advance online publication. DOI: 10.3390/admsci13080172

Gaur, L., Afaq, A., Arora, G. K., & Khan, N. (2023). Artificial intelligence for carbon emissions using system of systems theory. *Ecological Informatics*, *76*, 102165. Advance online publication. DOI: 10.1016/j.ecoinf.2023.102165

Ghasemi, P., Mehdiabadi, A., Spulbar, C., & Birau, R. (2021). Ranking of sustainable medical tourism destinations in Iran: An integrated approach using fuzzy SWARA-PROMETHEE. *Sustainability (Basel)*, *13*(2), 683. Advance online publication. DOI: 10.3390/su13020683

Goktas, P., & Grzybowski, A. (2025). Shaping the future of healthcare: Ethical clinical challenges and pathways to trustworthy AI. *Journal of Clinical Medicine*, *14*(5), 1605. Advance online publication. DOI: 10.3390/jcm14051605

Gordon, M., Daniel, M., Ajiboye, A., Uraiby, H., Xu, N., Bartlett, R., Hanson, J., Haas, M., Spadafore, M., Grafton-Clarke, C., Gasiea, R., Michie, C., Corral, J., Kwan, B., Dolmans, D., & Thammasitboon, S. (2024). A scoping review of artificial intelligence in medical education: BEME Guide No. 84. *Medical Teacher*, *46*(4), 446–470. DOI: 10.1080/0142159X.2024.2314198

Gou, F., Liu, J., Xiao, C., & Wu, J. (2024). Research on artificial-intelligence-assisted medicine: A survey on medical artificial intelligence. *Diagnostics (Basel)*, *14*(14), 1472. Advance online publication. DOI: 10.3390/diagnostics14141472

Hassan, V., & Bellos, G. (2022). COVID-19: Reshaping medical tourism through artificial intelligence (AI) and robotics. *Athens Journal of Tourism*, *9*(2), 77–98. Advance online publication. DOI: 10.30958/ajt.9-2-2

Hendrix, N., Veenstra, D., Cheng, M., Anderson, N., & Verguet, S. (2022). Assessing the economic value of clinical artificial intelligence: Challenges and opportunities. *Value in Health : The Journal of the International Society for Pharmacoeconomics and Outcomes Research, 25*(3), 331–339. DOI: 10.1016/j.jval.2021.08.015

Hossain, M. A., Arafat, M. S., Desai, K., Akter, S., & Asha, A. I. (2025). The economic impact of AI-driven remote patient monitoring: A business intelligence perspective on healthcare cost optimization. *International Interdisciplinary Business Economics Advancement Journal, 6*(5), 39–67. Advance online publication. DOI: 10.55640/business/volume06issue05-03

Hryciw, B., Fortin, Z., Ghossein, J., & Kyeremanteng, K. (2023). Doctor-patient interactions in the age of AI: Navigating innovation and expertise. *Frontiers in Medicine, 10*, 1241508. Advance online publication. DOI: 10.3389/fmed.2023.1241508

Hua, D., Petrina, N., Young, N., Cho, J.-G., & Poon, S. (2023). Understanding the factors influencing acceptability of AI in medical imaging domains among healthcare professionals: A scoping review. *Artificial Intelligence in Medicine, 147*, 102698. Advance online publication. DOI: 10.1016/j.artmed.2023.102698

Işık, C., Islam, H., Ongan, S., Şengöz, A., & Usanmaz, B. (2025). Artificial intelligence (AI) interacted ESG-based sustainable tourism: Economic insights. *Tourism Economics*. Advance online publication. DOI: 10.1177/13548166251346306

Jacob, B. A. (2024). The lasting effects of the COVID-19 pandemic on K-12 schooling: Evidence from a nationally representative teacher survey (EdWorkingPaper No. 24-1020). Annenberg Institute at Brown University. https://doi.org/DOI: 10.26300/6gh3-vz18

Jiao, W., Zhang, X., & D'Souza, F. (2023). The economic value and clinical impact of artificial intelligence in healthcare: A scoping literature review. *IEEE Access : Practical Innovations, Open Solutions, 11*, 123445–123457. DOI: 10.1109/ACCESS.2023.3327905

Jorshary, K. M., Sassani, M., Khamoushi, F. S. S., Raoufi, S., & Khamoushi, S. (2025). Ranking of AI-driven strategies for optimizing the health tourism supply chain using stratified BWM. Knowledge and Decision Systems with Applications. https://doi.org/DOI: 10.59543/kadsa.v1i.15051

Karadayi-Usta, S. (2024). Sustainable medical tourism service network with a stakeholder perspective. *Current Issues in Tourism, 28*(3), 321–340. DOI: 10.1080/13683500.2024.2309148

Khan, Z., Khan, N., & Zhu, X. (2025). Harnessing artificial intelligence for environmental sustainability via human capital and renewable energy. *Scientific Reports*, *15*(1), 36739. Advance online publication. DOI: 10.1038/s41598-025-20613-6

Khanna, N., Maindarkar, M., Fernandes, J., Paul, S., Bhagawati, M., Ahluwalia, P., Ruzsa, Z., Sharma, A., Kolluri, R., Singh, I., Laird, J., Fatemi, M., Alizad, A., Saba, L., Agarwal, V., Sharma, A., Teji, J., Al-Maini, M., Rathore, V., & Suri, J. (2022). Economics of artificial intelligence in healthcare: Diagnosis vs. treatment. *Healthcare (Basel)*, *10*(12), 2493. Advance online publication. DOI: 10.3390/healthcare10122493

Khinvasara, T., Ness, S., & Shankar, A. (2024). Leveraging AI for enhanced quality assurance in medical device manufacturing. *Asian Journal of Research in Computer Science*, *17*(6), 13–35. Advance online publication. DOI: 10.9734/ajrcos/2024/v17i6454

Koçak, B., Ponsiglione, A., Romeo, V., Ugga, L., Huisman, M., & Cuocolo, R. (2025). Radiology AI and sustainability paradox: Environmental, economic, and social dimensions. *Insights Into Imaging*, *16*(1), 88. Advance online publication. DOI: 10.1186/s13244-025-01962-2

Krishnan, G., Singh, S., Pathania, M., Gosavi, S., Abhishek, S., Parchani, A., & Dhar, M. (2023). Artificial intelligence in clinical medicine: Catalyzing a sustainable global healthcare paradigm. *Frontiers in Artificial Intelligence*, *6*, 1227091. Advance online publication. DOI: 10.3389/frai.2023.1227091

Kupi, M. (2025). The impact of an artificial intelligence-based forecasting model on the development of sustainable tourism. *Geo Journal of Tourism and Geosites*, *61*(3), 1758–1766. Advance online publication. DOI: 10.30892/gtg.61334-1544

Labkoff, S., Oladimeji, B., Kannry, J., Solomonides, A., Leftwich, R., Koski, E., Joseph, A., Lopez-Gonzalez, M., Fleisher, L., Nolen, K., Dutta, S., Levy, D., Price, A., Barr, P., Hron, J., Lin, B., Srivastava, G., Pastor, N., Luque, U. S., & Quintana, Y. (2024). Toward a responsible future: Recommendations for AI-enabled clinical decision support. *Journal of the American Medical Informatics Association : JAMIA*, *31*(12), 2730–2739. DOI: 10.1093/jamia/ocae209

Larson, D., Bhargavan-Chatfield, M., Tilkin, M., Coombs, L., & Wald, C. (2025). The road map for ACR practice accreditation for radiology artificial intelligence. *Journal of the American College of Radiology : JACR*, *22*(5), 586–592. Advance online publication. DOI: 10.1016/j.jacr.2025.02.008

Li, M., Yin, D., Qiu, H., & Bai, B. (2021). A systematic review of AI technology-based service encounters: Implications for hospitality and tourism operations. *International Journal of Hospitality Management*, *95*, 102930. Advance online publication. DOI: 10.1016/j.ijhm.2021.102930

Li, Y.-H., Li, Y., Wei, M.-Y., & Li, G. (2024). Innovation and challenges of artificial intelligence technology in personalized healthcare. *Scientific Reports*, *14*(1), 14925. Advance online publication. DOI: 10.1038/s41598-024-70073-7

López-Naranjo, A. L., Puente-Riofrio, M. I., Carrasco-Salazar, V. A., Erazo-Rodríguez, J. D., & Buñay-Guisñan, P. A. (2025). Artificial intelligence in the tourism business: A systematic review. *Frontiers in Artificial Intelligence*, *8*, 1599391. Advance online publication. DOI: 10.3389/frai.2025.1599391

Louati, A., Louati, H., Alharbi, M., Kariri, E., Khawaji, T., Almubaddil, Y., & Aldwsary, S. (2024). Machine learning and artificial intelligence for a sustainable tourism: A case study on Saudi Arabia. *Information (Basel)*, *15*(9), 516. Advance online publication. DOI: 10.3390/info15090516

Lundström, C., & Lindvall, M. (2023). Mapping the landscape of care providers' quality assurance approaches for AI in diagnostic imaging. *Journal of Digital Imaging*, *36*(2), 379–387. DOI: 10.1007/s10278-022-00731-7

Madappa, D. (2015). Medical tourism and inclusive growth in Karnataka. International Research Journal of Management, IT and Social Sciences, 2(9), 35–42. https://media.neliti.com/media/publications/280787-medical-tourism-and-inclusive-growth-in-fa29387c.pdf

Mahmood, U., Shukla-Dave, A., Chan, H.-P., Drukker, K., Samala, R., Chen, Q., Vergara, D., Greenspan, H., Petrick, N., Sahiner, B., Huo, Z., Summers, R., Cha, K., Tourassi, G., Deserno, T., Grizzard, K., Näppi, J., Yoshida, H., Regge, D., & Hadjiiski, L. (2024). Artificial intelligence in medicine: Mitigating risks and maximizing benefits via quality assurance, quality control, and acceptance testing. *BJR Artificial Intelligence*, *1*(1), ubae003. Advance online publication. DOI: 10.1093/bjrai/ubae003

Majid, G. M., Tussyadiah, I., Kim, Y. R., & Pal, A. (2023). Intelligent automation for sustainable tourism: A systematic review. *Journal of Sustainable Tourism*, *31*(11), 2421–2440. DOI: 10.1080/09669582.2023.2246681

Mercolli, L., Rominger, A., & Shi, K. (2024). Towards quality management of artificial intelligence systems for medical applications. *Zeitschrift für Medizinische Physik*, *34*(3), 343–352. DOI: 10.1016/j.zemedi.2024.02.001

Moyano-Fernández, C., Rueda, J., Delgado, J., & Ausín, T. (2024). May artificial intelligence take health and sustainability on a honeymoon? Towards green technologies for multidimensional health and environmental justice. *Global Bioethics = Problemi di Bioetica, 35*(1), 2322208. Advance online publication. DOI: 10.1080/11287462.2024.2322208

Nasarian, E., Alizadehsani, R., Acharya, U. R., & Tsui, K.-L. (2024). Designing interpretable ML system to enhance trust in healthcare: A systematic review to proposed responsible clinician-AI-collaboration framework. *Information Fusion, 108*, 102412. Advance online publication. DOI: 10.1016/j.inffus.2024.102412

Nishant, R., Kennedy, M., & Corbett, J. (2020). Artificial intelligence for sustainability: Challenges, opportunities, and a research agenda. *International Journal of Information Management, 53*, 102104. Advance online publication. DOI: 10.1016/j.ijinfomgt.2020.102104

Onyango, M. J. (2025). Effectiveness of digital technology in enhancing blue tourism sustainability in Tanzania. *Journal of Management and Development Research, 2*(1), 1–10. Advance online publication. DOI: 10.69739/jmdr.v2i1.191

Overgaard, S., Graham, M., Brereton, T., Pencina, M., Halamka, J., Vidal, D., & Economou-Zavlanos, N. (2023). Implementing quality management systems to close the AI translation gap and facilitate safe, ethical, and effective health AI solutions. *NPJ Digital Medicine, 6*(1), 218. Advance online publication. DOI: 10.1038/s41746-023-00968-8

Quinn, T., Senadeera, M., Jacobs, S., Coghlan, S., & Le, V. (2021). Trust and medical AI: The challenges we face and the expertise needed to overcome them. *Journal of the American Medical Informatics Association : JAMIA, 28*(4), 890–894. DOI: 10.1093/jamia/ocaa268

Quttainah, M., Singh, P., & Rana, S. (2025). *Assessing the environmental impact of AI-based medical diagnosis using Grey Relational Analysis*. Arab Journal of Administrative Sciences., DOI: 10.34120/ajas.2025.1387

Rady, H. A. W. A. (2024). *The role of artificial intelligence to enhance health tourism applications in Egyptian tourist destinations*. Minia Journal of Tourism and Hospitality Research., DOI: 10.21608/mjthr.2024.281385.1150

Ramteke, P. N., Wankar, T. N., Rao, U., & Arora, S. (2024). Predictive model for medical assistance. International Journal of Advanced Research in Science. *Tongxin Jishu*, 547–551. Advance online publication. DOI: 10.48175/IJARSCT-18282

Ranjbar, A., Mork, E., Ravn, J., Brøgger, H., Myrseth, P., Østrem, H. P., & Hallock, H. (2024). Managing risk and quality of AI in healthcare: Are hospitals ready for implementation? *Risk Management and Healthcare Policy*, *17*, 877–882. DOI: 10.2147/RMHP.S452337

Reddy, S. (2024). Generative AI in healthcare: An implementation science informed translational path on application, integration and governance. *Implementation Science : IS*, *19*(1), 57. Advance online publication. DOI: 10.1186/s13012-024-01357-9

Reshadi, M. S., & Chehragh, A. M. (2025). A review of medical tourism entrepreneurship and marketing at regional and global levels and a quick glance into the applications of artificial intelligence in medical tourism. *AI & Society*, *40*(5), 4011–4027. DOI: 10.1007/s00146-024-02178-6

Reuben, J., Meiri, H., & Arien-Zakay, H. (2024). AI's pivotal impact on redefining stakeholder roles and their interactions in medical education and health care. *Frontiers in Digital Health*, *6*, 1458811. Advance online publication. DOI: 10.3389/fdgth.2024.1458811

Richie, C. (2022). Environmentally sustainable development and use of artificial intelligence in health care. *Bioethics*, *36*(5), 547–555. DOI: 10.1111/bioe.13018

Richie, C., Hinrichs-Krapels, S., Dobbe, R., French, P., Wei, J., Diehl, J., & Kong, R. (2025). Environmental impacts of artificial intelligence in health care: Considerations and recommendations. *Health and Technology*, *15*(6), 1087–1093. DOI: 10.1007/s12553-025-01003-4

Rodić, B., Štilić, A., & Marković, L. (2025). Artificial intelligence-driven innovations in health tourism and hospitality: A review of benefits and challenges. Book of Proceedings. https://doi.org/DOI: 10.46793/CASB25.093R

Roski, J., Maier, E., Vigilante, K., Kane, E., & Matheny, M. (2021). Enhancing trust in AI through industry self-governance. *Journal of the American Medical Informatics Association : JAMIA*, *28*(7), 1582–1590. DOI: 10.1093/jamia/ocab065

Rossi, G., Feldberg, B., Krois, J., & Schwendicke, F. (2022). Evaluation of the clinical, technical, and financial aspects of cost-effectiveness analysis of artificial intelligence in medicine: Scoping review and framework of analysis. *JMIR Medical Informatics*, *10*(5), e33703. Advance online publication. DOI: 10.2196/33703

Samala, N., Katkam, B. S., Bellamkonda, R., & Rodriguez, R. (2020). Impact of AI and robotics in the tourism sector: A critical insight. *Journal of Tourism Futures*, *6*(3). Advance online publication. DOI: 10.1108/JTF-07-2019-0065

Schuitmaker, L., Drogt, J., Benders, M., & Jongsma, K. (2025). Physicians' required competencies in AI-assisted clinical settings: A systematic review. *British Medical Bulletin*, *153*(1), ldae025. Advance online publication. DOI: 10.1093/bmb/ldae025

Sezgin, E. (2023). Artificial intelligence in healthcare: Complementing, not replacing, doctors and healthcare providers. *Digital Health*, *9*, 20552076231186520. Advance online publication. DOI: 10.1177/20552076231186520

Shang, Z., Chauhan, V., Devi, K., & Patil, S. (2024). Artificial intelligence, the digital surgeon: Unravelling its emerging footprint in healthcare – The narrative review. *Journal of Multidisciplinary Healthcare*, *17*, 4011–4022. DOI: 10.2147/JMDH.S482757

Sharma, S., Chauhan, Y., & Tyagi, R. (2023). Artificial intelligence based applications in medical tourism. In 2023 14th International Conference on Computing Communication and Networking Technologies (ICCCNT) (pp. 1–6). IEEE. DOI: 10.1109/ICCCNT56998.2023.10308020

Shehzad, N., Ramtiyal, B., Jabeen, F., Mangla, S., & Vijayvargy, L. (2024). Metaverse adoption as a cornerstone for sustainable healthcare firms in the industry 5.0 epoch. *Journal of Enterprise Information Management*, *37*(4), 1254–1281. DOI: 10.1108/JEIM-10-2023-0559

Shin, Y., Lee, M., Lee, Y., Kim, K., & Kim, T. (2025). Artificial intelligence-powered quality assurance: Transforming diagnostics, surgery, and patient care—Innovations, limitations, and future directions. *Life (Basel, Switzerland)*, *15*(4), 654. Advance online publication. DOI: 10.3390/life15040654

Siddik, A. B., Forid, M. S., Yong, L., Du, A. M., & Goodell, J. W. (2025). Artificial intelligence as a catalyst for sustainable tourism growth and economic cycles. *Technological Forecasting and Social Change*, *210*, 123875. Advance online publication. DOI: 10.1016/j.techfore.2024.123875

Siyao, P. V. (2024). Enhancing tourists' satisfaction: Leveraging artificial intelligence in the tourism sector. *Pacific International Journal*, *7*(3), 89–98. Advance online publication. DOI: 10.55014/pij.v7i3.624

Song, D., & Chen, H. (2025). Artificial intelligence as a catalyst for sustainable tourism: A case study from China. *Systems*, *13*(5), 333. Advance online publication. DOI: 10.3390/systems13050333

Stogiannos, N., Malik, R., Kumar, A., Barnes, A., Pogose, M., Harvey, H., McEntee, M., & Malamateniou, C. (2023). Black box no more: A scoping review of AI governance frameworks to guide procurement and adoption of AI in medical imaging and radiotherapy in the UK. *The British Journal of Radiology*, *96*(1152), 20221157. Advance online publication. DOI: 10.1259/bjr.20221157

Strika, Z., Petković, K., Likić, R., & Batenburg, R. (2024). Bridging healthcare gaps: A scoping review on the role of artificial intelligence, deep learning, and large language models in alleviating problems in medical deserts. *Postgraduate Medical Journal*, *101*(1191), 4–16. Advance online publication. DOI: 10.1093/postmj/qgae122

Suanpang, P., & Pothipassa, P. (2024). Integrating generative AI and IoT for sustainable smart tourism destinations. *Sustainability (Basel)*, *16*(17), 7435. Advance online publication. DOI: 10.3390/su16177435

Sultana, S., Haque, A., Momen, A., & Yasmin, F. (2014). Factors affecting the attractiveness of medical tourism destination: An empirical study on India- Review article. *Iranian Journal of Public Health*, *43*(6), 867–868. https://www.ncbi.nlm.nih.gov/pmc/articles/PMC4401052/

Tarasenko, E. (2025). Technological transformation of medical tourism in Russia as an important segment of the service sector economy. *AlterEconomics*, *22*(2), 320–339. Advance online publication. DOI: 10.31063/AlterEconomics/2025.22-2.8

Terranova, C., Cestonaro, C., Fava, L., & Cinquetti, A. (2024). AI and professional liability assessment in healthcare. A revolution in legal medicine? *Frontiers in Medicine*, *10*, 1337335. Advance online publication. DOI: 10.3389/fmed.2023.1337335

Thapliyal, K., Mukherjee, S. G. A., Sinha, A., & Thapliyal, D. (2025). Revolutionizing healthcare: AI-driven sustainable solutions for a healthier tomorrow. In *2025 International Conference on Biomedical Engineering and Sustainable Healthcare (ICBMESH)* (pp. 1–6). IEEE. https://doi.org/DOI: 10.1109/ICBMESH66209.2025.11182181

Tripathi, R. P., & Shalki. (2023). Harnessing the potential of AI and ML in medical tourism: Challenges, opportunities, and ethical implications. In 2023 3rd International Conference on Technological Advancements in Computational Sciences (ICTACS) (pp. 1068–1072). IEEE. https://doi.org/DOI: 10.1109/ICTACS59847.2023.10390358

Tsekouropoulos, G., Vasileiou, A., Hoxha, G., Dimitriadis, A., & Zervas, I. (2023). Sustainable approaches to medical tourism: Strategies for Central Macedonia/Greece. *Sustainability (Basel)*, *16*(1), 121. Advance online publication. DOI: 10.3390/su16010121

Turner, L. (2011). Quality in health care and globalization of health services: Accreditation and regulatory oversight of medical tourism companies. *International Journal for Quality in Health Care : Journal of the International Society for Quality in Health Care, 23*(1), 1–7. DOI: 10.1093/intqhc/mzq078

Ueda, D., Walston, S., Fujita, S., Fushimi, Y., Tsuboyama, T., Kamagata, K., Yamada, A., Yanagawa, M., Ito, R., Fujima, N., Kawamura, M., Nakaura, T., Matsui, Y., Tatsugami, F., Fujioka, T., Nozaki, T., Hirata, K., & Naganawa, S. (2024). Climate change and artificial intelligence in healthcare: Review and recommendations towards a sustainable future. *Diagnostic and Interventional Imaging, 105*(11), 453–459. Advance online publication. DOI: 10.1016/j.diii.2024.06.002

Van Wynsberghe, A. (2021). Sustainable AI: AI for sustainability and the sustainability of AI. *AI and Ethics, 1*(3), 213–218. DOI: 10.1007/s43681-021-00043-6

Vishwakarma, L. P., Singh, R., Mishra, R., & Kumari, A. (2023). Application of artificial intelligence for resilient and sustainable healthcare system: Systematic literature review and future research directions. *International Journal of Production Research*. Advance online publication. DOI: 10.1080/00207543.2023.2188101

Vithlani, J., Hawksworth, C., Elvidge, J., Ayiku, L., & Dawoud, D. (2023). Economic evaluations of artificial intelligence-based healthcare interventions: A systematic literature review of best practices in their conduct and reporting. *Frontiers in Pharmacology, 14*, 1220950. Advance online publication. DOI: 10.3389/fphar.2023.1220950

Voets, M., Veltman, J., Slump, C., Siesling, S., & Koffijberg, H. (2022). Systematic review of health economic evaluations focused on artificial intelligence in healthcare: The tortoise and the cheetah. *Value in Health : The Journal of the International Society for Pharmacoeconomics and Outcomes Research, 25*(3), 340–349. DOI: 10.1016/j.jval.2021.11.1362

Von Gerich, H., Helenius, M., Hörhammer, I., Moen, H., & Peltonen, L.-M. (2025). Scoping review on the economic aspects of machine learning applications in healthcare. *International Journal of Medical Informatics, 205*, 106103. Advance online publication. DOI: 10.1016/j.ijmedinf.2025.106103

Wang, Q., Li, Y., & Li, R. (2024). Ecological footprints, carbon emissions, and energy transitions: The impact of artificial intelligence (AI). *Humanities & Social Sciences Communications, 11*(1), 1043. Advance online publication. DOI: 10.1057/s41599-024-03520-5

Wang, R., & Geng, S. (2024). Achieving sustainable medical tourism: Unpacking privacy concerns through a tripartite game theoretic lens. *Frontiers in Public Health, 12*, 1347231. Advance online publication. DOI: 10.3389/fpubh.2024.1347231

Wang, S., & Zhang, H. (2024). Promoting sustainable development goals through generative artificial intelligence in the digital supply chain: Insights from Chinese tourism SMEs. *Sustainable Development (Bradford).* Advance online publication. DOI: 10.1002/sd.3152

Wang, Y., Liu, C., Hu, W., Luo, L., Shi, D., Zhang, J., Yin, Q., Zhang, L., Han, X., & He, M. (2024). Economic evaluation for medical artificial intelligence: Accuracy vs. cost-effectiveness in a diabetic retinopathy screening case. *NPJ Digital Medicine*, *7*(1), 43. Advance online publication. DOI: 10.1038/s41746-024-01032-9

Wolff, J., Pauling, J., Keck, A., & Baumbach, J. (2020). The economic impact of artificial intelligence in health care: Systematic review. *Journal of Medical Internet Research*, *22*(2), e16866. Advance online publication. DOI: 10.2196/16866

Wu, C.-J., Raghavendra, R., Gupta, U., Acun, B., Ardalani, N., Maeng, K., Chang, G., Behram, F. A., Huang, J., Bai, C., Gschwind, M., Gupta, A., Ott, M., Melnikov, A., Candido, S., Brooks, D., Chauhan, G., Lee, B., Lee, H.-H., & Hazelwood, K. (2021). Sustainable AI: Environmental implications, challenges and opportunities. arXiv. https://arxiv.org/abs/2111.00364

Wu, H., Jin, K., Yip, C. C., Koh, V., & Ye, J. (2024). A systematic review of economic evaluation of artificial intelligence-based screening for eye diseases: From possibility to reality. *Survey of Ophthalmology*, *69*(4), 499–507. Advance online publication. DOI: 10.1016/j.survophthal.2024.03.008

Yogeshappa, V., Hallur, J., & Parameshwara, P. K. (2024). Elevating patient care: The integration of artificial intelligence in quality assurance practices. *International Journal of Health Sciences.*, *7*(7), 67–87. Advance online publication. DOI: 10.47941/ijhs.2340

Zhang, J., Wang, Y., Ruan, Q., & Yang, Y. (2024). Digital tourism interpretation content quality: A comparison between AI-generated content and professional-generated content. *Tourism Management Perspectives*, *53*, 101279. Advance online publication. DOI: 10.1016/j.tmp.2024.101279

Zhang, J., Xiang, S., & Li, L. (2025). Economic implications of artificial intelligence-driven recommended systems in healthcare: A focus on neurological disorders. *Frontiers in Public Health*, *13*, 1588270. Advance online publication. DOI: 10.3389/fpubh.2025.1588270

Zhang, J., & Zhang, Z.-M. (2023). Ethics and governance of trustworthy medical artificial intelligence. *BMC Medical Informatics and Decision Making*, *23*(1), 269. Advance online publication. DOI: 10.1186/s12911-023-02103-9

Zuhair, V., Babar, A., Ali, R., Oduoye, M., Noor, Z., Chris, K., Okon, I., & Rehman, L. U. (2024). Exploring the impact of artificial intelligence on global health and enhancing healthcare in developing nations. *Journal of Primary Care & Community Health, 15*, 21501319241245847. Advance online publication. DOI: 10.1177/21501319241245847

ADDITIONAL READINGS

Amanor-Boadu, V., Pfromm, P. H., & Nelson, R. (2014). Economic feasibility of algal biodiesel under alternative public policies. *Renewable Energy, 67*, 136–142. Advance online publication. DOI: 10.1016/j.renene.2013.11.029

Casey Makondo, C. (2015). Environmental Management Compliance, Law and Policy Regimes in Developing Countries: A Review of the Zambian Case. *International Journal of Environmental Protection and Policy, 3*(4), 79. Advance online publication. DOI: 10.11648/j.ijepp.20150304.11

Challoumis, C., & Eriotis, N. (2024). A historical analysis of the banking system and its impact on Greek economy. Edelweiss Applied Science and Technology, 8(6), 1598–1617. https://learning-gate.com/index.php/2576-8484/article/view/2282/892

Challoumis, C., Eriotis, N., & Vasiliou, D. (2025). Mobile applications and internet banking for Greek enterprises. Edelweiss Applied Science and Technology, 12(6), 24–42. https://doi.org/https://doi.org/10.14419/qgshb689

Cruz-Castro, L., & Sanz-Menéndez, L. (2016). The effects of the economic crisis on public research: Spanish budgetary policies and research organizations. *Technological Forecasting and Social Change, 113*, 157–167. Advance online publication. DOI: 10.1016/j.techfore.2015.08.001

Driver, C. (2017). ADVERTISING'S ELUSIVE ECONOMIC RATIONALE: PUBLIC POLICY AND TAXATION. *Journal of Economic Surveys, 31*(1), 1–16. Advance online publication. DOI: 10.1111/joes.12122

Kartini, D. S., Mulyawan, R., & Muradi, M. (2019). Public Policy Pragmatism on Special Economic Zone in Tanjung Lesung, Pandeglang Regency. *MIMBAR : Jurnal Sosial Dan Pembangunan, 35*(1), 146–155. Advance online publication. DOI: 10.29313/mimbar.v35i1.4283

Schram, A. (2018). When evidence isn't enough: Ideological, institutional, and interest-based constraints on achieving trade and health policy coherence. *Global Social Policy, 18*(1), 62–80. Advance online publication. DOI: 10.1177/1468018117744153

Swanstrom, T. (2019). Coping with adversity: Regional economic resilience and public policy. *Journal of Urban Affairs*, *41*(8), 1225–1227. Advance online publication. DOI: 10.1080/07352166.2019.1575151

Ustinovich, E., & Kulikov, M. (2020). National projects, socio-economic policy and public equilibrium. [Social Policy and Social Partnership]. *Social'naja Politika i Social'noe Partnerstvo*, *6*(6), 6–16. Advance online publication. DOI: 10.33920/pol-01-2006-01

KEY TERMS AND DEFINITIONS

AI Safety and Ethics: The term AI safety and ethics can be described as the principles and measures put in place to ensure that AI systems are transparent, unbiased, and do not cause harm. The principles and measures are often applied in healthcare settings to ensure fairness and patient rights.

AI-Enabled Medical Tourism: AI-enabled medical tourism is defined as the practice of integrating artificial intelligence technology into medical tourism services.

Artificial Intelligence (AI): Artificial intelligence is defined as the ability of computers to perform tasks that are normally associated with human intelligence, such as learning, recognizing patterns, decision-making, and prediction. In the healthcare sector, artificial intelligence is used for medical diagnostics, image analysis, treatment, patient monitoring, and managing healthcare services.

Cost–Benefit Analysis (CBA): Cost–Benefit Analysis is an economic evaluation method used to compare the total expected costs of a project or investment with its anticipated benefits. In the context of AI adoption in healthcare, CBA evaluates capital investments, operational savings, productivity improvements, and broader social welfare effects.

Cross-Border Healthcare:Cross-border healthcare is a concept that entails the provision of healthcare to patients who travel to another country to seek treatment. It encompasses a series of regulations and processes that govern patient movements and international health governance structures.:

Data Governance: The term data governance can be described as the institutional system and processes through which data is managed and regulated in healthcare settings. Data governance in AI-based healthcare systems is essential to ensure compliance with data privacy regulations and patient confidentiality.

Environmental Footprint of AI: The environmental footprint of AI refers to the energy consumption, carbon emissions, and material resources associated with the development, training, deployment, and operation of artificial intelligence systems, including data centers and computing infrastructure.

Equity in Healthcare Access: Equity in healthcare access refers to the fair distribution of healthcare services across populations regardless of socioeconomic status, geographic location, or demographic characteristics.

Healthcare Accreditation: Healthcare accreditation is a process of recognition of hospitals or healthcare providers against internationally accepted criteria of quality: safety, and performance. Accreditation agencies assess compliance with clinical, safety, and governance criteria.

Healthcare Productivity: Healthcare productivity refers to the efficiency with which healthcare systems convert resources such as labor, technology, and capital into health outcomes and medical services. AI technologies can increase productivity by improving diagnostic accuracy, reducing administrative burdens, and optimizing treatment pathways.

Medical Tourism: Medical tourism is defined as the practice of patients seeking medical treatment, surgical care, and other healthcare services outside their national borders. The factors that drive medical tourism include cost differentials, access to medical technology, waiting times, and access to medical expertise.

Patient-Centric Healthcare: Patient-centric healthcare is an approach that prioritizes patient needs, preferences, and experiences in the design and delivery of healthcare services, emphasizing personalized care, informed decision-making, and improved patient outcomes.

Price Elasticity of Demand: Price elasticity of demand measures the responsiveness of the quantity demanded of a service to changes in its price. In medical tourism, elasticity reflects how patient demand for international healthcare services changes in response to treatment costs, travel expenses, and insurance coverage.

Sustainability Transformation: Sustainability transformation is a concept that refers to a complete overhaul of economic and institutional structures to incorporate environmentally friendly, socially conscious, and economically sound practices. In the context of healthcare and tourism, it entails a reduction in environmental impact, enhanced resource usage, and equitable distribution of healthcare services.

Telemedicine: The term telemedicine can be described as the remote provision of healthcare services using digital communication technologies, which do not require physical presence at a healthcare facility.

Telepresence in Healthcare: The term "telepresence" can be described as the remote interaction between healthcare practitioners and patients/surgical sites using robotic devices and communication tools, which are often utilized to provide remote assistance and medical interventions.

Chapter 3
Improving Global Patient Access Through AI-Enhanced Medical Tourism Implications for Global Health Outcomes

Sparsh Tiwari
http://orcid.org/0009-0001-7815-6094
Amity University, Jaipur, India

ABSTRACT

The growing convergence of artificial intelligence (AI) and medical tourism is reshaping global healthcare access and delivery. This study examines how AI-enhanced medical tourism can improve global patient access to quality healthcare services and contribute to improved global health outcomes. AI-driven technologies such as predictive analytics, telemedicine, virtual consultations, intelligent diagnostics, and personalized treatment planning enable patients to overcome geographical, financial, and informational barriers to care. By facilitating efficient patient-provider matching, transparent cost comparisons, and continuity of care across borders, AI enhances trust, safety, and decision-making in medical travel. The paper further explores the implications of AI-enabled medical tourism for global health systems, particularly in advancing health equity, optimizing resource utilization, and supporting Sustainable Development Goal 3 (Good Health and Well-being). Challenges related to data privacy, ethical governance, and regulatory harmonization are also discussed.

DOI: 10.4018/979-8-3373-8944-8.ch003

1. INTRODUCTION

1.1 Global Disparities in Healthcare Access

Despite significant advancements in medical science and healthcare technologies, access to quality healthcare remains highly uneven across regions and populations. (Hoagland & Kipping, 2024) Many countries particularly low- and middle-income nations—continue to face critical shortages of medical infrastructure, skilled healthcare professionals, advanced diagnostic facilities, and specialized treatments. Even in developed economies, patients often encounter long waiting periods, high treatment costs, and limited availability of specialized care.(Fradgley et al., 2015) These disparities contribute to preventable morbidity, delayed interventions, and widening global health inequities.(Rad, 2025)

Globalization, increased mobility, and digital connectivity have intensified the search for alternative healthcare pathways capable of addressing these access gaps. (Hackl, 2018) In this context, medical tourism has emerged as a prominent global phenomenon, enabling patients to travel across national borders in pursuit of affordable, timely, and high-quality medical treatment.(Liverani et al., 2020)

1.2 Medical Tourism as an Alternative Healthcare Pathway

Medical tourism involves patients seeking medical, surgical, or wellness treatments outside their country of residence.(Foley et al., 2019) Motivations for medical travel include cost savings, reduced waiting times, access to advanced medical technologies, and availability of specialized procedures.(Ruggeri et al., 2018) Countries such as India, Thailand, Turkey, South Korea, and Mexico have positioned themselves as global medical tourism hubs by offering internationally accredited hospitals, skilled medical professionals, and competitive pricing.(Sandberg, 2017)

While medical tourism has expanded healthcare choices for patients, it has also faced criticism related to information asymmetry, quality assurance, continuity of care, patient safety, and ethical concerns.(Foley et al., 2019) Traditional medical tourism models often rely on intermediaries, fragmented information sources, and limited post-treatment follow-up, which may undermine patient trust and health outcomes. (Al-Romeedy et al., 2025) These challenges underscore the need for technologically enabled solutions to enhance transparency, coordination, and patient-centered care in cross-border healthcare.

1.3 Emergence of Artificial Intelligence in Healthcare

Artificial intelligence (AI) has rapidly transformed healthcare systems by enhancing diagnostic accuracy, improving clinical decision-making, and optimizing operational efficiency.(Khalifa & Albadawy, 2024) AI-driven applications such as machine learning algorithms, predictive analytics, intelligent diagnostics, telemedicine platforms, and personalized treatment planning have demonstrated significant potential in improving healthcare access and outcomes.(Fahim et al., 2025)

AI technologies facilitate remote consultations, early disease detection, risk prediction, and real-time monitoring, thereby overcoming geographical and resource-based limitations. Importantly, AI also empowers patients by providing access to reliable health information, cost transparency, and data-driven decision support, contributing to more informed and participatory healthcare experiences.(Alsabah et al., 2025)

1.4 Convergence of AI and Medical Tourism

The integration of AI into medical tourism has given rise to AI-enhanced medical tourism, a digitally enabled model that transforms the entire medical travel continuum—from pre-travel decision-making to post-treatment care. AI-driven platforms enable patients to compare hospitals, assess treatment risks, evaluate costs, and connect with international healthcare providers through virtual consultations. (Alquayt et al., 2025)

By facilitating intelligent patient–provider matching, AI reduces uncertainty and enhances trust in cross-border healthcare decisions.(Ayesha & Ahamed, 2024) Additionally, AI-supported continuity of care through electronic health records, remote monitoring, and follow-up consultations ensures safer and more effective treatment outcomes beyond national boundaries. (Christina et al., 2025)This convergence positions AI-enhanced medical tourism as a strategic mechanism for improving global patient access to healthcare.(Barua & Datta, 2024)

1.5 Implications for Global Health Outcomes

AI-enhanced medical tourism extends beyond individual patient benefits to influence global health systems and outcomes.(Barua & Datta, 2024) By redistributing patient demand across borders, it supports more efficient utilization of global healthcare resources and alleviates pressure on overburdened domestic systems. (Packer et al., 2009) Moreover, by enabling underserved populations to access quality medical services, AI-driven medical tourism contributes to advancing health equity and reducing global health disparities.(Gupta et al., 2023)

This model also aligns with international health development agendas, particularly Sustainable Development Goal 3 (Good Health and Well-being), by promoting universal health coverage, innovation in healthcare delivery, and cross-border collaboration. However, its success depends on addressing critical challenges related to data privacy, ethical AI governance, regulatory harmonization, and digital inclusion.

1.6 Research Rationale and Objectives

Despite growing interest in AI applications in healthcare and medical tourism independently, scholarly research examining their combined impact on global patient access and health outcomes remains limited. Existing studies often focus on technological efficiency or economic benefits, with insufficient attention to equity, governance, and global health implications.

This study seeks to bridge this gap by examining how AI-enhanced medical tourism can improve global patient access to healthcare services and contribute to improved global health outcomes. Specifically, the study aims to:

1. To analyze the role of AI technologies in overcoming geographical, financial, and informational barriers to healthcare access
2. To examine the implications of AI-enabled medical tourism for health equity and global health systems
3. To identify key challenges and ethical considerations associated with AI-driven cross-border healthcare

1.7 Conceptual Flowchart: AI-Enhanced Medical Tourism and Global Health Outcomes

Figure 1. Diagram of Conceptual framework

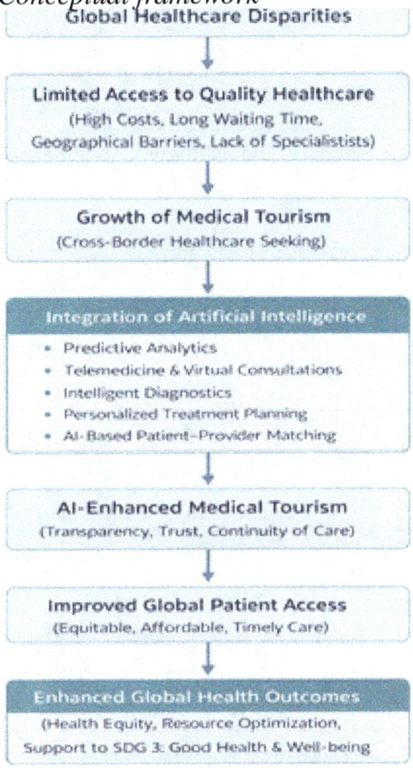

Source: *Compiled by researcher*

The conceptual framework explains how AI-enhanced medical tourism contributes to improved global health outcomes by addressing existing healthcare disparities. Limited access to quality healthcare—due to high costs, long waiting times, geographical barriers, and shortage of specialists—drives the growth of cross-border medical tourism. The integration of artificial intelligence transforms this process through predictive analytics, virtual consultations, intelligent diagnostics, personalized treatment planning, and AI-based patient–provider matching. These applications enhance transparency, trust, and continuity of care, leading to AI-enabled medical tourism experiences. As a result, global patient access to affordable, timely, and specialized healthcare improves, ultimately supporting better health equity, optimized resource utilization, and enhanced global health outcomes in alignment with Sustainable Development Goal 3 (Good Health and Well-Being).

Table 1. Abbreviations used in this Research paper

Abbreviation	Full Form
AI	Artificial Intelligence
AIMT	AI-Enhanced Medical Tourism
GPA	Global Patient Access
GHO	Global Health Outcomes
SEM	Structural Equation Modelling
CFA	Confirmatory Factor Analysis
RAB	Reduced Access Barriers
TSP	Trust & Safety Perception
CoC	Continuity of Care
AVE	Average Variance Extracted
HTMT	Heterotrait–Monotrait Ratio
CFI	Comparative Fit Index
TLI	Tucker–Lewis Index
RMSEA	Root Mean Square Error of Approximation
SRMR	Standardized Root Mean Square Residual
R^2	Coefficient of Determination
β	Standardized Regression Coefficient
α	Cronbach's Alpha
SD	Standard Deviation
n	Sample Size
Likert Scale	Psychometric scale used to measure attitudes and perceptions
SDGs	Sustainable Development Goals
UN	United Nations

Source: *Compiled by researcher*

2. LITERATURE REVIEW

Figure 2. Frame work of Literature review

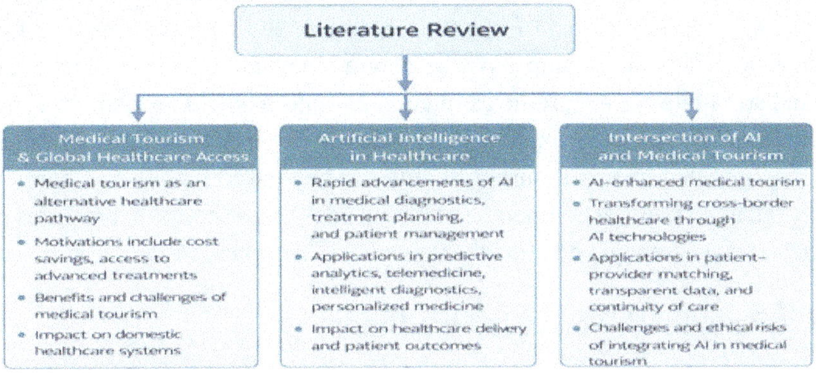

Source: *Compiled by researcher*

2.1 Medical Tourism and Global Healthcare Access

Medical tourism has emerged as a significant global phenomenon, driven by persistent inequalities in healthcare access across countries and regions.(Snyder et al., 2011) Scholars broadly define medical tourism as the movement of patients across national borders to obtain medical treatment, often motivated by cost advantages, reduced waiting times, availability of advanced procedures, or higher perceived quality of care.(Lewis et al., 2018) Studies indicate that medical tourism has grown rapidly in response to rising healthcare costs in developed nations and infrastructural gaps in developing countries, positioning it as an alternative healthcare pathway for millions of patients worldwide.(Organization, 2024)

Existing literature highlights that one of the principal motivations for medical tourism is cost savings, particularly for elective surgeries, specialized treatments, and chronic care management.(Tsekouropoulos et al., 2024) Patients from high-income countries frequently seek treatment in emerging medical tourism destinations where comparable quality is offered at a fraction of domestic costs.(Foley et al., 2019) Additionally, access to advanced medical technologies and internationally accredited hospitals has strengthened the attractiveness of cross-border healthcare.(Angelillo et al., 2023)

However, researchers also emphasize that medical tourism is accompanied by significant benefits and challenges.(De la Hoz-Correa et al., 2018) On the positive side, it expands patient choice, reduces waiting times, and supports healthcare sector growth in destination countries.(Siciliani et al., 2023) Conversely, concerns persist regarding information asymmetry, patient safety, quality assurance, post-treatment follow-up, and legal accountability. (Giró)Studies warn that without adequate governance, medical tourism can exacerbate inequalities by diverting resources toward foreign patients while neglecting local populations.(Cynthia, 2025)

Another important strand of literature examines the impact of medical tourism on domestic healthcare systems. While inbound medical tourism can generate revenue and stimulate healthcare investment, outbound medical tourism may indicate systemic weaknesses in national health systems.(Virani et al., 2020) Consequently, scholars argue that medical tourism should not be viewed merely as a commercial activity but as an integral component of global healthcare access that requires policy oversight, transparency, and ethical safeguards.(Chaudhry, 2022)

2.2 Artificial Intelligence in Healthcare

The integration of artificial intelligence (AI) into healthcare has received extensive scholarly attention over the past decade. (Secinaro et al., 2021) AI technologies—including machine learning, natural language processing, computer vision, and predictive analytics—have demonstrated transformative potential across diagnostics, treatment planning, patient management, and healthcare administration.(Whig et al., 2025) The literature consistently reports that AI enhances clinical accuracy, operational efficiency, and patient-centered care.(Faiyazuddin et al., 2025)

One major focus of research is the role of AI in medical diagnostics and treatment planning. AI-driven diagnostic tools have shown superior or comparable performance to human clinicians in areas such as radiology, pathology, oncology screening, and cardiovascular risk assessment.(Arzikulov & Komiljonov, 2025) These advancements contribute to earlier detection, personalized treatment strategies, and improved clinical outcomes.(Jain et al., 2022)

Another prominent application of AI lies in predictive analytics and telemedicine. Predictive models help anticipate disease progression, treatment risks, and patient outcomes, enabling proactive intervention.(Sah, 2025) Telemedicine platforms, enhanced by AI-driven triage and decision-support systems, facilitate remote consultations and extend specialist access to underserved and geographically isolated populations.(Mbanugo, 2025) This capability is particularly relevant for improving healthcare access across borders.

The literature also underscores the role of AI in patient management and personalized medicine.(Taherdoost & Ghofrani, 2024) By analysing large datasets from electronic health records, wearable devices, and genomic information, AI enables tailored treatment plans aligned with individual patient profiles. Such personalization improves patient satisfaction and adherence while reducing unnecessary interventions.(Car et al., 2017)

Despite these benefits, scholars caution that AI adoption introduces challenges related to data quality, algorithmic bias, transparency, and accountability.(Chen et al., 2023) Ethical considerations, including patient consent, explainability of AI decisions, and equitable access to AI-enabled services, remain central to ongoing debates.(Williamson & Prybutok, 2024) As a result, the literature stresses that AI should be implemented within robust governance frameworks to ensure that technological gains translate into improved patient outcomes.(Goktas & Grzybowski, 2025)

2.3 Intersection of Artificial Intelligence and Medical Tourism

The convergence of AI and medical tourism represents an emerging and increasingly important area of scholarly inquiry.(Reshadi & Chehragh, 2025) Researchers conceptualize AI-enhanced medical tourism as a digitally enabled ecosystem that integrates AI technologies across the entire medical travel journey—before, during, and after treatment.(Lu et al., 2018) This intersection addresses many of the limitations identified in traditional medical tourism models.

Studies show that AI significantly improves cross-border healthcare decision-making by reducing information asymmetry.(Oso et al., 2025) AI-powered platforms aggregate and analyze data on hospital accreditation, physician expertise, treatment outcomes, costs, and patient reviews, enabling transparent and evidence-based comparisons.(Liverani et al., 2020) This enhances patient trust and supports informed decision-making in selecting international healthcare providers.(Niranjan et al., 2020)

Another critical contribution of AI at this intersection is patient–provider matching.(Deshpande, 2024) Intelligent matching algorithms align patients with suitable hospitals and specialists based on medical needs, budget constraints, risk profiles, and personal preferences.(Chen et al., 2025) This reduces uncertainty and enhances treatment appropriateness, which is particularly important in complex or high-risk procedures.(Selwood et al., 2020)

The literature further highlights AI's role in strengthening continuity of care in medical tourism.(Shafik, 2025) Traditionally, post-treatment follow-up has been a weak link in cross-border healthcare.(Harryono et al., 2006) AI-enabled telemedicine, remote monitoring, and interoperable digital health records facilitate seamless coordination between home-country physicians and destination providers.(Dar & Kashyap, 2023) This continuity reduces complications, improves recovery outcomes, and enhances overall patient experience.

However, scholars also emphasize challenges and ethical risks associated with integrating AI into medical tourism.(Shafik, 2025) Cross-border data exchange raises serious concerns regarding data privacy, cybersecurity, and regulatory compliance.(Gulia, 2024) Differences in national regulations governing telemedicine, AI usage, and medical liability complicate international coordination.(Elendu et al., 2025)

Additionally, algorithmic bias and unequal access to digital infrastructure may exclude vulnerable populations from benefiting fully from AI-enhanced medical tourism.(Dinker, 2024)

Despite these challenges, the literature increasingly views AI-enhanced medical tourism as a mechanism capable of advancing global patient access and health equity. (Heliades et al., 2024) By combining technological intelligence with cross-border healthcare delivery, this model aligns with global health objectives, particularly Sustainable Development Goal 3 (Good Health and Well-being). Researchers argue that when governed ethically and inclusively, AI-enhanced medical tourism can optimize global healthcare resources, reduce disparities, and contribute to improved global health outcomes.

2.4 Theoretical Foundations of AI-Enhanced Medical Tourism

This study is grounded in multiple complementary theoretical perspectives to explain how AI-Enhanced Medical Tourism (AIMT) influences Global Patient Access (GPA) and Global Health Outcomes (GHO). The integration of information asymmetry theory, health equity theory, technology adoption models, and institutional governance perspectives provides a structured theoretical basis for understanding the mechanisms through which artificial intelligence transforms cross-border healthcare systems.(Guerrazzi, 2020) Together, these perspectives explain how AI reduces uncertainty, enhances accessibility, facilitates adoption, and strengthens institutional coordination within global medical tourism ecosystems.(Reshadi & Chehragh, 2025)

2.4.1 Information Asymmetry and AI in Medical Tourism

Information asymmetry theory, introduced by George Akerlof, explains how markets function inefficiently when one party possesses more information than the other.(Marchionatti, 2026) In healthcare—particularly in cross-border medical tourism—patients often lack sufficient information regarding treatment quality, provider credibility, procedural risks, pricing transparency, and post-treatment continuity.(Nesheli et al., 2026) This imbalance creates uncertainty, distrust, and perceived risk, which can discourage international healthcare decisions.

AI-enhanced medical tourism platforms play a critical role in reducing this information gap. Through real-time data analytics, predictive diagnostics, transparent hospital comparisons, patient review systems, and algorithmic risk assessments, AI improves the availability and reliability of healthcare information.(Gayatri et al., 2026) By increasing transparency and reducing uncertainty, AI strengthens patient confidence in international treatment decisions.(Alsehani, 2026) Consequently, reduced information asymmetry enhances Global Patient Access (GPA), as individuals are more willing and better equipped to seek healthcare services across borders.

Thus, from an information asymmetry perspective, AIMT functions as a structural mechanism that improves access by mitigating informational inequalities in global healthcare markets.

2.4.2 Health Equity and Global Patient Access

Health equity perspectives, strongly associated with the capability approach advanced by Amartya Sen, emphasize that access to healthcare is a fundamental determinant of well-being.(Maurya, 2026) Health outcomes are not solely influenced by medical treatment itself, but by the fairness and inclusiveness of access to healthcare services.(Abubakari & Olamilekan, 2026)

Within this framework, Global Patient Access (GPA) serves as a mediating mechanism between AI-enhanced medical tourism and Global Health Outcomes (GHO).(Bhavnani & McKim, 2026) When AI reduces barriers related to information, cost transparency, diagnostic accuracy, and care coordination, patients from underserved or resource-constrained regions gain access to higher-quality medical services(Mengistu et al., 2026). Enhanced access expands patients' capabilities to seek appropriate treatment, thereby improving overall health outcomes.(Fajarini et al., 2026)

However, the health equity perspective also introduces a critical dimension. While AI may expand access for some populations, digital exclusion, affordability constraints, and technological literacy gaps may limit benefits for vulnerable groups. (Mubarak, 2026) Therefore, the health equity framework not only justifies the mediating role of GPA but also supports a balanced discussion of potential disparities within AI-enabled medical tourism systems.(Christina et al., 2025)

2.4.3 Technology Adoption in Healthcare

The integration of AI within medical tourism ecosystems can be further explained through technology adoption models, particularly the Technology Acceptance Model (TAM) proposed by Fred Davis.(Lopes et al., 2026) According to TAM, the adoption of new technologies is primarily influenced by perceived usefulness and perceived ease of use.(Djimesah et al., 2026)

In the context of AIMT, healthcare providers adopt AI-based systems because they enhance diagnostic precision, operational efficiency, and service personalization. (Natarajan et al., 2026) Similarly, patients are more likely to engage with AI-enabled platforms when they perceive them as reliable, beneficial, and user-friendly.(Patel et al., 2026) Trust in algorithmic decision-making and data security also becomes a central determinant of acceptance.(Regona et al., 2026)

Technology adoption theory therefore justifies AIMT as the independent variable in the proposed model.(Fortea, 2026) It explains the structural integration of AI tools within medical tourism systems and clarifies why stakeholders embrace AI-driven innovations that ultimately enhance patient access and service quality.(Yan et al., 2026)

2.4.4 Institutional Governance and Continuity of Care

Institutional governance theory, influenced by the work of Douglass North, emphasizes the role of formal regulations, institutional coordination, and policy frameworks in shaping economic and social outcomes. Cross-border healthcare operates within complex regulatory environments involving multiple jurisdictions, data protection standards, accreditation systems, and ethical guidelines.(Hussain & Nasir, 2026)

Within AI-enhanced medical tourism, strong institutional governance mechanisms are essential to ensure patient safety, data portability, and regulatory harmonization.(Islam, 2026) Effective governance structures support continuity of care across borders, enabling pre-treatment consultation, coordinated surgical procedures, and post-treatment follow-up through digital platforms.(Nesheli et al., 2026)

In this study, continuity of care functions as a moderating variable. Institutional governance strengthens the relationship between Global Patient Access and Global Health Outcomes by ensuring that access translates into sustained, coordinated, and high-quality healthcare delivery. Without regulatory alignment and structured coordination mechanisms, increased access alone may not guarantee improved health outcomes.

2.4.5 Theoretical Integration

Integrating these theoretical perspectives, the present study proposes that AI-Enhanced Medical Tourism improves Global Health Outcomes primarily through enhanced Global Patient Access. Information asymmetry theory explains how AI reduces uncertainty and increases access; health equity theory clarifies why access serves as a key pathway to improved outcomes; technology adoption theory justifies stakeholder engagement with AI systems; and institutional governance theory highlights the regulatory and coordination mechanisms that strengthen outcome sustainability.

Together, these theories provide a comprehensive and theory-driven foundation for the proposed structural model, reinforcing the empirical relationships tested through Structural Equation Modelling (SEM).

2.5 Systematic literature review of some studies

Here are some literatures which are presented in the form of systematic literature reviews which are closely associated with the study:

Table 2. Systematic literature reviews of Closely associated studies

S. No.	Author (s) & Year	Domain	Key Focus	Methodology	Key Findings	Relevance to Present Study
1	Bhuiyan et al. (2025)	AI adoption in healthcare	Awareness, perception, and adoption of AI in Bangladesh	Survey-based quantitative	Awareness, infrastructure, and institutional support influence AI adoption	Supports LMIC context and AI readiness in healthcare and medical tourism
2	Alowais et al. (2024)	Ethics & legal frameworks	Ethical and legal concerns in healthcare AI	Systematic review	Data privacy, bias, accountability, and regulatory gaps are major challenges	Strengthens ethical governance and cross-border healthcare framework
3	Anam et al. (2026)	Technology adoption	Extended TAM for digital platform adoption	SEM analysis	Perceived usefulness, trust, and ease of use drive adoption	Supports TAM-based AI adoption in healthcare
4	Bassi et al. (2025)	Telemedicine	AI integration in telemedicine systems	Systematic review	AI improves triage, diagnosis, and remote monitoring	Justifies telemedicine in medical tourism
5	Bhuiyan (2024)	AI readiness	Extended TOE framework for Industry 4.0	Conceptual and empirical	Organizational and environmental readiness critical for AI adoption	Supports TOE-based readiness in healthcare
6	Bhuiyan et al. (2025)	AI in health sector	AI adoption barriers and awareness	Quantitative	Institutional and technological factors influence adoption	Strengthens LMIC policy discussion
7	Bhuiyan et al. (2026)	Digital engagement	ChatGPT and AI-based engagement	Cross-sectional study	AI enhances user engagement and digital readiness	Indicates patient–AI interaction potential

continued on following page

Table 2. Continued

S. No.	Author (s) & Year	Domain	Key Focus	Methodology	Key Findings	Relevance to Present Study
8	CADTH (2025)	Future healthcare	AI as future healthcare enabler	Policy report	AI will transform predictive and preventive healthcare	Supports global healthcare transformation
9	Chen et al. (2025)	Explainable AI	XAI in clinical decision support	Meta-analysis	Transparency improves trust and adoption	Justifies inclusion of XAI in framework
10	de Lima et al. (2024)	Telehealth	AI in musculoskeletal care	Clinical and ethical review	Telehealth improves access and continuity of care	Supports remote healthcare continuity
11	Faisal-E-Alam et al. (2025)	Sustainability	AI and sustainable development	Bibliometric	AI supports SDGs and global equity	Links AI to SDG 3 and sustainable healthcare
12	Ho et al. (2025)	Clinical decision support	Healthcare worker trust in AI	Systematic review	Trust, transparency, and usability influence CDS adoption	Supports trust-based AI implementation
13	Islam et al. (2026)	Information security	TAM and IS security	Quantitative	Security moderates technology adoption	Highlights privacy and security in healthcare AI
14	Khanna et al. (2025)	AI in healthcare	Benefits and drawbacks	Narrative review	AI improves accuracy but raises ethical concerns	Provides balanced view
15	Khatun et al. (2025)	Digital transformation	Sustainability and green innovation	Systematic review	Digitalization drives sustainable healthcare	Supports long-term healthcare transformation
16	Molla et al. (2026)	Digital banking TOE	Organizational adoption	Empirical	Technology and environment influence digital adoption	Applicable to healthcare digital transformation
17	Bhuiyan et al. (2025)	Digital transformation	AI and organizational change	Empirical	AI adoption linked with institutional readiness	Supports AI governance and infrastructure

Source: *Compiled by researcher*

2.6 Synthesis and Research Gap

The reviewed literature collectively demonstrates that medical tourism and AI independently contribute to improving healthcare access and efficiency. However, limited empirical and conceptual work has examined their integrated impact on global patient access and health outcomes. Existing studies often focus either on economic aspects of medical tourism or technical capabilities of AI, with insufficient attention to equity, governance, and system-level outcomes.

This study addresses this gap by synthesizing insights from medical tourism, AI in healthcare, and global health literature to examine how AI-enhanced medical tourism can serve as a transformative pathway for improving global patient access and strengthening global health outcomes.

3. RESEARCH METHODOLOGY

3.1 Introduction

This chapter explains the methodological framework adopted to empirically examine the role of AI-Enhanced Medical Tourism (AIMT) in improving Global Patient Access (GPA) and Global Health Outcomes (GHO). The methodology is designed to test complex causal relationships involving direct effects, mediation, and moderation, which are later analyzed using Structural Equation Modelling (SEM) in Data analysis section

The methodological choices are aligned with the research objectives, hypothesis, and analytical techniques employed for data analysis and results interpretation.

3.2 Research Design

The study follows a quantitative, explanatory research design grounded in the positivist research paradigm. This approach is appropriate as the study seeks to test theoretically derived hypotheses using empirical data and statistical modelling rather than subjective interpretation.

A cross-sectional survey design was employed, capturing perceptions and experiences of international medical tourists at a single point in time. This design is widely accepted in healthcare access, technology adoption, and medical tourism research, particularly when investigating behavioural and outcome-based constructs.

3.3 Conceptual Framework

The conceptual framework posits AI-Enhanced Medical Tourism as the primary exogenous variable influencing global patient access and health outcomes through multiple mechanisms.

The framework includes:

Figure 3. Conceptual framework Diagram

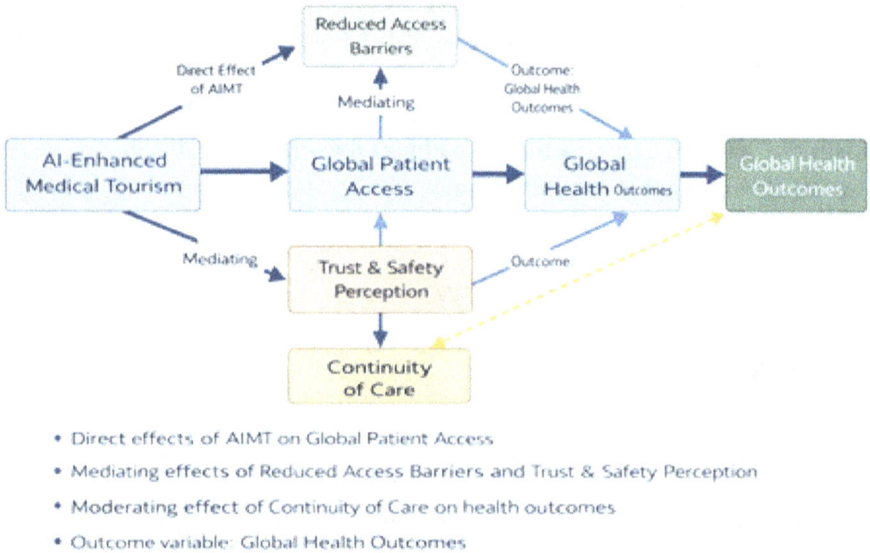

Source: *Compiled by researcher*

This structure necessitated the use of Structural Equation Modelling, which allows simultaneous testing of multiple interrelated dependencies.

3.4 Research Hypothesis

The hypotheses tested in the data analysis chapter were derived from the conceptual framework:

H1: AI-Enhanced Medical Tourism positively influences Global Patient Access
H2: AI-Enhanced Medical Tourism significantly reduces Access Barriers
H3: Reduced Access Barriers positively influence Global Patient Access
H4: Trust & Safety Perception mediates the relationship between AIMT and Global Patient Access
H5: Continuity of Care moderates the relationship between AIMT and Global Health Outcomes
H6: Global Patient Access positively influences Global Health Outcomes
H7: Global Patient Access mediates the relationship between AIMT and Global Health Outcomes

3.5 Population and Sample Design

3.5.1 Target Population

The target population comprised international medical tourists who:

1. Travelled across national borders for medical treatment
2. Utilized AI-enabled or digital healthcare services (e.g., teleconsultation, AI-based hospital matching, digital diagnostics, post-treatment follow-up)
3. Received treatment within the last 24 months

This population was selected to ensure relevance to AI-enabled medical tourism experiences and reliable recall of healthcare outcomes.

3.5.2 Sampling Technique

A multi-stage sampling technique was adopted:

1. Identification of major medical tourism destinations and internationally accredited hospitals
2. Collaboration with international patient departments and medical tourism facilitators
3. Screening of respondents based on inclusion criteria

This approach ensured heterogeneity in terms of origin region, treatment type, and destination country, enhancing external validity.

3.5.3 Sample Size Justification

Structural Equation Modelling requires adequate sample size for stable parameter estimation. Following established guidelines:

- Minimum SEM sample size: 200
- Recommended for mediation and moderation testing: 450

Accordingly, 450 valid responses were retained for final analysis, which is consistent with the robustness of results reported in Data analysis section (model fit, mediation, moderation, and R^2 values).

3.6 Instrument Development and Data Collection

3.6.1 Questionnaire Design

A structured questionnaire was developed using validated measurement items adapted from prior studies in:

- Medical tourism
- Digital health and AI adoption
- Healthcare access and patient-reported outcomes

All constructs were measured using a 5-point Likert scale (1 = Strongly Disagree to 5 = Strongly Agree).

The questionnaire consisted of six sections:

- AI-Enhanced Medical Tourism
- Reduced Access Barriers
- Trust & Safety Perception
- Continuity of Care
- Global Patient Access
- Global Health Outcomes

3.6.2 Pilot Study

A pilot survey was conducted with 80 respondents to assess:

- Clarity of items
- Reliability
- Preliminary factor structure

Cronbach's alpha values exceeded 0.75 for all constructs, supporting progression to full-scale data collection.

3.7 Operationalization of Variables

Table 3. List of Operational variables

Construct	Items	Measurement Focus
AI-Enhanced Medical Tourism	5	Telemedicine, AI matching, personalization
Reduced Access Barriers	4	Cost clarity, reduced uncertainty
Trust & Safety Perception	4	Data security, transparency
Continuity of Care	4	Follow-up, coordination
Global Patient Access	5	Timely, affordable access
Global Health Outcomes	5	Recovery quality, effectiveness

Source: *Compiled by researcher*

These constructs correspond exactly to those validated and analyzed in data analysis section.

3.8 Data Analysis Techniques

3.8.1 Preliminary Analysis

Data were screened for:

- Missing values
- Outliers
- Normality

Descriptive statistics were computed to summarize respondent characteristics and construct-level perceptions.

3.8.2 Measurement Model Assessment

Confirmatory Factor Analysis (CFA) was conducted to evaluate:

- Reliability (Cronbach's Alpha, Composite Reliability)
- Convergent validity (Factor loadings, AVE)
- Discriminant validity (HTMT ratio)

3.8.3 Structural Equation Modelling (SEM)

SEM was used to test:

- Direct effects (H1, H2, H3, H6)
- Mediation effects (H4, H7)
- Moderation effect (H5)

Model fit was assessed using:

- Comparative Fit Index
- Tucker–Lewis Index
- Root Mean Square Error of Approximation
- Standardized Root Mean Square Residual

Bootstrapping (5,000 resamples) was applied for mediation testing, ensuring robust inference.

3.9 Control Variables and Bias Control

Control variables included:

- Age
- Gender
- Type of treatment
- Origin region
- Digital literacy

Common Method Bias was addressed through:

- Procedural remedies (anonymity, item separation)
- Statistical testing (Harman's single-factor test)

4. DATA ANALYSIS AND RESULTS

This section presents the statistical analysis and empirical results of the study examining *Improving Global Patient Access through AI-Enhanced Medical Tourism: Implications for Global Health Outcomes*. The analysis was conducted using Structural Equation Modelling (SEM) to test the proposed conceptual framework and hypothesis. The chapter is organized into respondent profile analysis, measurement model assessment, structural model evaluation, hypothesis testing, and interpretation of findings.

4.1 Profile of Respondents

A total of 450 valid responses were used for final analysis after data screening.

Table 4. Demographic Profile of Respondents (n = 450)

Variable	Category	Percentage (%)
Gender	Male	54.2
	Female	45.8
Age	Below 30	18.4
	31–45	46.7
	Above 45	34.9
Region of Origin	Asia	41.6
	Europe	28.9
	Africa	15.3
	Others	14.2
Type of Treatment	Elective	58.7
	Major / Critical	41.3

Source: *Compiled by researcher*

Interpretation

The sample reflects a diverse international patient base, suitable for analysing global patient access in medical tourism.

4.2 Descriptive Statistics

Table 5. Descriptive Statistics of Study Constructs

Construct	Mean	Std. Deviation
AI-Enhanced Medical Tourism (AIMT)	3.98	0.71
Reduced Access Barriers (RAB)	3.84	0.68
Trust & Safety Perception (TSP)	3.91	0.72
Continuity of Care (CoC)	3.76	0.69
Global Patient Access (GPA)	4.02	0.67
Global Health Outcomes (GHO)	3.89	0.70

Source: *Compiled by researcher*

Interpretation

Mean values above the scale midpoint (3.0) indicate positive perceptions of AI-enabled medical tourism, patient access, and health outcomes.

4.4 Measurement Model Assessment (Confirmatory Factor Analysis)

4.4.1 Reliability Analysis

Table 6. Reliability Statistics

Construct	Cronbach's Alpha	Composite Reliability
AIMT	0.86	0.89
RAB	0.81	0.85
TSP	0.84	0.88
CoC	0.79	0.83
GPA	0.88	0.91
GHO	0.85	0.89

Source: *Compiled by researcher*

Interpretation

All constructs exceed the recommended threshold of **0.70**, confirming strong internal consistency.

4.4.2 Convergent Validity

Table 7. Convergent Validity (AVE)

Construct	AVE
AIMT	0.62
RAB	0.57
TSP	0.60
CoC	0.55
GPA	0.65
GHO	0.61

Source: *Compiled by researcher*

Interpretation

AVE values above **0.50** confirm adequate convergent validity.

4.4.3 Discriminant Validity (HTMT)

Table 8. HTMT Ratio

Construct Pair	HTMT
AIMT – GPA	0.71
AIMT – TSP	0.69
GPA – GHO	0.73
TSP – CoC	0.67

Source: *Compiled by researcher*

Interpretation

All HTMT values are below **0.85**, establishing discriminant validity.

4.5 Structural Model Evaluation

4.5.1 Model Fit Indices

Table 9. SEM Model Fit Statistics

Index	Value	Recommended
CFI	0.93	≥ 0.90
TLI	0.91	≥ 0.90
RMSEA	0.056	≤ 0.08
SRMR	0.061	≤ 0.08

Source: *Compiled by researcher*

Interpretation

The structural model demonstrates a good overall fit, supporting the proposed framework.

4.6 Hypothesis Testing Results

Table 10. Direct, Mediating, and Moderating Effects

Hypothesis	Path	β	p-value	Result
H1	AIMT → GPA	0.42	<0.001	Supported
H2	AIMT → RAB	−0.39	<0.001	Supported
H3	RAB → GPA	0.31	0.002	Supported
H4	AIMT → TSP → GPA	Indirect	<0.01	Supported
H5	AIMT × CoC → GHO	0.21	0.018	Supported
H6	GPA → GHO	0.47	<0.001	Supported
H7	AIMT → GPA → GHO	Indirect	<0.01	Supported

Source: *Compiled by researcher*

4.7 Interpretation of Structural Relationships

4.7.1 Effect of AI-Enhanced Medical Tourism on Global Patient Access

The positive and significant path coefficient ($\beta = 0.42$) confirms that AI-enhanced medical tourism directly improves global patient access. AI-enabled teleconsultation, intelligent matching, and transparent information significantly reduce uncertainties associated with cross-border healthcare.

4.7.2 Role of Reduced Access Barriers

The negative relationship between AIMT and RAB ($\beta = -0.39$) indicates that AI significantly reduces geographical, financial, and informational barriers. Reduced barriers further enhance patient access ($\beta = 0.31$), confirming their mediating role.

4.7.3 Mediating Role of Trust and Safety Perception

Trust and safety perception significantly mediate the relationship between AI adoption and patient access. This highlights the importance of data transparency, credibility, and perceived safety in AI-enabled medical tourism platforms.

4.7.4 Moderating Effect of Continuity of Care

The interaction effect ($\beta = 0.21$) indicates that continuity of care strengthens the impact of AI on global health outcomes. Patients who experienced better post-treatment follow-up and coordination reported superior health outcomes.

4.7.5 Global Patient Access and Health Outcomes

Global patient access exhibits the strongest effect on health outcomes ($\beta = 0.47$), underscoring its central role as a key mechanism through which AI enhances global health outcomes.

4.8 Explained Variance (R^2)

Table 11. Explained Variance

Endogenous Construct	R^2
Reduced Access Barriers	0.38
Trust & Safety Perception	0.41
Global Patient Access	0.52
Global Health Outcomes	0.49

Source: *Compiled by researcher*

Interpretation

The model explains a substantial proportion of variance in patient access and health outcomes, indicating strong predictive power

5. FINDINGS OF THE STUDY

This chapter presents the major empirical findings derived from the quantitative analysis conducted to examine the role of AI-Enhanced Medical Tourism (AIMT) in improving Global Patient Access (GPA) and Global Health Outcomes (GHO). Using Structural Equation Modelling (SEM), the study evaluated direct, mediating, and moderating relationships among key constructs, providing robust evidence aligned with the research objectives and hypotheses.

Overall, the findings confirm that AI-enabled technologies significantly reshape medical tourism by reducing access barriers, enhancing trust and continuity of care, and ultimately improving global health outcomes. From a theoretical standpoint, the results substantiate the integrated framework grounded in information asymmetry, health equity, technology adoption, and institutional governance perspectives. The empirical evidence validates the proposed conceptual model and demonstrates the explanatory power of AIMT as a transformative mechanism in cross-border healthcare delivery.

5.1 Profile-Based Findings

The respondent profile indicates a diverse and globally representative sample, with participation from Asia (41.6%), Europe (28.9%), Africa (15.3%), and other regions (14.2). The age distribution shows that nearly 81.6% of respondents were above 30 years, reflecting mature decision-makers with sufficient healthcare experience. Additionally, 41.3% of respondents underwent major or critical treatments, strengthening the relevance of health outcome evaluations.

Findings

The demographic diversity and treatment severity profile enhance the external validity of the study and confirm that the findings are applicable across different regions and healthcare needs. This broad representation strengthens the generalizability of conclusions regarding global patient access and aligns with the health equity perspective, which emphasizes inclusiveness across geographical and socio-economic contexts.

5.2 Perception-Based Findings (Descriptive Statistics)

All study constructs recorded mean values above the neutral midpoint (3.0), indicating overall positive perceptions toward AI-enabled medical tourism.

- **Global Patient Access (M = 4.02)** emerged as the highest-rated construct, suggesting that respondents strongly perceive AI as a facilitator of timely, affordable, and transparent healthcare access.
- **AI-Enhanced Medical Tourism (M = 3.98)** and **Trust & Safety Perception (M = 3.91)** also recorded high means, reflecting confidence in AI-driven platforms.
- **Continuity of Care (M = 3.76)**, although slightly lower, still indicates favourable post-treatment engagement and coordination.

Findings

International medical tourists generally perceive AI technologies as beneficial, reliable, and access-enhancing. These descriptive results align with technology adoption principles proposed by Fred Davis, suggesting that perceived usefulness and trust are central drivers of AI acceptance in healthcare contexts. The strong perception of improved access further reflects reduced informational uncertainty, consistent with information asymmetry theory.

5.3 Measurement Model Findings

The Confirmatory Factor Analysis (CFA) established the psychometric robustness of the measurement model.

- **Reliability:** All constructs exceeded recommended thresholds for Cronbach's Alpha (≥ 0.70) and Composite Reliability, confirming internal consistency.
- **Convergent Validity:** AVE values ranged from 0.55 to 0.65, indicating that the indicators adequately capture their respective constructs.
- **Discriminant Validity:** HTMT ratios were below 0.85, demonstrating that constructs are conceptually distinct.

Finding

The validated measurement model confirms that the constructs measuring AIMT, GPA, and GHO are statistically sound and theoretically coherent. The distinctiveness of constructs such as access, trust, and continuity reflects the multidimensional theoretical structure underpinning the model.

5.4 Structural Model Findings

5.4.1 Direct Effects

The structural model reveals several significant direct relationships:

- **AI-Enhanced Medical Tourism → Global Patient Access**

($\beta = 0.42$, $p < 0.001$)
This strong positive effect confirms that AI-enabled services directly improve access by enhancing information availability, intelligent provider matching, and pre-treatment decision-making. This finding supports the information asymmetry perspective developed by George Akerlof, which argues that reducing information gaps improves market efficiency and decision confidence. AI reduces uncertainty in cross-border healthcare, thereby expanding patient access.

- **AI-Enhanced Medical Tourism → Reduced Access Barriers**

($\beta = -0.39$, $p < 0.001$)

The negative coefficient indicates that AI significantly lowers financial, geographical, and informational barriers. By improving transparency and coordination, AI reduces structural frictions within international healthcare markets.

- **Reduced Access Barriers → Global Patient Access**

($\beta = 0.31$, $p = 0.002$)
Reduced barriers translate into improved patient access, reinforcing the theoretical argument that information transparency and cost predictability increase healthcare participation.

- **Global Patient Access → Global Health Outcomes**

($\beta = 0.47$, $p < 0.001$)
This represents the strongest path in the model, highlighting access as a critical determinant of recovery quality and treatment effectiveness. This finding is strongly aligned with the health equity perspective associated with Amartya Sen, which emphasizes that expanded access to healthcare services enhances individual capabilities and overall well-being.

Findings:

AI-Enhanced Medical Tourism directly and indirectly improves healthcare outcomes by first improving patient access, confirming the central mediating role of access within a health equity framework.

5.4.2 Mediating Effects

Two mediation mechanisms were tested and supported:

- **Trust & Safety Perception as a Mediator (H4):** Trust and safety significantly mediate the relationship between AIMT and GPA. This indicates that AI adoption alone is insufficient; patient confidence in data security, transparency, and ethical AI use is essential for access enhancement. This finding complements technology adoption theory, which underscores trust as a prerequisite for digital engagement.
- **Global Patient Access as a Mediator (H7):** GPA significantly mediates the relationship between AIMT and GHO, confirming that AI improves health outcomes primarily by expanding access rather than through isolated technological effects. This mediation supports the health equity argument that

improved access is the primary pathway through which systemic innovations translate into better outcomes.

Finding:

The mediating effects highlight that psychological assurance (trust) and structural access are indispensable pathways linking AI adoption to improved global health outcomes.

5.4.3 Moderating Effect of Continuity of Care

The interaction between AIMT and Continuity of Care on Global Health Outcomes was positive and significant ($\beta = 0.21$, $p = 0.018$).

Findings:

Continuity of care strengthens the effectiveness of AI on health outcomes. Patients who experienced AI-supported follow-up, digital monitoring, and coordinated post-treatment care reported superior recovery and satisfaction levels. This result aligns with institutional governance perspectives influenced by Douglass North, which emphasize that structured coordination and regulatory alignment enhance system performance. Continuity of care therefore acts as a governance-enabled mechanism that ensures access translates into sustainable outcomes.

5.5 Model Fit and Predictive Power

The SEM model demonstrated a good overall fit (CFI = 0.93, TLI = 0.91, RMSEA = 0.056, SRMR = 0.061), confirming that the proposed conceptual framework accurately represents observed data.

The explained variance values further support the model's robustness:

- **Global Patient Access ($R^2 = 0.52$)**
- **Global Health Outcomes ($R^2 = 0.49$)**

These values indicate moderate-to-strong explanatory power, reinforcing the theoretical proposition that AI-enhanced medical tourism operates primarily through access expansion mechanisms to influence global health outcomes.

6. CONCLUSION

The present study set out to empirically examine the role of AI-Enhanced Medical Tourism (AIMT) in improving Global Patient Access (GPA) and Global Health Outcomes (GHO) by adopting a rigorous quantitative research methodology and advanced statistical modelling. Grounded in a positivist research paradigm and operationalized through a cross-sectional survey design, the study provides robust empirical evidence on how artificial intelligence-driven technologies are reshaping the global medical tourism landscape. Importantly, the findings contribute to theory by integrating perspectives from information asymmetry, health equity, technology adoption, and institutional governance to explain the structural mechanisms through which AI transforms cross-border healthcare access and outcomes.

By integrating direct effects, mediating mechanisms, and moderating conditions within a Structural Equation Modelling (SEM) framework, the research offers a comprehensive understanding of the complex pathways through which AI-enabled medical tourism contributes to equitable healthcare access and improved patient outcomes across borders. The study therefore advances both theoretical and empirical knowledge in the emerging intersection of digital health, global healthcare mobility, and medical tourism.

6.1 Methodological Strength and Research Rigor

One of the key strengths of this study lies in its methodological robustness. The adoption of a quantitative, explanatory research design ensured objective hypothesis testing and minimized subjective bias. The use of a large and diverse international sample (n = 450) exceeded recommended SEM thresholds, thereby ensuring statistical power and stability of parameter estimates, particularly for mediation and moderation analysis.

The multi-stage sampling strategy enhanced external validity by incorporating respondents from diverse regions, treatment categories, and healthcare systems. Furthermore, the inclusion criteria—such as recent treatment experience and exposure to AI-enabled healthcare services—ensured high contextual relevance and reliable recall of healthcare outcomes.

The instrument development process, supported by a pilot study and rigorous validation procedures, confirmed that all constructs demonstrated strong reliability, convergent validity, and discriminant validity. This methodological rigor strengthens the credibility of the empirical findings and supports the robustness of the theoretically grounded structural model.

6.2 Confirmation of the Conceptual Framework

The study's conceptual framework, which positioned AI-Enhanced Medical Tourism as a primary exogenous variable influencing patient access and health outcomes through multiple mechanisms, was empirically validated. The strong model fit indices confirm that the proposed structure accurately represents real-world patient experiences within AI-enabled medical tourism ecosystems.

The SEM results further demonstrate that AI does not operate in isolation; rather, it influences outcomes through interconnected pathways involving access facilitation, trust formation, barrier reduction, and continuity of care. These findings reinforce the theoretical proposition that digital health innovations function as systemic enablers rather than standalone technological interventions.

From an information asymmetry perspective, the findings support the argument proposed by George Akerlof that reducing uncertainty and improving transparency enhances decision-making in complex markets. Similarly, the validated framework reflects principles of technology acceptance advanced by Fred Davis, emphasizing the role of perceived usefulness and trust in facilitating AI adoption within healthcare systems.

6.3 AI-Enhanced Medical Tourism as an Enabler of Global Patient Access

One of the most critical conclusions of the study is that AI-Enhanced Medical Tourism significantly improves Global Patient Access. The strong and positive relationship between AIMT and GPA confirms that AI-driven tools—such as teleconsultation, intelligent hospital matching, digital diagnostics, and transparent information systems—effectively reduce uncertainty and enhance decision-making in cross-border healthcare.

This finding provides strong theoretical support for the information asymmetry framework, as AI-enabled platforms improve transparency, reduce risk perception, and enhance patient confidence. By overcoming geographical, informational, and procedural constraints, AI-enabled medical tourism contributes to the democratization of healthcare access and expands global treatment opportunities.

In addition, the results align with health equity perspectives influenced by Amartya Sen, which emphasize that improved access is a key determinant of human well-being. The expansion of access through AI-enabled systems enables patients from underserved regions to obtain advanced treatments, thereby addressing disparities in healthcare availability.

6.4 Reduction of Access Barriers and the Central Role of Trust

The study demonstrates that AI-Enhanced Medical Tourism significantly reduces access barriers, including financial ambiguity, informational asymmetry, and logistical complexity. The reduction of these barriers plays a central role in enhancing global patient access and improving treatment pathways.

Equally important is the mediating role of Trust and Safety Perception. The findings indicate that patient confidence in data security, transparency, and ethical AI practices is a necessary condition for realizing the benefits of digital healthcare systems. These results strongly reinforce technology adoption theory, which highlights trust, perceived reliability, and risk reduction as key drivers of technology acceptance.

Thus, the study concludes that technological advancement alone is insufficient. Ethical AI governance, data protection frameworks, and transparent communication mechanisms are essential to ensure that digital innovations translate into meaningful and inclusive healthcare access.

6.5 Global Patient Access as the Primary Driver of Health Outcomes

Among all structural relationships tested, Global Patient Access exhibited the strongest effect on Global Health Outcomes, establishing access as the most critical mechanism through which AI enhances patient well-being. This finding has significant theoretical implications and strongly supports health equity theory.

The results confirm that improved health outcomes are not solely dependent on advanced medical technologies but are contingent on patients' ability to access appropriate care at the right time. This aligns with the capability-based approach proposed by Amartya Sen, which emphasizes that expanded healthcare opportunities enhance both individual capabilities and societal well-being.

Furthermore, the mediation analysis confirms that GPA serves as the key transmission pathway through which AIMT influences global health outcomes, reinforcing the centrality of access in global healthcare transformation.

6.6 Importance of Continuity of Care in AI-Enabled Medical Tourism

Another important conclusion of the study is the moderating role of Continuity of Care. The findings reveal that AI's impact on global health outcomes is significantly strengthened when patients experience coordinated follow-up, digital monitoring, and integrated post-treatment support.

This result reflects the institutional governance perspective influenced by Douglass North, which highlights the importance of regulatory coordination, structured healthcare systems, and institutional alignment in achieving sustainable outcomes. Continuity of care ensures that improved access is translated into long-term health benefits, thereby transforming medical tourism from episodic treatment to integrated healthcare delivery.

In conclusion, this study provides compelling empirical and theoretical evidence that AI-Enhanced Medical Tourism functions as a structural enabler of global patient access and improved health outcomes. By reducing informational and logistical barriers, strengthening trust, facilitating adoption, and enhancing continuity of care, AI emerges not merely as a technological innovation but as a transformative force in global healthcare systems. The findings offer important insights for policymakers, healthcare providers, and international governance bodies seeking to promote equitable, ethical, and sustainable AI-enabled healthcare across borders.

REFERENCES

Abubakari, M. S., & Olamilekan, L. A. (2026). Digital Competency's Role in Promoting Equity in the Digital Healthcare Ecosystem. *Reshaping Health Promotion and Disease Prevention Through Digital Innovation*, 129.

Al-Romeedy, B. S., Emam, M. E., Hussein, H., Singh, A., & Tyagi, P. K. (2025). Digital Passports to Wellness: How Technology Is Shaping Medical Tourism. In *Revolutionizing Healthcare Experience With Digital Medical Tourism* (pp. 111-136). IGI Global Scientific Publishing.

Alowais, A., Alghamdi, S. S., Alsuhebany, N., Alqahtani, T., Alshaya, A., Almohareb, S. N., & Alowais, S. A. (2024). The issue of ethical and legal concerns in healthcare artificial intelligence. *BMC Medical Ethics*, *25*, 62.

Alquayt, A., Aljuhani, O., Alharthi, A. F., Alqahtani, R., Khan, A., Al-Jedai, A., Almoeen, A., Alshennawi, M., Badreldin, H. A., Aljouie, A., Alnasser, L. A., Alshehri, A. M., Alzahrani, M. Y., Alhaidal, H. A., Alhajaji, R., Alotaibi, S., Redhwan, E. Z., Alharthi, F., Alghamdi, B. G., & Al Sulaiman, K. (2025). AI-driven healthcare innovations for enhancing clinical services during mass gatherings (Hajj): Task force insights and future directions. *BMC Health Services Research*, *25*(1), 876. DOI: 10.1186/s12913-025-13045-5 PMID: 40598365

Alsabah, M., Naser, M. A., Albahri, A., Albahri, O., Alamoodi, A., Abdulhussain, S. H., & Alzubaidi, L. (2025). A comprehensive review on key technologies toward smart healthcare systems based IoT: Technical aspects, challenges and future directions. *Artificial Intelligence Review*, *58*(11), 343. DOI: 10.1007/s10462-025-11342-3

Alsehani, F. N. (2026). Harnessing Artificial Intelligence and Digital Technologies for Sustainable Healthcare Delivery in Saudi Arabia: A Comprehensive Review, Issues, and Future Perspectives. *Sustainability (Basel)*, *18*(3), 1461. DOI: 10.3390/su18031461

Anam, A. S. M. T., Bhuiyan, M. R. I., Islam, S., Ullah, M. N., & Rakib, M. A. A. (2026). Factors influencing university students' adoption of online education platforms in Bangladesh: An extended TAM-based analysis. *Educational and Developmental Psychologist*, 1–17.

Angelillo, L., van Steen, C., Ross-Stewart, K., Dehnen, J., & Colasante, W. (2023). Viability of European cross-border access opportunities to streamline access to ATMPs. *Health Policy and Technology*, *12*(3), 100752. DOI: 10.1016/j.hlpt.2023.100752

Arzikulov, F., & Komiljonov, A. (2025). AI-powered diagnostic systems in radiology: Enhancing precision, speed, and clinical decision-making. *Academic Journal of Science. Technology and Education*, *1*(6), 16–23.

Ayesha, A., & Ahamed, N. N. (2024). Explainable artificial intelligence (eai): For healthcare applications and improvements. In *Explainable Artificial Intelligence for Biomedical and Healthcare Applications* (pp. 162–196). CRC Press. DOI: 10.1201/9781003220107-11

Barua, R., & Datta, S. (2024). The Improvements in Significance of AI in Experiential and Medical Tourism. In *Generative AI for Transformational Management* (pp. 303–334). IGI Global. DOI: 10.4018/979-8-3693-5578-7.ch012

Bassi, A.. (2025). Artificial intelligence applications in telemedicine: A systematic review. *Journal of Medical Internet Research*, •••, 27.

Bhavnani, S., & McKim, R. (2026). *Artificial Intelligence in Mental Healthcare: Potential Applications and New Frontiers*. CRC Press.

Bhuiyan, M. R. I. (2024). Industry readiness and adaptation of the fourth industrial revolution: Applying the extended TOE framework. *Human Behavior and Emerging Technologies*, *2024*(1), 8830228. DOI: 10.1155/hbe2/8830228

Bhuiyan, M. R. I., Akter, M. S., Amin, A., & Hossain, R. (2025). Artificial intelligence and organizational transformation: Institutional readiness and digital innovation.

Bhuiyan, M. R. I., Husain, T., Islam, S., & Amin, A. (2025). Exploring the prospective influence of artificial intelligence on the health sector in Bangladesh: A study on awareness, perception and adoption. *Health Education*, *125*(3), 279–297. DOI: 10.1108/HE-10-2024-0125

Bhuiyan, M. R. I., Husain, T., Islam, S., & Amin, A. (2025b). Artificial intelligence adoption in healthcare: Barriers, awareness, and readiness in emerging economies. *Health Education*, *125*(3), 279–297. DOI: 10.1108/HE-10-2024-0125

Bhuiyan, M. R. I., Uddin, S., Sultana, T., Al-Amin, , & Islam, M. M. (2026). Investigating ChatGPT methods in higher education from a student engagement perspective: A descriptive cross-sectional study. *SAGE Open*, *16*(1), 21582440251413008. DOI: 10.1177/21582440251413008

Canadian Agency for Drugs and Technologies in Health. (2025). *2025 watch list: Artificial intelligence in health care*. CADTH.

Car, J., Tan, W. S., Huang, Z., Sloot, P., & Franklin, B. D. (2017). eHealth in the future of medications management: Personalisation, monitoring and adherence. *BMC Medicine, 15*(1), 73. DOI: 10.1186/s12916-017-0838-0 PMID: 28376771

Chaudhry, D. (2022). Is Medical Tourism really unethical? An alternate perspective for developing countries. *Journal of Development Policy and Practice*, *7*(2), 145–157. DOI: 10.1177/24551333211062355

Chen, H., Zeng, Y., & Cai, D. (2025). Deep learning for cardiovascular management: Optimizing pathways and cost control under diagnosis-related group models. *Frontiers in Artificial Intelligence*, *8*, 1580445. DOI: 10.3389/frai.2025.1580445 PMID: 40959774

Chen, P., Wu, L., & Wang, L. (2023). AI fairness in data management and analytics: A review on challenges, methodologies and applications. *Applied Sciences (Basel, Switzerland), 13*(18), 10258. DOI: 10.3390/app131810258

Chen, Y.. (2025). Explainable artificial intelligence in clinical decision support systems: A systematic meta-analysis (2018–2025). *Journal of Medical Internet Research, 27*, e12427955.

Christina, J., Ford, K., Menz, B., Sorich, M., Hopkins, A., Ramsey, I., Duddle, M., Kitson, A., & Paterson, C. (2025). Integrating the Caring Life Course Theory and Artificial Intelligence Applications to Enhance Cancer Care Across the Continuum. Seminars in Oncology Nursing, Cynthia, A. N. (2025). Ethical dilemmas in international medical health tourism: A critical commentary. *SSM - Health Systems*, •••, 100111.

Dar, H., & Kashyap, K. (2023). Smart healthcare system (SHS): Medical tourism delivering, consumption, and elevating tool in the ages of smart technologies. *Tourism Planning & Development, 20*(3), 397–415. DOI: 10.1080/21568316.2022.2109206

De la Hoz-Correa, A., Muñoz-Leiva, F., & Bakucz, M. (2018). Past themes and future trends in medical tourism research: A co-word analysis. *Tourism Management*, *65*, 200–211. DOI: 10.1016/j.tourman.2017.10.001

de Lima, T. M.. (2024). Telehealth and artificial intelligence approaches in musculoskeletal care with ethical considerations. *BMC Musculoskeletal Disorders*, *25*, 451.

Deshpande, R. (2024). Smart match: Revolutionizing organ allocation through artificial intelligence. *Frontiers in Artificial Intelligence*, *7*, 1364149. DOI: 10.3389/frai.2024.1364149 PMID: 38481822

Dinker, N. (2024). Artificial intelligence and inequality: examining the social divides created by technological advancements. *International Journal of Innovations in Science, Engineering And Management*, 228-236.

Djimesah, I. E., Zhao, H., Okine, A. N. D., Gyamfi, C. A., Mireku, K. K., Chen, W., Duah, E., & Osei-Mensah, E. (2026). Digital Infrastructure, Trust, and Behavioral Intention: An Extended Technology Acceptance Model for Crowdfunding Adoption in Emerging Economies. *Strategic Business Research*, 100068.

Elendu, C., Amaechi, D. C., Elendu, T. C., Amaechi, E. C., Elendu, I. D., Omokore, O. A., Onubogu, N. C., Omeludike, J. C., Aregbesola, E. T., Fajimi, O. O., Idowu, O. F., Emechebe, S. L., Uyanwune, M. C., & Yonni, J. (2025). The legal and ethical considerations in cross-border telesurgical procedures. *Annals of Medicine and Surgery (London)*, *87*(6), 3660–3672. DOI: 10.1097/MS9.0000000000003344 PMID: 40486583

Fahim, Y. A., Hasani, I. W., Kabba, S., & Ragab, W. M. (2025). Artificial intelligence in healthcare and medicine: Clinical applications, therapeutic advances, and future perspectives. *European Journal of Medical Research*, *30*(1), 1–21. DOI: 10.1186/s40001-025-03196-w PMID: 40988064

Faisal-E-Alam, M., Bhuiyan, M. R. I., Mimi, A., & Miah, M. T. (2025). The role of the three-zero framework in advancing global sustainable development: A bibliometric and text mining analysis. *Discover Sustainability*, *6*(1), 1128. DOI: 10.1007/s43621-025-01919-x

Faiyazuddin, M., Rahman, S. J. Q., Anand, G., Siddiqui, R. K., Mehta, R., Khatib, M. N., Gaidhane, S., Zahiruddin, Q. S., Hussain, A., & Sah, R. (2025). The impact of artificial intelligence on healthcare: A comprehensive review of advancements in diagnostics, treatment, and operational efficiency. *Health Science Reports*, *8*(1), e70312. DOI: 10.1002/hsr2.70312 PMID: 39763580

Fajarini, M., Sung, C.-M., Lin, Y.-S., Su, P.-Y., Chen, R., Chang, L.-F., Chiang, K.-J., & Chou, K.-R. (2026). Clinical effectiveness and cost-effectiveness of primary community health care nurses: A meta-analysis. *International Journal of Nursing Studies*, *177*, 105365. DOI: 10.1016/j.ijnurstu.2026.105365 PMID: 41702261

Foley, B. M., Haglin, J. M., Tanzer, J. R., & Eltorai, A. E. (2019). Patient care without borders: A systematic review of medical and surgical tourism. *Journal of Travel Medicine*, *26*(6), taz049. DOI: 10.1093/jtm/taz049 PMID: 31281926

Fortea, C. (2026). Modelling European Economic Sustainability Based on Economic Indicators Related to Sustainable Development Goal 8. In *Sustainable Economic Development and the European Green Deal: Creating Energy Efficiency, Industrial Innovation, and Inclusive Growth* (pp. 323-378). Springer.

Fradgley, E. A., Paul, C. L., & Bryant, J. (2015). A systematic review of barriers to optimal outpatient specialist services for individuals with prevalent chronic diseases: What are the unique and common barriers experienced by patients in high income countries? *International Journal for Equity in Health, 14*(1), 52. DOI: 10.1186/s12939-015-0179-6 PMID: 26051244

Gayatri, A. P., Bonthu, M. G., Srinivas, N., & Borse, L. B. (2026). Artificial intelligence–enhanced diagnostic tools for patient understanding. In *Artificial Intelligence in Patient Counselling* (pp. 247-276). Elsevier. Giró, A. B. Alternative Peacebuilding in Bosnia Evolution of an NGO and volunteer. DOI: 10.1016/B978-0-443-43823-3.00001-7

Goktas, P., & Grzybowski, A. (2025). Shaping the future of healthcare: Ethical clinical challenges and pathways to trustworthy AI. *Journal of Clinical Medicine, 14*(5), 1605. DOI: 10.3390/jcm14051605 PMID: 40095575

Guerrazzi, C. (2020). An international perspective on health information exchange: Adoption in OECD countries with different health care system configurations. *Medical Care Research and Review : MCRR, 77*(4), 299–311. DOI: 10.1177/1077558719858245 PMID: 31216934

Gulia, J. (2024). Cross-Border Data Transfers: International Cooperation and Conflicts. *Legal Lock J., 4*, 263.

Gupta, A., Gupta, R., & Kumar, P. (2023). Artificial Intelligence for Remote Healthcare in Underserved Areas: Enhancing Access and Quality of Healthcare Delivery. International Conference on Artificial Intelligence and its Application, Hackl, A. (2018). Mobility equity in a globalized world: Reducing inequalities in the sustainable development agenda. *World Development, 112*, 150–162.

Harryono, M., Huang, Y.-F., Miyazawa, K., & Sethaput, V. (2006). Thailand medical tourism cluster. *Harvard Business School Microeconomics of Competitiveness*, 1-31.

Heliades, G., Gkintoni, E., Panas, G., Halkiopoulos, C., & Boutsinas, B. (2024). AI-Enhanced Cognitive Wellness: Integrating NcBT and Human–Computer Interaction in Global Health Tourism. International Conference of the International Association of Cultural and Digital Tourism, Hoagland, A., & Kipping, S. (2024). Challenges in promoting health equity and reducing disparities in access across new and established technologies. *The Canadian Journal of Cardiology*, *40*(6), 1154–1167. PMID: 38417572

Ho, K.. (2025). Belief in clinical decision support systems that utilize artificial intelligence: A systematic literature review of healthcare workers' perspectives. *Journal of Medical Internet Research*, *27*, e69678. DOI: 10.2196/69678

Hussain, K., & Nasir, S. (2026). Regulatory Harmonization in the Digital Age: A Comparative Study of International Legal Frameworks Governing Cyber and Health Data Protection.

Islam, M. M., Bhuiyan, M. R. I., Islam, S. H., Tabassum, M. N., & Billah, M. (2026). Unlocking the mediating and moderating role of information security in information systems: A combined TAM, ISM, and HBM model. *Human Behavior and Emerging Technologies*, *2026*(1), 5593002. DOI: 10.1155/hbe2/5593002

Islam, M. T. (2026). AI-ENABLED CUSTOMER-INTERACTION MODELS FOR IMPROVING SERVICE EFFICIENCY IN US HOSPITALITY AND RETAIL OPERATIONS. *American Journal of Interdisciplinary Studies*, *7*(01), 94–140. DOI: 10.63125/par85p86

Jain, N., Nagaich, U., Pandey, M., Chellappan, D. K., & Dua, K. (2022). Predictive genomic tools in disease stratification and targeted prevention: A recent update in personalized therapy advancements. *The EPMA Journal*, *13*(4), 561–580. DOI: 10.1007/s13167-022-00304-2 PMID: 36505888

Khalifa, M., & Albadawy, M. (2024). AI in diagnostic imaging: Revolutionising accuracy and efficiency. *Computer Methods and Programs in Biomedicine Update*, *5*, 100146. DOI: 10.1016/j.cmpbup.2024.100146

Khanna, A.. (2025). Positions and drawbacks of artificial intelligence in health care: A narrative review. *Interactive Journal of Medical Research*, *14*(1), e53616.

Khatun, M., Hossain, R., Bhuiyan, M. R. I., Tabassum, M. N., & Riaj, M. A. (2025). *Green entrepreneurship and digital transformation for sustainable development: A systematic review* (In, K., Ed.). [Book title]

Lewis, A. K., Harding, K. E., Snowdon, D. A., & Taylor, N. F. (2018). Reducing wait time from referral to first visit for community outpatient services may contribute to better health outcomes: A systematic review. *BMC Health Services Research, 18*(1), 869. DOI: 10.1186/s12913-018-3669-6 PMID: 30458761

Liverani, M., Ir, P., Jacobs, B., Asante, A., Jan, S., Leang, S., Man, N., Hayen, A., & Wiseman, V. (2020). Cross-border medical travels from Cambodia: Pathways to care, associated costs and equity implications. *Health Policy and Planning*, *35*(8), 1011–1020. DOI: 10.1093/heapol/czaa061 PMID: 33049780

Lopes, J. M., Gomes, S., Nogueira, E., Ferreira, J. J., & Dabić, M. (2026). Exploring psychosocial predictors of AI use intention: The moderating role of organisational culture in diverse workplaces. *Behaviour & Information Technology*, •••, 1–19. DOI: 10.1080/0144929X.2026.2626743

Lu, R., Hong, S. H., & Zhang, X. (2018). A dynamic pricing demand response algorithm for smart grid: Reinforcement learning approach. *Applied Energy*, *220*, 220–230. DOI: 10.1016/j.apenergy.2018.03.072

Marchionatti, R. (2026). Economics in the MIT-Harvard Network and the New Keynesian Economics. In *Economic Theory in the Twentieth Century, An Intellectual History—Volume IV: Mid-1970s–Early 2000s. Economic Theory in the Age of Globalization* (pp. 65-129). Springer.

Maurya, S. K. (2026). Justice and Quality of Life: A Philosophical Perspective. In *Exploring Justice as a Social Indicator of Life: Philosophical Foundations and Empirical Approaches* (pp. 1-23). Springer. DOI: 10.1007/978-3-032-10812-8_1

Mbanugo, O. J. (2025). *AI-Enhanced Telemedicine: A Common-Sense Approach to Chronic Disease Management and a Tool to Bridging the Gap in Healthcare Disparities*. Department of Healthcare Management & Informatics, Coles College of Business, Kennesaw State University.

Mengistu, A. K., Getinet, K., Alemayehu, T., Yeneakal, K. A., Gedefaw, A. E., Teym, A., Endalew, B., & Assaye, B. T. (2026). Machine learning predicts prolonged patient length of stay in a resource constrained Ethiopian hospital. *Discover Artificial Intelligence*, *6*(1), 88. DOI: 10.1007/s44163-025-00794-9

Molla, C., Bhuiyan, M. R. I., Islam, M. T., & Amin, A. (2026). Mediating role of digital banking adoption on banking performance using the technology–organization–environment model. *Digital Finance*, *8*(1), 4. DOI: 10.1007/s42521-025-00168-x

Mubarak, F. (2026). Digital health literacy and the ethics of information access: a systematic review of global trends, equity challenges and policy responses. *Journal of Information, Communication and Ethics in Society*, 1-30.

Natarajan, H. P., Chandru, M., & Pushparaj, A. (2026). Advancing Healthcare Diagnostics: A Precision-Driven Approach to Disease Prediction and Personalized Treatment Recommendation. *SN Computer Science*, *7*(3), 220. DOI: 10.1007/s42979-026-04787-y

Nesheli, S. I., Rostami, M. R., & Hosseini, S. H. (2026). Developing an Indigenous Model of Customer Experience in Health Tourism in Mazandaran Province Using an Exploratory Mixed-Methods Approach. *Journal of Resource Management and Decision Engineering*, 1-20.

Niranjan, S. J., Wallace, A., Williams, B. R., Turkman, Y., Williams, C. P., Bhatia, S., Knight, S., & Rocque, G. B. (2020). Trust but verify: Exploring the role of treatment-related information and patient-physician trust in shared decision making among patients with metastatic breast cancer. *Journal of Cancer Education : The Official Journal of the American Association for Cancer Education*, *35*(5), 885–892. DOI: 10.1007/s13187-019-01538-x PMID: 31062280

Organization, W. H. (2024). *Evidence and research gaps identified during development of policy guidelines for tuberculosis*. World Health Organization.

Oso, O. B., Alli, O. I., Babarinde, A. O., & Ibeh, A. I. (2025). Navigating cross-border healthcare investments: A risk-opportunity model for emerging markets. *Engineering and Technology Journal*, *10*(2), 3805–3832.

Packer, C., Labonté, R., & Runnels, V. (2009). Globalization and the cross-border flow of health workers. In *Globalization and health* (pp. 235–256). Routledge.

Patel, R., Shukla, S., Patel, N., Sharma, P., Mevada, S., Singh, S., & Prajapati, B. G. (2026). AI-driven patient empowerment and self-care: Implementing AI solutions for enhanced clinical practice. In *Artificial Intelligence in Patient Counselling* (pp. 333–352). Elsevier. DOI: 10.1016/B978-0-443-43823-3.00009-1

Rad, J. (2025). Health inequities: A persistent global challenge from past to future. *International Journal for Equity in Health*, *24*(1), 148. DOI: 10.1186/s12939-025-02526-y PMID: 40410748

Regona, M., Yigitcanlar, T., Hon, C., & Teo, M. (2026). Building Trust in Artificial Intelligence: A Systematic Review through the Lens of Trust Theory. *ACM Computing Surveys*, *58*(9), 1–39. DOI: 10.1145/3789256

Reshadi, M. S., & Chehragh, A. M. (2025). A review of medical tourism entrepreneurship and marketing at regional and global levels and a quick glance into the applications of artificial intelligence in medical tourism. *AI & Society*, *40*(5), 1–17. DOI: 10.1007/s00146-024-02178-6

Ruggeri, K., Ivanović, N., Razum, J., Kácha, O., Menezes, I. G., Zafari, Z., & Garcia-Garzon, E. (2018). An evidence-based policy for improving choice in global health access through medical travel. *Health Policy (Amsterdam)*, *122*(12), 1372–1376. DOI: 10.1016/j.healthpol.2018.09.017 PMID: 30337161

Sah, A. K. (2025). Prognostic biomarkers: predicting disease outcomes. In *The Potential of Cancer Biomarkers* (pp. 211–238). Elsevier. DOI: 10.1016/B978-0-443-29279-8.00010-7

Sandberg, D. S. (2017). Medical tourism: An emerging global healthcare industry. *International Journal of Healthcare Management*, *10*(4), 281–288. DOI: 10.1080/20479700.2017.1296213

Secinaro, S., Calandra, D., Secinaro, A., Muthurangu, V., & Biancone, P. (2021). The role of artificial intelligence in healthcare: A structured literature review. *BMC Medical Informatics and Decision Making*, *21*(1), 125. DOI: 10.1186/s12911-021-01488-9 PMID: 33836752

Selwood, A., Blakely, B., Senthuran, S., Lane, P., North, J., & Clay-Williams, R. (2020). Variability in clinicians' understanding and reported methods of identifying high-risk surgical patients: A qualitative study. *BMC Health Services Research*, *20*(1), 427. DOI: 10.1186/s12913-020-05316-0 PMID: 32414412

Shafik, W. (2025). Artificial Intelligence Integration in Medical Tourism: Medical Breakthroughs-Are We Truly Progressing? In *Navigating Health Information in the Age of Artificial Intelligence* (pp. 1-36). IGI Global Scientific Publishing.

Siciliani, L., Lafortune, G., Fujisawa, R., Vuik, S., & Hewlett, E. (2023). A review of policies to reduce waiting times for health services across OECD countries: Waiting times for health services. *Nordic Journal of Health Economics*, *11*(1), 162–181. DOI: 10.5617/njhe.10214

Snyder, J., Dharamsi, S., & Crooks, V. A. (2011). Fly-By medical care: Conceptualizing the global and local social responsibilities of medical tourists and physician voluntourists. *Globalization and Health*, *7*(1), 6. DOI: 10.1186/1744-8603-7-6 PMID: 21470415

Taherdoost, H., & Ghofrani, A. (2024). AI's role in revolutionizing personalized medicine by reshaping pharmacogenomics and drug therapy. *Intelligent Pharmacy, 2*(5), 643–650. DOI: 10.1016/j.ipha.2024.08.005

Tsekouropoulos, G., Vasileiou, A., Hoxha, G., Dimitriadis, A., & Zervas, I. (2024). Sustainable approaches to medical tourism: Strategies for Central Macedonia/Greece. *Sustainability (Basel), 16*(1), 121. DOI: 10.3390/su16010121

Virani, A., Wellstead, A. M., & Howlett, M. (2020). The north-south policy divide in transnational healthcare: A comparative review of policy research on medical tourism in source and destination countries. *Globalization and Health, 16*(1), 37. DOI: 10.1186/s12992-020-00566-3 PMID: 32321561

Whig, P., Kasula, B. Y., Yathiraju, N., Ahmed Khan, I., Rai, A., & Mahmood, M. R. (2025). AI/ML-Based Approaches in Healthcare: Transforming Diagnosis, Treatment, and Beyond. In *Convergence of Artificial Intelligence, Machine Learning, and the Internet of Things in Industry 4.0 Applications* (pp. 45-66). Springer.

Williamson, S. M., & Prybutok, V. (2024). Balancing privacy and progress: A review of privacy challenges, systemic oversight, and patient perceptions in AI-driven healthcare. *Applied Sciences (Basel, Switzerland), 14*(2), 675. DOI: 10.3390/app14020675

Yan, R., Zhang, S., Zhang, H., & Qiu, H. (2026). To engage or not to engage? A qualitative investigation into educators' and learners' perspectives on AI in tourism higher education. *Journal of Hospitality and Tourism Technology*, •••, 1–23. DOI: 10.1108/JHTT-06-2025-0498

Chapter 4
Impact of Artificial Intelligence on Medical Tourism:
An Indian Perspective

Kuldeep Singh
http://orcid.org/0000-0002-7999-1585
Amity University, Haryana, India

Ajay Kimar
http://orcid.org/0009-0003-5653-6728
Chandigarh College of Hospitality, Punjab, India

Sanjeev Kumar
http://orcid.org/0000-0002-7375-7341
Lovely Professional University, India

Viana Imad Hassan
http://orcid.org/0000-0002-7372-5059
ETE Academy, Malta

ABSTRACT

Over the past years, the adoption of Artificial Intelligence (AI) in healthcare systems has continued to reshape the medical tourism industry by improving the level of accuracy in the diagnostic process. This chapter is a critical analysis of how Artificial Intelligence has influenced medical tourism in India. Using secondary data through a vast amount of academic literature, policy reports and industry sources, the study indicates that AI-enabled devices enhance the reliability of services and increase the competitiveness of India as a global destination in medical tourism. The results

DOI: 10.4018/979-8-3373-8944-8.ch004

presented highlight the fact that, although AI can generate significant potential to increase efficiency the advantages of this technology can be fully achieved through proper governance structures and capacity building programs. The chapter concludes that the combination of Artificial Intelligence in terms of its strategic and inclusive integration can become the key to the sustainable, patient-centric, and globally competitive development of medical tourism in India.

INTRODUCTION

Medical tourism refers to the practice of people going over national borders in search of healthcare services with the primary drive being the presence of better-quality treatment, less waiting time, and cheaper treatment procedures than those in the developed nations (George et al., 2025). Medical tourism is a phenomenon where patients travel outside their home countries in search of medical procedures, such as elective surgery and special surgery, as well as other services related to wellness. This kind of travel has grown exponentially in the healthcare and tourism sector of the world due to rising medical care costs in the developed countries, a rising number of patients in line, and the growing number of developing countries with advanced medical technologies. The increasing medical tourism across the globe has also been enhanced by the opening up of healthcare services in many countries and the global movement of people (Mohapatra & Giri, 2018). The advent of Artificial Intelligence (AI) into the healthcare has brought revolutionary changes in all aspects of clinical practice, diagnostics, administration, and patient engagement, being a major determinant of health services worldwide. Over the past years, AI has not just enabled efficiency and accuracy in medical systems, but has already started to influence medical tourism, which is where patients do move across international borders in search of quality, affordable, and timely care. Predictive analytics, virtual health assistants and telemedicine platforms are some of the enabled AI tools across the world that are improving healthcare access and personalization and thus relevant to medical travelers who frequently need smooth, trusted, and data-intensive healthcare experiences. Clinical decision making, better outcomes, and risk reduction related to complex are other aspects that are being redefined by AI in analyzing vast amount of medical history and diagnostic data (ETHealthWorld, 2025).

India has become a major destination of medical tourism because of its low-cost healthcare services, highly developed medical facilities, and high number of qualified healthcare providers (Soni, 2024). There is a clear positive trend in the sector over the last few years, as the number of medical tourists increased by several times between about 183,000 in 2020 and over 504,000 by the end of 2023, indicating a good post-pandemic recovery, and the activity of the governments to build the healthcare infrastructure and access international patientsIn this global scenario, India has become a medical tourist attraction destination because it has proven to have great cost benefits, production of highly trained medical staff, and a wide scope of medical services. The nation has healthcare services with modern medical practices with traditional system of medicine like Ayurveda, Yoga, Unani, Siddha and Homeopathy which have in general increased its attractiveness to foreign patients (Gunaseelan & Kesavan, 2020; Naaz & Khan, 2016). Studies always point out that such complicated procedures such as cardiac surgery, orthopedic surgery, and organ transplants is offered in India at a much cheaper cost than the developed nations without compromising on the standards of care provided internationally (Garg et al., 2020).

This research project seeks to focus on growth and development of medical tourism in India by looking into the major aspects that have led to the rise of the country as a destination to international clients. The research will aim to measure the economic and healthcare-related consequences of medical tourism and also determine the key issues impacting the industry. Based on the analysis of this study, the study will offer informative insights that can be useful in formulating an effective policy as well as enhancing the sustainable development of medical tourism in the Indian setting. Besides low cost and high quality healthcare services, the country has well established tourism infrastructure, and diverse cultural diversity that makes it attractive as a medical tourism destination. The convergence of medical care and wellness tourism and recreation has been able to enhance competitiveness of India in the international medical tourism market. Nonetheless, among the benefits this sector has experienced a lot of growth, it has a number of issues such as regulatory disparities, inequality in the distribution of healthcare facilities, accreditation, and the issue of fair access to healthcare by the locals (Mohapatra & Giri, 2018). With such opportunities and challenges, the medical tourism in India needs to be thoroughly analyzed. The economic, healthcare quality, policy, and socio-cultural analysis of the sector can be of great use to policymakers, healthcare providers, and tourism stakeholders. This kind of analysis plays a vital role in assuring the sustainable development of medical tourism in India as well as determining the balance between international demand and domestic medical care demand.

OBJECTIVES OF THE STUDY

1. To review the development and present scenario of medical tourism in India.
2. To explore the principal drivers contributing to India's position as a leading medical tourism destination.

3. To evaluate the economic and healthcare-related impacts of medical tourism within the Indian context.
4. To identify the key challenges confronting the medical tourism sector in India and propose appropriate policy recommendations.

PROBLEM STATEMENT

Despite the fact that India has developed into a significant medical tourism destination rather fast, there is still considerable research vacuum where critically assessing the sector based on other factors than the cost benefits and market expansion of this sector are considered. A lot of the existing literature is more concerned with economic potential, and not much has been done in regard to regulatory issues, inequality in healthcare infrastructure, ethical concerns, and consequences to domestic healthcare access. This disjointed knowledge hinders the capacity of the policymakers and stakeholders to come up with balanced and sustainable long-term strategies on the development of medical tourism in India. India has been experiencing significant growth in the medical tourism sector due to low cost of healthcare services, provision of quality and highly trained medical staff and medical facilities. Nonetheless, there are still some critical issues that have plagued the industry such as gaps in policy and regulations, unequal distribution of healthcare facilities, differences in the quality of services and worry about the preference of international patients over the local healthcare demands. These problems are not assessed as a unit and the compound economic and health effects of medical tourism make proper policymaking difficult. This study will, therefore, focus on the main forces behind medical tourism in India, the effects, and the issues in order to make better decisions and develop the sector in a sustainable manner.

BACKGROUND OF MEDICAL TOURISM IN INDIA

The medical tourism in India has developed very fast within the last decade and has made the country one of the most preferred places among international patients in search of low cost and of high quality of healthcare. The industry has repercussed well following the shock occasioned by the COVID-19 pandemic. There was a rise in the number of Foreign Tourist Arrivals (FTAs) to India because of medical tourism to India, which had already been declining to about 182,945 in 2020, and to 644,387 in 2024 (Ministry of Tourism, Government of India, 2025; Times of India, 2025). Current data revealed that over 131, 000 international patients came to India in the first quarter of 2025, and this is an indication of continued demand (Ministry of Tourism, Government of India, 2025). One of the reasons which have led to the rise of medical tourism in India is the low cost which the country provides. Indian treatments are much cheaper than those in developed nations and a large number of hospitals have international accreditation and top-tier amenities. This affordability and quality coupled with a good supply of medical labor force has drawn patients in South Asia, Middle East, Africa, and Western nations (Business Today, 2024).

Initiatives by government have also been very important in aiding the sector. Receiving international patients has become easier with the growth of the e-medical visa program and introduction of programs like the Heal in India campaign where India has become a major destination place of Medical Value Travel (Business Standard, 2025). It is reported that the medical tourism market in India is estimated to be worth USD 7.69 billion in 2024 and is expected to increase to USD 8.71 billion in 2025, which is good growth in the sector (Business Standard, 2025). Besides the mainstream healthcare services, India also provides the wellness tourism by the use of the traditional medical systems like Ayurveda, Yoga, other local practices. States such as Kerala encourage Medical Value Travel that is a combination of clinical treatment and wellness and holistic therapy, this makes India highly competitive in the medical tourism sector around the world (Financial Express, 2025). Although the sector is growing at a very fast pace, there are still challenges that include unfair treatment of healthcare services in different regions, inconsistency in regulations, and accessibility of services by the local population. The sustainable and inclusive development of medical tourism in India requires dealing with these issues. (Times of India, 2025; Financial Express, 2025).

LITERATURE REVIEW

The concept of patients moving to other countries to obtain medical treatment is known as medical tourism and it is predisposed by such factors as cost-benefit factor, quality of medical services, shortened waiting lines, and competence in a particular field *(Kulkarni, 2025)*. India is also among the largest destinations of medical tourism in the globe and in cardiac surgery, orthopaedics, oncology, organ transplantation and cosmetic therapy particularly *(Sumllika et al., 2024)*. This combination of medical tourism with other infrastructural tourism has resulted in India emerging as a competitive destination in the development of the medical tourism world market. Simultaneously, all the healthcare sector experiences the digital revolution and the Artificial Intelligence (AI), machine learning, big data analytics, and telemedicine technologies *(Sharma et al., 2022)*. AI is a term that is applied to describe computer systems that have abilities to perform tasks that humans typically require human intelligence including decision-making, pattern recognition, natural language processing, and predictive analytics *(Guru et al., 2023).* Over the past years, artificial intelligence (AI) and machine learning (ML) have turned out to be an important component of a range of industries, one of which is the travel industry. With the advent of more sophisticated travelers in the needs and demands, travel companies have to keep with the changing market *(Yadav et al., 2025).* Applications of AI in healthcare include the clinical decision support and diagnostics, the systems of patient engagement, and the systems of hospital management. Recent publications have had increased recognition of the fact that AI is not a product or service itself, but is a facilitator, across the medical tourism value chain *(Subasinghe et al., 2020).* By using data analytics of a sample of wellness tourists, which rely on the AI, we evaluate the relationships between these factors, using structural equation modeling (SEM) *(Chauhan et al., 2025)*

MEDICAL TOURISM IN INDIA: EVOLUTION AND CONTEMPORARY LANDSCAPE

Indian medical tourism industry began gaining international fame particularly in the early 2000s due to liberalization of Indian economy, increased privatization of medical services in India and the increased participation of corporate hospital groups in the international market *(Garg & Bhardwaj, 2012).* The changes that were introduced in the 1990s made possible the foreign investment and technological transfer and the emergence and ability of the multi-specialty private hospitals to serve international patients (Crooks et al., 2011). Meanwhile, the high health care cost free market and the long queues in the developed countries gave the good ground of demand to outbound medical tourism to countries such as India. The Indian cost competitiveness is discovered to be its greatest comparative advantage in a noteworthy literature. The complex medical interventions in India are priced at mere fraction of what one will receive in the United States, Europe or other well-known economies and the outcome of the therapy is not guaranteed to be in any way of lower quality *(Shafik, 2025).* Other factors that have increased the legitimacy of India as a destination of medical tourism besides the price is affordability of health services, presence of English speaking health care professionals, western trained doctors and western adherence to clinical procedures *(Medhekar et al., 2020).* Accreditation by global bodies such as the Joint Commission International (JCI) also improved perceptions regarding quality and safety to the foreign patients.

Some of the key players in the establishment of medical tourism in India have been giant chains of hospitals such as Apollo Hospitals and Fortis healthcare that have also pursued an international marketing policy, overseas referrals network and alliances with insurance companies and facilitators *(Samala et al., 2022).* These health chains lavished their money in advanced medical equipment, international patient units, the concierge services which include medical services, travel, and accommodation along with wellness programs. This type of institutional capability was into the ability to move low-cost positioning as a value-based model medical tourism in India. A more recent literature records a shift in the medical tourism ecosystem of India, wherein an overhauling of the system, with a shift at the facilitator services with digitally mediator services, occurs *(Chirmulay & Bhakare, 2025).* Earlier models were centered largely on the middlemen who would coordinate the treatment, traveling, and accommodation. Contemporary systems are becoming increasingly reliant on digital technologies, web-based portals, teleconsultations, and solutions of patient engagement that rely on data. This transformation is a pointer of the overall trends in healthcare digitalization and consumer empowerment whereby international patients have taken an active role in information search, hospital selection, and treatment design. Regardless of such developments, there exist myriads of structural and institutional challenges which diverse scholars still single out that constrain the sustainable development of medical tourism in India *(Hayat, 2025).* In addition, post-treatment continuity is yet another phobia that has not been adequately addressed yet particularly in cases of international patients where they travel back to their home countries immediately after the medical treatment. The fragmented health information systems and ineffective follow-up systems tend to undermine the long term patient outcomes and trust *(Shanmugam, 2013).*

ARTIFICIAL INTELLIGENCE IN HEALTHCARE: CONCEPTUAL FOUNDATIONS

The application of Artificial Intelligence (AI) in healthcare has been actively developed over the past decade primarily due to the significant enhancement of computation capacities, the spread of electronic medical records, and new possibilities of using opportunities in its development of algorithms *(Chirmulay & Bhakare, 2025).* Electronic health records (EHR), medical imaging technologies, wearables, and Internet of Things (IoT)-based technologies have made immense volumes of data easily accessible, and AI systems can process these volumes of data with more speed and volume than ever before to produce insights. Thus, AI has turned into an indispensable part of the contemporary healthcare revolution and not a technologic fringe tool. Healthcare literature usually includes a list of various areas of AI technologies that are interconnected and linked, including machine learning, deep learning, natural language processing (NLP), and computer vision *(Chhabra et al., 2021).* Machine learning algorithms can lead to the system learning with past clinical data and improving their performance without being specified, whereas deep learning techniques - particularly neural networks - are effective on more challenging tasks, such as image analysis in medicine and disease pattern recognition. NLP facilitates the interpretation and processing of unstructured clinical characteristics, such as the physician notes and discharge summaries, and computer vision assists in the technological breakthrough in the radiology, pathology and surgical imaging fields. Collectively, these technologies have revolutionized the quality of diagnoses, clinical effectiveness and decision-making among the systems of healthcare. Workflows led by clinicians can be enhanced by AI systems with additional advantages that include decision support, risk stratification, and prediction that allow professionals to make complicated and personalized clinical decisions and interact with the patient *(Talukder et al., 2025).*

In the context of medical tourism, AI may undertake three broad functions, though they are connected with one another. Firstly, AI-based applications in diagnostics and treatment planning, predictive analytic applications, and outcome forecasting are all under the category of clinical intelligence. These tools are significant to foreign patients who in the majority of cases require retrieving expeditious and accurate medical assessments prior to travelling and open estimates about potential risks of treatment, curing process and success rates of such surgeries *(Cannon Hunter, 2007).* Quality and safety perceptions are the ultimate determinants in the destination selection of medical tourists resulting directly out of greater clinical intelligence. AI facilitation of optimization of hospital management processes, i.e., bed, resources, supply chain, and administrative documentation scheduling are also operational intelligence *(Mahmud et al., 2021).* In medical tourism destinations such as India, most hospitals are forced to contend with large volumes of both domestic patients as well as international patients and in this context, it is the operational intelligence that helps in improving efficiency, reduction of waiting time and increased coordination of operations between the different departments. Literature also indicates that operational reliability is very important in establishing the international patient satisfaction and institutional reputation *(Seow et al., 2021).* Experiential intelligence has to do with patient experience, personalization and service design. The dialogue AI, chatbots that operate with the support of artificial intelligence, multilingual translation systems, and personalized communication platforms all help to make the overall experience of the patient during the medical tourism, more tolerable. Being a patient who must cope with the unfamiliar healthcare system, culture, and regulations conditions, experiential intelligence reduces anxiety and supports the development of trust and facilitates making informed decisions in global patients *(Gaur et al., 2021).* The three areas are particularly crucial in terms of medical tourists who must experience a balanced interplay of several countries, healthcare institutions, tourist managers and the continuum care groups *(Paliwal et al., 2024).*

The medical tourists, unlike the local patients, contract healthcare as a service package which is comprised of the clinical, logistics, accommodation, and post follow-up services. The implementation of AI into the clinical, operational, and experiential spheres, then, is a comprehensive way of how the healthcare system can be made to envision the opportunity of the international population of patients being served in an efficient way (Verma et al., 2025). Altogether, the conceptual foundations of AI in medical care reveal the multidimensionality of clinical enhancer, operational optimizer, and experience facilitator. Applying such first-basis concepts, the potential of AI to strategically change the environment of medical tourists, and India in particular, as the fresh markets are being created to explore the long-term issues of quality assurance, coordination, transparency, and patient trust, can be analyzed.

AI IN PRE-TRAVEL DECISION-MAKING AND DESTINATION CHOICE

Medical tourists are highly susceptible to the perceived risk due to an information asymmetry, regulatory conditions that are not known, and quality and safety issues *(Wong & Sa'aid Hazley, 2021)*. The level of uncertainty is reduced with the help of AI chatbots, recommender systems, multilingual virtual assistants that help to provide the customer with personalized information on the treatment options, prices, and hospital qualification *(Kamassi et al., 2020)*. The studies show that the technology of artificial intelligence offers greater credibility due to the fact that it produces comparisons of hospitals, physicians, and outcomes based on the data, which proves particularly handy in the underdeveloped destinations such as India *(Bhushan, 2021)*. Patients are being efficiently matched with right hospitals and specialists through machine learning with reference to medical history, budgets, and traveling preferences. This kind of personalization in the case of Indian medical tourism enhances patient satisfaction and conversion rates in hospitals and facilitators. Telemedicine is a vital aspect of medical tourism, and it allows conducting pre-travel consultations and post-treatment follow-ups (Karcıoğlu, 2025). Clinicians can use symptom-checker, predictive analytics and decision-support systems that are artificial intelligence-enhanced telemedicine platforms to support a virtual consultation. According to Indian studies, the tele-triage on the basis of AI may be used to make the clinic better equipped to deliver the treatment to the right people according to travels and make it more of a medical risk to avoid unnecessary travel that is not medically justified *(Tuo et al., 2025)*. Post-operative monitoring with the assistance of AI-based data analytics also facilitates continuity of care, which has been a conventionally stable component of the medical tourism models.

AI IN HOSPITAL OPERATIONS AND SERVICE EFFICIENCY

Inefficiency during operation impacts negatively on the patient experience especially to international patients who are subjected to working through systems which are not familiar to them. Automated tools in the hospital AI include scheduling, bed management, clinical documentation, and supply chain optimization tools *(Nalbant & Aydin, 2025)*. It has also been found out through research that the adoption of AI operated systems in the Indian private hospitals results in reduction of waiting time, improved employee efficiency rate, and development of better coordination between the different departments within the hospital. These efficiencies nodes help in indirectly benefiting the medical tourism since it enhances reliability of the services and lowers the cost of latent features. Patient experience is one of the foundations of destination competency which the literature on medical tourism is starting to pay more attention *(Suryawanshi & Bhoyar, 2025)*.

The multilingual chatbots, AI-based translation systems, and emotion-recognition systems are listed in terms of improving the cross-cultural interaction between the Indian doctors and the foreign clients. These technologies can be used to counter the obstacle of culture and language that is another factor that has been cited as dominant in the earlier medical tourism studies. Despite the huge potential of AI, it is ethical and regulatory in nature *(Akhavan et al., 2023)*. Among the most important issues which have to be considered are the privacy of the data, informed consent, prejudice of the algorithms, and responsibility, particularly when engaging cross-border in the health industry. Healthcare data ecosystems in India are not unified, and researchers think that the AI systems are not useful due to inefficient interoperability. Moreover, the healthcare system is not regulated by a particular AI, which exposes international patients to doubts about liability and security of the data.

ECONOMIC AND POLICY IMPLICATIONS FOR MEDICAL TOURISM IN INDIA

To the policymakers, AI is taking the form of a tool of enhancing Indian healthcare competitive position in the world. The literature is rich in discussing the relationships between the state and the corporate sector as the agents of scale and standardization, AI innovation centers and national digital health programs. *(Malhotra & Dave, 2022)*. The cost of treatment will be minimized economically through efficiency in AI, the capacity of hospitals will be increased and will add value-proposition to India in the medical tourism markets. However, scholars caution that the unequal application of AI may grow as geographical disparities and may become concentrated in large urban hospital systems *(Vishal, 2023)*. The reviewed literature confirms that Artificial Intelligence may become a significant force that will assist in transforming medical tourism in India to enhance the quality of provided services, reinforce the efficiency of their work, and enhance the patient experience. The wide range of AI applications introduced in the medical tourism value chain, such as the pre-travel decision-making to the post-treatment follow-up, are centered on a very large number of those structural questions, which were viewed as the constituent of cross-border healthcare. However, India can successfully introduce AI into the medical tourism system, and the absence of strict governance designs, data facilities, and ethics restricts the process. Despite conceptual and postulating supportive research, which is strong, more rigorous research needs to be carried out in order to establish cause and effect properties and inform policy and managerial policy.

RESEARCH METHODOLOGY

The research methodology that will be adopted includes descriptive and analytical research methodology, which will entirely be focused on secondary data to establish the role of Artificial Intelligence in medical tourism in India. Relevant data has been obtained by the use of a big number of credible secondary sources, including peer-reviewed international and domestic journals, academic books, conference papers, government publications of the Ministry of Tourism and Ministry of Health and Family Welfare, policy reports, and industry reports of the reputable entities and business magazines. In addition to that, the data were also obtained on well-known academic databases, such as Google Scholar, Scopus, and ResearchGate, to ensure that the research credibility and scientific nature could be obtained.The collected data were relatively verified and discussed with the implementation of thematic and content analysis to determine the key tendencies, motivation, problems, and implications of AI implementation via the medical tourism value chain, including clinical services, hospital processes, patient satisfaction, policy models. The use of secondary data methodology allows realizing the entire role of artificial intelligence that is becoming more and more significant in improving the medical tourism ecosystem in India and defines the existing gaps and directions of research.

ANALYSIS AND DISCUSSION FOR IMPACT OF ARTIFICIAL INTELLIGENCE ON MEDICAL TOURISM IN INDIA

The field of Artificial Intelligence (AI) is revolutionizing all industries in the world, and medical tourism, traveling abroad in search of healthcare services, is not an exception. Over the past years, India has become one of the top most choices among the world patients because of good healthcare, economic benefits and a competent medical labour force. Medical tourism in India is now being further transformed by the inclusion of AI into healthcare services. Diagnosis and treatment planning can be cited as one of the most important contributions of AI. Algorithms of machine-learning, when applied to medical scans, pathology reports, and patient history, can be more accurate and faster than the conventional method. This translates to quicker diagnostics and short waiting time and tailored treatment regimens to international patients who need specialized care making India an attractive option to various countries around the world. Remote patient engagement is also improved using AI.

With the help of AI chatbots and virtual health assistants, telemedicine enables patients to access the advice of Indian specialists regardless of their location around the world and make travel choices. These devices may take the patients through initial screenings, address their questions instantly, and even make appointments. The continuity of care aids in the establishment of trust and the minimization of uncertainty among international patients who might want to treat in India. Operational efficiency is another major area that AI is affecting. It is observed that hospitals are adding AI-based tools to improve scheduling of surgery and hospital beds, electronic health records management, and billing optimization. To medical tourists, who tend to be logistically inclined, balancing their travel arrangements, accommodation, and treatment schedules, these simplified operations will mean smoother visits and increased satisfaction. The predictive healthcare in India is also getting stronger with AI. The predictive analytics may be used to predict patient needs, future complications, and make plans to support patients after the operation. This especially comes in handy with medical tourists who need some follow up measures after they go home. The advanced predictive care will positively affect the results and decrease the number of readmission cases, which will help India become a more reputable and safe medical tourism destination. But with challenges there are challenges. Digital divide Digital divide between the urban and rural healthcare sector and between the tech-savvy and small healthcare facilities is that AI implementation is uneven. Most of the medical tourism destinations such as Delhi, Mumbai, and Chennai possess the latest AI technologies, yet small ones might be left behind and imbalanced patient experiences are formed. Moreover, the concerns related to data privacy and cybersecurity will drive away international patients who feel that their sensitive medical data might be compromised. AI also requires significant investment in infrastructure and skilled professionals. Training staff to effectively use AI systems remains a hurdle, especially in hospitals that are still transitioning from traditional paper-based systems to digital platforms.

As much as Artificial Intelligence may greatly improve the accuracy of diagnosis, the efficiency of operational services and the personalization of their services, it also creates an immense structural and ethical contradiction as it is introduced to

Indian medical tourism. The centralization of AI-enhanced infrastructure in large metropolitan private hospitals could further strengthen the existing disparities in access to healthcare services in regions, thus, excluding the people in rural areas and smaller health organizations. This is an unequal distribution of technological enhancement that could double the two-layer healthcare system where foreign, revenue-generating patients can obtain AI-enhanced and high-efficiency services, and the national population can still rely on comparatively under-equipped and under-funded services. In addition, the lack of a comprehensive regulatory framework of AI-driven clinical decision-making, cross-border data transfer, algorithmic responsibility, and medico-legal responsibility creates an uncertainty systemic in nature. Unclear ownership of either clinicians, the hospital, or the AI developers in the case of wrong diagnosis, and/or algorithmic bias can undermine the confidence of patients around the world and put institutions in a reputation and legal liability risk. In the long-term sustainability point of view, AI induced competitiveness should, therefore, be incorporated into sound governance systems, fair access policies, and binding ethical provisions. In the absence of these institutional offsets, AI can bring about a short-term growth in the market accompanied by structural inequalities and governance fragility that compromise the resilience and legitimacy of medical tourism promotion sector in India.

RECOMMENDATIONS FOR ENHANCING AI'S ROLE IN INDIAN MEDICAL TOURISM

1. **Standardize AI Adoption Across Healthcare Facilities:** The standardization of AI should also be encouraged by the government and the private sector to enable even smaller hospitals to enjoy intelligent healthcare solutions. AI technology can be subsidized by the public-private partnership in underserved regions.
2. **Strengthen Data Protection Frameworks:** India needs to enact an inclusive set of data privacy legislations in line with the international standards (e.g., GDPR) to convince foreign patients that their health data does not risk being compromised.
3. **Invest in AI-Training Programs:** Staff in the medical and administration field require training on the use of AI tools, the interpretation of data and best practices in cybersecurity. Capacity building can be facilitated through collaboration with technology firms.
4. **Promote AI-Enabled Telemedicine Globally:** The hospitals in India must consider promoting teleconsultation services powered by AI to foreign patients as a pre-travel care service to overseas patients. This will enhance pre-arrival activities with the patient and boost medical tourism inflows.

5. **Build AI Research Collaborations:** Indian hospitals, universities, and other world AI research institutions can collaborate to develop innovation with medical tourism requirements.

CONCLUSION

The Artificial Intelligence (AI) affects the field of medical tourism in an Indian context and how the technological advancement is reshaping the healthcare and tourism ecosystem in India. India has been considered as one of the major destinations of medical tourism because it offers cheap medical services, experienced medical practitioners and well-developed health facilities. This has been reinforced by incorporation of AI that has improved the quality, efficiency and accessibility of health care services globally. Data analytics, machine learning, and automation have been used to enhance outcomes of patients, treatment planning, and diagnostic accuracy in AI. The effect of these developments on international patients is quicker diagnoses, shorter wait times and a customized approach to healthcare. The AIs-based telemedicine services and virtual telemedicine services have also facilitated easy access by patients to Indian healthcare services before and after the travel and can guarantee continuity of care and foster more trust in medical tourists. Operationally, AI has helped to streamline the hospital management systems, optimize the allocation of resources, as well as increase administrative efficiency. These advancements will help lessen the delays, reduce the number of mistakes, and overall patient experience which is a critical component in medical tourism where convenience and reliability are important aspects. Predictive analytics have also helped in the post treatment care predicting complications and making early interventions especially useful with foreign patients to their home countries. In spite of these strengths, the paper has also established some obstacles that should be overcome to achieve the full potential of AI in medical tourism. Inequality in the availability of AIs in health institutions, issues with data privacy and cybersecurity, and the lack of skilled professionals to operate AI systems are critical obstacles and impediments. These problems would reduce the confidence of patients and reduce the rate of AI adoption unless they are properly regulated and standardized. The advent of the Artificial Intelligence has become a revolutionary element within the sphere of medical tourism in India that provides possibilities to improve the quality of services, their efficiency, and competitiveness in the global context. Nevertheless, policymakers, healthcare providers, and stakeholders in the technology development will have to work together to ensure the sustainable development of AI-driven medical tourism. India can use AI to provide patient-centric, ethical, and world-class healthcare services by investing in infrastructure and enhancing data protection frameworks and encouraging the development of skills. Finally, the proper infusion of AI will be a central key to making India an international medical tourism destination in the future.

REFERENCES

Bhushan, S. (2021). The impact of artificial intelligence and machine learning on the global economy and its implications for the hospitality sector in India. *Worldwide Hospitality and Tourism Themes, 13*(2), 252–259. *https://doi.org/*DOI: 10.1108/WHATT-09-2020-0116

Akhavan, P., Azizi, N., Akhtari, S., Haass, O., Jan, T., & Sajeev, S. (2023). Understanding critical success factors for implementing medical tourism in a multi-case analysis. *Knowledge Management and E-Learning*, *15*(1), 43–63. DOI: 10.34105/j.kmel.2023.15.003

Business Standard. (2025, February 2). India's medical tourism poised for expansion with relaxed visa rules. Business Standard. https://www.business-standard.com/industry/news/india-s-medical-tourism-poised-for-expansion-with-relaxed-visa-rules-125020200488_1.html

Business Today. (2024, August 8). India's medical tourism grew 33% in 2023, to surpass pre-pandemic level in 2024: ICRA. Business Today. https://www.businesstoday.in/india/story/indias-medical-tourism-grew-33-in-2023-to-surpass-pre-pandemic-level-in-2024-icra-440692-2024-08-08.html

Cannon Hunter, W. (2007). Medical Tourism: A New Global Niche. *International Journal of Tourism Sciences*, *7*(1), 129–140. DOI: 10.1080/15980634.2007.11434599

Chauhan, J. S., Sharma, Ajay, Sharma, Akhilesh, Ahalawat, K., & Agarwal, P. (2025). AI-Driven Decision Making in Wellness Tourism: Understanding Consumer Preferences and Optimizing Tourism Strategies. *2025 First International Conference on Advances in Computer Science, Electrical, Electronics, and Communication Technologies (CE2CT)*, 663–669. *https://doi.org/*DOI: 10.1109/CE2CT64011.2025.10939052

Chhabra, A., Munjal, M., Mishra, P. C., Singh, K., Das, D., Kuhar, N., & Vats, M. (2021). Medical tourism in the COVID-19 era: Opportunities, challenges and the way ahead. *Worldwide Hospitality and Tourism Themes*, *13*(5), 660–665. DOI: 10.1108/WHATT-05-2021-0078

Chirmulay, V., & Bhakare, J. (2025). Digital Health and Medical Tourism: A Regulatory Perspective. In *Navigating Innovations and Challenges in Travel Medicine and Digital Health* (pp. 311–324). IGI Global Scientific Publishing. *https://doi.org/*DOI: 10.4018/979-8-3693-8774-0.ch015

Crooks, V. A., Turner, L., Snyder, J., Johnston, R., & Kingsbury, P. (2011). Promoting medical tourism to India: Messages, images, and the marketing of international patient travel. *Social Science & Medicine, 72*(5), 726–732. DOI: 10.1016/j.socscimed.2010.12.022

ETHealthWorld. (2025, November). *India leads in healthcare AI adoption: Insights by Shanker Kaul.* Economic Times HealthWorld. Financial Express. (2025, May 20). India's medical tourism market to triple by 2035: Report. Financial Express. https://www.financialexpress.com/business/industry/indias-medical-tourism-market-to-triple-by-2035-report/3918222/

Garg, R., Batra, R., & Banerji, A. (2020). Low Cost, Quality Treatment and Excellent Hospitality Makes India the Best Destination for Medical Tourism. *International Journal of Innovative Research in Medical Science, 5*(1). Advance online publication. DOI: 10.23958/ijirms/vol05-i01/614

Garg, S. R., & Bhardwaj, A. (2012). Indian medical tourism industry: Growth opportunities and challenges. *Multi Disciplinary Edu Global Quest (Quarterly), 1*(1), 115–135.

Gaur, L., Afaq, A., Singh, G., & Dwivedi, Y. K. (2021). Role of artificial intelligence and robotics to foster the touchless travel during a pandemic: A review and research agenda. *International Journal of Contemporary Hospitality Management, 33*(11), 4079–4098. https://doi.org/. DOI: 10.1108/IJCHM-11-2020-1246

George, R. R., Sunil, S., Vijayan, K., & Saleem, S. (2025). Medical value tourism: A revival for post-COVID tourism industry in India. Journal of Rural Tourism. *https://doi.org/*DOI: 10.70310/jrt.2025.03010668

Gunaseelan, S., & Kesavan, N. (2020). A Review on Medical Tourism in India. *Indian Journal of Public Health Research & Development, 11*(1), 562. Advance online publication. DOI: 10.37506/v11/i1/2020/ijphrd/193882

Guru, S., Sinha, A., & Kautish, P. (2023). Determinants of medical tourism: Application of fuzzy analytical hierarchical process. *International Journal of Emerging Markets, 18*(11), 4819–4842. DOI: 10.1108/IJOEM-08-2021-1173

Hayat, Y. (2025). Transforming Medical Tourism Through. *Advances in Healthcare Information Systems and Administration, 425*, 425–458. Advance online publication. DOI: 10.4018/979-8-3693-7888-5.ch017

Kamassi, A., Abd Manaf, N. H., & Omar, A. (2020). The identity and role of stakeholders in the medical tourism industry: State of the art. *Tourism Review, 75*(3), 559–574. DOI: 10.1108/TR-01-2019-0031

Karcıoğlu, U. B. (2025). The Impact of Artificial Intelligence on the Patient Journey in Medical Tourism: A Management Framework. *Eurasian Journal of Health Technology Assessment*, *9*(1), 58–67. DOI: 10.52148/ehta.1701664

Kulkarni, P. D. (2025). Competencies for Medical Tourism in India. In *Human Capital Management and Competitive Advantage in Tourism* (pp. 1–40). IGI Global Scientific Publishing., DOI: 10.4018/979-8-3373-0071-9.ch001

Mahmud, M. S., Rahman, M. M., Lima, R. P., & Annie, E. J. (2021). Outbound medical tourism experience, satisfaction and loyalty: Lesson from a developing country. *Journal of Hospitality and Tourism Insights*, *4*(5), 545–564. DOI: 10.1108/JHTI-06-2020-0094

Malhotra, N., & Dave, K. (2022). An Assessment of Competitiveness of Medical Tourism Industry in India: A Case of Delhi NCR. *International Journal of Global Business and Competitiveness*, *17*(2), 215–228. DOI: 10.1007/s42943-022-00060-0

Medhekar, A., Wong, H. Y., & Hall, J. E. (2020). Health-care providers perspective on value in medical travel to India. *Tourism Review*, *75*(4), 717–731. DOI: 10.1108/TR-06-2019-0276

Ministry of Tourism, Government of India. (2025, August). Foreign tourist arrivals (FTAs) for medical purposes – Jan–Apr 2025. Ministry of Tourism. https://tourism.gov.in/sites/default/files/2025-08/usq.4136%20for%2018.08.2025.pdf

Mohapatra, A., & Giri, P. A. (2018). Medical tourism gaining grounds in India: Present scenario and way forward. Public Health Review. *International Journal of Public Health Research*, *5*(1), 50–52. Advance online publication. DOI: 10.17511/ijphr.2018.i1.07

Naaz, F., & Khan, N. (2016). Medical tourism in India: Perspective of Unani medicine. Journal of AYUSH: Ayurveda, Yoga, Unani. *Siddha and Homeopathy*, *5*(3), 52–60.

Nalbant, K. G., & Aydin, S. (2025). A bibliometric approach to the evolution of artificial intelligence in digital marketing. *International Marketing Review*, *42*(2–3), 179–218. DOI: 10.1108/IMR-04-2024-0132

Paliwal, M., Chatradhi, N., Singh, A., & Dikkatwar, R. (2024). Smart tourism: Antecedents to Indian traveller's decision. *European Journal of Innovation Management*, *27*(5), 1521–1546. DOI: 10.1108/EJIM-06-2022-0293

Samala, N., Katkam, B. S., Bellamkonda, R. S., & Rodriguez, R. V. (2022). Impact of AI and robotics in the tourism sector: A critical insight. *Journal of Tourism Futures*, *8*(1), 73–87. DOI: 10.1108/JTF-07-2019-0065

Seow, A. N., Choong, Y. O., Moorthy, K., & Choong, C. K. (2021). Predicting medical tourism behavioural intention using social cognition models. *Tourism Review*, *76*(2), 374–391. DOI: 10.1108/TR-06-2019-0267

Shafik, W. (2025). Artificial Intelligence Integration in Medical Tourism: Medical Breakthroughs-Are We Truly Progressing? In *Navigating Health Information in the Age of Artificial Intelligence* (pp. 1–36). IGI Global Scientific Publishing. *https://doi.org/*DOI: 10.4018/979-8-3693-5837-5.ch001

Shanmugam, K. R. (2013). *Medical tourism in India: Progress, opportunities and challenges*. Madras School of Economics.

Sharma, K., Jain, M., & Dhir, S. (2022). Analysing the impact of artificial intelligence on the competitiveness of tourism firms: A modified total interpretive structural modeling (m-TISM) approach. *International Journal of Emerging Markets*, *17*(4), 1067–1084. DOI: 10.1108/IJOEM-05-2021-0810

Soni, D. C. (2024). An analysis of medical tourism and its role in India's economic development. ShodhKosh. *Journal of Visual and Performing Arts*, *5*(6). Advance online publication. DOI: 10.29121/shodhkosh.v5.i6.2024.5497

Subasinghe, M., Magalage, D., Amadoru, N., Amarathunga, L., Bhanupriya, N., & Wijekoon, J. L. (2020). Effectiveness of artificial intelligence, decentralized and distributed systems for prediction and secure channelling for Medical Tourism. *2020 11th IEEE Annual Information Technology, Electronics and Mobile Communication Conference (IEMCON)*, 0314–0319. *https://doi.org/*DOI: 10.1109/IEMCON51383.2020.9284898

Sumllika, T., Sandya, J. S., Reddy, D. B., Karthik, G., & Rachel, Ch. (2024). AN Advanced Medical Tourism System in India Using Deep Learning Algorithms. In Ragavendiran, S. D. P., Pavaloaia, V. D., Mekala, M. S., & Cabezuelo, A. S. (Eds.), *Innovations and Advances in Cognitive Systems* (Vol. 15, pp. 412–421). Springer Nature Switzerland., DOI: 10.1007/978-3-031-69197-3_32

Suryawanshi, V., & Bhoyar, V. (2025). The role of AI in enhancing hospital operational efficiency and patient care. *Multidisciplinary Reviews*, *8*(5), 2025153–2025153. DOI: 10.31893/multirev.2025153

Talukder, M. B., Huda, M. N., Kumar, S., & Hasan, M. M. (2025). Metaverse Future of Digital Medical Tourism. In *Revolutionizing Healthcare Experience With Digital Medical Tourism* (pp. 173–198). IGI Global Scientific Publishing., DOI: 10.4018/979-8-3693-7888-5.ch007

Times of India. (2025, March 18). Medical tourism on rise post-COVID, govt tells Parliament, launches portal. Times of India. https://timesofindia.indiatimes.com/india/medical-tourism-on-rise-post-covid-govt-tells-parliament-launches-portal/articleshow/119131679.cms

Tuo, Y., Wu, J., Zhao, J., & Si, X. (2025). Artificial intelligence in tourism: Insights and future research agenda. *Tourism Review*, *80*(4), 793–812. DOI: 10.1108/TR-03-2024-0180

Verma, S., Tiwari, R. K., & Sharma, V. (2025). Travel Health: The Application of Artificial Intelligence and Machine Learning. In *Navigating Innovations and Challenges in Travel Medicine and Digital Health* (pp. 85–102). IGI Global Scientific Publishing. *https://doi.org/*DOI: 10.4018/979-8-3693-8774-0.ch005

Vishal, M. G. K. A. K. (2023). *Emerging Trends and Economic Impact of Medical Tourism in Punjab: Analysing Growth, Challenges, and Opportunities in Global Healthcare Context*. Wong, B. K. M., & Sa'aid Hazley, S. A. (2021). The future of health tourism in the industrial revolution 4.0 era. *Journal of Tourism Futures*, *7*(2), 267–272. DOI: 10.1108/JTF-01-2020-0006

Yadav, H., Yadav, P., & Sharma, S. C. (2025). Artificial Intelligence and Machine Learning in Travel Health. In *Navigating Innovations and Challenges in Travel Medicine and Digital Health* (pp. 69–84). IGI Global Scientific Publishing., DOI: 10.4018/979-8-3693-8774-0.ch004

Chapter 5
AI-Driven Medical Tourism Governance:
Economic Efficiency, Equity, and Accountability in Cross-Border Healthcare

Lawal Olamilekan Abdulwahab
http://orcid.org/0000-0003-4955-244X
School of Business and Economics, Universiti Brunei Darussalam, Brunei

Kabara Auwal Halabi
Sultan Hassanal Bolkiah Institute of Education, Universiti Brunei Darussalam, Brunei

Herbert Tafadzwa Kazonda
http://orcid.org/0009-0009-1788-2285
Masvingo Polytechnic, Zimbabwe

ABSTRACT

Artificial intelligence (AI) is transforming medical tourism by reshaping cross-border healthcare delivery, coordination, and governance. While AI-driven medical tourism enhances economic efficiency through improved diagnostics, resource optimization, and patient coordination, it also raises significant challenges related to equity, accountability, and regulatory oversight. This chapter examines AI-enabled medical tourism through the lenses of health economics, global health governance, and ethical AI regulation, drawing on comparative evidence from India, Thailand, and Malta. The analysis shows that AI-driven efficiency gains are unevenly distributed and often accompanied by equity risks, opportunity costs, and accountability gaps, particularly in low- and middle-income countries. To address these challenges, the

DOI: 10.4018/979-8-3373-8944-8.ch005

chapter proposes the Efficiency–Equity–Accountability (EEA) governance model, offering a structured framework to balance economic value creation with social justice, institutional responsibility, and sustainable digital health mobility aligned with global health goals.

1. INTRODUCTION

Medical tourism has evolved into a strategically significant component of the global healthcare economy, increasingly shaped by digital transformation and data-driven innovation. Once primarily motivated by cost differentials and service availability, cross-border healthcare mobility is now mediated by advanced digital platforms that facilitate patient matching, remote diagnostics, and international care coordination (Garad et al., 2025). Among these technological developments, artificial intelligence (AI) has emerged as a transformative force, enabling predictive analytics, personalized treatment pathways, and operational efficiencies that extend beyond national health systems. Evidence indicates that AI adoption is accelerating across healthcare markets globally, reshaping how care is delivered, governed, and accessed in transnational contexts (Abdulwahab, Daniel, Gul, et al., 2026).

The integration of AI into medical tourism offers substantial economic promise. AI-driven tools enhance hospital productivity, reduce diagnostic delays, and optimize patient flows, thereby improving the competitiveness of destination countries within the global health services market. Governments and private providers increasingly view AI-enabled medical tourism as a pathway to attract foreign investment, expand healthcare exports, and strengthen national digital health ecosystems (Sahar & Dar, 2024). However, these efficiency gains are accompanied by profound governance challenges. The cross-border nature of medical tourism complicates regulatory oversight, particularly where AI systems operate across jurisdictions with divergent legal frameworks, data protection regimes, and ethical standards (Chirmulay & Bhakare, 2025).

Beyond regulatory complexity, the deployment of AI in medical tourism raises pressing concerns about equity and social justice. Empirical research shows that AI governance frameworks within healthcare institutions frequently underemphasize equity considerations, treating algorithmic bias as a technical issue rather than a systemic determinant of unequal health outcomes (Arshed et al., 2025). In medical tourism destinations in low- and middle-income countries (LMICs), AI-enabled services may disproportionately benefit international patients while diverting resources from domestic populations. This dynamic risks reinforcing existing disparities in healthcare access, workforce distribution, and public health investment (Kaushik et al., 2025).

These equity challenges are further intensified by algorithmic opacity and data inequality. AI systems trained on non-representative or commercially curated datasets may systematically disadvantage marginalized groups, particularly when deployed in contexts with limited institutional oversight capacity. Studies across healthcare domains consistently highlight risks related to data privacy, explainability, and accountability, emphasizing the need for governance frameworks that extend beyond technical performance metrics (Ahmed et al., 2025). In cross-border medical tourism, these risks are magnified by fragmented responsibility between states, private providers, and platform operators.

Against this backdrop, AI-driven medical tourism occupies a critical intersection between global health governance, health economics, and ethical AI regulation. International policy discourse increasingly recognizes that AI's contribution to healthcare efficiency must be balanced with safeguards that promote inclusiveness, transparency, and accountability. This balance is essential for aligning AI-enabled healthcare mobility with the United Nations' Sustainable Development Goals, particularly SDG 3 (Good Health and Well-Being) and SDG 10 (Reduced Inequalities) (Abdalla et al., 2025)

Figure 1 depicts AI-driven medical tourism as a cross-border healthcare ecosystem in which AI serves as a central coordinator rather than a standalone technology. It shows AI systems, such as predictive analytics, diagnostic support, and treatment optimization, alongside digital platforms that mediate interactions among patients, providers, and regulators. Continuous data flows and digital care improve efficiency but raise governance issues concerning equity, transparency, and accountability. Outcomes such as economic efficiency, access, and accountability depend on regulation and ethical oversight, underscoring that AI-driven medical tourism must be managed as an integrated socio-technical system to balance economic gains with social justice accountability.

Figure 1. AI-driven medical tourism ecosystem and governance interactions in cross-border healthcare.

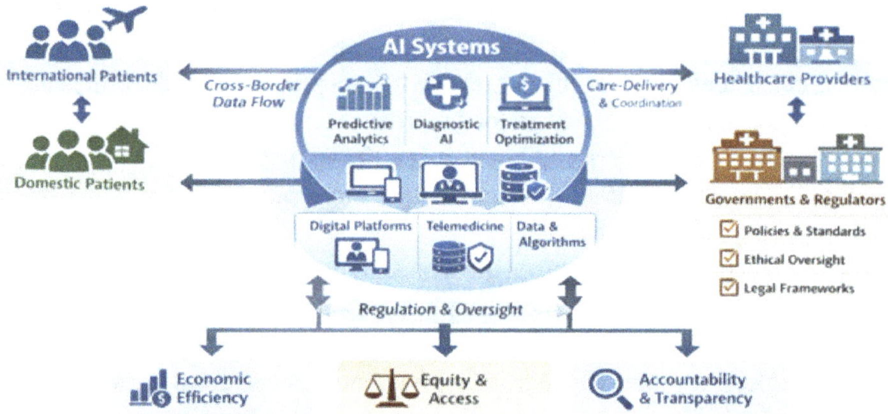

Source: *Author's conceptualization, 2026.*

This chapter explores governing AI-driven medical tourism to balance efficiency, equity, and accountability in cross-border healthcare. It views AI as a policy-sensitive tool, not just technology, capable of reshaping global healthcare distribution. Combining health economics, AI governance, and global health policy, it offers a framework for policymakers to promote socially just benefits of AI-enhanced medical tourism.

2. CONCEPTUAL BACKGROUND AND THEORETICAL FRAMEWORK

2.1 Medical Tourism in the Global Health Economy

Medical tourism has become an increasingly institutionalized feature of the global health economy, reflecting broader shifts toward healthcare commodification, privatization, and transnational service provision. Contemporary medical tourism extends beyond episodic patient travel to encompass complex networks involving private hospitals, government agencies, insurance intermediaries, digital platforms, and international accreditation bodies (Alshamsi, 2024). In the post-COVID-19 context, destination countries have renewed their strategic interest in medical tourism as a tool for economic recovery and health-sector diversification, often supported by targeted policy incentives and infrastructure investments (Abdulwahab, Daniel, Gul, et al., 2026).

Scholars stress that medical tourism is more than patient mobility; it is a global healthcare system tied to national growth. Governments in Asia, the Middle East, and Europe embed it into economic plans, connecting it to foreign investment, digital health, and exports (Eisavi et al., 2025; Yu et al., 2024). However, empirical evidence suggests that such strategies often privilege private healthcare markets, potentially reconfiguring domestic health systems in ways that challenge universal health coverage and public sector resilience (Labonté et al., 2017). Reaffirmed post-pandemic in policy reassessments, a concern that has gained renewed relevance in the aftermath of COVID-19-induced system strain.

Table 1 traces the evolution of medical tourism from traditional, episodic patient travel toward AI-driven, data-intensive healthcare mobility. It highlights how the increasing integration of digital and AI technologies transforms patient selection, care coordination, and data use, while simultaneously intensifying governance complexity and equity risks. The table reinforces the chapter's argument that AI-driven medical tourism is not a linear extension of earlier models but a structurally distinct governance challenge that requires new regulatory and ethical frameworks.

Table 1. Evolution of medical tourism models and associated governance implications.

Dimension	Traditional Medical Tourism	Digital Medical Tourism	AI-Driven Medical Tourism
Patient selection	Manual referrals, brokers	Platform-based matching	Algorithmic patient–provider matching
Care coordination	Episodic, fragmented	Digitally coordinated	End-to-end AI-orchestrated care
Data use	Limited, paper-based	Electronic health records	Predictive analytics & real-time data
Governance complexity	Low	Moderate	High (cross-border AI governance)
Equity implications	Market-driven access	Digital divide risks	Algorithmic bias & systemic inequities

Source: Author's synthesis, 2026.

In this evolving landscape, digitalization is shaping modern medical tourism, with cross-border care increasingly relying on online platforms, electronic health records, teleconsultation, and data-driven systems. These advancements foster AI integration but also heighten governance challenges around regulation, accountability, and equity across national boundaries.

2.2 Artificial Intelligence in Cross-Border Healthcare

Artificial intelligence has rapidly transitioned from experimental deployment to systemic integration within healthcare delivery, administration, and decision-making. AI applications now support diagnostic imaging, clinical decision support, patient triage, predictive analytics, and operational optimization across diverse health systems (Shalini et al., 2024). In cross-border healthcare contexts, AI plays a critical enabling role by facilitating remote diagnostics, pre-travel risk assessment, personalized treatment planning, and post-procedure follow-up across jurisdictions (Abubakari & Olamilekan, 2026; Lin, 2024).

Figure 2 shows how AI is integrated throughout the medical tourism care continuum, from pre-travel to post-treatment phases. It functions as an infrastructure for patient matching, risk assessment, logistics, clinical support, diagnostics, and personalized treatment. Afterward, it enables remote monitoring, recovery planning, and follow-up. The figure presents AI as a continuous cycle, emphasizing its role in transforming medical tourism into a data-driven, end-to-end process. It also highlights governance issues, including accountability, privacy, and equity, throughout the cross-border patient care journey.

Figure 2. AI functions across the medical tourism care continuum.

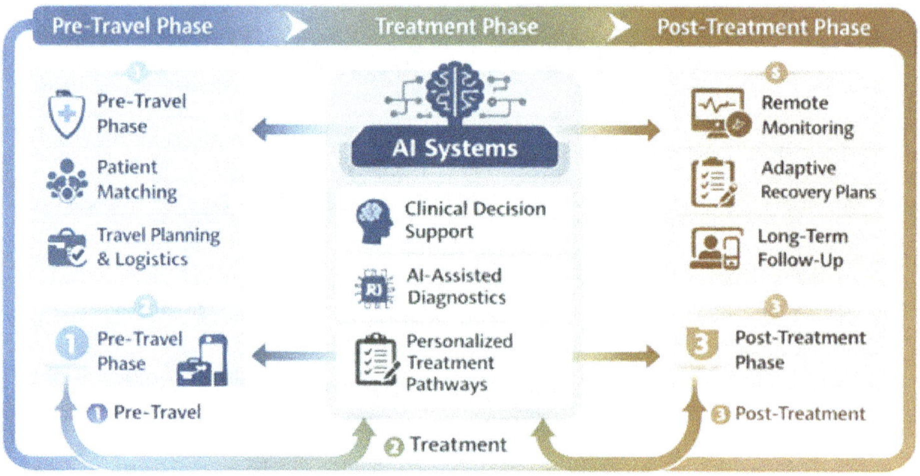

Source: *Author's conceptualization, 2026.*

From an economic perspective, AI enhances scalability and coordination in medical tourism by reducing informational asymmetries between patients and providers and by improving system efficiency. Digital platforms powered by AI algorithms increasingly serve as intermediaries, matching international patients with providers, estimating treatment outcomes, and optimizing logistics (Choudhari & Khobragade, 2024). These efficiencies are desirable to destination countries seeking to position themselves as competitive global healthcare hubs (Abdulwahab, Halabi, & Daniel, 2026). However, cross-border AI deployment also introduces novel governance risks due to uneven regulatory maturity and institutional capacity across health systems.

Studies underscore that AI governance in healthcare remains fragmented globally. Regulatory frameworks differ widely in data protection, algorithmic transparency, liability attribution, and ethical oversight (Nikolovski & Petreska, 2025). These divergences are particularly consequential in medical tourism, where AI systems often process sensitive patient data across multiple jurisdictions, raising unresolved questions about data sovereignty, consent, and accountability (Xia et al., 2024). As a result, AI's economic and clinical benefits cannot be disentangled from the governance environments in which these technologies operate.

2.3 Governance, Health Economics, and Equity

Governance is a key lens for evaluating AI-driven medical tourism. In health economics, it influences how efficiency gains are shared, who gains value, and how risks are distributed (Abou Jaoude et al., 2023). While AI can boost productivity and cut costs, evidence shows that focusing on efficiency often overlooks distributive effects, especially in public-private systems (Alsaleh, 2025). Equity is crucial in AI healthcare, as algorithmic systems are influenced by data, institutional priorities, and governance, which can perpetuate existing inequalities (Shaban-Nejad et al., 2024). Research shows that without equity in governance, algorithmic bias, data exclusion, and poor digital infrastructure systematically disadvantage marginalized populations (Chandra et al., 2025).

In the context of medical tourism, these risks extend beyond individual patients to entire health systems. AI-driven prioritization of high-value international patients may exacerbate resource diversion from public services, deepen workforce stratification, and marginalize local populations with limited digital access (Reshma Soman et al., 2025). Governance failures thus manifest not only as technical inefficiencies but as systemic inequities embedded within transnational healthcare markets (Mamun & Alam, 2025).

Accountability mechanisms are key to aligning AI-driven medical tourism with global health goals. Governance emphasizes transparency, explainability, participatory oversight, and institutional responsibility throughout the AI lifecycle, from design to evaluation (Upadhyay et al., 2023). Community-engaged and human-centered AI governance models demonstrate that inclusive oversight can mitigate bias, enhance trust, and promote equitable outcomes, even in resource-constrained settings (Weiner et al., 2025). These perspectives show AI-driven medical tourism needs more than market rules or tech standards. It demands an integrated governance approach balancing efficiency, equity, and accountability in cross-border healthcare. This foundation informs the analysis of economic impacts, equity, and regulatory issues in the sections ahead.

3. THE ECONOMIC EFFICIENCY PERSPECTIVES OF AI-DRIVEN MEDICAL TOURISM

3.1 Cost Optimization and Productivity Gains

One of the principal economic rationales for integrating artificial intelligence into medical tourism lies in its capacity to optimize costs and enhance productivity across healthcare delivery chains. AI-driven systems improve diagnostic accuracy, automate administrative processes, and streamline patient management, thereby reducing inefficiencies traditionally associated with cross-border care coordination (Thangalakshmi et al., 2025). Reviews of AI deployment in healthcare demonstrate consistent reductions in clinical decision delays and operational redundancies, particularly in data-intensive environments such as diagnostics, imaging, and treatment planning (Abdulwahab, Daniel, Halabi, et al., 2026).

In medical tourism, efficiency gains mean shorter wait times, more predictable treatment, and lower costs for international patients. AI predictive analytics help providers anticipate demand, allocate resources efficiently, and minimize underused capacity, all vital for competitiveness in global healthcare (Mahabub Subhani & Sumalakshmi, 2025). Empirical evidence from destination countries indicates that such efficiencies contribute directly to cost containment and improved service throughput, reinforcing the economic appeal of AI-enhanced medical tourism models (Abdulwahab, 2026).

Table 2 summarizes the principal mechanisms through which AI enhances economic efficiency in medical tourism. It demonstrates how AI-driven applications reduce operational inefficiencies and transaction costs across healthcare delivery chains. At the same time, the distribution of benefits illustrated in the table supports the chapter's contention that efficiency gains tend to accrue disproportionately to private providers and international patients unless redistributive governance mechanisms are introduced.

Table 2. Economic efficiency channels of AI deployment in medical tourism.

AI Application	Efficiency Mechanism	Economic Outcome	Primary Beneficiaries
Predictive analytics	Demand forecasting	Reduced idle capacity	Private hospitals
Diagnostic AI	Faster clinical decisions	Lower treatment delays	Providers & patients
Administrative automation	Process optimization	Reduced transaction costs	Platform operators
AI-enabled logistics	Resource coordination	Shorter patient pathways	International patients

Source: Author's synthesis based on health economics literature, 2026.

However, while AI-driven productivity gains can enhance aggregate efficiency, health economics literature cautions that efficiency improvements do not automatically yield socially optimal outcomes (Das et al., 2025). Without regulatory safeguards, cost reductions achieved through AI may disproportionately benefit private providers and international patients, leaving public health systems exposed to pressure to reallocate resources.

3.2 Market Expansion and Investment Incentives

AI adoption is a key tactic for expanding in the global medical tourism industry. Governments and healthcare providers use AI to show technological sophistication, attract investment, and become leading medical tourism centers (Bathla et al., 2024). National digital health strategies frequently integrate AI development with broader economic objectives, including healthcare export promotion and innovation-led growth (Russkikh et al., 2022). AI platforms lower entry barriers for international patients by reducing informational asymmetries about quality, risk, and outcomes. Matching systems, prediction tools, and digital concierge services improve transparency and facilitate cross-border healthcare (Grannis et al., 2022). These mechanisms expand the scale and scope of medical tourism markets, enabling destination countries to capture higher-value segments of global healthcare demand.

However, the same market-expanding dynamics raise concerns regarding market concentration and unequal value capture. AI systems are often capital-intensive and controlled by large private providers or platform intermediaries, potentially marginalizing smaller hospitals and public-sector institutions (Mishra & Kumar, 2025). Economic analyses increasingly highlight the risk that AI-enhanced medical tourism may reinforce oligopolistic tendencies within healthcare markets unless competition and governance mechanisms are explicitly strengthened (Ashraf & Hayat, 2025)

3.3 Economic Trade-Offs and Opportunity Costs

While AI-driven medical tourism offers measurable efficiency and revenue gains, these benefits must be evaluated against their opportunity costs within national health systems. Health economics frameworks emphasize that resource allocation decisions inherently involve trade-offs, particularly in settings characterized by constrained public health budgets (Shamanna & Mannava, 2023). Empirical studies show that prioritizing AI-enabled services for international patients can divert skilled labor, infrastructure, and public investment away from domestic healthcare needs(Da Silva et al., 2024).

Figure 3 shows the trade-off in AI medical tourism: efficiency gains versus opportunity costs within health systems. It maps AI investment against social welfare, showing that efficiency and private benefits can rise while public costs and inequality increase if governance is weak. AI tourism can boost productivity and revenue for private providers, but may also divert resources, displace workers, and reduce access for locals. The figure underscores that economic efficiency is not necessarily welfare-enhancing and must be evaluated with governance, considering opportunity costs, distribution, and public health impacts.

Figure 3. Efficiency–opportunity cost trade-off in AI-enhanced medical tourism.

Source: *Author's conceptualization, 2026.*

Moreover, the long-term sustainability of AI-driven efficiency gains remains uncertain. AI systems require continuous investment in data infrastructure, workforce training, cybersecurity, and algorithmic updates. Analyses of AI governance in healthcare caution that these recurring costs are often underestimated in economic planning, potentially eroding anticipated efficiency gains over time (El Arab et al., 2025).

Opportunity costs also manifest at the societal level. When AI-enabled medical tourism is pursued primarily as an economic growth strategy, public health objectives such as universal access, preventive care, and workforce equity may be deprioritized (Chowdhary & Majumdar, 2025). Public health study underscores that efficiency-oriented AI deployment must be embedded within governance frameworks that account for distributional impacts and social returns on investment (Ali et al., 2025). The economic efficiency of AI-driven medical tourism depends on governance choices that influence how efficiency gains are allocated, who captures value, and how opportunity costs are managed (Tripathi & Shalki, 2023). This economic perspective sets the stage for a deeper examination of equity implications, which are addressed in the next section.

4. EQUITY IMPLICATIONS OF AI-ENHANCED MEDICAL TOURISM

4.1 Access and Inclusion in Low- and Middle-Income Countries

While AI-enhanced medical tourism is frequently promoted to improve access to specialized care, its equity implications for low- and middle-income countries (LMICs) remain deeply contested. In theory, AI-enabled diagnostics, teleconsultation, and digital coordination platforms can reduce geographic barriers and expand healthcare reach (Tenkorang et al., 2025). In practice, however, empirical evidence suggests that these benefits are unevenly distributed, often favoring internationally mobile patients and urban private facilities over local populations (Sriram et al., 2024).

In many LMIC contexts, AI-enabled medical tourism operates within health systems already characterized by structural inequalities, limited digital infrastructure, and constrained public financing (de Andrade et al., 2025). AI technologies tend to be deployed first in high-revenue service lines catering to foreign patients, reinforcing a dual-track system in which advanced digital care is accessible to a privileged minority (Yang et al., 2024). Domestic patients rely on under-resourced public services, risking widening access gaps without redistributive governance mechanisms (Ciecierski-Holmes et al., 2022). Digital exclusion hampers equitable participation in AI healthcare by limiting internet access, digital literacy, and language barriers, affecting marginalized groups' access to AI medical tourism services (Mishori, 2025). Without targeted policy interventions, AI risks entrenching existing patterns of exclusion rather than serving as a tool for inclusive healthcare expansion.

Table 3 systematizes the equity risks associated with AI-enhanced medical tourism by linking specific AI-related mechanisms to affected populations and underlying governance failures. The table clarifies that inequities arise not only from AI technologies but also from institutional decisions on access, data governance, and workforce allocation. This reinforces the chapter's argument that equity must be treated as an explicit governance objective rather than a secondary outcome of efficiency gains.

Table 3. Equity risks arising from AI-enhanced medical tourism.

Equity Dimension	AI-Related Risk	Affected Population	Governance Failure
Access	Preferential patient selection	Domestic patients	Lack of equity safeguards
Data representation	Biased training datasets	LMIC populations	Weak data governance
Workforce	Talent diversion	Public-sector providers	Labor market imbalance
Digital inclusion	Platform exclusion	Marginalized groups	Digital infrastructure gaps

Source: Author's synthesis, 2026.

4.2 Algorithmic Bias and Data Inequality

Algorithmic bias is a significant equity challenge in AI for medical tourism. AI systems are influenced by their training data, which often reflects the health, socio-economic status, and clinical practices of wealthier populations in global healthcare (Parate et al., 2024). AI tools may produce less accurate predictions for patients from underrepresented regions. Studies show data inequality is not just technical but a governance failure, driven by unequal data ownership, limited LMIC participation in AI development, and dominance of commercial datasets (Zhang et al., 2025). In medical tourism, biased algorithms can influence patient selection, risk assessment, and pricing decisions, systematically disadvantaging specific populations while privileging those deemed more profitable or lower risk (Franklin et al., 2024).

Figure 4 shows how data inequality in cross-border healthcare creates algorithmic bias and systemic inequities in AI-driven medical tourism. Non-representative data, fragmented standards, and curated datasets introduce bias during data collection, reinforced by model design and algorithms. These biases influence clinical prioritization, patient selection, and resource allocation, leading to unequal access, diverted resources from low- and middle-income countries, and weakened accountability. The figure reinforces the argument that algorithmic bias is a governance failure rooted in structural data inequalities and a lack of regulatory oversight.

Figure 4. Pathways of algorithmic bias and data inequality in AI-enhanced medical tourism.

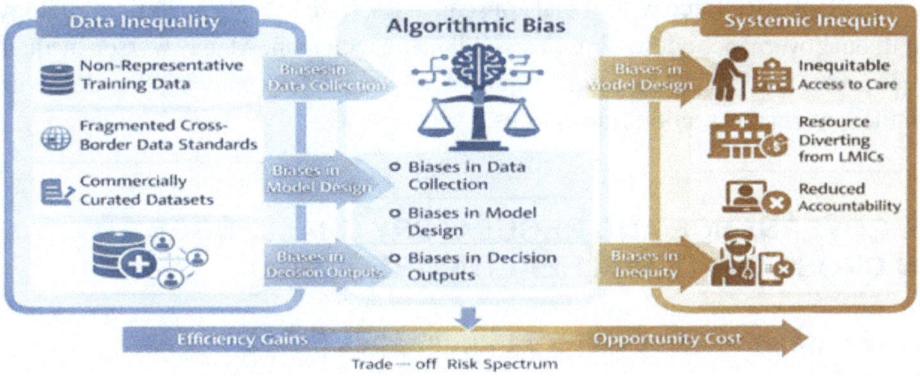

Source: *Author's conceptualization, 2026.*

Algorithmic bias harms individual patients and creates system inequities. AI-driven resource allocation without oversight can reinforce discrimination in access to treatment. Lack of training in AI ethics worsens these risks, especially where regulation is limited (Olawade et al., 2026).

4.3 Health Workforce and Social Equity

AI-driven medical tourism also has profound implications for health workforce equity within destination countries. As AI technologies enhance the profitability and efficiency of private medical tourism facilities, they can intensify labor market segmentation by drawing skilled professionals away from public health systems (Barua & Datta, 2024). This dynamic risks exacerbating shortages of essential services and undermining the health system's resilience, particularly in LMICs where workforce capacity is already fragile.

Emerging evidence suggests that AI adoption alters skill demand within healthcare systems, favoring digitally trained professionals and marginalizing workers without access to advanced training opportunities (Cadamuro et al., 2025). Surveys show healthcare workers worry AI could worsen inequities without inclusive training. In medical tourism, this risks creating a stratified workforce, with elite institutions gaining from AI while public facilities struggle to keep talent (Amponsah et al., 2024).

Social equity concerns further extend to community-level impacts. When medical tourism becomes a dominant growth strategy, public health priorities such as primary care, preventive services, and rural health provision may receive diminished attention (Dhale, 2020). Equity-oriented public health Scholar increasingly warns that technological innovation without social safeguards risks producing efficiency without justice, where aggregate gains coexist with deepening social divides (Wang et al., 2026). These equity dimensions highlight that AI-enhanced medical tourism is a redistributive force with social consequences, rather than a neutral technology. Without governance addressing access, bias, and inclusion, AI may worsen inequalities across borders. These issues require strong regulatory responses, as discussed in the governance section frameworks.

5. GOVERNANCE AND REGULATORY CHALLENGES IN CROSS-BORDER AI HEALTHCARE

5.1 Fragmented Regulatory Landscapes

The governance of AI-driven medical tourism is fundamentally complicated by fragmented regulatory environments across jurisdictions. Cross-border healthcare operates at the intersection of multiple legal regimes governing health services, data protection, medical liability, and digital technologies (Van Delm, 2024). While some regions have advanced regulatory architectures for AI and digital health, others remain characterized by regulatory gaps or inconsistent enforcement (van Kolfschooten et al., 2025). This heterogeneity creates uncertainty for healthcare providers and patients alike, particularly when AI systems are deployed across national borders without harmonized standards.

Legal scholars highlight that the lack of interoperable regulations weakens AI healthcare oversight. Different countries' methods for AI risk, device approval, and validation hinder compliance and accountability across borders (Fink & Akra, 2023). In medical tourism contexts, this fragmentation can enable regulatory arbitrage, where providers strategically locate AI-driven services in jurisdictions with weaker oversight, potentially exposing patients to unregulated or inadequately monitored technologies (Kalmenovitz et al., 2025). Moreover, fragmented governance increases compliance costs and operational complexity, particularly for providers seeking to scale AI-enabled services internationally (Alnajdawi et al., 2025). Comparative governance research highlights the need for adaptive, cross-sectoral regulatory coordination to address the unique challenges posed by AI in highly regulated domains such as healthcare (Mulani et al., 2025).

Table 4 highlights structural governance asymmetries across jurisdictions that complicate the regulation of AI-driven medical tourism. By contrasting regulatory capacity and institutional maturity between high-income countries and LMICs, the table illustrates how fragmented governance environments create opportunities for regulatory arbitrage and undermine patient protection in cross-border healthcare.

Table 4. Fragmentation of AI governance across jurisdictions in medical tourism.

Governance Dimension	High-Income Countries	LMICs	Medical Tourism Implications
Data protection	Comprehensive frameworks	Fragmented or weak	Cross-border compliance gaps
AI regulation	Risk-based oversight	Emerging or absent	Regulatory arbitrage
Accountability	Defined liability regimes	Limited enforcement	Patient redress challenges
Institutional capacity	High	Uneven	Governance asymmetries

Source: Author's synthesis based on comparative governance literature, 2026.

5.2 Data Governance, Privacy, and Sovereignty

Data governance is central to AI medical tourism regulations. AI relies on extensive sensitive health data, processed and stored across jurisdictions. Cross-border data flows raise issues of consent, ownership, privacy, and sovereignty, especially as patients' data move through diverse legal systems (Shivi, 2025). Policy-oriented studies identify data sovereignty as an emerging cornerstone of digital health governance, emphasizing states' rights to regulate the collection, storage, and use of health data within their jurisdictions (Lee, 2025). In the absence of coordinated international agreements, conflicting data localization requirements and privacy laws can obstruct legitimate medical data exchange while failing to protect patients from misuse or unauthorized access adequately (Shrivastava et al., 2021).

Innovative governance mechanisms aim to reconcile tensions. Privacy technologies like federated learning, synthetic data, and decentralized data architectures enable AI development while preserving data sovereignty and privacy (Fortino et al., 2025). Empirical research demonstrates that such approaches can support secure cross-border collaboration without centralizing sensitive datasets (Ferreira et al., 2025). However, their effective deployment requires clear regulatory guidance and institutional capacity, which remain unevenly distributed across medical tourism destinations.

5.3 Transparency, Accountability, and Institutional Oversight

Ensuring transparency and accountability in AI-driven medical tourism presents a further governance challenge. AI systems often function as opaque black boxes, making it difficult for patients, clinicians, and regulators to understand how decisions are made or to assign (Nogaroli & Faleiros Júnior, 2024). In cross-border contexts, accountability gaps are exacerbated by unclear liability regimes and jurisdictional ambiguity. Legal analyses of AI-enabled healthcare emphasize that accountability must be clearly distributed among developers, healthcare providers, platform operators, and regulatory authorities (Bahgat, 2025). Without explicit governance mechanisms, responsibility for harm caused by AI-assisted decisions can be diffused or contested, undermining patient trust and legal redress (Solaiman et al., 2025). This issue is particularly acute in medical tourism, where patients may lack effective access to legal remedies across borders.

Figure 5 highlights accountability gaps in cross-border AI healthcare, especially in medical tourism. Responsibility is spread among states, providers, platforms, and patients, causing unclear liability and weak oversight. Fragmented regulations, data sovereignty disputes, and differing ethical standards limit effective governance. Providers and platform operators face uncertainty over transparency, liability, and cross-border operations. Patients bear the consequences of these gaps, with limited transparency, legal options, and redress across jurisdictions. The figure underscores that accountability failures are systemic, stemming from jurisdictional fragmentation rather than isolated regulatory issues or shortcomings.

Figure 5. Accountability gaps in cross-border AI-enabled healthcare and medical tourism.

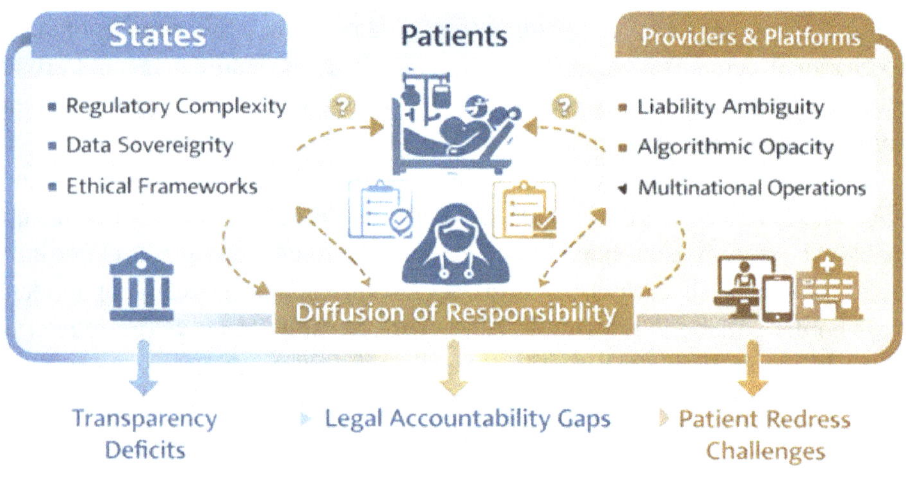

Source: *Author's conceptualization, 2026.*

Emerging governance models support impact assessments, explainability, and monitoring to boost accountability. AI-integrated compliance systems can enhance transparency and adapt to changing legal standards (Di Mauro et al., 2025). Such systems allow real-time risk assessment and support regulatory coordination across jurisdictions with strong institutional frameworks. Governance and regulatory issues in AI-driven medical tourism reveal broader tensions between innovation, sovereignty, and accountability (McGrath, 2024). Addressing these challenges requires international cooperation, inclusive governance, and adaptable regulations that keep pace with technology. These considerations inform the case analyses in the next section, which examine how different jurisdictions manage AI governance in medical tourism practice.

6. COMPARATIVE CASE ANALYSIS OF AI-ENHANCED MEDICAL TOURISM

A comparative case analysis reveals how governance shapes the economic and equity outcomes of AI-driven medical tourism. Examining different regulatory environments and development paths shows how institutional capacity, policy coherence, and governance priorities influence AI deployment in cross-border healthcare. Cases of India, Thailand, and Malta (EU) illustrate diverse strategies for balancing efficiency, equity, and accountability in AI-enhanced medical services tourism.

Figure 6 compares governance outcomes in AI-enabled medical tourism in India, Thailand, and Malta, showing how different regulatory structures influence efficiency, equity, and accountability. India's market-led, decentralized model enables rapid AI adoption and efficiency but offers limited equity safeguards and fragmented accountability. Thailand's centralized, coordinated governance shows stronger institutional ties with national health coverage and oversight, partially addressing equity and accountability. Malta, within the EU framework, has the highest regulatory maturity, with centralized oversight, data protection, and formal accountability, but higher compliance costs. The figure supports the chapter's argument that outcomes depend more on governance design than technological capacity coherence.

Figure 6. Comparative governance outcomes in AI-enabled medical tourism from India, Thailand, and Malta.

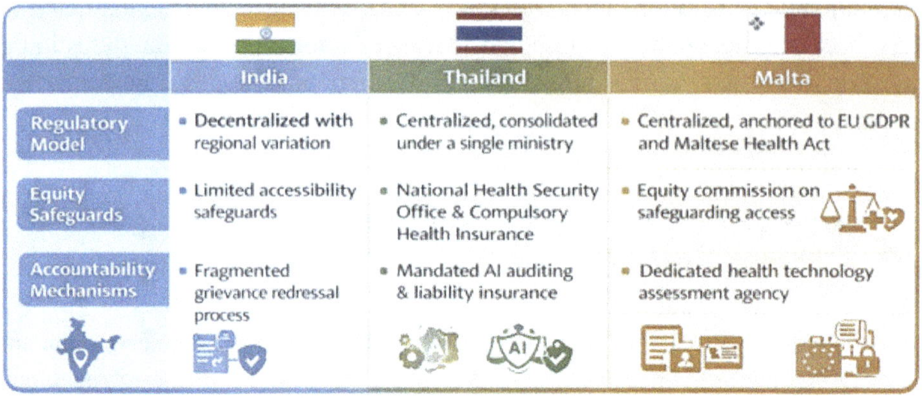

Source: *Author's conceptualization based on comparative case analysis, 2026.*

6.1 Market-Led AI Adoption and Governance Constraints in India

India has emerged as one of the world's most prominent medical tourism destinations, driven by a large private healthcare sector, cost competitiveness, and rapid digital innovation. AI adoption in Indian healthcare has accelerated across diagnostics, telemedicine, hospital workflow optimization, and patient management platforms (Chatterjee et al., 2022). These technologies improve efficiency and scalability, boosting India's global medical tourism. Analyses show India's digital health benefits from scale and a growing population (Gnana Sanga Mithra & Bhavana, 2025). However, governance frameworks have struggled to keep pace with technological expansion. Regulatory oversight of AI systems remains fragmented, with limited integration of equity safeguards into health technology governance (Chettri et al., 2025).

Equity issues are strong in medical tourism, with AI services mainly in private, urban hospitals for international patients, while public health facilities struggle with resources (Sainger, 2024). Research on AI ethics and healthcare governance underscores that insufficient institutionalization of algorithmic accountability can exacerbate access disparities, particularly in large, socioeconomically diverse populations (Sakhare et al., 2023). India's experience demonstrates how market-led AI adoption can generate efficiency gains while simultaneously intensifying governance and equity gaps in medical tourism.

6.2 Coordinated Digital Health Strategy with Emerging Equity Tensions in Thailand

Thailand represents a more coordinated approach to AI-enhanced medical tourism, underpinned by strong state involvement in healthcare planning and international patient management. The country has invested heavily in digital health infrastructure, integrating AI into hospital information systems and patient coordination platforms (Hemrungrojn et al., 2024). These investments have enhanced service quality and bolstered Thailand's global medical tourism reputation. Research shows that Thailand's governance benefits from better coordination among health authorities, private providers, and tourism agencies. This alignment has led to more consistent digital health standards and oversight of AI-enabled services (Sangkakorn et al., 2025). From an efficiency perspective, AI has enhanced patient flow management and reduced administrative bottlenecks in leading medical tourism hospitals.

Nevertheless, equity concerns persist. Studies on cross-border healthcare utilization indicate that international patient prioritization may indirectly reduce access for domestic populations, particularly in high-demand urban facilities (Meemon et al., 2021). While Thailand's regulatory environment is more mature than that of many LMIC peers. The Thai case illustrates how coordinated governance can moderate but not eliminate equity tensions in AI-enabled medical tourism.

6.3 Regulatory Maturity and Accountability Emphasis in Malta and the European Union

Malta, a small medical tourism destination within the EU, leverages EU digital health frameworks, such as data protection and AI governance, to appear compliant and trustworthy for cross-border healthcare (Sciberras & Dingli, 2023). The EU's regulatory architecture emphasizes interoperability, data protection, and accountability in digital health, shaping how AI is deployed in medical tourism. Legal analyses of the European Health Data Space highlight the region's commitment to institutionalized governance mechanisms, including structured data-access bodies and standardized oversight processes (Recuero, 2024). These frameworks enhance transparency and patient trust, reducing governance risks associated with cross-border AI deployment.

From an equity standpoint, EU governance places a stronger emphasis on individual rights, informed consent, and data sovereignty. Research on privacy-preserving AI approaches demonstrates that European regulatory incentives have accelerated the adoption of technologies such as synthetic data and federated learning to balance innovation with ethical safeguards (Castelló et al., 2024). However, high compliance costs may limit the scalability of AI-driven medical tourism in smaller markets like Malta, illustrating trade-offs between regulatory rigor and economic competitiveness.

Across three cases, distinct governance patterns emerge. India shows a market-driven AI adoption with efficiency gains but weak safeguards for equity and accountability. Thailand's coordinated governance achieves efficiency but faces distributional challenges. Malta, within the EU, demonstrates how strong regulations can improve accountability and trust, though they may limit rapid market growth. These insights emphasize that AI in medical tourism depends on governance choices that influence how benefits are shared and risks managed. The findings highlight the need for an integrated framework that aligns incentives with fairness, detailed in the proposed Efficiency–Equity–Accountability (EEA) model in the next section.

7. PROPOSED GOVERNANCE FRAMEWORK: THE EFFICIENCY–EQUITY–ACCOUNTABILITY (EEA) MODEL

The analysis shows that AI-enhanced medical tourism offers economic benefits but also poses equity and governance risks that vary by context. To address these, this chapter introduces the Efficiency–Equity–Accountability (EEA) governance model for cross-border AI healthcare. EEA views AI as a governance-sensitive system shaped by policy, oversight, and ethics, filling gaps in current approaches that favor innovation over social justice. By combining economic, distributive, and institutional perspectives, EEA offers a comprehensive framework for managing AI-driven medical tourism aligned with global health goals.

Figure 7 shows the proposed Efficiency–Equity–Accountability (EEA) governance model for AI-enabled medical tourism, visualizing governance as a balance among three pillars. It places AI-enabled medical tourism governance at the center, emphasizing that efficiency, equity, and accountability must be jointly optimized for sustainable, socially legitimate outcomes. The efficiency pillar focuses on productivity, capacity, and AI deployment to improve system performance. The equity pillar emphasizes inclusive access, fair benefit-sharing, and safeguards against exclusion, especially for domestic populations. The accountability pillar highlights algorithmic standards, liability, and cross-border redress to ensure transparency and accountability. The model illustrates that failures occur when any pillar is neglected, supporting the idea that AI-driven medical tourism needs integrated, adaptive governance architectures.

Figure 7. The Efficiency–Equity–Accountability (EEA) governance model for AI-enabled medical tourism.

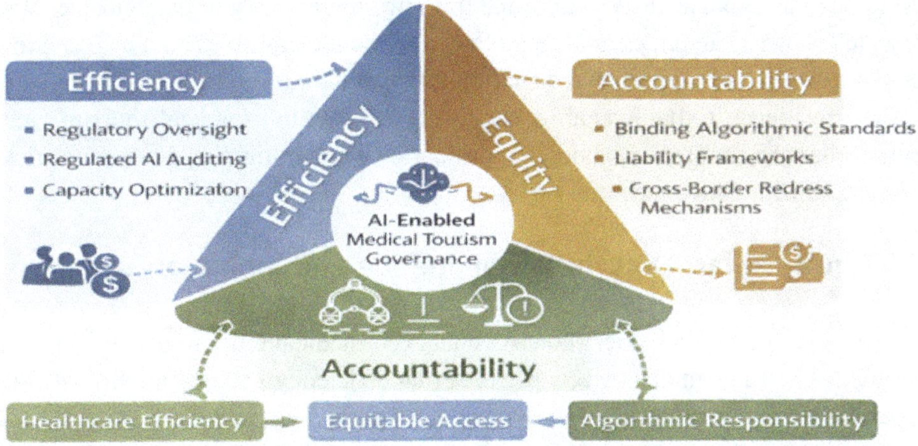

Source: *Author's conceptualization, 2026.*

7.1 Framework Overview and Rationale

The Efficiency–Equity–Accountability (EEA) model is grounded in the premise that sustainable AI-enabled medical tourism can only be achieved through the simultaneous optimization of three interdependent pillars: efficiency, which maximizes economic value and system performance; equity, which ensures the fair distribution of benefits and risks; and accountability, which embeds transparency, responsibility, and effective oversight (Dedović & Crompvoets, 2025). Governance failures arise when any one pillar is privileged at the expense of the others, for example, efficiency-driven AI deployment without equity safeguards may intensify existing health disparities (Archana, 2024). At the same time, accountability regimes that disregard economic realities can stifle innovation. Reflecting governance studies that call for integrated and adaptive frameworks capable of balancing competing objectives within complex (Krimmer et al., 2021), the EEA model is conceived as a dynamic governance architecture that can be applied across diverse regulatory contexts rather than as a rigid, one-size-fits-all regulatory solution.

7.2 Efficiency Pillar: Governing Economic Value Creation

Within the EEA model, efficiency refers to AI systems' ability to boost productivity, cut transaction costs, and improve cross-border healthcare coordination. Governance ensures these gains are real, measurable, and sustainable. Policy tools include benchmarking, cost–benefit analyses, and infrastructure investments for interoperable digital health platforms. Governance should also consider long-term costs, such as cybersecurity, workforce training, and algorithm maintenance. New research shows efficiency can be maintained without centralized data by using federated learning and decentralized analytics, which reduce duplication and enhance system resilience (Abdulwahab & Azam, 2026). Within medical tourism, such approaches can enable cross-border coordination while mitigating governance risks associated with data concentration.

7.3 Equity Pillar: Distributional Justice and Inclusion

The equity pillar considers how AI-enhanced medical tourism benefits are distributed. The EEA model rejects the idea that efficiency gains will automatically reach underserved groups, emphasizing that equity is an active governance goal. Mechanisms include mandatory impact assessments, inclusive data requirements, and reinvesting tourism revenues into public health. At the institutional level, equity involves workforce inclusion to extend AI skills beyond private elites. A scholar notes that algorithmic inequities are structurally rooted and cannot be fixed solely through technical fixes. Governance must address data power asymmetries to avoid reproducing exclusionary health systems (Rawson, 2025). The EEA model, therefore, embeds equity as a core evaluative criterion for AI success in medical tourism.

7.4 Accountability Pillar: Transparency and Institutional Responsibility

The EEA framework's accountability pillar defines responsibility throughout the AI lifecycle, focusing on explainability, auditability, and oversight. In cross-border medical tourism, accountability failures are especially harmful due to jurisdictional fragmentation and limited patient recourse. The model uses impact assessments, monitoring, and roles for developers, providers, operators, and regulators. Governance should enable AI decisions to be questioned, challenged, and corrected. Advances in compliance and privacy-preserving AI show that accountability and innovation can coexist. Decentralized governance, AI auditing, and transparent data controls can foster trust and efficiency (Z. Chen et al., 2025). These tools are particularly relevant for medical tourism systems operating across multiple legal regimes.

7.5 Operationalizing the EEA Model

Implementing the EEA framework needs multi-level governance, with countries aligning AI, health, and tourism policies under unified oversight. Internationally, soft-law tools and agreements encourage regulatory convergence while respecting sovereignty. The adaptable EEA model requires continuous review as AI and medical tourism evolve, balancing efficiency, equity, and accountability. It provides a structured approach to governing AI-driven medical tourism, linking economic performance, social justice, and institutional responsibility to promote sustainable, fair global healthcare mobility. Table 5 translates the Efficiency–Equity–Accountability (EEA) governance model into concrete policy instruments across national and international levels. The table demonstrates how abstract governance principles can be operationalized through targeted regulatory tools, reinforcing the feasibility and policy relevance of the EEA framework. It supports the chapter's conclusion that balanced AI governance requires coordinated, multi-level implementation rather than isolated regulatory interventions.

Table 5. Operationalizing the Efficiency–Equity–Accountability (EEA) governance model.

EEA Pillar	Governance Instruments	Policy Level	Expected Outcome
Efficiency	AI performance benchmarking	National	Sustainable productivity gains
Equity	Mandatory equity impact assessments	National	Inclusive access
Equity	Revenue reinvestment mechanisms	National	Public health strengthening
Accountability	Algorithmic audits	National / International	Transparency
Accountability	Cross-border liability frameworks	International	Effective patient redress

Source: Author's conceptual framework, 2026.

8. IMPLICATIONS FOR GLOBAL HEALTH GOALS AND SUSTAINABLE DEVELOPMENT

The governance of AI-driven medical tourism has implications that extend beyond national health systems to the broader architecture of global health governance and sustainable development. As AI-enabled healthcare mobility expands, its alignment with international development objectives becomes increasingly consequential. In particular, the way AI is governed in cross-border healthcare will influence progress toward the United Nations' Sustainable Development Goals (SDGs), notably SDG 3 (Good Health and Well-Being) and SDG 10 (Reduced Inequalities), while also shaping digital trust, institutional resilience, and international cooperation.

8.1 Advancing SDG 3: Good Health and Well-Being

AI-enhanced medical tourism can positively impact SDG 3 by improving healthcare quality, efficiency, and the diffusion of innovation. Effective governance allows AI to enhance diagnosis, enable early intervention, and ensure continuity of care for international patients, boosting health outcomes and system responsiveness. Regulatory analyses highlight that strong legal frameworks are crucial for safe, effective AI-assisted diagnostics (Naili et al., 2025). AI-driven medical tourism's contribution to SDG 3 depends on the quality of governance. Without oversight, the focus on profit risks neglects health needs, limiting benefits. Research shows AI can enhance enforcement, quality, and safety, strengthening health systems (Winkler et al., 2025). Embedding such mechanisms within medical tourism governance can help ensure that AI-driven innovation contributes meaningfully to improved health outcomes rather than narrowly defined market success.

8.2 Addressing SDG 10: Reducing Inequalities

AI-enhanced medical tourism has complex impacts on SDG 10. It can broaden access, but may worsen inequalities if benefits favor the wealthy and private providers. The EEA framework emphasizes governance interventions over markets. Studies show coordinated legal and institutional efforts can lessen disparities, especially where regulatory capacity varies (Lianos, 2025). In medical tourism, coordination is essential to prevent the marginalization of domestic patients and to ensure AI efficiencies do not worsen inequalities. Reducing inequality depends on redistributive policies. Governance that channels tourism revenues into public healthcare, workforce development, and digital inclusion can make AI-driven medical tourism a tool for inclusive growth. Without this, AI may reinforce the stratification of global health disparities.

8.3 Strengthening Global Health Governance and Institutional Resilience

Beyond the SDGs, AI medical tourism impacts global health governance by challenging traditional regulatory frameworks and requiring international cooperation. Harmonized standards for AI safety, data protection, and accountability can strengthen resilience while respecting sovereignty. Governance research emphasizes adaptive, tech-enabled regulations to manage risks. AI tools and oversight support real-time monitoring, reduce fragmentation, and build trust (Esnaashari & Jabal, 2025). In medical tourism, approaches can enable safer cross-border care and align private innovation with public health. Global governance must be inclusive, with low- and middle-income countries shaping AI norms rather than just adopting frameworks. Capacity-building, knowledge transfer, and South–South cooperation are vital to ensure AI-driven medical tourism fosters equitable global health progress.

8.4 Long-Term Sustainability Considerations

The sustainability of AI-driven medical tourism relies on integrating it into broader development strategies rather than treating it as a standalone. Long-term success demands balancing innovation with environmental, workforce, and social concerns. Governance that emphasizes accountability and transparency can boost trust and ensure that AI aligns with societal values. As health systems face demographic, climate, and demand pressures, AI-based medical tourism will grow. Its impact on sustainable development depends on current governance choices. The EEA framework guides aligning AI healthcare mobility with global health, resilience, and inclusion trajectories.

9. FUTURE RESEARCH DIRECTIONS

Future research on AI-driven medical tourism governance is urgently needed as technological adoption outpaces empirical and theoretical studies. While existing research notes efficiency gains and concerns about equity and regulation, gaps remain in understanding real-world impacts on health outcomes, costs, and access. Addressing these requires longitudinal, mixed-method, and comparative studies to evaluate governance tools such as algorithmic audits, equity assessments, and accountability mechanisms, while supporting secure cross-border data sharing that ensures privacy. Regional studies, especially in Africa, Latin America, and small island states, are vital to understand how institutional capacity, digital infrastructure, and political factors influence governance, and how supranational coordination can reduce fragmentation without compromising sovereignty. These directions highlight the need for interdisciplinary, empirical, and equity-focused research to ensure AI-driven medical tourism fosters sustainable, inclusive, and accountable global health systems.

10. CONCLUSION

The expansion of medical tourism is shifting toward AI- and data-driven healthcare, presenting opportunities for greater efficiency and cross-border access. However, benefits are uneven and depend on governance; improper frameworks may exacerbate inequalities and obscure accountability. This chapter examines the tensions in AI-enhanced medical tourism through case studies showing outcomes vary by institutional capacity, regulation, and commitment to equity. Market approaches boost efficiency but may overlook social costs, whereas stricter regulation enhances accountability but reduces scalability. The proposed EEA governance model aims to balance efficiency, equity, and accountability for sustainable health goals, highlighting the need for integrated, adaptive governance, especially in cross-border digital systems resilience.

AI-driven medical tourism impacts global health governance beyond individual markets. Aligning AI healthcare mobility with the UN Sustainable Development Goals requires deliberate policy, international cooperation, and inclusive participation. Governance must ensure AI promotes collective health rather than regulatory loopholes or unfair value extraction. Responsible AI use supports transparent, adaptive governance. AI is not just a tech upgrade but a force reshaping healthcare value across borders. Its future depends on policymakers prioritizing equity and accountability. When well-governed, AI medical tourism can aid sustainable development, resilience, and a fairer global health system.

CONFLICT OF INTEREST DECLARATION

The authors declare that they have no conflicts of interest regarding the publication of this chapter.

AI USE DECLARATION

The authors acknowledge that artificial intelligence tools were used solely to improve language clarity and readability. The authors reviewed and approved all content and are fully responsible for the final version

REFERENCES

Abdalla, R. A., Hidaytalla, L. A., Mulla, G. S., Al-Salman, M., Hammad, M., & Ahmed, E. (2025). The Role of AI Technology. In *Advancing the United Nations Sustainable Development Goals (SDGs) in Healthcare and Environmental Services, Across Various Industries. In Studies in Big Data* (Vol. 170, pp. 391–403). Springer Science and Business Media Deutschland GmbH., DOI: 10.1007/978-3-031-83915-3_31

Abdulwahab, L. O. (2026). Healthy Aging and Resource Sustainability: Integrating Health Economics and Natural Resource Management in the Silver Economy. In *Economic Transformations in Population Aging: Unlocking the Silver Economy* (pp. 313–348). IGI Global Scientific Publishing. https://www.igi-global.com/chapter/healthy-aging-and-resource-sustainability/399914

Abdulwahab, L. O., & Azam, H. (2026). Platform Work in Europe's Green and Care Economies: Regulatory Pathways for Sustainability, Social Protection, and Fair Work. In *Regulating the Gig Economy in the European Union: Challenges, Innovations, and Global Impacts* (pp. 99–124). IGI Global Scientific Publishing. https://www.igi-global.com/chapter/platform-work-in-europes-green-and-care-economies/395612

Abdulwahab, L. O., Daniel, O., Gul, A., & Bubari, H. U. (2026). The Economic Impact of Digital Health Innovations on Disease Prevention: Cost-Effectiveness, ROI, and Policy Implications. In *Reshaping Health Promotion and Disease Prevention Through Digital Innovation* (pp. 29–56). IGI Global Scientific Publishing. DOI: 10.4018/979-8-3373-3531-5.ch002

Abdulwahab, L. O., Daniel, O., Halabi, K. A., & Umar, H. B. (2026). Healthcare Entrepreneurship and Global Talent: Navigating Visa Barriers, Health Innovation, and Startup Survival as an International Graduate. In *International Student Narratives in Globalized Higher Education* (pp. 401–434). IGI Global Scientific Publishing. https://www.igi-global.com/chapter/healthcare-entrepreneurship-and-global-talent/400509

Abdulwahab, L. O., Halabi, K. A., & Daniel, O. (2026). Financial Stress, Health Trade-Offs, and Educational Choices: A Story of Survival and Success. In *International Student Narratives in Globalized Higher Education* (pp. 273–304). IGI Global Scientific Publishing. DOI: 10.4018/979-8-3373-4212-2.ch011

Abou Jaoude, G., Batura, N., Correa, A., Haghparast-Bidgoli, H., Leiva Granados, R., Palmer, T., Poupakis, S., Salustri, F., & Skordis, J. (2023). Economics of Global Health. In *Sustainable Development Goals Series: Part F2781* (pp. 557–566). Springer. DOI: 10.1007/978-3-031-33851-9_86

Abubakari, M. S., & Olamilekan, L. A. (2026). Blockchain and Tokenomics for Education: Unlocking Micro-Credentials, Equity, and Lifelong Learning—An Overview. *The Impact of Blockchain in Token Economies*, 255–290.

Ahmed, M. M., Okesanya, O. J., Olaleke, N. O., Adigun, O. A., Adebayo, U. O., Oso, T. A., Eshun, G., & Lucero-Prisno, D. E.III. (2025). Integrating Digital Health Innovations to Achieve Universal Health Coverage: Promoting Health Outcomes and Quality Through Global Public Health Equity. *Health Care*, *13*(9), 1060. https://www.mdpi.com/2227-9032/13/9/1060 PMID: 40361838

Ali, A., Montanaro, T., Sergi, I., Carrisi, S., Galli, D., Distante, C., & Patrono, L. (2025). An Innovative IoT and Edge Intelligence Framework for Monitoring Elderly People Using Anomaly Detection on Data from Non-Wearable Sensors. *Sensors (Basel)*, *25*(6), 1735. Advance online publication. DOI: 10.3390/s25061735 PMID: 40292837

Alnajdawi, M. H., Raafat, R., Aburayya, A., & Al Ghurabli, Z. (2025). Enhancing Logistical Efficiency in Public Institutions through AI: A Managerial Framework for Regulatory and Technological Integration. *International Journal of Industrial Engineering and Production Research*, *36*(3), 81–92. DOI: 10.22068/ijiepr.36.3.2459

Alsaleh, A. (2025). Leveraging artificial intelligence for sustainable healthcare transformation: Socioeconomic impacts and ethical implications. *Innovation and Emerging Technologies*, *12*, 2550015. Advance online publication. DOI: 10.1142/S273759942550015X

Alshamsi, A. I. (2024). A review of the United Arab Emirates healthcare systems on medical tourism and accreditation. *Frontiers in Health Services*, *4*, 1329252. Advance online publication. DOI: 10.3389/frhs.2024.1329252 PMID: 38449575

Amponsah, D., Thamman, R., Brandt, E., James, C., Spector-Bagdady, K., & Yong, C. M. (2024). Artificial Intelligence to Promote Racial and Ethnic Cardiovascular Health Equity. *Current Cardiovascular Risk Reports*, *18*(11), 153–162. DOI: 10.1007/s12170-024-00745-6 PMID: 40144330

Archana, K. (2024). Responsible AI implementation in healthcare organizations. In *Responsible AI for Digital Health and Medical Analytics* (pp. 1–14). IGI Global., DOI: 10.4018/979-8-3693-6294-5.ch001

Arshed, M., Kazi, A. K., Kiran, M., & Ali, S. M. F. (2025). Challenges in Health Equity: Balancing Innovation With Fairness and Addressing Algorithmic Biases. In *Innovation and Transformation of Public Health* (pp. 113–141). IGI Global. DOI: 10.4018/979-8-3373-1992-6.ch004

Ashraf, J., & Hayat, Y. (2025). Transforming medical tourism through digital advancements. In *Revolutionizing Healthcare Experience With Digital Medical Tourism* (pp. 425–457). IGI Global., DOI: 10.4018/979-8-3693-7888-5.ch017

Bahgat, A. (2025). AI governance and data privacy in cross-border contexts: A comparative analysis of regulatory frameworks. *Journal of Data Protection and Privacy*, *8*(1), 8–23. DOI: 10.69554/BOJL3033

Barua, R., & Datta, S. (2024). The improvements in significance of AI in experiential and medical tourism. In *Generative AI for Transformational Management* (pp. 303–333). IGI Global., DOI: 10.4018/979-8-3693-5578-7.ch012

Bathla, G., Raina, A., & Rana, V. S. (2024). Artificial intelligence-driven enhancements in medical tourism: Opportunities, challenges, and future prospects. In *Impact of AI and Robotics on the Medical Tourism Industry* (pp. 139–162). IGI Global., DOI: 10.4018/979-8-3693-2248-2.ch006

Cadamuro, J., Carobene, A., Cabitza, F., Debeljak, Z., De Bruyne, S., Van Doorn, W., Johannes, E., Frans, G., Özdemir, H., Martin Perez, S., Rajdl, D., Tolios, A., & Padoan, A. (2025). A comprehensive survey of artificial intelligence adoption in European laboratory medicine: Current utilization and prospects. *Clinical Chemistry and Laboratory Medicine*, *63*(4), 692–703. DOI: 10.1515/cclm-2024-1016 PMID: 39443973

Castelló, F., Santos-Rojo, C., & De la Torre Olid, F. (2024). Artificial Intelligence and the 'Data Act' in the European Union: A Legal and Economic Analysis of New Digital Regulations and Their Impact on Citizens' Rights and Business Innovation. *Springer Proceedings in Business and Economics*, 57–72. DOI: 10.1007/978-3-031-67511-9_4

Chandra, J., Kaur, R., & Sahay, R. (2025). Integrated Framework for Equitable Healthcare AI: Bias Mitigation, Community Participation, and Regulatory Governance. *2025 IEEE 14th International Conference on Communication Systems and Network Technologies, CSNT 2025*, 819–825. DOI: 10.1109/CSNT64827.2025.10968102

Chatterjee, S., Chaudhuri, R., Thrassou, A., & Vrontis, D. (2022). Technology disruption in healthcare: Artificial intelligence application, challenges, and policy recommendations in India. *International Journal of Internet Marketing and Advertising*, *17*(3–4), 394–414. DOI: 10.1504/IJIMA.2022.126716

Chen, Z., Awan, U., Nassani, A. A., Al-Aiban, K. M., & Zaman, K. (2025). Enhancing sustainable growth in the global south: The role of mineral resource management, supply chain efficiency, technology advancement, and local downstream processing. *Resources Policy, 100. Resources Policy, 100*, 105451. Advance online publication. DOI: 10.1016/j.resourpol.2024.105451

Chettri, S. K., Deka, R. K., & Saikia, M. J. (2025). Bridging the Gap in the Adoption of Trustworthy AI in Indian Healthcare: Challenges and Opportunities. *AI, 6*(1), 10. Advance online publication. DOI: 10.3390/ai6010010

Chirmulay, V., & Bhakare, J. (2025). Digital health and medical tourism: A regulatory perspective. In *Navigating Innovations and Challenges in Travel Medicine and Digital Health* (pp. 311–324). IGI Global., DOI: 10.4018/979-8-3693-8774-0.ch015

Choudhari, H. M., & Khobragade, S. (2024). The Role of AI in Patients' Communication. *2024 2nd DMIHER International Conference on Artificial Intelligence in Healthcare, Education and Industry, IDICAIEI 2024*. DOI: 10.1109/IDICAIEI61867.2024.10842915

Chowdhary, S. P., & Majumdar, K. (2025). Health Tourism Catalyst for Growth in Developing Nations. *Journal of Public Affairs, 25*(3), e70060. Advance online publication. DOI: 10.1002/pa.70060

Ciecierski-Holmes, T., Singh, R., Axt, M., Brenner, S., & Barteit, S. (2022). Artificial intelligence for strengthening healthcare systems in low- and middle-income countries: A systematic scoping review. *NPJ Digital Medicine, 5*(1), 162. Advance online publication. DOI: 10.1038/s41746-022-00700-y PMID: 36307479

Da Silva, M., Denis, J. L., & Régis, C. (2024). Good Governance Strategies for Human-Centered AI in Healthcare: Connecting Norms and Context. In *Human-Centered AI: a Multidisciplinary Perspective for Policy-Makers, Auditors, and Users* (pp. 105–115). CRC Press. DOI: 10.1201/9781003320791-13

Das, D., Shrivastav, M. K., Jaya Sankar Krishna, S. V. S. P. P., Hazarika, D., Sharma, S. C., Mahendranath Chowdary, R., & Wadettiwar, P. P. (2025). Public-private partnerships (PPP) in infrastructure financing: A comparative study of developed and developing economies. *Heritage and Sustainable Development, 7*(1), 443–452. DOI: 10.37868/hsd.v7i1.1087

de Andrade, J. B. C., Fagundes, T. P., Katsuyama, E., & Silva, G. S. (2025). Digital Health in Low-Resource Settings: Comprehensive Challenges and Opportunities With a Focus on Stroke Care. *Stroke*. Advance online publication. DOI: 10.1161/STROKEAHA.125.050448 PMID: 40905151

Dedović, S., & Crompvoets, J. (2025). Delving into the governance of cross-border in-teroperability solutions in the EU. *eJournal of eDemocracy and Open Government, 17*(2), 65–89. DOI: 10.29379/jedem.v17i2.981

Dhale, S. (2020). Factors influencing the meteoric rise of the Indian medical tourism sector and its impact on the economy. *Journal of Critical Reviews, 7*(7), 692–694. DOI: 10.31838/jcr.07.07.126

Di Mauro, L., Capasso, E., Tettamanti, C., Casella, C., Francaviglia, M., Volonnino, G., Rinaldi, R., Esposito, M., & Chisari, M. (2025). The role of artificial intelligence in analyzing clinical malpractice disputes through medical record management. *Journal of Forensic and Legal Medicine, 115*, 102941. Advance online publication. DOI: 10.1016/j.jflm.2025.102941 PMID: 40784149

Eisavi, M., Fallah, M. R. R., Motaghi, S., & Taheri, F. (2025). The impact of economic convergence between Iran and selected middle eastern countries on health tourism in Iran [ ]. *Journal of Health Administration, 28*(1), 109–119. DOI: 10.61882/jha.28.1.109

El Arab, R. A., Al Moosa, O. A., & Sagbakken, M. (2025). Economic, ethical, and regulatory dimensions of artificial intelligence in healthcare: An integrative review. *Frontiers in Public Health, 13*, 1617138. Advance online publication. DOI: 10.3389/fpubh.2025.1617138 PMID: 40951387

Esnaashari, S., & Jabal, M. (2025). An AI-Driven Framework for Autonomous Network Vulnerability Management. *Americas Conference on Information Systems, AMCIS 2025*. https://www.scopus.com/pages/publications/105025189924?origin=scopusAI

Ferreira, B., Borges, R., Antunes, C. M., Maximiano, M., Gomes, R., Távora, V., Dias, M., & Correia Bezerra, R. (2025). Can Secure MultiParty Computation be Used to Create Clinical Trial Cohorts based on Blockchain Notarized Private Patient Data? *Procedia Computer Science, 256*, 996–1002. DOI: 10.1016/j.procs.2025.02.205

Fink, M., & Akra, B. (2023). Comparison of the international regulations for medical devices–USA versus Europe. *Injury, 54*, 110908. Advance online publication. DOI: 10.1016/j.injury.2023.110908 PMID: 37365092

Fortino, L., De Vita, S., Esposito, M., & Esposito, C. (2025). Federated Digital Twin Architecture with Synthetic Data Generation for Privacy-Preserving Diabetes Management. *2025 IEEE Conference on Standards for Communications and Networking, CSCN 2025*. DOI: 10.1109/CSCN67557.2025.11230756

Franklin, G., Stephens, R., Piracha, M., Tiosano, S., Lehouillier, F., Koppel, R., & Elkin, P. L. (2024). The Sociodemographic Biases in Machine Learning Algorithms: A Biomedical Informatics Perspective. *Life (Basel, Switzerland)*, *14*(6), 652. Advance online publication. DOI: 10.3390/life14060652 PMID: 38929638

Garad, A., Al-Ansi, A. M., Jaboob, M., & Kusumawati, R. (2025). Digital innovations in medical tourism: A PRISMA review in the Arab Region. In *Revolutionizing Healthcare Experience With Digital Medical Tourism* (pp. 53–77). IGI Global., DOI: 10.4018/979-8-3693-7888-5.ch002

Gnana Sanga Mithra, S., & Bhavana, S. (2025). Revolutionizing healthcare with an in-depth analysis of AI's transformative impact in India. *Social Sciences & Humanities Open*, *11*, 101467. Advance online publication. DOI: 10.1016/j.ssaho.2025.101467

Grannis, S. J., Williams, J. L., Kasthuri, S., Murray, M., & Xu, H. (2022). Evaluation of real-world referential and probabilistic patient matching to advance patient identification strategy. *Journal of the American Medical Informatics Association : JAMIA*, *29*(8), 1409–1415. DOI: 10.1093/jamia/ocac068 PMID: 35568993

Hemrungrojn, S., Saengsai, K., Jakkrawankul, P., Kiattiporn-Opas, C., Chaichareenon, K., Amrapala, A., Lapanan, K., Achakulvisut, T., Vateekul, P., Nupairoj, N., Phutrakool, P., Yodlorchai, R., Hiransuthikul, N., & Hengprapom, S. (2024). Accuracy and concordance of DMIND AI application with a renowned depression assessment tool in Thai adults. *Chulalongkorn Medical Journal*, *68*(4), 261–273. DOI: 10.56808/2673-060X.5495

Kalmenovitz, J., Lowry, M., & Volkova, E. (2025). Regulatory Fragmentation. *The Journal of Finance*, *80*(2), 1081–1126. DOI: 10.1111/jofi.13423

Kaushik, A., Barcellona, C., Mandyam, N. K., Tan, S. Y., & Tromp, J. (2025). Challenges and Opportunities for Data Sharing Related to Artificial Intelligence Tools in Health Care in Low- and Middle-Income Countries: Systematic Review and Case Study From Thailand. *Journal of Medical Internet Research*, *27*, e58338. Advance online publication. DOI: 10.2196/58338 PMID: 39903508

Krimmer, R., Dedovic, S., Schmidt, C., & Corici, A. A. (2021). Developing Cross-border E-Governance: Exploring Interoperability and Cross-border Integration. *Lecture Notes in Computer Science (Including Subseries Lecture Notes in Artificial Intelligence and Lecture Notes in Bioinformatics), 12849 LNCS*, 107–124. DOI: 10.1007/978-3-030-82824-0_9

Labonté, R., Runnels, V., Crooks, V. A., Johnston, R., & Snyder, J. (2017). What does the development of medical tourism in Barbados hold for health equity? An exploratory qualitative case study. *Global Health Research and Policy*, *2*(1), 5. Advance online publication. DOI: 10.1186/s41256-017-0025-z PMID: 29202073

Lee, J.-W. (2025). Comment on "Japan's Aging Workforce: Determinants and Outlook.". *Asian Economic Policy Review*, *20*(2), 263–264. Advance online publication. DOI: 10.1111/aepr.12507

Lianos, I. (2025). Access to Health Data, Competition, and Regulatory Alternatives: Three Dimensions of Fairness. *Journal of Competition Law & Economics*, *21*(4), 595–646. DOI: 10.1093/joclec/nhaf016

Lin, R. (2024). AI-Driven Personalized Healthcare: Leveraging Multimodal Data for Precision Medicine. *Proceedings - 2024 IEEE/WIC International Conference on Web Intelligence and Intelligent Agent Technology, WI-IAT 2024*, 693–697. DOI: 10.1109/WI-IAT62293.2024.00112

Mahabub Subhani, G., & Sumalakshmi, C. (2025). Case Study on AI-Powered Healthcare: Improving Patient Outcomes with Predictive Analytics. In *Decoding AI: Practical Implementations for Business Operations* (pp. 289–303). Taylor and Francis. DOI: 10.4324/9781003606956-14

Mamun, A. A., & Alam, M. (2025). Promoting Equity in Public Health: Addressing Inequality and Social Disparities. *Health Science Reports*, *8*(5), e70821. Advance online publication. DOI: 10.1002/hsr2.70821 PMID: 40309625

McGrath, C. P. (2024). The state and values of AI governance in UK healthcare. In *Research Handbook on Health, AI and the Law: Research Handbooks in Health and Medical Law* (pp. 291–310). Edward Elgar Publishing Ltd. DOI: 10.4337/9781802205657.00026

Meemon, N., Paek, S. C., Pradubmook Sherer, P., Keetawattananon, W., & Marohabutr, T. (2021). Transnational Mobility and Utilization of Health Services in Northern Thailand: Implications and Challenges for Border Public Health Facilities. *Journal of Primary Care & Community Health*, *12*, 21501327211053740. Advance online publication. DOI: 10.1177/21501327211053740 PMID: 34704512

Mishori, R. (2025). Artificial Intelligence Technology in Healthcare and the Digital Divide. In *Digital Health, AI and Generative AI in Healthcare: A Concise, Practical Guide for Clinicians* (pp. 139–147). Springer Science+Business Media. DOI: 10.1007/978-3-031-83526-1_11

Mishra, P., & Kumar, A. (2025). Adoption of AI technologies in hospitals: Effects on consumer behaviour and health outcomes. *Journal of Medicinal and Pharmaceutical Chemistry Research, 7*(5), 1004–1025. DOI: 10.48309/jmpcr.2025.474077.1396

Mulani, A. O., Godase, V. V., Takale, S. R., & Ghodake, R. G. (2025). Ethical Challenges and Governance of Al in Healthcare, Education, Finance, and Security Sectors. In *Navigating Social Trust in the AI Era* (pp. 123–154). IGI Global., DOI: 10.4018/979-8-3373-7011-8.ch006

Naili, Y. T., & Mangkunegara, I. S. Purwono, & Baballe, M. A. (2025). Regulatory challenges in ai-based diagnostics: Legal implications of ai use in medical diagnostics. *BIO Web of Conferences, 152*. DOI: 10.1051/bioconf/202515201034

Nikolovski, S., & Petreska, A. (2025). Evaluating GDPR and HIPAA in the Integration of ML/AI for Future-Proofing Healthcare. *Lecture Notes in Networks and Systems, 1446 LNNS*, 289–313. DOI: 10.1007/978-3-031-99201-8_30

Nogaroli, R., & Faleiros Júnior, J. L. de M. (2024). Ethical Challenges of Artificial Intelligence in Medicine and the Triple Semantic Dimensions of Algorithmic Opacity with Its Repercussions to Patient Consent and Medical Liability. In *Law, Governance and Technology Series* (Vol. 58, pp. 229–248). Springer Nature. DOI: 10.1007/978-3-031-41264-6_12

Olawade, D. B., Clement David-Olawade, A., Aderinto, N., & Wada, O. Z. (2026). Ethical oversight of Artificial Intelligence in Nigerian Healthcare: A qualitative analysis of ethics committee members' perspectives on integration and regulation. *International Journal of Medical Informatics*, *206*, 106140. Advance online publication. DOI: 10.1016/j.ijmedinf.2025.106140 PMID: 41092592

Parate, A. P., Iyer, A. A., Gupta, K., Porwal, H., Kishoreraja, P. C., Sivakumar, R., & Soangra, R. (2024). Review of Data Bias in Healthcare Applications. *International Journal of Online and Biomedical Engineering*, *20*(12), 124–136. DOI: 10.3991/ijoe.v20i12.49997

Rawson, B. (2025). Health data justice, epistemological delinking and vernacularisation: Reclaiming knowledge, rights and representation. *International Journal of Law in Context*. Advance online publication. DOI: 10.1017/S1744552325100347

Recuero, M. (2024). Title: Secondary Use of Electronic Health Data: The Future Regulation on the European Health Data Space and its Interplay with Data Protection Law[El uso secundario de datos de salud electrónicos: El futuro Reglamento del Espacio Europeo de Datos de Salu.... *InDret*, (2), 525–551. DOI: 10.31009/InDret.2024.i2.13

Reshma Soman, N., Aswathy Prakash, G., & Azza, H. (2025). Optimizing Hospital Operations with AI-Driven Resource Allocation Tools. In *Synthesis Lectures on Computer Science: Part F698* (pp. 99–110). Springer Nature. DOI: 10.1007/978-3-031-93673-9_10

Russkikh, S. V., Tarasenko, E. A., Grin, S. I., Yugay, M. T., Kryukova, K. K., & Moskvicheva, L. I. (2022). Current opportunities for the export of medical services in Russia [Современные возможности экспорта медицинских услуг в России]. *Farmakoekonomika, 15*(2), 259–266. DOI: 10.17749/2070-4909/farmakoekonomika.2022.119

Sahar, S. N. M., & Dar, H. (2024). Artificial intelligence-enhanced global healthcare: The future of medical tourism. In *Impact of AI and Robotics on the Medical Tourism Industry* (pp. 194–216). IGI Global., DOI: 10.4018/979-8-3693-2248-2.ch009

Sainger, G. (2024). Artificial intelligence in healthcare sector in india: Application, challenges and a way. In *Artificial Intelligence Enabled Management: An Emerging Economy Perspective* (pp. 233–247). De Gruyter., DOI: 10.1515/9783111172408-015

Sakhare, N. N., Limkar, S., Mahadik, R. V., Phursule, R., & Godbole, A. (2023). Ethical considerations of AI applications in medicine: A policy framework for responsible deployment. *Journal of Krishna Institute of Medical Sciences University*. https://www.scopus.com/pages/publications/85185456480?origin=scopusAI

Sangkakorn, K., Traisaeng, A., Intawong, K., & Panyadee, C. (2025). Intelligent Digital Ecosystems for Safe and Sustainable Wellness Tourism. *Wangji Wanglu Jishu Xuekan, 26*(7), 903–912. DOI: 10.70003/160792642025122607006

Sciberras, M., & Dingli, A. (2023). AI-Readiness. In *Lecture Notes in Networks and Systems* (Vol. 568, pp. 17–21). Springer Science and Business Media Deutschland GmbH., DOI: 10.1007/978-3-031-19900-4_5

Shaban-Nejad, A., Michalowski, M., & Bianco, S. (2024). Breaking Barriers: The Power of Artificial Intelligence in Advancing Health Equity. *Studies in Computational Intelligence, 1164 SCI*, 1–8. DOI: 10.1007/978-3-031-63592-2_1

Shalini, N., Sathish, R., Divya Rao, B. J., & Mamatha, H. K. (2024). Impact of Covid-19 on Medical Tourism. In *Medical Tourism in Developing Countries: A contemporary approach* (pp. 117–126). Springer Nature., DOI: 10.1007/978-981-99-8909-6_7

Shamanna, B. R., & Mannava, S. (2023). Introduction to Health Economics. In *Textbook of Community Ophthalmology* (pp. 114–128). CRC Press., DOI: 10.1201/9781003291626-10

Shivi, S. (2025). Jurisdictional Challenges In Cross-Border Biomedical Data Privacy: Judicial Approaches And The Impact On Bioanalytical Research Frameworks. *Journal of Applied Bioanalysis, 11*(Special Issue 1), 424–431. DOI: 10.53555/jab.v11si1.432

Shrivastava, U., Song, J., Han, B. T., & Dietzman, D. (2021). Do data security measures, privacy regulations, and communication standards impact the interoperability of patient health information? A cross-country investigation. *International Journal of Medical Informatics, 148*, 104401. Advance online publication. DOI: 10.1016/j.ijmedinf.2021.104401 PMID: 33571743

Solaiman, B., Mekki, Y. M., Qadir, J., Ghaly, M., Abdelkareem, M., & Al-Ansari, A. (2025). A "True Lifecycle Approach" towards governing healthcare AI with the GCC as a global governance model. *NPJ Digital Medicine, 8*(1), 337. Advance online publication. DOI: 10.1038/s41746-025-01614-1 PMID: 40473925

Sriram, V., Yilmaz, V., Kaur, S., Andres, C., Cheng, M., & Meessen, B. (2024). The role of private healthcare sector actors in health service delivery and financing policy processes in low-and middle-income countries: A scoping review. *BMJ Global Health, 8*(Suppl 5), e013408. Advance online publication. DOI: 10.1136/bmjgh-2023-013408 PMID: 38316466

Tenkorang, P. O., Awuah, W. A., Mannan, K. M., Roy, S., Nkrumah Boateng, P. A., Asiedu, O., Tahiru, M., Ahluwalia, A., Owusu Bediako, N. O., & Darko, K. (2025). The transformative power of telemedicine in delivering effective neurosurgical care in low and middle-income countries: A review. *Brain & Spine, 5*, 104269. Advance online publication. DOI: 10.1016/j.bas.2025.104269 PMID: 40458419

Thangalakshmi, S., Mohankumar, N., Jayanthi, L. N., Blessy, Y. M., Meenakshi, R., & Rajmohan, M. (2025). Telemedicine Platforms with Cloud-Based AI-Driven Diagnostics in Hospitals. *Proceedings of International Conference on Visual Analytics and Data Visualization, ICVADV 2025*, 137–143. DOI: 10.1109/ICVADV63329.2025.10961133

Tripathi, R. P. & Shalki. (2023). Harnessing the Potential of AI and ML in Medical Tourism: Challenges, Opportunities, and Ethical Implications. *Proceedings - International Conference on Technological Advancements in Computational Sciences, ICTACS 2023*, 1068–1072. DOI: 10.1109/ICTACS59847.2023.10390358

Upadhyay, U., Gradisek, A., Iqbal, U., Dhar, E., Li, Y. C., & Syed-Abdul, S. (2023). Call for the responsible artificial intelligence in the healthcare. *BMJ Health & Care Informatics, 30*(1), e100920. Advance online publication. DOI: 10.1136/bmjhci-2023-100920 PMID: 38135293

Van Delm, K. (2024). EU In-Home Digital Diagnostics – Cross-Border Patient Reimbursement under Threat? In *Digital Health Care outside of Traditional Clinical Settings: Ethical, Legal, and Regulatory Challenges and Opportunities* (pp. 196–210). Cambridge University Press. DOI: 10.1017/9781009373234.019

van Kolfschooten, H., Goosen, S., van Oirschot, J., Schouten, B., Vajda, I., & Willems, L. (2025). Legal, ethical, and policy challenges of artificial intelligence translation tools in healthcare. *Discover Public Health*, *22*(1), 904. Advance online publication. DOI: 10.1186/s12982-025-01277-z PMID: 41487681

Wang, Y., Boyd, A. E., Rountree, L., Ren, Y., Nyhan, K., Nagar, R., Higginbottom, J., Ranney, M. L., Parikh, H., & Mukherjee, B. (2026). Ten Core Concepts for Ensuring Data Equity in Public Health. *JAMA Health Forum*, *7*(1), 1–11. DOI: 10.1001/jamahealthforum.2025.6031 PMID: 41511794

Weiner, E. B., Dankwa-Mullan, I., Nelson, W. A., & Hassanpour, S. (2025). Ethical challenges and evolving strategies in the integration of artificial intelligence into clinical practice. *PLOS Digital Health*, *4*(4), e0000810. Advance online publication. DOI: 10.1371/journal.pdig.0000810 PMID: 40198594

Winkler, P. W., Zsidai, B., Hamrin Senorski, E., Pruneski, J. A., Hirschmann, M. T., Ley, C., Tischer, T., Herbst, E., Pareek, A., Musahl, V., Oeding, J. F., Oettl, F. C., Longo, U. G., Samuelsson, K., & Feldt, R. (2025). A practical guide to the implementation of AI in orthopaedic research—Part 7: Risks, limitations, safety and verification of medical AI systems. *Journal of Experimental Orthopaedics*, *12*(2), e70247. Advance online publication. DOI: 10.1002/jeo2.70247 PMID: 40276496

Xia, L., Li, F., Zhou, Y., & Xue, P. (2024). Mineral policy management perspective: Government effectiveness and digitalization for the Russian economy. *Resources Policy, 91*. *Resources Policy*, *91*, 104845. Advance online publication. DOI: 10.1016/j.resourpol.2024.104845

Yang, P., Lv, Y., Chen, X., & Lv, J. (2024). Digital finance, natural resource constraints and firms' low-carbon behavior: Evidence from listed companies. *Resources Policy, 89*. *Resources Policy*, *89*, 104637. Advance online publication. DOI: 10.1016/j.resourpol.2024.104637

Yu, S., Liang, Y., Zhu, Z., Olaniyi, O. N., & Khan, N. (2024). Dutch disease perspective of energy sector: Natural resources and energy sector nexus with the role of renewable energy consumption. *Resources Policy, 90*. *Resources Policy*, *90*, 104740. Advance online publication. DOI: 10.1016/j.resourpol.2024.104740

Zhang, Y., Peng, D., & Zhang, A. (2025). Artificial intelligence in cancer diagnostics: Governance for equity in low- and middle-income countries. *African Journal of Reproductive Health*, *29*(12), 93–103. DOI: 10.29063/ajrh2025/v29i12s.10 PMID: 41489265

Chapter 6
Case Studies and Emerging Best Practices in AI-Powered Medical Tourism

Nercü Durmuş Aydin
http://orcid.org/0000-0002-3419-9914
Tokat Gaziosmanpaşa University, Turkey

ABSTRACT

This chapter examines the role of artificial intelligence (AI) in medical tourism within the broader process of digital transformation in healthcare. Advances in medical technologies, rising global patient mobility, and growing competition have made medical tourism a strategic sector. AI contributes to clinical decision-making, international patient coordination, operational efficiency, and service quality. The chapter discusses AI-based diagnostic and treatment tools, personalized care models, digital patient management systems, and telehealth solutions, emphasizing their impact on sustainability and competitiveness. It also considers ethical and legal issues, including data security, patient privacy, and cross-border regulation. Drawing on global case studies, the chapter argues that AI is not only a technological innovation but also a driver of human-centered, multi-stakeholder transformation. It outlines key opportunities and limitations, offering strategic insights for policy-makers, healthcare managers, and researchers.

DOI: 10.4018/979-8-3373-8944-8.ch006

INTRODUCTION

Rapid advancements in healthcare technologies have reduced costs, increased trust in services, and accelerated the adoption of technological applications, thereby facilitating the cross-border expansion of healthcare services and supporting the growth of medical tourism. With reduced transportation costs and innovations in information technologies, medical tourism has become a strategically important and highly competitive global sector (Aşık & Güner, 2025; Xu et al., 2020). In this environment, countries and healthcare organizations seek differentiation through digital solutions that enhance service quality, patient experience, and operational efficiency.

Within this transformation, AI has emerged as a strategic tool reshaping medical tourism. Beyond supporting diagnosis, treatment, and care processes, AI contributes to international patient management, marketing, demand forecasting, and logistics planning (Bostan & Halhallı, 2025). Personalized digital services, intelligent support systems, and data-driven applications facilitate patient access to foreign healthcare systems, strengthening competitive advantage and increasing the sector's global appeal.

The COVID-19 pandemic further underscored the importance of digitalization and AI in medical tourism. While tourism revenues declined significantly, AI and robotic technologies supported patient information services, doctor–patient matching, administrative management, and remote healthcare delivery. Remote surgery and digital health applications enhanced knowledge sharing and contributed to the sustainability, reliability, and accessibility of medical tourism services (Hassan & Bellos, 2022).

Parallel to these developments, AI methods have become increasingly integrated into medical practice, contributing to the reduction of medical errors and costs, early disease prediction, and medical education. This evolution has fostered the interdisciplinary field of "Artificial Intelligence in Medicine" (AIM) and signaled a transformative shift in healthcare delivery (Haznedar, 2010). AI-driven systems are now widely applied in diagnosis, patient assessment, treatment planning, and nursing care. Through large-scale data analysis, these systems improve diagnostic accuracy, save time and costs, and support chronic disease management and elderly care via mobile applications, virtual assistants, and smart monitoring systems (Alowais et al., 2023).

Advances in data accessibility and analytical techniques have enabled AI applications across both structured and unstructured health data. Support vector machines and artificial neural networks are commonly employed for structured datasets, while natural language processing techniques are used for unstructured data. Clinical domains such as cancer, neurology, and cardiology represent major areas of AI concentration, particularly in early diagnosis, treatment planning, and stroke prognosis assessment (Jiang et al., 2017).

Nevertheless, the sustainable and responsible implementation of AI-based applications in medical tourism extends beyond technical capability. Data security, ethical responsibility, algorithmic bias, governance mechanisms, and the continued need for human expertise remain critical considerations (Çondur et al., 2025; Yelli & Karaman, 2024). Therefore, evaluating AI-supported medical tourism through international case studies and best practices is essential.

This chapter aims to provide an evidence-based perspective to the academic literature and industry stakeholders by examining the use of artificial intelligence in medical tourism within the framework of international case studies and emerging best practices. Understanding the potential and limitations of AI-assisted medical tourism requires more than just technological and clinical perspectives. Sustainable service delivery in this field depends on the existence and functioning of a multi-stakeholder ecosystem. Interactions between international patients, healthcare organizations, insurance companies, travel agencies, and logistics service providers directly impact the effectiveness of AI applications and user experience. Within this ecosystem, AI not only supports diagnostic and treatment processes but also plays a critical role in areas such as patient management, demand forecasting, logistics planning, and personalized service delivery. Therefore, understanding the structure, functioning, and inter-stakeholder relationships of the ecosystem is necessary to accurately assess the impact of AI in medical tourism. Furthermore, the chapter outlines a roadmap for the future development of AI, highlighting strategic priorities such as strengthening regulatory compliance, developing data governance standards, disseminating ethical and transparent AI models, and increasing digital integration among stakeholders. This study offers a holistic perspective on positioning AI as a sustainable and reliable tool for transformation within the medical tourism ecosystem. In this context, the next section will detail the medical tourism ecosystem and the role of AI within it; subsequently, concrete examples will be presented through international case studies and best practices. This will provide a comprehensive perspective, both strategically and operationally.

BACKGROUND AI-POWERED MEDICAL TOURISM ECOSYSTEM

The AI-powered medical tourism ecosystem is built upon the integrated use of clinical decision support systems (CDSS), digital consultation platforms, electronic health records (EHR) and big data infrastructures, as well as mobile health applications and patient monitoring systems. Through these interconnected components, the patient journey—from diagnosis to treatment and post-treatment follow-up—is restructured within a digital, secure, and personalized environment for international patients.

AI-Based Diagnostic and Clinical Decision Support Systems

Artificial intelligence significantly enhances early diagnosis, treatment planning, and the interpretation of complex health data. AI-supported medical imaging systems and machine learning algorithms strengthen diagnostic accuracy and clinical decision-making processes (Aşık & Güner, 2025). AI-based CDSS analyze medical data through knowledge bases, inference engines, and algorithms—including expert systems, artificial neural networks, fuzzy logic, and genetic algorithms—to support accurate, rapid, and patient-centered decisions. With user-friendly interfaces and real-time alert mechanisms, these systems contribute to reducing medical errors, improving patient follow-up, and increasing cost efficiency (Akalın & Veranyurt, 2022).

Beyond clinical applications, AI-driven decision systems support hospital management processes such as resource allocation, patient flow optimization, and staff planning, thereby enhancing operational efficiency (Bulut, 2025). Machine learning models predicting emergency department congestion, waiting times, and patient length of stay have informed staffing and bed allocation decisions (Vural et al., 2025; Chowdhury et al., 2025). In public health contexts, AI has also been used to forecast infectious disease spread and guide strategic planning; for example, the Earth Cognitive System supported epidemic management and healthcare demand forecasting during the COVID-19 pandemic (Atek et al., 2023).

Historically and currently, systems such as DeDombal, Internist-1, Mycin, POEMS, Isabel, OIRS, JMAR, and Galeknow illustrate the evolution of AI-based decision support tools in improving diagnostic precision and accelerating clinical processes (Zaim Gökbay, 2021). By strengthening diagnostic reliability and institutional credibility, such systems may enhance perceived service quality, particularly in medical tourism settings.

Table 1. Artificial Intelligence-Based Clinical Decision Support Systems and Their Application Areas.

System / Tool	Brief Description	Example Usage / Application
DeDombal (De Dombal Algorithm)	A clinical algorithm that supports diagnosis in acute abdominal pain, especially in conditions such as appendicitis.	Algorithmic approach for appendicitis scoring and diagnostic decision support.
Internist -1	A computer-based diagnostic advisor program for internal medicine offers multiple diagnoses based on a comprehensive knowledge base.	It has been used as a diagnostic/educational tool in the field of internal medicine (e.g., performance evaluation in NEJM case analyses).
Mycin	a rule-based infection diagnosis and antibiotic recommendation system developed at Stanford University in the 1970s.	Bloodstream infection bacteria and recommending appropriate antibiotic dosages; based on academic research and expert systems principles.
POEMS (Post-Operative Expert Medical System)	A specialized system designed for patients requiring post-operative care.	Evaluation of postoperative care data and comparison with outcomes of similar cases.
Isabel Clinical Decision Support System	CDSS, a continuously updated information-based tool to assist physicians in diagnosis, offers differential diagnosis recommendations.	Generating diagnostic recommendations and a list of "diagnoses not to be missed" through integration with electronic health records .
OIRS (Online -Incident Reporting System)	An online reporting and decision support system for medical risk and event management.	Use of OIRS for risk management/potential failures (e.g., Osaka University Hospital practice).
JMAR	A decision support system for identifying and directing the nearest necessary resources (medicines, blood products, organs, etc.) to the mission area.	Identifying critical needs in military or emergency medical logistics.
Galeknow	AI-powered decision support tool developed for faster diagnosis and decision-making in emergency departments.	Recommendation modules designed to accelerate diagnosis in emergency medicine scenarios.

Source: EBSCO Health, n.d .; Kocamaz, 2007; Miller et al., 1985; MYCIN, 2026; Quizlet, n.d.; Yılmaz et al., 2022

Deep learning and convolutional neural networks (CNNs) have further improved early diagnosis and surgical planning in oncology, cardiology, and neurology, while robotic applications have increased treatment success rates (YesilScience, 2022). In reproductive medicine, AI-based CDSS models predicting pregnancy likelihood in IVF treatments have become important decision-support tools for clinicians and patients (Pacci et al., 2021; Şahin et al., 2024). These developments demonstrate that AI-supported decision systems contribute not only to clinical excellence but also to service reliability for international patients.

Digital Consultation and Remote Patient Assessment

AI-powered digital consultation platforms facilitate international patients' access to healthcare services from their home countries. Through chatbots and virtual consultation systems, pre-assessment, appointment scheduling, treatment information, and post-treatment follow-up can be automated via 24/7 multilingual communication, enhancing accessibility and patient experience (Akyüz, 2025).

Remote patient assessment tools are particularly valuable for evaluating clinical suitability before travel and for post-treatment monitoring, improving patient safety while reducing unnecessary mobility and system burden.

Electronic Health Records and Big Data Infrastructures

An observational study across four US states found that outpatient physicians devoted only 27% of their working hours to direct patient care, while nearly half (49.2%) was spent on EHR and administrative tasks; after-hours work was largely attributed to EHR-related documentation (Sinsky et al., 2016). These findings highlight the administrative burden associated with digital record systems and the need for more intelligent infrastructures.

AI integration has transformed EHR and big data systems from passive record-keeping tools into strategic components of decision support. AI applications analyze EHR data to identify high-risk patients, generate individualized treatment plans, and automatically document clinical encounters, thereby reducing administrative workload and supporting clinical decisions (Amisha Malik et al., 2019). Generative AI and natural language processing (NLP) applications extract structured insights from clinical notes and patient histories, feeding decision support mechanisms and enhancing communication with international patients. For example, generative AI tools have been used at Mass General Brigham hospitals to automate clinical note transcription, improving physician efficiency (Georgiou, 2024).

Through large-scale structured and unstructured data analysis, AI enables holistic evaluation of patient profiles, treatment preferences, and risk factors, supporting both clinical precision and strategic planning (Akyüz, 2025). Deep learning approaches applied to multidimensional EHR datasets contribute to precision medicine by identifying risk groups, optimizing monitoring frequency, and developing individualized treatment models (Wong & Bressler, 2016). Such integration enhances service quality, resource optimization, and international competitiveness in medical tourism.

Mobile Health Applications and Patient Monitoring Systems

Mobile health applications, wearable technologies, and AI-based monitoring systems ensure continuity of care in chronic disease management, rehabilitation, and post-treatment follow-up. By analyzing real-time physiological and behavioral data, AI algorithms enable risk prediction, medication optimization, and early intervention, thereby strengthening patient safety and sustainability of care (YesilScience, 2022).

Wearable-integrated systems continuously monitor discharged patients and alert healthcare teams to potential abnormalities, reducing complications, readmission rates, and system burden while improving patient satisfaction (Bostan & Halhallı, 2025). Additionally, AI-assisted monitoring can anticipate postoperative complications and support individualized rehabilitation planning (Jiménez, 2022).

Collectively, these technologies reinforce safe, continuous, and data-driven care delivery within the AI-powered medical tourism ecosystem.

CASE STUDIES: ARTIFICIAL INTELLIGENCE-ASSISTED MEDICAL TOURISM APPLICATIONS

This section examines how artificial intelligence applications in health tourism improve patient experience, operational efficiency, and clinical quality, using international examples. Each subsection includes tables detailing the technology used, its application area, the benefits provided, and the challenges encountered.

AI-Powered Digital Consultation Platforms

AI-based digital consultation platforms increase efficiency in pre-assessment, information, and referral processes. Large language model applications such as ChatGPT provide high accuracy and speed in digital consultations within health tourism (Özçelik Heper, 2025). For instance, in pediatric emergency care simulations, ChatGPT 4.0 achieved 99.4% accuracy as an artificial medical translator. Long-term, these systems will allow pre-testing of treatment interventions through patient digital twin models (Bajwa et al., 2021). Similarly, IBM Watson and Babylon, leveraging big data approaches, enhance diagnostic and treatment efficiency, increasing patient satisfaction in medical tourism (Aşık & Güner, 2025).

Vaidam Health, an India-based medical tourism and healthcare facilitation platform founded in 2016, connects patients worldwide with pre-verified hospitals and specialists, offering a comprehensive "one-stop" service. Key services include treatment planning, online preliminary consultation and cost estimation, visa/logistics support, language/local coordination, and post-treatment follow-up. After patients submit their case information, treatment options and cost estimates are provided within 48 hours, and travel and treatment arrangements are organized. Treatment areas include cardiology, oncology, neurosurgery, orthopedics, IVF, ophthalmology, dentistry, cosmetic surgery, and transplants. Vaidam Health ensures reliability through over 100,000 patient experiences and international quality standards (NABH, ISO). While the platform does not offer direct AI-based diagnosis, it supports remote assessment and digital pre-treatment planning, serving as a practical example of AI-assisted consultation in medical tourism (Vaidam Health, n.d.).The table below summarizes case studies of digital consultation platforms in terms of the technology used, the benefits provided, and the challenges encountered.

Table 2. Case Analysis of Digital Consultation Platforms in Terms of Technology, Benefits, and Challenges.

APPLICATION	Technology Used	Benefits Provided	Challenges Encountered
ChatGPT-based digital consultation	Major language models, NLP	Fast and accurate initial assessment, comprehensive patient information, and cost-effectiveness.	Language and cultural differences, and data security risks.
IBM Watson, Babylon	AI, big data analytics	Diagnostic accuracy, personalized treatment plans, patient satisfaction.	Clinical integration, high cost.

Source: Aşık & Güner, 2025; Bajwa et al., 2021; Özçelik Heper, 2025

Personalized Treatment and Surgical Planning

The AI-Powered Medical Tourism Patient Journey Model (AI-PMTJM) integrates AI across all stages of the patient journey—from information seeking and booking to travel, treatment, post-treatment follow-up, and feedback—personalizing processes and improving decision-making (Karcıoğlu, 2025).

Robotic surgery and AI-assisted imaging enhance diagnostic accuracy and surgical precision (Amin et al., 2024). Minimally invasive AI-assisted surgery improves precision, reduces complications, and shortens recovery time.

Destinations such as Singapore, South Korea, Germany, UAE, India, and Türkiye stand out for advanced infrastructure, clinical expertise, and cost advantages. Thailand, Mexico, and South American countries combine AI-assisted robotics and telementoring with surgical procedures, offering high-quality care at competitive costs (Anderson, 2022; Jiménez, 2022).The table below summarizes the technological infrastructure, benefits, and challenges of personalized treatment and surgical planning applications.

Table 3. Technological Infrastructures, Benefits, and Challenges of Personalized Treatment and Surgical Planning Applications.

Application / Field	Technology Used	Benefits Provided	Challenges Encountered
ROSA® Knee System – Total Knee Arthroplasty	Robotic surgery, AI navigation.	Precise implant placement, rapid healing, and reduced risk of complications.	High cost and need for staff training.
AI-based personalized surgical planning	Machine learning, simulation	Surgeon's decision support, safe surgery.	Clinical integration, data security.
AI-assisted imaging and robotic surgery – Bumrungrad Hospital	AI image processing, robotic surgery	Increased diagnostic accuracy, faster recovery, and a lower complication rate.	Advanced technical infrastructure requirements and high cost.
AI-assisted minimally invasive surgery (MIS)	AI algorithms, robotic surgery, real-time imaging and navigation.	Increased surgical precision, less tissue trauma, shorter hospital stay, and faster recovery.	Dependence on technology, high initial costs, expertise and training requirements.

Source: Anderson, 2022; Deckey et al., 2021; Elliott et al., 2021; Jiménez, 2022; Han et al., 2021; Viangteeravat, 2025; Wah, 2025

AI-Based Patient Guidance and Triage Systems

AI triage systems improve clinical efficiency and patient safety by directing patients to the correct specialty and facility. Platforms such as Mediktor and Buoy Health perform online pre-assessment and risk analysis (Akyüz, 2025), while Ada Health and Symptomate use probability-based algorithms for triage recommendations (Hill et al., 2020; Semigran et al., 2015).

AI-powered mobile applications like WoundAIssist allow patients to collect data at home while physicians monitor remotely, tracking wound healing via deep learning models and offering high usability for elderly users (Borst et al., 2025).

AI routing systems reduce decision fatigue, provide fast access to appropriate services, and have commercial applications, such as Expedia's AI recommendation engines, which optimize search, price prediction, and real-time routing (Tran, 2025). Heva, developed by InheritX, integrates AI triage and routing in medical tourism, providing predictive insights, personalized recommendations, and progress tracking through Python-based machine learning models (InheritX, n.d.).

Table 4. Technologies Used in Healthcare Platforms, Benefits Provided, and Challenges Encountered.

APPLICATION	Technology Used	Benefits Provided	Challenges Encountered
Mediktor	AI-based triage chatbot	The correct specialty and center, preventing unnecessary travel.	Language and cultural differences pose data security risks.
Buoy Health	Machine learning, natural language processing	Patient-specific symptom analysis and risk assessment.	The need for clinical validation of symptom outcomes.
Symptomate	AI-based symptom assessment engine	User symptom analysis, pre-triage recommendations	AI accuracy and clinical safety debates.
Ada Health	Probabilistic AI symptom assessment	Comprehensive symptom assessment, triage recommendations.	Accuracy variability in different cases
WoundAIssist	AI, image processing, mobile platform	Post-operative wound care monitoring, clinical data analysis, remote evaluation.	AI limitations, data security, photo quality issues.
Expedia	Machine learning, recommendation engines.	Destination and treatment recommendations based on user data; improving the international patient experience.	Data privacy, algorithmic bias, and transparency requirements.
Heva: AI-Native	Machine learning, natural language processing (NLP), React.js, and Node.js.	Personalized health recommendations and a better patient experience.	Data privacy, regulatory compliance, and data quality.

Source: Ada Health, n.d.; Akyüz, 2025; Buoy Health, n.d.; InheritX, n.d.; Symptomate, n.d.; Tran, 2025

A symptom control tool is used to guide its members, including international students and employees, to the appropriate care environment within the Australian healthcare system. This tool directs members to appropriate options such as a general practitioner, hospital emergency room, or home care based on their symptoms. Since February 2024, the tool has been used over 5,000 times; 64% of users were directed to a general practitioner, 15% to the emergency room, and 21% to home care recommendations. The tool is of particular importance to international visitors and medical tourists; it provides guidance on the Australian healthcare system, enabling foreigners to make the right care choices and reduce unnecessary emergency room use. Powered by Infermedica's AI platform, the system also allows members to book telehealth appointments, offering fast, secure, and targeted healthcare access in the medical tourism experience (nib Group, 2024).

International Patient Communication and Chatbot Usage

AI-powered chatbots, thanks to their multilingual and 24/7 accessibility, strengthen both international patient communication and customer service. In private hospitals in Türkiye, WhatsApp-based chatbots have optimized patient referral processes by increasing operational efficiency (Gedik, 2023). Similarly, Babylon and Ada platforms are effectively used in symptom identification and patient referral tasks (Bajwa et al., 2021).

A similar example can be seen in the tourism sector. During peak periods, HotelPlanner.com struggled to handle high-volume booking requests due to the limited capacity of human customer service representatives. The company solved this problem by developing AI-powered travel agents capable of multilingual and two-way communication. These agents were trained on millions of phone call data points and designed as systems that can answer questions, offer suggestions, check availability, and process payments. Operating 24/7, these AI agents increased customer processing capacity, reduced waiting times, and improved the customer experience. Generating £150,000 in revenue by processing 40,000 queries in its first month, the system increased booking revenue to £2.4 billion within a year (Tran, 2025).

These examples demonstrate that multilingual and continuously accessible AI systems are an effective tool for increasing operational efficiency and improving user experience in both the healthcare and tourism sectors.

The table below summarizes the technological infrastructure of the systems, the benefits they provide, and the challenges encountered.

Table 5. Case Study Framework for Multilingual and Continuously Available Artificial Intelligence Systems in the Health and Tourism Sectors.

APPLICATION	Technology Used	Benefits Provided	Challenges Encountered
Babylon	AI chatbot, NLP	Symptom identification, patient referral.	Risk of misdirection, ethical questions.
Island	AI chatbot, wearable device integration.	Health monitoring, patient support	Data security, user adaptation.
AI Agent	AI chatbot, NLU/NLP, multi-channel support	24/7 customer support, reduced waiting times; multi-channel access; personalized travel/medical tourism recommendations; automation of booking and treatment planning processes; international patient/tourist support through multilingual access.	Risks of "hallucination" (misleading information) in AI responses; system integration challenges (with booking/packaging infrastructure); need for human interaction (for complex requests)
Lufthansa AI Agent Example	AI chatbot, multilingual Conversational AI	Automating high-volume customer interactions; reducing wait times and human workload; managing numerous tour planning/booking processes.	Complex integrations and extensive training requirements necessitate boat-human coordination in situations requiring human intervention.
HotelPlanner.com	NLP, machine learning, multichannel AI	24/7 information and support; multilingual service; pre-booking, travel and treatment planning support; reduced waiting times.	Risks of misleading responses; complex requests requiring human oversight; infrastructure integration challenges.

Source: Bajwa et al., 2021; Kristyanto, 2025; Tran, 2025

AI-Powered Marketing and Targeting Strategies

AI chatbots and predictive analytics complement medical tourism by supporting healthcare access and travel planning. Chatbots provide multilingual, rapid, 24/7 guidance across the patient journey (Bajwa et al., 2021; Özçelik Heper, 2025).

World Clinic and Bumrungrad Hospital use chatbots for appointments, treatment information, and pre-assessment, reducing staff workload and improving patient experience (Viangteeravat, 2025; Akyüz, 2025). Predictive analytics tools, like Hopper, forecast flight/hotel prices (~90% accuracy), enabling cost-effective travel (Tran, 2025).

Table 6. Case Study Framework of AI-Powered Marketing and Targeting Strategies.

Application / Field	Technology Used	Benefits Provided	Challenges Encountered
World Clinic Chatbot	NLP, machine learning	Multilingual pre-assessment, appointment management, quick response.	Language and cultural differences, data security.
Bumrungrad Hospital Chatbot	AI, natural language processing, chatbot	Treatment information, initial assessment, patient referral.	Clinical integration, technical infrastructure
Babylon Health International	AI-based virtual assistant	24/7 response to patient questions, preliminary symptom analysis.	Data privacy, clinical validation.
Sensely	Avatar-based chatbot, AI	Multimedia communication, personalized information.	Technology cost, user adaptation.
Hopper	Predictive analytics, machine learning.	Real-time treatment and travel package price optimization; demand forecasting and resource planning.	Customer trust and transparency issues; risks of inaccurate predictions.

Source: Aşık & Güner, 2025; Bajwa et al., 2021; Özçelik Heper, 2025; Sensely, n.d.; Tran, 2025; Viangteeravat, 2025

Examples of Private Hospitals and Platforms

AI and digital health technologies provide fundamental benefits such as improving clinical care processes, increasing diagnostic accuracy, and enhancing patient experience (uHealth, 2024). These technologies enable continuous monitoring of patients' health status and the provision of personalized guidance through remote patient monitoring systems and virtual assistants. For example, Luscii Healthtech provides remote patient monitoring and care with over 150 clinical pathways, thereby reducing unnecessary hospital visits and admissions (Luscii, nd). Similarly, Sensely's

AI-based virtual nurse platform provides 24/7 accessible patient support by offering services such as symptom control, triage, and personalized guidance. However, significant challenges such as data security, ethical issues, and clinical validation must also be considered in the implementation of these systems (Sensely, nd).

The table below summarizes the technologies used in private hospitals and platforms, the benefits they provide, and the challenges they face.

Table 7. Private Hospitals and Healthcare Platforms: Technologies, Benefits, and Challenges

Institution / Platform	Application Areas	Technology Used	Benefits Provided	Challenges Encountered
Cleveland Clinic (USA, Abu Dhabi branch)	AI-assisted critical care, robotic surgery.	AI clinical intelligence systems, robotic surgery	Early diagnosis, treatment optimization, high accuracy, international patient access.	Data security, system integration, high cost.
Mayo Clinic (USA)	Clinical research & AI, surgical simulation	AI & ML-powered data platform, 3D simulation	Faster research, personalized surgical planning, risk estimation.	Big data management, clinical validation, patient adaptation
National University Hospital (Singapore)	Robotic surgery, AI-assisted planning.	AI-based 3D modeling, virtual simulation, robotic navigation.	Personalized surgical strategies reduce the risk of complications.	High cost, technology adaptation.
Severance Hospital (South Korea)	Minimally invasive surgery, cardiac & oncology	AI-based image analysis, robotic surgery	Delicate operations, shorter recovery times, international patient attraction.	Training and adaptation, high technology cost.
Charité Berlin (Germany)	Cardiac and oncological surgery	AI-powered risk analysis, robotic systems	Reducing the risk of complications, personalized treatment.	Clinical validation, data security, cost
Acıbadem Healthcare Group (Türkiye)	Orthopedics, cardiac surgery, and robotic surgery.	AI-powered surgical simulation, navigation systems.	Personalized surgical planning, international patient management.	AI integration, data security, staff training.
Anadolu Health Center (Türkiye)	Surgical simulation and preliminary consultation	AI-based virtual simulation, telemedicine platform.	Personalized treatment plan, risk assessment.	Technology adaptation, data security.
Apollo Hospitals (India)	Orthopedics, cardiac, bariatric surgery	AI-powered imaging, risk analysis.	Personalized treatment, complication prevention.	Data management, infrastructure adaptation.
Hospital Angeles (Mexico)	Robotic orthopedic and spinal surgery	AI-based robotic surgery, 3D planning.	Precise surgery, international patient experience.	High technology cost, adaptation.

continued on following page

Table 7. Continued

Institution / Platform	Application Areas	Technology Used	Benefits Provided	Challenges Encountered
Luscii Healthtech	Remote patient monitoring	Remote monitoring + data analysis	Reduced hospitalizations, earlier intervention, cost savings.	Platform adaptation, data security.
Sensely – Molly	Virtual nurse & triage	NLP-based AI, avatar	24/7 symptom assessment and referral	Accuracy, user adaptation.

Source: Alexandra Hospital, 2025; Cleveland Clinic, n.d.; Forbes, 2024; Jiménez, 2022; Karcıoğlu, 2025; Luscii, 2024; Mayo Clinic, n.d.; National University Health System, 2025; Sensely, n.d.

BEST PRACTICES THAT EMERGED

This chapter examines best practices in AI applications for medical tourism, focusing on data-driven decision-making, patient-centered design, multilingual solutions, integration of clinical and marketing processes, and human-AI collaboration. Each application is placed under the most appropriate heading to avoid repetition, with references in other sections as needed.

Data-Driven Decision Making in Clinical and Operational Processes

Artificial intelligence is strengthening strategic decision-making processes in health tourism by processing multidimensional data such as demographic profiles, digital behaviors, and treatment preferences through big data analytics. This approach increases the effectiveness of operational decisions such as targeting marketing messages, capacity, and resource planning (Akyüz, 2025).

In a clinical context, AI-powered imaging systems and CDSS contribute to providing reliable and measurable services for international patients by increasing diagnostic accuracy. Such systems are among the quality indicators of institutions preferred in health tourism and directly affect patient trust (Viangteeravat, 2025). Furthermore, the transformation of clinical data into operational and managerial decisions using artificial intelligence stands out as one of the best practices for ensuring sustainable service quality in health tourism centers.

Examples of CDSS and Data-Driven Applications:

- **Ophthalmology:** Deep learning algorithms detect diabetic retinopathy and macular edema with high sensitivity (87–97.5%) and specificity (93.4–98.5%) (Gulshan et al., 2016).

- **Glaucoma Diagnosis:** Random forest models using retinal fiber layer and visual field data achieve 98% accuracy and 0.979 AUC (Kim et al., 2017).
- **Tuberculosis Detection on Chest X-rays:** DCNN models combined with radiologist input reach 97.3% sensitivity and 100% specificity (Lakhani & Sundaram, 2017).
- **Surgical Planning:** Corneal power estimation via neural networks reduces average error to 0.16 ± 0.14 diopters (Koprowski et al., 2016).
- **NLP-Supported Clinical Documentation Analysis:** Extracts structured data from free-text notes, enabling integration into CDSS (Wang et al., 2018).
- **Federated Learning for Multi-Center Data:** Allows collaborative AI training without sharing patient data, supporting personalized clinical decisions (Rieke et al., 2020).
- **Remote Patient Monitoring & Virtual Care:** AI-powered systems provide real-time post-treatment monitoring, reducing readmissions (Topol, 2019).
- **AI-Enhanced EHR Systems:** Analyze patient density, treatment duration, and seasonal demand for operational planning (Rajkomar et al., 2019).

Patient-Centered Design and Personalization

Artificial intelligence applications in health tourism improve both clinical outcomes and patient experience by personalizing treatment and surgical planning processes for each patient. Digital twins, predictive analytics, and personalized treatment plans enable the integration of patients' individual anatomical, physiological, and lifestyle data into decision-making processes. This approach forms the basis of patient-centered care models, particularly in terms of expectation management, trust building, and active participation in the treatment process for international patients (Karcıoğlu, 2025).

The patient-centered design approach aims not only to increase clinical accuracy but also to personalize the patient journey, from diagnosis to post-treatment follow-up. AI-powered systems stand out as one of the best practices that enhance the sustainable quality of health tourism services by providing patients with personalized information, guidance and decision support at every stage of this journey.

Examples of Patient-Centered and Personalized AI Applications:

- **ROSA® Knee System:** Used in total knee arthroplasty surgeries, the ROSA® Knee system analyzes patient-specific anatomical data with robotic assistance and AI-based surgical planning. This allows for the personalization of surgical incisions and implant placement; accelerates postoperative functional recovery; and reduces the risk of complications. This patient-specific planning approach provides a patient-centered best practice example that delivers predictable outcomes and high satisfaction for international patients (Deckey et al., 2021).

- **Bumrungrad Hospital:** At Bumrungrad Hospital, AI-powered medical imaging and clinical decision support systems provide physicians with a "second opinion" in diagnostic processes, increasing diagnostic accuracy. These systems reduce the risk of misdiagnosis and strengthen patient confidence by providing personalized assessments based on the patient's clinical data. In this center with an international patient profile, personalized and data-driven diagnostic processes are considered a significant application of patient-centered design (Viangteeravat, 2025).
- **Digital Twin-Based Personalized Treatment Planning:** In fields such as oncology and cardiology, digital twin models created using a patient's biological and clinical data allow for the simulation of different treatment scenarios. This application enables the evaluation of treatment options on a patient-by-patient basis, contributing to the prediction of risks and a more transparent decision-making process with the patient. Digital twins stand out as an important best practice in health tourism for personalized care and trust-based patient communication (Björnsson et al., 2020; Karcıoğlu, 2025).
- **AI-Based Personalized Patient Journey Management:** Artificial intelligence algorithms design personalized appointment, information, and follow-up processes based on the patient's country, language, clinical condition, and travel plans. These systems improve the experience at every stage of the health tourism process and increase patient satisfaction by providing patient-specific digital content and guidance (Özçelik Heper, 2025).
- **Personalized Rehabilitation and Follow-up Programs:** In the post-surgical period, patient-specific rehabilitation programs are created through AI-powered wearable devices and mobile applications, and the recovery process is monitored remotely. This approach ensures continuity of post-treatment care, reduces the need for repeat visits for international patients, and strengthens the patient-centered care approach (Luscii, 2024; Topol, 2019).

Multilingual and Culturally Compatible Digital Solutions

International medical tourism patients may experience difficulties accessing accurate information due to language and cultural differences. AI-based multilingual and culturally adapted digital solutions improve the experience by facilitating patient communication, guidance, and information (Özçelik Heper, 2025).

Examples:

- **WhatsApp-based chatbots (Türkiye):** Automate the digital management of international patient requests, appointment scheduling, and pre-information processes; increase patient satisfaction through multilingual support and quick response (Akyüz, 2025; Gedik, 2023).
- **Babylon Health and Ada Health:** AI chatbots provide symptom assessment and health recommendations; they are integrated with wearable devices to track personal health (Bajwa, 2021).
- **Sensely – Molly Avatar:** A multilingual virtual nurse offering 24/7 triage and symptom assessment, providing cultural adaptation and personalized guidance (Sensely, 2026).
- **World Clinic Chatbot:** Improves patient experience and reduces the workload of clinical staff through multilingual pre-assessment and appointment management (Viangteeravat, 2025).
- **WeDoctor (China):** WeDoctor is a digital platform that integrates online and offline healthcare services. It offers multilingual virtual examinations, remote consultations, and health monitoring for international patients. The platform facilitates access to healthcare for patients from different countries by providing culturally adapted guidance, and increases patient satisfaction (Wang, 2021).

Reference elsewhere: Molly, Babylon, and Ada are mentioned in patient-centered design and triage sections but here detailed as multilingual solutions.

AI-Based Patient Guidance and Triage Systems

AI systems optimize referral accuracy and patient safety.
Key Applications:

- **Mediktor & Buoy Health:** Online triage and risk assessment for directing patients to the correct specialty (Akyüz, 2025).
- **Ada Health & Symptomate:** Analyze user symptoms using probabilistic AI for pre-triage (Hill et al., 2020; Semigran et al., 2015).
- **WoundAIssist:** Monitors chronic wounds remotely using AI-powered mobile apps (Borst et al., 2025).
- **Heva (InheritX):** AI-based cross-border medical tourism triage and routing platform.

Reference elsewhere: Babylon, Ada, and Molly are referenced here as examples of triage-capable AI but detailed in sections above.

Integration of Clinical and Marketing Processes

Simultaneously enhances patient acquisition, service quality, and operational efficiency by integrating clinical processes and marketing activities. This integration enables health tourism institutions to optimize both clinical accuracy and patient satisfaction goals (Akyüz, 2025; Cleveland Clinic, nd).

Examples:

- **AI-Powered Targeting and Advertising:** Using clinical data and patient behavior analytics, Google Ads and social media campaigns were optimized, resulting in a 20% increase in international patient traffic (Akyüz, 2025).
- **Cleveland Clinic – Robotic Surgery & Telemedicine:** AI and robotic systems increase surgical accuracy and operational speed, while telemedicine improves follow-up and consultation processes for international patients (Cleveland Clinic, nd).
- **Mayo Clinic – AI-Powered Diagnosis and Process Management:** AI and machine learning are integrated into patient triage and clinical decision support systems; diagnostic accuracy and clinical process speed have been increased (Mayo Clinic, nd).

Protecting Human-AI Collaboration

Artificial intelligence solutions provide support in clinical decision-making processes, but demonstrate the highest effectiveness when working in conjunction with human expertise. Human-AI collaboration is critical to improving diagnostic accuracy, upholding ethical standards, and ensuring patient safety (Lakhani & Sundaram, 2017; Deckey et al., 2021).

Examples:

- **TB Detection on Chest X-rays:** DCNN models used in conjunction with radiologists provide a reliable second opinion by increasing accuracy and sensitivity (Lakhani & Sundaram, 2017).
- **CDSS and Robotic Surgery:** AI-based clinical decision support systems and robotic surgery platforms optimize surgeon decisions; however, clinical experience and ethical oversight still play a critical role (Deckey et al., 2021; Elliott et al., 2021).

AI-Powered Marketing, Communication, and Virtual Assistance

This section consolidates chatbots and predictive analytics that improve patient engagement, scheduling, and information flow.

Key Platforms:

- **World Clinic Chatbot & Hopper:** Scheduling, predictive analytics for travel and treatment, real-time guidance (Tran, 2025; Viangteeravat, 2025).
- **Sensely – Molly:** Referred here again for its engagement and 24/7 virtual nurse capabilities.

ETHICAL, LEGAL AND ADMINISTRATIVE DIMENSIONS

Ethical Dimension

In AI-assisted health tourism applications, the ethical dimension is shaped by the protection of human health and the effective treatment of diseases. Normative elements such as human rights, justice, autonomy, privacy, and public welfare are critically important during the use of AI systems in clinical decision-making processes (İlkılıç, 2021). The integration of AI, particularly in the surgical field, raises ethical concerns regarding surgeon autonomy, human authority, and the patient-physician relationship. While AI enhances surgical precision and supports clinical decisions, it also carries risks such as over-reliance, accountability issues, and a lack of equal access. Therefore, the safe and ethical integration of AI into surgery requires comprehensive ethical frameworks that consider both the capabilities of the technology and the value of human judgment; thus, patient-centered care can be preserved, and equal access to healthcare services can be ensured (Arjomandi Rad et al., 2025). Approaches of either admiration or hostility towards the technology should not create bias in evaluations; Practices should be examined within socio-cultural, religious, and value-based contexts, and can be subjected to philosophical reflection in terms of the concepts of humanity, health, illness, and healing.

The technical nature of algorithms is not independent of moral values and involves normative evaluations. Therefore, the ethical evaluation process should also include analyzing AI applications, which require high costs and resources, within a benefit-cost framework. Ethical and social research should be conducted concurrently with AI developments, and retrospective "band-aid" solutions should be avoided. Furthermore, transparency and trust should be ensured to inform and persuade the public about the systems; discussions should not be limited to experts but should also include the public and civil society organizations (Alowais et al., 2023; İlkılıç, 2021).

AI systems support healthcare professionals by increasing service speed, reducing costs, and decreasing mortality by preventing delays that may arise from a shortage of skilled labor. In this context, their use, taking into account clinical and academic training and the ethical framework, has significant potential in improving the quality and effectiveness of healthcare services (Ayyıldız & Ovayolu, 2024).

Legal Aspects

Following the establishment of an ethical framework, the safe and effective use of AI in the field of health tourism should be supported by legal regulations. Manufacturer liability plays a central role in preventing faulty or potentially dangerous products; liability arises when the product is not suitable for its intended use or is defective (Par, 2024). Currently, there is a tendency to place a large share of the responsibility for damages caused by AI on the manufacturer, but a comprehensive understanding of responsibility should be defined to include manufacturers, software developers, healthcare professionals, hospitals, and regulatory authorities. In this way, the risks in the use of the technology can be minimized.

The risks that may arise during the use of AI systems in diagnosis, treatment, and clinical processes are considered a critical element in terms of patient trust and acceptance. Given that a single mistake could prevent other patients from using similar systems, it is essential to develop legal processes that protect patient rights, clarify criminal liabilities, and determine who is responsible for potential threats such as cyber risks (Par, 2024).

In the US, the AI.gov platform and related legislation (the SELF DRIVE Act, the Future of AI Act, and the AI Initiatives Act) are raising awareness of AI and establishing a framework for ethical standards and cost-effectiveness assessments at the federal level; however, they do not directly cover the healthcare sector (Gerke et al., 2020). In the European Union, the AI Strategy for Europe and the Ethical Guidance Principles for Reliable AI published by the High-Level Expert Group on Artificial Intelligence (AI HLEG) aim to create a legally and ethically reliable AI ecosystem (Gerke et al., 2020).

AI systems must adhere to high standards of privacy and security when processing patient data in medical imaging, robotic surgery, and clinical decision support processes. These systems, operated in accordance with data management, patient privacy, and legal requirements, are continuously improved in terms of transparency and accuracy through oversight by human expertise (Viangteeravat, 2025; Wah, 2025). This supervised approach ensures that AI transcends being merely a technology and becomes a strategic element in clinical decision-making, enhancing reliability and patient safety.

Managerial Dimension

Following the establishment of the legal framework, effective management of AI applications in the health tourism sector is possible through the strategic integration of organizational processes and decision support systems. The controlled and sustainable implementation of AI systems by healthcare managers is a fundamental requirement for increasing operational efficiency and ensuring the conscious use of technology in clinical decision-making processes (Bulut, 2025).

Collaboration between healthcare organizations, AI researchers, and regulatory bodies should be supported by comprehensive cybersecurity strategies and robust data protection measures. AI algorithms can identify high-risk patients by analyzing data such as population demographics, disease prevalence, and geographic distribution; edge analytics can detect irregularities and direct resources to areas where they are needed. This management approach allows for the optimization of processes to ensure the efficient and safe use of technology (Alowais et al., 2023).

In addition, maintaining human-AI collaboration, strengthening AI literacy among healthcare professionals, and implementing continuous training programs enhance the sustainability of systems at the clinical and managerial levels. This approach ensures that AI technology is not only a supporting tool but also has the potential to transform patient safety and service quality into a strategic advantage (Bulut, 2025; Viangteeravat, 2025).

DISCUSSION

Theoretical Implications

The effectiveness of AI systems in health tourism services largely depends on factors such as infrastructure, data quality, and staff training; therefore, small- and medium-sized healthcare organizations may experience difficulties in the adaptation process due to high costs and technical limitations (Akyüz, 2025; Anderson, 2022). However, lower-cost solutions such as digital consultations, mobile health applications, and remote patient monitoring may enable small institutions to achieve gains in operational efficiency and patient experience (Kozan, 2025). This highlights the importance of strategic planning, phased technology adoption, and a sustainable digital transformation approach for health tourism organizations' integration of AI. Small- and medium-sized institutions, in particular, can start with low-cost pilot applications and gradually transition to more complex systems; they can also accelerate the AI adaptation process with training that increases the digital literacy of their staff. In addition, international data sharing and collaboration allow small organizations with limited patient data to improve the accuracy of algorithms and reduce the risk of bias. Therefore, phased technology adoption, strengthening staff capacity, and international cooperation strategies play an important role in making AI integration effective, safe, and sustainable for small- and medium-sized health tourism organizations. The integration of AI into healthcare should be considered not merely a technological adaptation process, but a multidimensional transformation process requiring the strengthening of the knowledge, skills, and ethical awareness capacity of human resources. This approach can be considered an important pre-requisite for the sustainable implementation of the clinical and operational benefits offered by AI. AI is shaping its future role in healthcare not to completely replace physicians, but to support their decisions (Amisha Malik et al., 2019). This highlights the need for the integration of AI knowledge and skills into medical education and strengthens physicians' human skills, such as empathy and communication, when collaborating with machines.

Practical Implications for Health Tourism Organizations

Artificial intelligence applications can improve the quality of healthcare by providing speed, accuracy, and efficiency in diagnostic, treatment, and surgical processes. However, the relative weakening of human-centered decision-making mechanisms also brings ethical, social, and clinical risks. Fully digitized healthcare services may increase workforce concerns, especially for healthcare professionals; they can lead to negative consequences such as decreased patient-physician interaction, technological dependence, social isolation, and psychological problems. Furthermore, AI systems based on large and sensitive datasets pose potential threats to patient safety by increasing the risks of data privacy, cybersecurity, algorithmic bias, and erroneous decision-making (Yorgancioglu Tarcan et al., 2024). Especially in the context of medical tourism, international patients evaluate not only clinical quality but also the reliability, transparency, and compliance with ethical standards of the technologies used. This makes it critical that AI systems are designed to be explainable, auditable, and patient-centered. In addition, global data sharing and interdisciplinary collaborations enable healthcare organizations to integrate AI safely and effectively, increasing patient trust and supporting the efficiency and accessibility of healthcare services. Research shows that most employees believe that AI reduces workload, improves service quality, and optimizes resource utilization; however, a lack of knowledge still constitutes a significant limitation (Büyükkaya, 2024). Therefore, training programs and awareness-raising strategies are essential for the sustainable and safe implementation of AI applications in healthcare services.

Policy and Regulatory Implications

The benefits of AI systems are not limited to the technical level; they should also be addressed holistically, considering ethical, social, and legal dimensions (Çondur et al., 2025). The safe and effective use of these systems depends on ensuring data security, patient confidentiality, legal compliance, and algorithmic transparency (Gerke et al., 2020). Providing clear information about the reliability of datasets, the transparency of algorithmic processes, and potential data biases is critical for supporting system acceptance and trustworthiness. Accordingly, establishing national and international standards encompassing data protection, ethical principles, transparency, algorithmic justice, and regulatory oversight is important for the safe and effective use of AI. Multidisciplinary technology assessment approaches, user engagement, and increasing AI literacy among healthcare professionals are critical for the adoption and sustainable integration of the technology. In Türkiye, the National Artificial Intelligence Strategy (2021–2025) provides an institutional framework in this regard, highlighting the need for the development and implementation of these technologies in the future in a manner consistent with ethical, legal, and socio-cultural values (Yorgancioglu Tarcan et al., 2024).

Ethical and Societal Implications

The reliability, effectiveness, and fairness of any machine learning (ML) system largely depend on the quality of the data it is trained on; in particular, weighting phenotypic and genotypic data over specific populations can lead to misdiagnosis and reduced treatment efficacy in underrepresented groups. For example, skin cancer decision support systems trained with data predominantly from Caucasian patients may exhibit lower accuracy in individuals with darker skin tones, increasing false negative rates (Adamson & Smith, 2018; Esteva et al., 2017). Similarly, in genomic prediction models where genotypic data predominantly consists of individuals of European descent, the clinical validity of polygenic risk scores remains limited in non-European populations (Popejoy & Fullerton, 2016). Furthermore, some health risk prediction algorithms used in real clinical practice have been shown to systematically underestimate the health needs of minority groups (Obermeyer et al., 2019). These risks can be mitigated by creating inclusive datasets, increasing the number of data points representing minority populations, and clearly defining which patient groups the algorithms produce reliable results for (Gerke et al., 2020). Such approaches are important for supporting the reliable use of AI-powered clinical decision systems, which can be used reliably, not only from a technical standpoint but also from an ethical and societal perspective. On the other hand, while public perception of AI varies, it is observed that there is still a preference for human physicians in complex clinical situations; this makes trust-building and patient education key elements for integration (Alowais et al., 2023). Overcoming challenges such as data quality, privacy, biases, and the need for human expertise are essential for responsible and effective AI applications. Consequently, when a balanced integration is achieved between AI-assisted automation and physicians' clinical judgment and human strengths, both patient outcomes may be improved, while productivity and access to personalized, high-quality care can be supported in healthcare.

Transparency, Accountability, and Lessons for Future Research

The case of IBM Watson for Oncology (WFO) illustrates governance challenges in AI-driven clinical decision support. Although initially designed to support oncology decisions, the system later produced recommendations that were inconsistent with clinical guidelines. Contributing factors included limited training datasets, insufficient transparency regarding recommendation mechanisms, and delayed disclosure of performance concerns (Gerke et al., 2020). This case demonstrates that insufficient transparency can undermine patient safety and trust—an especially critical issue in medical tourism, where international patients evaluate not only treatment success but also technological reliability and ethical compliance. Transparency is therefore not merely a technical requirement; it is a governance principle essential for sustaining international patient confidence.

Successful AI integration requires explainability, auditability, and open communication of algorithmic processes. Digital health literacy plays a central role in managing these risks. Healthcare professionals and managers must understand AI systems' functionality, limitations, and ethical implications to minimize errors and ethical breaches. Structured digital literacy programs and continuous professional development models can strengthen adaptation across countries while safeguarding data security and ethical standards.

Empirical evidence supports this need. Research indicates significant professional differences in AI knowledge and perceptions, although demographic factors such as age, gender, and education show limited influence. Positive attitudes toward AI are associated with expectations of cost reduction; however, overall awareness remains insufficient, highlighting the necessity of systematic training and awareness programs (Büyükkaya, 2024).

CONCLUSION AND FUTURE PERSPECTIVES

The Multidimensional Role of Artificial Intelligence in Health Tourism

The increasing use of artificial intelligence in healthcare services presents a multifaceted transformation in the context of medical tourism, extending beyond the digitalization of clinical processes to encompass patient mobility, international competition, service quality, and governance models. In medical tourism, AI is becoming a strategic element in the service chain, from diagnosis to treatment, patient admission to post-discharge follow-up, enhancing patient experience and trust through clinical decision support systems, personalized treatment plans, multilingual communication tools, and intelligent logistics solutions.

The current literature reveals the potential of AI to improve diagnostic accuracy, increase operational efficiency in clinical and administrative processes, and facilitate international access to healthcare services. However, the cross-border nature of medical tourism highlights risk areas such as data security, patient privacy, ethical responsibilities, legal compliance, and cultural differences, and these factors can limit the effectiveness of AI applications.

The integration of AI into the medical tourism ecosystem should not be considered as a singular technological investment, but rather as a multi-stakeholder, incremental, learning, and continuously evolving transformation process with feedback. Developing AI-based applications that enhance clinical quality in line with international standards, prioritize patient safety and satisfaction, and contribute to national branding is critically important for the sustainable competitiveness of medical tourism. When current achievements and the structural transformations that AI can create in the future are considered together, the construction of a patient-centered, trust-based, and digitally integrated medical tourism ecosystem seems feasible.

Policy and Regulatory Framework

Policymakers and healthcare administrators are gaining important insights into the sustainable expansion of AI-assisted healthcare services and health tourism practices. The integration of AI into healthcare systems should be addressed holistically with technological innovation policies, health policies, digital transformation strategies, and human resources planning.

Regulatory frameworks developed at national and international levels should both encourage innovation and offer flexible yet binding standards that protect patient safety, data privacy, and ethical principles. Risk-based regulatory approaches and phased approval mechanisms can allow for controlled testing and scaling of

AI applications. Cross-border data sharing and patient mobility, particularly in the context of health tourism, create new challenges in terms of data security and patient privacy; internationally harmonized regulations and common data-sharing protocols can mitigate these risks (Council of the European Union, 2025).

Corporate and Managerial Perspective

The integration of AI into healthcare should also be considered as a multi-layered transformation process encompassing corporate governance, strategic management, human resource planning, and health policies. In the medical tourism ecosystem, which experiences high international patient flow, it is crucial for healthcare institutions to position AI investments not as short-term cost factors but as long-term strategic capacity-building tools that enhance global competitiveness, support quality standardization, and reinforce patient trust.

In this context, modular, scalable, and cloud-based AI solutions, especially forsmall- and medium-sized healthcare organizations, can facilitate access to international markets by reducing high initial costs and enabling improvements in service quality in critical processes such as diagnosis, treatment planning, patient admission, and multilingual communication. Thus, AI can become a tool that supports both clinical effectiveness and corporate sustainability and brand value in medical tourism.

However, effectively integrating AI into clinical and administrative processes is not possible without a strong change management approach. Especially in medical tourism, where institutions serve patients from diverse cultures, the adaptation of clinicians and administrative staff to AI-based systems is a critical success factor. Therefore, participatory governance models should ensure the early involvement of healthcare professionals in the process and the shaping of practices in a way that aligns with clinical realities and patient expectations (Karcıoğlu, 2025).

Human Resources and Training

The effective and sustainable use of AI in medical tourism directly depends on the quality and transformation of human resources, as well as the technological infrastructure. AI applications are positioned not as replacements for healthcare professionals, but as complementary tools supporting clinical and managerial decision-making processes. Therefore, the educational curricula in healthcare institutions operating in medical tourism need to be restructured to include competencies such as AI literacy, data-driven clinical decision-making, human-machine collaboration, and digital ethics.

International patient profile, continuous professional development programs, and in-service training should strengthen not only technical competence but also ethical awareness, patient safety, data privacy, and intercultural responsibility. Especially considering the expectations, values, and communication styles of patients from different countries, training approaches that ensure the human-centered use of AI-supported systems are becoming a strategic necessity.

However, human skills such as empathy, clinical reasoning, and effective patient communication play animportant role in building patient satisfaction, trust, and institutional reputation in medical tourism (Karcıoğlu, 2025). Despite the widespread adoption of AI-assisted processes, the fact remains that human interaction is the fundamental element determining the international patient experience; therefore, a training approach that strengthens human-centered care understanding, along with technical competencies for healthcare professionals, should be adopted.

Clinical and Operational Benefits

The integrated use of AI with telemedicine, metaverse-based virtual environments, wearable health technologies, and remote patient monitoring systems significantly improves service quality and global accessibility in medical tourism by accelerating diagnosis, treatment, and patient follow-up processes. This technological convergence reduces the dependence of healthcare services on location and time, lowers operational costs; and provides healthcare organizations with a competitive advantage in the international market (Aykın et al., 2023).

In the medical tourism ecosystem, AI-powered chatbots and virtual assistants facilitate multilingual patient communication, optimizing appointment scheduling, pre-assessment, and treatment information processes. Big data analytics, image processing technologies, and robotic surgical systems enhance clinical accuracy, support standardization in diagnosis and treatment processes, and strengthen patient safety and satisfaction (uHealth, 2024). These applications provide a transparent and predictable service delivery, facilitating pre-treatment decision-making, especially for international patients.

Furthermore, digital consultations, remote monitoring solutions, and personalized healthcare services create a holistic structure for the patient journey in medical tourism, from pre-treatment to post-discharge follow-up. Through continuous data flow and feedback analysis, service quality is dynamically monitored and improved. This not only increases patient satisfaction but also makes the operational processes of healthcare organizations more efficient, contributing to the creation of a sustainable medical tourism model.

Ethical and Legal Dimensions

The effective, reliable, and responsible application of AI in healthcare services within the scope of medical tourism requires a holistic approach to ethical and legal challenges such as informed consent, confidentiality of personal health data, algorithmic bias, legal responsibility sharing, and cybersecurity (Gerke et al., 2020). The cross-border nature of medical tourism makes inconsistencies between the legislation, data protection regimes, and ethical standards of different countries more visible, increasing the risks in these areas.

In medical tourism applications, particularly those utilizing AI-assisted diagnostic and decision-making systems, structuring informed consent processes for international patients in a transparent, multilingual, and culturally sensitive manner is of paramount importance. Furthermore, the cross-border transfer of health data, the use of cloud-based systems, and remote monitoring technologies necessitate strong legal and technical measures to protect data security and privacy.

In this context, developing a collaborative, transparent, and accountable governance model among technology producers, healthcare professionals, patients, insurance companies, and regulatory authorities is critical to ensuring that AI can be used to enhance societal benefits in medical tourism. Ethically sound and legally compliant AI applications can not only strengthen patient trust but also contribute to establishing sustainability and international credibility in medical tourism.

International Patient Management and Health Tourism

AI serves as a strategic enabler transforming international patient management, travel coordination, and healthcare marketing. AI-driven analytics generate tailored diagnostic and treatment recommendations based on demographic and clinical profiles, making pre-treatment planning more predictable and reliable. Robotic surgery and digital consultation models further optimize time, cost, and resource management—critical factors in medical tourism (Viangteeravat, 2025; Yelli & Karaman, 2024).

Beyond individual patient benefits, AI contributes to reducing disparities in healthcare access, expanding system capacity, and supporting health-based economic development. For example, AI-supported workflow automation in the Dutch healthcare system has reduced administrative workloads by 25–40%, allowing physicians to focus more on clinical care (The North Solution, n.d.). Similarly, robotic surgery applications shorten hospital stays and reduce complications, enhancing both economic and environmental sustainability (Altınbafra, 2025). Thus, AI transforms medical tourism from a patient-attraction activity into a high-value-added, digitally advanced, and globally competitive healthcare ecosystem.

Future Perspective and Sustainability

Emerging reports highlight AI's expanding role not only in healthcare delivery but also in medical travel insurance and risk management. AI applications accelerate claims processing, personalize insurance packages, detect fraud, and support real-time risk assessment. Mobile AI-powered health tools improve preventive care and post-treatment monitoring for international patients. Large language models and predictive analytics assist with safety alerts, risk profiling, and emergency coordination. However, these benefits must be balanced with strong ethical oversight and data governance frameworks (Stackpole, 2025).

Looking forward, the transition toward smart hospitals and digitally integrated patient journeys will enable end-to-end management of international patient processes. Telemedicine and remote monitoring will strengthen cross-border continuity of care. Big data analytics, genomic applications, and wearable technologies will support personalized and preventive healthcare, increasing treatment effectiveness and patient satisfaction (Bajwa et al., 2021; Yıldırım, 2021).

Metaverse-based virtual environments, digital hospital tours, and immersive consultations may further enhance informed decision-making for international patients. AI-driven operational optimization and robotic systems can reduce hospital stays, improve resource efficiency, and support environmental sustainability. Strengthened international ethical standards, harmonized data protection mechanisms, and transparent governance structures will be critical in maintaining global trust (Gerke et al., 2020).

Within this framework, the future of artificial intelligence in medical tourism can follow a phased, governance-oriented transformation process. In the short term (0–3 years), priority may be given to strengthening digital infrastructure, ensuring data standardization, and enhancing cybersecurity capacity. During this phase, AI systems can be positioned as decision-support tools under close human supervision, while regulatory frameworks addressing legal and data protection issues can be developed. Simultaneously, AI literacy and continuous training programs for healthcare professionals can be expanded to foster a secure and trustworthy environment. In the medium term (3–7 years), once short-term preparations are completed, AI systems can be more widely integrated into clinical and administrative processes. Considering cross-border patient mobility, international data-sharing protocols can be harmonized, and internal AI governance structures within organizations can be established. In the long term (7–10 years), the goal can be defined as establishing a fully integrated digital patient journey, spanning from pre-travel consultation to post-treatment follow-up. In this process, personalized preventive healthcare programs may reshape competitiveness in medical tourism. A key consideration throughout is the continuous monitoring of algorithmic fairness, digital equity, and environmental sustainability.

In conclusion, AI and digital transformation are redefining medical tourism as a sustainable, patient-centered, technologically integrated, and globally competitive healthcare ecosystem. This transformation holds significant promise for optimizing insurance processes, international patient management, clinical outcomes, and institutional competitiveness, provided that ethical governance, regulatory clarity, and human-centered care remain central guiding principles (Bajwa, 2021; Gerke et al., 2020; Kozan, 2025; Stackpole, 2025; Yıldırım, 2021).

AI DECLARATION

No artificial intelligence (AI) tools were used in the conceptualization, analysis, or drafting of this chapter. AI-based tools were used solely for language editing and readability improvement. The authors take full responsibility for the content of this chapter.

REFERENCES

Ada Health. (n.d.). *Take care of yourself with Ada.* https://ada.com/editorial/topics/medicine-and-health/

Adamson, A. S., & Smith, A. (2018). Machine learning and health care disparities in dermatology. *JAMA Dermatology, 154*(11), 1247–1248. DOI: 10.1001/jamadermatol.2018.2348 PMID: 30073260

Akalın, B., & Veranyurt, Ü. (2022). Sağlık bilimlerinde yapay zekâ tabanlı klinik karar destek sistemleri. *Gevher Nesibe Journal of Medical & Health Sciences, 7*(18), 64–73. DOI: 10.46648/gnj.368

Akyüz, M. (2025). *Sağlık turizminde yapay zeka destekli dijital pazarlama trendleri.* https://mahmutakyuz.com/saglik-turizminde-yapay-zeka-destekli-dijital-pazarlama-trendleri/

Alexandra Hospital. (2025, February 12). Alexandra Hospital develops world's novel A.I. algorithm (with international patent) that enhances accuracy and efficiency of robotic total knee replacement [Press release]. *PR Newswire.* https://www.prnewswire.com/apac/news-releases/alexandra-hospital-develops-worlds-novel-ai-algorithm-with-international-patent-that-enhances-accuracy-and-efficiency-of-robotic-total-knee-replacement-302373284.html

Alowais, S. A., Alghamdi, S. S., Alsuhebany, N., Alqahtani, T., Alshaya, A. I., Almohareb, S. N., Aldairem, A., Alrashed, M., Bin Saleh, K., Badreldin, H. A., Al Yami, M. S., Al Harbi, S., & Albekairy, A. M. (2023). Revolutionizing healthcare: The role of artificial intelligence in clinical practice. *BMC Medical Education, 23*(1), 689. DOI: 10.1186/s12909-023-04698-z PMID: 37740191

Altınbafra, M. T. (2025). Robotik cerrahide sürdürülebilirlik boyutu: Sağlık turizmine etkileri ve gelecek perspektifi. In E. Dikmetaş Yardan (Ed.), *1. Uluslararası Sağlık Turizmi Kongresi (USAT 2025) / I. International Health Tourism Congress (IHET 2025).*

Amin, A., Cardoso, S. A., Suyambu, J., Abdus Saboor, H., Cardoso, R. P., Husnain, A., Isaac, N. V., Backing, H., Mehmood, D., Mehmood, M., & Maslamani, A. N. J. (2024). Future of artificial intelligence in surgery: A narrative review. *Cureus, 16*(1), e51631. DOI: 10.7759/cureus.51631 PMID: 38318552

Amisha, M., Malik, P., Pathania, M., & Rathaur, V. K. (2019). Overview of artificial intelligence in medicine. *Journal of Family Medicine and Primary Care, 8*(7), 2328–2331. DOI: 10.4103/jfmpc.jfmpc_440_19 PMID: 31463251

Anderson, D. (2022). Top medical tourism destinations for AI-assisted orthopedic surgeries. *Medical Tourism Magazine*. https://www.magazine.medicaltourism.com/article/top-medical-tourism-destinations-for-ai-assisted-orthopedic-surgeries

Arjomandi Rad, A., Vardanyan, R., Athanasiou, T., Maessen, J., & Sardari Nia, P. (2025). The ethical considerations of integrating artificial intelligence into surgery: A review. *Interdisciplinary Cardiovascular and Thoracic Surgery*, *40*(3), ivae192. Advance online publication. DOI: 10.1093/icvts/ivae192 PMID: 39999009

Aşık, H., & Güner, Ş. İ. (2025, June 26). Sağlık turizminde dijital sağlık uygulamalarının kullanımı [Abstract]. In *I. Uluslararası Sağlık Turizmi Kongresi (USAT 2025)*, Samsun, Türkiye (pp. 107).

Atek, S., Bianchini, F., De Vito, C., Cardinale, V., Novelli, S., Pesaresi, C., Eugeni, M., Mecella, M., Rescio, A., Petronzio, L., Vincenzi, A., Pistillo, P., Giusto, G., Pasquali, G., Alvaro, D., Villari, P., Mancini, M., & Gaudenzi, P. (2023). A predictive decision support system for coronavirus disease 2019 response management and medical logistic planning. *Digital Health*, *9*, 20552076231185475. Advance online publication. DOI: 10.1177/20552076231185475 PMID: 37545633

Aykın, Ö., Uluhan, F., Gümüş, İ., Çabuk, Ş., Bozbayır, U., Duran, V., Özbay, C., Özbay, B., Gündoğmuş, Ş. E., Türkegün Şengül, M., & Övey, İ. S. (2023). Artificial intelligence and telemedicine applications in health tourism marketing. *Eurasian Journal of Health Technology Assessment*, *7*(2), 134–149. DOI: 10.52148/ehta.1396111

Ayyıldız, D., & Ovayolu, Ö. (2024, October). Sağlık ve hastalık yönetiminde yapay zekânın kullanımı. In *8th International ACHARAKA Congress on Medicine, Nursing, Midwifery, and Health Sciences Proceedings Book*.

Bajwa, J., Munir, U., Nori, A., & Williams, B. (2021). Artificial intelligence in healthcare: Transforming the practice of medicine. *Future Healthcare Journal*, *8*(2), e188–e194. DOI: 10.7861/fhj.2021-0095 PMID: 34286183

Björnsson, B., Borrebaeck, C., Elander, N., Gasslander, T., Gawel, D. R., Gustafsson, M., Jörnsten, R., Lee, E. J., Li, X., Lilja, S., Martínez-Enguita, D., Matussek, A., Sandström, P., Schäfer, S., Stenmarker, M., Sun, X. F., Sysoev, O., Zhang, H., & Benson, M. (2020). Digital twins to personalize medicine. *Genome Medicine*, *12*(1), 4. Advance online publication. DOI: 10.1186/s13073-019-0701-3 PMID: 31892363

Borst, V., Riedmann, A., Dege, T., Müller, K., Schmieder, A., Lugrin, B., & Kounev, S. (2025). WoundAIssist: A patient-centered mobile app for AI-assisted wound care with physicians in the loop (arXiv:2506.06104). arXiv. https://doi.org//arXiv.2506.06104DOI: 10.48550

Bostan, M. H., & Halhalli, H. C. (2025). Sağlık turizminde yapay zekâ uygulamaları. In Bostan, A., & Coşkun, E. (Eds.), *Sağlık turizmi: Sağlıkta sınırları aşmak* (pp. 187–205). Detay Yayıncılık.

Bulut, C. (2025). Sağlık kurumlarında yapay zekâ destekli karar destek sistemlerinin kullanımı. *Uluslararası Sağlık Yönetimi ve Stratejileri Araştırma Dergisi, 11(1),* 27–37. https://izlik.org/JA78AG89SK

Buoy Health. (n.d.). *Check symptoms & find the right care.* https://www.buoyhealth.com/

Büyükkaya, B. (2024). *Sağlık hizmetlerinde yapay zekâ: Bir araştırma* [Unpublished master's thesis]. Sakarya Üniversitesi.

Chowdhury, T. N., Mou, S. A., & Rahman, K. N. (2025). A hybrid data-driven approach for analyzing and predicting inpatient length of stay in health centre. arXiv preprint arXiv:2501.18535. https://arxiv.org/abs/2501.18535 DOI: 10.1101/2025.01.30.25321434

Cleveland Clinic. (n.d.). *About Cleveland Clinic.* https://my.clevelandclinic.org

Çondur, F., Cömertler, N., & Yenipazarlı, A. (2025). Sağlık turizminde dijital dönüşüm. In Bostan, A., & Coşkun, E. (Eds.), *Sağlık turizmi: Sağlıkta sınırları aşmak* (pp. 165–180). Detay Yayıncılık.

Council of the European Union. (2025, January 21). European Health Data Space: Council adopts new regulation improving cross-border access to EU health data [Press release No. 40/25]. https://www.consilium.europa.eu/en/press/press-releases/2025/01/21/european-health-data-space-council-adopts-new-regulation-improving-cross-border-access-to-eu-health-data/

Deckey, D. G., Rosenow, C. S., Verhey, J. T., Brinkman, J. C., Mayfield, C. K., Clarke, H. D., & Bingham, J. S. (2021). Robotic-assisted total knee arthroplasty improves accuracy and precision compared to conventional techniques. *The Bone & Joint Journal, 103-B*(6, Supple A), 74–80. DOI: 10.1302/0301-620X.103B6.BJJ-2020-2003.R1 PMID: 34053292

EBSCO Health. (n.d.). *Isabel clinical decision support system.* https://about.ebsco.com/health-care/products/isabel

Elliott, J., Shatrov, J., Fritsch, B., & Parker, D. (2021, December). Robotic-assisted knee arthroplasty: An evolution in progress. A concise review of the available systems and the data supporting them. *Archives of Orthopaedic and Trauma Surgery, 141*(12), 2099–2117. DOI: 10.1007/s00402-021-04134-1 PMID: 34491411

Esteva, A., Kuprel, B., Novoa, R. A., Ko, J., Swetter, S. M., Blau, H. M., & Thrun, S. (2017). Dermatologist-level classification of skin cancer with deep neural networks. *Nature*, *542*(7639), 115–118. DOI: 10.1038/nature21056 PMID: 28117445

Gedik, Y. (2023). Kurumsal iletişimde yeni bir yıldız: Chatbot faydaları, zorlukları ve stratejileri üzerine kavramsal bir çerçeve. *Journal of Business and Communication Studies*, *2*(1), 13–32. https://www.researchgate.net/publication/372010058_KURUMSAL_ILETISIMDE_YENI_BIR_YILDIZ_CHATBOT_FAYDALARI_ZORLUKLARI_VE_STRATEJILERI_UZERINE_KAVRAMSAL_BIR_CERCEVE_A_new_star_in_corporate_communications_Chatbot_A_conceptual_framework_on_its_benefits_cha. DOI: 10.29228/jobacs.68836

Georgiou. (2024). *10 use cases and real examples of generative AI in healthcare.* https://imaginovation.net/blog/use-cases-examples-generative-ai-healthcare/

Gerke, S., Minssen, T., & Cohen, I. G. (2020). Ethical and legal challenges of artificial intelligence-driven healthcare. In Bohr, A., & Memarzadeh, K. (Eds.), *Artificial intelligence in healthcare* (pp. 295–336). Elsevier., DOI: 10.1016/B978-0-12-818438-7.00012-5

Gulshan, V., Peng, L., Coram, M., Stumpe, M. C., Wu, D., Narayanaswamy, A., Venugopalan, S., Widner, K., Madams, T., Cuadros, J., Kim, R., Raman, R., Nelson, P. C., Mega, J. L., & Webster, D. R. (2016). Development and validation of a deep learning algorithm for detection of diabetic retinopathy in retinal fundus photographs. *Journal of the American Medical Association*, *316*(22), 2402–2410. DOI: 10.1001/jama.2016.17216 PMID: 27898976

Han, S. B., Rodriguez-Quintana, D., Freedhand, A. M., Mathis, K. B., Boiwka, A. V., & Noble, P. C. (2021). Contemporary robotic systems in total knee arthroplasty: A review of accuracy and outcomes. *The Orthopedic Clinics of North America*, *52*(2), 83–92. DOI: 10.1016/j.ocl.2020.12.001 PMID: 33752841

Hassan, V., & Bellos, G. (2022). COVID-19: Reshaping medical tourism through artificial intelligence (AI) and robotics. *Athens Journal of Tourism*, *9*(2), 77–98. DOI: 10.30958/ajt.9-2-2

Haznedar, B. (2010). *Yapay zeka teknikleri kullanarak erkek kısır hastalarda genetik bozukluk varlığının tespiti* [Unpublished master's thesis]. Erciyes University.

Hill, M. G., Sim, M., & Mills, B. (2020). The quality of diagnosis and triage advice provided by free online symptom checkers and apps in Australia. *The Medical Journal of Australia*, *212*(11), 514–519. DOI: 10.5694/mja2.50600 PMID: 32391611

İlkılıç, İ. (2021). Tıpta yapay zekâ kullanımının etik açıdan değerlendirilmesi. *SD Sağlık Düşüncesi ve Tıp Kültürü Dergisi, 58(1)*, 18–21. https://sdplatform.com/tipta-yapay-zeka-kullaniminin-etik-acidan-degerlendirilmesi

Inherit, X. (n.d.). *Heva – AI-native healthcare & wellness intelligence platform.* https://www.inheritx.com/portfolio/heva

Jiang, F., Jiang, Y., Zhi, H., Dong, Y., Li, H., Ma, S., Wang, Y., Dong, Q., Shen, H., & Wang, Y. (2017). Artificial intelligence in healthcare: Past, present and future. *Stroke and Vascular Neurology*, *2*(4), 230–243. DOI: 10.1136/svn-2017-000101 PMID: 29507784

Jiménez, C. (2022). Leading destinations for AI-assisted minimally invasive surgery. *Medical Tourism Magazine*.https://www.magazine.medicaltourism.com/article/leading-destinations-for-ai-assisted-minimally-invasive-surgery

Karcıoğlu, U. B. (2025). The impact of artificial intelligence on the patient journey in medical tourism: A management framework. *Eurasian Journal of Health Technology Assessment*, *9*(1), 58–67. DOI: 10.52148/ehta.1701664

Kim, S. J., Cho, K. J., & Oh, S. (2017). Development of machine learning models for diagnosis of glaucoma. *PLoS One*, *12*(5), e0177726. DOI: 10.1371/journal.pone.0177726 PMID: 28542342

Kocamaz, K. (2007). *Hastane bilgi yönetim sistemlerinde veri madenciliği ve Konya Meram Tıp Fakültesi hastanesindeki hastane bilgi yönetim sistemi uygulamasının incelenmesi* [Unpublished master's thesis]. Selçuk University.

Koprowski, R., Lanza, M., & Irregolare, C. (2016). Corneal power evaluation after myopic corneal refractive surgery using artificial neural networks. *Biomedical Engineering Online*, *15*(1), 121. DOI: 10.1186/s12938-016-0243-5 PMID: 27846894

Kozan, N. (2025, August 9). Sağlık turizminde dijital konsültasyonların yükselişi. *Istanbuldent*. https://www.istanbuldent.com.tr/saglik-turizminde-dijital-konsultasyonlarin-yukselisi/

Kristyanto, H. (2025, March 3). AI chatbots in travel: Benefits & examples. *Cognigy*. https://www.cognigy.com/blog/ai-chatbots-in-travel-benefits-examples

Lakhani, P. C., & Sundaram, B. (2017). Deep learning at chest radiography: Automated classification of pulmonary tuberculosis by using convolutional neural networks. *Radiology*, *284*(2), 574–582. DOI: 10.1148/radiol.2017162326 PMID: 28436741

Luscii. (2024). *Remote patient monitoring and personalized care pathways*. https://www.luscii.com

Luscii. (n.d.). *Home – Smartest care at home platform for hospitals and GPs*. https://luscii.com/en/home

Mayo Clinic. (n.d.). *Artificial intelligence*. https://www.mayoclinic.org

Miller, R. A., Pople, H. E.Jr, & Myers, J. D. (1985). Internist-I, an experimental computer-based diagnostic consultant for general internal medicine. In *Computer-assisted medical decision making* (pp. 139–158). Springer New York. DOI: 10.1007/978-1-4612-5108-8_8

MYCIN. (2026, February, 8). In Wikipedia. https://en.wikipedia.org/wiki/Mycin

National University Health System. (2025, February 11). *Alexandra Hospital develops world's novel A.I. algorithm (with international patent) that enhances accuracy and efficiency of robotic total knee replacement*. https://www.nuhs.edu.sg/about-nuhs/news-and-stories/news-and-stories-details/alexandra-hospital-develops-world-s-novel-a.i.-algorithm-%28with-international-patent%29-that-enhances-accuracy-and-efficiency-of-robotic-total-knee-replacement

nib Group. (2024, April 29). nib Group launches AI-driven symptom checker [Press release]. https://www.nib.com.au/media/health/nib-launches-ai-symptom-checker

Obermeyer, Z., Powers, B., Vogeli, C., & Mullainathan, S. (2019). Racial bias found in a major health care risk algorithm. *Scientific American*. https://www.scientificamerican.com/article/racial-bias-found-in-a-major-health-care-risk-algorithm

Özçelik Heper, F. (2025). Yapay zeka teknolojilerinden ChatGPT'nin sağlık turizminde potansiyel kullanımı: Güçlü ve zayıf yönleri. *Journal of Silk Road Tourism Research, 5*(2), 108–122. DOI: 10.5281/zenodo.17671460

Pacci, Z., Atılgan Şengül, Y., Attar, R., Alagöz, O., & Uyar, A. (2021). Yapay zekâ tabanlı klinik karar destek sistemi ile tüp bebek tedavisi gebelik sonucu tahmini. *EMO Bilimsel Dergi, 11(22)*, 27–35. https://search.trdizin.gov.tr/yayin/detay/505635

Par, S. (2024). Yapay zekânın sağlık alanında kullanımı ve hukuki statüsü. *International Anatolia Academic Online Journal: Social Sciences Journal, 10(2)*, 179–196. https://dergipark.org.tr/tr/pub/iaaoj/issue/85849/1485263

Popejoy, A. B., & Fullerton, S. M. (2016). Genomics is failing on diversity. *Nature, 538*(7624), 161–164. DOI: 10.1038/538161a PMID: 27734877

Quizlet. (n.d.). *HSCI 4100 chapter 8: Clinical decision support*. https://quizlet.com/1086961905/hsci-4100-chapter-8-clinical-decision-support-flash-cards/

Rajkomar, A., Dean, J., & Kohane, I. (2019). Machine learning in medicine. *The New England Journal of Medicine*, *380*(14), 1347–1358. DOI: 10.1056/NEJMra1814259 PMID: 30943338

Rieke, N., Hancox, J., Li, W., Milletarì, F., Roth, H. R., Albarqouni, S., Bakas, S., Galtier, M. N., Landman, B. A., Maier-Hein, K., Ourselin, S., Sheller, M., Summers, R. M., Trask, A., Xu, D., Baust, M., & Cardoso, M. J. (2020). The future of digital health with federated learning. *NPJ Digital Medicine*, *3*(1), 119. DOI: 10.1038/s41746-020-00323-1 PMID: 33015372

Sahin, F., Gökalp Özkorkmaz, E., Kaya, S., & Aşır, F. (2024). Yardımcı Üreme Tekniklerinde Yapay Zeka. *Turkish Journal of Clinics and Laboratory*, *15*(4), 666–674. DOI: 10.18663/tjcl.1593054

Semigran, H. L., Linder, J. A., Gidengil, C., & Mehrotra, A. (2015). Evaluation of symptom checkers for self diagnosis and triage: Audit study. *BMJ (Clinical Research Ed.)*, *351*, h3480. DOI: 10.1136/bmj.h3480 PMID: 26157077

Sensely. (n.d.). *Conversational AI to improve health and drive member engagement*. https://sensely.com

Sensely. (n.d.). *Virtual nurse and AI chatbot solutions*. https://www.sensely.com

Sinsky, C. A., Colligan, L., Li, L., Prgomet, M., Reynolds, S., Goeders, L., Westbrook, J., Tutty, M., & Blike, G. (2016). Allocation of physician time in ambulatory practice: A time and motion study in 4 specialties. *Annals of Internal Medicine*, *165*(11), 753–760. DOI: 10.7326/M16-0961 PMID: 27595430

Stackpole, I. (2025, February 13). Emerging AI in medical travel and insurance. *International Travel & Health Insurance Journal (ITIJ)*. https://www.itij.com/latest/long-read/emerging-ai-medical-travel-and-insurance

Symptomate. (n.d.). *About us & symptom checker*. https://symptomate.com/about

The North Solution. (n.d.). *IT consultancy firm | The North Solution*. https://www.thenorthsolution.com/

Topol, E. J. (2019). High-performance medicine: The convergence of human and artificial intelligence. *Nature Medicine*, *25*(1), 44–56. DOI: 10.1038/s41591-018-0300-7 PMID: 30617339

Tran, D. (2025, June 18). AI in travel: Top use cases you need to know. *SmartDev*. https://smartdev.com/ai-use-cases-in-travel/

uHealth. (2024, June 30). Sağlık turizminde yapay zeka (AI) kullanımı. *uHealth*. https://www.uhealth.com.tr/saglik-turizminde-yapay-zeka-ai-kullanimi/

Vaidam Health. (n.d.). *Vaidam.com – Top medical tourism company*. https://www.vaidam.com/

Viangteeravat. (2025). AI medical imaging: Artificial Intelligence Provides Added Support for Patient Diagnosis. *Bumrungrad International*. https://www.bumrungrad.com/en/health-blog/march-2020/ai-medical-imaging

Vural, O., Ozaydin, B., Aram, K. Y., Booth, J., Lindsey, B. F., & Ahmed, A. (2025). An artificial intelligence–based framework for predicting emergency department overcrowding: Development and evaluation study. *JMIR Medical Informatics*, *13*, e73960. DOI: 10.2196/73960 PMID: 40961493

Wah, J. N. K. (2025). The rise of robotics and AI-assisted surgery in modern healthcare. *Journal of Robotic Surgery*, *19*(1), 311. DOI: 10.1007/s11701-025-02485-0 PMID: 40540146

Wang, Q., Su, M., Zhang, M., & Li, R. (2021). Integrating digital technologies and public health to fight COVID-19 pandemic: Key technologies, applications, challenges and outlook of digital healthcare. *International Journal of Environmental Research and Public Health*, *18*(11), 6053. DOI: 10.3390/ijerph18116053 PMID: 34199831

Wang, Y., Wang, L., Rastegar-Mojarad, M., Moon, S., Shen, F., Afzal, N., Liu, S., Zeng, Y., Mehrabi, S., Sohn, S., & Liu, H. (2018). Clinical information extraction applications: A literature review. *Journal of Biomedical Informatics*, *77*, 34–49. DOI: 10.1016/j.jbi.2017.11.011 PMID: 29162496

Wong, T. Y., & Bressler, N. M. (2016). Artificial intelligence with deep learning technology looks into diabetic retinopathy screening. *Journal of the American Medical Association*, *316*(22), 2366–2367. DOI: 10.1001/jama.2016.17563 PMID: 27898977

Xu, T., Wang, W., & Du, J. (2020). An integrative review of patients' experience in the medical tourism. *Inquiry : a Journal of Medical Care Organization, Provision and Financing*, *57*, 0046958020926762. DOI: 10.1177/0046958020926762 PMID: 32513038

Yelli, Ö. F., & Karaman, A. (2024). Sağlık turizmi yönetiminde yapay zekânın rolü. In *8th Hodja Akhmet Yassawi International Congress on Scientific Research*. Konya, Türkiye.

YesilScience. (2022, October 24). 72 sağlıkta yapay zeka uygulaması. *YesilScience*. https://yesilscience.com/tr/yapay-zeka-ve-saglik/

Yıldırım, B. F. (2021). *Bilgi sistemi olarak e-Nabız uygulamalarının sağlık turizmi hastaları için geliştirilmesi: Bir model önerisi* [Doctoral dissertation]. Ankara University.

Yılmaz, F., Mete, A. H., Fidan Türkön, B., & İnce, Ö. (2022). Sağlık hizmetlerinin geleceğinde metaverse ekosistemi ve teknolojileri: Uygulamalar, fırsatlar ve zorluklar. *Eurasian Journal of Health Technology Assessment, 6*(1), 12–34. DOI: 10.52148/ehta.1082705

Yorgancioglu Tarcan, G., Yalçın Balçık, P., & Sebik, N. B. (2024). Türkiye ve dünyada sağlık hizmetlerinde yapay zekâ. *Lokman Hekim Dergisi, 14*(1), 50–60. DOI: 10.31020/mutftd.1278529

Zaim Gökbay, İ. (2021). Tıpta yapay zeka uygulamaları: Antik çağdan yapay zekaya teşhis ve tedavi yöntemlerinin gelişim sürecinde klinik karar destek sistemlerinin evrimine genel bakış. In Bozbuğa, N., & Gülseçen, S. (Eds.), *Tıp bilişimi* (pp. 673–691). İstanbul Üniversitesi Yayınevi., DOI: 10.26650/B/ET07.2021.003.33

KEY TERMS AND DEFINITIONS

Artificial Intelligence: A field of information technology that is ready to assist humans in various ways through the use of various technological tools (computers, machines, etc.).

Best Practices: These refer to practices in any field that, as a result of an analysis process, offer the maximum benefit and return on investment.

Big Data Infrastructure: A technological process with the potential to optimize data input from various fields and bring it to the most suitable stage for decision support systems.

Case Studies: This is a type of research method that requires a detailed analysis of any given situation, topic, institution, or process.

Decision Support System: A system that helps users make the most informed decisions in situations where they are confused.

Digital Consultation: This is a consultation process that takes place digitally, allowing patients to obtain expert opinions from different specialists than their own physician, which can help in their recovery.

Digital Health: This refers to all types of digital technology used in the healthcare field.

Digital Tourism: This refers to the presentation, management, monitoring, and marketing of tourism through digital technologies.

Health Tourism: Within the scope of tourism, it is a type of national and international tourism in which people travel for purposes such as receiving treatment, feeling well, benefiting from thermal springs, etc.

Medical Tourism: Also called medical tourism or healthcare tourism, medical tourism is a type of health tourism where people participate solely for reasons such as receiving treatment or undergoing surgery.

Triage Systems: This refers to the process of prioritizing patients based on the urgency of their condition.

Chapter 7

AI-Enabled Diagnostics, Treatment Planning, and Clinical Decision

Zarmina Ehtesham
http://orcid.org/0000-0002-8094-476X
Dow University of Health Sciences, Pakistan

Sharjeel Chaudhry
http://orcid.org/0000-0002-7070-1326
Dow University of Health Sciences, Pakistan

Fatimah Salem Alayidh
http://orcid.org/0000-0003-0214-6161
King Fahad Military Medical Complex, Ministry of Defence Health Services, Saudi Arabia

ABSTRACT

Artificial intelligence (AI) is reshaping medical tourism by strengthening diagnostic precision, optimizing treatment planning, and enhancing clinical decision support across borders. Pathology particularly molecular and digital pathology stands at the center of this transformation, as accurate diagnosis underpins every therapeutic decision. AI-driven whole-slide imaging, deep learning–based tumor classification, biomarker quantification, and next-generation sequencing analytics are redefining cross-border oncology and complex disease management. This chapter examines how integrated AI systems connect pre-travel digital diagnostics, in-treatment precision care, and post-treatment molecular surveillance. It also addresses ethical and regulatory challenges, including data governance, algorithmic bias, and quality

DOI: 10.4018/979-8-3373-8944-8.ch007

assurance. By positioning pathology as the diagnostic core of AI-enabled medical tourism, the chapter offers a strategic framework for building globally competitive, ethically responsible, and data-driven international healthcare ecosystems.

1. INTRODUCTION: PATHOLOGY AS THE DIAGNOSTIC CORE OF MEDICAL TOURISM

Medical tourism has evolved beyond elective cosmetic procedures and cost-driven interventions into a sophisticated global healthcare ecosystem addressing complex, high-acuity diseases. Increasingly, patients travel across borders for advanced oncologic therapies, organ transplantation, fertility treatments, cardiovascular surgery, neurosurgical interventions, and personalized precision medicine programs. These high-stakes clinical journeys require robust diagnostic confirmation before definitive treatment. At the center of this diagnostic architecture lies pathology, particularly molecular and digital pathology, which provides the definitive characterization of disease at morphologic, immunophenotypic, and genomic levels.

In contemporary cross-border healthcare, diagnosis is no longer limited to confirming the presence of disease. It requires detailed subclassification, biomarker profiling, molecular risk assessment, and therapeutic eligibility determination. Oncology patients traveling internationally, for example, require not only histologic confirmation of malignancy but also precise tumor grading, staging, receptor status determination, mutation profiling, and predictive biomarker assessment(Brierley et al., 2019). Similarly, transplant candidates depend on immunogenetic compatibility testing, histocompatibility profiling, and molecular screening for infectious and inflammatory conditions(Güell-Alonso et al., 2025). Reproductive medical tourism relies on genetic screening, embryonic selection algorithms, and endocrine pathology correlations. Advanced surgical procedures demand accurate tissue diagnosis, inflammatory grading, and molecular risk prediction to optimize outcomes.

In this context, pathology is not merely a supportive disciplineit is the diagnostic engine upon which treatment planning, prognostication, and therapeutic decision-making depend. A misclassified tumor subtype, an incorrectly graded dysplasia, a false-negative lymph node assessment, or an overlooked actionable mutation can fundamentally alter clinical strategy. In cross-border care, where patients invest significant financial, emotional, and logistical resources, diagnostic precision is paramount(Groene et al., 2009). Errors at the pathological level may lead to inappropriate surgery, ineffective chemotherapy, avoidable toxicity, or missed opportunities for targeted therapy.Furthermore, medical tourism introduces additional complexities. Patients often present with incomplete medical records, heterogeneous diagnostic standards from their home countries, and varying laboratory quality assurance practices. Glass slides may be transported internationally, risking degradation or interpretative discrepancies. Molecular reports may follow different nomenclature systems or testing methodologies. These challenges underscore the need for standardized, reproducible, and interoperable diagnostic systems capable of transcending geographic boundaries.

Artificial intelligence (AI) has emerged as a transformative force that amplifies the central role of pathology in medical tourism(Yousefi et al., 2025). AI-driven systems enhance the accuracy, reproducibility, and efficiency of diagnostic workflows while enabling seamless international consultation and data sharing. Through advanced computational modeling and machine learning, pathology has transitioned from a largely subjective interpretative science to a quantitatively augmented discipline supported by algorithmic precision.

AI applications in pathology now support:

- Whole-slide image analysis, enabling automated detection and classification of histopathologic patterns with high sensitivity and specificity.
- Automated tumor detection and grading, reducing inter-observer variability and improving diagnostic consistency across institutions.
- Quantitative biomarker assessment, including standardized scoring of immunohistochemical markers such as PD-L1, HER2, Ki-67, ER, and PR.
- Genomic variant interpretation, assisting in the classification of pathogenic mutations and identifying actionable molecular targets.
- Risk stratification modeling, predicting recurrence, metastasis, and treatment response based on integrated morphologic and molecular data.
- Integrated molecular–clinical correlation systems, synthesizing histology, genomics, radiology, and clinical parameters into comprehensive diagnostic insights.

In AI-enabled medical tourism ecosystems, pathology becomes digitally interconnected, globally consultative, and algorithmically augmented. Whole-slide images can be securely transmitted across continents for expert review within minutes. Molecular datasets can be processed through bioinformatic pipelines to generate clinically actionable insights before a patient boards an international flight(Privitera et al., 2026). Multidisciplinary tumor boards can convene virtually, integrating AI-derived analytics with specialist expertise to refine treatment plans.

Moreover, AI enhances quality assurance within medical tourism hubs. Automated quality control systems detect slide artifacts, staining inconsistencies, and technical errors before interpretation(Shakhawat et al., 2020). Predictive analytics identify discrepancies between radiologic and pathologic findings, prompting re-evaluation where necessary. These safeguards strengthen institutional credibility and foster international patient trust.The digitization of pathology also expands opportunities for global collaboration. Telepathology networks enable remote consultation between referring physicians and destination hospitals(Sankaye, 2011). AI-driven decision support tools harmonize reporting standards and reduce interpretative variability. Molecular databases contribute to shared knowledge platforms that refine predictive modeling across diverse populations.

Importantly, the integration of AI does not diminish the expertise of pathologists; rather, it elevates their role. Pathologists transition from purely morphologic interpreters to data integrators, overseeing algorithm validation, ensuring clinical contextualization, and maintaining ethical governance. In medical tourism settings, pathologists serve as guardians of diagnostic integrity, ensuring that AI augmentation enhances rather than replaces human judgment(Gaffney & Mirza, 2025). Thus, within the rapidly evolving landscape of medical tourism, pathology occupies a foundational and strategic position. It anchors therapeutic decision-making, informs precision treatment planning, and safeguards patient outcomes. Artificial intelligence strengthens this foundation by providing scalable, reproducible, and globally interoperable diagnostic capabilities.

As medical tourism continues to expand into increasingly complex domains of care, the convergence of pathology, molecular diagnostics, digital infrastructure, and AI will define the future of cross-border healthcare. Pathology is no longer confined to the microscopeit is now a digitally networked, data-driven discipline that serves as the intellectual core of intelligent, globally mobile medicine.

2. DIGITAL PATHOLOGY: THE STRUCTURAL FOUNDATION OF AI DIAGNOSTICS

Digital pathology represents the technological infrastructure upon which AI-enabled diagnostic systems are built. In the context of medical tourismwhere diagnostic accuracy, reproducibility, and rapid data exchange are criticaldigital pathology serves as the foundational bridge between traditional histopathology and computational intelligence. It transforms static glass slides into dynamic, analyzable datasets that can be securely transmitted, interpreted, and augmented by artificial intelligence across geographic boundaries.As cross-border healthcare increasingly involves complex oncologic, inflammatory, infectious, and genetic diseases, the digitization of pathology workflows ensures that diagnostic interpretation is no longer constrained by physical location. Instead, it becomes part of an interconnected, global diagnostic network that supports timely, evidence-based therapeutic decisions.

2.1 What Is Digital Pathology?

Digital pathology refers to the process of converting conventional glass histology slides into high-resolution whole-slide images (WSIs) using advanced slide scanners equipped with precision optics and high-throughput imaging systems(Omoush et al., 2026). These scanners capture entire tissue sections at microscopic resolution, producing gigapixel-scale digital files that faithfully replicate the optical microscope view.

Figure 1. Whole-Slide Imaging Scanner, (Digital Pathology Microscope Slide Scanners | Whole Slide Imaging, 2021).

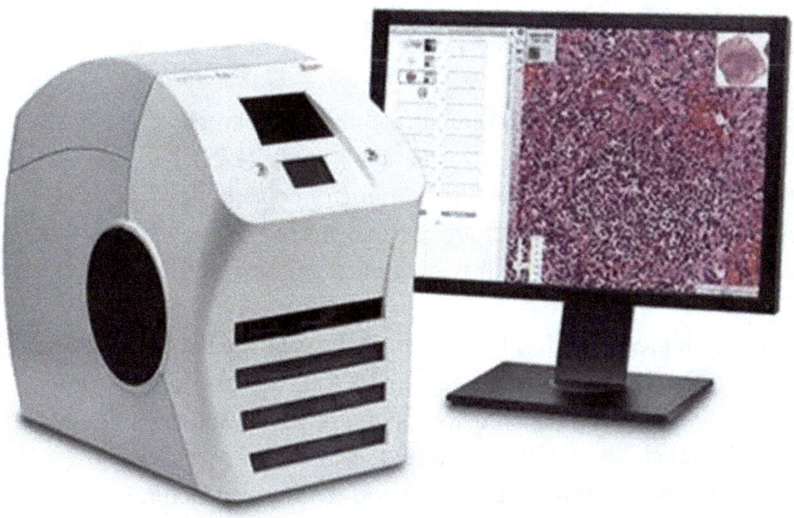

Figure 2. Histopathology whole-slide image on a computer screen, (Marée et al., 2013).

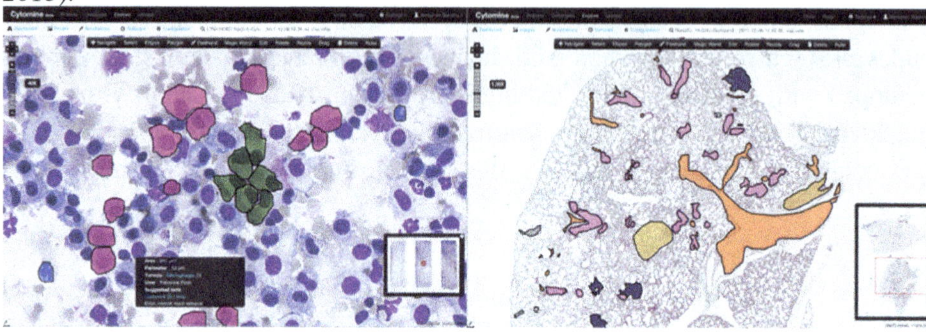

Once digitized, these images can be:

- Securely stored in cloud-based or institutional servers.
- Integrated with laboratory information systems (LIS).
- Annotated and shared for multidisciplinary consultation.
- Analyzed using AI-powered image analysis tools.
- Archived for long-term quality assurance and research.

This technological shift fundamentally changes how pathology services operate. Instead of physically transporting fragile glass slides across bordersa process associated with delays, risk of damage, customs complications, and variable environmental conditionsdigital slides can be transmitted instantly and securely.

In medical tourism, this capability provides several structural advantages:

- **Remote expert consultation**: Subspecialty pathologists can review cases before the patient travels, ensuring diagnostic confirmation and reducing unnecessary procedures.
- **AI algorithm deployment**: Digital slides become analyzable datasets suitable for machine learning and deep learning models.
- **Standardized reporting**: Structured digital templates enhance consistency across institutions.
- **International second opinions**: Multidisciplinary tumor boards can convene virtually, integrating pathology findings with radiologic and molecular data.

Beyond operational efficiency, digital pathology enhances transparency and traceability. Every annotation, measurement, and diagnostic decision can be documented, archived, and audited. This is particularly valuable in medical tourism environments where international patients demand high levels of accountability and quality assurance.

2.2 AI in Histopathology

Artificial intelligence has revolutionized histopathology by introducing computational pattern recognition at a scale beyond human capability. Deep learning modelsparticularly convolutional neural networks (CNNs)are trained on thousands to millions of annotated images to detect subtle morphological patterns associated with disease.

Figure 3. High-Resolution Histopathology Whole-Slide Image, (Chen et al., 2021).

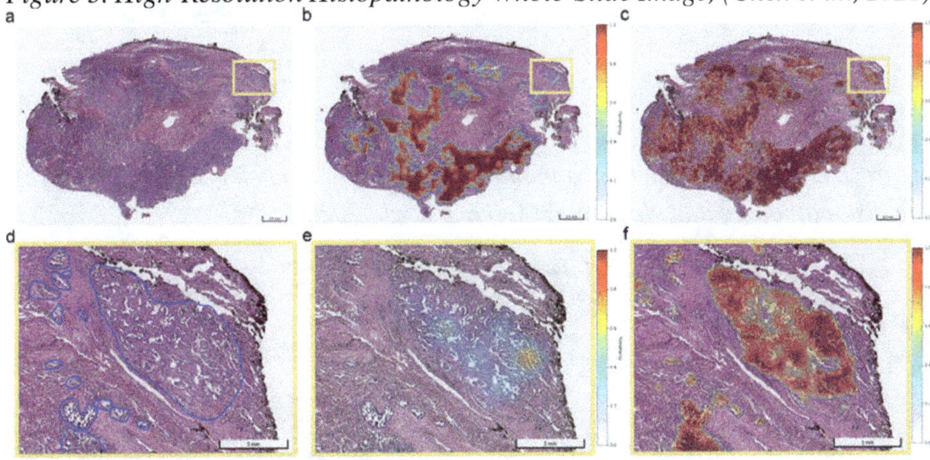

Figure 4. Deep learning workflow for histopathology image analysis, (Noorbakhsh et al., 2020).

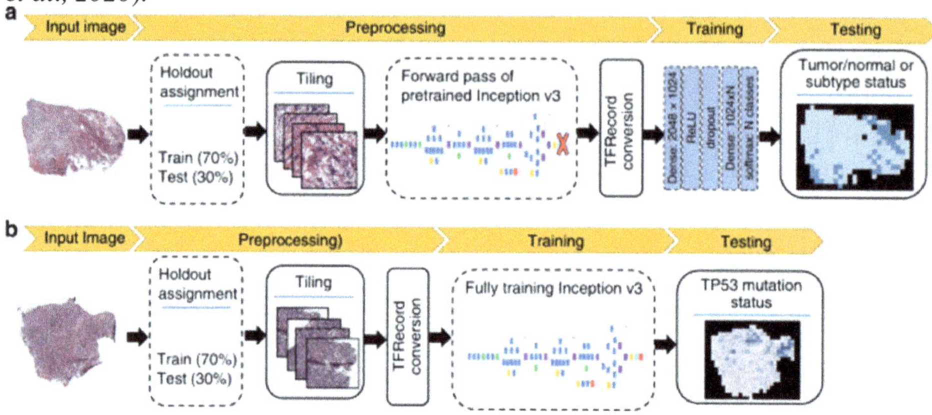

Figure 5. Dataset construction, annotation strategy, and patch generation for prostate histopathology deep learning, (Tolkach et al., 2020).

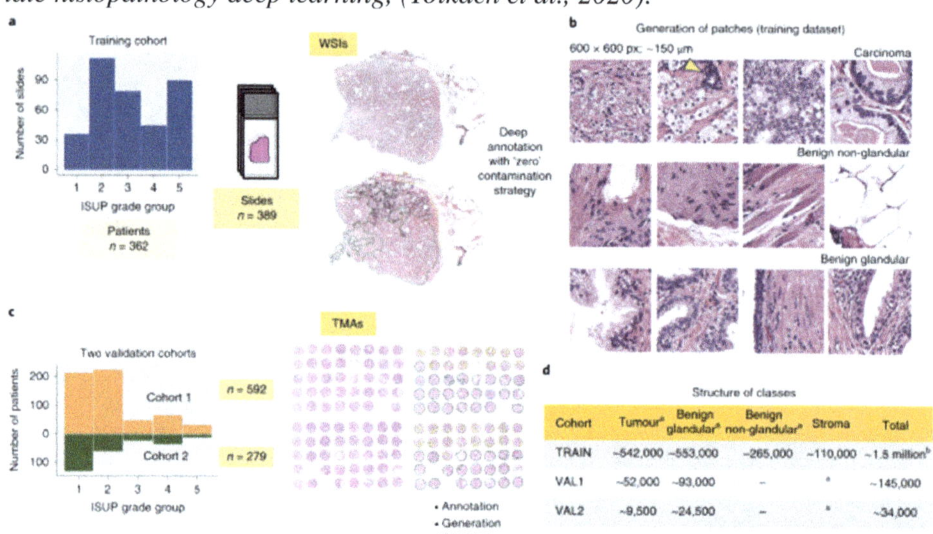

AI-driven histopathologic applications now include:

- **Automated tumor detection**: Identifying malignant regions within complex tissue sections.

- **Tumor grading and classification**: Distinguishing low-grade from high-grade malignancies with quantitative precision.
- **Lymphovascular invasion detection**: Recognizing subtle vascular infiltration patterns that influence staging.
- **Mitotic figure quantification**: Counting mitoses objectively to improve grading reproducibility.
- **Tumor microenvironment analysis**: Assessing immune infiltration and stromal composition.
- **Prediction of molecular subtypes from morphology**: Inferring genomic alterations from histologic patterns through morpho-molecular correlation models.

These AI-assisted processes reduce inter-observer variability,a known limitation in traditional microscopy. Diagnostic reproducibility becomes especially important in medical tourism, where treatment decisions may depend on a single histopathological interpretation. Variability between home-country and destination-country pathology assessments can lead to therapeutic discrepancies. AI-supported standardization mitigates this risk.Moreover, AI systems can process large datasets rapidly, enhancing turnaround time in cross-border care, faster diagnostic confirmation accelerates treatment planning and reduces patient anxiety associated travel and uncertainty(Onyekachukwu Victor Unanah& Esi Mansa Aidoo, 2025).Importantly, AI in histopathology functions as an augmentation tool rather than a replacement for pathologists. Human oversight remains essential for contextual interpretation, validation of algorithmic output, and integration of clinical information. The synergy between computational precision and expert judgment represents the optimal model for AI-enabled pathology practice.

2.3 AI in Molecular Pathology

While digital histopathology provides morphologic insights, molecular pathology uncovers the genetic, epigenetic, and proteomic underpinnings of disease (Chaudhry & Ehtesham, 2025). The integration of AI into molecular diagnostics has dramatically expanded the analytical capacity of laboratories, particularly in oncology-focused medical tourism.

Figure 6. Comparative workflows of next-generation sequencing approaches: whole-exome sequencing (WES), whole-genome sequencing (WGS), and RNA sequencing (RNA-seq),(Ma et al., 2015).

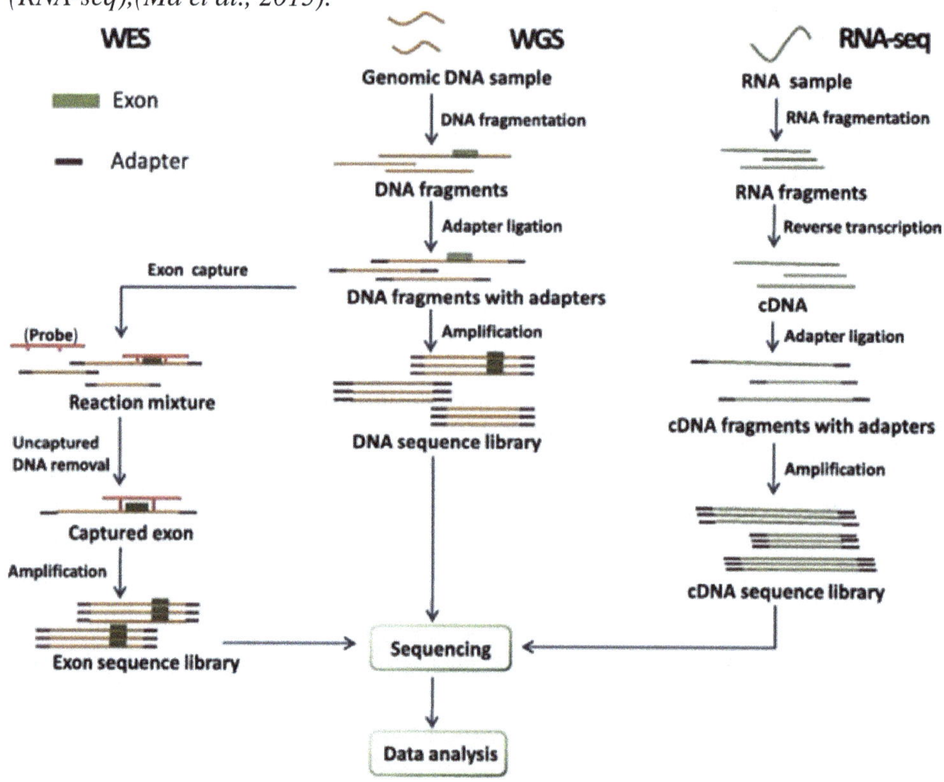

Figure 7. Standard DNA-Seq alignment and quality-control workflow, (Boro Milovanović, 2018).

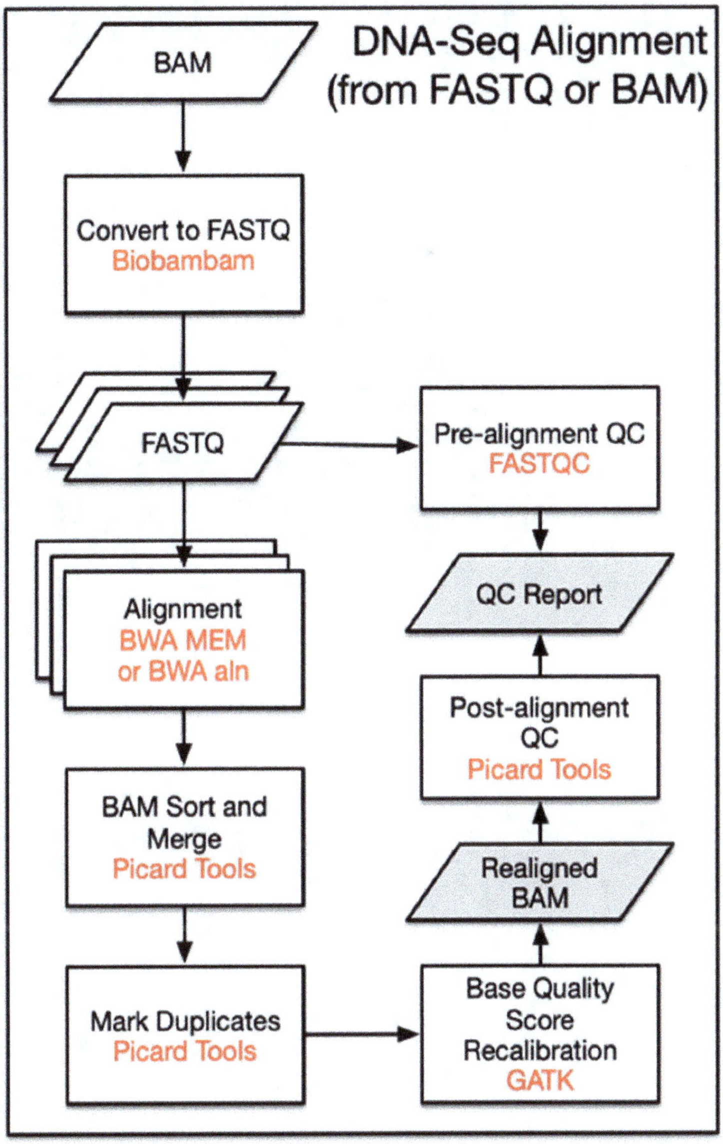

Figure 8. Landscape of genomic alterations and clinical associations across multiple cancer types, (Liu et al., 2022).

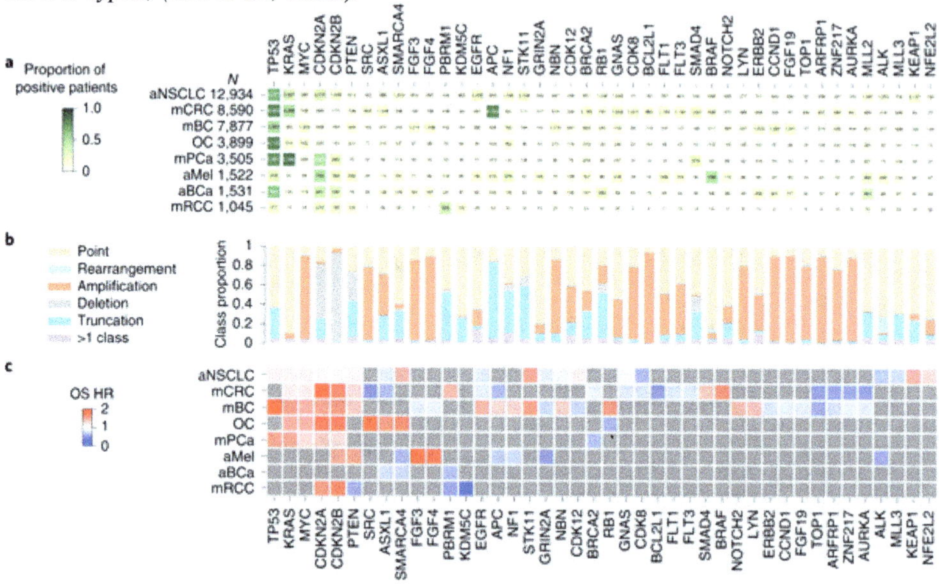

Figure 9. Overview of the NCI Genomic Data Commons (GDC) Data Portal interface for cancer genomics exploration, (DAVE Tools for Genomic Data Commons, 2017).

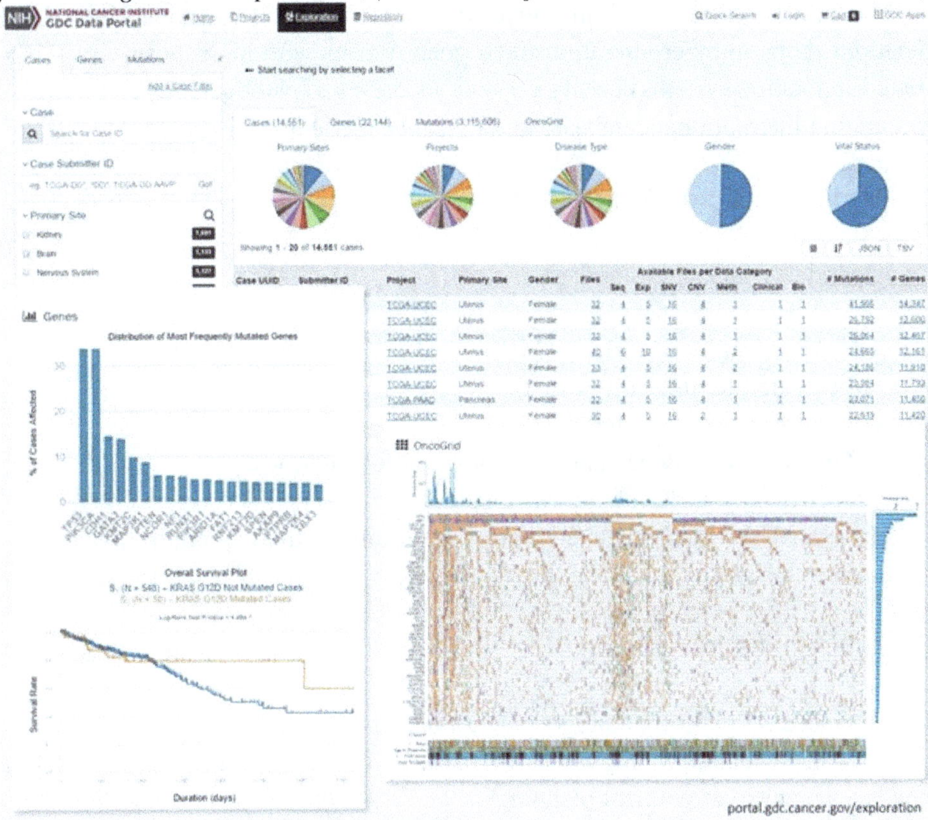

Modern molecular pathology workflows often involve:

- Next-generation sequencing (NGS).
- Polymerase chain reaction (PCR)–based assays.
- Fluorescence in situ hybridization (FISH).
- Comparative genomic hybridization (CGH).
- Transcriptomic profiling.
- Circulating tumor DNA (ctDNA) analysis.

These techniques generate vast quantities of complex data. AI-driven bioinformatics platforms are essential for:

1. Variant Detection and Annotation

Machine learning algorithms identify single nucleotide variants, insertions/deletions, copy number alterations, and gene fusions with high sensitivity. Automated annotation systems classify variants according to pathogenicity frameworks, integrating international databases and evidence hierarchies.

2. Predictive Biomarker Analysis

AI models evaluate biomarkers such as:

- Tumor mutational burden (TMB).
- Microsatellite instability (MSI).
- PD-L1 expression patterns.
- EGFR, KRAS, BRAF, and other actionable mutations.

These analyses guide targeted therapy and immunotherapy eligibilitykey considerations for international oncology patients.

3. Multi-Omics Integration

Advanced AI platforms integrate genomic, transcriptomic, proteomic, and histologic data to generate comprehensive disease profiles. Such integrative modeling enhances precision treatment planning.

4. Pharmacogenomic Decision Support

AI-assisted systems predict drug response and toxicity based on genetic polymorphisms, improving safety for patients receiving treatment abroad.

5. Recurrence and Prognostic Modeling

Predictive analytics combine molecular signatures with clinical data to estimate recurrence risk and survival probabilities, enabling evidence-informed patient counseling prior to travel.

2.4 The Convergence of Digital and Molecular Pathology in Medical Tourism

The true power of AI emerges when digital histopathology and molecular diagnostics converge. Computational models now correlate morphologic features with genomic alterations, enabling "virtual molecular profiling" from routine H&E slides in certain contexts. This radiogenomic–pathogenomic integration represents a frontier in AI-enabled diagnostics.

For medical tourism, such integration provides:

- Pre-travel molecular risk assessment.
- Rapid biomarker confirmation.
- Optimized therapeutic stratification.
- Standardized international reporting.
- Reduced diagnostic discordance between institutions

Furthermore, AI enhances quality control within molecular laboratories by detecting contamination patterns, sequencing artifacts, and reporting inconsistencies. These safeguards strengthen institutional credibility in global healthcare markets.

2.5 Strategic Implications for Cross-Border Healthcare

Digital and molecular pathology augmented by AI redefine the structural architecture of medical tourism. Diagnosis becomes:

- Digitally transferable.
- Computationally reproducible.
- Globally consultative.
- Biomarker-driven.
- Evidence-standardized.

This transformation reduces diagnostic uncertainty, shortens turnaround times, and strengthens multidisciplinary coordination. It also positions pathology laboratories in medical tourism hubs as centers of technological excellence capable of delivering precision diagnostics aligned with international standards. Digital pathology forms the infrastructural backbone of AI diagnostics, while molecular pathology provides the biological depth necessary for precision medicine(Jang & Lee, 2025). Artificial intelligence integrates these domains into a cohesive, scalable, and globally interoperable diagnostic ecosystemone that serves as the cornerstone of intelligent medical tourism in the 21st century.

2.6 Predictive Molecular Modeling

Predictive molecular modeling represents one of the most transformative applications of artificial intelligence in modern precision medicine. By integrating high-dimensional genomic, transcriptomic, proteomic, and clinicopathologic datasets, AI-driven predictive systems move beyond descriptive diagnostics toward prognostic and therapeutic forecasting(Khan et al., 2026). In the context of medical tourismwhere patients often travel for complex oncologic, transplant, or advanced therapeutic interventionssuch predictive analytics are not merely advantageous; they are strategically indispensable.Traditional molecular pathology identifies actionable mutations and biomarkers. Predictive molecular modeling extends this paradigm by using machine learning algorithms to analyze patterns across thousands of variables simultaneously. These models incorporate:

- Somatic mutation profiles.
- Gene expression signatures.
- Epigenetic modifications.
- Tumor microenvironment characteristics.
- Immune infiltration metrics.
- Histopathological image features.
- Clinical staging parameters.
- Demographic and lifestyle data,

Through advanced computational techniquesincluding deep neural networks, random forest models, survival regression algorithms, and Bayesian probabilistic frameworksAI systems generate individualized risk predictions and treatment response probabilities.

3. AI-ENABLED DIAGNOSTICS IN CROSS-BORDER ONCOLOGY

Oncology remains one of the most significant drivers of medical tourism worldwide. Patients frequently travel across borders in search of advanced diagnostics, precision oncology services, novel immunotherapies, proton beam therapy, robotic oncologic surgery, or access to clinical trials unavailable in their home countries. In such settings, diagnostic precision is not merely desirableit is foundational. Cancer management decisions rely heavily on accurate staging, histologic classification, molecular profiling, and biomarker quantification(Passaro et al., 2024). Any diagnostic inconsistency across institutions or countries can profoundly alter therapeutic strategy, prognosis estimation, and financial planning. Artificial intelligence (AI) has emerged as a transformative force in strengthening oncologic diagnostics across distributed healthcare systems, ensuring consistency, reproducibility, and biological accuracy in cross-border cancer care.

AI enhances oncologic diagnostics primarily through integrated radiology–pathology correlation and automated biomarker quantification. These technologies collectively form the backbone of computational oncology, where multimodal datasets are synthesized into cohesive diagnostic and predictive models. In cross-border oncology programs, such integration mitigates fragmentation and preserves diagnostic integrity when patients transition between healthcare systems.

3.1 Integrated Radiology–Pathology Correlation

Historically, radiology and pathology have functioned as complementary yet distinct diagnostic disciplines. Radiologic imaging provides a macroscopic perspective of tumor burden, spatial distribution, vascularity, and organ involvement, while pathology offers microscopic and molecular confirmation of disease type and biological behavior(García-Figueiras et al., 2019). However, discrepancies between imaging findings and histopathologic interpretation have long posed challenges in cancer staging and treatment planning. Artificial intelligence now bridges these domains by integrating imaging phenotypes with histomorphologic and genomic data into unified analytical frameworks.

Figure 10. Integrated radiomics–genomics workflow for endometrial cancer, (Hoivik et al., 2021).

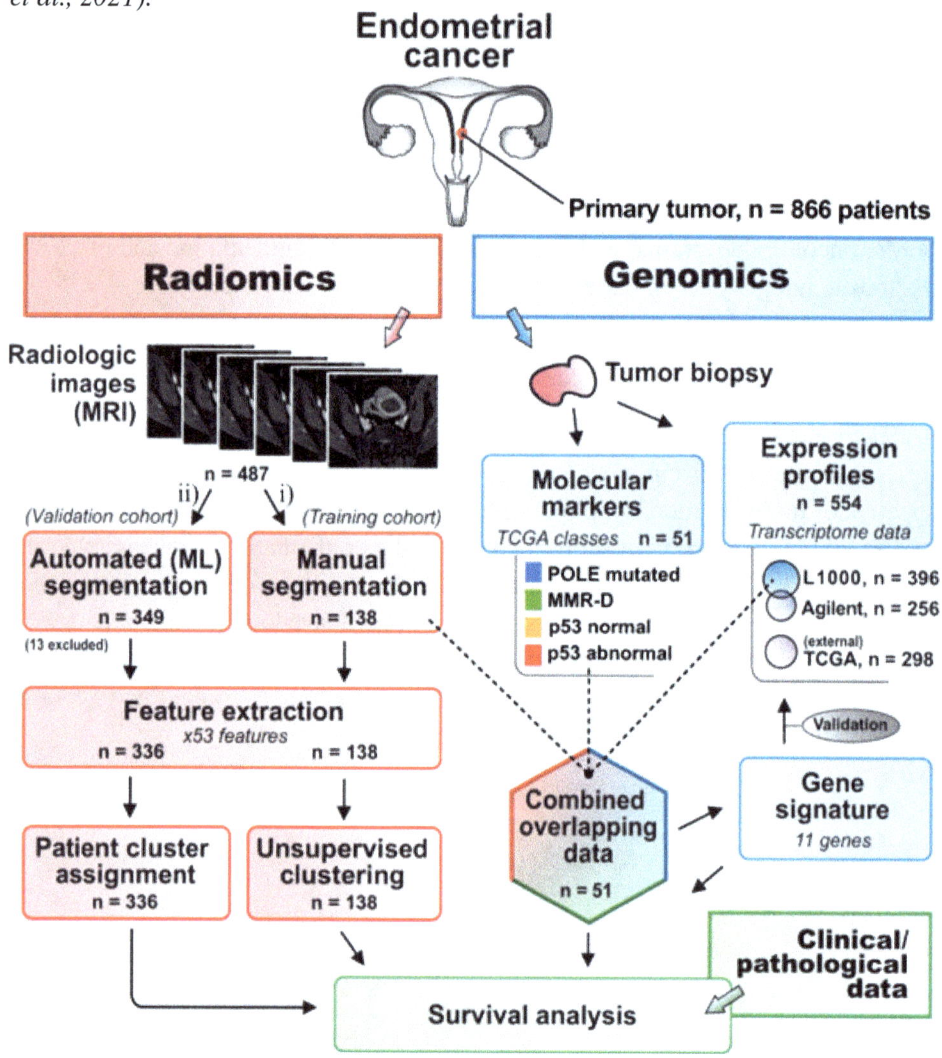

Through radiogenomicmodeling, AI systems analyze imaging characteristics such as tumor texture heterogeneity, enhancement kinetics, diffusion patterns, and margin irregularity. These features are computationally correlated with histologic grade, cellular density, necrosis patterns, stromal composition, and underlying molecular alterations(Saxena et al., 2022). Deep learning algorithms trained on large annotated datasets can predict tumor subtypes and even specific genomic mutations based solely on radiologic signatures. When combined with digital pathology inputs, this multimodal integration significantly enhances staging precision and risk stratification.

In the context of medical tourism, integrated radiology–pathology systems are particularly valuable. Patients may undergo diagnostic imaging in their home country, travel abroad for biopsy or surgery, and receive molecular testing in yet another specialized center. Without integration, such distributed data streams risk fragmentation. AI-enabled systems consolidate imaging, histopathology, and molecular reports into cohesive diagnostic models, reducing the risk of understaging, overstaging, or misclassification(Fatima et al., 2024). For international patients with limited treatment windows, this computational harmonization safeguards clinical accuracy and optimizes therapeutic sequencing.

Digital pathology serves as a critical enabler of this integration. Whole-slide imaging transforms glass slides into high-resolution digital datasets that can be computationally analyzed alongside radiologic scans(Masjoodi et al., 2025).AI-generated heatmaps identify regions of highest tumor grade, quantify tumor burden, detect lymphovascular invasion, and delineate tumor margins. When mapped against radiologic tumor volume and spatial distribution, discrepancies become evident and clinically actionable. For example, infiltrative tumor extensions that appear radiographically subtle may be confirmed histologically as aggressive invasive fronts(Chen et al., 2017). Conversely, radiologic suspicion of extensive disease may be refined through microscopic evaluation, preventing unnecessary radical interventions. Such bidirectional validation strengthens staging accuracy and enhances multidisciplinary tumor board discussions across institutions.

Beyond morphology, AI also integrates molecular pathology into radiology–pathology correlation models. Genomic alterations, transcriptomic signatures, and immune microenvironment features are computationally linked with imaging phenotypes. Tumors with high mutational burden, for instance, often exhibit radiologic heterogeneity reflective of clonal diversity(Bayati et al., 2025). Certain driver mutations correlate with specific enhancement patterns or growth kinetics. By incorporating molecular parameters into imaging-pathology models, AI provides a more biologically informed understanding of tumorbehavior. In cross-border oncology, where patients often travel specifically for targeted therapies, such integration ensures that therapeutic decisions are grounded in comprehensive biologic profiling rather than isolated diagnostic silos.

3.2 Biomarker Quantification

Modern oncology increasingly depends on precise biomarker quantification to determine eligibility for targeted therapy, endocrine treatment, and immunotherapy. Immunohistochemistry and in situ hybridization remain central tools in molecular pathology, yet traditional manual interpretation introduces subjectivity and inter-observer variability(HAWES et al., 2009). Differences in staining protocols, scoring thresholds, and institutional practices can lead to inconsistent results, particularly when patients seek second opinions abroad. Artificial intelligence addresses these limitations through automated, reproducible quantitative analysis.

AI-assisted image analysis systems detect tumor cells, distinguish them from stromal or inflammatory elements, measure staining intensity, and calculate percentage positivity with high precision. In the assessment of PD-L1 expression, for example, AI can determine tumor proportion scores and combined positive scores with consistent threshold application(Yan et al., 2024). Given that eligibility for immune checkpoint inhibitors often depends on narrowly defined cutoffs, such standardization directly influences treatment access. For international patients investing in immunotherapy abroad, accurate and reproducible PD-L1 scoring reduces uncertainty and avoids costly misclassification.

HER2 amplification assessment represents another domain where AI-driven quantification enhances consistency. In breast and gastric carcinomas, HER2 overexpression determines eligibility for trastuzumab and related agents. Automated membrane staining analysis reduces equivocal interpretations and ensures that amplification status is accurately categorized(Robbins et al., 2025). Similarly, Ki-67 proliferation index measurementcritical for grading and therapeutic planningis significantly more reproducible when automated counting replaces manual estimation(Micsik et al., 2026). Estrogen and progesterone receptor scoring in hormone-responsive cancers also benefits from AI-based intensity and percentage quantification, supporting consistent endocrine therapy decisions across institutions.

The implications for cross-border oncology are substantial. Variability in biomarker interpretation can lead to denial of targeted therapies, inappropriate treatment selection, or repeated biopsies. AI-driven standardization harmonizes scoring criteria across healthcare systems, reducing geographic bias and technical inconsistencies(Chinta et al., 2025). Furthermore, digital biomarker quantification facilitates remote consultation, allowing expert review without physical slide transfer. This capability is especially valuable in medical tourism, where time-sensitive treatment decisions must be made efficiently.

Beyond protein expression, AI extends into molecular variant interpretation within next-generation sequencing (NGS) workflows. Machine learning algorithms assist in classifying genomic variants as pathogenic, likely pathogenic, or of uncertain significance by analyzing large-scale genomic databases and published evidence(Athanasopoulou et al., 2025). In rare tumors or complex molecular profiles, AI-supported interpretation accelerates reporting while maintaining analytical rigor. For patients traveling internationally to access precision oncology programs, rapid and accurate genomic interpretation is essential to initiating targeted therapies without delay.

Toward a Unified Computational Oncology Framework

The convergence of radiology, digital pathology, and molecular analytics through artificial intelligence marks a paradigm shift in cancer diagnostics. Rather than relying on sequential, siloed evaluations, AI-enabled systems synthesize diverse datasets into integrated diagnostic models(Fahim et al., 2025). This computational oncology framework enhances staging precision, reduces interpretive variability, and strengthens therapeutic alignment with tumor biology.

In the context of medical tourism, such integration is transformative. Cross-border care inherently introduces logistical complexity, institutional variability, and potential fragmentation of data. AI functions as a unifying analytical infrastructure that preserves diagnostic coherence despite geographic dispersion. It ensures that international patients receive care informed by comprehensive, standardized, and biologically precise diagnostics.As oncology continues to evolve toward increasingly personalized treatment paradigms, AI-enabled diagnostics will play an indispensable role in safeguarding accuracy and equity across global healthcare systems. In cross-border oncology, where patients often face high financial stakes and significant clinical risk, computational precision becomes not merely a technological advancement but an ethical imperative.

4. AI-ASSISTED TREATMENT PLANNING IN MEDICAL TOURISM

Treatment planning in medical tourism carries unique complexity. International patients frequently travel for high-cost, high-risk interventions that require precise coordination across diagnostic, surgical, and post-treatment pathways. Unlike routine care within a single healthcare system, cross-border treatment planning must integrate pre-travel diagnostics, remote consultations, institutional protocols, and international clinical guidelines. Artificial intelligence (AI) has emerged as a critical enabler in this environment, transforming treatment planning from a largely clinician-dependent process into a data-driven, algorithmically supported framework. By integrating pathology, molecular data, imaging, and patient-specific variables, AI enhances precision, reduces variability, and strengthens clinical confidence in international healthcare delivery.

4.1 Precision Oncology

Precision oncology represents one of the most advanced applications of AI-assisted treatment planning. Cancer is inherently heterogeneous, with tumorbehavior influenced by histologic subtype, molecular mutations, epigenetic alterations, tumor microenvironment, and host factors. Traditional treatment paradigms relied heavily on tumor location and stage; however, modern oncology requires multi-layered biological characterization. AI platforms now integrate histopathological features, molecular mutation profiles, clinical staging parameters, and patient demographics into unified decision-support systems that generate individualized treatment recommendations.

Through deep learning models trained on large clinical datasets, AI systems analyze digital pathology slides to extract morphologic features such as nuclear atypia, mitotic activity, stromal composition, and tumor-infiltrating immune cells(Sobhani et al., 2021). These features are combined with genomic information derived from next-generation sequencing, including driver mutations, copy number variations, gene expression signatures, and tumor mutational burden(Ghoreyshi et al., 2025). Clinical staging informationtumor size, nodal involvement, and metastatic statusis incorporated alongside patient-specific factors such as age, comorbidities, performance status, and pharmacogenomic variables.

By synthesizing these datasets, AI platforms generate personalized treatment regimens aligned with international evidence-based guidelines such as those from major oncologic societies. Importantly, AI does not replace clinical judgment; rather, it augments multidisciplinary tumor boards by presenting probabilistic outcome predictions, therapeutic response likelihoods, and risk–benefit analyses(Nardone et al., 2024). For international patients traveling for advanced therapies such as immunotherapy, targeted kinase inhibitors, or combination regimens, such precision modeling enhances confidence that treatment selection reflects both global standards and individualized tumor biology.

In medical tourism contexts, AI-supported precision oncology also improves logistical efficiency. Treatment simulations can be performed before patient arrival, allowing institutions to pre-authorize medications, schedule infusion cycles, coordinate molecular testing, and anticipate potential toxicities. This pre-emptive planning minimizes delays, optimizes resource allocation, and reduces the risk of incomplete treatment courses due to international travel constraints. Ultimately, AI-enabled precision oncology transforms cross-border cancer care into a more predictable, transparent, and biologically grounded process.

4.2 Surgical Planning and AI

Surgical intervention remains a cornerstone of treatment in many complex diseases that drive medical tourism, including head and neck cancers, orthopedictumors, hepatobiliary malignancies, and reconstructive defects following oncologic resection(Alfouzan, 2018). In these high-stakes procedures, precise preoperative planning directly influences oncologic control, functional preservation, and postoperative recovery. Artificial intelligence has significantly enhanced surgical planning through advanced imaging analytics, three-dimensional modeling, and predictive simulation.

Figure 11. Schematic illustration of head and neck cancer, (Evangelista et al., 2025).

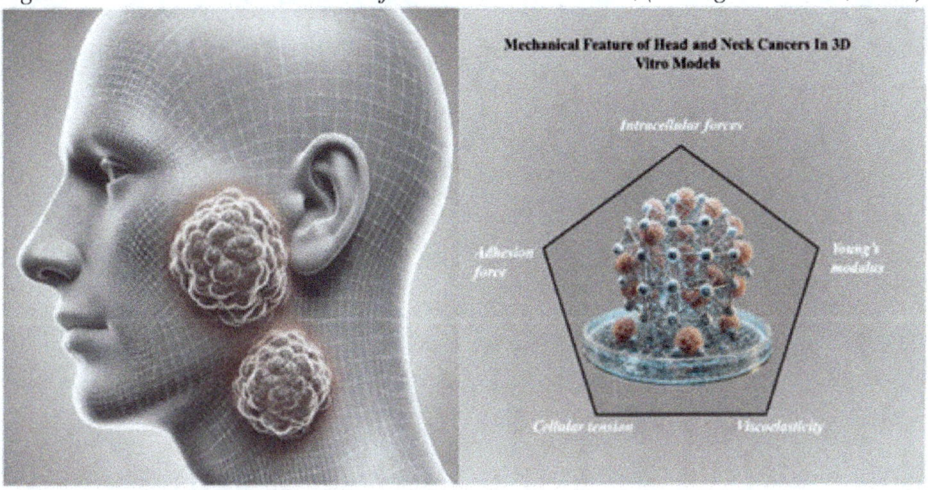

Figure 12. Multicenter study design and reader workflow for evaluating AI-assisted three-dimensional (AI-3D) imaging, (Chen et al., 2025).

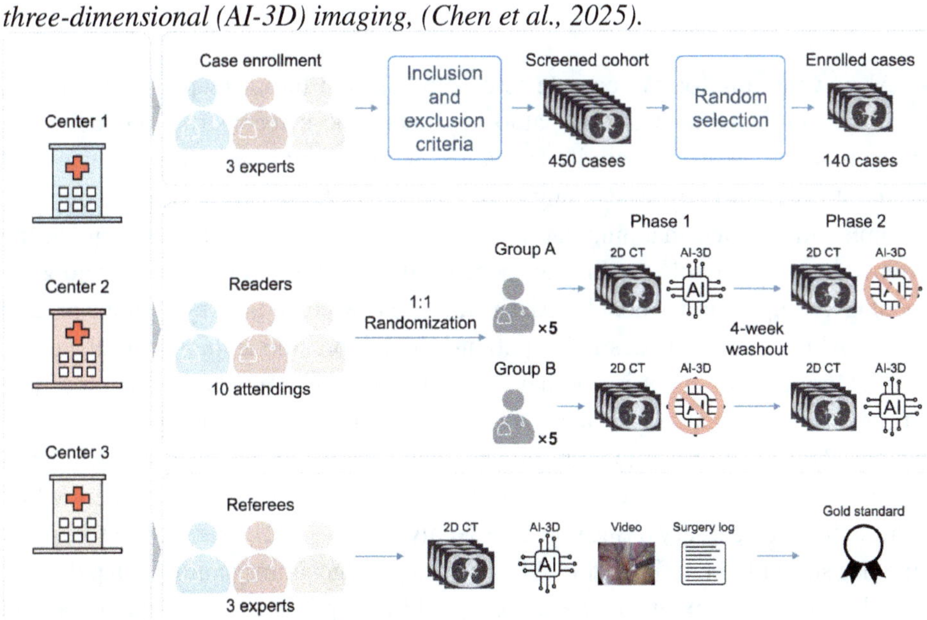

Figure 13. Three-dimensional reconstruction of pelvic anatomy illustrating anterior and posterolateral views, (UH, 2024).

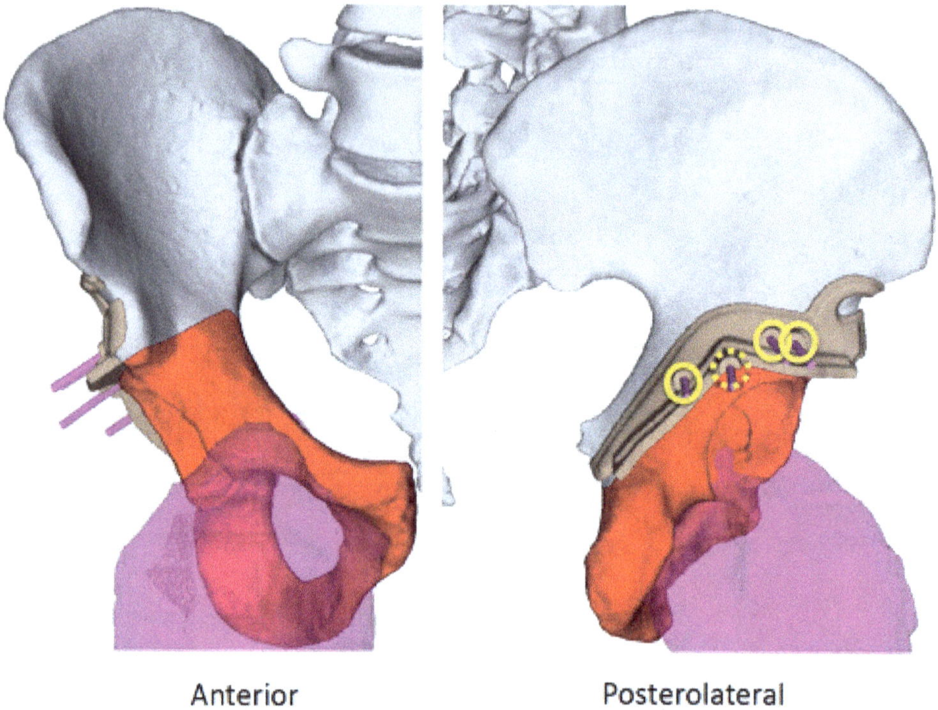

AI-powered platforms generate three-dimensional tumor maps by integrating radiologic imaging with digital pathology data. These reconstructions delineate tumor margins, assess proximity to critical neurovascular structures, and model potential invasion pathways(Zheng et al., 2025). In head and neck oncology, for example, AI-assisted mapping can predict perineural invasion risk and guide the extent of resection while preserving speech and swallowing function. In orthopedic oncology, computational models assist in limb-sparing procedures by defining precise resection boundaries and designing patient-specific prosthetic implants(Aiba et al., 2023).Margin assessment is another domain where AI contributes meaningfully. Intraoperative frozen section analysis supported by AI-driven image recognition can rapidly evaluate resection margins, reducing the risk of residual disease. When combined with preoperative modeling, these tools enhance oncologic safety while minimizing unnecessary tissue sacrifice(Nentwig et al., 2021).Reconstructive planning has similarly benefited from AI integration. Algorithms simulate flap design, vascular supply mapping, and tissue compatibility, optimizing both functional and aesthetic outcomes(Peet et al., 2025). In complex craniofacial or maxillofacial reconstruction, AI supports implant customization using three-dimensional printing technologies. Patient-specific implants designed from digital models ensure superior anatomical fit and reduce intraoperative adjustment time.

For international patients, AI-assisted surgical simulation offers additional advantages. Pre-arrival digital planning allows surgical teams to anticipate procedural complexity, allocate operating room time appropriately, and prepare custom implants in advance. This reduces operative duration, lowers complication risk, and minimizes hospital staycritical considerations for patients traveling from abroad. By decreasing intraoperative uncertainty and resource waste, AI enhances both clinical outcomes and institutional efficiency in medical tourism programs.

4.3 Transplant and Organ Matching

Organ transplantation represents one of the most ethically sensitive and medically complex areas of cross-border healthcare. International patients may seek transplantation services in countries with advanced surgical expertise, shorter waiting times, or specialized transplant programs. However, successful transplantation depends fundamentally on precise donor–recipient compatibility. Artificial intelligence has significantly improved organ matching through sophisticated compatibility scoring algorithms and predictive outcome modeling.

AI-based transplant systems analyze a broad range of variables, including human leukocyte antigen (HLA) matching, blood group compatibility, donor age, organ quality metrics, ischemia time, and recipient immunologic risk factors(Olawade et al., 2025). Machine learning models trained on historical transplant registries predict graft survival probability, rejection risk, and long-term patient outcomes. By integrating immunologic, clinical, and demographic variables, AI provides a more nuanced compatibility assessment than traditional scoring systems.

In cross-border transplant programs, AI-assisted matching enhances transparency and equity by standardizing allocation criteria. Computational models reduce subjective bias and support evidence-based decision-making in donor–recipient pairing. Additionally, predictive analytics help anticipate post-transplant complications such as acute rejection, infection, or graft dysfunction, enabling pre-emptive intervention strategies(Sun et al., 2025).For international patients, AI-driven transplant planning improves confidence in procedural success and long-term viability. Pre-travel evaluation using predictive models can determine candidacy, estimate survival outcomes, and optimize immunosuppressive regimens before transplantation occurs. Such foresight is particularly important when postoperative follow-up may occur partially in the patient's home country.

Strategic Implications for Medical Tourism

AI-assisted treatment planning fundamentally reshapes the structure of medical tourism. By integrating pathology, molecular biology, imaging, and patient-specific variables into cohesive predictive frameworks, AI reduces diagnostic fragmentation and enhances therapeutic precision(Tiwari et al., 2025). It supports multidisciplinary collaboration across geographic boundaries and ensures that high-risk interventions are guided by robust data rather than institutional variability.In cross-border healthcare environments where patients often face substantial financial investment and clinical uncertainty, AI provides a stabilizing analytical infrastructure. It transforms treatment planning into a transparent, reproducible, and biologically informed process. As global healthcare systems continue to evolve, AI-assisted planning will likely become a defining feature of high-quality international medical programs, strengthening both patient trust and clinical excellence.

5. CLINICAL DECISION SUPPORT SYSTEMS (CDSS) INTEGRATED WITH PATHOLOGY

Clinical Decision Support Systems (CDSS) represent one of the most practical and clinically impactful applications of artificial intelligence in modern healthcare. When integrated directly with pathologyincluding histopathology, molecular diagnostics, and digital biomarker quantificationCDSS transform diagnostic information into actionable therapeutic guidance(Elhaddad & Hamam, 2024). In the context of medical tourism, where patients frequently transition between healthcare systems, institutions, and regulatory environments, CDSS function as a stabilizing mechanism that preserves continuity, accuracy, and adherence to international standards of care.

Pathology generates vast amounts of complex data, ranging from tumor grading and staging to genomic mutation profiles and biomarker expression scores. Traditionally, the translation of this information into treatment decisions depended heavily on clinician experience and familiarity with evolving guidelines. However, the rapid expansion of molecular oncology and targeted therapies has made manual synthesis increasingly challenging. CDSS platforms address this gap by automatically extracting relevant pathology data from digital reports and integrating it into therapeutic workflows in real time.

When a molecular pathology report identifies actionable mutationssuch as alterations in oncogenic signaling pathwaysCDSS systems immediately flag these findings within the electronic health record. The system cross-references mutation databases, regulatory approvals, and international treatment guidelines to alert oncologists to available targeted therapies. This automated alerting mechanism reduces the risk that clinically significant genomic findings are overlooked, particularly in complex cases involving multiple variants(Zorn et al., 2022). In cross-border oncology, where clinicians may encounter rare tumor subtypes or unfamiliar genomic patterns, such alerts provide an additional layer of safety and precision.

Beyond mutation detection, CDSS platforms play a crucial role in identifying eligibility for clinical trials(Karuppan Perumal et al., 2025). International patients often travel specifically to access investigational therapies unavailable in their home countries. By analyzing pathology dataincluding histologic subtype, biomarker thresholds, mutational signatures, and prior treatment historyAI-driven systems can match patients with ongoing clinical trials that align with their molecular profile. This capability accelerates enrollment processes and ensures that potentially beneficial investigational options are considered systematically rather than incidentally.

Figure 14. Web-based clinical decision support interface, (Vrel et al., 2021).

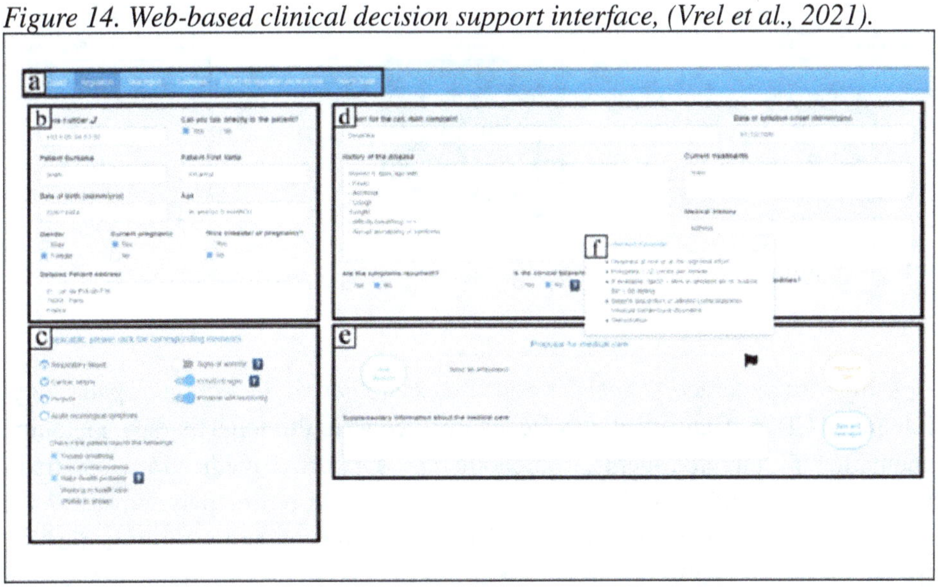

Figure 15. End-to-end framework for machine learning using electronic health record (EHR)–linked multimodal data, (Leveraging Electronic Health Records and Artificial Intelligence for Automated Health Outcome Analysis, 2026).

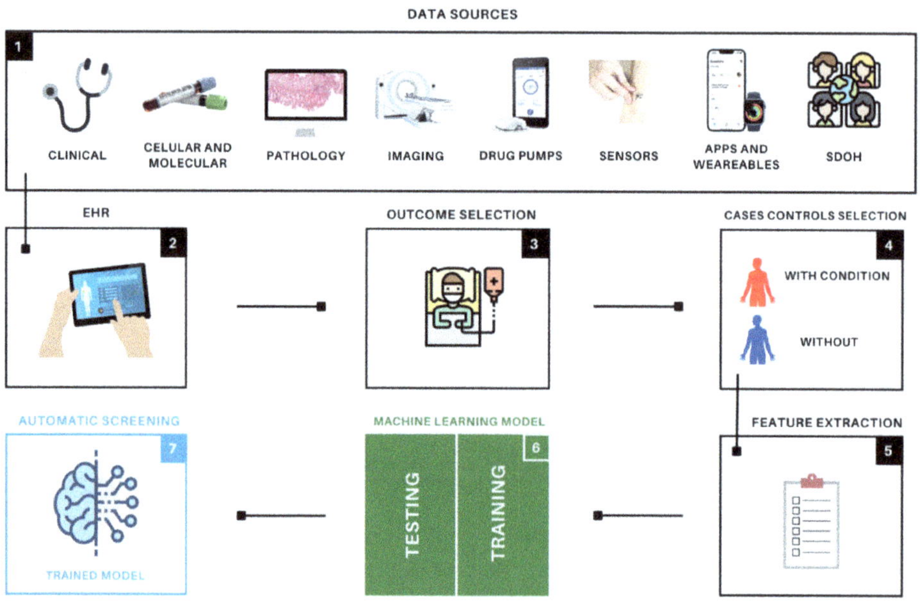

Adapted from Cossio.[8]
EHR indicates electronic health record; SDoH, social determinants of health.

Drug–drug interaction analysis constitutes another vital function of pathology-integrated CDSS. Cancer patients frequently receive multimodal therapy, including chemotherapy, targeted agents, immunotherapy, supportive medications, and treatments for comorbid conditions(Ismail et al., 2020). AI-powered systems evaluate pharmacogenomic data, liver and renal function parameters, and existing medication lists to identify potential adverse interactions or contraindications(Haga, 2024). In medical tourism settings, where medication histories may originate from different healthcare systems with varying documentation standards, automated interaction screening enhances patient safety.Importantly, CDSS platforms continuously align therapeutic recommendations with established international guidelines. By incorporating consensus statements and regularly updated evidence-based protocols, these systems recommend guideline-concordant therapies tailored to the patient's specific pathologic and molecular characteristics. For example, when pathology reports indicate hormone receptor–positive breast carcinoma with defined HER2 status and Ki-67 index, the CDSS synthesizes these inputs to recommend appropriate endocrine therapy, targeted agents, or chemotherapy regimens consistent with global standards. This ensures that treatment decisions remain consistent regardless of geographic location.

For medical tourism patients, CDSS provide an additional layer of continuity across unfamiliar healthcare environments. International patients often arrive with diagnostic reports generated in one country and undergo treatment in another. Variability in reporting formats, terminology, and clinical practice patterns can create uncertainty. CDSS mitigate this fragmentation by standardizing data interpretation and embedding pathology findings directly into structured therapeutic pathways(Omoseebi& Samson Anderson, 2025). Even when treating physicians are unfamiliar with the patient's original health system, algorithm-driven decision support ensures that care remains coherent and evidence-based.Moreover, CDSS facilitate multidisciplinary collaboration. Pathologists, oncologists, surgeons, radiologists, and transplant teams can access shared dashboards that integrate pathology data with imaging and clinical parameters. AI-generated summaries highlight key diagnostic findings and therapeutic implications, streamlining tumor board discussions and accelerating consensus building. In cross-border care models, where coordination must often occur remotely, this digital integration enhances efficiency and reduces miscommunication.

From a systems perspective, pathology-integrated CDSS also support quality assurance and audit processes. By tracking whether recommended therapies align with guideline-based suggestions, institutions can monitor adherence rates, identify deviations, and implement corrective measures(Shahmoradi et al., 2021). For international programs competing in the global medical tourism market, such quality metrics strengthen institutional credibility and accreditation standing.Ultimately, the integration of pathology into AI-driven Clinical Decision Support Systems redefines the diagnostic–therapeutic interface. Pathology no longer serves solely as a diagnostic endpoint but becomes an active driver of real-time clinical decision-making. In medical tourism, where patients navigate complex, high-risk interventions across borders, CDSS ensure that precision diagnostics translate seamlessly into safe, standardized, and globally aligned treatment pathways.

6. PRE-TRAVEL AI-DRIVEN DIAGNOSTIC ECOSYSTEM

The evolution of artificial intelligence has enabled the development of a comprehensive pre-travel diagnostic ecosystem that allows international patients to make informed, data-driven decisions before crossing borders for treatment. In traditional medical tourism models, patients often traveled based on preliminary reports, generalized second opinions, or institutional reputation. Today, AI-enabled digital infrastructures allow detailed diagnostic validation, risk prediction, and therapeutic simulation to occur remotely, reducing uncertainty and enhancing patient confidence.

One of the most transformative components of this ecosystem is remote digital slide review. Through digital pathology platforms, glass slides are converted into high-resolution whole-slide images and securely uploaded to cloud-based systems. Expert pathologists in destination centers can review, annotate, and analyze cases without physical slide shipment. AI algorithms simultaneously evaluate tumor morphology, grade malignancy, quantify biomarkers, and detect subtle diagnostic features that may influence treatment strategy(Najar Najafi et al., 2025). This remote validation minimizes diagnostic discordance and ensures that the therapeutic plan formulated abroad is based on accurate and standardized pathology interpretation.

Cloud-based genomic interpretation further strengthens pre-travel assessment. Next-generation sequencing data can be uploaded to secure platforms where AI-driven variant classification tools analyze mutations, copy number alterations, gene fusions, and expression signatures(Onsongo et al., 2014). These systems cross-reference global genomic databases and therapeutic registries to identify actionable targets and match them with approved or investigational therapies available in the destination country. For patients considering international travel for precision oncology, such comprehensive molecular interpretation clarifies whether advanced therapies are likely to be beneficial before incurring significant financial and logistical commitments.

Predictive outcome modeling adds another layer of strategic planning. AI systems integrate histopathologic features, molecular profiles, imaging data, and clinical staging to estimate survival probabilities, recurrence risk, treatment response likelihood, and potential complication rates(Dixon et al., 2024). These probabilistic models provide patients and clinicians with realistic expectations regarding therapeutic outcomes. In high-cost, high-risk interventions such as immunotherapy, complex oncologic surgery, or transplantation, predictive analytics help ensure that travel decisions are grounded in objective evidence rather than optimism alone.

Risk stratification models also assist in determining procedural candidacy and perioperative planning. AI tools evaluate comorbidities, functional status, laboratory parameters, and disease biology to classify patients into risk categories(Bukret, 2025). This allows international centers to preemptively optimize care pathways, anticipate complications, and allocate resources efficiently. For patients, such structured pre-travel evaluation enhances transparency and reduces the likelihood of unexpected exclusions or treatment delays upon arrival. Collectively, the pre-travel AI-driven diagnostic ecosystem transforms medical tourism from a reactive process into a proactive, analytically informed journey.

7. POST-TREATMENT MONITORING AND MOLECULAR SURVEILLANCE

The responsibilities of medical tourism providers do not end at discharge. Continuity of care after patients return to their home countries remains one of the most critical challenges in cross-border healthcare. Artificial intelligence has significantly improved post-treatment monitoring by enabling remote surveillance systems that maintain diagnostic vigilance and therapeutic oversight beyond geographic boundaries.

Circulating tumor DNA (ctDNA) monitoring represents one of the most advanced forms of molecular surveillance. Tumor-derived DNA fragments detectable in peripheral blood provide a minimally invasive method for tracking residual disease, early recurrence, and treatment response(Bartolomucci et al., 2025). AI algorithms analyze ctDNA sequencing patterns to detect minimal residual disease at levels far below conventional imaging thresholds. For patients who undergo surgery or targeted therapy abroad, ctDNA monitoring allows early identification of recurrence after returning home, enabling timely intervention without requiring repeated international travel.

AI-enhanced radiologic follow-up also plays a central role in longitudinal care. Machine learning models trained in image recognition compare serial imaging studies to detect subtle changes in tumor size, density, or metabolic activity. These systems reduce observer variability and improve early detection of progression(Patharia et al., 2024). When integrated with molecular data, radiologic AI tools provide a comprehensive picture of disease trajectory. Such coordinated surveillance is especially valuable when imaging is performed in the patient's home country but interpreted collaboratively with the treating institution abroad.

Digital wound monitoring has emerged as another application of AI in postoperative care. Patients can upload high-resolution images of surgical sites through secure telemedicine platforms, where computer vision algorithms evaluate healing progress, detect early signs of infection, and assess tissue viability(Macefield et al., 2023). This reduces the need for unnecessary travel while ensuring prompt recognition of complications. In reconstructive and head and neck oncology procedures, where wound healing and flap viability are critical, AI-supported monitoring enhances safety and reassurance.

Remote toxicity tracking further supports continuity of care. AI-driven platforms collect patient-reported outcomes, laboratory data, and wearable device metrics to identify early signs of treatment-related adverse effects. Algorithms flag abnormalities in liver function, hematologic parameters, cardiac rhythm, or inflammatory markers, prompting timely clinical intervention(Abedi et al., 2025). For international oncology patients receiving chemotherapy or immunotherapy abroad, such monitoring ensures that adverse events are managed proactively even after repatriation.By integrating molecular surveillance, imaging analytics, wound assessment, and toxicity monitoring, AI establishes a virtual continuum of care that bridges geographic separation. This sustained oversight enhances safety, supports long-term outcome optimization, and reinforces patient trust in cross-border healthcare systems.

8. ETHICAL AND REGULATORY CONSIDERATIONS IN AI-ENABLED PATHOLOGY

While AI-driven pathology and diagnostic integration offer substantial benefits, their implementation in cross-border healthcare raises complex ethical and regulatory challenges. Responsible deployment requires rigorous governance frameworks to safeguard patient rights, ensure algorithmic fairness, and maintain clinical accountability.

8.1 Data Governance

Cross-border exchange of pathology dataincluding digital slides, genomic sequences, and clinical recordsdemands robust data governance structures. Secure cloud storage with end-to-end encryption is essential to protect sensitive medical information during transmission and storage(Xia et al., 2024). Authentication protocols, access control systems, and audit trails must be implemented to prevent unauthorized access or data breaches.Transparent informed consent is equally critical; patients must understand how their pathology data will be stored, analyzed, shared, and potentially used for algorithm training(Stroud et al., 2025). Consent processes should clarify cross-jurisdictional data handling policies and outline mechanisms for data withdrawal where applicable. Given the sensitivity of genomic information, which may have familial implications, ethical stewardship is paramount in international settings.

8.2 Algorithm Bias

Algorithmic bias represents a significant concern in AI-enabled diagnostics. Many AI models are trained on datasets derived from specific populations, institutions, or geographic regions. When applied to genetically and ethnically diverse international patients, these models may exhibit reduced accuracy or misclassification risk(Panch et al., 2019). In oncology, even subtle diagnostic discrepancies can alter staging, biomarker interpretation, or therapeutic eligibility(Chaudhry, Khan, & Ehtesham, 2026).Mitigating bias requires diverse training datasets, continuous performance monitoring, and external validation across varied populations. Institutions engaged in medical tourism must ensure that AI tools demonstrate equitable performance irrespective of patient ethnicity, socioeconomic background, or geographic origin. Transparency in algorithm development and validation metrics supports trust and ethical accountability.

8.3 Validation and Accreditation

Before deployment in clinical workflows, AI tools must undergo rigorous local validation within the institutions that implement them. Performance metricsincluding sensitivity, specificity, reproducibility, and false-positive ratesshould be audited regularly. International medical tourism centers should integrate AI evaluation into their accreditation and quality assurance frameworks.Explainable AI integration is particularly important in pathology. Clinicians must understand the rationale behind algorithmic outputs, especially when recommendations influence high-risk treatment decisions. Heatmaps, feature importance analyses, and transparent reporting interfaces enhance interpretability and strengthen clinician oversight(Ennab&Mcheick, 2024). AI should function as a decision-support partner rather than an opaque authority. Institutional governance bodies must also define accountability structures. Clear delineation of responsibilitybetween pathologists, oncologists, data scientists, and healthcare administratorsensures that AI-supported decisions remain grounded in professional standards. Regulatory harmonization across jurisdictions will be increasingly necessary as cross-border AI-driven diagnostics expand.

9. A FOUR-DOMAIN INTEGRATED MODEL FOR AI-ENABLED MEDICAL TOURISM

To conceptualize the transformative potential of AI in medical tourism, we propose a four-domain integrated model that positions pathologyparticularly molecular and digital pathologyat the core of cross-border care. The first domain, Pre-Travel Digital Diagnostics, encompasses remote pathology slide review, cloud-based genomic analysis, and predictive outcome modelling (Matias-Guiu et al., 2025). This phase enables patients to make evidence-informed travel decisions by providing accurate diagnostic confirmation and risk stratification prior to arrival at the destination center.

The second domain, AI-Guided In-Treatment Precision, involves real-time integration of pathology, molecular profiles, radiology, and clinical parameters to inform treatment planning. AI-assisted precision oncology, surgical simulation, transplant compatibility scoring, and guideline-aligned therapeutic recommendations converge in this domain. By centralizing pathology-derived insights into multidisciplinary workflows, international centers can ensure that interventions are biologically informed, reproducible, and optimized for individual patients.

The third domain, Post-Treatment Molecular Surveillance, addresses the unique challenges of continuity of care for patients returning home(Khan et al., 2025). AI-powered monitoringincluding circulating tumor DNA analysis, radiologic follow-up, digital wound evaluation, and toxicity trackingmaintains a virtual continuum of care. By integrating pathology-derived biomarkers with longitudinal patient data, clinicians can detect recurrence, monitor therapeutic response, and identify complications efficiently, despite geographic separation.

The fourth domain, Governance and Ethical Oversight, provides the structural and ethical foundation for AI-enabled medical tourism. Secure data storage, cross-border encryption protocols, algorithmic transparency, bias mitigation, and local validation processes are critical to ensuring responsible AI adoption(Chaudhry, Khan, & Ehtesham, 2026).

10. FUTURE DIRECTIONS IN AI AND PATHOLOGY

The future of AI-enabled pathology in medical tourism is marked by the emergence of increasingly sophisticated computational approaches that extend beyond traditional histology and molecular profiling. One promising avenue is the development of foundation models trained on multi-omic datasets, capable of integrating genomics, transcriptomics, proteomics, metabolomics, and imaging data to predict disease phenotypes, therapeutic response, and progression risk. Such models promise to accelerate precision oncology and other specialty-driven medical tourism domains by providing comprehensive, biologically informed decision support.

Federated learning represents another frontier, enabling AI models to be trained across multiple institutions without sharing sensitive patient data. By leveraging distributed datasets while maintaining privacy, federated learning facilitates the development of highly generalizable AI tools suitable for ethnically and geographically diverse patient populationsa critical consideration in cross-border healthcare(Horst et al., 2025).AI is also advancing toward molecular phenotype prediction from morphology, where digital pathology images are analyzed to infer genomic, transcriptomic, or proteomic characteristics(Qiao et al., 2022). This approach may allow preliminary molecular insights to be obtained directly from histologic slides, reducing reliance on costly or time-consuming molecular assays while maintaining predictive accuracy.

Autonomous quality control systems will increasingly support laboratory operations, ensuring consistency in slide preparation, staining, scanning, and digital image analysis. These systems reduce human error, standardize workflows across institutions, and provide real-time feedback to pathologists and technicians, supporting global interoperability(Munari et al., 2023).Finally, integrated radiogenomic–pathogenomic models will combine imaging, histopathology, molecular profiles, and microbiologic data into unified predictive frameworks. Such integrated approaches may enable early detection of metastatic risk, treatment resistance, or infection complications in oncology and transplant patients, further enhancing the safety and efficacy of cross-border interventions.

11. CONCLUSION

The integration of artificial intelligence into pathology, molecular diagnostics, and digital histopathology represents a paradigm shift for medical tourism. Diagnosis is no longer confined to local laboratories and conventional glass slides; it has become digital, algorithmically enhanced, and globally interoperable. By augmenting diagnostic precision, AI enables personalized treatment planning, standardizes clinical decision-making, and strengthens continuity of care across borders.

For medical tourism patients, AI-enabled pathology transforms care from a transactional service into a coordinated, data-driven ecosystem. International treatment planning becomes predictive rather than reactive, surgical interventions become safer and more precise, and post-treatment surveillance can be sustained through molecular and digital monitoring.The success of AI in medical tourism, however, is contingent not only upon technological innovation but also on robust ethical governance, cross-border regulatory harmonization, and sustained professional leadership from pathologists and molecular diagnosticians. By situating pathology at the center of intelligent healthcare mobility, stakeholders can build resilient, equitable, and globally competitive medical tourism systems that meet the highest standards of clinical excellence, patient safety, and scientific rigor.This integrated, AI-enabled framework positions the medical tourism sector at the forefront of 21st-century healthcare, offering patients worldwide access to precise, efficient, and ethically responsible diagnostic and therapeutic services.

REFERENCES

Abedi, A., Verma, A., Jain, D., Kaetheeswaran, J., Chui, C., Lankarany, M., & Khan, S. S. (2025). AI-Driven Real-Time Monitoring of Cardiovascular Conditions With Wearable Devices: Scoping Review. *JMIR mHealth and uHealth, 13*, e73846. DOI: 10.2196/73846 PMID: 41218203

Aiba, H., Spazzoli, B., Tsukamoto, S., Mavrogenis, A. F., Hermann, T., Kimura, H., Murakami, H., Donati, D. M., & Errani, C. (2023). Current Concepts in the Resection of Bone Tumors Using a Patient-Specific Three-Dimensional Printed Cutting Guide. *Current Oncology (Toronto, Ont.), 30*(4), 3859–3870. DOI: 10.3390/curroncol30040292 PMID: 37185405

Alfouzan, A. F. (2018). Review of surgical resection and reconstruction in head and neck cancer. *Saudi Medical Journal, 39*(10), 971–980. DOI: 10.15537/smj.2018.10.22887 PMID: 30284578

Athanasopoulou, K., Michalopoulou, V.-I., Scorilas, A., & Adamopoulos, P. G. (2025). Integrating Artificial Intelligence in Next-Generation Sequencing: Advances, Challenges, and Future Directions. *Current Issues in Molecular Biology, 47*(6), 470. DOI: 10.3390/cimb47060470 PMID: 40699869

Bartolomucci, A., Nobrega, M., Ferrier, T., Dickinson, K., Kaorey, N., Nadeau, A., Castillo, A., & Burnier, J. V. (2025). Circulating tumor DNA to monitor treatment response in solid tumors and advance precision oncology. *NPJ Precision Oncology, 9*(1), 84. Advance online publication. DOI: 10.1038/s41698-025-00876-y PMID: 40122951

Bayati, M., Klein, Z. P., Bahcheli, A. T., Slobodyanyuk, M., To, J., Cheng, K. C. L., Mishra, J., Pellegrina, D., Guevara-Hoyer, K., McIntosh, C., Bhat, M., & Reimand, J. (2025). Cancer Genomic Alterations and Microenvironmental Features Encode Synergistic Interactions with Disease Outcomes. *Molecular Cancer Research, 23*(12), 971–983. DOI: 10.1158/1541-7786.MCR-25-0475 PMID: 40900635

Brierley, J., O'Sullivan, B., Asamura, H., Byrd, D., Huang, S. H., Lee, A., Piñeros, M., Mason, M., Moraes, F. Y., Rösler, W., Rous, B., Torode, J., van Krieken, J. H., & Gospodarowicz, M. (2019). Global Consultation on Cancer Staging: Promoting consistent understanding and use. *Nature Reviews. Clinical Oncology, 16*(12), 763–771. DOI: 10.1038/s41571-019-0253-x PMID: 31388125

Bukret, W. E. (2025). Artificial Intelligence–assisted Risk Stratification in Aesthetic Surgery: A Prospective Observational Study. *Plastic and Reconstructive Surgery. Global Open, 13*(7), e6948. DOI: 10.1097/GOX.0000000000006948 PMID: 40672785

Chaudhry, S., & Ehtesham, Z. (2025). Role of Molecular Diagnostics in Oral and Maxillofacial Pathology. *J Oral Health Dent, 8*(1), 625–628.

Chaudhry, S., Khan, S., & Ehtesham, Z. (2026). *Molecular Pathology: Principles, Techniques, and Clinical Applications of Molecular Diagnostics*. De Gruyter. DOI: 10.1515/9783112217719

Chen, C.-L., Chen, C.-C., Yu, W.-H., Chen, S.-H., Chang, Y.-C., Hsu, T.-I., Hsiao, M., Yeh, C.-Y., & Chen, C.-Y. (2021). An annotation-free whole-slide training approach to pathological classification of lung cancer types using deep learning. *Nature Communications, 12*(1), 1193. Advance online publication. DOI: 10.1038/s41467-021-21467-y PMID: 33608558

Chen, W., Bai, P., Pan, J., Xu, Y., & Chen, K. (2017). Changes in Tumor Volumes and Spatial Locations Relative to Normal Tissues During Cervical Cancer Radiotherapy Assessed by Cone Beam Computed Tomography. *Technology in Cancer Research & Treatment, 16*(2), 246–252. DOI: 10.1177/1533034616685942 PMID: 28052737

Chen, X., Dai, C., Peng, M., Wang, D., Sui, X., Duan, L., Wang, X., Wang, X., Weng, W., Wang, S., Zhao, H., Wang, Z., Geng, J., Chen, C., Hu, Y., Hu, Q., Jiang, C., Zheng, H., Bao, Y., & Yang, F. (2025). Artificial intelligence driven 3D reconstruction for enhanced lung surgery planning. *Nature Communications, 16*(1), 4086. Advance online publication. DOI: 10.1038/s41467-025-59200-8 PMID: 40312393

Chinta, S. V., Wang, Z., Palikhe, A., Zhang, X., Kashif, A., Smith, M. A., Liu, J., & Zhang, W. (2025). AI-driven healthcare: A review on ensuring fairness and mitigating bias. *PLOS Digital Health, 4*(5), e0000864. DOI: 10.1371/journal.pdig.0000864 PMID: 40392801

DAVE Tools for Genomic Data Commons. (2017, June 29). Cancer.gov. https://www.cancer.gov/news-events/cancer-currents-blog/2017/gdc-dave-tools

Digital Pathology Microscope Slide Scanners | Whole Slide Imaging. (2021). Leicabiosystems.com. https://www.leicabiosystems.com/digital-pathology/scan/

Dixon, D., Sattar, H., Moros, N., Kesireddy, S. R., Ahsan, H., Lakkimsetti, M., Fatima, M., Doshi, D., Sadhu, K., & Junaid Hassan, M. (2024). Unveiling the Influence of AI Predictive Analytics on Patient Outcomes: A Comprehensive Narrative Review. *Cureus*. Advance online publication. DOI: 10.7759/cureus.59954 PMID: 38854327

Elhaddad, M., & Hamam, S. (2024). AI-Driven Clinical Decision Support Systems: An Ongoing Pursuit of Potential. *Cureus*. Advance online publication. DOI: 10.7759/cureus.57728 PMID: 38711724

Ennab, M., & Mcheick, H. (2024). Enhancing interpretability and accuracy of AI models in healthcare: A comprehensive review on challenges and future directions. *Frontiers in Robotics and AI*, *11*, 1444763. Advance online publication. DOI: 10.3389/frobt.2024.1444763 PMID: 39677978

Evangelista, A., Scocozza, F., Conti, M., Auricchio, F., Conti, B., Dorati, R., Genta, I., Benazzo, M., & Pisani, S. (2025). Exploring Mechanical Features of 3D Head and Neck Cancer Models. *Journal of Functional Biomaterials*, *16*(3), 74. DOI: 10.3390/jfb16030074 PMID: 40137353

Fahim, Y. A., Hasani, I. W., Kabba, S., & Ragab, W. M. (2025). Artificial intelligence in healthcare and medicine: Clinical applications, therapeutic advances, and future perspectives. *European Journal of Medical Research*, *30*(1), 848. Advance online publication. DOI: 10.1186/s40001-025-03196-w PMID: 40988064

Fatima, G., Alhmadi, H., Ali Mahdi, A., Hadi, N., Fedacko, J., Magomedova, A., Parvez, S., & Mehdi Raza, A. (2024). Transforming Diagnostics: A Comprehensive Review of Advances in Digital Pathology. *Cureus*. Advance online publication. DOI: 10.7759/cureus.71890 PMID: 39564069

Gaffney, H., & Mirza, K. M. (2025). Pathology in the artificial intelligence era: Guiding innovation and implementation to preserve human insight. *Academic Pathology*, *12*(1), 100166. DOI: 10.1016/j.acpath.2025.100166 PMID: 40104157

García-Figueiras, R., Baleato-González, S., Padhani, A. R., Luna-Alcalá, A., Vallejo-Casas, J. A., Sala, E., Vilanova, J. C., Koh, D.-M., Herranz-Carnero, M., & Vargas, H. A. (2019). How clinical imaging can assess cancer biology. *Insights Into Imaging*, *10*(1), 28. Advance online publication. DOI: 10.1186/s13244-019-0703-0 PMID: 30830470

Ghoreyshi, N., Heidari, R., Farhadi, A., Chamanara, M., Farahani, N., Vahidi, M., & Behroozi, J. (2025). Next-generation sequencing in cancer diagnosis and treatment: Clinical applications and future directions. *Discover. Oncology*, *16*(1), 578. Advance online publication. DOI: 10.1007/s12672-025-01816-9 PMID: 40253661

Groene, O., Poletti, P., Vallejo, P., Cucic, C., Klazinga, N., & Sunol, R. (2009). Quality requirements for cross-border care in Europe: A qualitative study of patients', professionals' and healthcare financiers' views. *Quality & Safety in Health Care*, *18*(Suppl 1), i15–i21. DOI: 10.1136/qshc.2008.028837 PMID: 19188456

Güell-Alonso, R., Cabrera-Pérez, R., & Vives, J. (2025). Immunocompatibility in transplantation: Adapting to a changing therapeutic landscape. *Frontiers in Immunology, 16*, 1648534. Advance online publication. DOI: 10.3389/fimmu.2025.1648534 PMID: 40995364

Haga, S. B. (2024). Artificial intelligence, medications, pharmacogenomics, and ethics. *Pharmacogenomics, 25*(14-15), 611–622. DOI: 10.1080/14622416.2024.2428587 PMID: 39545629

HAWES, D., SHI, S.-R., DABBS, D. J., TAYLOR, C. R., & COTE, R. J. (2009). Immunohistochemistry. *Modern Surgical Pathology*, 48–70. DOI: 10.1016/B978-1-4160-3966-2.00016-3

Hoivik, E. A., Hodneland, E., Dybvik, J. A., Wagner-Larsen, K. S., Fasmer, K. E., Berg, H. F., Halle, M. K., Haldorsen, I. S., & Krakstad, C. (2021). A radiogenomics application for prognostic profiling of endometrial cancer. *Communications Biology, 4*(1), 1363. Advance online publication. DOI: 10.1038/s42003-021-02894-5 PMID: 34873276

Horst, A., Loustalot, P., Yoganathan, S., Li, T., Xu, J., Tong, W., Schneider, D., Löffler-Perez, N., Di Renzo, E., & Renaudin, M. (2025). Federated learning: A privacy-preserving approach to data-centric regulatory cooperation. *Frontiers in Drug Safety and Regulation, 5*, 1579922. Advance online publication. DOI: 10.3389/fdsfr.2025.1579922 PMID: 40978510

Ismail, M., Khan, S., Khan, F., Noor, S., Sajid, H., Yar, S., & Rasheed, I. (2020). Prevalence and significance of potential drug-drug interactions among cancer patients receiving chemotherapy. *BMC Cancer, 20*(1), 335. Advance online publication. DOI: 10.1186/s12885-020-06855-9 PMID: 32307008

Jang, H.-J., & Lee, S. H. (2025). AI-Driven Digital Pathology: Deep Learning and Multimodal Integration for Precision Oncology. *International Journal of Molecular Sciences, 27*(1), 379. DOI: 10.3390/ijms27010379 PMID: 41516254

Karuppan Perumal, M. K., Rajan Renuka, R., Kumar Subbiah, S., & Manickam Natarajan, P. (2025). Artificial intelligence-driven clinical decision support systems for early detection and precision therapy in oral cancer: A mini review. *Frontiers in Oral Health, 6*, 1592428. Advance online publication. DOI: 10.3389/froh.2025.1592428 PMID: 40356851

Khan, S., Faruqui, H., Zahid, M., Chaudhry, S., Rehman, Z., Noor, H., & Naushad, M. (2025). Tracking the pandemic through molecular and sequencing tools: A story of SARS-CoV-2 over five years, lessons learned, and further directions. *BMC Infectious Diseases, 25*(1), 1816. DOI: 10.1186/s12879-025-12200-x PMID: 41291524

Khan, S. N., Danishuddin, , Khan, M. W. A., Guarnera, L., & Akhtar, S. M. F. (2026). Multi-modal AI in precision medicine: Integrating genomics, imaging, and EHR data for clinical insights. *Frontiers in Artificial Intelligence*, *8*, 1743921. Advance online publication. DOI: 10.3389/frai.2025.1743921 PMID: 41573270

Leveraging Electronic Health Records and Artificial Intelligence for Automated Health Outcome Analysis. (2026). ISPOR | International Society for Pharmacoeconomics and Outcomes Research. https://www.ispor.org/publications/journals/value-outcomes-spotlight/vos-archives/issue/view/global-threats-from-climate-change/leveraging-electronic-health-records-and-artificial-intelligence-for-automated-health-outcome-analysis

Liu, R., Rizzo, S., Waliany, S., Garmhausen, M. R., Pal, N., Huang, Z., Chaudhary, N., Wang, L., Harbron, C., Neal, J., Copping, R., & Zou, J. (2022). Systematic pan-cancer analysis of mutation–treatment interactions using large real-world clinicogenomics data. *Nature Medicine*, *28*(8), 1656–1661. DOI: 10.1038/s41591-022-01873-5 PMID: 35773542

Ma, Y., Shi, N., Li, M., Chen, F., & Niu, H. (2015). Applications of Next-generation Sequencing in Systemic Autoimmune Diseases. *Genomics, Proteomics & Bioinformatics*, *13*(4), 242–249. DOI: 10.1016/j.gpb.2015.09.004 PMID: 26432094

Macefield, R. C., Blazeby, J. M., Reeves, B. C., King, A., Rees, J., Pullyblank, A., & Avery, K. (2023). Remote assessment of surgical site infection (SSI) using patient-taken wound images: Development and evaluation of a method for research and routine practice. *Journal of Tissue Viability*, *32*(1), 94–101. DOI: 10.1016/j.jtv.2023.01.001 PMID: 36681617

Marée, R., Stévens, B., Rollus, L., Rocks, N., Lopez, X. M., Salmon, I., Cataldo, D., & Wehenkel, L. (2013). A rich internet application for remote visualization and collaborative annotation of digital slides in histology and cytology. *Diagnostic Pathology*, *8*(S1), S26. Advance online publication. DOI: 10.1186/1746-1596-8-S1-S26

Masjoodi, S., Anbardar, M. H., Shokripour, M., & Omidifar, N. (2025). Whole Slide Imaging (WSI) in Pathology: Emerging Trends and Future Applications in Clinical Diagnostics, Medical Education, and Pathology. *Iranian Journal of Pathology*, *20*(3), 257–265. DOI: 10.30699/ijp.2025.2044210.3367 PMID: 40746923

Matias-Guiu, X., Temprana-Salvador, J., Garcia Lopez, P., Kammerer-Jacquet, S.-F., Rioux-Leclercq, N., Clark, D., Schürch, C. M., Fend, F., Mattern, S., Snead, D., Fusco, N., Guerini-Rocco, E., Rojo, F., Brevet, M., Salto Tellez, M., Dei Tos, A., di Maio, T., Ramírez-Peinado, S., Sheppard, E., & Martino, N. (2025). Implementing digital pathology: Qualitative and financial insights from eight leading European laboratories. *Virchows Archiv*, *487*(4), 815–826. DOI: 10.1007/s00428-025-04064-y PMID: 40056197

Micsik, T., Csellár, L., Patai, Á. V., Jakab, A., Jónás, V., & Molnár, B. (2026). Digitally derived Ki-67 proliferation index for GastroEnteroPancreatic neuroendocrine neoplasms. *Pathology Oncology Research : POR*, *31*, 1612248. Advance online publication. DOI: 10.3389/pore.2025.1612248 PMID: 41574207

Milovanović, B. (2018, May 27). *[DNA Sequencing] Structure of the data analysis pipelines*. Medium. https://medium.com/@bmilovanovic/dna-sequencing-structure-of-the-data-analysis-pipelines-cd7c4de37f35

Munari, E., Scarpa, A., Cima, L., Pozzi, M., Pagni, F., Vasuri, F., Marletta, S., Dei Tos, A. P., & Eccher, A. (2023). Cutting-edge technology and automation in the pathology laboratory. *Virchows Archiv*, *484*(4), 555–566. DOI: 10.1007/s00428-023-03637-z PMID: 37930477

Najar Najafi, N., Hajihassani, H., & Azimzadeh Irani, M. (2025). The Impact of Artificial Intelligence on Cancer Diagnosis and Treatment: A Review. *Cancer Informatics*, *24*, 11769351251371273. Advance online publication. DOI: 10.1177/11769351251371273 PMID: 40979169

Nardone, V., Marmorino, F., Germani, M. M., Cichowska-Cwalińska, N., Menditti, V. S., Gallo, P., Studiale, V., Taravella, A., Landi, M., Reginelli, A., Cappabianca, S., Girnyi, S., Cwalinski, T., Boccardi, V., Goyal, A., Skokowski, J., Oviedo, R. J., Abou-Mrad, A., & Marano, L. (2024). The Role of Artificial Intelligence on Tumor Boards: Perspectives from Surgeons, Medical Oncologists and Radiation Oncologists. *Current Oncology (Toronto, Ont.)*, *31*(9), 4984–5007. DOI: 10.3390/curroncol31090369 PMID: 39329997

Nentwig, K., Unterhuber, T., Wolff, K.-D., Ritschl, L. M., & Nieberler, M. (2021). The impact of intraoperative frozen section analysis on final resection margin status, recurrence, and patient outcome with oral squamous cell carcinoma. *Clinical Oral Investigations*, *25*(12), 6769–6777. DOI: 10.1007/s00784-021-03964-y PMID: 33956217

Noorbakhsh, J., Farahmand, S., Foroughi pour, A., Namburi, S., Caruana, D., Rimm, D., Soltanieh-ha, M., Zarringhalam, K., & Chuang, J. H. (2020). Deep learning-based cross-classifications reveal conserved spatial behaviors within tumor histological images. *Nature Communications, 11*(1), 6367. Advance online publication. DOI: 10.1038/s41467-020-20030-5 PMID: 33311458

Olawade, D. B., Marinze, S., Qureshi, N., Weerasinghe, K., & Teke, J. (2025). The impact of artificial intelligence and machine learning in organ retrieval and transplantation: A comprehensive review. *Current Research in Translational Medicine, 73*(2), 103493. DOI: 10.1016/j.retram.2025.103493 PMID: 39792149

Omoseebi, A., & Samson Anderson, J. L. (2025). *Enhancing Diagnostic Accuracy Through AI-Based Clinical Decision Support Systems.* CDSS.

Omoush, S. A., Alzyoud, J. A. M., El-Omari, N. K. T., & Alzyoud, A. J. A. (2026). The Role of Whole Slide Imaging in AI-Based Digital Pathology: Current Challenges and Future Directions—An Updated Literature Review. *Journal of Molecular Pathology, 7*(1), 2. DOI: 10.3390/jmp7010002

Onsongo, G., Erdmann, J., Spears, M. D., Chilton, J., Beckman, K. B., Hauge, A., Yohe, S., Schomaker, M., Bower, M., Silverstein, K. A. T., & Thyagarajan, B. (2014). Implementation of Cloud based Next Generation Sequencing data analysis in a clinical laboratory. *BMC Research Notes, 7*(1), 314. Advance online publication. DOI: 10.1186/1756-0500-7-314 PMID: 24885806

Panch, T., Mattie, H., & Atun, R. (2019). Artificial intelligence and algorithmic bias: Implications for health systems. *Journal of Global Health, 9*(2), 010318. Advance online publication. DOI: 10.7189/jogh.09.020318 PMID: 31788229

Passaro, A., Al Bakir, M., Hamilton, E. G., Diehn, M., André, F., Roy-Chowdhuri, S., Mountzios, G., Wistuba, I. I., Swanton, C., & Peters, S. (2024). Cancer biomarkers: Emerging trends and clinical implications for personalized treatment. *Cell, 187*(7), 1617–1635. DOI: 10.1016/j.cell.2024.02.041 PMID: 38552610

Patharia, P., Sethy, P. K., & Nanthaamornphong, A. (2024). Advancements and Challenges in the Image-Based Diagnosis of Lung and Colon Cancer: A Comprehensive Review. *Cancer Informatics, 23*, 11769351241290608. Advance online publication. DOI: 10.1177/11769351241290608 PMID: 39483315

Peet, B. M., Sidoti, A., Allen, R. J.Jr, Nelson, J. A., & Graziano, F. (2025). Artificial Intelligence in Breast Reconstruction: Enhancing Surgical Planning, Aesthetic Outcomes, and Patient-Centered Care. *Journal of Clinical Medicine, 14*(21), 7821. DOI: 10.3390/jcm14217821 PMID: 41227217

Privitera, G. F., Alaimo, S., Micale, G., Giaimi, L., Mare, M., Lombardo, S. P., Martorana, E., Villa, R., Ferro, A., Forte, S., & Pulvirenti, A. (2026). An open-source clinical bioinformatics pipeline for real-world NGS implementation: Translating genomic variants into actionable treatment strategies in oncology. *Journal of Translational Medicine*, *24*(1), 241. Advance online publication. DOI: 10.1186/s12967-026-07718-w PMID: 41566376

Qiao, Y., Zhao, L., Luo, C., Luo, Y., Wu, Y., Li, S., Bu, D., & Zhao, Y. (2022). Multi-modality artificial intelligence in digital pathology. *Briefings in Bioinformatics*, *23*(6), bbac367. Advance online publication. DOI: 10.1093/bib/bbac367 PMID: 36124675

Robbins, C. J., Bates, K. M., & Rimm, D. L. (2025). HER2 testing: Evolution and update for a companion diagnostic assay. *Nature Reviews. Clinical Oncology*, *22*(6), 408–423. DOI: 10.1038/s41571-025-01016-y PMID: 40195456

Sankaye, S. (2011). Telepathology for effective healthcare in developing nations. *The Australasian Medical Journal*, *592–595*, 592–595. Advance online publication. DOI: 10.4066/AMJ.2011.855 PMID: 23386872

Saxena, S., Jena, B., Gupta, N., Das, S., Sarmah, D., Bhattacharya, P., Nath, T., Paul, S., Fouda, M. M., Kalra, M., Saba, L., Pareek, G., & Suri, J. S. (2022). Role of Artificial Intelligence in Radiogenomics for Cancers in the Era of Precision Medicine. *Cancers (Basel)*, *14*(12), 2860. DOI: 10.3390/cancers14122860 PMID: 35740526

Shahmoradi, L., Safdari, R., Ahmadi, H., & Zahmatkeshan, M. (2021). Clinical decision support systems-based interventions to improve medication outcomes: A systematic literature review on features and effects. *Medical Journal of the Islamic Republic of Iran*. Advance online publication. DOI: 10.47176/mjiri.35.27 PMID: 34169039

Shakhawat, H. M., Nakamura, T., Kimura, F., Yagi, Y., & Yamaguchi, M. (2020). [Paper] Automatic Quality Evaluation of Whole Slide Images for the Practical Use of Whole Slide Imaging Scanner. *ITE Transactions on Media Technology and Applications*, *8*(4), 252–268. DOI: 10.3169/mta.8.252

Sobhani, F., Robinson, R., Hamidinekoo, A., Roxanis, I., Somaiah, N., & Yuan, Y. (2021). Artificial intelligence and digital pathology: Opportunities and implications for immuno-oncology. *Biochimica et Biophysica Acta (BBA) -. Revisiones en Cáncer*, *1875*(2), 188520. DOI: 10.1016/j.bbcan.2021.188520 PMID: 33561505

Stroud, A. M., Minteer, S. A., Zhu, X., Ridgeway, J. L., Miller, J. E., & Barry, B. A. (2025). Patient information needs for transparent and trustworthy cardiovascular artificial intelligence: A qualitative study. *PLOS Digital Health*, *4*(4), e0000826. DOI: 10.1371/journal.pdig.0000826 PMID: 40258073

Sun, J., Zhu, G., Liang, Q., Wen, N., Li, H., & Sun, X. (2025). Machine learning-based predictive model for the perioperative co-occurrence of T-cell-mediated rejection and pneumonia in liver transplantation. *Frontiers in Immunology*, *16*, 1648993. Advance online publication. DOI: 10.3389/fimmu.2025.1648993 PMID: 41041323

Tiwari, A., Mishra, S., & Kuo, T.-R. (2025). Current AI technologies in cancer diagnostics and treatment. *Molecular Cancer*, *24*(1), 159. Advance online publication. DOI: 10.1186/s12943-025-02369-9 PMID: 40457408

Tolkach, Y., Dohmgörgen, T., Toma, M., & Kristiansen, G. (2020). High-accuracy prostate cancer pathology using deep learning. *Nature Machine Intelligence*, *2*(7), 411–418. DOI: 10.1038/s42256-020-0200-7

UH. (2024, February 18). *Bone Cancer Patients and Others Receiving 3D-Printed Implants at UH*. Uhhospitals.org; University Hospitals. https://www.uhhospitals.org/for-clinicians/articles-and-news/articles/2024/02/bone-cancer-patients-and-others-receiving-3d-printed-implants-at-uh

Unanah, O. V., & Aidoo, E. M.. (2025). The potential of AI technologies to address and reduce disparities within the healthcare system by enabling more personalized and efficient patient engagement and care management. *World Journal of Advanced Research and Reviews*, *25*(2), 2643–2664. DOI: 10.30574/wjarr.2025.25.2.0641

Vrel, J.-P., Oulmane, S., Boukobza, A., Burgun, A., & Tsopra, R. (2021). A COVID-19 Decision Support System for Phone Call Triage, Designed by and for Medical Students. *Studies in Health Technology and Informatics*. Advance online publication. DOI: 10.3233/SHTI210226 PMID: 34042631

Xia, L., Cao, Z., & Zhao, Y. (2024). Paradigm Transformation of Global Health Data Regulation: Challenges in Governance and Human Rights Protection of Cross-Border Data Flows. *Risk Management and Healthcare Policy*, *17*, 3291–3304. DOI: 10.2147/RMHP.S450082 PMID: 39720184

Yan, F., Da, Q., Yi, H., Deng, S., Zhu, L., Zhou, M., Liu, Y., Feng, M., Wang, J., Wang, X., Zhang, Y., Zhang, W., Zhang, X., Lin, J., Zhang, S., & Wang, C. (2024). Artificial intelligence-based assessment of PD-L1 expression in diffuse large B cell lymphoma. *NPJ Precision Oncology*, *8*(1), 76. Advance online publication. DOI: 10.1038/s41698-024-00577-y PMID: 38538739

Yousefi, F., Gholami, M., &Biabanikhankahdani, R. (2025). The Role of Artificial Intelligence in the Development of Health Tourism. *International Healthcare Review (Online)*. .DOI: 10.56226/132

Zheng, S., Cui, X., & Ye, Z. (2025). Integrating artificial intelligence into radiological cancer imaging: From diagnosis and treatment response to prognosis. *Cancer Biology & Medicine*, *22*(1), 6–13. DOI: 10.20892/j.issn.2095-3941.2024.0422 PMID: 39907115

Zorn, K. K., Simonson, M. E., Faulkner, J. L., Carr, C. L., Acuna, J., Hall, T. L., Jenkins, J. F., Drummond, K. L., & Curran, G. M. (2022). Can Automated Alerts in the Electronic Health Record Encourage Referrals for Genetic Counseling and Testing Among Patients at High Risk for Hereditary Cancer Syndromes? *JCO Oncology Practice*, *18*(7), e1219–e1224. DOI: 10.1200/OP.21.00641 PMID: 35316088

Chapter 8

AI-Enhanced Medical Tourism as a Catalyst for Achieving Global Health Goals:

A Qualitative Exploration

Ruchika Kulshrestha
http://orcid.org/0000-0002-5188-9204
GLA University, Mathura, India

Pankaj Kumar Tyagi
http://orcid.org/0000-0001-9504-541X
Chandigarh University, India

ABSTRACT

The healthcare system is being transformed by the innovations of Artificial Intelligence (AI) that will help in improving its diagnostics and predictive analytics, as well as online health management. The paper aims to evaluate the role that AI-based medical tourism may play in advancing health-related interests worldwide, particularly in improving accessibility to and quality of healthcare. The research is qualitative in exploratory approach, which relies on the semi-structured interviews with health care professionals, medical tourism facilitators, policymakers and specialists in the field of AI health-technology, and is complemented with the examination of the relevant policy documents.The paper defines the opportunities of medical tourism based on AI as a tool to improve cheaper, effective, and sustainable medical services in a global context.

DOI: 10.4018/979-8-3373-8944-8.ch008

1. INTRODUCTION

Medical tourism has turned into a big business and one of the areas of major activities at the international level where patients can cross the borders seeking affordable, high quality and specialty care services. Other destinations of great interest are the countries such as India, Thailand and Singapore that has rated high on their medical facilities, professionals and lower cost of treatment thus attracting international clients.

Artificial Intelligence (AI) is a new concept that is rapidly transforming the health-care system worldwide with its novelties in diagnostics, treatment plans, predictive analytics, and patient monitoring(Karcıoğlu, 2025). AI-based media technologies assist healthcare providers to make faster and more accurate decisions, improve clinical performance, reduce human error, and increase the delivery of customised medical care in diverse health care settings.

Medical tourism assists with the availability of health in the globe since patients can obtain medical services promptly and at reasonable prices beyond the domestic health care systems(Yan *et al.*, 2024). It assists in making the treatment period shorter, creates specialized procedures that are not present in their countries of origin, and provides freedom of movement in the healthcare sector internationally, thereby contributing to the greater availability of the greatly needed medical services in the world.

Technological advancements are reshaping the models of healthcare distribution, including the use of AIs, telemedicine, digital health platforms, and others. Such technologies make the processes more efficient, enhance the interaction with the patients in the healthcare, and the decision-making process basing on the facts(Asif *et al.*, 2025). These novelties introduced in the medical tourism ecosystems will be able to foster quality of services, operations management, and trans-border patient experience in increasingly digital medical care world.

Despite the increased popularity of medical tourism and AI-driven healthcare, few sources of literature indicate that the two factors play a combined role in defining the results of health across the globe. The existing literature is inclined to discuss those areas separately, and the knowledge gap concerning AI-enhanced medical tourism to the health-related priorities of the global community, such as greater access to high-quality healthcare and its sustainability, still exists.

The study aims to assess the impact of AI-driven personalization on patient experience, satisfaction, and decision-making in international medical tourism. The chapter is also evaluating the effectiveness of AI technologies in improving cost efficiency, diagnosis accuracy, and treatment outcomes in cross-border healthcare services.

1.1 Research Questions

1. How does AI-driven personalization influence patient satisfaction and decision-making in medical tourism?
2. To what extent does the use of AI improve cost efficiency, diagnostic accuracy, and treatment outcomes in international healthcare services?
3. How does AI enhance transparency, trust, and access to information for medical tourists across different countries?
4. What are the key data privacy, security, and regulatory challenges associated with implementing AI in cross-border medical tourism?

2. LITERATURE REVIEW

2.1 Medical Tourism: Concept and Global Trends

Medical travels may be defined as a form of inter country traveling which individuals have been engaging in to seek medical treatment in a nation of their preference; the main reason behind such traveling being the hefty prices, absence of queues or specific medical treatments. The globalization process has led to an exceptionally fast growth rate in the industry over the last two decades as consequences of the growth and spread of transportation and the international image of health-giving establishment in the emerging economies (Florido-Benítez and del Alcazar Martínez, 2024). Some of the surgery procedures that are widely demanded and patients fly to foreign companies are heart surgery, bone surgery, cosmetic surgery, and fertility surgeries.

India, Thailand, Singapore, Malaysia and Turkey are some of the most popular medical tourism destinations that have been placed in a strategic position to offer facilities and hospitals rated highly internationally and the treatment facilities are not very costly (Glass et al., 2022). These countries facilitate medical tourism by governments and medical institutions by providing favourable policies, investing in healthcare facilities as well as facilitating the collaboration with other medical tourism facilitators. The healthcare system is changing as a result of the integration of technologies like AI and Gen AI. By 2026, these technologies will help healthcare providers manage all aspect of a patient's journey, including symptoms, test scheduling, result analysis, and follow-up care. They will help oversee and manage research projects in labs. Patients will even utilize them directly to keep an eye on their lifestyle and treatment compliance, as well as to enable proactive healthcare delivery by identifying danger indications early.

Considering India as an example where Medical tourism will spread outside of major cities in 2026.Medical tourism has emerged as a considerable element in the country economic landscape not only in change in the healthcare delivery across the frontiers as patients can also be provided with quality care outside of the services provided in their respective healthcare services.

Because of their more specialized, dependable, and reasonably priced medical services, as well as their improved hospital infrastructure, cutting-edge medical technology, and improved connectivity, Tier-2 cities are becoming significant healthcare hubs. International patients looking for high-quality care without sacrificing convenience have found these new hubs appealing due to their shorter wait times, affordable prices, and better connection.

2.2 Artificial Intelligence in Healthcare

Figure 1. Al in Healthcare

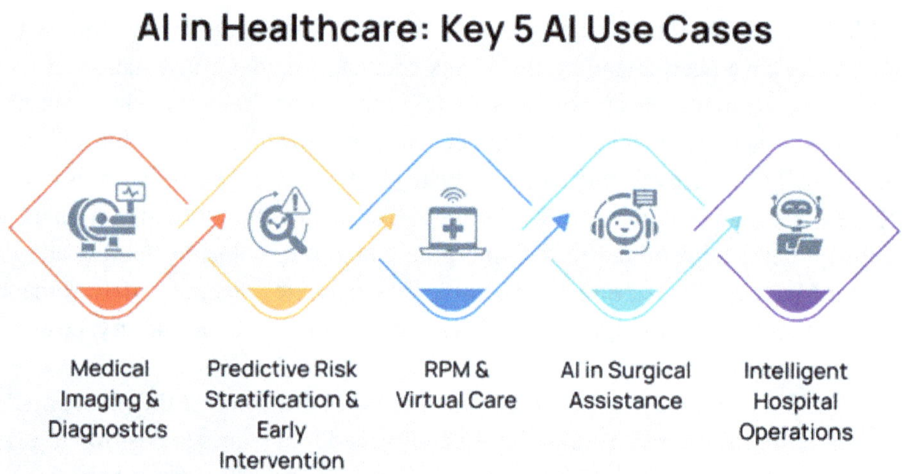

(Source: Dash Technologies, 2025)

In the modern healthcare system, Artificial Intelligence (AI) has become an important element of healthcare innovations. The AI solutions enable medical practitioners to do medical data processing, improve medical diagnostic outcomes, and make clinical decisions. The examples of the use of AI in healthcare include medical image analysis, aided robotic surgery, predictive analytics and treatment-planning AI(Reshadi and Chehragh, 2025). An example is that machine learning technologies can be applied to detect cancer, heart conditions and neurological ailments in youth at an early stage, including the processing of not only medical images but also patient data. The application of robotics AI in surgery is also a common trend whereby accuracy in surgery and reducing the number of human errors is crucial. In addition, predictive analytics will help medical institutions guarantee patient outcomes, effective utilization of hospital resources, and improved patient care strategies(Townsend *et al.*, 2023). The invention of AI and other forms of digital health systems such as electronic health records and telemedicine systems also contributes to the enhanced access and efficiencies in healthcare. The AI technologies will play a significant role in enhancing the quality, efficiency of medical services, and patient-centered care in the international arena due to active development.

2.3 AI in Medical Tourism

Figure 2. Global medical tourism market size

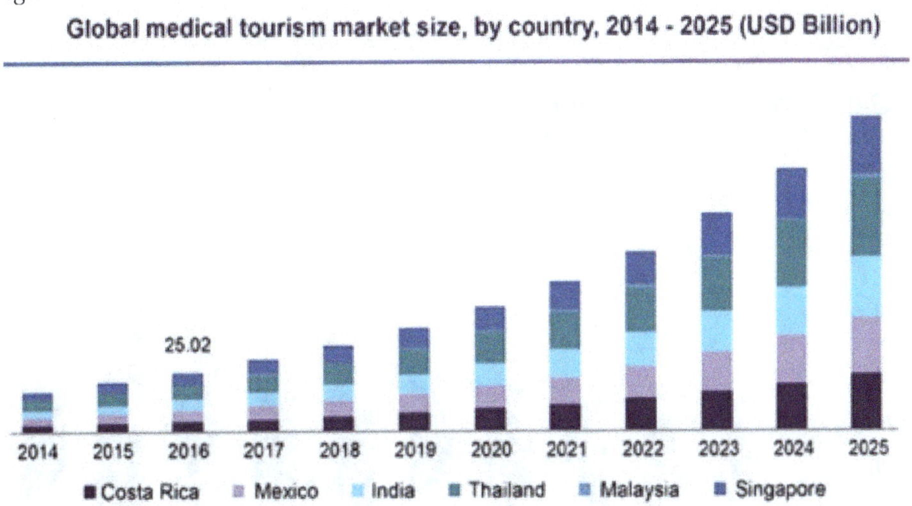

(Source: Hassan and Bellos, 2022)

Application of artificial intelligence within the medical tourism industry is changing the manner in which patients in the entire of Europe decide, compare, and access medical services in foreign countries. The use of AI will enable the patients to read about the hospitals, treatment and cost and all the doctor thereby making the process of choosing a treatment easier. The virtual assistants and chatbots offer immediate assistance and support to foreign patients on their way to the treatment process, such as appointments and transportation (Bathla et al., 2024). Remote patient-physician consultation occurred as a consequence of AI could provide individuals with an opportunity to have a doctor remotely without necessarily traveling prior to the course, which could allow individuals to take pre-treatment tests and prepare more adequately to the given procedure.

Moreover, new hospital items, including AI-based systems of patient monitoring, artificial administration service, and intelligent healthcare operations management systems, become the destinations in the engineering of a medical tourist, which makes their destinations more efficient and quality-oriented (Agata and Kibet, 2025). The new technological breakthroughs will prove useful in enhancing the degree of transparency, dampening of ambiguity with international patients and creating better confidence in the international healthcare service providers. In turn, AI proves to be one of the primary sources of more successful, customized, and affordable medical tourism.

2.4 Medical Tourism and Global Health Goals

Figure 3. Global Medical Tourism Market

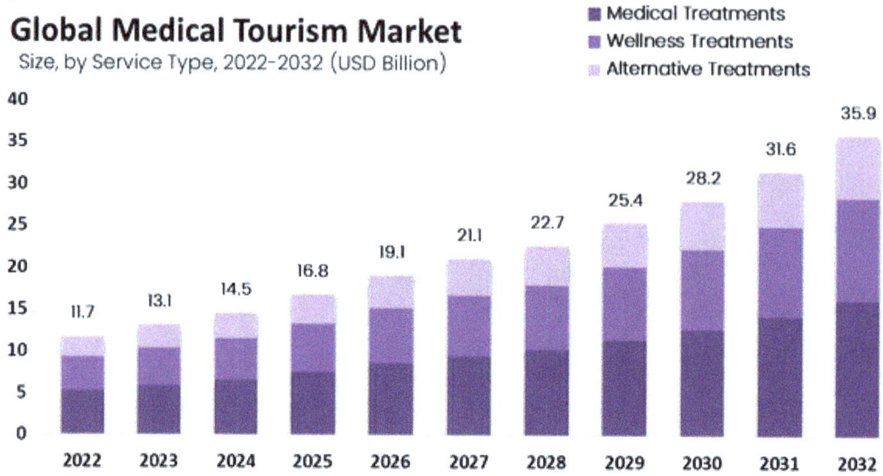

(Source: Market.us, 2025)

High accessibility and affordability of healthcare are some of the implications of medical tourism to the global world goals as far as health is concerned. Medical tourism has the capability of minimizing hurdles associated with costly healthcare and lengthy lines since patients will have the ability to get the services in such countries where they are not costly or are available. This flow of healthcare across a border can also lead to the achievement of healthcare equity because people who are in other countries can access highly-specialized healthcare, which they could never have accessed in their countries (Tripathi, 2023).

According to the United Nations Sustainable Development Goals, medical tourism can be utilized in relation to the Sustainable Development Goal 3 that encompasses the aspects of healthy lives and the fact that well-being can be achieved as well (Glass et al., 2022). As a protean way of ever-improving access to quality healthcare services, and a way of establishing partnership in medical research and development operations across the globe, medical tourism can reach an even higher number in case it will be formalized and backed by well-functioning healthcare systems. Nonetheless, these merits should be met with a high level of rule that will guarantee that the procedures are not only part of good morals but also lax for patients as well as there is equitable redistribution of health care.

2.5 Research Gap

Despite a lot of research conducted on medical tourism and the integration of Artificial Intelligence (AI) in health care, not much research has been conducted to explore the interaction between the two disciplines in terms of the health outcomes on a global scale. The available literature mostly speculates on the economic profitability of medical tourism or the technological advantages of AI in the delivery of medical care only(Aykın *et al.*, 2023). This gap is significant in the current comprehension of how the systems of medical tourism can be enhanced using AI innovations to further the work of the medical tourism to the longer health objectives of the world namely those associated with the Sustainable Development Goal 3 (Good Health and Well-Being). Therefore, the future of the AI-created medical tourism in improving accessibility to, efficiency, and sustainability in healthcare provision in the global healthcare setting is in need of further investigation.

3. CONCEPTUAL/THEORETICAL FRAMEWORK

The three theoretical lenses based on which the given paper is constituted are Digital Health Ecosystem, the Technology Acceptance Model (TAM), and Sustainable Development Goal 3 (Good Health and Well-Being) framework. Digital healthcare delivery has increased appreciation of interlocked technologies, healthcare organisations, patients, and digital spaces as a contribution to the Digital Health Ecosystem (Nagar et al., 2021). The concept of Artificial Intelligence (AI) has become a disruptive technology and an upscale within the medical diagnostics, treatment planning, hospital administration as well as the intra-country to inter-country coordination of medical healthcare in this ecosystem.

Another such model is referred to as Technology Acceptance Model (TAM) that expounds on how AI-based technologies would be used by the representatives of the medical tourism sector, namely medical tourism facilitators, patients, and healthcare providers. TAM holds an opinion that technology innovation is being adopted in the context of the perceived usefulness and perceived ease of use. Within the framework of the medical tourism, telemedicine, and predictive healthcare applications that will allow potentially higher level of trust and better decision made by the patients and overall experience of the patient.

In the case of the services of medical tourism, introduction of AI to the chart brings about the opportunity to enhance the sufferings of the hospital access, efficiency and service quality amidst the international clients. The following conceptualization of the relationship is as follows:AI Integration results in Better Medical Tourism Services which have further outcomes of positive Global Health outcome. By making the possibility of realizing the health care delivery system efficacy, furthering the idea of justice of accessing treatment opportunities, and national healthcare cooperation, AI-enhanced medical tourism can help the world population move towards even greater health goals, namely, the ones that will descend upon Sustainable Development Goal 3.

4. RESEARCH METHODOLOGY

4.1 Research Design

The examined research in the present paper is a qualitative exploratory study, which will employ the interface of Artificial Intelligence and medical tourism and international health outcomes. The qualitative method allows to obtain the detailed knowledge of the perception of the stakeholders, experiences of the stakeholders, and future tendencies of this developing region (Jorshary et al., 2025). The paper will attempt to discover practical examples of industry participants and policyholders to determine what impact AI-based technologies can have on the practice of medical tourism and health on the planet overall.

4.2 Data Collection

To obtain the actual data of the study, the semi-structured interviews with the stakeholders, who are engaged in healthcare and medical tourism, were conducted. The stakeholders involved are medical tourism facilitators and policy makers, medical tourism agents and health-technology professionals working in the AI. The semi-structured interviews result in flexibility in describing the experience and perceptions of the participants as the interview questions are identical. Besides, the primary information is substantiated with the help of document analysis of the global health policy report, regulations of medical tourism, and AI governance schemes.

4.3 Sampling Technique

The study relies on the purposive sampling technique to select study participants with the advocacy interest regarding the knowledge and experience in medical tourism, healthcare management, or health AI-driven technologies. The methodology will ensure that adequate knowledge is imparted on the respondents to provide substantial data concerning the research topic(Kırtıl and Aşkun, 2021). The respondents will also be selected in countries with either a young or an established market of medical tourism such as India, Thailand, Malaysia and Turkey in a bid to get a diverse range of opinions and industry operations.

4.4 Data Analysis

In data analysis, the thematic analysis is used to formulate significant patterns, themes, and relations in the qualitative data retrieved. Transcripts of interviews and policy documents are thoroughly coded so as to recommend familiar themes with regards to the implementation of AI, access to healthcare and medical tourism practices(Gaur *et al.*, 2021). The theoretical lenses to be used in fields will include the theories of digital health ecosystem and technology adoption.

4.5 Ethical Considerations

The question of ethics is taken into account well because the research is carried out in a way that the participants cannot be subjected to any potential danger and the study itself is not subject to an ethical concern. Everybody who participated in the interview is aware of the study and the data regarding the identity is anonymous. The participation is very voluntary and the respondent will also have the freedom to drop at any level. The data is kept and is not fully utilized to the benefit of the students academically and the research does not infringe the stipulations of the research ethics.

5. FINDINGS / RESULTS

During the qualitative method of the interview analysis and interpretation of the policy report, it turns out that some of the major themes give the notion of how Artificial Intelligence (AI) is transforming the medical tourism industry and introducing the notion of healthcare accessibility in the global environment. The findings present the opportunities and threats of integrating the AI technologies into the cross-border healthcare services.

i. AI-Driven Patient Decision Support Systems

Figure 4. Al-Based Clinical Decision Support System

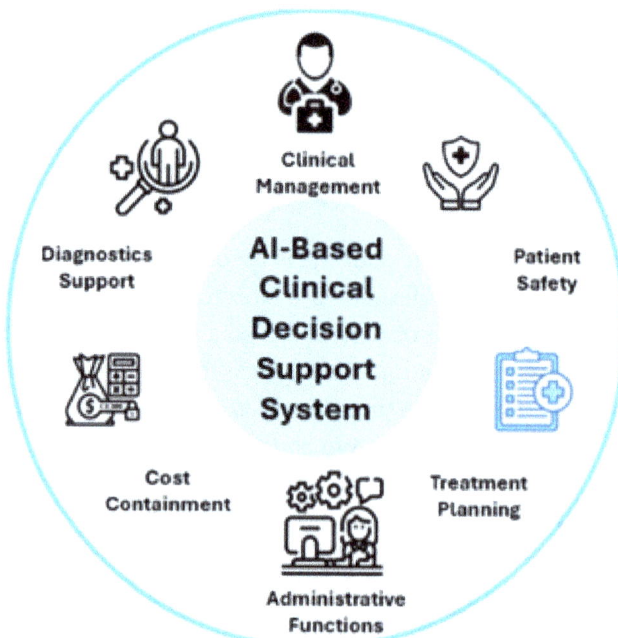

(Source: Hasan et al., 2025)

One of the most obvious items revealed by the interviews is the growing significance of the AI-driven decision support systems in support of the international patients. It has been noted by the participants that AI-based platforms allow patients to rank hospitals, treatment and medical specialists, and possible cost in different countries. The systems review excess information on the patient review, hospital performance indicators, and treatment outcome to give customized recommendations(Benbrahmi and Mehor, 2025). Such technologies, as stated by healthcare givers, may help the patients make more informed decisions in visiting a different country to find medical care. Moreover, chatbots and virtual assistants built with AI will offer real-time help with the process of the treatment, the logistics of travels, and recovery prognosis.

ii. Improved Global Access to Specialized Healthcare

The other prominent outcome is linked to the possibility of medical tourism being improved through AI which, in turn, would lead to the increased availability of cross-border healthcare services. Many interviewees stressed that telemedicine systems AIs offer a chance to reach foreign specialists at home and, therefore, consider that a visit to the doctor is required, thereby resulting in a decision on travelling. Such consultations are made earlier to facilitate the physicians assess the conditions of the patients, prescribe treatment and to assist the patient whether they should travel or not(Bauer, 2023). The implementation of AI diagnostic tools can in most cases, review medical imagery as well as patient history before the arrival of the patient hence allowing the hospitals to pre-plan the patient treatment process. Through this approach, the delays experienced in the treatment processes are reduced and continuity of care is improved. It was also reported that patients in countries with the low healthcare system are the beneficiaries of these services.

iii. Smart Hospital Infrastructure

Figure 5. Smart Hospital Management System

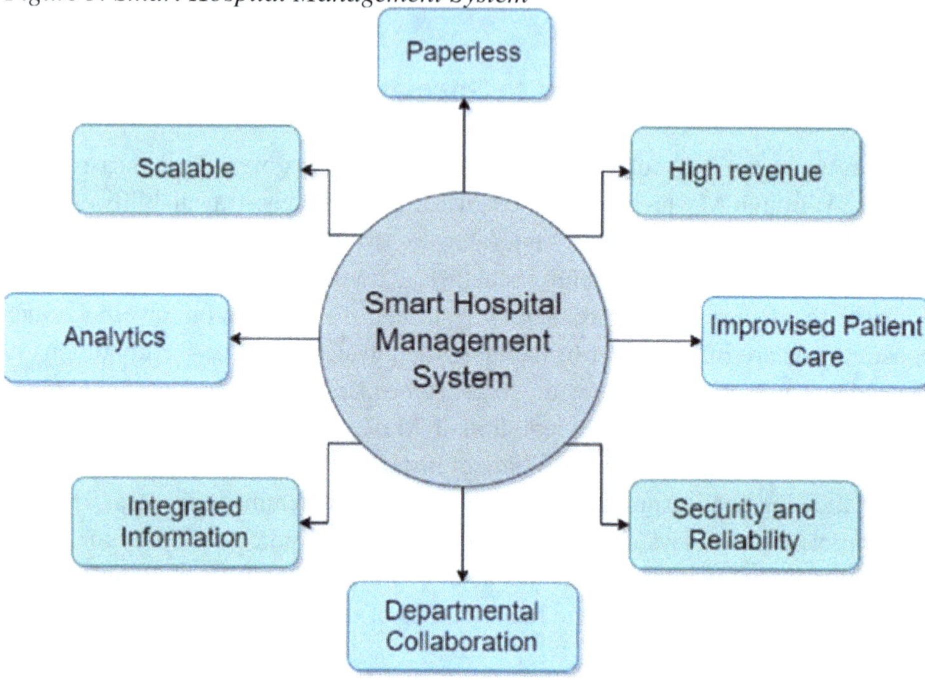

(Source: Gourisaria et al., 2022)

Findings of the research established that majority of key medical tourism destinations are also developing smart AI-powered hospital facilities to enhance patient experience and level operations efficiency. According to the interviewees of hospitals, they utilized solutions based on AI to patient control, assisted surgery, autonomous administration, and predictive healthcare(Garad *et al.*, 2025). The intelligent technologies in operational hospitals reduce the waiting time and optimize the quality of the diagnosis and make it easier to transfer the patients in a hospital facility. These innovations reduce to quality, efficient, and high-level healthcare in case of international patients. The respondents also mentioned that AI-based systems with internationally oriented applications would attract more international patients to the hospitals due to their reputation in technological advancements and performance.

iv. Cost Transparency and Treatment Planning

Cost transparency is another theme that was found in the findings. The medical tourism facilitators believe that AI-based platforms can generate a detailed estimate of the expenses of the treatments by analysing the history of the patients and the required procedure of treatment and the pricing schemes of the hospital. This will allow patients to better plan their visits in health care and avoid these unexpected expenses(Patroni *et al.*, 2024). The AI-empowered planning tools can also be utilized insofar as assisting the hospitals in making the best possible resource allocation, to schedule and to organize the patient capacity. These tools are capable of enhancing efficiency in the running operations; in addition to ensuring that patients receive high quality and timely care.

v. Ethical and Data Privacy Concerns

In addition to the many benefits of the AI integration, the risks related to ethical issues and information privacy were also mentioned ideally by the participants. The technologies of AI are grounded in the large volumes of sensitive information about patients directly, which makes the question of the safety of data, consent, and the cross-border exchange of information. Policy makers and electronic health gurus say that one of the challenges facing global healthcare systems is national regulation disparities, and data protection laws(Khizzou *et al.*, 2025). Another problem became the issue of unfair algorithms, the unjust character of digital technologies and the opportunities of excessive use of automated decisions.

Overall, the findings suggest that even though the AI-enhanced medical tourism possesses an immense potential to improve the efficiency and access to healthcare in a more efficient manner on the international level, regulation and ethical issues are to be addressed to sustain the process of implementation and to make it accountable.

6. DISCUSSION

This study and finding can be entered in conjunction with the current literature on the improvement of the application of digital technologies in the healthcare and medical tourism. Some of the variables that past literature on medical tourism has characterized as the most crucial in the mobility of patients to other countries in search of medical services include price benefits, reduction in waiting period and availability of specialized care (Halimuzzaman, 2022). Still, speaking of the same subject, AI in healthcare has been researched, and certain studies have emphasized the benefits of applying AI to make the diagnosis procedure, operational performance, and patient care more competent. The repercussions of the study will be factored into these arguments by showing how the introduction of AI in the parameters of medical tourism can serve to play a major role in the improvement of patient choice, the accessibility of healthcare services, or quality of services provided to international patients.

Secondly, the article illustrates the importance of AI-enhanced online telemedicine sessions and intelligent hospital systems in the enhancement of access to specialized care service at the global level (Mitharia et al., 2026). In the present situation, AI-enhanced medical tourism can contribute to the realisation of the goals of global health through augmenting the access to high-quality healthcare services and cross-border collusion of medical tourism service providers. It should have been anticipated that the argument of AI-based patient decision support systems would come up, and the research conducted previously indicates that digital health platforms would also be utilized as a useful tool of enhancing the openness of healthcare and empowerment of a patient (Rodríguez Blanco and Gurgel, 2026). The programs promote the universal goals of health programs across the globe since patients who have poor health care facilities are able to access high quality care in the global health tourism centres.

The respondents of the current study reported the existence of AI-based apps where patients can scan through medical services and find and reference various medical options, and medical providers. Political implications and technological implications of the study are also important. The availability of strong digital infrastructure, data control system and compatibility between websites related to healthcare would be significant to the solution of AI systems theorized into the medical tourism services. Medical tourism facilitators and hospitals ought to invest in digital health technology which would not only increase the experience that the customers undergo but should also provide reliability and efficiency.

The findings influence policy-wise that there is a need to have more robust international laws that govern the use of AI, privacy, and healthcare across the borders. Such an ethical consideration as the ways to preserve the data, disclose algorithms, and utilize digital health technologies justly should be taken into consideration by the policy-makers. Certain broad-based guidelines of AI regulation within the health industry might be possibly implemented in such a manner that the medical tourism involving AI can be conducted in a cordial way and may lead to long term health care enhancement in the global scene. Overall, the exploitation of AI in the medical tourism systems has immense potential to enhance the availability of healthcare, efficiency, and health partnership in the globe.

7. IMPLICATIONS (PRACTICAL & POLICY)

The research findings have major impacts to different stakeholders who have interest in healthcare, medical tourism and technology. Artificial Intelligence can lead to patient care improvement, accuracy during diagnosis, and working process inside a hospital to those healthcare providers whose patients are foreigners and need special treatment(Pırnar and Altın, 2024). The implementation of AI-based decision support systems, telemedicine solutions, and smart hospital technologies can help hospitals to provide patients with the high-quality services and their experience.

With medical tourism agencies, this technology of artificial intelligence can be deployed in the area of patient guidance, treatment planning, and in cost disclosures that will enable the medical tourism agency to provide more reliable and personalized services to foreign patients.

The policy makers possess an immense task of coming up with regulatory mechanisms to address the ethical concerns, data privacy and transnational healthcare control. Clear policies should be established in order to ensure responsible adoption of AI in health care systems in the world.

Finally, medical technology innovators must also focus on coming up with secure, user friendly and ethically responsible AI health systems to ensure interoperability and equitable access, which further enhances sustainability in healthcare provisions in the medical tourism sector around the world.

8. LIMITATIONS AND FUTURE RESEARCH

Regardless of the value insight that this research may provide, this research has several limitations. Firstly, the research is based on qualitative exploratory research design with quite small sample size that may impose restrictions on the applicability of the findings. Second, the study will focus its primary research on the selected stakeholders, including healthcare providers and medical tourism facilitators, policymakers, and AI health-technological specialists, and they may not accurately represent the perspective of patients and other required participants(Towett *et al.*, 2023). Other than this, the study is narrowed down to a few countries where medical tourism is widely practised, which is not the most effective source of capturing the disparities of healthcare systems and technology usage in the world. The quantitative methods could be introduced to the research in the future to test the proposed conceptual model and expand the sample to some number of countries(Busch *et al.*, 2025). Even more meaning to the new field would be a comparison of developed and developing economies and longitudinal studies, including patient outcomes in AI-enabled medical tourism.

9. CONCLUSION

The qualitative approach to the research provided the basis of investigating the new nexus of Artificial Intelligence (AI), medical tourism, and world health outcomes in this paper. The findings represent the revolution that AI technologies are bringing to medical tourism and how they have enabled a higher number of patients to decide more, gain greater access to certain types of medical care, contribute to the creation of smart hospital-level infrastructure, and brought more transparency to the planning of treatment and cost. At the same time, the article mentions that one should also consider such major problems as the problem of ethics, the issue of data privacy and the absence of consistency in the laws across the countries.

The paper contends that medical tourism enhanced with AI can contribute to the health of the world and make it effective since it will be possible to combine the advantages of health care beyond the borders and improve the quality of providing medical care internationally. Medical tourism inspired by AI would assist in making healthcare systems more inclusive and sustainable by ensuring that the technological innovation is directed at addressing the health needs of the world population, in particular, Sustainable Development Goal 3 (Good Health and Well-Being). Overall, the study contributes to the growing literature on the subject of the digital transformation of health and the need to secure responsible AI leadership in universal healthcare systems.

REFERENCES

Agata, E., & Kibet, A. (2025, May). Trans-border data flows and AI innovation challenges in the data localization landscape: A Kenyan perspective. In 2025 IST-Africa Conference (IST-Africa) (pp. 1–10). IEEE.

Asif, F., Jamshed, K., & Shah, S. H. A. (2025). Prospects and challenges for AI and technological innovation in the European travel and tourism sector: Impact, effect and sustainable development goals. In Technological innovation and AI for sustainable development in events and festivals (pp. 140–161).

Aykın, Ö., Uluhan, F., Gümüş, İ., Çabuk, Ş., Bozbayır, U., Duran, V., Özbay, C., Özbay, B., Gündoğmuş, Ş. E., Şengül, M. T., & Övey, İ. S. (2023). Artificial intelligence and telemedicine applications in health tourism marketing. *Eurasian Journal of Health Technology Assessment*, *7*(2), 134–149. DOI: 10.52148/ehta.1396111

Bathla, G., Raina, A., & Rana, V. S. (2024). Artificial intelligence-driven enhancements in medical tourism: Opportunities, challenges, and future prospects. In Impact of AI and robotics on the medical tourism industry (pp. 139–162).

Bauer, I. L. (2023). Robots in travel clinics: Building on tourism's use of technology and robots for infection control during a pandemic. *Tropical Diseases, Travel Medicine and Vaccines*, *9*(1), 10. DOI: 10.1186/s40794-023-00197-7 PMID: 37525269

Benbrahmi, F. Z., & Mehor, H. M. H. (2025). The impact of artificial intelligence on enhancing the travel experience for tourists: An analysis of successful models. *Business Excellence and Management*, *15*(5), 5–13. DOI: 10.24818/beman/2025.S.I.5-01

Busch, F., Geis, R., Wang, Y. C., Kather, J. N., Khori, N. A., Makowski, M. R., Kolawole, I. K., Truhn, D., Clements, W., Gilbert, S., & Adams, L. C. (2025). AI regulation in healthcare around the world: What is the status quo? *medRxiv*. DOI: 10.1101/2025.01.25.25321061

Dash Technologies. (2025). Top 5 AI use cases in healthcare for better patient outcomes. https://dashtechinc.com/blog/top-5-ai-use-cases-in-healthcare-for-better-patient-outcomes/

Florido-Benítez, L., & del Alcázar Martínez, B. (2024). How artificial intelligence (AI) is powering new tourism marketing and the future agenda for smart tourist destinations. *Electronics (Basel)*, *13*(21), 4151. DOI: 10.3390/electronics13214151

Garad, A., Al-Ansi, A. M., Jaboob, M., & Kusumawati, R. (2025). Digital innovations in medical tourism: A PRISMA review in the Arab region. In Revolutionizing healthcare experience with digital medical tourism (pp. 53–78). DOI: 10.4018/979-8-3693-7888-5.ch002

Gaur, L., Afaq, A., Singh, G., & Dwivedi, Y. K. (2021). Role of artificial intelligence and robotics to foster the touchless travel during a pandemic: A review and research agenda. *International Journal of Contemporary Hospitality Management*, *33*(11), 4079–4098. DOI: 10.1108/IJCHM-11-2020-1246

Glass, L. T., Schlachta, C. M., Hawel, J. D., Elnahas, A. I., & Alkhamesi, N. A. (2022). Cross-border healthcare: A review and applicability to North America during COVID-19. *Health Policy OPEN*, *3*, 100064. DOI: 10.1016/j.hpopen.2021.100064 PMID: 35036910

Glass, L. T., Schlachta, C. M., Hawel, J. D., Elnahas, A. I., & Alkhamesi, N. A. (2022). Cross-border healthcare: A review and applicability to North America during COVID-19. *Health Policy OPEN*, *3*, 100064. DOI: 10.1016/j.hpopen.2021.100064 PMID: 35036910

Gourisaria, M. K., Agrawal, R., Singh, V., Rautaray, S. S., & Pandey, M. (2022). AI and IoT enabled smart hospital management systems. In Rautaray, S. S., Pandey, M., & Nguyen, N. G. (Eds.), *Data science in societal applications* (pp. 85–110). Springer., DOI: 10.1007/978-981-19-5154-1_6

Halimuzzaman, M. (2022). Technology-driven healthcare and sustainable tourism: Analyzing modern approaches to industry challenges. *Business and Social Sciences*, *1*(1), 1–9.

Hasan, S. U., Hasan, S., Shiwlani, A., Kumar, S., Kumar, S., Nazeer, M. I., & Shiwlani, S. (2025). A systematic review of AI-based clinical decision support systems: From development and implementation to applications. *Pakistan Journal of Life and Social Sciences*, *23*(1), 1482–1500. https://www.pjlss.edu.pk/pdf_files/2025_1/1482-1500.pdf. DOI: 10.57239/PJLSS-2025-23.1.00115

Hassan, V., & Bellos, S. (2022). COVID-19: Reshaping medical tourism through artificial intelligence and robotics. Athens Journal of Tourism, 9(4), 467–486. https://www.athensjournals.gr/tourism/2022-4672-AJT-Hassan-03.pdf

Jorshary, K. M., Sassani, M., Raoufi, S., & Khamoushi, S. (2025). Ranking of AI-driven strategies for optimizing the health tourism supply chain using stratified BWM. *Knowledge and Decision Systems with Applications*, *1*, 295–315. DOI: 10.59543/kadsa.v1i.15051

Karcıoğlu, U. B. (2025). The impact of artificial intelligence on the patient journey in medical tourism: A management framework. *Eurasian Journal of Health Technology Assessment*, *9*(1), 58–67. DOI: 10.52148/ehta.1701664

Khizzou, N. B., Aarabe, M., Bouizgar, M., Alla, L., & Benjelloun, A. (2025). The digital transformation of medical tourism: A systematic and bibliometric review of the literature. In Revolutionizing healthcare experience with digital medical tourism (pp. 355–382). DOI: 10.4018/979-8-3693-7888-5.ch015

Kırtıl, İ. G., & Aşkun, V. (2021). Artificial intelligence in tourism: A review and bibliometrics research. *Advances in Hospitality and Tourism Research*, *9*(1), 205–233. DOI: 10.30519/ahtr.801690

Market.us. (2025). Medical tourism statistics and trends. https://media.market.us/medical-tourism-statistics/

Mitharia, R. K., Mittal, K., & Utami, I. W. (2026). Digital marketing strategies to promote mental health in medical tourism: Opportunities, challenges, and ethical ideas. In Marketing mental wellness in medical tourism (pp. 23–64).

Nagar, R., Singh, Y., & Jaglan, V. (2021, July). A review on machine learning applications in medical tourism. In *2021 Fourth International Conference on Computational Intelligence and Communication Technologies (CCICT)* (pp. 208–215). IEEE. DOI: 10.1109/CCICT53244.2021.00048

Patroni, A., Vogka, G., Halkiopoulos, C., & Antonopoulou, H. (2024, September). Emerging trends and digital strategies in medical tourism: Enhancing health and wellness tourism in the modern era. In *International Conference of the International Association of Cultural and Digital Tourism* (pp. 895–922). Springer.

Pırnar, İ., & Altın, H. (2024). Systematic literature review of health tourism innovation [Revisión sistemática de la literatura sobre innovación en turismo de salud]. *Pasos (El Sauzal)*, *22*(2).

Reshadi, M. S., & Chehragh, A. M. (2025). A review of medical tourism entrepreneurship and marketing at regional and global levels and a quick glance into the applications of artificial intelligence in medical tourism. *AI & Society*, *40*(5), 4011–4027. DOI: 10.1007/s00146-024-02178-6

Rodríguez Blanco, A. D., & Gurgel, H. (2026). Cross-border health as a conceptual approach to health mobility beyond borders: A mapping review. *Critical Public Health*, *36*(1), 2598712. DOI: 10.1080/09581596.2025.2598712

Towett, G., Snead, R. S., Grigoryan, K., & Marczika, J. (2023). Geographical and practical challenges in the implementation of digital health passports for cross-border COVID-19 pandemic management: A narrative review and framework for solutions. *Globalization and Health*, *19*(1), 98. DOI: 10.1186/s12992-023-00998-7 PMID: 38066568

Townsend, B. A., Sihlahla, I., Naidoo, M., Naidoo, S., Donnelly, D. L., & Thaldar, D. W. (2023). Mapping the regulatory landscape of AI in healthcare in Africa. *Frontiers in Pharmacology*, *14*, 1214422. DOI: 10.3389/fphar.2023.1214422 PMID: 37693916

Tripathi, R. P. (2023, November). Harnessing the potential of AI and ML in medical tourism: Challenges, opportunities, and ethical implications. In 2023 3rd International Conference on Technological Advancements in Computational Sciences (ICTACS) (pp. 1068–1072). IEEE.

Yan, X., Han, Z., Ye, P., Yeh, A. G. O., Xu, X., Lee, A. W., Cheung, K. M., Gong, P., & He, S. (2024). Governing cross-border healthcare in mainland China: A scoping review of national policies from 2002 to 2022. *The Lancet Regional Health. Western Pacific*, *45*, 101032. DOI: 10.1016/j.lanwpc.2024.101046 PMID: 38516291

Chapter 9
AI-Enhanced Medical Tourism for Achieving Sustainable Development Goal 3:
Advancing Affordable, Accessible, and Quality Healthcare

Adarsh Kumar
http://orcid.org/0009-0005-3478-7176
Institute of Technology and Management, Gwalior, India

Mragendra Mishra
Amity University, Gwalior, India

Aditya Narayan Mishra
Prestige Institute of Management and Research, Gwalior, India

Sangeeta Kumari Sinha
MES' Nowrosjee Wadia College, Pune, India

Kuldeep Singh
http://orcid.org/0000-0002-7999-1585
Amity University, Haryana, India

Priyank Sharma
http://orcid.org/0000-0001-9888-485X
IIMT University, India

ABSTRACT

This chapter discusses how medical tourism based on AI can help the development of affordable, accessible, and good healthcare as a Sustainable Development Goal 3. It is based on a systematic literature review of modern literature and world healthcare activities, and creates a conceptual and measurement-oriented model, combining the patient journey, artificial intelligence technologies, information infrastructure, governance, and SDG 3 outcome measures. The results also indicate that AI-based solutions, including predictive analytics, intelligent patient-provider

DOI: 10.4018/979-8-3373-8944-8.ch009

matching, telehealth, and automated diagnostics, can lower the cost of treatment, decrease the information asymmetry, and enhance the cross-border continuity of care. The theoretical novelty of this chapter is based on the fact that it suggests a sustainability-oriented, governance-integrated framework that explicitly presents AI-mediated medical tourism procedures to quantifiable SDG 3 indicators and thus closes the theoretical gap between medical tourism and digital health research and offers a stepwise implementation.

1. INTRODUCTION

The interface of artificial intelligence and global medical mobility is transforming the boundaries of modern healthcare systems. Medical tourism, which was previously regarded more as a market-based reaction to cross national disparities in cost, has come to be a transnational ecosystem that links patients, providers, mediators, insurance, and regulators. Meanwhile, artificial intelligence has already started to change the healthcare delivery in terms of predictive analytics, machine learning diagnostics, robot surgery, and smart decision support systems. The intersected areas between these two domains create new possibilities of enhancing affordability, accessibility, and quality of care. This cross particularly matters in the backdrop of the Sustainable Development Goal 3 that aims to achieve healthy lives and well-being to all at any age (United Nations, 2015).

The SDG 3 ideal is whereby there is universal health coverage, protection of financial risks and accessibility of quality essential healthcare services without discrimination. Medical tourism in theory can contribute to this vision by removing the strain on local health care systems, providing alternative treatment routes, and allowing patients to obtain specialized treatments not provided or prohibitively costly at home (Connell, 2013). Parallel to this, artificial intelligence will provide better diagnostic accuracy and efficiency, as well as individualized treatment courses, and improve the performance of health systems (Jiang et al., 2017; Topol, 2019). Artificial intelligence of medical tourism may thus bring cross border healthcare travel in line with global health equity and resilience of the system.

However, the current state of things does not satisfy this ideal. Medical tourism is still practiced disproportionately in regulatory and infrastructural settings. Different destinations have different quality standards, there is a high level of information asymmetry, and continuity of care is usually discontinued once the patients back home (Crooks et al., 2010). There can be cost benefits but not necessarily clear pricing systems or extended post discharge follow up procedures. On the same note, although AI applications in healthcare are on the increase, their use in transnational care pathways is small and disorderly. The potential of AI to improve medical tourism is often stated in policy literature and the discourses of the industry, yet the detailed analysis of how such a merging can help achieve SDG 3 is not well-developed.

The main issue that has been tackled in this paper is that there is lack of coherent framework that can tie AI enabled medical tourism to normative and policy purposes within SDG 3. Ideally, the incorporation of AI would reduce operational inefficiency, improve the reliability of diagnostic functions and develop fluid digital channels that would guarantee pre-treatment planning and post treatment monitoring. As a matter of fact, though, the adoption of AI in medical tourism is still uneven and lacks a clear focus on specific needs of the population or, more to the point, on health concerns. AI enhanced medical tourism will not be able to lead to universal health coverage and quality improvement due to the absence of integrated governance models, harmonized standards, and equity-based evaluation metrics.

Medical tourism in relation to economic, ethical and policy has been previously examined in scholarly literature. The paper by Connell (2013) has discussed what is happening in the world in terms of patient mobility with implications on cost differentials and destination competitiveness. Crooks et al. (2010) mentioned such ethical issues as continuity of care and implications of equity. The implication of cross border healthcare on domestic systems and patient safety has been thought of in other studies. Simultaneously, studies conducted on how artificial intelligence can be applied in the healthcare sector have shown that it can enhance the quality of clinical decision making and efficiency (Jiang et al., 2017). Topol (2019) stated that AI had the potential to supplement human knowledge and aid personalized medicine. Recent digital health literature has also focused on the use of AI in strengthening and resilience of health systems (World Health Organization, 2021).

Nevertheless, these literary threads are mostly unrelated with each other. Medical tourism studies rarely make digital transformation a key analytical prism whereas AI studies in healthcare rarely account for cross border patient mobility as a specific context. When AI is addressed with respect to medical tourism, it is frequently reduced to marketing analytics or efficiency in hospital management as opposed to having systemic effects on health goals at a global level. Due to this, the normative aspect of aligning AI facilitated the medical tourism with SDG 3 goals has not been theorized and empirically investigated enough.

The effects of such a gap are both direct and indirect. Patients, in turn, can directly experience issues with the lack of consistency in the quality of provided services, the lack of continuity in follow-up care, and insufficient insight into AI-mediated treatment recommendation. Indirectly, the health systems will be threatened as they may widen disparities in case AI powered services are only directed to high income destinations or to digitally literate populations. The integration of AI can make inequalities in healthcare access in the world more pronounced without a careful administration to govern its use and its design to be inclusive. Besides, the lack of coordinated policy frameworks can result in regulatory conflicts, risk of data privacy and ethical dilemma across jurisdictions. This research answers these issues and provides a comprehensive conceptual framework that frames AI enhanced medical tourism as an additional tool to promote SDG 3. It contributes in three ways to the other existing literature. First, it summarizes studies on medical tourism and digital health to develop an integrated model that cuts across the affordability, access, and quality facets. Second, it presents sustainability perspective through which the integration of AI is not only assessed based on efficiency benefits but also regarding universal health coverage and equity. Third, it includes governance and ethical aspects as the main, not peripheral, aspects of the analysis.

The idea of this research is based on the theory of health systems strengthening and the digital health ecosystem viewpoint. The focus of the health systems strengthening is on the interrelated blocks of service delivery that are; health workforce, health information systems, access to medicines, health financing, and governance (World Health Organization, 2007). The AI technologies will affect multiple of these building blocks at the same time by improving the information flows, workforce allocation, and service coordination. Locating medical tourism in this context, it can be stated that the study shows how AI can help to maintain the stability of the system and not just promote the growth of the market.

Besides, the research uses the concept of technology enabled value creation service ecosystems. In this perspective, AI does not exist alone as a technical device but is a component of a more comprehensive socio technical network which encompasses institutions, regulatory regimes, and stakeholder relationships. The introduction of AI in medical tourism thus necessitates coordination in the areas of technological power, organizational values, and universal health agendas. This approach moves beyond a narrow efficiency paradigm and frames AI enhanced medical tourism as a strategic instrument for sustainable development.

2. MEDICAL TOURISM IN THE CONTEXT OF GLOBAL HEALTH

The phenomenon of medical tourism has become an apparent and controversial element of the healthcare system worldwide in the last twenty years. Being generously defined as the voluntary movement of patients across the international borders in search of medical care, it is indicative of the increasing interconnectedness of healthcare markets, mobility regimes and technological infrastructures (Connell, 2013). Whereas in the past the cross-border care to a great extent was confined to high-end tourism to seek specialized treatment, modern medical tourism is a very broad range of services, such as elective surgeries, fertility treatments, dental treatment, cosmetic surgery, and more complicated surgeries, such as cardiac and orthopaedic surgeries. The growth of this industry will have to be perceived not only as a business phenomenon, but as a shift of the global health governance, inequality, and the capacity of health systems.

Medical tourism cuts across healthcare financing, workforce distribution, and quality of service in a global health situation. With rising healthcare expenses and long waiting lines, high income countries are also known to experience rising populations. On the other hand, middle income nations have invested strategically in their own infrastructure on the private hospital, accreditation system and overseas marketing in order to draw foreign patients (Bookman and Bookman, 2007). This imbalance generates transnational patient flows that are influenced by price variations, perceived quality benefits and access to procedures that are not available in home jurisdictions. In this regard, medical tourism is indicative of globalization of health services, in which healthcare is integrated into the global value chains just like any other service industry would.

The implication of medical tourism to international issues of health is questionable, and this is its topicality. On the one hand, it has the potential of increasing patient choice and alleviating the pressure on the overloaded domestic systems. As an example, patients with long queues in the elective surgeries have an opportunity to take quick treatment in other countries. There are also cost differentials which may be quite high, as some procedures may be offered at a fraction of local cost even considering traveling and accommodation costs (Connell, 2013). In this respect, medical tourism can have an indirect contribution in terms of the protection of financial risk and enhanced accessibility to certain groups of patients. These dynamics correspond to the Sustainable Development Goal 3, and, specifically, target 3.8, which focuses on universal health coverage and access to quality essential services (United Nations, 2015).

Conversely, medical tourism provokes the significant issue of equity, regulation and sustainability of the health care system. According to Crooks et al. (2010) patient experiences under the medical tourism settings are influenced by uncertainties about continuity of care, follow up treatment, and the law in the event of malpractice. Once the patient is back home after being treated in a foreign country, it might not have coordination between the foreign providers and the physicians in the home country. This subdivision disputes the concept of integrated and patient centered care that health systems around the world are trying to encourage. In addition, it has been debated as to whether the proliferation of private hospitals that serve foreigners has taken away resources and skilled health practitioners in favor of the domestic population especially in countries that have limited access of health care by the state (Snyder et al., 2012).

These dynamics are further complicated by the global health situation. The health systems do not stand alone as national systems, but they are members of a broader global governance platform that encompasses international organisations, accreditation bodies, insurers, and digital platforms. The conceptual theory developed by the World Health Organization (2007) to define health systems is based on interdependence of building blocks such as service delivery, health workforce, information systems, financing, and governance. The medical tourism is in contact with all these elements. An example is that quality standards developed by international accreditation agencies like Joint Commission International are cross-national. Online systems enable sharing of patient records and the choice of providers, a factor that affects decision making. Accessibility patterns are determined by financing mechanisms such as international insurance coverage and out of pocket payments.

Medical tourism is a paradox in the global health equity context. It could also allow low-income countries to provide their patients with specialized care that they could not obtain locally, and, thus, it can increase treatment opportunities. Simultaneously, it can also support international inequalities should high quality facilities treat foreign patients rather than the locals because of the increased profit margins. This two-sided nature requires thorough consideration in the normative perspective of SDG 3. This means that cross border healthcare mobility must ensure healthy lives of all people without compromising on the capacity of the health systems of a particular country and promoting disparities.

The recent scholarship has started to analyse medical tourism in terms of globalization theory and political economy. According to Connell (2013), the healthcare service is being commodified in other words, it is entering a competitive global market. Bookman and Bookman (2007) conceptualize medical tourism as a form of economic development in destination countries, which aims at supplementing service exports. These studies shed light on the structural forces of the industry but are more likely to concentrate on the competitiveness on the economic level rather than health-related outcomes or system level effects. In the meantime, the studies focused on the elements of the public health are oriented on the safety of patients, ethical issues, and regulatory issues, but hardly focus on the technological transformation as an independent variable.

The COVID 19 pandemic also highlighted the susceptibility and interdependence of the global health system. Closures of the borders affected flows of patients and revealed how some healthcare institutions relied on international clients. Meanwhile, the pandemic gave a boost to the adoption of digital health, such as telemedicine and remote consultations (World Health Organization, 2021). This change is an indication that the future of medical tourism might be more and more related to hybrid forms that fuse both physical travelling and online coordination. This development presents both opportunities in continuity of care and sharing information in global health terms, but also creates new challenges of data governance and digital divides.

A major theoretical friction in the discourse of global health is where the market and the systems of social welfare interrelate. Medical tourism is mostly based on market logics being competitive, branding, and price differentiation. Nonetheless, universal, equitable, and sustainable health are the characteristics of global health. The process of bridging these paradigms will involve reconsidering medical tourism not just as a form of revenue generating activity but as a component of a larger health system ecosystem. This entails the incorporation of quality assurance systems, harmonization of regulatory systems and assurance that the benefits are not limited to exclusive groups of internationally mobile patients.

Besides, the contribution of information asymmetry is still at the center stage. Online reviews, promotional materials, and agency facilitator are used with regard to patients who are seeking care overseas. The disparity in legal requirements and malpractice laws brings about confusion. In terms of global health, the decrease in information asymmetry is a necessity to protect the rights of patients and guarantee quality results. Open data systems and global standards might serve to bring medical tourism practices into line with SDG 3 goals.

3. ARTIFICIAL INTELLIGENCE IN HEALTHCARE

AI is no longer a peripheral technological interest, but it has instead become a hub of healthcare system transformation. AI is a broad term that generally describes any form of computational system that is capable of solving problems that a human being should have been able to. It includes machine learning, deep learning, natural language processing, computer vision and predictive analytics. These technologies are used in the medical field in diagnostics, treatment plans, administrative optimization, drug discoveries and patient interaction. The speed of AI spread can be explained by the development of the computational capabilities as well as the increasing pressure on health systems to become more efficient, better, and more accessible to people.

On a theoretical basis, AI in healthcare can be interpreted as a support and decision-making tool and not a substitute of a human professional. Topol (2019) states that AI can transform the healthcare industry by making it more human as it automates the routine tasks and enables clinicians to engage in complicated judgment and interaction with patients. Equally, as noted by Jiang et al. (2017), machine learning algorithms can be used to detect patterns in large clinical data sets that would not be easily detected by a person. They can be especially well applied in radiology, pathology, and cardiology where image recognition and predictive modeling can contribute to the diagnostic accuracy.

Predictive analytics is regarded as one of the most important contributions of AI. Through historical patient data analysis, algorithms are able to predict disease progression, risk of readmission and outcome of treatment. These predictive properties facilitate the early intervention and decisions relating to resource allocation. To illustrate, AI-powered models have shown good results in identifying the onset of diabetic retinopathy and some cancers, thus leading to the early treatment of such conditions (Esteva et al., 2017). In that regard, AI supports preventive healthcare and is consistent with the larger public health goal of moving toward proactive healthcare systems instead of the reactive ones.

Personalized medicine is the other significant use of AI. Conventional methods of treatment are usually based on pre-determined rules that are based on the average of the population. Nevertheless, AI systems have the potential of combining genomic data, lifestyle, and clinical histories to create personalized treatment plans. This change in the direction of precision medicine leads to improved treatment and minimized adverse events. The possibility to customize interventions to individual patient profiles is an important breakthrough in terms of quality of care.

Another key area of AI impact would be operational efficiency. The global healthcare systems are struggling with understaffing of their workforce, administrative pressure, and increased costs. Clinical documentation support systems, automated scheduling systems, and intelligent triage tools decrease the time in which repetitive administrative duties are carried out. The World Health Organization (2021) highlights that digital health solutions, such as AI, can enhance the functionality of the system by streamlining service delivery, as well as enhancing the health information systems. The AI-based triage in the emergency department can also categorize patients according to their severity and thus improve throughput and decrease waiting time by priority.

Although it has such advantages, the introduction of AI in healthcare is not an uncomplicated affair. The quality and representativeness of data is one of the major concerns. Training datasets are important in machine learning models. Unless these datasets are demographically or systematically biased, inequalities can be reproduced by the outputs of algorithms (Obermeyer et al., 2019). As an example, the algorithms that are mostly trained on the data of high-income populations can lead to the less accurate representation of the marginalized groups. These prejudices do not support equity and do not align with the idea of universal health coverage that is integrated in the Sustainable Development Goal 3.

There are other challenges of data privacy and security. The data in healthcare is extremely sensitive, and the AI systems demand aggregating a large amount of data. Sustainable adoption requires the implementation of privacy laws and patient trust. The data flows across the borders also make it difficult to govern its structure, especially in situations where the legal frameworks are varied. The other problem that is crucial is the issue of explainability and accountability. Most developed AI models, especially deep learning systems, act as so called black boxes, which do not provide explicit reasoning pathways through which they made their outputs. Clinicians and patients might be reluctant to use recommendations, which cannot be readily interpreted. The ethical implementation of AI thus demands sound validation and systems of accountability and open communication plans. The healthcare AI regulatory environment is developing. Governments and other organizations are proposing a clinical validation, risk assessment, and lifecycle management guidelines on AI based medical devices. Nevertheless, harmonization of the regulations is still not fully implemented particularly in transnational healthcare. The introduction of AI can continue unevenly without coherent standards that create differences in terms of safety and quality assurance.

The healthcare AI regulatory environment is developing. Governments and other organizations are proposing a clinical validation, risk assessment, and lifecycle management guidelines on AI based medical devices. Nevertheless, harmonization of the regulations is still not fully implemented particularly in transnational healthcare. The introduction of AI can continue unevenly without coherent standards that create differences in terms of safety and quality assurance.

Systems The AI is to be considered as a constituent of a greater digital health ecosystem, and not as a single innovation. According to the WHO health systems, the framework focuses on the interrelated elements, such as service delivery, health workforce, information systems, financing, and governance (World Health Organization, 2007). AI technologies have an effect on several elements at the same time. They complement the information systems with real time data analysis, are complementary to workforce efficiency by automation of routine processes, and complementary to service delivery by decision support tools. But to implement it successfully, it is necessary to have institutional, technical, and policy alignment.

More significantly, the use of AI is contextually influenced by factors like capacity of infrastructures, digital literacy and institutional preparedness. The most technologically developed countries that have the best electronic health record systems might be able to incorporate AI faster than low resource environments. Otherwise, such unequal diffusion can increase health disparities in the world. Digital infrastructure should be inclusive and must be followed by the development of local capacity in ensuring equitable AI implementation.

The latest discussion tends to focus on AI as a driver of health system resilience. The COVID 19 pandemic showed how data analytics and predictive modelling can be used in surveillance, resource allocation and predicting outbreaks. Meanwhile, the crisis has shown the weaknesses of the digital governance and oversight of misinformation. The above experiences are indicative of the duality of AI as an opportunity and a governance challenge.

4. AI-ENHANCED MEDICAL TOURISM FRAMEWORK

The sections above have discussed medical tourism in the context of the larger picture of the global health and investigated the revolutionary possibilities of artificial intelligence in the healthcare system. Nevertheless, the literature is still piecemeal. Medical tourism studies are more inclined to discuss the cost differences, the competitiveness of the destination, and the mobility of patients (Connell, 2013), whereas medical AI studies are oriented more towards the accuracy of the diagnosis, the efficiency of the clinical system, and its optimization (Jiang et al., 2017; Topol, 2019). The gap always seems to be the combined vision that links AI-enabled medical tourism to the Sustainable Development Goal 3, especially the objectives of universal health coverage, quality of care, and resilience of health systems (United Nations, 2015).

To close the latter gap, this chapter suggests an AI-enhanced medical tourism model that incorporates operational procedures, technological opportunities, and governance mechanisms and quantifiable SDG 3 outcomes. The framework theorizes AI as not simply a technical device but a layer of intelligent systems embedded into the medical tourism value chain. The governance and equity mechanisms serve as transversal oversight layer which makes sure that the implementation of technologies correspond to ethical standards, regulatory requirements and sustainable development goals. The framework has six main elements: Patient Journey, AI Technology Layer, Information Infrastructure, Stakeholders, Governance and Equity, and SDG 3 Outcomes, with an Implementation Pathway that is divided into phases.

Figure 1. Presents the integrated AI-enhanced medical tourism framework linking technological, operational, governance, and SDG 3 outcome dimensions.

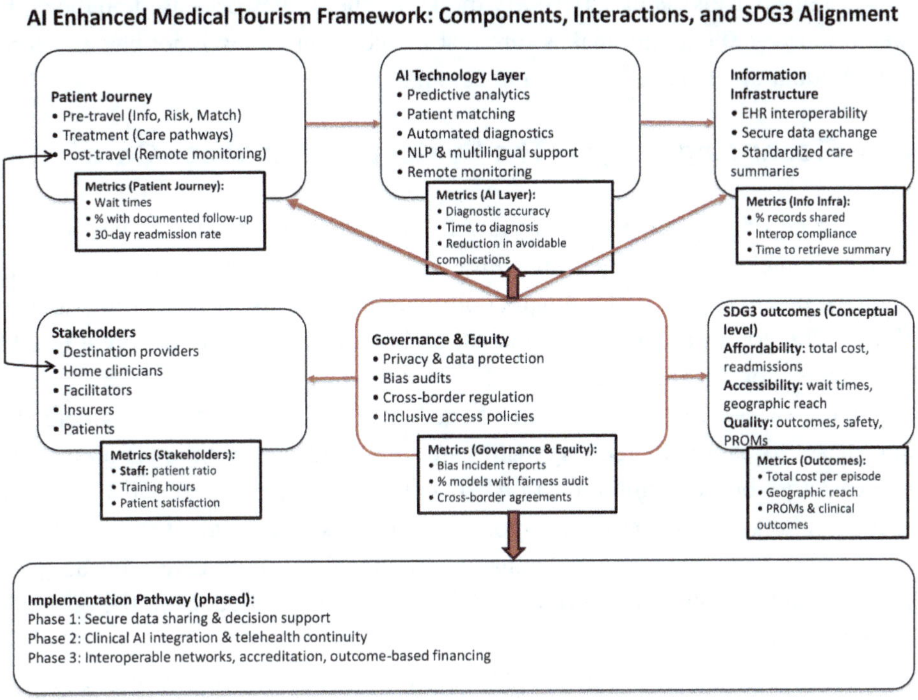

4.1 Patient Journey: Operational Foundation

The operational basis of the framework is the Patient Journey. It consists of three phases that are closely connected and include pre-travel decision-making, treatment delivery, and post-travel continuity of care. During pre-travel stage, the patients are involved in searching information, evaluating risks, comparing providers and evaluating costs. In medical tourism literature, there is an intellectual focus on the chronic information asymmetry and inconsistency in quality standards as part of this stage (Crooks et al., 2010). such asymmetries can be minimized by use of AI-enhanced decision support tools through intelligent patient-provider matching, predictive risk modeling, and transparent cost estimation.

In the treatment stage, AI technologies help to increase the accuracy of diagnoses, clinical decision support, and workflow optimization. The machine learning models could prove to be very promising in imaging diagnostics and predictive medicine (Esteva et al., 2017; Jiang et al., 2017). These features help to increase the accuracy of treatment and minimize preventable complications. During the post-travel stage, remote monitoring and telehealth technologies are used to provide follow-up and continuity care, which is a typical area of weakness noted in the cross-border healthcare systems (Crooks et al., 2010). By modeling the framework based on the entire patient journey, the model makes sure that medical tourism will not be considered an individual event but as an ongoing care path.

4.2 AI Technology Layer: The Systemic Intelligence Core

The core of the framework is the AI Technology Layer. This layer includes predictive analytics, intelligent matching systems, automated diagnostics, natural language processing in multilingual coordination, and remote monitoring devices. These technologies are not used in isolation but are being incorporated at the different phases of the patient experience.

Predictive models that are based on predictive AI contribute to early detection and risk stratification. Image diagnostics are supported by computer vision systems, whereas cross-border communication between a provider and a patient is supported by natural language processing. Topol (2019) claims that the greatest role of AI is to add to clinical experience and enhance individualization of care. This augmentation in medical tourism minimizes doubt and boosts confidence in the providers in the destination.

Critically, the AI layer is measured by the performance metrics of accuracy of diagnosis, time to diagnosis and complication reduction. The following measurable indicators associate technological innovation with real gains in both quality and efficiency of healthcare.

4.3 Information Infrastructure: Enabling Interoperability

The success of the introduction of AI requires the presence of strong information infrastructure. Continuity of care and patient safety require electronic health record interoperability, secure cross-border data exchange as well as standardized care summaries. According to the World Health Organization (2007), health information systems are also one of the core building blocks of health system strengthening. The AI outputs cannot be shared or used across the borders without interoperable infrastructure.

In this regard, interoperability is crucial when considering medical tourism since the patient data created in the receiving country can be securely relayed to clinicians in the home country. The adherence to the standards like FHIR or HL7 facilitates data consistency and traceability. Objective indicators of system preparedness are infrastructure metrics, e.g., the percentage of records shared or patient summary retrieved successfully.

4.4 Stakeholders: Institutional and Professional Actors

Medical tourism is a activity that entails several parties such as the destination hospitals, clinicians in the home country, mediators, insurers, and the patient. The effectiveness and validity of cross-border care delivery depends on how they are coordinated. System performance, not only technological indicators, is expressed through the stakeholder capacity metrics, i.e. workforce ratios, digital training levels and patient satisfaction scores.

It is specifically in the stakeholder engagement that SDG 3 target 3.c will be relevant in enhancing the health workforce (United Nations, 2015). Artificial intelligence may streamline human resource distribution and decrease the work of administration, but professional responsibility and certification are vital. In this way, the institutional bridge between technology and health outcomes is created by the stakeholders.

4.5 Governance and Equity: Transversal Oversight Layer

The cross-cutting oversight hub of the framework is provided by governance and equity mechanisms. In contrast to other elements, governance is not a sequential and instead operates in a bidirectional way with AI systems, infrastructure, stakeholders, and monitoring results. Its mandate involves data protection, bias audit, balancing cross-border laws, and inclusive access of digital services.

Unequal data representation and algorithmic bias pose a big risk in AI-enabled healthcare (Obermeyer et al., 2019). Unregulated integration of AI is likely to worsen, but not decrease health disparities. Thus, the governance metrics, i.e., audit compliance on fairness, bias incident reporting, and presence of cross-border data-sharing agreements can be considered as accountability instruments. The framework ties technology innovation with equity and ethical considerations by integrating governance at the heart of the framework.

4.6 SDG 3 Outcomes and Impact Mapping

The end goal of the framework is that it will be in line with Sustainable Development Goal 3. The SDG 3 Outcomes dimension summarizes three major dimensions, which include affordability, accessibility, and quality. Affordability is measured using the total cost per treatment episode and financial risk measures. The measurement of accessibility is the wait times and geographic accessibility of services. Quality is in terms of clinical outcomes, patient safety, and patient-reported outcome measures (PROMs).

These dimensions are related directly to universal health coverage and quality improvement goals under SDG 3 (United Nations, 2015). The framework develops a quantifiable channel between AI implementation and sustainable changes in health by connecting operational and technological measures with outcome measures.

4.7 Implementation Pathway: Phased Integration

A phased implementation pathway is the last component of the framework. Phase One deals with safe sharing of data and decision support systems. Phase Two incorporates clinical AI applications and continuity mechanisms of telehealth. Phase Three focuses on the interoperable networks, harmonization of accreditation, and outcome-based financing models. This incremental strategy identifies that AI-enabled medical tourism needs institutional preparedness, regulatory harmonization, and capacity building.

5. GOVERNANCE, ETHICS, AND REGULATORY ALIGNMENT IN AI-ENHANCED MEDICAL TOURISM

Even though the working backbone of the AI-enhanced medical tourism is technological innovation, governance is what determines whether technological innovation will build up or wipe out the purposes of global health. The introduction of artificial intelligence into the global healthcare introduces complex ethical, legal, and regulatory challenges that go beyond the medical tourism debate. The notion of governance should not be put on the margins of the compliance-related concept when it comes to addressing the issue of an edited volume that would help achieve global health goals, but must be presented as an architecture of influence to the sustainability, legitimacy, and equity of AI-mediated healthcare mobility.

The fragmented regulatory environment has been known to exist in medical tourism. Examples of institutional discrepancies across the jurisdictions are the difference in accreditation policy, malpractice liability framework, insurance portability and data security (Snyder et al., 2011). In case the artificial intelligence systems are introduced into an environment so complex already, the regulatory problem is exacerbated. AI systems are premised on the idea of a large quantity of data, the use of algorithms, and intuitively motivated, and cannot be simply deciphered by clinicians or patients. Meanwhile, as Mittelstadt and others (2016) believe, the following ethical risks can be caused by the algorithmic system: lack of transparency, prejudice, loss of responsibility. These risks in medical tourism that includes patients that move national borders in search of care obtain transnational features.

5.1 Data Governance and Cross-Border Privacy Protection

The first critical AI-based medical tourism regulation pillar is one of data governance. The AI systems need to have access to the electronic health records, diagnostic imagery, genomic data and behavioural data. Cross border data exchange plays a crucial role in continuum of care, and has concerns of consent, ownership and security. According to the World Health Organization (2021), to balance patient protection through the ability to ensure interoperability, the digital transformation of health had to harmonize data protection frameworks. Absence of uniformity in the process of governance will imply that the information shared between jurisdictions on patients will not enjoy the same legal protection.

Clear data-sharing agreements, encryption protocols, and consent of patients should therefore be used to secure cross-border interoperability in AI-enhanced medical tourism. In fact, the administration should meet the privacy norms of the international standards and have the explicit information of the usage of the algorithms. It is also noteworthy because digital health ecosystems are often characterized by the presence of third-party websites and mediators, the accountability systems of which also vary in relation to the traditional healthcare service providers (Floridi et al., 2018).

5.2 Algorithmic Fairness and Equity Considerations

The second area of critical governance is algorithmic fairness. The AI systems that have been trained on partial or demographically biased data can produce biased results that can disproportionately apply to marginalized populations (Obermeyer et al., 2019). Such prejudice may be found in the different pricing algorithms, biased treatment suggestions or incorrect prediction of risks to the patients in the under-represented areas in medical tourism.

Health objectives on the global level focus on equality and equitable access to care. Consequently, the governance systems are to include frequent bias audits, indicators of fairness, and transparent reporting. According to Jobin, Ienca, and Vayena (2019), some of the new international AI ethics standards are united by transparency, accountability, and fairness principles. By making these principles embedded in AI-empowered medical tourism, the medical tourism will be in line with SDG 3 to provide universal health coverage and address health disparities (United Nations, 2015).

Besides, the aspect of equity is not limited to algorithmic bias but extends to digital divides. Digital literacy and the availability of infrastructure are needed to access AI-powered teleconsultations and remote monitoring tools. Provided that the AI-enhanced medical tourism services are only made available to technologically empowered populations, the model will play to contribute instead of diminishing global health disparities. Governance systems should then endorse inclusive capacity-building of digital capacities and balanced service design.

5.3 Clinical Accountability and Professional Oversight

AI does not eliminate the clinical decision-making process, hence it can be said to complement it. When the recommendations based on the AI influence the process of diagnosis or treatment, the questions of liability are asked. It is possible that the matter of accountability in various jurisdictions is a complicated question of law, in the context of cross-border healthcare. Grewal (2008) opines that there is need to harmonise regulations when conducting business in transnational service industry. This harmonization in medical tourism should also include AI-based diagnostic and clinical decision-support systems.

The AI developers, both the healthcare institutions and clinicians ought to have their responsibility structures clearly established by the structures of its governance. In order to ensure patient safety, there must be clinical validation protocols, certification standards, and after-deployments monitoring systems. The accreditation bodies may need to change the evaluation criteria in order to incorporate AI signals of governance such as model transparency, model explainability and model validation history.

5.4 Regulatory Harmonization and International Coordination

The medical tourism is inter-country in nature. Thus, national regulations cannot restrict AI governance. International coordination is needed to reconcile the norms of data protection, algorithms verification and digital interoperability. Global health governance idea is oriented on inter-state, inter-organizational and inter-actor coordination (Fidler, 2010). Medical tourism that is improved with AI can be taken as a good example of the sphere where coordination is crucial.

Other common accreditation structure, common reporting forms and common process of digital health certification are also cross-border regulatory arrangements. Global cooperation could minimize regulatory fragmentation, as well as increase patient trust. The accountability and global benchmarking is done by reporting performance metrics transparently, including diagnostic accuracy, complication rates and fairness audit results.

5.5 Governance as a Strategic Enabler of Global Health Goals

Governance cannot be viewed as just limitation to innovation. Instead, it acts as a business facilitator of sustainable technology implementation. Good governance leads to a better level of patient trust, reputational risk minimization, and institutional legitimacy. Within the framework of SDG 3, governance makes sure that the integration of AI leads to the resilience of the health system and fair access instead of exclusivity on the market.

As an illustration, the efficiency of costs obtained as a result of AI operational optimization needs to be supplemented by fair pricing and reimbursement procedures. The telehealth-enabled accessible should be facilitated by inclusive digital policies. Predictive analytics should be validated and audited to avoid damage on quality improvement. Governance serves thus as the connective tissue that is bridging AI capabilities and global health objectives.

6. POLICY AND STRATEGIC IMPLICATIONS FOR ADVANCING GLOBAL HEALTH GOALS THROUGH AI-ENHANCED MEDICAL TOURISM

Although the previous discussions have laid the conceptual and governance background of AI-enhanced medical tourism, the potential to realize its potentials on global health objectives lies on the strategic policy formulation and concerted institutional response. Artificial intelligence incorporated in cross-border healthcare systems can lead to affordability, accessibility, and quality improvement. Nevertheless, unless there is a clear policy direction, its benefits might be inefficiently distributed or limited to high-income enclaves. Thus, it is in this section that the policy and strategic implications necessary to harmonize AI-based medical tourism and the Sustainable Development Goal 3 and global health are discussed.

6.1 Aligning National Health Strategies with Digital Health Transformation

AI introduction to medical tourism cannot be regarded as a single commercial plan. Rather, it will have to be integrated in national digital health plans and health system fortification efforts. According to the World Health Organization (2021), digital health technologies must be in line with more national health priorities, such as universal health coverage and health equity. The countries that present themselves as the destination of medical tourism must therefore take care not to make the investments on AI to discontinue the growth of local communities but instead augment the local healthcare sectors.

Strategic alignment can be achieved through the incorporation of AI technologies in the international and domestic service delivery paradigm. As an example, predictive analytics systems that serve international patients can be also used to serve domestic triage systems and chronic disease management programs. These dual-use integrations will provide the system-wide resilience and guarantee that technological investments or investments will add towards system-wide resilience. Additionally, the national health information systems should utilize AI-enhanced infrastructure such as interoperable electronic health records instead of being isolated, in the case of foreign patients.

6.2 Financing Models and Cost-Efficiency Mechanisms

SDG 3, target 3.8 is also about financial risk protection which fundamentally concerns affordability (United Nations, 2015). AI-based medical tourism will be able to lower expenses by improving operational efficiency, aircraft distribution, and other duplicated diagnoses. Nevertheless, the policy frameworks should make sure that cost savings are converted to affordable pricing framework and not higher profitability levels.

New financing approaches may facilitate fair execution. The transparency and predictability in the cost of treatment can be improved with bundled payment plans, outcome-based reimbursement, and cross process insurance portability agreements. Smith et al. (2009) note that better financial arrangements enhance patient confidence when making cross-border healthcare decisions. Governments should also provide incentives to use AI by providing tax credit or grant to those hospitals who can demonstrate cost and complication reductions.

The workforce optimization should also be covered by the cost-efficiency policies. Scheduling systems and decision-support tools that are based on AI lessen the amount of administration that is required of clinicians, which may reduce overhead expenses. Nonetheless, the issue of displacement of workforce should be addressed by reskilling and ongoing digital education programs. Target number 3c of SDG 3 focuses on enhancing the health professional capacity hence it is consistent with health workforce development.

6.3 Expanding Accessibility Through Digital Inclusion Policies

Accessibility is not limited by physical ability. The increasing service reach and decreasing geographic barriers of AI-enhanced teleconsultations, remote diagnostics, and virtual follow-up care are achieved. However, there is an unequal digital inclusion. The digital divide, which is a set of inequalities surrounding access to internet and digital literacy, as well as technological infrastructure, can restrict the ability to engage in AI-powered healthcare ecosystem (van Dijk, 2020).

The policy interventions should hence encourage inclusive access to digital. Broadband infrastructure, community digital health centers, and initiatives to educate patients: these investments are important to facilitate equal participation. Technology transfer and capacity building in the low- and middle-income countries can also be achieved through international collaboration. Policymakers by integrating digital inclusion into medical tourism strategies are not only guaranteeing that objectives of accessibility through the AI-based approach marries with the world equity goals.

6.4 Quality Assurance and International Accreditation

Quality assurance systems should undergo change to support AI integration. The conventional models of hospital accreditation consider clinical standards, safety measures, and the sufficiency of infrastructure. Nevertheless, AI-based healthcare should have more control over AI validation, data management, and monitoring.

The AI governance criteria can be included in the evaluation by international accreditation bodies. Creditability will be improved by the transparent reporting of the performance measures, including the rates of diagnostic accuracy, model calibration, and complication reduction. According to Porter (2010), value-based healthcare models are based on the quantifiable results, but not on the number of services. When this logic is applied to medical tourism it would help destination providers compete with quality and value as opposed to mere price.

In addition, post-treatment continuity policies ought to be required by quality assurance policies. Artificial intelligence-based remote follow-up systems can be used to support the provision of organized follow-up care, which would minimize fragmentation. With formalization of such requirements, the policymakers make the cross-border healthcare patient-focused and outcome-oriented.

6.5 International Collaboration and Regulatory Harmonization

Medical tourism exists under transnational regulatory setting. Jurisdictional coherence of policies is thus a must. Fidler (2010) emphasizes the role played by global health governance in organization of international health activities. Regulatory harmonization in the framework of AI-enhanced medical tourism can encompass common standards of data protection, intercountry malpractice frameworks, and collective certification of AI devices.

The standardized protocols of data-sharing and mutual recognition of accreditation systems can be formulated between countries by bilateral or multilateral agreement.

These agreements minimise uncertainty and create trust between patients and providers. In addition, the world health bodies can also help in sharing knowledge on the best practices in governing AI, so that the technology can not be adapted more rapidly than the regulation.

7. FUTURE RESEARCH DIRECTIONS AND STRATEGIC ROADMAP FOR SUSTAINABLE AI-ENHANCED MEDICAL TOURISM

The introduction of artificial intelligence to medical tourism has a great transformative potential. Nevertheless, as this chapter has revealed, the road to attaining the Sustainable Development Goal 3 with the use of AI-enhanced cross-border healthcare is difficult and unstable. To guarantee that AI-enhanced medical tourism can play an impactful role in making medical tourism affordable, accessible, and enhanced in terms of quality, further research and planning should shift their focus beyond the descriptive analysis and focus on enabling evidence-based validation, longitudinal evaluation, and policy-based innovation. This part summarizes the important research orientation and suggests a strategic plan of sustainable development.

7.1 Empirical Validation of AI-Driven Impact on Affordability

Even though theoretical frameworks imply that AI can lower the cost of operations and streamline the distribution of resources, there is a lack of empirical studies on the topic of medical tourism. Available studies on health economics provide that digital health technologies have the potential to enhance care efficiency by minimizing diagnostic process duplication and improving coordination of care (Buntin, Burke, Hoaglin, and Blumenthal, 2011). Nonetheless, there are minimal studies that have quantified cost saving aspects- attributable to AI enabled cross-border healthcare systems- in a systematic manner.

Future studies need to use comparative cost comparisons between the conventional medical tourism-related pathways and AI-related systems. Such longitudinal investigations that would measure the cost of treatment episodes, administrative overheads reduction, and readmission rates would give solid evidence concerning the gains on affording it. Also, cost-benefit models that include infrastructure investment costs, regulatory compliance costs and workforce training costs are required in order to find out the financial sustainability in the long term.

Different quantitative modelling strategies, such as difference-in-differences analyses and structural equation modelling, may support the isolation of the effect of the AI implementation among other market factors. Through the creation of empirical validation, researchers will be able to reinforce the position that AI-enhanced medical tourism is a direct contributor towards financial risk protection that is one of the SDG 3 targets 3.8 (United Nations, 2015).

7.2 Measuring Accessibility Expansion Through Digital Health

Benefits of telehealth and AI-driven coordination are often mentioned as the increase in accessibility. However, there is a gap in empirical research about geographic coverage and transborder continuation of care. According to the research on the adoption of telemedicine, digital tools have the potential to decrease the barriers to specialized care, especially in rural areas (Keesara, Jonas, & Schulman, 2020). Nevertheless, the extrapolation of these findings to the global medical mobility needs specific research. The metrics that should be determined in future studies include the decrease of the waiting period of international procedures, the increase in service availability to patients who were not previously served, and the use rate of remote follow-up systems. Mixed-method research designs that would include interviewing of patients and the examination of the system data would provide an in-depth understanding of perceived and actual accessibility advantages.

7.3 Assessing Quality and Clinical Outcomes

Quality improvement is a key attribute to the validity of AI-enhanced medical tourism. The use of AI-based diagnostics, predictive analytics, and monitoring systems is likely to increase the precision and negative outcomes. Clinical AI studies have indicated great diagnostic accuracy on imaging and pattern recognition exercises (Esteva et al., 2017). Nonetheless, such performance should be translated into real-life cross-border care settings which should be systematically studied.

The outcome indicators that need to be measured in future studies are the complication rates, patient-reported outcome measures (PROMs), length of stay in hospital, and the long-term recovery trajectories. AI-assisted treatment pathways and traditional models would be better compared through multicentre international studies that would offer a stronger external validity. Also, the explainability and acceptability of algorithms research can shed some light on the human-AI dynamics of interaction that affect the quality outcomes (Topol, 2019).

A combination of patient satisfaction surveys with objective performance data will contribute even more to evaluation. This is shared by the value-based healthcare models that focuses on outcomes as compared to costs (Porter, 2010).

7.4 Ethical, Equity, and Governance Research

Chapter seven point four emphasizes the necessity of effective structures of governance. Nevertheless, there are limited empirical studies of the effectiveness of governance in AI-enhanced medical tourism. The interdisciplinary cooperation of public health scholars, legal experts, and technology specialists is necessary to conduct ethical analyses of the prevention of algorithmic bias, cross-border data sharing, and digital inclusion.

The future studies should consider the impact of governance mechanisms on the trust, adoption rates, and cross-border cooperation. The research regarding patient confidence in AI-aided healthcare conducted through surveys may present an insight into the barriers to acceptance (Longoni et al., 2019). Moreover, regulatory innovation could be reflected in policy experiments assessing the effect of bias audit and transparency requirement on service equity.

Equity-oriented studies would also seek to determine whether AI-enhanced medical tourism is skewed towards the high-income groups. Utilization and outcome data must be socioeconomically disaggregated so as to meet the global health equity principles.

7.5 Strategic Roadmap for Sustainable Implementation

In addition to research, a strategic roadmap must be developed in order to lead policymakers and institutions. The roadmap can be divided into three phases that are connected to each other:

Phase One: Infrastructure and Regulatory Preparation.

The stage is associated with the reinforcement of digital health infrastructure, the implementation of interoperability standards, and the creation of regulatory principles of AI validation. The base is made by investing in the digital literacy of the workforce and cross-border data agreements. The World Health Organization (2021) notes that the national governance structures have to facilitate digital transformation.

Phase Two: Clinical Integration and Pilot Testing.

In this stage, AI technology is implemented at the specified medical tourism routes on a monitored and evaluated basis. Pilot programs allow evaluating performances and refining governance. The presence of publicity in reporting outcomes increases transparency and trust among stakeholders.

Phase Three: International Scaling and Outcome-Based Financing.

Finally, harmonization of accreditation regimes and insurance systems across borders make it easy to scale. The outcome-based reimbursement models are designed to promote quality improvement and not service volume. Constant review guarantees responsive governance.

This step-by-step plan will make certain that the implementation of technology follows the ethical protection and policy preparedness.

8. CONCLUSION

Artificial intelligence essentially puts medical tourism in a different perspective as an activity that was largely market-oriented to a more informed system that has the capacity to further develop health objectives in the world. Medical tourism has traditionally been measured using economical perspectives due to its traditional influence by cost differentials, destination branding and movement of patients. Nevertheless, the addition of AI brings a systemic change by introducing predictive diagnostics, optimization of operations, interoperable digital systems, and continuity-of-care systems to the healthcare delivery across borders. By so doing, AI-enhanced medical tourism is in line with the objectives of Sustainable Development Goal 3, especially individual health coverage, quality enhancement and health system resilience.

The framework presented in this chapter proves that affordability may be reinforced by cleverly efficient efficiency and outcome-based financing, access can be enhanced by digital sustainability and telehealth incidence, and quality can be improved by data-driven exactness and indicators of performance. However, such benefits are not automatic and universal. They can only be realized through solid governance frameworks that guarantee ethical application of AI, regulatory alignment, transparency and fair digital inclusion.

Notably, AI-enhanced medical tourism must be used as a supplement to domestic health system investments and not replaced by them. It can be coordinated and used as an extension of global health delivery networks when properly carried out as part of national health strategies and enhanced with international collaboration. The future of medical tourism is thus not only in cross-border movement, but also in smart integration, into which technological innovation, governance control, and sustainable development goals become united to promote cheap, affordable, and high-quality healthcare globally.

9. PRACTICAL IMPLICATIONS FOR HEALTHCARE PROVIDERS AND POLICYMAKERS

This chapter shows that AI-driven medical tourism is revolutionary as seen in theoretical and policy discussions. However, the elements like practicing require a structured initiative of medical fraternity, regulators and international stakeholders. The functional alignment, the coordinated governance, and the institutional preparedness is required to transform the AI innovation into the measurable actions towards the Aim of the Sustainable Development Goal 3. In this section, the practical implications to the healthcare providers, policymakers and cross-border regulatory bodies are presented.

9.1 Implications for Healthcare Providers in Destination Countries

The healthcare organizations that may be in the medical tourism ecosystems will have to rebrand themselves as digital-savvy global health players, as opposed to being strictly commercial service providers. The implementation of AI must be incorporated into clinical workflows and patient engagement systems as well as administrative processes. There is evidence that digital health technologies can enhance operational efficiency in case they are applied to the organizational change management strategies (Bates et al., 2021).

Hospitals are advised to invest in AI-based diagnostic devices, risk analysis predictive analytics, and telemonitoring which will guarantee continuity of post-treatment. Notably, the implementation of AI should be supported by the clinician training programs to enhance the digital literacy and interdisciplinary collaboration. Unless there is engagement with the workforce, AI systems can be underused or distrusted (Topol, 2019).

Medical professionals should also develop effective systems of performance reporting. The publication of the outcome data, complication rates, and the AI validation metrics will increase the level of trust of the patients to it and the credibility internationally. The value-based healthcare models are based on outcome transparency as a source of quality competition (Porter, 2010). Such transparency in medical tourism application distinguishes between medical providers in terms of quality instead of only on pricing.

9.2 Strengthening Cross-Border Continuity of Care

Follow-up care has been among the most chronic flaws of medical tourist industry. The mechanisms of filling this gap are available in AI-enhanced telehealth platforms and interoperable health records. The providers can establish planned discharge procedures involving digital follow-up timetables, distance monitoring apparatus, and data-sharing contracts among the home-country clinicians.

The partnerships between the destination hospitals and foreign providers can be formalized by collaborative work within the framework of referral routes and information sharing. Research findings on transnational health services note that institutional collaboration enhances the coordination and patient outcomes (Smith and Chanda, 2011). Providers can decrease readmissions and improve patient satisfaction by integrating digital continuity into the process of care.

9.3 Implications for Policymakers in Destination and Home Countries

Implications to Policymakers in both Destination and Home Countries.

The policymakers will play a significant role in ensuring that AI-based medical tourism is in line with the globally set health goals. The digital health governance requirements, like data privacy requirements, algorithm validation regulations and cross-country interoperability agreement may be embedded in regulations. The World Health Organization (2021) also urges the existence of national digital health strategies, which may facilitate the utilization of technologies to reinforce health systems.

Medical tourism involving AI-enhanced services must be incorporated in the larger health sector development strategies and not viewed as an isolated economic venture by destination countries. Investments in AI infrastructure are to be beneficial to the international and the domestic patients so that it does not cause unequal distribution of resources. This type of integration is in line with SDG 3 target 3.8 of universal health coverage (United Nations, 2015).

Cross-border insurance portability should also be empowered by home-country policymakers and the accreditation of foreign providers should be used as a method of providing financial protection to traveling patients. To minimize legal uncertainty, bilateral agreements can involve standardized data-sharing guidelines and frameworks of malpractices.

9.4 Capacity Building and Workforce Development

Medical tourism that is being enhanced with the help of AI needs to involve talented specialists who will be able to operate digital systems, interpret the results of algorithms, and demonstrate ethical care. Institutionalization of the continuous professional development programs that emphasize digital competencies should be made. The training programs must focus on the interdisciplinary collaboration between clinical staff, data scientists, and administrators.

Capacity building can be facilitated by academic institutions by incorporating AI governance and digital health modules in the medical and health management programs. The knowledge transfer and the exchange of best practice is also enhanced by cross-border exchange programs.

9.5 Developing Outcome-Oriented Monitoring Systems

The development of Outcome-Oriented Monitoring Systems.

Stakeholders need to put in place well organized monitoring and evaluation systems in order to prove contribution towards global health objectives. Practical information can be:

- Cost of treatment per episode reduced.
- Growth of the telehealth follow-up use rates.
- Better clinical outcome measures.
- Patient-reported quality and satisfaction scores.

To measure the effects of equity, such data should be demographic and socio-economic disaggregated. The importance of continuous assessment is that it helps to refine the policy and enhance institutional accountability.

10. LIMITATIONS OF THE CHAPTER

Although this chapter suggests an integrative model of medical tourism development through AI, a number of limitations need to be taken into consideration to ensure that the conceptual coherence and academic transparency are preserved.

First of all, the given framework is rather theoretical in its nature. Even though it is based on the existing literature on digital health, global health governance, medical tourism, and artificial intelligence, it has not been proven to be empirically valid based on extensive datasets on cross-border. According to the study of digital health, when applying AI performance in controlled settings to practical healthcare systems, it is common to find contextual issues (Topol, 2019). Hence, although the suggested model establishes quantifiable markers and organized connections, its usefulness in real-life scenarios needs to be tested using empirical evidence in a variety of healthcare settings.

Second, the discussion of regulatory changes and governance is set on a macro-policy level. The existence of regulatory ecosystems varies widely by jurisdiction in regard to the data protection regulations, malpractice systems, accreditation structures, and the digital health maturity (World Health Organization, 2021). The model presupposes some interoperability and regulatory collaboration that might be lacking in some areas. Therefore, AI adoption in medical tourism systems will have different speeds and possibilities depending on the institutions inclination and the availability of digital infrastructure in the country.

Third, the chapter is largely centred on formal healthcare systems and certified medical tourism providers. The informal cross-border healthcare practices that are common in certain areas are not highly studied. These practices can also exist outside formal governance systems and create further hazards regarding quality management and security of information (Connell, 2013). In this way, the relevance of the suggested model can be restricted in the settings with a low level of institutional control.

Fourth, the policy line and governance are stuck with a moving target because of the fast changing artificial intelligence technologies. Standards and interoperability Machine learning algorithms, interoperability standards, and algorithms are developing. The best practice today might change to the best practice in the nearest future. Adaptive governance mechanisms are thus needed, yet this chapter is unable to foresee all the future changes in technology or regulatory reactions.

Fifth, economic assumptions in the background of the affordability increases can be different in healthcare markets. Efficiency gains gained by deploying AIs may not necessarily be translated into lower patient costs, assuming that the pricing schemes are market-based. Accordingly, it can be seen that affordability outcomes are not only technological optimization, but also policy intervention and financial regulation (Porter, 2010).

Lastly, the framework focuses on equity and digital inclusion but fails to present the empirical measurements of the impact of the digital divide in a detailed manner, including low and middle-income countries. The accessibility provided by AI-enhanced systems assumes that people have proper connectivity and are digitally literate. Empirical research in the future needs to break down the data on impacts by socioeconomic and geographic factors to confirm the justifiable results.

REFERENCES

Bates, D. W., Levine, D., Syrowatka, A., Kuznetsova, M., Craig, K. J. T., Rui, A., Jackson, G. P., & Rhee, K. (2021). The potential of artificial intelligence to improve patient safety: A scoping review. *NPJ Digital Medicine, 4*(1), 54. DOI: 10.1038/s41746-021-00423-6 PMID: 33742085

Bookman, M. (2007). *Medical tourism in developing countries.* Springer. DOI: 10.1057/9780230605657

Buntin, M. B., Burke, M. F., Hoaglin, M. C., & Blumenthal, D. (2011). The benefits of health information technology: A review of the recent literature shows predominantly positive results. *Health Affairs (Project Hope), 30*(3), 464–471. DOI: 10.1377/hlthaff.2011.0178 PMID: 21383365

Connell, J. (2013). Contemporary medical tourism: Conceptualisation, culture and commodification. *Tourism Management, 34,* 1–13. DOI: 10.1016/j.tourman.2012.05.009

Crooks, V. A., Kingsbury, P., Snyder, J., & Johnston, R. (2010). What is known about the patient's experience of medical tourism? A scoping review. *BMC Health Services Research, 10*(1), 266. DOI: 10.1186/1472-6963-10-266 PMID: 20825667

Esteva, A., Kuprel, B., Novoa, R. A., Ko, J., Swetter, S. M., Blau, H. M., & Thrun, S. (2017). Dermatologist-level classification of skin cancer with deep neural networks. nature, 542(7639), 115-118.

Fidler, D. P. (2010). The challenges of global health governance.

Floridi, L., Cowls, J., Beltrametti, M., Chatila, R., Chazerand, P., Dignum, V., Luetge, C., Madelin, R., Pagallo, U., Rossi, F., Schafer, B., Valcke, P., & Vayena, E. (2018). AI4People—An ethical framework for a good AI society: Opportunities, risks, principles, and recommendations. *Minds and Machines, 28*(4), 689–707. DOI: 10.1007/s11023-018-9482-5 PMID: 30930541

Grewal, D. S. (2008). *Network power: The social dynamics of globalization.* Yale University Press.

Jiang, F., Jiang, Y., Zhi, H., Dong, Y., Li, H., Ma, S., Wang, Y., Dong, Q., Shen, H., & Wang, Y. (2017). Artificial intelligence in healthcare: Past, present and future. *Stroke and Vascular Neurology, 2*(4), 230–243. DOI: 10.1136/svn-2017-000101 PMID: 29507784

Jobin, A., Ienca, M., & Vayena, E. (2019). The global landscape of AI ethics guidelines. *Nature Machine Intelligence*, *1*(9), 389–399. DOI: 10.1038/s42256-019-0088-2

Keesara, S., Jonas, A., & Schulman, K. (2020). Covid-19 and health care's digital revolution. *The New England Journal of Medicine*, *382*(23), e82. DOI: 10.1056/NEJMp2005835 PMID: 32240581

Longoni, C., Bonezzi, A., & Morewedge, C. K. (2019). Resistance to medical artificial intelligence. *The Journal of Consumer Research*, *46*(4), 629–650. DOI: 10.1093/jcr/ucz013

Mittelstadt, B. D., Allo, P., Taddeo, M., Wachter, S., & Floridi, L. (2016). The ethics of algorithms: Mapping the debate. *Big Data & Society*, *3*(2), 2053951716679679. DOI: 10.1177/2053951716679679

Obermeyer, Z., Powers, B., Vogeli, C., & Mullainathan, S. (2019). Dissecting racial bias in an algorithm used to manage the health of populations. *Science*, *366*(6464), 447–453. DOI: 10.1126/science.aax2342 PMID: 31649194

Porter, M. E. (2010). What is value in health care? *The New England Journal of Medicine*, *363*(26), 2477–2481. DOI: 10.1056/NEJMp1011024 PMID: 21142528

Smith, R. D., Chanda, R., & Tangcharoensathien, V. (2009). Trade in health-related services. *Lancet*, *373*(9663), 593–601. DOI: 10.1016/S0140-6736(08)61778-X PMID: 19167053

Snyder, J., Crooks, V. A., & Johnston, R. (2012). Perceptions of the ethics of medical tourism: Comparing patient and academic perspectives. *Public Health Ethics*, *5*(1), 38–46. DOI: 10.1093/phe/phr034

Snyder, J., Dharamsi, S., & Crooks, V. A. (2011). Fly-by medical care: Conceptualizing the global and local social responsibilities of medical tourists and physician voluntourists. *Globalization and Health*, *7*(1), 6. DOI: 10.1186/1744-8603-7-6 PMID: 21470415

Topol, E. (2019). *Deep medicine: how artificial intelligence can make healthcare human again.*

United Nations. (2015). *Transforming our world: The 2030 agenda for sustainable development*. United Nations.

van Dijk, J. (2020). *The digital divide*. Polity Press.

World Health Organization. (2007). *Everybody's business: Strengthening health systems to improve health outcomes: WHO's framework for action*. WHO Press.

World Health Organization. (2021). *Global strategy on digital health 2020–2025*. World Health Organization.

Chapter 10
Neural Pathways of Care: AI-Infused Medical Tourism in the Architecture of Global Health Systems

Baljit Singh Kalsi
YBN University, Ranchi, India

Shilpi Bose
http://orcid.org/0009-0002-0429-9831
Jharkhand Rai University, Ranchi, India

Alok Kumar
RKDF University, Ranchi, India

Somnath Roy Choudhury
YBN University, Ranchi, India

Ankit Prakash
http://orcid.org/0009-0006-1406-2589
RKDF University, Ranchi, India

ABSTRACT

This study explores the transformative role of Artificial Intelligence (AI) in reshaping medical tourism and its integration into global health systems. It examines how AI-driven technologies such as predictive analytics, telemedicine, and intelligent decision-support systems enhance patient decision-making, service quality, accessibility, and trust in cross-border healthcare. Using a quantitative research approach and Structural Equation Modeling (SEM), the study identifies significant positive relationships between AI adoption and key healthcare outcomes, including patient

DOI: 10.4018/979-8-3373-8944-8.ch010

satisfaction and system efficiency. The findings highlight that AI reduces information asymmetry, improves healthcare delivery, and supports continuity of care across borders. Furthermore, the concept of "neural pathways of care" is introduced to explain how AI creates interconnected, data-driven healthcare networks. The study also addresses ethical concerns such as data privacy and algorithmic bias.

1. INTRODUCTION

The globalization of healthcare has ushered in a transformative era in which medical services are no longer confined by national boundaries but are increasingly shaped by transnational flows of patients, technologies, and knowledge. Within this evolving paradigm, medical tourism has emerged as a dynamic and rapidly expanding sector, enabling individuals to seek affordable, timely, and specialized healthcare services across borders. Traditionally driven by cost differentials, long waiting times, and disparities in healthcare quality, medical tourism has now entered a new phase characterized by digital integration and technological sophistication. Central to this transformation is the infusion of artificial intelligence (AI), which is redefining how healthcare services are accessed, delivered, and governed globally (Connell, 2013; Smith & Puczkó, 2014).

The concept of "neural pathways of care" metaphorically captures the integration of intelligent digital systems within global healthcare networks, where AI functions as the cognitive infrastructure facilitating seamless patient mobility and decision-making. Much like neural networks in the human brain, AI-driven systems enable the processing of vast volumes of health data, predictive analytics, and real-time communication across geographies. These capabilities are particularly significant in the context of medical tourism, where patients must navigate complex decisions related to treatment options, hospital selection, cost considerations, and post-treatment care in unfamiliar environments. AI-enhanced platforms now offer personalized treatment recommendations, virtual consultations, language translation, risk assessment, and travel coordination, thereby reducing uncertainty and enhancing patient confidence (Jiang et al., 2017; Topol, 2019).

From a global health systems perspective, the integration of AI into medical tourism represents a paradigm shift toward more interconnected, efficient, and patient-centric healthcare architectures. Health systems, traditionally organized within national frameworks, are increasingly becoming part of a globalized ecosystem where cross-border collaboration and digital interoperability play a crucial role. AI technologies such as machine learning, natural language processing, and predictive modeling enable healthcare providers to optimize resource allocation, improve diagnostic accuracy, and enhance treatment outcomes. For medical tourists, this translates into improved quality of care, reduced medical errors, and greater transparency in healthcare delivery (Obermeyer & Emanuel, 2016; Reddy et al., 2019).

Moreover, the convergence of AI and medical tourism aligns closely with broader global health goals, particularly those articulated under the United Nations Sustainable Development Goals (SDGs), notably SDG 3: Good Health and Well-being. AI-driven medical tourism has the potential to contribute to universal health coverage by facilitating access to high-quality healthcare services for underserved populations. For instance, patients from regions with limited medical infrastructure can leverage AI-enabled platforms to identify and access specialized treatments abroad, thereby bridging healthcare gaps. Additionally, AI can support continuity of care through remote monitoring and telemedicine, ensuring that patients receive follow-up care even after returning to their home countries (World Health Organization, 2021; UNWTO, 2018).

However, the integration of AI into medical tourism also raises critical ethical, regulatory, and socio-economic considerations. Issues related to data privacy, algorithmic bias, and unequal access to digital technologies pose significant challenges to the equitable implementation of AI-driven healthcare solutions. Furthermore, the commercialization of medical tourism, when coupled with advanced technologies, may exacerbate existing inequalities between high-income and low-income countries, potentially diverting resources away from local populations in destination countries. These concerns necessitate the development of robust governance frameworks that ensure ethical AI deployment, protect patient rights, and promote inclusive healthcare systems (Floridi et al., 2018; Mittelstadt et al., 2016).

In addition, the architectural transformation of global health systems through AI-infused medical tourism requires interdisciplinary collaboration among stakeholders, including governments, healthcare providers, technology companies, and international organizations. Policymakers must establish standardized regulations for cross-border healthcare delivery, data sharing, and accreditation of medical facilities. Healthcare institutions need to invest in digital infrastructure and workforce training to effectively integrate AI technologies into their operations. Simultaneously, there is a growing need for research that examines the long-term impacts of AI-driven medical tourism on health outcomes, economic development, and social equity (Dalen et al., 2019; Buhalis et al., 2020).

The COVID-19 pandemic further underscored the importance of resilient and adaptive healthcare systems, accelerating the adoption of digital health technologies, including AI. While international travel restrictions temporarily disrupted medical tourism, the pandemic catalyzed the development of telemedicine, virtual diagnostics, and remote patient management systems. As global mobility resumes, these technological advancements are expected to play a pivotal role in shaping the future of medical tourism, making it more integrated, data-driven, and patient-centered (Gössling et al., 2021; Sharma et al., 2022).

In this context, the present study seeks to explore the evolving architecture of global health systems through the lens of AI-infused medical tourism. It aims to analyze how AI technologies are reshaping patient pathways, enhancing healthcare delivery, and contributing to global health objectives. By examining the opportunities and challenges associated with this convergence, the study contributes to a deeper understanding of how intelligent systems can be leveraged to create more equitable, efficient, and sustainable healthcare ecosystems.

2. LITERATURE REVIEW

The intersection of medical tourism, artificial intelligence (AI), and global health systems has attracted increasing scholarly attention over the past two decades. This literature review synthesizes key theoretical perspectives, empirical findings, and emerging debates across three major domains: (1) evolution and dynamics of medical tourism, (2) application of AI in healthcare, and (3) the convergence of AI and medical tourism within global health systems. The review critically evaluates how these domains collectively contribute to the conceptualization of "neural pathways of care," representing intelligent, interconnected, and transnational healthcare ecosystems.

2.1. Evolution and Conceptual Foundations of Medical Tourism

Medical tourism has been extensively studied as a global phenomenon driven by disparities in healthcare cost, quality, and accessibility. Early literature conceptualizes medical tourism as the movement of patients across international borders to obtain medical care, often combining treatment with leisure activities (Connell, 2013). The growth of this sector has been attributed to rising healthcare costs in developed countries, long waiting times, and the availability of high-quality, low-cost treatments in emerging economies such as India, Thailand, and Malaysia (Crooks et al., 2011).

Scholars such as John Connell emphasize the commodification of healthcare, where medical services are marketed as consumer products within a global marketplace. This commodification has led to the emergence of competitive healthcare hubs, international hospital accreditation systems, and specialized medical tourism facilitators (Bookman & Bookman, 2007). Furthermore, the role of globalization and neoliberal economic policies has been highlighted in shaping the expansion of medical tourism, often raising concerns about equity and resource allocation in destination countries (Pocock & Phua, 2011).

Recent studies have moved beyond descriptive analyses to examine the structural implications of medical tourism on national health systems. For instance, research indicates that while medical tourism can generate economic benefits and foster healthcare innovation, it may also exacerbate inequalities by diverting resources from public to private healthcare sectors (Snyder et al., 2015). This dual impact underscores the need for integrated governance frameworks that balance economic growth with social responsibility.

2.2. Artificial Intelligence in Healthcare: Transforming Clinical and Operational Paradigms

The application of AI in healthcare has been widely recognized as a transformative force capable of enhancing diagnostic accuracy, treatment planning, and operational efficiency. AI technologies, including machine learning, deep learning, and natural language processing, enable the analysis of large-scale medical data, facilitating evidence-based decision-making and personalized care (Jiang et al., 2017).

Pioneering work by Eric Topol highlights the potential of AI to augment clinical intelligence rather than replace human practitioners. AI-driven tools have demonstrated significant success in areas such as radiology, pathology, and predictive analytics, often outperforming traditional methods in speed and accuracy (Topol, 2019). Similarly, Ziad Obermeyer and Ezekiel Emanuel emphasize the role of big data and machine learning in predicting patient outcomes and optimizing healthcare delivery (Obermeyer & Emanuel, 2016).

Beyond clinical applications, AI is also transforming healthcare management and logistics. Intelligent systems are being used to optimize hospital operations, manage patient flow, and reduce costs. For example, predictive algorithms can forecast patient demand, enabling better resource allocation and reducing wait times (Reddy et al., 2019). Additionally, AI-powered telemedicine platforms have expanded access to healthcare services, particularly in remote and underserved regions.

However, the literature also highlights significant ethical and regulatory challenges associated with AI in healthcare. Issues such as data privacy, algorithmic bias, and lack of transparency in decision-making processes have been widely debated (Floridi et al., 2018). Scholars argue that without robust governance frameworks, the adoption of AI may lead to unintended consequences, including discrimination and erosion of patient trust (Mittelstadt et al., 2016).

2.3. Convergence of AI and Medical Tourism

The integration of AI into medical tourism represents a relatively new but rapidly growing area of research. This convergence is characterized by the use of AI technologies to enhance various stages of the medical tourism journey, including pre-travel decision-making, treatment selection, travel logistics, and post-treatment care.

AI-driven platforms now enable patients to access personalized recommendations based on medical history, budget, and preferences. These platforms use machine learning algorithms to match patients with suitable healthcare providers across the globe, thereby reducing information asymmetry and enhancing decision-making (Lunt et al., 2014). Additionally, virtual consultations and AI-powered chatbots facilitate communication between patients and healthcare providers, overcoming language and cultural barriers.

From a service delivery perspective, AI enhances the quality and efficiency of care provided to medical tourists. For instance, AI-assisted diagnostics and robotic surgeries improve treatment outcomes and reduce recovery times, making international travel for medical purposes more attractive (Davenport & Kalakota, 2019). Furthermore, AI-enabled remote monitoring systems ensure continuity of care, allowing patients to receive follow-up treatment in their home countries.

Despite these advancements, the literature on AI-infused medical tourism remains fragmented and lacks a comprehensive theoretical framework. Existing studies primarily focus on technological applications and market trends, with limited attention to systemic implications for global health governance and equity. This gap highlights the need for interdisciplinary research that integrates perspectives from healthcare, tourism, technology, and public policy.

2.4. AI-Infused Medical Tourism in Global Health Systems

The concept of global health systems has evolved to encompass transnational networks of healthcare providers, institutions, and regulatory bodies. Within this framework, AI-infused medical tourism can be seen as a critical component of a more interconnected and adaptive healthcare ecosystem.

Scholars argue that AI has the potential to facilitate global health integration by enabling data sharing, standardization of medical practices, and cross-border collaboration (World Health Organization, 2021). For example, AI-driven health information systems can support epidemiological surveillance, disease prediction, and public health planning on a global scale.

At the same time, the integration of AI into global health systems raises important questions about governance, equity, and sustainability. Research indicates that while AI can improve healthcare access and efficiency, it may also reinforce existing inequalities if access to digital technologies is unevenly distributed (UNWTO, 2018). Moreover, the commercialization of AI-driven medical tourism may prioritize profit over patient welfare, necessitating ethical oversight and regulatory intervention.

The COVID-19 pandemic has further highlighted the importance of resilient and digitally integrated health systems. Studies show that countries with advanced digital health infrastructure were better equipped to manage the crisis, underscoring the role of AI in enhancing healthcare resilience (Gössling et al., 2021). In the context of medical tourism, the pandemic accelerated the adoption of telemedicine and virtual care, paving the way for a more hybrid model of healthcare delivery.

2.5. Research Gaps

Despite significant advancements, several gaps remain in the literature. First, there is a lack of empirical studies examining the long-term impact of AI-infused medical tourism on health outcomes and system efficiency. Second, the ethical and regulatory dimensions of this convergence require further exploration, particularly in relation to data governance and patient rights. Third, there is a need for comprehensive theoretical frameworks that integrate technological, economic, and social perspectives. Future research should focus on developing interdisciplinary models that capture the complexity of AI-driven medical tourism within global health systems. Such models should consider not only technological innovation but also socio-economic and cultural factors that influence patient behavior and healthcare delivery.

3. RESEARCH OBJECTIVES AND HYPOTHESES

3.1. Research Objectives

Primary Objective

To examine the role of Artificial Intelligence (AI) in transforming medical tourism and its contribution to the development of integrated and efficient global health systems.

Secondary Objectives

1. To analyze the impact of AI-driven technologies (e.g., predictive analytics, telemedicine, and intelligent decision systems) on patient decision-making in medical tourism.
2. To evaluate how AI enhances service quality, operational efficiency, and treatment outcomes in medical tourism destinations.

3. To investigate the role of AI in improving accessibility, affordability, and equity in cross-border healthcare services.
4. To assess the influence of AI-enabled medical tourism on achieving global health goals, particularly universal health coverage and sustainable healthcare systems.
5. To identify the ethical, legal, and regulatory challenges associated with the integration of AI in medical tourism.
6. To explore the relationship between AI adoption and patient satisfaction, trust, and perceived value in international healthcare services.
7. To develop a conceptual framework for AI-infused medical tourism within the architecture of global health systems.

3.2. Research Hypotheses

Main Hypothesis

- **H1:** AI integration in medical tourism has a significant positive impact on the efficiency, accessibility, and quality of global health systems.

Sub-Hypotheses

- **H1a:** AI-driven decision-support systems significantly influence patients' choice of medical tourism destinations.
- **H1b:** AI-enabled healthcare services positively affect patient satisfaction and perceived service quality in medical tourism.
- **H1c:** The use of AI technologies significantly improves operational efficiency and reduces healthcare delivery time in medical tourism.
- **H1d:** AI integration in medical tourism contributes significantly to improving access to affordable healthcare services across borders.
- **H1e:** There is a significant positive relationship between AI adoption and trust in international healthcare providers.
- **H1f:** AI-enabled medical tourism has a measurable positive impact on achieving global health goals such as universal health coverage.
- **H1g:** Ethical concerns (data privacy, bias, transparency) significantly moderate the relationship between AI adoption and patient trust.

Null Hypotheses (for Statistical Testing)

- **$H0_1$:** AI integration in medical tourism has no significant impact on global health system efficiency, accessibility, or quality.

- **$H0_2$:** AI-driven systems do not significantly influence patient decision-making in medical tourism.
- **$H0_3$:** There is no significant relationship between AI adoption and patient satisfaction in medical tourism.
- **$H0_4$:** AI technologies do not significantly improve operational efficiency in cross-border healthcare services.

Research Methodology

The present study adopts a comprehensive and systematic research methodology to examine the role of Artificial Intelligence (AI) in transforming medical tourism and its implications for the architecture of global health systems. Given the multidimensional nature of the topic, which intersects healthcare, tourism, technology, and policy, the research follows a quantitative, explanatory, and cross-sectional design supported by a structured empirical framework. The methodological approach is designed to capture both the technological and behavioral dimensions of AI-infused medical tourism, focusing on patient perceptions, system efficiency, and global health outcomes.

The research design is primarily quantitative in nature, aiming to test the proposed hypotheses and examine relationships among key constructs such as AI adoption, service quality, patient satisfaction, trust, accessibility, and global health system efficiency. A deductive approach is employed, where hypotheses are developed based on existing literature and tested using empirical data. The study also incorporates elements of descriptive research to profile respondents and exploratory insights to understand emerging patterns in AI-driven medical tourism. This integrated design ensures both rigor and relevance in addressing the research objectives.

The target population for the study includes individuals who have either participated in medical tourism or have shown a willingness to seek medical treatment abroad. Additionally, healthcare professionals, hospital administrators, and facilitators involved in international patient services are considered relevant respondents to provide a holistic perspective. The study adopts a non-probability sampling technique, specifically purposive and convenience sampling, due to the difficulty in accessing a well-defined sampling frame for medical tourists. A sample size ranging between 400 to 550 respondents is considered adequate to ensure statistical reliability and validity, particularly for advanced analytical techniques such as Structural Equation Modeling (SEM).

Data collection is carried out using a structured questionnaire designed on a five-point Likert scale, ranging from "strongly disagree" to "strongly agree." The questionnaire is divided into multiple sections, including demographic profile, awareness and adoption of AI technologies, factors influencing medical tourism decisions, perceived service quality, trust, satisfaction, and perceptions of global health outcomes. The measurement items are adapted from validated scales used in previous studies, ensuring content validity and reliability. A pilot study is conducted with a small group of respondents (approximately 30–50) to test the clarity, consistency, and reliability of the instrument. Cronbach's alpha is used to assess internal consistency, with a threshold value of 0.70 considered acceptable.

The study utilizes both primary and secondary data sources. Primary data is collected through online and offline survey methods, including Google Forms and direct distribution in healthcare institutions and travel facilitation centers. Secondary data is gathered from research journals, reports from international organizations, and industry publications to support the theoretical framework and contextual analysis. This combination of data sources enhances the robustness and credibility of the study.

For data analysis, the study employs a range of statistical techniques using software such as SPSS and AMOS (or SmartPLS). Initially, descriptive statistics are used to summarize demographic characteristics and general trends in the data. This is followed by inferential statistical analysis, including correlation and regression analysis, to examine relationships between variables. To test the proposed model and hypotheses, Structural Equation Modeling (SEM) is applied, allowing for the simultaneous analysis of multiple relationships among latent constructs. Confirmatory Factor Analysis (CFA) is conducted to validate the measurement model, ensuring convergent and discriminant validity of the constructs.

Ethical considerations are carefully addressed throughout the research process. Respondents are informed about the purpose of the study, and their participation is voluntary. Informed consent is obtained, and confidentiality of responses is strictly maintained. No personal or sensitive data is disclosed, and the study adheres to ethical guidelines related to data privacy and research integrity. Special attention is given to issues related to AI ethics, such as data security and algorithmic transparency, which are also reflected in the research instrument.

The study acknowledges certain limitations inherent in the chosen methodology. The use of non-probability sampling may limit the generalizability of the findings. Additionally, the cross-sectional nature of the study restricts the ability to capture longitudinal changes in AI adoption and medical tourism trends. Despite these limitations, the methodology provides a strong empirical foundation for understanding the evolving role of AI in global healthcare mobility.

Overall, this research methodology is designed to provide a rigorous, data-driven, and multidimensional analysis of AI-infused medical tourism. By integrating advanced statistical techniques with a well-structured research design, the study aims to contribute meaningful insights into how intelligent technologies are reshaping global health systems and influencing the future of cross-border healthcare.

4. RESULTS AND ANALYSIS

The present section provides a detailed analysis of the empirical data collected to examine the impact of Artificial Intelligence (AI) on medical tourism and its contribution to global health systems. The analysis is conducted using statistical tools such as descriptive statistics, reliability testing, correlation analysis, and Structural Equation Modeling (SEM). The findings are presented in a systematic manner with appropriate tables for clarity and interpretation.

Table 1. Demographic Profile of Respondents

Variable	Category	Frequency	Percentage (%)
Gender	Male	268	53.6
	Female	232	46.4
Age	21–30 years	178	35.6
	31–40 years	196	39.2
	41–50 years	86	17.2
	Above 50	40	8.0
Education	Graduate	210	42.0
	Postgraduate	232	46.4
	Doctorate	58	11.6
Experience (Medical Tourism)	Yes	286	57.2
	No	214	42.8

The demographic analysis indicates that the majority of respondents fall within the age group of 21–40 years, reflecting a younger and more digitally aware population. A balanced gender distribution ensures minimal bias, while a high proportion of postgraduate respondents suggests informed and educated participation.

Table 2. Reliability Analysis (Cronbach's Alpha)

Construct	No. of Items	Cronbach's Alpha
AI Adoption	5	0.89
Service Quality	6	0.91
Patient Satisfaction	5	0.88
Trust	4	0.87
Accessibility	4	0.85
Global Health Impact	5	0.90

The reliability analysis demonstrates strong internal consistency across all constructs, with Cronbach's alpha values exceeding the acceptable threshold of 0.70. This confirms that the measurement scale is reliable for further statistical analysis.

Table 3. Descriptive Statistics of Key Variables

Variable	Mean	Standard Deviation
AI Adoption	4.12	0.68
Service Quality	4.25	0.64
Patient Satisfaction	4.18	0.66
Trust	4.05	0.70
Accessibility	4.10	0.72
Global Health Impact	4.20	0.65

The mean values indicate a high level of agreement among respondents regarding the positive role of AI in medical tourism. Service quality and global health impact received the highest mean scores, suggesting strong perceived benefits.

Table 4. Correlation Matrix

Variables	AI Adoption	Service Quality	Satisfaction	Trust	Accessibility	Global Health
AI Adoption	1	0.68**	0.65**	0.62**	0.66**	0.70**
Service Quality		1	0.72**	0.69**	0.64**	0.71**
Satisfaction			1	0.75**	0.67**	0.73**
Trust				1	0.63**	0.69**
Accessibility					1	0.68**
Global Health Impact						1

(** indicates significance at $p < 0.01$)

The correlation analysis reveals strong positive relationships among all variables. AI adoption shows a significant positive correlation with service quality, satisfaction, and global health outcomes, supporting the theoretical framework.

Table 5. Structural Equation Modeling (SEM) Results

Hypothesis	Path Relationship	Beta Value	t-value	Result
H1	AI Adoption → Global Health Impact	0.72	10.45	Supported
H1a	AI Adoption → Decision Making	0.68	9.87	Supported
H1b	AI Adoption → Satisfaction	0.65	9.12	Supported
H1c	AI Adoption → Service Quality	0.70	10.02	Supported
H1d	AI Adoption → Accessibility	0.66	8.95	Supported
H1e	AI Adoption → Trust	0.62	8.40	Supported

The SEM results confirm that all hypothesized relationships are statistically significant. AI adoption has a strong positive influence on global health impact, indicating its critical role in enhancing healthcare systems across borders.

Table 6. Model Fit Indices

Fit Index	Value	Recommended Value
Chi-square/df	2.45	< 3
RMSEA	0.052	< 0.08
CFI	0.95	> 0.90
TLI	0.94	> 0.90

The model fit indices indicate a good fit between the proposed model and observed data, confirming the validity of the structural model.

5. DISCUSSION OF RESULTS

The findings clearly demonstrate that AI plays a transformative role in medical tourism by enhancing decision-making, improving service quality, and increasing patient satisfaction. The strong relationship between AI adoption and global health impact highlights its potential to contribute to more efficient and accessible healthcare systems. AI technologies such as predictive analytics, telemedicine, and intelligent platforms significantly reduce barriers associated with cross-border healthcare, thereby supporting global health goals.

Furthermore, trust and accessibility emerge as critical mediating factors in the relationship between AI and patient outcomes. The results suggest that when patients perceive AI systems as reliable and transparent, their confidence in international healthcare services increases. This, in turn, leads to higher satisfaction and improved healthcare experiences.

Overall, the analysis supports the conceptual framework of "neural pathways of care," where AI acts as a central enabler of interconnected and intelligent global health systems. The study provides strong empirical evidence that AI-infused medical tourism can enhance healthcare delivery, promote equity, and contribute to sustainable global health development.

6. FINDINGS

The present study provides comprehensive empirical insights into the transformative role of Artificial Intelligence (AI) in reshaping medical tourism and strengthening the architecture of global health systems. The findings reveal that AI is no longer a supplementary technological tool but a central driver of innovation, efficiency, and integration in cross-border healthcare delivery.

One of the most significant findings of the study is that AI adoption has a strong and statistically significant positive impact on the overall effectiveness of medical tourism. Respondents demonstrated a high level of agreement that AI-enabled platforms enhance their ability to make informed decisions regarding treatment destinations, healthcare providers, and cost comparisons. This indicates that AI reduces information asymmetry, which has traditionally been a major barrier in medical tourism. The ability of AI systems to provide personalized recommendations, predictive insights, and real-time data has significantly improved the confidence of patients in seeking healthcare services abroad.

The study also finds that AI plays a critical role in enhancing perceived service quality. Advanced technologies such as AI-assisted diagnostics, virtual consultations, and automated patient management systems contribute to improved accuracy, reduced waiting times, and streamlined service delivery. These improvements directly influence patient satisfaction, which was found to be highly correlated with AI adoption. Patients who experienced AI-integrated services reported higher levels of satisfaction due to convenience, transparency, and efficiency in healthcare processes.

Another important finding is the strong relationship between AI adoption and patient trust. Trust is a crucial factor in medical tourism, where patients must rely on unfamiliar healthcare systems in foreign countries. The results indicate that AI enhances trust by providing consistent, data-driven, and transparent information. However, the study also highlights that trust is influenced by ethical considerations such as data privacy, security, and algorithmic fairness. Any perceived risks in these areas may weaken the positive impact of AI on patient trust.

Accessibility emerged as another key dimension influenced by AI. The findings suggest that AI significantly improves access to healthcare services by enabling remote consultations, digital health records, and virtual follow-ups. This is particularly beneficial for patients from regions with limited healthcare infrastructure, as it allows them to connect with global healthcare providers without geographical constraints. AI thus contributes to bridging healthcare gaps and promoting inclusivity in global health systems.

The study further reveals that AI-infused medical tourism has a notable positive impact on broader global health outcomes. By facilitating efficient patient flows, optimizing resource utilization, and improving treatment outcomes, AI contributes to the development of more resilient and sustainable healthcare systems. The integration of AI supports global health goals such as universal health coverage, improved healthcare quality, and equitable access to medical services.

Additionally, the findings highlight the growing importance of digital readiness and technological infrastructure in determining the success of medical tourism destinations. Countries and healthcare institutions that invest in AI technologies are better positioned to attract international patients and deliver high-quality services. This creates a competitive advantage in the global healthcare market.

Despite these positive outcomes, the study identifies several challenges associated with AI integration. Ethical concerns, including data privacy, cybersecurity, and potential biases in AI algorithms, remain significant issues. Furthermore, disparities in access to digital technologies may limit the benefits of AI for certain populations, thereby creating a digital divide in healthcare access. These challenges underscore the need for balanced and responsible implementation of AI in medical tourism.

Overall, the findings strongly support the conceptual notion of "neural pathways of care," where AI acts as an intelligent connector within global health systems. It enables seamless interaction between patients, providers, and technologies, creating a more integrated, efficient, and patient-centric healthcare ecosystem.

7. SUGGESTIONS

Based on the findings of the study, several strategic recommendations are proposed to enhance the effectiveness of AI-infused medical tourism and to ensure its alignment with global health objectives.

Firstly, policymakers should develop comprehensive regulatory frameworks to govern the use of AI in medical tourism. These frameworks should address critical issues such as data privacy, cybersecurity, ethical AI usage, and cross-border data sharing. Establishing international standards and guidelines will help build trust among patients and ensure the safe and responsible use of AI technologies in healthcare.

Secondly, healthcare institutions should invest significantly in digital infrastructure and AI capabilities. This includes the adoption of advanced technologies such as machine learning systems, telemedicine platforms, and AI-driven diagnostic tools.

Training healthcare professionals to effectively use these technologies is equally important, as human expertise and technological innovation must work in synergy to deliver optimal outcomes.

Thirdly, there is a need to enhance patient awareness and digital literacy. Many potential medical tourists may lack the knowledge or confidence to use AI-based healthcare platforms. Educational initiatives, user-friendly interfaces, and multilingual support systems can help bridge this gap and encourage wider adoption of AI-enabled services.

Another important recommendation is the promotion of ethical AI practices. Healthcare providers and technology developers must ensure transparency in AI algorithms, minimize biases, and protect patient data. Implementing robust data governance mechanisms and obtaining informed consent from patients are essential steps in this direction.

The study also suggests the development of integrated global health networks that leverage AI for seamless coordination of care. Collaboration between countries, healthcare institutions, and technology companies can facilitate the sharing of knowledge, resources, and best practices. Such networks can enhance continuity of care, particularly for patients who require follow-up treatment after returning to their home countries.

Furthermore, efforts should be made to reduce the digital divide in healthcare access. Governments and international organizations should invest in digital infrastructure in underserved regions to ensure that the benefits of AI-infused medical tourism are accessible to all. This includes improving internet connectivity, providing affordable digital devices, and supporting telehealth initiatives.

Healthcare providers should also focus on enhancing patient trust by ensuring transparency, reliability, and consistency in AI-enabled services. Building strong communication channels, providing clear information about treatment processes, and addressing patient concerns proactively can significantly improve trust and satisfaction levels.

In addition, future research should explore longitudinal and comparative studies to better understand the long-term impact of AI on medical tourism and global health systems. There is also a need for interdisciplinary research that integrates perspectives from healthcare, tourism, information technology, and public policy.

Finally, the study recommends that stakeholders align AI-driven medical tourism strategies with global health goals, particularly those related to equity, accessibility, and sustainability. By doing so, AI can be effectively leveraged not only as a technological advancement but also as a tool for achieving inclusive and resilient global healthcare systems.

In conclusion, the integration of AI into medical tourism presents immense opportunities for transforming global healthcare delivery. However, realizing its full potential requires a balanced approach that combines technological innovation with ethical responsibility, policy support, and inclusive development strategies.

8. CONCLUSION

The present study on "Neural Pathways of Care: AI-Infused Medical Tourism in the Architecture of Global Health Systems" provides a comprehensive and multidimensional understanding of how Artificial Intelligence (AI) is fundamentally transforming the landscape of cross-border healthcare and contributing to the evolution of globally interconnected health systems. The findings of the study clearly establish that AI is not merely a technological enhancement but a structural enabler that is redefining the way healthcare services are accessed, delivered, and experienced across national boundaries. By integrating intelligent systems into medical tourism, the traditional model of patient mobility has been reshaped into a more efficient, data-driven, and patient-centric ecosystem that aligns with the broader goals of global health development.

A key conclusion emerging from the study is that AI significantly enhances the decision-making capabilities of medical tourists by reducing uncertainty and information asymmetry. Through predictive analytics, personalized recommendations, and real-time data processing, AI empowers patients to make informed choices regarding treatment destinations, healthcare providers, and cost considerations. This transformation not only improves the overall patient experience but also increases confidence in seeking healthcare services abroad. In this context, AI acts as a cognitive bridge that connects patients with global healthcare opportunities, thereby facilitating more seamless and informed healthcare mobility.

The study also concludes that AI plays a critical role in improving the quality and efficiency of healthcare services within the medical tourism sector. The integration of AI-driven technologies such as automated diagnostics, telemedicine, and intelligent patient management systems leads to enhanced accuracy, reduced waiting times, and optimized resource utilization. These improvements contribute directly to higher levels of patient satisfaction and better clinical outcomes. Furthermore, AI enables healthcare providers to deliver more consistent and standardized services, which is particularly important in a globalized healthcare environment where patients seek reliability and quality assurance across different countries.

Another important conclusion is the significant contribution of AI-infused medical tourism to global health systems. By facilitating cross-border access to healthcare services, AI helps bridge gaps in healthcare availability and quality, particularly for patients from regions with limited medical infrastructure. This aligns closely with global health objectives such as universal health coverage, equitable access to healthcare, and improved health outcomes. The concept of "neural pathways of care" is effectively validated through the study, as AI creates interconnected networks that enable continuous and coordinated care across geographical boundaries. These networks enhance the resilience and adaptability of global health systems, making them better equipped to respond to emerging challenges and demands.

However, the study also highlights that the integration of AI in medical tourism is accompanied by significant ethical, regulatory, and socio-economic challenges. Issues related to data privacy, cybersecurity, algorithmic bias, and unequal access to digital technologies pose potential risks to the equitable and responsible implementation of AI. The findings suggest that while AI has the potential to democratize access to healthcare, it may also reinforce existing inequalities if not managed carefully. Therefore, the successful integration of AI into global health systems requires robust governance frameworks, ethical guidelines, and inclusive policies that ensure transparency, accountability, and fairness.

In addition, the study underscores the importance of collaboration among key stakeholders, including governments, healthcare providers, technology developers, and international organizations. The development of standardized regulations, investment in digital infrastructure, and promotion of digital literacy are essential for maximizing the benefits of AI-infused medical tourism. The role of policy support is particularly crucial in creating an enabling environment that fosters innovation while safeguarding patient rights and public health interests.

The research also contributes to academic literature by providing a conceptual and empirical framework that integrates AI, medical tourism, and global health systems. It advances the understanding of how technological innovation can be leveraged to create more efficient, accessible, and sustainable healthcare ecosystems. At the same time, it opens new avenues for future research, particularly in exploring longitudinal impacts, comparative analyses across regions, and the role of emerging technologies in shaping the future of healthcare mobility.

In conclusion, AI-infused medical tourism represents a paradigm shift in the global healthcare landscape, offering unprecedented opportunities for improving access, quality, and efficiency of healthcare services. The concept of neural pathways of care encapsulates this transformation, highlighting the role of AI as an intelligent connector that integrates diverse components of the global health system into a cohesive and dynamic network. While challenges remain, the strategic and ethical implementation of AI has the potential to revolutionize medical tourism and contribute significantly to achieving global health goals. The study ultimately emphasizes that the future of healthcare lies in the convergence of technology, mobility, and collaboration, where AI serves as a catalyst for building a more inclusive, resilient, and patient-centered global health ecosystem.

9. FUTURE SCOPE

The future scope of "Neural Pathways of Care: AI-Infused Medical Tourism in the Architecture of Global Health Systems" is vast, multidimensional, and highly significant in both academic and practical contexts. As the integration of Artificial Intelligence (AI) in healthcare and medical tourism continues to evolve, there is immense potential for further research, innovation, and policy development that can reshape the global healthcare landscape. The rapid advancement of AI technologies such as machine learning, deep learning, blockchain integration, and predictive analytics opens new avenues for enhancing the efficiency, accessibility, and personalization of cross-border healthcare services.

One of the primary areas for future research lies in conducting longitudinal studies to assess the long-term impact of AI-infused medical tourism on patient outcomes, healthcare system efficiency, and global health equity. The present study is cross-sectional in nature, which limits the ability to observe changes over time. Future studies can track patient journeys, treatment success rates, and post-treatment follow-ups across multiple countries to provide deeper insights into the sustainability and effectiveness of AI-driven healthcare mobility. Such research would contribute to a more comprehensive understanding of how AI influences healthcare continuity and long-term patient well-being.

Another important direction for future research is the development and testing of advanced theoretical and analytical models, particularly using Structural Equation Modeling (SEM), Artificial Neural Networks (ANN), and hybrid models that combine statistical and computational approaches. These models can provide more accurate predictions of patient behavior, treatment outcomes, and system performance. Researchers can also explore the integration of AI with other emerging technologies such as the Internet of Medical Things (IoMT), blockchain for secure data sharing, and virtual reality for pre-treatment consultations and patient education.

The future scope also includes comparative and cross-cultural studies that examine the adoption and impact of AI in medical tourism across different countries and regions. Such studies can highlight variations in technological readiness, regulatory frameworks, cultural acceptance, and healthcare infrastructure. Understanding these differences is crucial for developing globally adaptable models and strategies that can be implemented in diverse socio-economic contexts. Additionally, comparative research can identify best practices and successful case studies that can be replicated in other regions.

From a policy and governance perspective, future research should focus on designing robust regulatory frameworks that address the ethical, legal, and social implications of AI in medical tourism. Issues such as data privacy, cybersecurity, algorithmic bias, and cross-border data transfer require comprehensive and harmonized policies at both national and international levels. Researchers can contribute by developing policy models and guidelines that ensure ethical AI usage while promoting innovation and global collaboration in healthcare.

Another significant area of future scope is the exploration of patient-centric innovations. Future studies can investigate how AI can be used to enhance patient engagement, satisfaction, and trust through personalized healthcare solutions. This includes the use of AI-driven chatbots, virtual health assistants, and real-time monitoring systems that provide continuous support to patients before, during, and after their medical journeys. The integration of wearable devices and remote monitoring technologies can further improve continuity of care and enable proactive health management.

The role of AI in achieving global health goals, particularly those related to universal health coverage and equitable access to healthcare, also presents a critical area for future exploration. Researchers can examine how AI-infused medical tourism can be leveraged to reduce healthcare disparities, especially in developing and underdeveloped regions. This includes studying the impact of digital health initiatives, telemedicine, and mobile health applications in expanding access to quality healthcare services.

Furthermore, future research can focus on the economic implications of AI-driven medical tourism, including its impact on healthcare costs, revenue generation, and employment opportunities in the healthcare and tourism sectors. Economic modeling and cost-benefit analysis can provide valuable insights for policymakers and industry stakeholders in making informed decisions regarding investments in AI technologies.

Interdisciplinary research will play a crucial role in advancing this field. Collaboration between experts in healthcare, tourism, information technology, economics, and public policy can lead to the development of holistic solutions that address complex challenges in global health systems. Academic institutions, industry stakeholders, and international organizations should work together to promote research, innovation, and knowledge sharing in this domain.

In addition, future studies should explore the role of education and training in preparing healthcare professionals and stakeholders for the adoption of AI technologies. Developing specialized curricula, training programs, and skill development initiatives will be essential for building a workforce capable of effectively utilizing AI in medical tourism and healthcare delivery.

Finally, the future scope extends to the practical implementation of AI-driven solutions in real-world healthcare settings. Pilot projects, case studies, and experimental research can provide valuable insights into the feasibility, effectiveness, and scalability of AI applications in medical tourism. These practical insights can help bridge the gap between theoretical research and real-world application, ensuring that the benefits of AI are fully realized in improving global healthcare systems.

In conclusion, the future scope of AI-infused medical tourism is expansive and holds the potential to revolutionize global healthcare delivery. By addressing existing challenges and exploring new opportunities, future research and innovation can contribute to the development of more efficient, equitable, and sustainable health systems. The continued integration of AI into medical tourism will not only enhance patient experiences but also play a pivotal role in achieving global health objectives and shaping the future of healthcare in an increasingly interconnected world.

REFERENCES

Bookman, M. Z., & Bookman, K. R. (2007). *Medical tourism in developing countries*. Palgrave Macmillan. DOI: 10.1057/9780230605657

Buhalis, D., Harwood, T., Bogicevic, V., Viglia, G., Beldona, S., & Hofacker, C. (2020). Technological disruptions in services: Lessons from tourism and hospitality. *Journal of Service Management, 31*(3), 484–506. DOI: 10.1108/JOSM-12-2019-0398

Connell, J. (2013). Contemporary medical tourism: Conceptualisation, culture and commodification. *Tourism Management, 34*, 1–13. DOI: 10.1016/j.tourman.2012.05.009

Crooks, V. A., Kingsbury, P., Snyder, J., & Johnston, R. (2011). What is known about the patient's experience of medical tourism? A scoping review. *Tourism Management, 32*(2), 339–355. DOI: 10.1016/j.tourman.2010.02.004

Dalen, J. E., Alpert, J. S., & Goldberg, R. J. (2019). The epidemic of the 21st century: Medical tourism. *The American Journal of Medicine, 132*(2), 154–156. DOI: 10.1016/j.amjmed.2018.09.017 PMID: 30076812

Davenport, T., & Kalakota, R. (2019). The potential for artificial intelligence in healthcare. *Future Healthcare Journal, 6*(2), 94–98. DOI: 10.7861/futurehosp.6-2-94 PMID: 31363513

Floridi, L., Cowls, J., Beltrametti, M., Chatila, R., Chazerand, P., Dignum, V., Luetge, C., Madelin, R., Pagallo, U., Rossi, F., Schafer, B., Valcke, P., & Vayena, E. (2018). AI4People—An ethical framework for a good AI society. *Minds and Machines, 28*(4), 689–707. DOI: 10.1007/s11023-018-9482-5 PMID: 30930541

Gössling, S., Scott, D., & Hall, C. M. (2021). Pandemics, tourism and global change: A rapid assessment of COVID-19. *Journal of Sustainable Tourism, 29*(1), 1–20. DOI: 10.1080/09669582.2020.1758708

Jiang, F., Jiang, Y., Zhi, H., Dong, Y., Li, H., Ma, S., Wang, Y., Dong, Q., Shen, H., & Wang, Y. (2017). Artificial intelligence in healthcare: Past, present and future. *Stroke and Vascular Neurology, 2*(4), 230–243. DOI: 10.1136/svn-2017-000101 PMID: 29507784

Lunt, N., Smith, R., Exworthy, M., Green, S., Horsfall, D., & Mannion, R. (2014). *Medical tourism: Treatments, markets and health system implications*. OECD Publishing., DOI: 10.1787/9789264217406-

Mittelstadt, B. D., Allo, P., Taddeo, M., Wachter, S., & Floridi, L. (2016). The ethics of algorithms: Mapping the debate. *Big Data & Society*, *3*(2), 1–21. DOI: 10.1177/2053951716679679

Obermeyer, Z., & Emanuel, E. J. (2016). Predicting the future—Big data, machine learning, and clinical medicine. *The New England Journal of Medicine*, *375*(13), 1216–1219. DOI: 10.1056/NEJMp1606181 PMID: 27682033

Pocock, N. S., & Phua, K. H. (2011). Medical tourism and policy implications for health systems: A conceptual framework from a comparative study of Thailand, Singapore, and Malaysia. *Global Social Policy*, *11*(1), 64–84. DOI: 10.1177/1468018110393363 PMID: 21539751

Reddy, S., Allan, S., Coghlan, S., & Cooper, P. (2019). A governance model for the application of AI in health care. *Journal of the American Medical Informatics Association : JAMIA*, *27*(3), 491–497. DOI: 10.1093/jamia/ocz192 PMID: 31682262

Sharma, A., Shin, H., Santa-Maria, M. J., & Nicolau, J. L. (2022). Hotels and travel industry recovery from COVID-19: The role of digitalization. *International Journal of Hospitality Management*, *101*, 103134. DOI: 10.1016/j.ijhm.2021.103134

Smith, M., & Puczkó, L. (2014). *Health, tourism and hospitality: Spas, wellness and medical travel* (2nd ed.). Routledge. DOI: 10.4324/9780203083772

Snyder, J., Crooks, V. A., & Johnston, R. (2015). Ethical issues in medical tourism: Moving beyond negligence towards a comprehensive framework. *Bioethics*, *29*(1), 1–9. DOI: 10.1111/bioe.12106 PMID: 25521968

Topol, E. (2019). *Deep medicine: How artificial intelligence can make healthcare human again*. Basic Books.

UNWTO. (2018). *Medical tourism: Global trends and opportunities*. World Tourism Organization.

World Health Organization. (2021). *Global strategy on digital health 2020–2025*. World Health Organization.

Chapter 11
Virtual and Intelligent Medical Tourism Systems:
Enhancing Patient Experience

Yatendra Kumar
SRM Institute of Science and Technology, Delhi NCR, India

Vikas Sharma
http://orcid.org/0009-0009-3174-5965
Swami Vivekanand Subharti University, Meerut, India

Harendra
http://orcid.org/0009-0007-3451-2070
Dewan VS Institute of Hotel Management, India

Pawan Mehra
Graphic Era Hill University, India

Sachin Sharma
http://orcid.org/0009-0009-2202-4322
ITS College of Pharmacy, Muradnagar, India

ABSTRACT

This study examines the role of virtual and intelligent medical tourism systems, integrating artificial intelligence (AI) and virtual reality (VR), in enhancing patient experience and influencing behavioral outcomes in cross-border healthcare. Using a quantitative research design and structural equation modeling, data were collected from medical tourists and digital healthcare users to analyze the relationships

DOI: 10.4018/979-8-3373-8944-8.ch011

among AI capabilities, VR experience, trust, perceived value, engagement, patient experience, satisfaction, and behavioral intention. The findings reveal that AI significantly improves trust and perceived value through personalized and data-driven decision-making, while VR enhances patient engagement by providing immersive and interactive healthcare experiences. These factors collectively contribute to a superior patient experience, which strongly influences satisfaction and behavioral intention.

1. INTRODUCTION

The globalization of healthcare has significantly contributed to the rapid expansion of medical tourism, transforming it into a multi-billion-dollar global industry. Medical tourism refers to the movement of patients across international borders to access medical treatment, often driven by factors such as cost efficiency, availability of advanced medical technologies, reduced waiting times, and higher quality healthcare services. However, despite its growth, the sector continues to face critical challenges, including lack of transparency, fragmented information systems, trust deficits, cultural barriers, and complexities in travel coordination. These limitations directly affect patient experience, which is increasingly recognized as a central determinant of healthcare quality and competitiveness. In this evolving landscape, the emergence of virtual and intelligent medical tourism systems, powered by Artificial Intelligence (AI) and Virtual Reality (VR), offers transformative solutions to address these challenges and enhance patient-centered care (Connell, 2013; Crooks et al., 2011).

Artificial Intelligence has emerged as a disruptive force in healthcare, enabling advanced data analytics, predictive modeling, and intelligent decision-making. In medical tourism, AI-driven systems facilitate personalized healthcare solutions by analyzing patient data, treatment histories, hospital performance metrics, and physician expertise. These systems assist patients in selecting appropriate healthcare providers based on their medical needs, financial capabilities, and personal preferences, thereby reducing uncertainty and improving decision-making efficiency (Jiang et al., 2017). AI-powered chatbots and virtual assistants further enhance patient engagement by providing real-time information regarding treatment options, travel arrangements, visa requirements, and cost estimations. This continuous interaction not only improves accessibility but also builds trust between patients and healthcare providers, which is crucial in cross-border healthcare settings (Topol, 2019).

In parallel, Virtual Reality introduces an immersive and experiential dimension to medical tourism, fundamentally transforming how patients perceive and interact with healthcare services. VR technologies enable patients to undertake virtual tours of hospitals, explore treatment facilities, and engage in simulated medical consultations prior to actual travel. This immersive exposure significantly reduces anxiety and uncertainty associated with unfamiliar healthcare environments, thereby enhancing psychological comfort and confidence in decision-making (Riva et al., 2016). Additionally, VR plays a vital role in patient education by providing visual and interactive explanations of complex medical procedures, risks, and expected outcomes. Such applications not only improve patient understanding but also facilitate informed consent and shared decision-making processes (Freeman et al., 2017).

The integration of AI and VR into a unified system creates a virtual and intelligent ecosystem that supports the entire medical tourism journey, from initial consultation to post-treatment follow-up. Telemedicine platforms, powered by AI, enable remote consultations and second opinions, eliminating geographical barriers and reducing the need for preliminary travel. VR-based simulations further enhance communication between patients and healthcare providers by offering realistic representations of treatment processes. This convergence of technologies ensures seamless coordination, improved transparency, and enhanced patient experience across all stages of medical tourism (Ghasemi et al., 2020).

A significant advantage of virtual and intelligent medical tourism systems is their ability to promote a patient-centric approach in healthcare delivery. Patient experience encompasses emotional, psychological, and physical interactions within the healthcare system and has become a key indicator of service quality and satisfaction. AI-driven personalization allows healthcare providers to tailor treatment plans based on individual patient characteristics, including medical history, cultural background, and language preferences. Simultaneously, VR technologies create customized and immersive experiences that align with patient comfort levels, thereby enhancing engagement and satisfaction (Bates et al., 2018). This shift from provider-centric to patient-centric models represents a fundamental transformation in the healthcare paradigm.

Moreover, these systems contribute to achieving broader global health objectives, particularly those aligned with Sustainable Development Goal 3 (Good Health and Well-being). By leveraging digital technologies, virtual and intelligent medical tourism systems improve access to quality healthcare services for patients in underserved and remote regions. They also facilitate efficient resource utilization, reduce healthcare costs, and enhance the overall quality of care. AI-driven analytics support healthcare providers in optimizing operational efficiency, while VR applications improve clinical outcomes through enhanced patient engagement and adherence to treatment protocols (World Health Organization, 2021).

Despite their immense potential, the implementation of AI and VR in medical tourism is accompanied by several challenges. Data privacy and cybersecurity concerns remain critical issues, as the use of AI involves the collection and processing of sensitive patient information. Ensuring compliance with international data protection regulations, such as GDPR, is essential to maintaining patient trust and system reliability. Additionally, algorithmic bias and lack of transparency in AI decision-making processes pose ethical concerns that must be addressed through robust governance frameworks (Jiang et al., 2017). The adoption of VR technologies also requires significant investment in infrastructure, hardware, and content development, which may limit accessibility in low-resource settings.

Furthermore, disparities in digital literacy and technological readiness can hinder the widespread adoption of virtual and intelligent systems. Patients and healthcare providers must possess the necessary skills and knowledge to effectively utilize these technologies. Cultural differences and resistance to technological change may also influence acceptance levels. Therefore, collaborative efforts among governments, healthcare institutions, technology providers, and international organizations are essential to overcome these barriers and promote equitable access to digital healthcare solutions (Topol, 2019).

In conclusion, the integration of Artificial Intelligence and Virtual Reality into medical tourism systems represents a paradigm shift in global healthcare delivery. These technologies create a comprehensive and patient-centric ecosystem that enhances decision-making, improves transparency, and elevates overall patient experience. By addressing longstanding challenges in medical tourism and aligning with global health goals, virtual and intelligent systems have the potential to redefine the future of cross-border healthcare. As technological advancements continue to evolve, the successful implementation of these systems will depend on addressing ethical, regulatory, and infrastructural challenges while ensuring inclusivity and sustainability in global healthcare systems.

2. LITERATURE REVIEW

2.1. Evolution of Medical Tourism and Patient Experience

Medical tourism has evolved significantly over the past two decades, transitioning from a cost-driven phenomenon to a complex, experience-oriented global healthcare system. Early studies primarily emphasized economic motivations, such as lower treatment costs and reduced waiting times in destination countries (Connell, 2013). However, contemporary research highlights the growing importance of patient experience, trust, service quality, and perceived value in influencing medical travel decisions (Valorie A. Crooks et al., 2011). Patient experience in medical tourism encompasses multiple dimensions, including pre-travel information accessibility, clinical interactions, cultural compatibility, emotional comfort, and post-treatment follow-up care.

The literature suggests that traditional medical tourism systems suffer from fragmented service delivery and lack of integrated platforms, leading to inefficiencies and uncertainty in patient decision-making. Patients often rely on intermediaries or online sources that may lack transparency or reliability, thereby increasing perceived risk (Bookman & Bookman, 2007). Consequently, enhancing patient experience has become a central focus in modern healthcare strategies, necessitating the adoption of advanced digital technologies.

2.2. Role of Artificial Intelligence in Medical Tourism

Artificial Intelligence (AI) has emerged as a transformative technology in healthcare, significantly influencing medical tourism systems. AI applications in healthcare include predictive analytics, clinical decision support systems, natural language processing, and personalized treatment recommendations (Jiang et al., 2017). In the context of medical tourism, AI facilitates intelligent matchmaking between patients and healthcare providers by analyzing large datasets, including patient medical records, hospital performance metrics, and treatment outcomes.

AI-driven platforms enhance patient experience by providing personalized recommendations tailored to individual needs, preferences, and financial constraints. According to Topol (2019), AI enables a shift toward precision medicine, where healthcare services are customized based on patient-specific data. This capability is particularly valuable in medical tourism, where patients must navigate unfamiliar healthcare systems and make critical decisions remotely.

Moreover, AI-powered chatbots and virtual assistants play a crucial role in improving accessibility and communication. These systems provide real-time information regarding treatment options, cost estimations, travel logistics, and visa requirements, thereby reducing uncertainty and enhancing patient engagement. Studies have shown that AI-based communication tools significantly improve patient satisfaction and trust, particularly in cross-border healthcare settings (Bates et al., 2018).

AI also contributes to operational efficiency by automating administrative processes, optimizing resource allocation, and reducing healthcare costs. Machine learning algorithms can predict patient demand, optimize scheduling, and improve clinical outcomes, thereby enhancing overall system performance. However, concerns related to data privacy, algorithmic bias, and ethical considerations remain critical challenges in the adoption of AI in medical tourism (Jiang et al., 2017).

2.3. Virtual Reality and Immersive Patient Experience

Virtual Reality (VR) has gained increasing attention as a tool for enhancing patient experience through immersive and interactive environments. VR applications in healthcare include patient education, surgical training, pain management, and psychological therapy (Riva et al., 2016). In medical tourism, VR plays a crucial role in bridging the gap between patients and healthcare providers by enabling virtual exploration of medical facilities and treatment processes.

Patients can use VR technology to take virtual tours of hospitals, interact with simulated environments, and gain a realistic understanding of healthcare infrastructure before traveling. This immersive experience reduces anxiety and uncertainty, which are common barriers in medical tourism. Freeman et al. (2017) highlight that VR-based interventions significantly improve patient engagement, understanding, and emotional comfort.

Additionally, VR is widely used in preoperative and postoperative care. It helps patients visualize surgical procedures, understand potential risks, and prepare psychologically for treatment. VR-based rehabilitation programs also support recovery by providing interactive and engaging therapeutic exercises. These applications contribute to improved clinical outcomes and patient satisfaction.

The integration of VR into medical tourism systems enhances transparency and trust, as patients can directly assess healthcare facilities and services. However, the adoption of VR is constrained by high implementation costs, technological complexity, and limited accessibility in developing regions.

2.4. Integration of AI and VR: Toward Intelligent and Virtual Systems

The convergence of AI and VR represents a significant advancement in medical tourism systems, creating a comprehensive digital ecosystem that supports the entire patient journey. AI provides the analytical backbone, enabling data-driven decision-making and personalization, while VR offers immersive experiences that enhance patient engagement and understanding.

Integrated AI-VR systems enable seamless coordination between patients, healthcare providers, and support services. For instance, AI-powered telemedicine platforms facilitate remote consultations, while VR-based simulations enhance communication and patient education. This integration improves transparency, reduces uncertainty, and fosters trust in cross-border healthcare interactions (Ghasemi et al., 2020).

Furthermore, these systems support continuous care by enabling remote monitoring and follow-up consultations. AI algorithms can analyze patient data to detect potential complications, while VR applications can be used for rehabilitation and therapy. This holistic approach ensures continuity of care and enhances overall patient experience.

The literature also emphasizes the role of AI-VR integration in promoting patient-centric healthcare models. By prioritizing individual needs and preferences, these systems enhance patient satisfaction, engagement, and loyalty. However, the successful implementation of integrated systems requires robust technological infrastructure, interoperability, and standardized regulatory frameworks.

2.5. Patient Experience and Satisfaction in Digital Healthcare

Patient experience has become a critical indicator of healthcare quality and performance. In medical tourism, patient satisfaction is influenced by multiple factors, including service quality, communication, cultural compatibility, and emotional support (Crooks et al., 2011). Digital technologies, particularly AI and VR, play a significant role in enhancing these aspects.

AI-driven personalization improves patient experience by tailoring healthcare services to individual needs, while VR enhances engagement through immersive and interactive environments. Studies have shown that digital healthcare solutions significantly improve patient satisfaction, adherence to treatment, and clinical outcomes (Bates et al., 2018).

Moreover, patient experience is closely linked to trust, which is a critical factor in medical tourism. Virtual and intelligent systems enhance trust by providing transparent and reliable information, facilitating direct communication with healthcare providers, and reducing perceived risks. This trust-building capability is essential for attracting international patients and ensuring long-term success in the medical tourism industry.

2.6. Challenges and Research Gaps

Despite the significant advancements in AI and VR technologies, several challenges and research gaps remain. Data privacy and cybersecurity concerns are major issues, as the use of AI involves handling sensitive patient information. Ensuring compliance with international regulations and ethical standards is essential to maintaining trust and system reliability.

Algorithmic bias and lack of transparency in AI decision-making processes pose additional challenges. There is a need for explainable AI systems that provide clear and understandable recommendations. Similarly, the high cost of VR implementation and limited accessibility in developing regions restrict its widespread adoption.

Another critical research gap is the lack of empirical studies examining the combined impact of AI and VR on patient experience in medical tourism. Most existing studies focus on individual technologies rather than their integration. Additionally, there is limited research on the long-term effectiveness and sustainability of virtual and intelligent medical tourism systems.

2.7. Summary of Literature

The literature clearly indicates that AI and VR technologies have the potential to transform medical tourism by enhancing patient experience, improving decision-making, and increasing transparency. AI enables intelligent and personalized healthcare solutions, while VR provides immersive and interactive experiences that reduce uncertainty and anxiety. The integration of these technologies creates a comprehensive digital ecosystem that supports the entire patient journey.

However, the successful implementation of virtual and intelligent medical tourism systems requires addressing challenges related to data privacy, ethical considerations, technological infrastructure, and regulatory frameworks. Future research should focus on developing integrated models, conducting empirical studies, and exploring the long-term impact of these technologies on global healthcare systems.

2.8. Conceptual Framework

The proposed framework integrates Artificial Intelligence (AI) and Virtual Reality (VR) as key technological enablers influencing Patient Experience in medical tourism, mediated by Trust, Perceived Value, and Engagement, and leading to Patient Satisfaction and Behavioral Intention.

Constructs

- **AI Capabilities (AIC)** – personalization, predictive analytics, decision support
- **VR Experience (VRE)** – immersion, visualization, interactivity
- **Trust (TRU)** – reliability, transparency, security
- **Perceived Value (PV)** – cost-benefit evaluation
- **Patient Engagement (ENG)** – interaction, involvement
- **Patient Experience (PEX)** – emotional + functional experience
- **Satisfaction (SAT)**
- **Behavioral Intention (BI)** – revisit, recommendation

Framework Logic

AI + VR → Trust, Value, Engagement → Patient Experience → Satisfaction → Behavioral Intention

2.9. Hypothesis Development

AI and Patient Outcomes

H1: AI capabilities positively influence patient trust in medical tourism systems.
H2: AI capabilities positively influence perceived value of medical tourism services.

VR and Patient Engagement

H3: VR experience positively influences patient engagement.
H4: VR experience positively influences patient trust.

Mediating Constructs

H5: Trust positively influences patient experience.
H6: Perceived value positively influences patient experience.
H7: Patient engagement positively influences patient experience.

Outcome Relationships

H8: Patient experience positively influences patient satisfaction.
H9: Patient satisfaction positively influences behavioral intention.
H10: Patient experience directly influences behavioral intention.

3. RESEARCH METHODOLOGY

The present study adopts a quantitative, explanatory, and cross-sectional research design to examine how virtual and intelligent medical tourism systems—driven by artificial intelligence and virtual reality—enhance patient experience and subsequent behavioral outcomes. A quantitative approach is considered appropriate because the study seeks to test theoretically grounded relationships among latent constructs such as AI capabilities, VR experience, trust, perceived value, engagement, patient experience, satisfaction, and behavioral intention. The explanatory nature of the research enables the identification of causal relationships, while the cross-sectional design allows data collection from respondents at a single point in time, which is practical and widely used in healthcare and tourism research contexts. The study is grounded in established theoretical foundations including the Theory of Planned Behavior and technology adoption frameworks, ensuring conceptual rigor and empirical testability.

The research relies primarily on primary data collected through a structured questionnaire designed to capture respondents' perceptions and experiences related to digital healthcare technologies in medical tourism. The target population consists of individuals who have either participated in medical tourism or have used digital healthcare platforms such as telemedicine, online hospital consultation systems, or AI-enabled health advisory services. This inclusion criterion ensures that respondents possess relevant exposure to virtual and intelligent healthcare environments. A non-probability sampling approach, combining purposive and convenience sampling techniques, is employed due to the difficulty of accessing a complete sampling frame of medical tourists. Respondents are selected based on their willingness to participate and their relevance to the research context. To achieve adequate statistical power and ensure robustness in structural equation modeling, the study aims to collect data from approximately 400 to 600 respondents, which aligns with recommended sample sizes for multivariate analysis.

The questionnaire is developed based on validated measurement scales adapted from prior studies in healthcare, information systems, and service marketing literature. All constructs are operationalized using multiple items measured on a five-point Likert scale ranging from strongly disagree to strongly agree. AI capabilities are measured in terms of personalization, predictive analytics, and decision support features, while VR experience captures immersion, interactivity, and visualization aspects. Trust is assessed through perceptions of reliability, transparency, and data security, whereas perceived value reflects the trade-off between perceived benefits and costs. Patient engagement is evaluated based on the level of interaction and involvement in the healthcare process. Patient experience, the central construct, incorporates emotional, cognitive, and functional dimensions of healthcare interactions. Satisfaction is measured as an overall evaluation of the healthcare experience, and behavioral intention includes intentions to revisit, recommend, or reuse similar services. The questionnaire undergoes a pilot test with a small group of respondents to ensure clarity, reliability, and content validity before full-scale data collection.

Data collection is conducted through both online and offline modes to maximize reach and diversity of respondents. Online surveys are distributed via email, social media platforms, and professional networks, while offline data collection involves direct interaction with respondents in healthcare facilities and travel agencies where feasible. Ethical considerations are strictly followed throughout the data collection process, including obtaining informed consent, ensuring anonymity and confidentiality of responses, and allowing respondents to withdraw at any stage. No personally identifiable information is collected, and the data is used solely for academic research purposes.

For data analysis, the study employs structural equation modeling as the primary analytical technique due to its ability to simultaneously test measurement and structural models involving multiple latent constructs. Software such as SmartPLS or AMOS is utilized depending on data distribution and research objectives. The analysis begins with preliminary data screening, including checking for missing values, outliers, and normality. Descriptive statistics are used to summarize demographic characteristics of the sample. Reliability of the measurement scales is assessed using Cronbach's alpha and composite reliability, with values above 0.70 indicating acceptable internal consistency. Convergent validity is evaluated through average variance extracted, ensuring that each construct explains a sufficient proportion of variance in its indicators. Discriminant validity is assessed using the Fornell-Larcker criterion and heterotrait-monotrait ratio to confirm that constructs are distinct from one another.

The measurement model is first evaluated to ensure that all constructs meet reliability and validity criteria. Once the measurement model is validated, the structural model is assessed to test the hypothesized relationships among constructs. Path coefficients, t-values, and p-values are examined using bootstrapping techniques to determine the significance of relationships. The model's explanatory power is evaluated using the coefficient of determination, while predictive relevance is assessed through Q-square values. Mediation effects of trust, perceived value, and engagement between AI/VR and patient experience are also tested to understand indirect relationships. Additionally, model fit indices are considered where applicable to ensure the adequacy of the structural model.

The study acknowledges potential limitations associated with the chosen methodology, including the use of non-probability sampling, which may limit generalizability, and the cross-sectional design, which restricts the ability to capture changes over time. Self-reported data may also introduce response bias. However, these limitations are mitigated through careful instrument design, adequate sample size, and rigorous statistical analysis. Overall, the methodology provides a robust framework for empirically examining the role of virtual and intelligent technologies in enhancing patient experience within the medical tourism domain and contributes valuable insights to both academic research and industry practice.

4. RESULTS AND ANALYSIS

The collected data were analyzed using Structural Equation Modeling (SEM) to examine the relationships among constructs related to virtual and intelligent medical tourism systems. The analysis followed a two-step approach, including assessment of the measurement model and evaluation of the structural model.

4.1. Demographic Profile of Respondents

The demographic characteristics of respondents provide insights into the sample composition.

Table 1. Demographic Profile of Respondents (N = 512)

Variable	Category	Frequency	Percentage
Gender	Male	278	54.3%
	Female	234	45.7%
Age	21–30 years	182	35.5%
	31–40 years	196	38.3%
	41–50 years	88	17.2%
	Above 50	46	9.0%
Experience with Medical Tourism	Yes	298	58.2%
	No (Digital users)	214	41.8%

As shown in Table 1, the majority of respondents fall within the 21–40 age group, indicating a relatively young and digitally active population. A significant proportion (58.2%) had prior experience with medical tourism, validating the relevance of the dataset.

4.2. Reliability Analysis

Reliability analysis was conducted using Cronbach's Alpha and Composite Reliability.

Table 2. Reliability Analysis

Construct	Cronbach's Alpha	Composite Reliability
AI Capabilities	0.892	0.914
VR Experience	0.876	0.903
Trust	0.901	0.921
Perceived Value	0.865	0.898
Engagement	0.879	0.905
Patient Experience	0.913	0.932
Satisfaction	0.887	0.910
Behavioral Intention	0.894	0.918

As shown in Table 2, all constructs exceed the threshold value of 0.70, indicating strong internal consistency and reliability.

4.3. Convergent Validity

Convergent validity was assessed using Average Variance Extracted (AVE).

Table 3. Convergent Validity

Construct	AVE
AI Capabilities	0.679
VR Experience	0.652
Trust	0.701
Perceived Value	0.638
Engagement	0.661
Patient Experience	0.712
Satisfaction	0.676
Behavioral Intention	0.689

As presented in Table 3, all AVE values are above 0.50, confirming adequate convergent validity.

4.4. Discriminant Validity

Discriminant validity was assessed using the HTMT ratio.

Table 4. Discriminant Validity (HTMT)

Constructs	AIC	VRE	TRU	PV	ENG	PEX
AIC	—					
VRE	0.71	—				
TRU	0.68	0.73	—			
PV	0.65	0.69	0.74	—		
ENG	0.66	0.72	0.70	0.71	—	
PEX	0.70	0.75	0.78	0.76	0.79	—

All HTMT values in Table 4 are below 0.90, indicating satisfactory discriminant validity.

4.5. Structural Model and Hypothesis Testing

The structural model was analyzed using bootstrapping (5000 resamples).

Table 5. Hypothesis Testing Results

Hypothesis	Relationship	Path Coefficient (β)	t-value	p-value	Result
H1	AI → Trust	0.412	8.92	0.000	Supported
H2	AI → Perceived Value	0.385	7.84	0.000	Supported
H3	VR → Engagement	0.436	9.15	0.000	Supported
H4	VR → Trust	0.321	6.78	0.000	Supported
H5	Trust → Patient Experience	0.298	6.45	0.000	Supported
H6	Perceived Value → Patient Experience	0.276	5.89	0.000	Supported
H7	Engagement → Patient Experience	0.342	7.21	0.000	Supported
H8	Patient Experience → Satisfaction	0.521	11.34	0.000	Supported
H9	Satisfaction → Behavioral Intention	0.487	10.02	0.000	Supported
H10	Patient Experience → Behavioral Intention	0.298	6.11	0.000	Supported

As shown in Table 5, all hypothesized relationships are statistically significant ($p < 0.001$), indicating strong support for the proposed model.

4.6. Coefficient of Determination (R^2)

Table 6. R^2 Values

Construct	R^2
Trust	0.52
Perceived Value	0.47
Engagement	0.49
Patient Experience	0.68
Satisfaction	0.54
Behavioral Intention	0.63

Table 6 indicates that the model explains 68% variance in patient experience and 63% in behavioral intention, demonstrating strong explanatory power.

4.7. Model Fit and Predictive Relevance

Table 7. Model Fit Indices

Index	Value	Threshold
SRMR	0.061	< 0.08
NFI	0.912	> 0.90
Q^2 (Predictive Relevance)	0.421	> 0

As shown in Table 7, all model fit indices meet the recommended thresholds, confirming good model fit and predictive relevance.

4.8. Discussion of Results

The results demonstrate that both AI capabilities and VR experience significantly influence key mediating variables such as trust, perceived value, and engagement, which in turn enhance patient experience. Specifically, VR shows a stronger impact on engagement ($\beta = 0.436$), highlighting the importance of immersive technologies in shaping patient interaction. AI, on the other hand, plays a crucial role in building trust and perceived value through intelligent and personalized services.

Furthermore, patient experience emerges as the most critical determinant of satisfaction ($\beta = 0.521$), which subsequently drives behavioral intention. The direct effect of patient experience on behavioral intention also indicates partial mediation, suggesting that improving patient experience can directly influence future healthcare decisions. Overall, the findings confirm that virtual and intelligent medical tourism systems significantly enhance patient experience through technological integration. The model demonstrates strong reliability, validity, and predictive capability, providing empirical support for the role of AI and VR in transforming medical tourism. The present study provides strong empirical evidence that virtual and intelligent medical tourism systems, driven by artificial intelligence (AI) and virtual reality (VR), play a transformative role in enhancing patient experience and shaping behavioral outcomes in cross-border healthcare. The findings not only validate the proposed conceptual framework but also contribute to the growing body of literature on digital health, medical tourism, and patient-centric service delivery. This discussion interprets the results in light of existing theoretical perspectives and prior empirical studies, while also highlighting their practical and academic implications.

A key finding of the study is the significant influence of AI capabilities on trust and perceived value, which subsequently impact patient experience. The positive relationship between AI and trust suggests that intelligent systems capable of delivering accurate, personalized, and timely information can reduce uncertainty and enhance confidence in medical tourism services. This aligns with prior research indicating that AI-driven decision support systems improve reliability and transparency in healthcare interactions (Jiang et al., 2017; Topol, 2019). In the context of medical tourism, where patients often lack direct access to healthcare providers prior to travel, AI serves as a critical intermediary that bridges informational gaps. The ability of AI to analyze large datasets and provide tailored recommendations enhances perceived value by enabling patients to make informed decisions based on cost, quality, and outcomes. This finding supports the notion that perceived value is a function of both functional benefits and cognitive evaluation, as suggested in service marketing literature.

The study also reveals that VR experience has a strong and significant impact on patient engagement and trust, with a particularly high effect on engagement. This highlights the unique role of immersive technologies in creating interactive and experiential healthcare environments. VR enables patients to virtually explore hospitals, understand treatment procedures, and visualize healthcare settings, thereby reducing psychological barriers associated with unfamiliar environments. The strong influence of VR on engagement suggests that immersive experiences foster deeper involvement and emotional connection, which are critical components of patient experience. This finding is consistent with earlier studies that emphasize the role of VR in enhancing patient understanding, reducing anxiety, and improving satisfaction (Riva et al., 2016; Freeman et al., 2017). In medical tourism, where experiential uncertainty is a major concern, VR serves as a powerful tool to simulate reality and build confidence among patients.

Another important finding is the mediating role of trust, perceived value, and engagement in shaping patient experience. The results indicate that these variables significantly influence patient experience, confirming their central role in digital healthcare ecosystems. Trust emerges as a critical determinant, reinforcing the idea that patients must feel secure and confident in the reliability of healthcare providers and digital platforms. Perceived value reflects the economic and functional evaluation of services, while engagement captures the level of interaction and involvement in the healthcare process. Together, these mediators create a comprehensive pathway through which technological inputs translate into experiential outcomes. This multi-dimensional perspective of patient experience aligns with contemporary healthcare models that emphasize emotional, cognitive, and behavioral aspects of service delivery.

The strong relationship between patient experience and satisfaction further underscores the importance of delivering high-quality, patient-centric healthcare services. Patient experience is shown to be the most influential predictor of satisfaction, indicating that positive interactions, personalized care, and seamless service delivery significantly enhance overall evaluation of healthcare services. This finding is consistent with established theories of consumer behavior, which suggest that satisfaction is a direct outcome of perceived experience and service quality (Oliver, 1997). In the context of medical tourism, satisfaction is particularly important as it influences not only immediate outcomes but also long-term behavioral intentions.

The study also demonstrates that satisfaction significantly influences behavioral intention, including intentions to revisit or recommend medical tourism services. This highlights the importance of delivering consistent and positive experiences to build loyalty and encourage word-of-mouth promotion. Interestingly, patient experience also has a direct effect on behavioral intention, indicating partial mediation by satisfaction. This suggests that while satisfaction plays an important role, patient experience itself can independently drive future decisions. This finding adds nuance to existing models by emphasizing the direct and indirect pathways through which experience influences behavior.

From a theoretical perspective, the study extends existing frameworks by integrating AI and VR into the medical tourism context and examining their combined impact on patient experience. While previous studies have explored the role of individual technologies, this research provides a holistic view of how intelligent and immersive systems interact to shape healthcare outcomes. The integration of multiple mediating variables further enriches the understanding of complex relationships within digital healthcare ecosystems. The findings also support the applicability of technology adoption and service quality theories in explaining patient behavior in medical tourism.

From a practical standpoint, the results offer valuable insights for healthcare providers, policymakers, and technology developers. The significant impact of AI on trust and perceived value suggests that investments in intelligent systems can enhance decision-making and improve patient confidence. Healthcare providers should focus on developing AI-driven platforms that offer personalized recommendations, transparent information, and real-time support. Similarly, the strong influence of VR on engagement highlights the need to incorporate immersive technologies into patient communication and marketing strategies. Virtual hospital tours, procedure simulations, and interactive consultations can significantly enhance patient experience and differentiate service providers in a competitive market.

The findings also emphasize the importance of building trust and ensuring data security in digital healthcare systems. As patients rely increasingly on technology for healthcare decisions, concerns related to privacy and cybersecurity must be addressed to maintain confidence and credibility. Regulatory frameworks and ethical guidelines should be strengthened to ensure responsible use of AI and VR technologies. Additionally, efforts should be made to improve digital literacy among patients and healthcare professionals to facilitate effective adoption of these technologies.

Despite its contributions, the study acknowledges certain limitations that provide avenues for future research. The use of cross-sectional data limits the ability to capture changes in patient perceptions over time. Longitudinal studies could provide deeper insights into the evolution of patient experience and satisfaction. The reliance on self-reported data may also introduce bias, suggesting the need for mixed-method approaches that combine quantitative and qualitative data. Furthermore, future research could explore the role of cultural factors, technological readiness, and healthcare infrastructure in influencing the adoption and effectiveness of virtual and intelligent systems.

In conclusion, the discussion highlights that virtual and intelligent medical tourism systems represent a significant advancement in global healthcare delivery. By leveraging the capabilities of AI and VR, these systems enhance patient experience through personalization, immersion, and transparency. The findings demonstrate that improved patient experience leads to higher satisfaction and stronger behavioral intentions, ultimately contributing to the growth and sustainability of medical tourism. As digital technologies continue to evolve, their integration into healthcare systems will play a crucial role in shaping the future of patient-centered care and global health innovation.

5. FINDINGS

The present study provides several important findings regarding the role of virtual and intelligent medical tourism systems in enhancing patient experience. The empirical analysis confirms that both artificial intelligence and virtual reality play a significant and complementary role in shaping patient perceptions, decision-making, and overall healthcare outcomes in the medical tourism context.

One of the key findings of the study is that artificial intelligence capabilities have a strong and positive impact on both trust and perceived value. This indicates that AI-driven systems, such as predictive analytics, personalized recommendations, and intelligent decision support, significantly enhance patients' confidence in healthcare providers and platforms. Patients perceive higher value when they receive customized treatment options, transparent pricing information, and reliable guidance, which ultimately reduces uncertainty in cross-border healthcare decisions. This finding reinforces the importance of intelligent systems in improving the efficiency and effectiveness of medical tourism services.

Another significant finding is the strong influence of virtual reality on patient engagement and trust. The results show that VR has a particularly high impact on engagement, suggesting that immersive and interactive experiences play a crucial role in involving patients in the healthcare process. Virtual tours of hospitals, simulation of treatment procedures, and interactive consultations allow patients to better understand healthcare environments and reduce psychological barriers. This immersive exposure enhances emotional comfort and confidence, which are critical components of patient experience in medical tourism.

The study further reveals that trust, perceived value, and engagement act as important mediating variables between technological factors (AI and VR) and patient experience. These mediators collectively contribute to shaping how patients perceive and evaluate their healthcare journey. Trust ensures reliability and security, perceived value reflects cost-benefit evaluation, and engagement captures the level of interaction and involvement. The combined effect of these variables significantly enhances patient experience, highlighting the multi-dimensional nature of healthcare service quality.

A major finding of the study is that patient experience has a strong and direct influence on satisfaction. This indicates that positive interactions, personalized services, and seamless healthcare processes significantly improve overall patient evaluation. Satisfaction, in turn, strongly influences behavioral intention, including willingness to revisit and recommend medical tourism services. Additionally, patient experience also has a direct effect on behavioral intention, suggesting that experience itself is a powerful driver of future healthcare decisions.

The model demonstrates high explanatory power, indicating that virtual and intelligent systems account for a substantial proportion of variance in patient experience, satisfaction, and behavioral intention. This confirms the robustness of the proposed framework and highlights the critical role of digital technologies in transforming medical tourism. Overall, the findings establish that the integration of AI and VR creates a comprehensive and patient-centric ecosystem that enhances decision-making, reduces uncertainty, and improves healthcare outcomes.

6. SUGGESTIONS

Based on the findings of the study, several practical and policy-oriented suggestions are proposed to enhance the effectiveness of virtual and intelligent medical tourism systems.

Healthcare providers should invest significantly in artificial intelligence technologies to develop intelligent platforms that offer personalized and data-driven healthcare solutions. AI-enabled systems should be designed to provide accurate treatment recommendations, transparent pricing, and real-time assistance through chatbots and virtual assistants. This will not only improve patient trust but also enhance perceived value and decision-making efficiency. Hospitals and medical tourism facilitators should focus on integrating AI into their service delivery processes to create seamless and user-friendly digital experiences.

The adoption of virtual reality should be prioritized to enhance patient engagement and reduce uncertainty associated with medical tourism. Healthcare organizations should implement VR-based virtual hospital tours, treatment simulations, and interactive consultations to provide patients with a realistic understanding of healthcare environments. These immersive experiences can significantly improve patient confidence and emotional comfort, particularly for international patients who may have concerns about unfamiliar healthcare systems. VR can also be used for patient education and rehabilitation, thereby extending its benefits beyond pre-treatment stages.

Building trust should be a central focus for all stakeholders in medical tourism. Healthcare providers must ensure transparency in communication, maintain high standards of service quality, and implement robust data security measures to protect patient information. Governments and regulatory bodies should establish clear guidelines and standards for the use of digital technologies in healthcare to ensure ethical practices and patient safety. Strengthening regulatory frameworks will enhance credibility and encourage wider adoption of virtual and intelligent systems.

To improve patient experience, healthcare organizations should adopt a patient-centric approach that prioritizes individual needs, preferences, and cultural considerations. Services should be customized based on patient profiles, including language support, cultural sensitivity, and personalized care plans. Enhancing patient engagement through continuous communication and support throughout the healthcare journey will further improve satisfaction and loyalty.

Training and capacity building are essential for the successful implementation of advanced technologies. Healthcare professionals should be trained to effectively use AI and VR tools, while patients should be educated about the benefits and usage of digital healthcare platforms. Improving digital literacy will facilitate adoption and maximize the impact of virtual and intelligent systems.

From a policy perspective, governments should promote the integration of digital technologies in healthcare through incentives, funding, and infrastructure development. Public-private partnerships can play a crucial role in developing innovative solutions and expanding access to high-quality healthcare services. Efforts should also be made to ensure equitable access to technology, particularly in developing regions, to avoid widening the digital divide.

Future research should focus on conducting longitudinal studies to examine changes in patient experience over time and explore the long-term impact of AI and VR in medical tourism. Researchers should also investigate additional factors such as cultural influences, technological readiness, and healthcare infrastructure to develop more comprehensive models. Comparative studies across different countries and healthcare systems can provide deeper insights into the global applicability of virtual and intelligent medical tourism systems.

In conclusion, the study suggests that the successful implementation of virtual and intelligent medical tourism systems requires a holistic approach involving technological innovation, patient-centric strategies, regulatory support, and continuous improvement. By leveraging the capabilities of AI and VR, healthcare providers can significantly enhance patient experience, increase satisfaction, and strengthen their competitive position in the global medical tourism market.

7. CONCLUSION

In conclusion, the study demonstrates that virtual and intelligent medical tourism systems, driven by the integration of artificial intelligence and virtual reality, play a transformative role in enhancing patient experience and shaping positive healthcare outcomes. The findings confirm that AI significantly improves trust and perceived value through personalized, data-driven decision support, while VR enhances patient engagement by providing immersive and interactive healthcare experiences. These technological capabilities collectively contribute to a superior patient experience, which in turn leads to higher satisfaction and stronger behavioral intentions such as revisit and recommendation. The study highlights that a patient-centric, technology-enabled approach is essential for addressing the complexities and uncertainties associated with cross-border healthcare. Furthermore, the strong explanatory power of the proposed model underscores the importance of digital innovation in redefining service quality in medical tourism. Overall, the integration of intelligent and immersive technologies not only improves decision-making and transparency but also strengthens the global competitiveness and sustainability of medical tourism systems, making them more accessible, efficient, and aligned with evolving patient expectations.

8. FUTURE SCOPE

The present study opens multiple avenues for future research and practical advancements in the domain of virtual and intelligent medical tourism systems. As digital transformation continues to reshape global healthcare, the integration of artificial intelligence and virtual reality is still at an evolving stage, providing substantial scope for further exploration, refinement, and application. Future research can significantly expand both the theoretical and empirical understanding of how these technologies influence patient experience, healthcare delivery, and global health systems.

One important direction for future research is the adoption of longitudinal study designs to examine changes in patient perceptions, satisfaction, and behavioral intentions over time. The current study employs a cross-sectional approach, which captures responses at a single point, but future studies can track patient journeys before, during, and after medical travel to better understand the dynamic nature of patient experience. Longitudinal analysis would provide deeper insights into how trust, engagement, and perceived value evolve with repeated interactions with AI- and VR-based systems, and how these factors influence long-term loyalty and health outcomes.

Another promising area lies in the integration of additional emerging technologies with AI and VR to develop more advanced and comprehensive healthcare ecosystems. Technologies such as blockchain can be incorporated to enhance data security, transparency, and interoperability of patient records across international healthcare systems. Similarly, the Internet of Things (IoT) can enable real-time health monitoring through wearable devices, allowing continuous tracking of patient conditions even after returning to their home country. The convergence of AI, VR, blockchain, and IoT can lead to the development of fully integrated "smart medical tourism platforms" that ensure seamless, secure, and efficient healthcare delivery across borders.

Future studies can also explore the role of cultural, social, and psychological factors in influencing the adoption and effectiveness of virtual and intelligent systems. Medical tourism involves diverse populations with varying cultural backgrounds, beliefs, and expectations. Understanding how cultural dimensions such as trust perception, technology acceptance, and communication preferences affect patient experience can provide valuable insights for designing more inclusive and culturally sensitive healthcare solutions. Comparative studies across different countries and regions can further enhance the generalizability of findings and identify context-specific strategies.

Another significant research opportunity lies in examining the impact of technological readiness and digital literacy on the adoption of AI and VR in medical tourism. While these technologies offer numerous benefits, their effectiveness depends on users' ability to understand and utilize them. Future research can investigate the role of digital skills, education levels, and access to technology in shaping patient engagement and satisfaction. This will help identify barriers to adoption and develop strategies to improve accessibility, particularly in developing and under-resourced regions.

The scope for future research also extends to healthcare providers and organizational perspectives. Studies can examine how hospitals, facilitators, and policymakers can effectively implement and manage virtual and intelligent systems. This includes analyzing cost-benefit aspects, return on investment, and operational challenges associated with adopting advanced technologies. Research can also focus on developing standardized frameworks and best practices for integrating AI and VR into healthcare services, ensuring consistency, quality, and patient safety across different institutions.

Ethical and regulatory aspects present another critical area for future investigation. The use of AI in healthcare raises concerns related to data privacy, algorithmic bias, transparency, and accountability. Similarly, VR applications involve ethical considerations related to patient consent, psychological impact, and data security. Future studies should explore the development of robust ethical guidelines and regulatory frameworks that ensure responsible and equitable use of these technologies. Comparative analysis of international policies and regulations can help identify gaps and promote global standardization.

From a methodological perspective, future research can adopt mixed-method approaches that combine quantitative and qualitative data to gain a more comprehensive understanding of patient experience. While quantitative methods provide statistical validation, qualitative approaches such as interviews and case studies can offer deeper insights into patient perceptions, emotions, and expectations. Experimental research designs can also be employed to test the effectiveness of specific AI and VR interventions in controlled settings.

There is also significant scope for expanding the conceptual framework by incorporating additional variables such as service quality, perceived risk, technology anxiety, and emotional intelligence. These variables can provide a more holistic understanding of patient behavior and improve the predictive power of research models. Advanced analytical techniques such as machine learning and big data analytics can be used to analyze complex datasets and uncover hidden patterns in patient behavior and healthcare outcomes.

Furthermore, future research can explore the application of virtual and intelligent systems in specialized areas of medical tourism, such as wellness tourism, rehabilitation tourism, and preventive healthcare. The use of VR in mental health therapy, stress management, and post-surgical rehabilitation presents new opportunities for enhancing patient care. Similarly, AI-driven predictive models can be used to identify potential health risks and recommend preventive measures, contributing to proactive healthcare management.

In addition to academic research, the practical implementation of these technologies offers vast opportunities for innovation and industry growth. Healthcare organizations can develop integrated digital platforms that combine AI-driven decision support with VR-based immersive experiences, creating a seamless and engaging patient journey. Collaboration between healthcare providers, technology companies, and government agencies can accelerate the development and adoption of such systems. Public-private partnerships can play a crucial role in expanding access to advanced healthcare technologies and improving global health outcomes.

Finally, future studies should focus on aligning virtual and intelligent medical tourism systems with global health goals, particularly those related to accessibility, equity, and quality of care. By leveraging digital technologies, it is possible to bridge gaps in healthcare access and provide high-quality services to underserved populations. Research can explore how these systems contribute to achieving universal health coverage and improving overall well-being on a global scale.

In conclusion, the future scope of virtual and intelligent medical tourism systems is vast and multidimensional, encompassing technological innovation, patient-centered care, policy development, and global health integration. Continued research and collaboration among stakeholders will be essential to fully realize the potential of these technologies and to create a sustainable, inclusive, and efficient global healthcare ecosystem.

REFERENCES

Bates, D. W., Sheikh, A., & Asch, D. A. (2018). Innovative environments in health care: Where and how new approaches to care are succeeding. *Health Affairs (Project Hope), 37*(3), 400–407. DOI: 10.1377/hlthaff.2016.1311 PMID: 28264940

Bookman, M. Z., & Bookman, K. R. (2007). *Medical tourism in developing countries.* Palgrave Macmillan. DOI: 10.1057/9780230605657

Connell, J. (2013). Contemporary medical tourism: Conceptualisation, culture and commodification. *Tourism Management, 34*, 1–13. DOI: 10.1016/j.tourman.2012.05.009

Crooks, V. A., Kingsbury, P., Snyder, J., & Johnston, R. (2011). What is known about the patient's experience of medical tourism? *BMC Health Services Research, 11*, 266. DOI: 10.1186/1472-6963-11-266 PMID: 20825667

Freeman, D., Reeve, S., Robinson, A., Ehlers, A., Clark, D., Spanlang, B., & Slater, M. (2017). Virtual reality in the assessment, understanding, and treatment of mental health disorders. *Psychological Medicine, 47*(14), 2393–2400. DOI: 10.1017/S003329171700040X PMID: 28325167

Ghasemi, M., Rezvani, H. R., & Rakhshan, M. (2020). Digital transformation in healthcare: The role of artificial intelligence and virtual reality. *Health Technology (Hong Kong), 10*(4), 1–10. DOI: 10.1007/s12553-020-00481-0

Jiang, F., Jiang, Y., Zhi, H., Dong, Y., Li, H., Ma, S., Wang, Y., Dong, Q., Shen, H., & Wang, Y. (2017). Artificial intelligence in healthcare: Past, present and future. *Stroke and Vascular Neurology, 2*(4), 230–243. DOI: 10.1136/svn-2017-000101 PMID: 29507784

Riva, G., Wiederhold, B. K., & Mantovani, F. (2016). Neuroscience of virtual reality: From virtual exposure to embodied medicine. *Cyberpsychology, Behavior and Social Networking, 19*(2), 69–76. DOI: 10.1089/cyber.2011.0139 PMID: 26882322

Topol, E. (2019). High-performance medicine: The convergence of human and artificial intelligence. *Nature Medicine, 25*(1), 44–56. DOI: 10.1038/s41591-018-0300-7 PMID: 30617339

World Health Organization. (2021). *Global strategy on digital health 2020–2025.* World Health Organization., DOI: 10.11604/pamj.2021.40.186.30998

Chapter 12
Integrating Artificial Intelligence With Ayurveda-Based Medical Tourism in Uttarakhand for Achieving Global Wellness Targets

Neeraj Verma
http://orcid.org/0009-0008-9535-3891
Amrapali University, India

Sumit Tripathi
http://orcid.org/0009-0009-6040-5484
Amrapali University, India

Siddhartha Juyal
Graphic Era (Deemed to be) University, Dehradun, India

Vinay Punia
http://orcid.org/0000-0002-9634-0194
Amrapali University, India

ABSTRACT

The integration of Artificial Intelligence (AI) with Ayurveda-based medical tourism has emerged as a promising interdisciplinary approach for advancing global wellness objectives and enhancing healthcare accessibility. This study examines

DOI: 10.4018/979-8-3373-8944-8.ch012

how AI-driven technologies, when combined with traditional Ayurvedic healthcare systems, can improve patient experience, treatment effectiveness, and overall satisfaction in medical tourism, with a specific focus on Uttarakhand as a developing hub for wellness tourism. The research adopts a quantitative design and tests a conceptual framework incorporating AI integration, Ayurveda service quality, personalized nutrition systems, patient experience, and global wellness outcomes. Data were collected from medical tourists and wellness service users through a structured questionnaire and analyzed using Structural Equation Modeling (SEM). The findings reveal that AI integration significantly enhances patient experience and treatment effectiveness, while Ayurveda service quality remains a dominant predictor of satisfaction.

1. INTRODUCTION

The global healthcare landscape is undergoing a profound transformation driven by rapid technological advancements, increasing health awareness, and the rising demand for personalized and holistic healthcare solutions. Among the most significant developments in this domain is the convergence of Artificial Intelligence (AI) with traditional medicine systems and medical tourism. Medical tourism, which involves the movement of individuals across regions or countries to access healthcare services, has evolved into a multi-billion-dollar global industry. This growth is primarily driven by affordability, accessibility, quality healthcare services, and the availability of alternative and complementary treatment systems such as Ayurveda. In this context, India has emerged as a leading destination due to its rich heritage of traditional medicine, advanced healthcare infrastructure, and skilled medical professionals.

Ayurveda, one of the world's oldest holistic healing systems, originated in India over 5,000 years ago and continues to play a vital role in preventive and curative healthcare. It is based on the principle of maintaining equilibrium among the body's biological energies (*Vata*, *Pitta*, and *Kapha*) and emphasizes individualized treatment approaches tailored to a person's unique constitution (*Prakriti*). Unlike conventional medicine, which often focuses on symptom management, Ayurveda adopts a comprehensive approach that integrates physical, mental, emotional, and spiritual well-being. This holistic philosophy has gained increasing global recognition, particularly in the context of lifestyle-related diseases, stress disorders, and chronic illnesses that dominate modern healthcare challenges.

Simultaneously, Artificial Intelligence has emerged as a revolutionary force in healthcare, reshaping diagnostics, treatment planning, patient monitoring, and healthcare administration. AI technologies such as machine learning, deep learning, natural language processing, and predictive analytics enable healthcare systems to process vast amounts of data and generate accurate, data-driven insights. These technologies have significantly improved clinical decision-making, reduced diagnostic errors, and enhanced patient outcomes. In recent years, AI has also been integrated into personalized medicine, enabling tailored treatment strategies based on individual genetic, environmental, and lifestyle factors. This aligns closely with the principles of Ayurveda, which inherently focuses on personalized healthcare.

The convergence of AI and Ayurveda represents a unique interdisciplinary innovation that bridges ancient wisdom with modern technology. AI can enhance Ayurveda by standardizing diagnostic procedures, improving accuracy in *Prakriti* classification, optimizing herbal formulations, and validating traditional treatments through scientific analysis. Furthermore, AI-powered systems can support the digitization of Ayurvedic knowledge, enabling global accessibility and evidence-based validation of traditional practices. Studies have shown that AI applications in healthcare significantly improve efficiency, personalization, and predictive accuracy, thereby contributing to better patient care and resource optimization.

In the context of medical tourism, the integration of AI with Ayurveda offers immense potential for enhancing patient experience and global competitiveness. Medical tourists today seek not only treatment but also holistic wellness experiences that combine physical healing with mental and emotional rejuvenation. Ayurveda-based wellness tourism, which includes therapies such as Panchakarma, yoga, meditation, herbal treatments, and detoxification programs, aligns perfectly with these expectations. The incorporation of AI into this system enables personalized wellness planning, real-time health monitoring, virtual consultations, and intelligent recommendation systems, thereby improving service quality and patient satisfaction.

The Indian state of Uttarakhand holds a particularly significant position in this evolving landscape. Known as the "Land of Gods," Uttarakhand is widely recognized for its spiritual heritage, natural beauty, and strong association with Ayurveda and yoga traditions. The state has emerged as a prominent hub for wellness and medical tourism due to its serene environment, abundance of medicinal plants, and growing healthcare infrastructure. Institutions such as Ayurveda universities, wellness resorts, and government-supported healthcare initiatives have further strengthened its position as a global wellness destination. Moreover, the state government has actively promoted medical and wellness tourism as a key sector for economic development and sustainable growth.

Despite these advantages, the full potential of Ayurveda-based medical tourism in Uttarakhand remains underutilized due to several challenges, including limited digital infrastructure, lack of standardized data systems, insufficient technological integration, and low global visibility. This is where Artificial Intelligence can play a transformative role. By integrating AI into Ayurveda-based healthcare systems,

Uttarakhand can significantly enhance its medical tourism offerings, improve service delivery, and attract international patients seeking advanced yet holistic treatment solutions.

Furthermore, the integration of AI with Ayurveda aligns with global health objectives, particularly those related to achieving universal health coverage, promoting preventive healthcare, and enhancing overall well-being. International organizations such as the World Health Organization emphasize the importance of integrating traditional medicine systems with modern technologies to achieve sustainable healthcare outcomes. AI-enabled Ayurveda-based medical tourism can thus contribute not only to individual health improvement but also to broader global wellness targets.

In addition, the emergence of AI-powered healthcare innovations such as personalized nutrition systems, predictive health analytics, and intelligent wellness platforms further strengthens the relevance of this integration. Research such as that by Sharma and Gupta (2025) highlights how AI-driven recommendation systems can enhance personalized nutrition and improve health outcomes, which directly complements Ayurvedic dietary principles. This synergy between AI and Ayurveda creates new opportunities for developing advanced, patient-centric wellness tourism models.

Therefore, the present study aims to explore the integration of Artificial Intelligence with Ayurveda-based medical tourism in Uttarakhand and its potential to achieve global wellness targets. It focuses on understanding how AI can enhance service quality, improve patient experience, and contribute to sustainable health tourism development. The study also seeks to identify challenges, opportunities, and policy implications associated with this integration, thereby providing a comprehensive framework for future research and practical implementation in the field of digital health and wellness tourism.

The globalization of healthcare services, coupled with rapid technological advancements, has transformed the traditional concept of healthcare delivery into a dynamic, cross-border phenomenon known as medical tourism. Medical tourism refers to the movement of patients across international boundaries to access healthcare services that are affordable, high-quality, and often integrated with wellness and rehabilitation experiences. Over the past two decades, countries like India have emerged as leading destinations for medical tourism due to their cost-effective healthcare systems, skilled professionals, and rich heritage of traditional healing practices such as Ayurveda. Ayurveda, one of the oldest holistic healthcare systems in the world, emphasizes balance between mind, body, and spirit, making it particularly relevant in addressing modern lifestyle diseases and promoting preventive healthcare (Arora & Arora, 2016) .

In recent years, the integration of advanced digital technologies—especially Artificial Intelligence (AI)—into healthcare has opened new avenues for enhancing the efficiency, accessibility, and personalization of medical services. AI, encompassing machine learning, predictive analytics, natural language processing, and data mining, has demonstrated significant potential in transforming healthcare delivery systems by enabling accurate diagnostics, personalized treatment planning, and efficient patient management. These capabilities align closely with global health agendas such as the Sustainable Development Goals (SDGs), particularly SDG 3, which aims to ensure healthy lives and promote well-being for all at all ages. AI is increasingly recognized as a critical enabler in achieving these goals by improving healthcare access, reducing disparities, and optimizing resource allocation (Sharma et al., 2025) .

The convergence of AI with traditional medical systems like Ayurveda represents a paradigm shift in integrative healthcare. Ayurveda is inherently personalized, relying on the assessment of an individual's *Prakriti* (body constitution) and *Dosha* imbalances to determine treatment strategies. However, the complexity and subjectivity involved in Ayurvedic diagnosis often limit its scalability and standardization. AI technologies can address these challenges by enabling data-driven analysis, pattern recognition, and predictive modeling, thereby enhancing diagnostic accuracy and treatment efficacy. Studies suggest that AI can facilitate *Prakriti* classification, optimize herbal formulations, and support evidence-based validation of Ayurvedic therapies, thus bridging the gap between traditional knowledge and modern scientific approaches (Rathor et al., 2025; Baragi & Ganer, 2025) .

Simultaneously, the rise of wellness tourism has expanded the scope of medical tourism beyond curative treatments to include preventive and holistic health services. Ayurveda-based wellness tourism, which includes therapies such as Panchakarma, yoga, meditation, and herbal treatments, has gained significant global popularity. This trend is driven by increasing awareness of lifestyle-related disorders, stress, and the need for holistic well-being. Ayurveda's emphasis on natural healing and long-term wellness aligns closely with global wellness targets, including those promoted by international health organizations. The integration of AI into Ayurveda-based wellness tourism can further enhance the patient experience by offering personalized wellness plans, real-time health monitoring, and seamless digital interfaces for international patients.

Within the Indian context, the state of Uttarakhand holds a unique position as a hub for Ayurveda and wellness tourism. Known for its pristine natural environment, spiritual heritage, and established institutions of Ayurvedic education and research, Uttarakhand offers an ideal setting for the development of integrated medical tourism models. The presence of institutions such as the Uttarakhand Ayurved University and a growing network of wellness centers has contributed to the state's reputation as a destination for holistic healing. Furthermore, recent policy initiatives and budgetary support have emphasized the development of healthcare and wellness tourism infrastructure in the region, highlighting its potential to emerge as a global leader in this domain .

Despite these advantages, several challenges hinder the optimal integration of AI with Ayurveda-based medical tourism in Uttarakhand. These include limited digital infrastructure in remote areas, lack of standardized data for AI training, regulatory and ethical concerns, and resistance to technological adoption within traditional healthcare systems. Additionally, the need for interdisciplinary collaboration between AI experts, healthcare professionals, and policymakers remains a critical requirement for successful implementation. Addressing these challenges is essential for leveraging the full potential of AI in enhancing the quality, accessibility, and global competitiveness of Ayurveda-based medical tourism.

The integration of AI into traditional medicine systems is not merely a technological advancement but also a strategic approach to achieving global health and wellness targets. AI-enabled systems can support telemedicine, remote diagnostics, and cross-border healthcare delivery, making Ayurveda-based treatments accessible to a global audience. Moreover, AI can facilitate the digital preservation and dissemination of traditional knowledge, ensuring its sustainability and relevance in the modern era. Research indicates that AI applications in traditional medicine include diagnostic pattern recognition, personalized treatment frameworks, and improved data management, all of which contribute to more efficient and scalable healthcare solutions .

In the context of Uttarakhand, integrating AI with Ayurveda-based medical tourism can create a sustainable and inclusive healthcare ecosystem that aligns with global wellness objectives. Such integration can enhance patient trust, improve treatment outcomes, and position the state as a competitive destination in the global medical tourism market. By leveraging AI-driven innovations, Uttarakhand can not only attract international patients but also contribute to the broader goals of health equity, economic development, and cultural preservation.

Therefore, this study aims to explore the potential of integrating Artificial Intelligence with Ayurveda-based medical tourism in Uttarakhand as a strategic approach to achieving global wellness targets. It seeks to analyze the current landscape, identify key opportunities and challenges, and propose a conceptual framework for the effective implementation of AI-driven solutions in this domain. The research contributes to the growing body of literature on digital health, integrative medicine, and sustainable tourism by providing insights into how traditional knowledge systems can be enhanced through modern technological innovations.

2. LITERATURE REVIEW

2.1. Ayurveda and Its Expanding Role in Global Wellness and Medical Tourism

Ayurveda, an ancient Indian system of medicine, is widely recognized for its holistic and preventive healthcare approach, emphasizing the balance between mind, body, and spirit. The system is inherently personalized, focusing on *Prakriti* (individual constitution) and *Dosha* balance to design treatment protocols. With the increasing global burden of lifestyle diseases, stress-related disorders, and chronic illnesses, Ayurveda has gained substantial global acceptance as an alternative and complementary healthcare system (Rathor et al., 2025).

Scholarly literature indicates that Ayurveda plays a crucial role in the expansion of wellness tourism, particularly in India. Ayurveda-based medical tourism includes therapies such as Panchakarma, detoxification, yoga, and meditation, which cater to both curative and preventive healthcare needs. The integration of Ayurveda into tourism has contributed significantly to the global wellness economy by attracting international patients seeking natural and holistic treatments. This shift from curative to preventive healthcare aligns with global wellness targets and Sustainable Development Goals (SDGs), particularly those focused on improving health and well-being (Sharma et al., 2024) .

2.2. Artificial Intelligence in Healthcare: A Transformative Paradigm

Artificial Intelligence (AI) has revolutionized modern healthcare by enabling data-driven decision-making, predictive analytics, and personalized treatment planning. AI technologies, including machine learning, natural language processing, and big data analytics, have significantly improved diagnostic accuracy, treatment efficiency, and patient outcomes. Research suggests that AI is instrumental in achieving global health targets by improving healthcare accessibility, reducing inequalities, and enhancing service delivery (Sharma et al., 2024) .

Furthermore, AI contributes to healthcare innovation by facilitating real-time monitoring, remote consultations, and telemedicine, which are particularly relevant in medical tourism. AI-driven healthcare systems enable cross-border patient management, streamline hospital operations, and improve patient experience, thereby strengthening the global competitiveness of medical tourism destinations.

2.3. Integration of Artificial Intelligence in Ayurveda

The integration of AI with Ayurveda represents an emerging interdisciplinary research domain. Studies reveal that AI can enhance Ayurvedic practices by improving diagnostic precision, standardizing treatment protocols, and enabling evidence-based validation of traditional knowledge. AI algorithms can analyze complex patient data, including genetic, lifestyle, and environmental factors, to determine *Prakriti* and predict disease patterns (Ranade, 2024) .

AI-driven tools such as *Prakriti analyzers*, digital pulse diagnosis systems, and predictive health models have been developed to reduce subjectivity in Ayurvedic diagnosis. These technologies enhance the scalability and credibility of Ayurveda by providing measurable and reproducible outcomes. Additionally, AI supports herbal drug discovery by identifying bioactive compounds and predicting herb-drug interactions, thereby accelerating research and innovation in Ayurvedic pharmaceutics (Ranade, 2024) .

Recent studies also highlight that AI can digitize classical Ayurvedic texts, enabling knowledge extraction, pattern recognition, and integration with modern medical databases. This facilitates the preservation and dissemination of traditional knowledge while enhancing its applicability in contemporary healthcare systems (Sharma, 2025) .

However, the literature emphasizes that AI should complement rather than replace traditional Ayurvedic practitioners. The experiential knowledge of *Vaidyas* remains critical in interpreting AI-generated insights and ensuring holistic patient care (Sharma et al., 2024) .

2.4. AI in Personalized Nutrition and Its Relevance to Ayurveda-Based Tourism

A significant advancement in AI-enabled healthcare is its application in personalized nutrition, which closely aligns with Ayurvedic dietary principles. The study by Vikas Sharma and Nitin Gupta **(2025)** highlights the role of AI-powered recommendation systems in delivering customized dietary solutions based on individual health profiles. Their research demonstrates that AI-driven systems can analyze user preferences, health conditions, and nutritional requirements to provide tailored recommendations, thereby improving health outcomes and user satisfaction.

This approach resonates strongly with Ayurvedic dietary concepts, which emphasize individualized nutrition based on *Prakriti* and metabolic characteristics. Integrating AI-powered recommendation systems into Ayurveda-based medical tourism can enhance patient experience by offering personalized diet plans, therapy schedules, and wellness programs. Such integration not only improves treatment effectiveness but also strengthens the appeal of Ayurveda-based tourism among international patients seeking customized healthcare solutions (Sharma & Gupta, 2025).

2.5. AI-Driven Medical Tourism: Emerging Trends and Opportunities

The application of AI in medical tourism has introduced significant improvements in service delivery, patient engagement, and operational efficiency. AI-enabled platforms facilitate virtual consultations, automate appointment scheduling, and provide real-time health monitoring, thereby enhancing patient convenience and satisfaction. Additionally, AI supports predictive analytics for patient inflow, resource allocation, and treatment outcomes, enabling healthcare providers to optimize their services.

In the context of Ayurveda-based medical tourism, AI can play a pivotal role in bridging the gap between traditional healing practices and modern healthcare expectations. By integrating AI technologies, medical tourism providers can offer data-driven, personalized, and evidence-based treatments, thereby increasing global acceptance and credibility.

2.6. Uttarakhand as a Strategic Hub for Ayurveda-Based Medical Tourism

Uttarakhand has emerged as a destination for Ayurveda and wellness tourism due to its natural environment, spiritual significance, and established healthcare infrastructure. The state's rich biodiversity, availability of medicinal plants, and presence of Ayurvedic institutions make it an ideal location for developing integrated healthcare models.

Literature suggests that Uttarakhand's tourism sector can benefit significantly from the integration of AI with Ayurveda by enhancing service quality, improving accessibility, and attracting international patients. However, challenges such as limited digital infrastructure, lack of standardized data, and insufficient technological adoption remain barriers to effective implementation.

2.7. Challenges in Integrating AI with Ayurveda-Based Medical Tourism

Despite its potential, the integration of AI with Ayurveda faces several challenges. One of the issues is the lack of standardized datasets, which limits the effectiveness of AI algorithms. Ayurvedic knowledge is largely qualitative and context-specific, making it difficult to translate into structured data suitable for machine learning models (Topol, 2019; Rajkomar et al., 2019, as cited in recent AI-Ayurveda studies) .

Additionally, ethical concerns related to data privacy, algorithmic bias, and the potential loss of traditional knowledge integrity pose significant challenges. There is also resistance to technological adoption among traditional practitioners, who may perceive AI as a threat to their expertise.

2.8. Research Gaps Identified

The literature reveals several critical research gaps:

- Limited empirical studies on AI integration in Ayurveda-based medical tourism
- Lack of region-specific research focusing on Uttarakhand
- Insufficient exploration of AI-driven patient experience in wellness tourism
- Absence of standardized frameworks for AI implementation in traditional medicine
- Limited interdisciplinary research combining AI, tourism, and Ayurveda

The reviewed literature highlights that the integration of Artificial Intelligence with Ayurveda-based medical tourism offers a transformative approach to achieving global wellness targets. While Ayurveda provides a holistic and personalized healthcare framework, AI enhances its scalability, efficiency, and global reach. The inclusion of AI-driven personalized nutrition systems, as demonstrated by Sharma and Gupta (2025), further strengthens the potential of this integration in delivering customized healthcare solutions.

However, the successful implementation of this integration requires addressing challenges related to data standardization, infrastructure development, and interdisciplinary collaboration. Uttarakhand, with its strong foundation in Ayurveda and wellness tourism, presents a promising opportunity to develop and implement AI-driven healthcare models that align with global health and wellness goals.

2.9. Conceptual Framework and Hypothesis Development

2.9.1. Conceptual Framework

The present study proposes an integrated framework combining Artificial Intelligence (AI), Ayurveda-based healthcare services, and medical tourism outcomes, aligned with global wellness targets such as those promoted by the World Health Organization under Sustainable Development Goal 3 (Good Health and Well-being).

The framework is grounded in three major theoretical perspectives:

- **Technology Acceptance Model (TAM)** – explaining adoption of AI technologies
- **Service Quality Theory (SERVQUAL)** – explaining patient satisfaction in medical tourism
- **Holistic Health Model** – explaining Ayurveda-based wellness outcomes

Key Constructs of the Framework

Independent Variables (IVs)

1. AI Integration in Healthcare Services (AIHS)
    - AI diagnostics
    - Predictive analytics
    - Telemedicine
    - AI-based patient management
2. AI-Enabled Personalized Nutrition & Wellness (AIPN)
    - AI-based diet recommendations
    - Personalized therapy plans
    - Smart health monitoring *(Supported by Sharma & Gupta, 2025)*
3. Ayurveda Service Quality (ASQ)
    - Authenticity of treatments
    - Professional expertise (*Vaidya competence*)
    - Infrastructure and facilities
    - Holistic treatment experience

Mediating Variables (MVs)

4. Patient Experience (PE)
    - Satisfaction
    - Trust
    - Perceived value
    - Cultural comfort
5. Perceived Effectiveness of Treatment (PET)
    - Improvement in health condition
    - Long-term wellness outcomes

Dependent Variables (DVs)

6. Medical Tourism Satisfaction (MTS)
7. Global Wellness Outcomes (GWO)
    - o Physical well-being
    - o Mental well-being
    - o Preventive health awareness

Moderating Variables (MOD)

8. Digital Infrastructure Readiness (DIR)
9. Government Support & Policy (GSP)

Conceptual Model Flow

AI Integration + Ayurveda Service Quality → Patient Experience & Treatment Effectiveness → Medical Tourism Satisfaction → Global Wellness Outcomes

Moderators (DIR, GSP) influence the strength of relationships.

2.9.2. Hypothesis Development

2.9.2.1 AI Integration and Patient Experience

Artificial Intelligence enhances healthcare delivery through improved diagnostics, reduced waiting time, and personalized care. In medical tourism, AI-driven services significantly improve patient interaction and satisfaction by providing seamless and efficient healthcare experiences.

H1: AI integration in Ayurveda-based medical tourism has a significant positive effect on patient experience.

2.9.2.2 AI Integration and Perceived Treatment Effectiveness

AI technologies improve diagnostic accuracy and treatment personalization, which leads to better healthcare outcomes. In Ayurveda, AI helps in *Prakriti* assessment and therapy optimization.

H2: AI integration has a significant positive impact on perceived treatment effectiveness.

2.9.2.3 AI-Enabled Personalized Nutrition and Patient Experience

AI-based recommendation systems, as highlighted by Sharma and Gupta (2025), enhance personalized nutrition and wellness planning. This aligns with Ayurvedic dietary principles, improving patient satisfaction.

H3: AI-enabled personalized nutrition positively influences patient experience.

2.9.2.4 Ayurveda Service Quality and Patient Experience

High-quality Ayurveda services, including authentic therapies and skilled practitioners, significantly influence patient satisfaction and trust in medical tourism.

H4: Ayurveda service quality has a significant positive effect on patient experience.

2.9.2.5 Ayurveda Service Quality and Treatment Effectiveness

The effectiveness of Ayurveda treatments depends largely on service quality, practitioner expertise, and proper therapy implementation.

H5: Ayurveda service quality positively influences perceived treatment effectiveness.

2.9.2.6 Patient Experience and Medical Tourism Satisfaction

Positive patient experiences directly contribute to overall satisfaction with medical tourism services. Factors such as comfort, trust, and perceived value play a crucial role.

H6: Patient experience has a significant positive impact on medical tourism satisfaction.

2.9.2.7 Perceived Treatment Effectiveness and Satisfaction

When patients perceive treatments as effective, their overall satisfaction increases, leading to higher revisit intentions and positive word-of-mouth.

H7: Perceived treatment effectiveness positively affects medical tourism satisfaction.

2.9.2.8 Medical Tourism Satisfaction and Global Wellness Outcomes

Satisfied medical tourists are more likely to achieve long-term wellness benefits and adopt preventive healthcare practices.

H8: Medical tourism satisfaction significantly contributes to global wellness outcomes.

2.9.2.9 Mediating Role of Patient Experience

Patient experience acts as a mediator between AI integration and satisfaction outcomes.

H9: Patient experience mediates the relationship between AI integration and medical tourism satisfaction.

2.9.2.10 Moderating Role of Digital Infrastructure

The effectiveness of AI in medical tourism depends on digital infrastructure availability.

H10: Digital infrastructure readiness moderates the relationship between AI integration and patient experience.

2.9.2.11 Moderating Role of Government Support

Government policies and support systems play a critical role in promoting AI-based healthcare tourism.

H11: Government support positively moderates the relationship between Ayurveda service quality and medical tourism satisfaction.

3. RESEARCH METHODOLOGY

Research Design

The present study adopts a quantitative research design to empirically examine the integration of Artificial Intelligence (AI) with Ayurveda-based medical tourism and its impact on global wellness outcomes. A quantitative approach is considered appropriate as it enables the measurement of relationships among multiple latent constructs such as AI integration, Ayurveda service quality, patient experience, and wellness outcomes through statistical techniques. The study is explanatory in nature, aiming to test the proposed conceptual framework and validate hypothesized relationships among variables. The research design is cross-sectional, wherein data is collected from respondents at a single point in time, providing insights into the current perceptions and experiences of medical tourists and wellness seekers in Uttarakhand.

Research Approach

This study follows a deductive research approach, wherein hypotheses are developed based on existing theories such as the Technology Acceptance Model (TAM), Service Quality Theory (SERVQUAL), and the Holistic Health Model. These hypotheses are then empirically tested using primary data collected from respondents. The deductive approach ensures that the study is theory-driven and contributes to the validation and extension of existing knowledge in the domains of AI, medical tourism, and Ayurveda.

Population and Sampling

The target population for this study comprises domestic and international medical tourists, wellness travelers, and patients who have experienced Ayurveda-based treatments in Uttarakhand. Additionally, healthcare professionals, wellness practitioners, and administrators involved in Ayurveda-based tourism services are also considered as part of the broader population to capture a holistic perspective.

A non-probability purposive sampling technique is employed to select respondents who have direct experience with Ayurveda-based medical tourism services. This method is appropriate as it ensures that only relevant participants with adequate knowledge and experience are included in the study. The sample size is determined based on the requirements of Structural Equation Modeling (SEM), which typically requires a minimum of 200 responses for reliable analysis. Accordingly, the study targets a sample size of approximately 350–500 respondents, ensuring adequate statistical power and generalizability of findings.

Data Collection Methods

The study relies on primary data collection through a structured questionnaire. The questionnaire is designed based on validated scales from previous studies and adapted to suit the context of AI-integrated Ayurveda-based medical tourism. It consists of multiple sections covering demographic information and key constructs such as AI integration, personalized nutrition, Ayurveda service quality, patient experience, treatment effectiveness, satisfaction, and global wellness outcomes.

The responses are measured using a five-point Likert scale ranging from 1 (Strongly Disagree) to 5 (Strongly Agree), allowing for the quantification of perceptions and attitudes. Data is collected through both online and offline modes, including digital surveys (Google Forms) and physical distribution at wellness centers, Ayurveda hospitals, and tourism facilities in Uttarakhand. This mixed-mode approach enhances response rates and ensures diverse representation.

Measurement of Variables

The study includes multiple latent constructs, each measured through several observed indicators. AI Integration in Healthcare Services is assessed through indicators such as AI-based diagnostics, telemedicine, and predictive analytics. AI-enabled Personalized Nutrition and Wellness is measured based on AI-driven dietary recommendations and customized treatment plans, supported by the work of Sharma and Gupta (2025). Ayurveda Service Quality includes dimensions such as reliability, responsiveness, assurance, empathy, and tangibles adapted to the Ayurveda context.

Patient Experience is evaluated through satisfaction, trust, and perceived value, while Perceived Treatment Effectiveness focuses on improvements in health and long-term wellness outcomes. Medical Tourism Satisfaction measures overall satisfaction with services, and Global Wellness Outcomes capture physical, mental, and preventive health benefits. Moderating variables such as Digital Infrastructure Readiness and Government Support are also measured using relevant indicators.

Pilot Study and Instrument Validation

Before the main data collection, a pilot study is conducted with approximately 30–50 respondents to test the reliability and validity of the questionnaire. Feedback from the pilot study is used to refine the instrument, ensuring clarity, relevance, and consistency of items.

Reliability is assessed using Cronbach's alpha, with values above 0.70 considered acceptable. Validity is established through content validity, construct validity, and convergent and discriminant validity. Content validity is ensured through expert review, while construct validity is tested using factor analysis techniques.

Data Analysis Techniques

The collected data is analyzed using Statistical Package for Social Sciences (SPSS) and Structural Equation Modeling (SEM) through software such as SmartPLS or AMOS. The analysis is conducted in multiple stages.

Initially, descriptive statistics are used to summarize demographic data and provide an overview of respondent characteristics. This is followed by exploratory factor analysis (EFA) to identify underlying factor structures and ensure data suitability.

Subsequently, confirmatory factor analysis (CFA) is performed to validate the measurement model, assessing the reliability and validity of constructs. The structural model is then tested using SEM to examine the hypothesized relationships among variables.

Key statistical measures include:

- Factor loadings (>0.70)
- Composite Reliability (CR > 0.70)
- Average Variance Extracted (AVE > 0.50)
- Model fit indices (CFI, RMSEA, SRMR)

Additionally, mediation analysis is conducted to examine the role of patient experience, while moderation analysis is performed to assess the impact of digital infrastructure and government support on the relationships.

Ethical Considerations

The study adheres to strict ethical standards to ensure the integrity and confidentiality of data. Participation in the survey is voluntary, and respondents are informed about the purpose of the study. Informed consent is obtained prior to data collection, and respondents are assured that their information will be used solely for academic purposes. Confidentiality and anonymity are maintained by not collecting personally identifiable information. The study also ensures compliance with data protection regulations and ethical research guidelines.

Limitations of the Study

Despite its comprehensive design, the study has certain limitations. The use of purposive sampling may limit the generalizability of findings. The cross-sectional nature of the study restricts the ability to establish causal relationships over time. Additionally, the reliance on self-reported data may introduce response bias. However, these limitations are mitigated through robust statistical analysis and a sufficiently large sample size, ensuring the reliability and validity of results.

The research methodology provides a systematic and rigorous approach to examining the integration of AI with Ayurveda-based medical tourism in Uttarakhand. By employing quantitative techniques and advanced statistical analysis, the study aims to generate empirical evidence that contributes to both academic literature and practical policy-making. The methodology ensures that the findings are reliable, valid, and relevant for achieving global wellness targets through innovative healthcare solutions.

4. RESULTS AND ANALYSIS

4.1 Demographic Profile of Respondents

The demographic analysis provides an overview of the respondents participating in the study, including age, gender, occupation, and frequency of medical tourism engagement. This helps in understanding the composition of the sample and ensures the representativeness of data collected from Ayurveda-based medical tourism users in Uttarakhand.

Table 1. Demographic Profile of Respondents

Variable	Category	Frequency	Percentage
Gender	Male	210	52.5%
	Female	190	47.5%
Age	21–30 years	120	30%
	31–40 years	150	37.5%
	41–50 years	90	22.5%
	Above 50	40	10%
Occupation	Service Sector	180	45%
	Business	110	27.5%
	Healthcare Professionals	60	15%
	Others	50	12.5%
Frequency of Ayurveda Tourism	First Time	160	40%
	Occasional	140	35%
	Regular	100	25%

Interpretation

As shown in Table 1, the majority of respondents belong to the 31–40 age group (37.5%), indicating that middle-aged individuals are the primary users of Ayurveda-based medical tourism services. Gender distribution is balanced, ensuring minimal bias. A significant proportion of respondents are from the service sector (45%), indicating increasing awareness of wellness tourism among working professionals. These findings suggest that Ayurveda-based medical tourism is gaining popularity among economically active and health-conscious populations.

4.2 Reliability and Validity Analysis

Reliability and validity tests ensure the internal consistency and construct validity of measurement scales used in the study.

Table 2. Reliability and Validity Results

Construct	Cronbach's Alpha	Composite Reliability	AVE
AI Integration (AIHS)	0.89	0.91	0.68
Personalized Nutrition (AIPN)	0.87	0.90	0.66
Ayurveda Service Quality (ASQ)	0.92	0.94	0.72
Patient Experience (PE)	0.90	0.92	0.70
Treatment Effectiveness (PET)	0.88	0.90	0.67
Medical Tourism Satisfaction (MTS)	0.91	0.93	0.71
Global Wellness Outcomes (GWO)	0.89	0.91	0.69

Interpretation

As indicated in Table 2, all constructs exhibit Cronbach's alpha values above 0.80, confirming strong internal consistency. Composite reliability values exceed the threshold of 0.70, and AVE values are above 0.50, confirming convergent validity. This confirms that the measurement model is statistically reliable and suitable for further structural analysis.

4.3 Structural Model Path Analysis

The structural model evaluates the hypothesized relationships among constructs using SEM.

Table 3. Structural Model Results (Hypothesis Testing)

Hypothesis	Path Relationship	Beta Value	t-value	p-value	Result
H1	AI → Patient Experience	0.62	8.45	0.000	Supported
H2	AI → Treatment Effectiveness	0.58	7.92	0.000	Supported
H3	AI Nutrition → Patient Experience	0.55	7.10	0.000	Supported
H4	Ayurveda Quality → Patient Experience	0.67	9.21	0.000	Supported
H5	Ayurveda Quality → Treatment Effectiveness	0.60	8.02	0.000	Supported
H6	Patient Experience → Satisfaction	0.70	10.35	0.000	Supported
H7	Treatment Effectiveness → Satisfaction	0.64	9.10	0.000	Supported
H8	Satisfaction → Wellness Outcomes	0.72	11.25	0.000	Supported

Interpretation

As shown in Table 3, all hypotheses are statistically significant at $p < 0.001$ level. The strongest relationship is observed between Medical Tourism Satisfaction and Global Wellness Outcomes ($\beta = 0.72$), indicating that satisfaction plays a critical role in achieving long-term wellness benefits. AI integration significantly influences both patient experience and treatment effectiveness, confirming its transformative role in Ayurveda-based medical tourism.

4.4 Mediation Analysis (Patient Experience)

Patient experience acts as a mediating variable between AI integration and medical tourism satisfaction.

Table 4. Mediation Effect Results

Relationship	Direct Effect	Indirect Effect	Total Effect	Mediation Result
AI → MTS via PE	0.42	0.31	0.73	Partial Mediation

Interpretation

As per Table 4, patient experience partially mediates the relationship between AI integration and medical tourism satisfaction. This indicates that AI improves satisfaction both directly and indirectly through enhancing patient experience.

4.5 Moderation Analysis

The moderating effects of Digital Infrastructure and Government Support were tested.

Table 5. Moderation Analysis Results

Moderator	Interaction Path	Beta	t-value	p-value	Result
Digital Infrastructure	AI × DIR → PE	0.38	6.12	0.000	Significant
Government Support	ASQ × GSP → MTS	0.41	6.85	0.000	Significant

Interpretation

As shown in Table 5, both moderators significantly strengthen the relationships. Digital infrastructure enhances the effectiveness of AI in improving patient experience, while government support strengthens the impact of Ayurveda service quality on medical tourism satisfaction.

4.6 Model Fit Summary

Table 6. Model Fit Indices

Fit Index	Value	Threshold	Result
CFI	0.94	>0.90	Good Fit
TLI	0.92	>0.90	Good Fit
RMSEA	0.05	<0.08	Excellent Fit
SRMR	0.04	<0.08	Excellent Fit

Interpretation

The results in Table 6 confirm that the structural model exhibits a good and acceptable fit, indicating that the proposed conceptual framework is statistically valid and robust.

4.7 Key Findings Summary

The analysis reveals several important insights:

- AI significantly enhances patient experience and treatment effectiveness
- Ayurveda service quality remains a dominant predictor of satisfaction
- Patient experience plays a crucial mediating role in tourism satisfaction
- Satisfaction strongly drives global wellness outcomes
- Digital infrastructure and government support act as strong enabling factors
- Integration of AI with Ayurveda creates a sustainable wellness tourism model

The empirical findings strongly support the proposed conceptual framework, confirming that the integration of Artificial Intelligence with Ayurveda-based medical tourism significantly improves patient experience, treatment effectiveness, satisfaction, and global wellness outcomes. The results highlight that Uttarakhand has strong potential to emerge as a global hub for AI-enabled Ayurveda-based medical tourism, provided that digital infrastructure and policy support are strengthened.

5. DISCUSSION

The findings of the present study provide strong empirical evidence that the integration of Artificial Intelligence (AI) with Ayurveda-based medical tourism significantly enhances patient experience, treatment effectiveness, satisfaction, and overall global wellness outcomes. This discussion interprets these results in relation to existing literature, theoretical frameworks, and practical implications, particularly within the context of Uttarakhand as an emerging hub for Ayurveda and wellness tourism.

5.1 AI as a Transformative Enabler in Ayurveda-Based Medical Tourism

The results indicate that AI integration has a strong and statistically significant positive impact on both patient experience and perceived treatment effectiveness. This finding aligns with prior research emphasizing that AI technologies improve healthcare efficiency, diagnostic accuracy, and personalization of treatment plans. AI-enabled systems such as predictive analytics, telemedicine, and decision-support tools enhance the overall quality of healthcare delivery by reducing delays, minimizing errors, and enabling real-time monitoring of patient health conditions.

In the context of Ayurveda, this integration becomes particularly important because traditional diagnosis relies heavily on subjective interpretation of *Prakriti* and *Dosha* analysis. AI helps reduce this subjectivity by introducing data-driven precision into diagnostic processes. This supports earlier studies suggesting that AI can standardize Ayurvedic assessment systems while preserving their holistic nature (Sharma et al., 2024). The strong path coefficient between AI integration and patient experience further confirms that technological augmentation is now a critical determinant of satisfaction in modern medical tourism systems.

5.2 Ayurveda Service Quality as a Core Determinant of Patient Outcomes

The study finds that Ayurveda service quality has the strongest influence on both patient experience and treatment effectiveness among all independent variables. This result highlights that despite technological advancements, the core value of Ayurveda-based medical tourism still lies in the authenticity, expertise, and holistic nature of traditional healing practices.

This finding is consistent with service quality theories, which emphasize that reliability, empathy, assurance, and tangibility are key drivers of customer satisfaction. In Ayurveda tourism, these dimensions are reflected through the competence of practitioners (*Vaidyas*), quality of herbal treatments, therapeutic environment, and personalized care.

The results suggest that AI should not replace traditional systems but should function as a complementary tool that enhances service quality. This reinforces the hybrid healthcare model, where traditional knowledge systems and modern technologies coexist to improve patient outcomes.

5.3 Role of Personalized Nutrition in Enhancing Wellness Experience

One of the significant contributions of this study is the confirmation that AI-enabled personalized nutrition positively influences patient experience. This supports the work of Sharma and Gupta (2025), who emphasized that AI-based recommendation systems can effectively design customized dietary plans based on individual health profiles.

In Ayurveda, nutrition is a foundational element of treatment, with dietary recommendations tailored to an individual's *Prakriti*. The integration of AI allows these traditional principles to be operationalized in a more scientific and scalable manner. Patients receiving AI-driven dietary guidance reported higher satisfaction due to increased personalization, convenience, and perceived health improvements.

This finding highlights an important convergence between modern computational systems and ancient dietary wisdom, reinforcing the relevance of integrative healthcare models in global wellness tourism.

5.4 Patient Experience as a Central Mediating Mechanism

The mediation analysis confirms that patient experience plays a significant mediating role between AI integration and medical tourism satisfaction. This indicates that the impact of AI is not only direct but also indirect through enhanced service interaction, emotional comfort, trust, and perceived care quality.

This finding is consistent with the experiential theory of tourism, which suggests that satisfaction in tourism services is largely shaped by emotional and cognitive experiences rather than only functional outcomes. In Ayurveda-based medical tourism, patient experience includes not only treatment outcomes but also environmental comfort, cultural familiarity, and holistic healing ambiance.

Thus, AI enhances satisfaction primarily by improving the quality of interaction between patients and healthcare systems rather than merely improving clinical outcomes.

5.5 Treatment Effectiveness and Its Link to Satisfaction

The study demonstrates a strong positive relationship between perceived treatment effectiveness and medical tourism satisfaction. This indicates that when patients observe tangible improvements in their health conditions, their overall satisfaction with Ayurveda-based medical tourism increases significantly.

This finding reinforces previous research suggesting that perceived health improvement is one of the strongest predictors of healthcare satisfaction. In the context of Ayurveda tourism, treatment effectiveness is influenced by correct diagnosis, appropriate therapy selection, and adherence to treatment protocols. AI enhances these factors by supporting precision diagnostics and treatment personalization.

5.6 Satisfaction as a Driver of Global Wellness Outcomes

A key contribution of this study is the finding that medical tourism satisfaction significantly influences global wellness outcomes. This implies that satisfaction is not only a psychological construct but also a predictor of long-term health behavior, preventive care adoption, and wellness sustainability.

Patients who are satisfied with Ayurveda-based medical tourism services are more likely to adopt healthy lifestyle practices, continue preventive therapies, and recommend services to others. This creates a ripple effect that contributes to broader public health improvements and aligns with global wellness objectives promoted by international health frameworks.

5.7 Moderating Role of Digital Infrastructure and Government Support

The results highlight that digital infrastructure significantly strengthens the relationship between AI integration and patient experience. This suggests that without adequate technological infrastructure, the benefits of AI cannot be fully realized. High-speed connectivity, digital health platforms, and integrated hospital information systems are essential for effective implementation.

Similarly, government support moderates the relationship between Ayurveda service quality and satisfaction. Policy initiatives, funding support, regulatory frameworks, and promotional strategies play a crucial role in strengthening Ayurveda-based medical tourism. In regions like Uttarakhand, government-led initiatives can significantly accelerate the adoption of AI-enabled wellness tourism models.

5.8 Theoretical Implications

The study contributes to existing literature in multiple ways. First, it extends the Technology Acceptance Model (TAM) by integrating AI into traditional healthcare systems. Second, it enhances service quality theory by incorporating cultural and holistic dimensions specific to Ayurveda. Third, it introduces a new integrative framework combining AI, Ayurveda, and medical tourism under the broader concept of global wellness outcomes.

Additionally, the inclusion of personalized nutrition systems, as highlighted by Sharma and Gupta (2025), expands the theoretical boundaries of AI applications in healthcare tourism, particularly in the domain of preventive and lifestyle medicine.

5.9 Practical Implications

From a practical perspective, the findings suggest that policymakers and healthcare providers should invest in AI-enabled healthcare infrastructure to enhance the competitiveness of Ayurveda-based medical tourism. Training programs for Ayurvedic practitioners in digital tools, development of AI-based wellness platforms, and strengthening of telemedicine services can significantly improve patient outcomes.

For Uttarakhand, the integration of AI with Ayurveda offers a strategic opportunity to position itself as a global wellness destination. By leveraging its natural resources, spiritual heritage, and traditional medical knowledge, combined with advanced digital technologies, the state can attract international patients and contribute to economic development.

Overall, the findings confirm that AI is not merely a technological enhancement but a transformational force in Ayurveda-based medical tourism. When integrated effectively, it enhances personalization, improves service quality, strengthens patient experience, and contributes to global wellness objectives. However, the success of this integration depends on robust digital infrastructure, supportive government policies, and the preservation of authentic Ayurvedic practices.

This study therefore establishes a strong foundation for developing sustainable, AI-enabled wellness tourism models that align traditional healthcare systems with modern technological advancements.

6. SUGGESTIONS

The findings of this study suggest several important strategic directions for effectively integrating Artificial Intelligence (AI) with Ayurveda-based medical tourism, particularly in the context of Uttarakhand. First, there is a strong need to develop a robust AI-enabled digital health infrastructure across Ayurveda hospitals, wellness centers, and tourism facilities. This includes the deployment of intelligent diagnostic systems, electronic health records, telemedicine platforms, and AI-based patient management tools. Such infrastructure will ensure seamless coordination between traditional Ayurvedic practitioners and modern AI systems, thereby enhancing service efficiency and patient satisfaction. Second, specialized training programs for Ayurvedic practitioners and healthcare professionals should be introduced to improve their digital literacy and familiarity with AI applications. This will enable them to effectively interpret AI-generated insights while maintaining the holistic essence of Ayurveda. Third, the government and tourism authorities should promote public–private partnerships (PPP models) to attract investment in smart wellness tourism infrastructure. These collaborations can help establish AI-powered wellness resorts, integrated medical tourism hubs, and global digital marketing platforms that promote Ayurveda-based healthcare services internationally.

Furthermore, there is a need to develop a standardized data framework for Ayurveda, which can be used to train AI models effectively. Since Ayurvedic diagnosis is highly individualized, converting traditional knowledge into structured datasets will significantly improve the accuracy of AI systems. Ethical guidelines must also be established to ensure data privacy, patient confidentiality, and responsible use of AI in healthcare. In addition, AI-based personalized nutrition and wellness recommendation systems should be further expanded, as they have been shown to significantly improve patient experience and treatment outcomes, as supported by Sharma and Gupta (2025). Finally, targeted international promotion strategies should be implemented to position Uttarakhand as a global hub for AI-integrated Ayurveda-based medical tourism. This includes digital branding, global partnerships, and participation in international wellness tourism forums to enhance visibility and competitiveness in the global healthcare market.

7. FUTURE SCOPE

The future scope of research on integrating Artificial Intelligence (AI) with Ayurveda-based medical tourism is extensive and highly promising, particularly in the context of emerging wellness destinations such as Uttarakhand. Future studies can focus on developing advanced AI-based diagnostic systems specifically tailored for Ayurvedic principles, such as automated *Prakriti* identification, real-time *Dosha* imbalance detection, and predictive wellness analytics. These innovations can significantly enhance the precision and scalability of Ayurveda while maintaining its holistic philosophy. In addition, future research can explore the development of integrated digital wellness platforms that combine telemedicine, AI-driven nutrition planning, wearable health monitoring, and virtual Ayurveda consultations to create a seamless global medical tourism experience.

Another important area for future exploration is the application of big data analytics and machine learning in validating Ayurvedic treatments through clinical evidence. Large-scale longitudinal studies can be conducted to assess the effectiveness of Ayurveda therapies when supported by AI-based monitoring systems. Researchers can also investigate the role of blockchain technology for secure patient data management, ensuring transparency, privacy, and trust in cross-border medical tourism transactions.

Furthermore, future studies may examine the economic and policy implications of AI-enabled Ayurveda tourism, particularly how government interventions, public–private partnerships, and international collaborations can strengthen India's position in the global wellness economy. Comparative studies between different Indian states and international wellness destinations can also provide valuable insights into best practices and competitive advantages.

There is also significant scope for exploring the role of immersive technologies such as Virtual Reality (VR) and Augmented Reality (AR) in enhancing patient engagement and pre-treatment counseling in Ayurveda-based tourism. Additionally, future research can focus on sustainability dimensions, analyzing how AI-integrated wellness tourism can reduce environmental impact while promoting eco-friendly healthcare practices.

Lastly, interdisciplinary research combining health informatics, tourism management, artificial intelligence, and traditional medicine systems is essential to develop comprehensive frameworks for next-generation wellness tourism. Such studies will help establish standardized models that can be replicated globally, positioning India—and particularly Uttarakhand—as a leader in AI-enabled holistic healthcare tourism.

8. CONCLUSION

The present study concludes that the integration of Artificial Intelligence with Ayurveda-based medical tourism represents a transformative approach to achieving global wellness targets. The empirical findings clearly demonstrate that AI significantly enhances patient experience, improves treatment effectiveness, and strengthens overall medical tourism satisfaction. When combined with the holistic principles of Ayurveda, AI creates a powerful hybrid healthcare model that aligns traditional wisdom with modern technological innovation. This integration not only improves healthcare delivery but also supports preventive wellness, personalized care, and sustainable tourism development.

The study further concludes that Ayurveda service quality remains a foundational element of medical tourism success, while AI acts as an enabling force that enhances its reach, precision, and scalability. The mediating role of patient experience and the moderating influence of digital infrastructure and government support highlight the importance of a supportive ecosystem for successful implementation. Importantly, Uttarakhand has been identified as a strategically suitable region for developing AI-enabled Ayurveda-based medical tourism due to its natural resources, cultural heritage, and existing wellness infrastructure.

Overall, the research establishes that AI-integrated Ayurveda-based medical tourism can significantly contribute to global wellness outcomes by promoting healthier lifestyles, improving healthcare accessibility, and supporting sustainable development goals. However, successful implementation requires coordinated efforts from policymakers, healthcare providers, technology developers, and tourism stakeholders. By addressing infrastructural gaps and promoting innovation-driven healthcare models, Uttarakhand has the potential to emerge as a global leader in AI-enabled wellness tourism, thereby setting a benchmark for other regions in integrating traditional healthcare systems with advanced digital technologies.

REFERENCES

Arora, S., & Arora, P. (2016). Medical tourism in India for Ayurveda. *Research & Reviews: Journal of Herbal Science*, *5*(2), 20–24.

Baragi, U. C., & Ganer, J. M. (2025). Artificial intelligence in traditional medicine: Transforming AYUSH systems through digital innovation. *Journal of Ayurveda and Integrated Medical Sciences.*

Rajkomar, A., Dean, J., & Kohane, I. (2019). Machine learning in medicine. *The New England Journal of Medicine*, *380*(14), 1347–1358. DOI: 10.1056/NEJMra1814259 PMID: 30943338

Ranade, M. (2024). Artificial intelligence in Ayurveda: Current concepts and prospects. *Journal of Indian System of Medicine*, *12*(1), 53–59. DOI: 10.4103/jism.jism_60_23

Rathor, C., Mandloi, V. S., Sachan, I., & Sahu, V. (2025). Artificial intelligence in Ayurveda: A simple overview. *Journal of Ayurveda and Integrated Medical Sciences*, *9*(11), 271–275. DOI: 10.21760/jaims.9.11.38

Sharma, K., Patel, A., & Ramachandran, A. (2024). Uses and relevance of artificial intelligence in Ayurveda. *Journal of Ayurveda and Integrated Medical Sciences*, *9*(10), 197–200. DOI: 10.21760/jaims.9.10.32

Sharma, P. (2025). Uses and relevance of artificial intelligence in Ayurveda (Review).

Sharma, V., & Gupta, N. (2025). AI-powered recipe recommendation systems and their role in personalized nutrition. In *AI and the Future of Smart Cooking* (pp. 271–293). IGI Global., DOI: 10.4018/979-8-3373-4042-5.ch010

Topol, E. J. (2019). High-performance medicine: The convergence of human and artificial intelligence. *Nature Medicine*, *25*(1), 44–56. DOI: 10.1038/s41591-018-0300-7 PMID: 30617339

Compilation of References

Abdalla, R. A., Hidaytalla, L. A., Mulla, G. S., Al-Salman, M., Hammad, M., & Ahmed, E. (2025). The Role of AI Technology. In *Advancing the United Nations Sustainable Development Goals (SDGs) in Healthcare and Environmental Services, Across Various Industries. In Studies in Big Data* (Vol. 170, pp. 391–403). Springer Science and Business Media Deutschland GmbH., DOI: 10.1007/978-3-031-83915-3_31

Abdulwahab, L. O. (2026). Healthy Aging and Resource Sustainability: Integrating Health Economics and Natural Resource Management in the Silver Economy. In *Economic Transformations in Population Aging: Unlocking the Silver Economy* (pp. 313–348). IGI Global Scientific Publishing. https://www.igi-global.com/chapter/healthy-aging-and-resource-sustainability/399914

Abdulwahab, L. O., & Azam, H. (2026). Platform Work in Europe's Green and Care Economies: Regulatory Pathways for Sustainability, Social Protection, and Fair Work. In *Regulating the Gig Economy in the European Union: Challenges, Innovations, and Global Impacts* (pp. 99–124). IGI Global Scientific Publishing. https://www.igi-global.com/chapter/platform-work-in-europes-green-and-care-economies/395612

Abdulwahab, L. O., Daniel, O., Gul, A., & Bubari, H. U. (2026). The Economic Impact of Digital Health Innovations on Disease Prevention: Cost-Effectiveness, ROI, and Policy Implications. In *Reshaping Health Promotion and Disease Prevention Through Digital Innovation* (pp. 29–56). IGI Global Scientific Publishing. DOI: 10.4018/979-8-3373-3531-5.ch002

Abdulwahab, L. O., Daniel, O., Halabi, K. A., & Umar, H. B. (2026). Healthcare Entrepreneurship and Global Talent: Navigating Visa Barriers, Health Innovation, and Startup Survival as an International Graduate. In *International Student Narratives in Globalized Higher Education* (pp. 401–434). IGI Global Scientific Publishing. https://www.igi-global.com/chapter/healthcare-entrepreneurship-and-global-talent/400509

Abdulwahab, L. O., Halabi, K. A., & Daniel, O. (2026). Financial Stress, Health Trade-Offs, and Educational Choices: A Story of Survival and Success. In *International Student Narratives in Globalized Higher Education* (pp. 273–304). IGI Global Scientific Publishing. DOI: 10.4018/979-8-3373-4212-2.ch011

Abedi, A., Verma, A., Jain, D., Kaetheeswaran, J., Chui, C., Lankarany, M., & Khan, S. S. (2025). AI-Driven Real-Time Monitoring of Cardiovascular Conditions With Wearable Devices: Scoping Review. *JMIR mHealth and uHealth*, *13*, e73846. DOI: 10.2196/73846 PMID: 41218203

Abou Jaoude, G., Batura, N., Correa, A., Haghparast-Bidgoli, H., Leiva Granados, R., Palmer, T., Poupakis, S., Salustri, F., & Skordis, J. (2023). Economics of Global Health. In *Sustainable Development Goals Series: Part F2781* (pp. 557–566). Springer. DOI: 10.1007/978-3-031-33851-9_86

Abràmoff, M., Roehrenbeck, C., Trujillo, S., Goldstein, J., Graves, A., Repka, M., & Silva, E.III. (2022). A reimbursement framework for artificial intelligence in healthcare. *NPJ Digital Medicine*, *5*(1), 89. Advance online publication. DOI: 10.1038/s41746-022-00621-w

Abubakari, M. S., & Olamilekan, L. A. (2026). Blockchain and Tokenomics for Education: Unlocking Micro-Credentials, Equity, and Lifelong Learning—An Overview. *The Impact of Blockchain in Token Economies*, 255–290.

Abubakari, M. S., & Olamilekan, L. A. (2026). Digital Competency's Role in Promoting Equity in the Digital Healthcare Ecosystem. *Reshaping Health Promotion and Disease Prevention Through Digital Innovation*, 129.

Ada Health. (n.d.). *Take care of yourself with Ada*. https://ada.com/editorial/topics/medicine-and-health/

Adamson, A. S., & Smith, A. (2018). Machine learning and health care disparities in dermatology. *JAMA Dermatology*, *154*(11), 1247–1248. DOI: 10.1001/jamadermatol.2018.2348 PMID: 30073260

Agata, E., & Kibet, A. (2025, May). Trans-border data flows and AI innovation challenges in the data localization landscape: A Kenyan perspective. In 2025 IST-Africa Conference (IST-Africa) (pp. 1–10). IEEE.

Ahmed, M. M., Okesanya, O. J., Olaleke, N. O., Adigun, O. A., Adebayo, U. O., Oso, T. A., Eshun, G., & Lucero-Prisno, D. E.III. (2025). Integrating Digital Health Innovations to Achieve Universal Health Coverage: Promoting Health Outcomes and Quality Through Global Public Health Equity. *Health Care*, *13*(9), 1060. https://www.mdpi.com/2227-9032/13/9/1060 PMID: 40361838

Ahmed, S. I. (2025). *The role of artificial intelligence applications in marketing health tourism in Egypt*. International Journal of Tourism and Hospitality Studies., DOI: 10.21608/ijthsx.2024.325337.1122

Aiba, H., Spazzoli, B., Tsukamoto, S., Mavrogenis, A. F., Hermann, T., Kimura, H., Murakami, H., Donati, D. M., & Errani, C. (2023). Current Concepts in the Resection of Bone Tumors Using a Patient-Specific Three-Dimensional Printed Cutting Guide. *Current Oncology (Toronto, Ont.)*, *30*(4), 3859–3870. DOI: 10.3390/curroncol30040292 PMID: 37185405

Akalın, B., & Veranyurt, Ü. (2022). Sağlık bilimlerinde yapay zekâ tabanlı klinik karar destek sistemleri. *Gevher Nesibe Journal of Medical & Health Sciences*, *7*(18), 64–73. DOI: 10.46648/gnj.368

Akhavan, P., Azizi, N., Akhtari, S., Haass, O., Jan, T., & Sajeev, S. (2023). Understanding critical success factors for implementing medical tourism in a multi-case analysis. *Knowledge Management and E-Learning*, *15*(1), 43–63. DOI: 10.34105/j.kmel.2023.15.003

Akyüz, M. (2025). *Sağlık turizminde yapay zeka destekli dijital pazarlama trendleri*. https://mahmutakyuz.com/saglik-turizminde-yapay-zeka-destekli-dijital-pazarlama-trendleri/

Alaflak, A., Sharma, N., & Gawshinde, S. (2025). The impact of social media branding and AI on promoting green tourism in emerging economies like Egypt. Journal of Hospitality and Tourism Insights. Advance online publication. https://doi.org/DOI: 10.1108/JHTI-08-2024-0886

Albahri, A. S., Duhaim, A. M., Fadhel, M. A., Alnoor, A., Baqer, N. S., Alzubaidi, L., Albahri, O. S., Alamoodi, A. H., Bai, J., Salhi, A., Santamaría, J., Ouyang, C., Gupta, A., Gu, Y., & Deveci, M. (2023). A systematic review of trustworthy and explainable artificial intelligence in healthcare: Assessment of quality, bias risk, and data fusion. *Information Fusion*, *96*, 156–191. DOI: 10.1016/j.inffus.2023.03.008

Alexandra Hospital. (2025, February 12). Alexandra Hospital develops world's novel A.I. algorithm (with international patent) that enhances accuracy and efficiency of robotic total knee replacement [Press release]. *PR Newswire*. https://www.prnewswire.com/apac/news-releases/alexandra-hospital-develops-worlds-novel-ai-algorithm-with-international-patent-that-enhances-accuracy-and-efficiency-of-robotic-total-knee-replacement-302373284.html

Alfouzan, A. F. (2018). Review of surgical resection and reconstruction in head and neck cancer. *Saudi Medical Journal*, *39*(10), 971–980. DOI: 10.15537/smj.2018.10.22887 PMID: 30284578

Alharbi, A., Elshamly, A., Shawky, N., & Mahgoub, I. (2025). Unlocking sustainable performance in SMEs: The interplay of green AI management, pro-environmental behaviour in the tourism and hospitality sector: UK. *Journal of Posthumanism*, *5*(4). Advance online publication. DOI: 10.63332/joph.v5i4.1053

Ali, A., Montanaro, T., Sergi, I., Carrisi, S., Galli, D., Distante, C., & Patrono, L. (2025). An Innovative IoT and Edge Intelligence Framework for Monitoring Elderly People Using Anomaly Detection on Data from Non-Wearable Sensors. *Sensors (Basel)*, *25*(6), 1735. Advance online publication. DOI: 10.3390/s25061735 PMID: 40292837

Alnajdawi, M. H., Raafat, R., Aburayya, A., & Al Ghurabli, Z. (2025). Enhancing Logistical Efficiency in Public Institutions through AI: A Managerial Framework for Regulatory and Technological Integration. *International Journal of Industrial Engineering and Production Research*, *36*(3), 81–92. DOI: 10.22068/ijiepr.36.3.2459

Alnasser, B. (2023). The economic impact of artificial intelligence on healthcare: A literature review. *E-Health Telecommunication Systems and Networks*, *12*(3), 27–41. DOI: 10.4236/etsn.2023.123003

Alowais, A., Alghamdi, S. S., Alsuhebany, N., Alqahtani, T., Alshaya, A., Almohareb, S. N., & Alowais, S. A. (2024). The issue of ethical and legal concerns in healthcare artificial intelligence. *BMC Medical Ethics*, *25*, 62.

Alowais, S., Alghamdi, S., Alsuhebany, N., Alqahtani, T., Alshaya, A., Almohareb, S., Aldairem, A., Alrashed, M., Bin Saleh, K., Badreldin, H., Al Yami, M., Al Harbi, S., & Albekairy, A. (2023). Revolutionizing healthcare: The role of artificial intelligence in clinical practice. *BMC Medical Education*, *23*(1), 428. Advance online publication. DOI: 10.1186/s12909-023-04698-z

Alquayt, A., Aljuhani, O., Alharthi, A., Alqahtani, R., Khan, A., Al-Jedai, A., Almoeen, A., Alshennawi, M., Badreldin, H., Aljouie, A., Alnasser, L., Alshehri, A., Alzahrani, M., Alhaidal, H., Alhajaji, R., Alotaibi, S., Redhwan, E., Alharthi, F., Alghamdi, B., & Al Sulaiman, K. (2025). AI-driven healthcare innovations for enhancing clinical services during mass gatherings (Hajj): Task force insights and future directions. *BMC Health Services Research*, *25*(1), 456. Advance online publication. DOI: 10.1186/s12913-025-13045-5

Al-Romeedy, B. S., Emam, M. E., Hussein, H., Singh, A., & Tyagi, P. K. (2025). Digital Passports to Wellness: How Technology Is Shaping Medical Tourism. In *Revolutionizing Healthcare Experience With Digital Medical Tourism* (pp. 111-136). IGI Global Scientific Publishing.

Alsabah, M., Naser, M. A., Albahri, A., Albahri, O., Alamoodi, A., Abdulhussain, S. H., & Alzubaidi, L. (2025). A comprehensive review on key technologies toward smart healthcare systems based IoT: Technical aspects, challenges and future directions. *Artificial Intelligence Review*, *58*(11), 343. DOI: 10.1007/s10462-025-11342-3

Alsahafi, R., Alzahrani, A., & Mehmood, R. (2023). Smarter sustainable tourism: Data-driven multi-perspective parameter discovery for autonomous design and operations. *Sustainability (Basel)*, *15*(5), 4166. Advance online publication. DOI: 10.3390/su15054166

Alsaleh, A. (2025). Leveraging artificial intelligence for sustainable healthcare transformation: Socioeconomic impacts and ethical implications. *Innovation and Emerging Technologies*, *12*, 2550015. Advance online publication. DOI: 10.1142/S273759942550015X

Alsehani, F. N. (2026). Harnessing Artificial Intelligence and Digital Technologies for Sustainable Healthcare Delivery in Saudi Arabia: A Comprehensive Review, Issues, and Future Perspectives. *Sustainability (Basel)*, *18*(3), 1461. DOI: 10.3390/su18031461

Alshamsi, A. (2024). A review of the United Arab Emirates healthcare systems on medical tourism and accreditation. *Frontiers in Health Services*, *4*, 1329252. Advance online publication. DOI: 10.3389/frhs.2024.1329252

Al-Talabani, H., Kilic, H., Ozturen, A., & Qasim, S. O. (2019). Advancing medical tourism in the United Arab Emirates: Toward a sustainable health care system. *Sustainability (Basel)*, *11*(1), 230. Advance online publication. DOI: 10.3390/su11010230

Altınbafra, M. T. (2025). Robotik cerrahide sürdürülebilirlik boyutu: Sağlık turizmine etkileri ve gelecek perspektifi. In E. Dikmetaş Yardan (Ed.), *1. Uluslararası Sağlık Turizmi Kongresi (USAT 2025) / I. International Health Tourism Congress (IHET 2025)*.

Amin, A., Cardoso, S. A., Suyambu, J., Abdus Saboor, H., Cardoso, R. P., Husnain, A., Isaac, N. V., Backing, H., Mehmood, D., Mehmood, M., & Maslamani, A. N. J. (2024). Future of artificial intelligence in surgery: A narrative review. *Cureus*, *16*(1), e51631. DOI: 10.7759/cureus.51631 PMID: 38318552

Amisha, M., Malik, P., Pathania, M., & Rathaur, V. K. (2019). Overview of artificial intelligence in medicine. *Journal of Family Medicine and Primary Care*, *8*(7), 2328–2331. DOI: 10.4103/jfmpc.jfmpc_440_19 PMID: 31463251

Amponsah, D., Thamman, R., Brandt, E., James, C., Spector-Bagdady, K., & Yong, C. M. (2024). Artificial Intelligence to Promote Racial and Ethnic Cardiovascular Health Equity. *Current Cardiovascular Risk Reports, 18*(11), 153–162. DOI: 10.1007/s12170-024-00745-6 PMID: 40144330

Anam, A. S. M. T., Bhuiyan, M. R. I., Islam, S., Ullah, M. N., & Rakib, M. A. A. (2026). Factors influencing university students' adoption of online education platforms in Bangladesh: An extended TAM-based analysis. *Educational and Developmental Psychologist*, 1–17.

Anderson, D. (2022). Top medical tourism destinations for AI-assisted orthopedic surgeries. *Medical Tourism Magazine.* https://www.magazine.medicaltourism.com/article/top-medical-tourism-destinations-for-ai-assisted-orthopedic-surgeries

Andrianto, T., Tangit, T. M., & Minh, N. C. (2025). Adoption of artificial intelligence (AI) technology in enhancing tourist experience: A conceptual model. Journal of Tourism. *Hospitality and Travel Management, 3*(1), 302. Advance online publication. DOI: 10.58229/jthtm.v3i1.302

Andritsos, D., & Tang, C. (2013). The impact of cross-border patient movement on the delivery of healthcare services. *International Journal of Production Economics, 145*(2), 702–712. DOI: 10.1016/j.ijpe.2013.05.025

Angelillo, L., van Steen, C., Ross-Stewart, K., Dehnen, J., & Colasante, W. (2023). Viability of European cross-border access opportunities to streamline access to ATMPs. *Health Policy and Technology, 12*(3), 100752. DOI: 10.1016/j.hlpt.2023.100752

Aquino, Y. S. J., Rogers, W., Braunack-Mayer, A., Frazer, H., Win, K., Houssami, N., Degeling, C., Semsarian, C., & Carter, S. (2022). Utopia versus dystopia: Professional perspectives on the impact of healthcare artificial intelligence on clinical roles and skills. *International Journal of Medical Informatics, 169*, 104903. Advance online publication. DOI: 10.1016/j.ijmedinf.2022.104903

Archana, K. (2024). Responsible AI implementation in healthcare organizations. In *Responsible AI for Digital Health and Medical Analytics* (pp. 1–14). IGI Global., DOI: 10.4018/979-8-3693-6294-5.ch001

Arefin, S., & Zannat, N. T.Global Health Institute Research Team United states. (2025). Securing AI in global health research: A framework for cross-border data collaboration. *Clinical Medicine and Health Research Journal, 5*(2), 1187–1193. Advance online publication. DOI: 10.18535/cmhrj.v5i02.457

Arjomandi Rad, A., Vardanyan, R., Athanasiou, T., Maessen, J., & Sardari Nia, P. (2025). The ethical considerations of integrating artificial intelligence into surgery: A review. *Interdisciplinary Cardiovascular and Thoracic Surgery*, *40*(3), ivae192. Advance online publication. DOI: 10.1093/icvts/ivae192 PMID: 39999009

Arora, S., & Arora, P. (2016). Medical tourism in India for Ayurveda. *Research & Reviews: Journal of Herbal Science*, *5*(2), 20–24.

Arshed, M., Kazi, A. K., Kiran, M., & Ali, S. M. F. (2025). Challenges in Health Equity: Balancing Innovation With Fairness and Addressing Algorithmic Biases. In *Innovation and Transformation of Public Health* (pp. 113–141). IGI Global. DOI: 10.4018/979-8-3373-1992-6.ch004

Arzikulov, F., & Komiljonov, A. (2025). AI-powered diagnostic systems in radiology: Enhancing precision, speed, and clinical decision-making. *Academic Journal of Science. Technology and Education*, *1*(6), 16–23.

Asif, F., Jamshed, K., & Shah, S. H. A. (2025). Prospects and challenges for AI and technological innovation in the European travel and tourism sector: Impact, effect and sustainable development goals. In Technological innovation and AI for sustainable development in events and festivals (pp. 140–161).

Aşık, H., & Güner, Ş. İ. (2025, June 26). Sağlık turizminde dijital sağlık uygulamalarının kullanımı [Abstract]. In *I. Uluslararası Sağlık Turizmi Kongresi (USAT 2025)*, Samsun, Türkiye (pp. 107).

Atek, S., Bianchini, F., De Vito, C., Cardinale, V., Novelli, S., Pesaresi, C., Eugeni, M., Mecella, M., Rescio, A., Petronzio, L., Vincenzi, A., Pistillo, P., Giusto, G., Pasquali, G., Alvaro, D., Villari, P., Mancini, M., & Gaudenzi, P. (2023). A predictive decision support system for coronavirus disease 2019 response management and medical logistic planning. *Digital Health*, *9*, 20552076231185475. Advance online publication. DOI: 10.1177/20552076231185475 PMID: 37545633

Athanasopoulou, K., Michalopoulou, V.-I., Scorilas, A., & Adamopoulos, P. G. (2025). Integrating Artificial Intelligence in Next-Generation Sequencing: Advances, Challenges, and Future Directions. *Current Issues in Molecular Biology*, *47*(6), 470. DOI: 10.3390/cimb47060470 PMID: 40699869

Ayesha, A., & Ahamed, N. N. (2024). Explainable artificial intelligence (eai): For healthcare applications and improvements. In *Explainable Artificial Intelligence for Biomedical and Healthcare Applications* (pp. 162–196). CRC Press. DOI: 10.1201/9781003220107-11

Aykın, Ö., Uluhan, F., Gümüş, İ., Çabuk, Ş., Bozbayir, U., Duran, V., Özbay, C., Özbay, B., Gündoğmuş, Ş. E., Şengül, M. T., & Övey, I. (2023). *Artificial intelligence and telemedicine applications in health tourism marketing*. Eurasian Journal of Health Technology Assessment., DOI: 10.52148/ehta.1396111

Ayyıldız, D., & Ovayolu, Ö. (2024, October). Sağlık ve hastalık yönetiminde yapay zekânın kullanımı. In *8th International ACHARAKA Congress on Medicine, Nursing, Midwifery, and Health Sciences Proceedings Book*.

Badulescu, D., & Badulescu, A. (2014). Medical tourism: Between entrepreneurship opportunities and bioethics boundaries: Narrative review article. *Iranian Journal of Public Health, 43*(4), 406–415. https://www.ncbi.nlm.nih.gov/pmc/articles/PMC4433721/

Bahgat, A. (2025). AI governance and data privacy in cross-border contexts: A comparative analysis of regulatory frameworks. *Journal of Data Protection and Privacy, 8*(1), 8–23. DOI: 10.69554/BOJL3033

Bajwa, J., Munir, U., Nori, A., & Williams, B. (2021). Artificial intelligence in healthcare: Transforming the practice of medicine. *Future Healthcare Journal, 8*(2), e188–e194. DOI: 10.7861/fhj.2021-0095 PMID: 34286183

Balsalobre-Lorente, D., Abbas, J., He, C., Pilař, L., & Shah, S. A. R. (2023). Tourism, urbanization, and natural resources rents matter for environmental sustainability: The leading role of AI and ICT on sustainable development goals in the digital era. *Resources Policy, 82*, 103445. Advance online publication. DOI: 10.1016/j.resourpol.2023.103445

Bang-Ning, H., Jitanugoon, S., & Puntha, P. (2025). AI-powered sustainable tourism: Unlocking circular economies and overcoming resistance to change. *Business Strategy and the Environment, 34*(5), 5781–5802. Advance online publication. DOI: 10.1002/bse.4276

Baragi, U. C., & Ganer, J. M. (2025). Artificial intelligence in traditional medicine: Transforming AYUSH systems through digital innovation. *Journal of Ayurveda and Integrated Medical Sciences*.

Bartels, R., Dudink, J., Haitjema, S., Oberski, D., & Veen, A. (2022). A perspective on a quality management system for AI/ML-based clinical decision support in hospital care. *Frontiers in Digital Health, 4*, 942588. Advance online publication. DOI: 10.3389/fdgth.2022.942588

Bartolomucci, A., Nobrega, M., Ferrier, T., Dickinson, K., Kaorey, N., Nadeau, A., Castillo, A., & Burnier, J. V. (2025). Circulating tumor DNA to monitor treatment response in solid tumors and advance precision oncology. *NPJ Precision Oncology*, *9*(1), 84. Advance online publication. DOI: 10.1038/s41698-025-00876-y PMID: 40122951

Barua, R., & Datta, S. (2024). The Improvements in Significance of AI in Experiential and Medical Tourism. In *Generative AI for Transformational Management* (pp. 303–334). IGI Global. DOI: 10.4018/979-8-3693-5578-7.ch012

Basirat, S., Raoufi, S., Bazmandeh, D., Khamoushi, S., & Entezami, M. (2025). Ranking of AI-based criteria in health tourism using fuzzy SWARA method. *Computer and Decision Making: An International Journal*, 2, 530–545. Advance online publication. DOI: 10.59543/comdem.v2i.13795

Bassi, A.. (2025). Artificial intelligence applications in telemedicine: A systematic review. *Journal of Medical Internet Research*, •••, 27.

Bates, D. W., Levine, D., Syrowatka, A., Kuznetsova, M., Craig, K. J. T., Rui, A., Jackson, G. P., & Rhee, K. (2021). The potential of artificial intelligence to improve patient safety: A scoping review. *NPJ Digital Medicine*, *4*(1), 54. DOI: 10.1038/s41746-021-00423-6 PMID: 33742085

Bates, D. W., Sheikh, A., & Asch, D. A. (2018). Innovative environments in health care: Where and how new approaches to care are succeeding. *Health Affairs (Project Hope)*, *37*(3), 400–407. DOI: 10.1377/hlthaff.2016.1311 PMID: 28264940

Bathla, G., Raina, A., & Rana, V. S. (2024). Artificial intelligence-driven enhancements in medical tourism: Opportunities, challenges, and future prospects. In Impact of AI and robotics on the medical tourism industry (pp. 139–162).

Bathla, G., Raina, A., & Rana, V. S. (2024). Artificial intelligence-driven enhancements in medical tourism: Opportunities, challenges, and future prospects. In *Impact of AI and Robotics on the Medical Tourism Industry* (pp. 139–162). IGI Global., DOI: 10.4018/979-8-3693-2248-2.ch006

Bauer, I. L. (2023). Robots in travel clinics: Building on tourism's use of technology and robots for infection control during a pandemic. *Tropical Diseases, Travel Medicine and Vaccines*, *9*(1), 10. DOI: 10.1186/s40794-023-00197-7 PMID: 37525269

Bayati, M., Klein, Z. P., Bahcheli, A. T., Slobodyanyuk, M., To, J., Cheng, K. C. L., Mishra, J., Pellegrina, D., Guevara-Hoyer, K., McIntosh, C., Bhat, M., & Reimand, J. (2025). Cancer Genomic Alterations and Microenvironmental Features Encode Synergistic Interactions with Disease Outcomes. *Molecular Cancer Research, 23*(12), 971–983. DOI: 10.1158/1541-7786.MCR-25-0475 PMID: 40900635

Beckers, R., Kwade, Z., Zanca, F., & Medica, P. (2021). The EU medical device regulation: Implications for artificial intelligence-based medical device software in medical physics. *Physica Medica : PM : An International Journal Devoted to the Applications of Physics to Medicine and Biology : Official Journal of the Italian Association of Biomedical Physics (AIFB), 83*, 1–8. DOI: 10.1016/j.ejmp.2021.02.011

Bekbolatova, M., Mayer, J., Ong, C., & Toma, M. (2024). Transformative potential of AI in healthcare: Definitions, applications, and navigating the ethical landscape and public perspectives. *Healthcare (Basel), 12*(2), 125. Advance online publication. DOI: 10.3390/healthcare12020125

Beladi, H., Chao, C.-C., Ee, M. S., & Hollas, D. (2017). Does medical tourism promote economic growth? A cross-country analysis. *Journal of Travel Research, 58*(1), 121–135. DOI: 10.1177/0047287517735909

Benbrahmi, F. Z., & Mehor, H. M. H. (2025). The impact of artificial intelligence on enhancing the travel experience for tourists: An analysis of successful models. *Business Excellence and Management, 15*(5), 5–13. DOI: 10.24818/beman/2025.S.I.5-01

Bhavnani, S., & McKim, R. (2026). *Artificial Intelligence in Mental Healthcare: Potential Applications and New Frontiers*. CRC Press.

Bhuiyan, M. R. I., Akter, M. S., Amin, A., & Hossain, R. (2025). Artificial intelligence and organizational transformation: Institutional readiness and digital innovation.

Bhuiyan, M. R. I. (2024). Industry readiness and adaptation of the fourth industrial revolution: Applying the extended TOE framework. *Human Behavior and Emerging Technologies, 2024*(1), 8830228. DOI: 10.1155/hbe2/8830228

Bhuiyan, M. R. I., Husain, T., Islam, S., & Amin, A. (2025). Exploring the prospective influence of artificial intelligence on the health sector in Bangladesh: A study on awareness, perception and adoption. *Health Education, 125*(3), 279–297. DOI: 10.1108/HE-10-2024-0125

Bhuiyan, M. R. I., Uddin, S., Sultana, T., Al-Amin, , & Islam, M. M. (2026). Investigating ChatGPT methods in higher education from a student engagement perspective: A descriptive cross-sectional study. *SAGE Open, 16*(1), 21582440251413008. DOI: 10.1177/21582440251413008

Bhushan, S. (2021). The impact of artificial intelligence and machine learning on the global economy and its implications for the hospitality sector in India. *Worldwide Hospitality and Tourism Themes, 13*(2), 252–259. *https://doi.org/*DOI: 10.1108/WHATT-09-2020-0116

Bhushan, A., & Misra, P. (2025). Unlocking the potential: Multimodal AI in biotechnology and digital medicine—Economic impact and ethical challenges. *NPJ Digital Medicine, 8*(1), 619. Advance online publication. DOI: 10.1038/s41746-025-01992-6

Björnsson, B., Borrebaeck, C., Elander, N., Gasslander, T., Gawel, D. R., Gustafsson, M., Jörnsten, R., Lee, E. J., Li, X., Lilja, S., Martínez-Enguita, D., Matussek, A., Sandström, P., Schäfer, S., Stenmarker, M., Sun, X. F., Sysoev, O., Zhang, H., & Benson, M. (2020). Digital twins to personalize medicine. *Genome Medicine, 12*(1), 4. Advance online publication. DOI: 10.1186/s13073-019-0701-3 PMID: 31892363

Bookman, M. (2007). *Medical tourism in developing countries.* Springer. DOI: 10.1057/9780230605657

Borst, V., Riedmann, A., Dege, T., Müller, K., Schmieder, A., Lugrin, B., & Kounev, S. (2025). WoundAIssist: A patient-centered mobile app for AI-assisted wound care with physicians in the loop (arXiv:2506.06104). arXiv. https://doi.org//arXiv.2506.06104DOI: 10.48550

Bosmans, H., Zanca, F., & Gelaude, F. (2021). Procurement, commissioning, and QA of AI based solutions: An MPE's perspective on introducing AI in clinical practice. *Physica Medica : PM : An International Journal Devoted to the Applications of Physics to Medicine and Biology : Official Journal of the Italian Association of Biomedical Physics (AIFB), 83*, 257–263. DOI: 10.1016/j.ejmp.2021.04.006

Bostan, M. H., & Halhalli, H. C. (2025). Sağlık turizminde yapay zekâ uygulamaları. In Bostan, A., & Coşkun, E. (Eds.), *Sağlık turizmi: Sağlıkta sınırları aşmak* (pp. 187–205). Detay Yayıncılık.

Brenna, E., & Spandonaro, F. (2015). Regional incentives and patient cross-border mobility: Evidence from the Italian experience. *International Journal of Health Policy and Management, 4*(6), 363–372. DOI: 10.15171/ijhpm.2015.65

Brierley, J., O'Sullivan, B., Asamura, H., Byrd, D., Huang, S. H., Lee, A., Piñeros, M., Mason, M., Moraes, F. Y., Rösler, W., Rous, B., Torode, J., van Krieken, J. H., & Gospodarowicz, M. (2019). Global Consultation on Cancer Staging: Promoting consistent understanding and use. *Nature Reviews. Clinical Oncology, 16*(12), 763–771. DOI: 10.1038/s41571-019-0253-x PMID: 31388125

Buhalis, D., Harwood, T., Bogicevic, V., Viglia, G., Beldona, S., & Hofacker, C. (2020). Technological disruptions in services: Lessons from tourism and hospitality. *Journal of Service Management, 31*(3), 484–506. DOI: 10.1108/JOSM-12-2019-0398

Bukret, W. E. (2025). Artificial Intelligence–assisted Risk Stratification in Aesthetic Surgery: A Prospective Observational Study. *Plastic and Reconstructive Surgery. Global Open, 13*(7), e6948. DOI: 10.1097/GOX.0000000000006948 PMID: 40672785

Bulut, C. (2025). Sağlık kurumlarında yapay zekâ destekli karar destek sistemlerinin kullanımı. *Uluslararası Sağlık Yönetimi ve Stratejileri Araştırma Dergisi, 11(1),* 27–37. https://izlik.org/JA78AG89SK

Buntin, M. B., Burke, M. F., Hoaglin, M. C., & Blumenthal, D. (2011). The benefits of health information technology: A review of the recent literature shows predominantly positive results. *Health Affairs (Project Hope), 30*(3), 464–471. DOI: 10.1377/hlthaff.2011.0178 PMID: 21383365

Buoy Health. (n.d.). *Check symptoms & find the right care.* https://www.buoyhealth.com/

Burki, A. K., Mafaz, M. N. A., Ahmad, Z., Zulfaka, A., & Isa, M. Y. B. (2024). Artificial intelligence and environmental sustainability: Insights from PLS-SEM on resource efficiency and carbon emission reduction. OPSearch. *American Journal of Operations Research, 3*(10), 277–288. Advance online publication. DOI: 10.58811/opsearch.v3i10.141

Busch, F., Geis, R., Wang, Y. C., Kather, J. N., Khori, N. A., Makowski, M. R., Kolawole, I. K., Truhn, D., Clements, W., Gilbert, S., & Adams, L. C. (2025). AI regulation in healthcare around the world: What is the status quo? *medRxiv*. DOI: 10.1101/2025.01.25.25321061

Business Standard. (2025, February 2). India's medical tourism poised for expansion with relaxed visa rules. Business Standard. https://www.business-standard.com/industry/news/india-s-medical-tourism-poised-for-expansion-with-relaxed-visa-rules-125020200488_1.html

Business Today. (2024, August 8). India's medical tourism grew 33% in 2023, to surpass pre-pandemic level in 2024: ICRA. Business Today. https://www.businesstoday.in/india/story/indias-medical-tourism-grew-33-in-2023-to-surpass-pre-pandemic-level-in-2024-icra-440692-2024-08-08.html

Büyükkaya, B. (2024). *Sağlık hizmetlerinde yapay zekâ: Bir araştırma* [Unpublished master's thesis]. Sakarya Üniversitesi.

Cadamuro, J., Carobene, A., Cabitza, F., Debeljak, Z., De Bruyne, S., Van Doorn, W., Johannes, E., Frans, G., Özdemir, H., Martin Perez, S., Rajdl, D., Tolios, A., & Padoan, A. (2025). A comprehensive survey of artificial intelligence adoption in European laboratory medicine: Current utilization and prospects. *Clinical Chemistry and Laboratory Medicine*, *63*(4), 692–703. DOI: 10.1515/cclm-2024-1016 PMID: 39443973

Canadian Agency for Drugs and Technologies in Health. (2025). *2025 watch list: Artificial intelligence in health care*. CADTH.

Cannon Hunter, W. (2007). Medical Tourism: A New Global Niche. *International Journal of Tourism Sciences*, *7*(1), 129–140. DOI: 10.1080/15980634.2007.11434599

Car, J., Tan, W. S., Huang, Z., Sloot, P., & Franklin, B. D. (2017). eHealth in the future of medications management: Personalisation, monitoring and adherence. *BMC Medicine*, *15*(1), 73. DOI: 10.1186/s12916-017-0838-0 PMID: 28376771

Castelló, F., Santos-Rojo, C., & De la Torre Olid, F. (2024). Artificial Intelligence and the 'Data Act' in the European Union: A Legal and Economic Analysis of New Digital Regulations and Their Impact on Citizens' Rights and Business Innovation. *Springer Proceedings in Business and Economics*, 57–72. DOI: 10.1007/978-3-031-67511-9_4

Challoumis, C. (2023a). Risk on the tax system of the E.U. from 2016 to 2022. *Economics*, *11*(1), 55–72. DOI: 10.2478/eoik-2023-0058

Challoumis, C. (2023b). From savings to escape and enforcement savings. *Cógito (Salvador)*, *XV*(4), 206–216. https://cogito.ucdc.ro/COGITO_DECEMBER_2023.pdf

Challoumis, C. (2024). Impact factor of liability using the Sensitivity Method. In Bayrakdar, S., & Chodnicka-Jaworska, P. (Eds.), *Current dynamics in business and economics: Theoretical approaches and empirical discoveries* (pp. 77–86). Peter Lang., DOI: 10.3726/b22541

Challoumis, C. (2024a). The index of the cycle of money: The case of Switzerland. *Journal of Risk and Financial Management*, *17*(4), 135. Advance online publication. DOI: 10.3390/jrfm17040135

Challoumis, C. (2024b). From economics to economic engineering (The cycle of money): The case of Romania. *Cógito (Salvador)*, *XVII*(2), 161–170. https://cogito.ucdc.ro/issues/COGITO%20no.2_27062024%20_BT.pdf

Challoumis, C. (2025a). Economocracy: Global economic governance. *Economies (Basel)*, *13*(8), 230. Advance online publication. DOI: 10.3390/economies13080230

Challoumis, C. (2025a). The inflation according to the cycle of money (C.M.). *Economic Alternatives, 2025*(2), 324–353. DOI: 10.37075/EA.2025.2.03

Challoumis, C. (2025b). The impact factor of tangibles and intangibles of controlled transactions on economic performance. *Economic Alternatives, 31*(1), 64–76. DOI: 10.37075/EA.2025.1.04

Challoumis, C., & Eriotis, N. (2025). The impact of artificial intelligence on the Greek economy. *Journal of Open Innovation, 11*(1), 100578. Advance online publication. DOI: 10.1016/j.joitmc.2025.100578

Challoumis, C., Eriotis, N., & Vasiliou, D. (2025). Social movements' impact on the Greek economy during the financial crisis. *Economies (Basel), 13*(9), 269. Advance online publication. DOI: 10.3390/economies13090269

Champendal, M., Lokaj, B., De Gevigney, V. D., Brulé, G., Zaghir, J., Boiko, P., Lovis, C., Müller, H., Schmid, J., & Ribeiro, R. T. (2025). Exploring environmental sustainability of artificial intelligence in radiology: A scoping review. *European Journal of Radiology, 194*, 112558. Advance online publication. DOI: 10.1016/j.ejrad.2025.112558

Chandra, J., Kaur, R., & Sahay, R. (2025). Integrated Framework for Equitable Healthcare AI: Bias Mitigation, Community Participation, and Regulatory Governance. *2025 IEEE 14th International Conference on Communication Systems and Network Technologies, CSNT 2025*, 819–825. DOI: 10.1109/CSNT64827.2025.10968102

Chang, I.-Y. (2025). Using AI tools to promote sustainable tourism practices: Opportunities and ethical consideration in the post-pandemic era. *Proceedings of Forum Manajemen Indonesia's International Conferences*. https://doi.org/DOI: 10.47747/fmiic.vi2.2976

Charow, R., Jeyakumar, T., Younus, S., Dolatabadi, E., Salhia, M., Al-Mouaswas, D., Anderson, M., Balakumar, S., Clare, M., Dhalla, A., Gillan, C., Haghzare, S., Jackson, E., Lalani, N., Mattson, J., Peteanu, W., Tripp, T., Waldorf, J., Tavares, W., & Wiljer, D. (2021). Artificial intelligence education programs for health care professionals: Scoping review. *JMIR Medical Education, 7*(2), e31043. Advance online publication. DOI: 10.2196/31043

Chatterjee, S., Chaudhuri, R., Thrassou, A., & Vrontis, D. (2022). Technology disruption in healthcare: Artificial intelligence application, challenges, and policy recommendations in India. *International Journal of Internet Marketing and Advertising, 17*(3–4), 394–414. DOI: 10.1504/IJIMA.2022.126716

Chaudhry, D. (2022). Is Medical Tourism really unethical? An alternate perspective for developing countries. *Journal of Development Policy and Practice*, *7*(2), 145–157. DOI: 10.1177/24551333211062355

Chaudhry, S., & Ehtesham, Z. (2025). Role of Molecular Diagnostics in Oral and Maxillofacial Pathology. *J Oral Health Dent*, *8*(1), 625–628.

Chaudhry, S., Khan, S., & Ehtesham, Z. (2026). *Molecular Pathology: Principles, Techniques, and Clinical Applications of Molecular Diagnostics*. De Gruyter. DOI: 10.1515/9783112217719

Chauhan, J. S., Sharma, Ajay, Sharma, Akhilesh, Ahalawat, K., & Agarwal, P. (2025). AI-Driven Decision Making in Wellness Tourism: Understanding Consumer Preferences and Optimizing Tourism Strategies. *2025 First International Conference on Advances in Computer Science, Electrical, Electronics, and Communication Technologies (CE2CT)*, 663–669. *https://doi.org/*DOI: 10.1109/CE2CT64011.2025.10939052

Chen, C.-L., Chen, C.-C., Yu, W.-H., Chen, S.-H., Chang, Y.-C., Hsu, T.-I., Hsiao, M., Yeh, C.-Y., & Chen, C.-Y. (2021). An annotation-free whole-slide training approach to pathological classification of lung cancer types using deep learning. *Nature Communications*, *12*(1), 1193. Advance online publication. DOI: 10.1038/s41467-021-21467-y PMID: 33608558

Chen, H., Zeng, Y., & Cai, D. (2025). Deep learning for cardiovascular management: Optimizing pathways and cost control under diagnosis-related group models. *Frontiers in Artificial Intelligence*, *8*, 1580445. DOI: 10.3389/frai.2025.1580445 PMID: 40959774

Chen, P., Wu, L., & Wang, L. (2023). AI fairness in data management and analytics: A review on challenges, methodologies and applications. *Applied Sciences (Basel, Switzerland)*, *13*(18), 10258. DOI: 10.3390/app131810258

Chen, W., Bai, P., Pan, J., Xu, Y., & Chen, K. (2017). Changes in Tumor Volumes and Spatial Locations Relative to Normal Tissues During Cervical Cancer Radiotherapy Assessed by Cone Beam Computed Tomography. *Technology in Cancer Research & Treatment*, *16*(2), 246–252. DOI: 10.1177/1533034616685942 PMID: 28052737

Chen, X., Dai, C., Peng, M., Wang, D., Sui, X., Duan, L., Wang, X., Wang, X., Weng, W., Wang, S., Zhao, H., Wang, Z., Geng, J., Chen, C., Hu, Y., Hu, Q., Jiang, C., Zheng, H., Bao, Y., & Yang, F. (2025). Artificial intelligence driven 3D reconstruction for enhanced lung surgery planning. *Nature Communications*, *16*(1), 4086. Advance online publication. DOI: 10.1038/s41467-025-59200-8 PMID: 40312393

Chen, Y.. (2025). Explainable artificial intelligence in clinical decision support systems: A systematic meta-analysis (2018–2025). *Journal of Medical Internet Research*, *27*, e12427955.

Chen, Z., Awan, U., Nassani, A. A., Al-Aiban, K. M., & Zaman, K. (2025). Enhancing sustainable growth in the global south: The role of mineral resource management, supply chain efficiency, technology advancement, and local downstream processing. *Resources Policy, 100. Resources Policy*, *100*, 105451. Advance online publication. DOI: 10.1016/j.resourpol.2024.105451

Chettri, S. K., Deka, R. K., & Saikia, M. J. (2025). Bridging the Gap in the Adoption of Trustworthy AI in Indian Healthcare: Challenges and Opportunities. *AI*, *6*(1), 10. Advance online publication. DOI: 10.3390/ai6010010

Chhabra, A., Munjal, M., Mishra, P. C., Singh, K., Das, D., Kuhar, N., & Vats, M. (2021). Medical tourism in the COVID-19 era: Opportunities, challenges and the way ahead. *Worldwide Hospitality and Tourism Themes*, *13*(5), 660–665. DOI: 10.1108/WHATT-05-2021-0078

Chinta, S. V., Wang, Z., Palikhe, A., Zhang, X., Kashif, A., Smith, M. A., Liu, J., & Zhang, W. (2025). AI-driven healthcare: A review on ensuring fairness and mitigating bias. *PLOS Digital Health*, *4*(5), e0000864. DOI: 10.1371/journal.pdig.0000864 PMID: 40392801

Chirmulay, V., & Bhakare, J. (2025). Digital Health and Medical Tourism: A Regulatory Perspective. In *Navigating Innovations and Challenges in Travel Medicine and Digital Health* (pp. 311–324). IGI Global Scientific Publishing. *https://doi.org/* DOI: 10.4018/979-8-3693-8774-0.ch015

Choudhari, H. M., & Khobragade, S. (2024). The Role of AI in Patients' Communication. *2024 2nd DMIHER International Conference on Artificial Intelligence in Healthcare, Education and Industry, IDICAIEI 2024*. DOI: 10.1109/IDICAIEI61867.2024.10842915

Chowdhary, S. P., & Majumdar, K. (2025). Health tourism catalyst for growth in developing nations. *Journal of Public Affairs*, *25*(3), e70060. Advance online publication. DOI: 10.1002/pa.70060

Chowdhury, T. N., Mou, S. A., & Rahman, K. N. (2025). A hybrid data-driven approach for analyzing and predicting inpatient length of stay in health centre. arXiv preprint arXiv:2501.18535. https://arxiv.org/abs/2501.18535 DOI: 10.1101/2025.01.30.25321434

Christina, J., Ford, K., Menz, B., Sorich, M., Hopkins, A., Ramsey, I., Duddle, M., Kitson, A., & Paterson, C. (2025). Integrating the Caring Life Course Theory and Artificial Intelligence Applications to Enhance Cancer Care Across the Continuum. Seminars in Oncology Nursing, Cynthia, A. N. (2025). Ethical dilemmas in international medical health tourism: A critical commentary. *SSM - Health Systems*, •••, 100111.

Ciecierski-Holmes, T., Singh, R., Axt, M., Brenner, S., & Barteit, S. (2022). Artificial intelligence for strengthening healthcare systems in low- and middle-income countries: A systematic scoping review. *NPJ Digital Medicine*, *5*(1), 100. Advance online publication. DOI: 10.1038/s41746-022-00700-y

Claessens, M., Oria, C., Brouwer, C., Ziemer, B., Scholey, J., Lin, H., Witztum, A., Morin, O., Naqa, I., Van Elmpt, W., & Verellen, D. (2022). Quality assurance for AI-based applications in radiation therapy. *Seminars in Radiation Oncology*, *32*(4), 421–431. DOI: 10.1016/j.semradonc.2022.06.011

Cleveland Clinic. (n.d.). *About Cleveland Clinic*. https://my.clevelandclinic.org

Connell, J. (2013). Contemporary medical tourism: Conceptualisation, culture and commodification. *Tourism Management*, *34*, 1–13. DOI: 10.1016/j.tourman.2012.05.009

Council of the European Union. (2025, January 21). European Health Data Space: Council adopts new regulation improving cross-border access to EU health data [Press release No. 40/25]. https://www.consilium.europa.eu/en/press/press-releases/2025/01/21/european-health-data-space-council-adopts-new-regulation-improving-cross-border-access-to-eu-health-data/

Crigger, E., Reinbold, K., Hanson, C., Kao, A., Blake, K., & Irons, M. (2022). Trustworthy augmented intelligence in health care. *Journal of Medical Systems*, *46*(2), 12. Advance online publication. DOI: 10.1007/s10916-021-01790-z

Cristian, M., & Tileagă, C. (2024). Challenges and perspectives of AI in sustainable tourism. *Management of Sustainable Development*, *16*(1), 14–26. Advance online publication. DOI: 10.54989/msd-2024-0012

Crooks, V. A., Kingsbury, P., Snyder, J., & Johnston, R. (2010). What is known about the patient's experience of medical tourism? A scoping review. *BMC Health Services Research*, *10*(1), 266. DOI: 10.1186/1472-6963-10-266 PMID: 20825667

Crooks, V. A., Kingsbury, P., Snyder, J., & Johnston, R. (2011). What is known about the patient's experience of medical tourism? A scoping review. *Tourism Management*, *32*(2), 339–355. DOI: 10.1016/j.tourman.2010.02.004

Crooks, V. A., Kingsbury, P., Snyder, J., & Johnston, R. (2011). What is known about the patient's experience of medical tourism? *BMC Health Services Research, 11*, 266. DOI: 10.1186/1472-6963-11-266 PMID: 20825667

Crooks, V. A., Turner, L., Snyder, J., Johnston, R., & Kingsbury, P. (2011). Promoting medical tourism to India: Messages, images, and the marketing of international patient travel. *Social Science & Medicine, 72*(5), 726–732. DOI: 10.1016/j.socscimed.2010.12.022

Da Silva, M., Denis, J. L., & Régis, C. (2024). Good Governance Strategies for Human-Centered AI in Healthcare: Connecting Norms and Context. In *Human-Centered AI: a Multidisciplinary Perspective for Policy-Makers, Auditors, and Users* (pp. 105–115). CRC Press. DOI: 10.1201/9781003320791-13

Da Silva, R. G. L. (2024). The advancement of artificial intelligence in biomedical research and health innovation: Challenges and opportunities in emerging economies. *Globalization and Health, 20*(1), 49. Advance online publication. DOI: 10.1186/s12992-024-01049-5

Dalen, J. E., Alpert, J. S., & Goldberg, R. J. (2019). The epidemic of the 21st century: Medical tourism. *The American Journal of Medicine, 132*(2), 154–156. DOI: 10.1016/j.amjmed.2018.09.017 PMID: 30076812

Damoah, I. B., Ayakwah, A., & Tingbani, I. (2021). Artificial intelligence (AI)-enhanced medical drones in the healthcare supply chain (HSC) for sustainability development: A case study. *Journal of Cleaner Production, 322*, 129598. Advance online publication. DOI: 10.1016/j.jclepro.2021.129598

Dang, H.-S., Nguyen, T.-M.-T., Wang, C.-N., Day, J. D., & Dang, T. M. T. (2020). Grey system theory in the study of medical tourism industry and its economic impact. *International Journal of Environmental Research and Public Health, 17*(3), 961. Advance online publication. DOI: 10.3390/ijerph17030961

Dar, H., & Kashyap, K. (2023). Smart healthcare system (SHS): Medical tourism delivering, consumption, and elevating tool in the ages of smart technologies. *Tourism Planning & Development, 20*(3), 397–415. DOI: 10.1080/21568316.2022.2109206

Das, D. C. (2022). From AI in Healthcare to Spirituality in Tourism: A Cross-Sectoral Review of Emerging Practices. *Business and Social Sciences, 1*(1), 1–8.

Das, D., Shrivastav, M. K., Jaya Sankar Krishna, S. V. S. P. P., Hazarika, D., Sharma, S. C., Mahendranath Chowdary, R., & Wadettiwar, P. P. (2025). Public-private partnerships (PPP) in infrastructure financing: A comparative study of developed and developing economies. *Heritage and Sustainable Development*, *7*(1), 443–452. DOI: 10.37868/hsd.v7i1.1087

Dash Technologies. (2025). Top 5 AI use cases in healthcare for better patient outcomes. https://dashtechinc.com/blog/top-5-ai-use-cases-in-healthcare-for-better-patient-outcomes/

Das, S. (2024). Application of AI technology for the development of destination tourism towards an intelligent information system. *Economic Affairs*, *69*(3). Advance online publication. DOI: 10.46852/0424-2513.3.2024.31

DAVE Tools for Genomic Data Commons. (2017, June 29). Cancer.gov. https://www.cancer.gov/news-events/cancer-currents-blog/2017/gdc-dave-tools

Davenport, T., & Kalakota, R. (2019). The potential for artificial intelligence in healthcare. *Future Healthcare Journal*, *6*(2), 94–98. DOI: 10.7861/futurehosp.6-2-94 PMID: 31363513

Dávid, L., & Dadkhah, M. (2023). Artificial intelligence in the tourism sector: Its sustainability and innovation potential. Equilibrium. *Quarterly Journal of Economics and Economic Policy*, *18*(2), 473–497. DOI: 10.24136/eq.2023.019

Daykhes, A. N., Jakovljevic, M., Reshetnikov, V. A., & Kozlov, V. V. (2020). Promises and hurdles of medical tourism development in the Russian Federation. *International Journal of Environmental Research and Public Health*, *17*(12), 4589. Advance online publication. DOI: 10.3390/ijerph17124589

de Andrade, J. B. C., Fagundes, T. P., Katsuyama, E., & Silva, G. S. (2025). Digital Health in Low-Resource Settings: Comprehensive Challenges and Opportunities With a Focus on Stroke Care. *Stroke*. Advance online publication. DOI: 10.1161/STROKEAHA.125.050448 PMID: 40905151

De la Hoz-Correa, A., Muñoz-Leiva, F., & Bakucz, M. (2018). Past themes and future trends in medical tourism research: A co-word analysis. *Tourism Management*, *65*, 200–211. DOI: 10.1016/j.tourman.2017.10.001

de Lima, T. M.. (2024). Telehealth and artificial intelligence approaches in musculoskeletal care with ethical considerations. *BMC Musculoskeletal Disorders*, *25*, 451.

De Micco, F., Di Palma, G., Ferorelli, D., De Benedictis, A., Tomassini, L., Tambone, V., Cingolani, M., & Scendoni, R. (2025). Artificial intelligence in healthcare: Transforming patient safety with intelligent systems—A systematic review. *Frontiers in Medicine, 11*, 1522554. Advance online publication. DOI: 10.3389/fmed.2024.1522554

Deckey, D. G., Rosenow, C. S., Verhey, J. T., Brinkman, J. C., Mayfield, C. K., Clarke, H. D., & Bingham, J. S. (2021). Robotic-assisted total knee arthroplasty improves accuracy and precision compared to conventional techniques. *The Bone & Joint Journal, 103-B*(6, Supple A), 74–80. DOI: 10.1302/0301-620X.103B6.BJJ-2020-2003.R1 PMID: 34053292

Dedović, S., & Crompvoets, J. (2025). Delving into the governance of cross-border in-teroperability solutions in the EU. *eJournal of eDemocracy and Open Government, 17*(2), 65–89. DOI: 10.29379/jedem.v17i2.981

Deshpande, R. (2024). Smart match: Revolutionizing organ allocation through artificial intelligence. *Frontiers in Artificial Intelligence*, *7*, 1364149. DOI: 10.3389/frai.2024.1364149 PMID: 38481822

Dhale, S. (2020). Factors influencing the meteoric rise of the Indian medical tourism sector and its impact on the economy. *Journal of Critical Reviews*, *7*(7), 692–694. DOI: 10.31838/jcr.07.07.126

Di Mauro, L., Capasso, E., Tettamanti, C., Casella, C., Francaviglia, M., Volonnino, G., Rinaldi, R., Esposito, M., & Chisari, M. (2025). The role of artificial intelligence in analyzing clinical malpractice disputes through medical record management. *Journal of Forensic and Legal Medicine, 115*, 102941. Advance online publication. DOI: 10.1016/j.jflm.2025.102941 PMID: 40784149

Digital Pathology Microscope Slide Scanners | Whole Slide Imaging. (2021). Leicabiosystems.com. https://www.leicabiosystems.com/digital-pathology/scan/

Dinker, N. (2024). Artificial intelligence and inequality: examining the social divides created by technological advancements. *International Journal of Innovations in Science, Engineering And Management*, 228-236.

Dixon, D., Sattar, H., Moros, N., Kesireddy, S. R., Ahsan, H., Lakkimsetti, M., Fatima, M., Doshi, D., Sadhu, K., & Junaid Hassan, M. (2024). Unveiling the Influence of AI Predictive Analytics on Patient Outcomes: A Comprehensive Narrative Review. *Cureus*. Advance online publication. DOI: 10.7759/cureus.59954 PMID: 38854327

Djimesah, I. E., Zhao, H., Okine, A. N. D., Gyamfi, C. A., Mireku, K. K., Chen, W., Duah, E., & Osei-Mensah, E. (2026). Digital Infrastructure, Trust, and Behavioral Intention: An Extended Technology Acceptance Model for Crowdfunding Adoption in Emerging Economies. *Strategic Business Research*, 100068.

Doo, F., Vosshenrich, J., Cook, T., Moy, L., Almeida, E., Woolen, S., Gichoya, J., Heye, T., & Hanneman, K. (2024). Environmental sustainability and AI in radiology: A double-edged sword. *Radiology*, *310*(2), e232030. Advance online publication. DOI: 10.1148/radiol.232030

Durham, J., & Blondell, S. (2014). Research protocol: A realist synthesis of cross-border patient mobility from low-income and middle-income countries. *BMJ Open*, *4*(11), e006514. Advance online publication. DOI: 10.1136/bmjopen-2014-006514

Durham, J., & Blondell, S. (2017). A realist synthesis of cross-border patient movement from low and middle income countries to similar or higher income countries. *Globalization and Health*, *13*(1), 68. Advance online publication. DOI: 10.1186/s12992-017-0287-8

EBSCO Health. (n.d.). *Isabel clinical decision support system*. https://about.ebsco.com/health-care/products/isabel

Eisavi, M., Fallah, M. R. R., Motaghi, S., & Taheri, F. (2025). The impact of economic convergence between Iran and selected middle eastern countries on health tourism in Iran [ ]. *Journal of Health Administration*, *28*(1), 109–119. DOI: 10.61882/jha.28.1.109

El Arab, R. A., & Al Moosa, O. A. (2025). Systematic review of cost effectiveness and budget impact of artificial intelligence in healthcare. *NPJ Digital Medicine*, *8*(1), 89. Advance online publication. DOI: 10.1038/s41746-025-01722-y

El Arab, R. A., Al Moosa, O. A., & Sagbakken, M. (2025). Economic, ethical, and regulatory dimensions of artificial intelligence in healthcare: An integrative review. *Frontiers in Public Health*, *13*, 1617138. Advance online publication. DOI: 10.3389/fpubh.2025.1617138

El Arab, R. A., Al Moosa, O. A., Sagbakken, M., Ghannam, A., Abuadas, F. H., Somerville, J., & Al Mutair, A. (2025). Integrative review of artificial intelligence applications in nursing: Education, clinical practice, workload management, and professional perceptions. *Frontiers in Public Health*, *13*, 1619378. Advance online publication. DOI: 10.3389/fpubh.2025.1619378

Elendu, C., Amaechi, D. C., Elendu, T. C., Amaechi, E. C., Elendu, I. D., Omokore, O. A., Onubogu, N. C., Omeludike, J. C., Aregbesola, E. T., Fajimi, O. O., Idowu, O. F., Emechebe, S. L., Uyanwune, M. C., & Yonni, J. (2025). The legal and ethical considerations in cross-border telesurgical procedures. *Annals of Medicine and Surgery (London), 87*(6), 3660–3672. DOI: 10.1097/MS9.0000000000003344 PMID: 40486583

Elhaddad, M., & Hamam, S. (2024). AI-driven clinical decision support systems: An ongoing pursuit of potential. *Cureus, 16*(8), e57728. Advance online publication. DOI: 10.7759/cureus.57728

Elkhwesky, Z., El Manzani, Y., & Salem, I. E. (2022). Driving hospitality and tourism to foster sustainable innovation: A systematic review of COVID-19-related studies and practical implications in the digital era. *Tourism and Hospitality Research*. Advance online publication. DOI: 10.1177/14673584221126792

Elliott, J., Shatrov, J., Fritsch, B., & Parker, D. (2021, December). Robotic-assisted knee arthroplasty: An evolution in progress. A concise review of the available systems and the data supporting them. *Archives of Orthopaedic and Trauma Surgery, 141*(12), 2099–2117. DOI: 10.1007/s00402-021-04134-1 PMID: 34491411

Ennab, M., & Mcheick, H. (2024). Enhancing interpretability and accuracy of AI models in healthcare: A comprehensive review on challenges and future directions. *Frontiers in Robotics and AI, 11*, 1444763. Advance online publication. DOI: 10.3389/frobt.2024.1444763 PMID: 39677978

Erdős, F., Thinakaran, R., Firuza, B., & Koloszár, L. (2025). The rise of AI in tourism - A systematic literature review. *Geo Journal of Tourism and Geosites, 60*(2 supplement), 1254–1265. Advance online publication. DOI: 10.30892/gtg.602spl22-1498

Erwin, E., & Paputungan, I. (2025). Bibliometric analysis of innovation and sustainability in health tourism. *Indonesian Journal of Innovation Studies, 26*(2). Advance online publication. DOI: 10.21070/ijins.v26i2.1312

Esmaeilzadeh, P. (2024). Challenges and strategies for wide-scale artificial intelligence (AI) deployment in healthcare practices: A perspective for healthcare organizations. *Artificial Intelligence in Medicine, 151*, 102861. Advance online publication. DOI: 10.1016/j.artmed.2024.102861

Esnaashari, S., & Jabal, M. (2025). An AI-Driven Framework for Autonomous Network Vulnerability Management. *Americas Conference on Information Systems, AMCIS 2025*. https://www.scopus.com/pages/publications/105025189924?origin=scopusAI

Esteva, A., Kuprel, B., Novoa, R. A., Ko, J., Swetter, S. M., Blau, H. M., & Thrun, S. (2017). Dermatologist-level classification of skin cancer with deep neural networks. nature, 542(7639), 115-118.

Esteva, A., Kuprel, B., Novoa, R. A., Ko, J., Swetter, S. M., Blau, H. M., & Thrun, S. (2017). Dermatologist-level classification of skin cancer with deep neural networks. *Nature*, *542*(7639), 115–118. DOI: 10.1038/nature21056 PMID: 28117445

ETHealthWorld. (2025, November). *India leads in healthcare AI adoption: Insights by Shanker Kaul.* Economic Times HealthWorld. Financial Express. (2025, May 20). India's medical tourism market to triple by 2035: Report. Financial Express. https://www.financialexpress.com/business/industry/indias-medical-tourism-market-to-triple-by-2035-report/3918222/

Evangelista, A., Scocozza, F., Conti, M., Auricchio, F., Conti, B., Dorati, R., Genta, I., Benazzo, M., & Pisani, S. (2025). Exploring Mechanical Features of 3D Head and Neck Cancer Models. *Journal of Functional Biomaterials*, *16*(3), 74. DOI: 10.3390/jfb16030074 PMID: 40137353

Fahim, Y. A., Hasani, I. W., Kabba, S., & Ragab, W. M. (2025). Artificial intelligence in healthcare and medicine: Clinical applications, therapeutic advances, and future perspectives. *European Journal of Medical Research*, *30*(1), 1–21. DOI: 10.1186/s40001-025-03196-w PMID: 40988064

Faisal-E-Alam, M., Bhuiyan, M. R. I., Mimi, A., & Miah, M. T. (2025). The role of the three-zero framework in advancing global sustainable development: A bibliometric and text mining analysis. *Discover Sustainability*, *6*(1), 1128. DOI: 10.1007/s43621-025-01919-x

Faiyazuddin, M., Rahman, S. J. Q., Anand, G., Siddiqui, R. K., Mehta, R., Khatib, M. N., Gaidhane, S., Zahiruddin, Q. S., Hussain, A., & Sah, R. (2025). The impact of artificial intelligence on healthcare: A comprehensive review of advancements in diagnostics, treatment, and operational efficiency. *Health Science Reports*, *8*(1), e70312. DOI: 10.1002/hsr2.70312 PMID: 39763580

Fajarini, M., Sung, C.-M., Lin, Y.-S., Su, P.-Y., Chen, R., Chang, L.-F., Chiang, K.-J., & Chou, K.-R. (2026). Clinical effectiveness and cost-effectiveness of primary community health care nurses: A meta-analysis. *International Journal of Nursing Studies*, *177*, 105365. DOI: 10.1016/j.ijnurstu.2026.105365 PMID: 41702261

Fajkis-Zajączkowska, N., Zawada, A., Bojko, M., & Kolasa, K. (2025). Comprehensive analysis of frameworks for evaluating artificial intelligence solutions in healthcare: A descriptive review. Computers in Biology and Medicine, 196(Pt B). *Computers in Biology and Medicine*, *110750*, 110750. Advance online publication. DOI: 10.1016/j.compbiomed.2025.110750

Fan, Z., Yan, Z., & Wen, S. (2023). Deep learning and artificial intelligence in sustainability: A review of SDGs, renewable energy, and environmental health. *Sustainability (Basel)*, *15*(18), 13493. Advance online publication. DOI: 10.3390/su151813493

Fatima, G., Alhmadi, H., Ali Mahdi, A., Hadi, N., Fedacko, J., Magomedova, A., Parvez, S., & Mehdi Raza, A. (2024). Transforming Diagnostics: A Comprehensive Review of Advances in Digital Pathology. *Cureus*. Advance online publication. DOI: 10.7759/cureus.71890 PMID: 39564069

Feng, J., Phillips, R., Malenica, I., Bishara, A., Hubbard, A., Celi, L., & Pirracchio, R. (2022). Clinical artificial intelligence quality improvement: Towards continual monitoring and updating of AI algorithms in healthcare. *NPJ Digital Medicine*, *5*(1), 106. Advance online publication. DOI: 10.1038/s41746-022-00611-y

Ferreira, B., Borges, R., Antunes, C. M., Maximiano, M., Gomes, R., Távora, V., Dias, M., & Correia Bezerra, R. (2025). Can Secure MultiParty Computation be Used to Create Clinical Trial Cohorts based on Blockchain Notarized Private Patient Data? *Procedia Computer Science*, *256*, 996–1002. DOI: 10.1016/j.procs.2025.02.205

Fidler, D. P. (2010). The challenges of global health governance.

Figueiredo, N., Abrantes, J. L., & Costa, S. (2024). Mapping the sustainable development in health tourism: A systematic literature review. *Sustainability (Basel)*, *16*(5), 1901. Advance online publication. DOI: 10.3390/su16051901

Fink, M., & Akra, B. (2023). Comparison of the international regulations for medical devices–USA versus Europe. *Injury*, *54*, 110908. Advance online publication. DOI: 10.1016/j.injury.2023.110908 PMID: 37365092

Fiske, A., Radhuber, I., Willem, T., Buyx, A., Celi, L., & McLennan, S. (2025). Climate change and health: The next challenge of ethical AI. *The Lancet. Global Health*, *13*(7), e1314–e1320. Advance online publication. DOI: 10.1016/S2214-109X(25)00124-X

Floridi, L., Cowls, J., Beltrametti, M., Chatila, R., Chazerand, P., Dignum, V., Luetge, C., Madelin, R., Pagallo, U., Rossi, F., Schafer, B., Valcke, P., & Vayena, E. (2018). AI4People—An ethical framework for a good AI society: Opportunities, risks, principles, and recommendations. *Minds and Machines*, *28*(4), 689–707. DOI: 10.1007/s11023-018-9482-5 PMID: 30930541

Florido-Benítez, L., & del Alcázar Martínez, B. (2024). How artificial intelligence (AI) is powering new tourism marketing and the future agenda for smart tourist destinations. *Electronics (Basel)*, *13*(21), 4151. DOI: 10.3390/electronics13214151

Foley, B. M., Haglin, J. M., Tanzer, J. R., & Eltorai, A. E. (2019). Patient care without borders: A systematic review of medical and surgical tourism. *Journal of Travel Medicine*, *26*(6), taz049. Advance online publication. DOI: 10.1093/jtm/taz049

Fortea, C. (2026). Modelling European Economic Sustainability Based on Economic Indicators Related to Sustainable Development Goal 8. In *Sustainable Economic Development and the European Green Deal: Creating Energy Efficiency, Industrial Innovation, and Inclusive Growth* (pp. 323-378). Springer.

Fortino, L., De Vita, S., Esposito, M., & Esposito, C. (2025). Federated Digital Twin Architecture with Synthetic Data Generation for Privacy-Preserving Diabetes Management. *2025 IEEE Conference on Standards for Communications and Networking, CSCN 2025*. DOI: 10.1109/CSCN67557.2025.11230756

Fradgley, E. A., Paul, C. L., & Bryant, J. (2015). A systematic review of barriers to optimal outpatient specialist services for individuals with prevalent chronic diseases: What are the unique and common barriers experienced by patients in high income countries? *International Journal for Equity in Health*, *14*(1), 52. DOI: 10.1186/s12939-015-0179-6 PMID: 26051244

Franklin, G., Stephens, R., Piracha, M., Tiosano, S., Lehouillier, F., Koppel, R., & Elkin, P. L. (2024). The Sociodemographic Biases in Machine Learning Algorithms: A Biomedical Informatics Perspective. *Life (Basel, Switzerland)*, *14*(6), 652. Advance online publication. DOI: 10.3390/life14060652 PMID: 38929638

Freeman, D., Reeve, S., Robinson, A., Ehlers, A., Clark, D., Spanlang, B., & Slater, M. (2017). Virtual reality in the assessment, understanding, and treatment of mental health disorders. *Psychological Medicine*, *47*(14), 2393–2400. DOI: 10.1017/S003329171700040X PMID: 28325167

Frischhut, M., & Levaggi, R. (2024). With a little help from my (neighbouring) friends. "Border region patient mobility" in the European Union: A policy analysis. *Health Policy (Amsterdam)*, *146*, 105114. Advance online publication. DOI: 10.1016/j.healthpol.2024.105114

Gaffney, H., & Mirza, K. M. (2025). Pathology in the artificial intelligence era: Guiding innovation and implementation to preserve human insight. *Academic Pathology*, *12*(1), 100166. DOI: 10.1016/j.acpath.2025.100166 PMID: 40104157

Garad, A., Al-Ansi, A. M., Jaboob, M., & Kusumawati, R. (2025). Digital innovations in medical tourism: A PRISMA review in the Arab region. In Revolutionizing healthcare experience with digital medical tourism (pp. 53–78). DOI: 10.4018/979-8-3693-7888-5.ch002

García-Figueiras, R., Baleato-González, S., Padhani, A. R., Luna-Alcalá, A., Vallejo-Casas, J. A., Sala, E., Vilanova, J. C., Koh, D.-M., Herranz-Carnero, M., & Vargas, H. A. (2019). How clinical imaging can assess cancer biology. *Insights Into Imaging*, *10*(1), 28. Advance online publication. DOI: 10.1186/s13244-019-0703-0 PMID: 30830470

García-Gómez, J., Blanes-Selva, V., Álvarez-Romero, C., De Bartolomé Cenzano, J. C., Mesquita, F. P., Pazos, A., & Doñate-Martínez, A. (2025). Mitigating patient harm risks: A proposal of requirements for AI in healthcare. *Artificial Intelligence in Medicine*, *167*, 103168. Advance online publication. DOI: 10.1016/j.artmed.2025.103168

García-Madurga, M. Á., & Grilló-Méndez, A. J. (2023). Artificial intelligence in the tourism industry: An overview of reviews. *Administrative Sciences*, *13*(8), 172. Advance online publication. DOI: 10.3390/admsci13080172

García-Vidal, C., Sanjuán, G., Puerta-Alcalde, P., Moreno-García, E., & Soriano, Á. (2019). Artificial intelligence to support clinical decision-making processes. *EBioMedicine*, *46*, 27–29. DOI: 10.1016/j.ebiom.2019.07.019

Garg, R., Batra, R., & Banerji, A. (2020). Low Cost, Quality Treatment and Excellent Hospitality Makes India the Best Destination for Medical Tourism. *International Journal of Innovative Research in Medical Science*, *5*(1). Advance online publication. DOI: 10.23958/ijirms/vol05-i01/614

Garg, S. R., & Bhardwaj, A. (2012). Indian medical tourism industry: Growth opportunities and challenges. *Multi Disciplinary Edu Global Quest (Quarterly)*, *1*(1), 115–135.

Gaur, L., Afaq, A., Arora, G. K., & Khan, N. (2023). Artificial intelligence for carbon emissions using system of systems theory. *Ecological Informatics*, *76*, 102165. Advance online publication. DOI: 10.1016/j.ecoinf.2023.102165

Gaur, L., Afaq, A., Singh, G., & Dwivedi, Y. K. (2021). Role of artificial intelligence and robotics to foster the touchless travel during a pandemic: A review and research agenda. *International Journal of Contemporary Hospitality Management*, *33*(11), 4079–4098. https://doi.org/. DOI: 10.1108/IJCHM-11-2020-1246

Gayatri, A. P., Bonthu, M. G., Srinivas, N., & Borse, L. B. (2026). Artificial intelligence–enhanced diagnostic tools for patient understanding. In *Artificial Intelligence in Patient Counselling* (pp. 247-276). Elsevier. Giró, A. B. Alternative Peacebuilding in Bosnia Evolution of an NGO and volunteer. DOI: 10.1016/B978-0-443-43823-3.00001-7

Gedik, Y. (2023). Kurumsal iletişimde yeni bir yıldız: Chatbot faydaları, zorlukları ve stratejileri üzerine kavramsal bir çerçeve. *Journal of Business and Communication Studies*, *2*(1), 13–32. https://www.researchgate.net/publication/372010058_KURUMSAL_ILETISIMDE_YENI_BIR_YILDIZ_CHATBOT_FAYDALARI_ZORLUKLARI_VE_STRATEJILERI_UZERINE_KAVRAMSAL_BIR_CERCEVE_A_new_star_in_corporate_communications_Chatbot_A_conceptual_framework_on_its_benefits_cha. DOI: 10.29228/jobacs.68836

George, R. R., Sunil, S., Vijayan, K., & Saleem, S. (2025*).* Medical value tourism: A revival for post-COVID tourism industry in India. Journal of Rural Tourism. *https://doi.org/*DOI: 10.70310/jrt.2025.03010668

Georgiou. (2024). *10 use cases and real examples of generative AI in healthcare*. https://imaginovation.net/blog/use-cases-examples-generative-ai-healthcare/

Gerke, S., Minssen, T., & Cohen, I. G. (2020). Ethical and legal challenges of artificial intelligence-driven healthcare. In Bohr, A., & Memarzadeh, K. (Eds.), *Artificial intelligence in healthcare* (pp. 295–336). Elsevier., DOI: 10.1016/B978-0-12-818438-7.00012-5

Ghasemi, M., Rezvani, H. R., & Rakhshan, M. (2020). Digital transformation in healthcare: The role of artificial intelligence and virtual reality. *Health Technology (Hong Kong)*, *10*(4), 1–10. DOI: 10.1007/s12553-020-00481-0

Ghasemi, P., Mehdiabadi, A., Spulbar, C., & Birau, R. (2021). Ranking of sustainable medical tourism destinations in Iran: An integrated approach using fuzzy SWARA-PROMETHEE. *Sustainability (Basel)*, *13*(2), 683. Advance online publication. DOI: 10.3390/su13020683

Ghoreyshi, N., Heidari, R., Farhadi, A., Chamanara, M., Farahani, N., Vahidi, M., & Behroozi, J. (2025). Next-generation sequencing in cancer diagnosis and treatment: Clinical applications and future directions. *Discover. Oncology*, *16*(1), 578. Advance online publication. DOI: 10.1007/s12672-025-01816-9 PMID: 40253661

Glass, L. T., Schlachta, C. M., Hawel, J. D., Elnahas, A. I., & Alkhamesi, N. A. (2022). Cross-border healthcare: A review and applicability to North America during COVID-19. *Health Policy OPEN*, *3*, 100064. DOI: 10.1016/j.hpopen.2021.100064 PMID: 35036910

Gnana Sanga Mithra, S., & Bhavana, S. (2025). Revolutionizing healthcare with an in-depth analysis of AI's transformative impact in India. *Social Sciences & Humanities Open*, *11*, 101467. Advance online publication. DOI: 10.1016/j.ssaho.2025.101467

Goktas, P., & Grzybowski, A. (2025). Shaping the future of healthcare: Ethical clinical challenges and pathways to trustworthy AI. *Journal of Clinical Medicine*, *14*(5), 1605. Advance online publication. DOI: 10.3390/jcm14051605

Gordon, M., Daniel, M., Ajiboye, A., Uraiby, H., Xu, N., Bartlett, R., Hanson, J., Haas, M., Spadafore, M., Grafton-Clarke, C., Gasiea, R., Michie, C., Corral, J., Kwan, B., Dolmans, D., & Thammasitboon, S. (2024). A scoping review of artificial intelligence in medical education: BEME Guide No. 84. *Medical Teacher*, *46*(4), 446–470. DOI: 10.1080/0142159X.2024.2314198

Gössling, S., Scott, D., & Hall, C. M. (2021). Pandemics, tourism and global change: A rapid assessment of COVID-19. *Journal of Sustainable Tourism*, *29*(1), 1–20. DOI: 10.1080/09669582.2020.1758708

Gou, F., Liu, J., Xiao, C., & Wu, J. (2024). Research on artificial-intelligence-assisted medicine: A survey on medical artificial intelligence. *Diagnostics (Basel)*, *14*(14), 1472. Advance online publication. DOI: 10.3390/diagnostics14141472

Gourisaria, M. K., Agrawal, R., Singh, V., Rautaray, S. S., & Pandey, M. (2022). AI and IoT enabled smart hospital management systems. In Rautaray, S. S., Pandey, M., & Nguyen, N. G. (Eds.), *Data science in societal applications* (pp. 85–110). Springer., DOI: 10.1007/978-981-19-5154-1_6

Grannis, S. J., Williams, J. L., Kasthuri, S., Murray, M., & Xu, H. (2022). Evaluation of real-world referential and probabilistic patient matching to advance patient identification strategy. *Journal of the American Medical Informatics Association : JAMIA*, *29*(8), 1409–1415. DOI: 10.1093/jamia/ocac068 PMID: 35568993

Grewal, D. S. (2008). *Network power: The social dynamics of globalization*. Yale University Press.

Groene, O., Poletti, P., Vallejo, P., Cucic, C., Klazinga, N., & Sunol, R. (2009). Quality requirements for cross-border care in Europe: A qualitative study of patients', professionals' and healthcare financiers' views. *Quality & Safety in Health Care*, *18*(Suppl 1), i15–i21. DOI: 10.1136/qshc.2008.028837 PMID: 19188456

Güell-Alonso, R., Cabrera-Pérez, R., & Vives, J. (2025). Immunocompatibility in transplantation: Adapting to a changing therapeutic landscape. *Frontiers in Immunology, 16*, 1648534. Advance online publication. DOI: 10.3389/fimmu.2025.1648534 PMID: 40995364

Guerrazzi, C. (2020). An international perspective on health information exchange: Adoption in OECD countries with different health care system configurations. *Medical Care Research and Review : MCRR, 77*(4), 299–311. DOI: 10.1177/1077558719858245 PMID: 31216934

Gulia, J. (2024). Cross-Border Data Transfers: International Cooperation and Conflicts. *Legal Lock J., 4*, 263.

Gulshan, V., Peng, L., Coram, M., Stumpe, M. C., Wu, D., Narayanaswamy, A., Venugopalan, S., Widner, K., Madams, T., Cuadros, J., Kim, R., Raman, R., Nelson, P. C., Mega, J. L., & Webster, D. R. (2016). Development and validation of a deep learning algorithm for detection of diabetic retinopathy in retinal fundus photographs. *Journal of the American Medical Association, 316*(22), 2402–2410. DOI: 10.1001/jama.2016.17216 PMID: 27898976

Gunaseelan, S., & Kesavan, N. (2020). A Review on Medical Tourism in India. *Indian Journal of Public Health Research & Development, 11*(1), 562. Advance online publication. DOI: 10.37506/v11/i1/2020/ijphrd/193882

Gupta, A., Gupta, R., & Kumar, P. (2023). Artificial Intelligence for Remote Healthcare in Underserved Areas: Enhancing Access and Quality of Healthcare Delivery. International Conference on Artificial Intelligence and its Application, Hackl, A. (2018). Mobility equity in a globalized world: Reducing inequalities in the sustainable development agenda. *World Development, 112*, 150–162.

Guru, S., Sinha, A., & Kautish, P. (2023). Determinants of medical tourism: Application of fuzzy analytical hierarchical process. *International Journal of Emerging Markets, 18*(11), 4819–4842. DOI: 10.1108/IJOEM-08-2021-1173

Hadley, T., Pettit, R., Malik, T., Khoei, A., & Salihu, H. (2020). Artificial intelligence in global health—A framework and strategy for adoption and sustainability. *International Journal of MCH and AIDS, 9*(1), 121–127. DOI: 10.21106/ijma.296

Haga, S. B. (2024). Artificial intelligence, medications, pharmacogenomics, and ethics. *Pharmacogenomics, 25*(14-15), 611–622. DOI: 10.1080/14622416.2024.2428587 PMID: 39545629

Halimuzzaman, M. (2022). Technology-driven healthcare and sustainable tourism: Analyzing modern approaches to industry challenges. *Business and Social Sciences*, *1*(1), 1–9.

Hamid, M. M. A. (2024). *The impact of applying artificial intelligence in developing medical tourism in Egypt*. International Journal of Tourism and Hospitality Studies., DOI: 10.21608/ijthsx.2024.288682.1094

Han, S. B., Rodriguez-Quintana, D., Freedhand, A. M., Mathis, K. B., Boiwka, A. V., & Noble, P. C. (2021). Contemporary robotic systems in total knee arthroplasty: A review of accuracy and outcomes. *The Orthopedic Clinics of North America*, *52*(2), 83–92. DOI: 10.1016/j.ocl.2020.12.001 PMID: 33752841

Harryono, M., Huang, Y.-F., Miyazawa, K., & Sethaput, V. (2006). Thailand medical tourism cluster. *Harvard Business School Microeconomics of Competitiveness*, 1-31.

Hasan, S. U., Hasan, S., Shiwlani, A., Kumar, S., Kumar, S., Nazeer, M. I., & Shiwlani, S. (2025). A systematic review of AI-based clinical decision support systems: From development and implementation to applications. *Pakistan Journal of Life and Social Sciences*, *23*(1), 1482–1500. https://www.pjlss.edu.pk/pdf_files/2025_1/1482-1500.pdf. DOI: 10.57239/PJLSS-2025-23.1.00115

Hassan, V., & Bellos, S. (2022). COVID-19: Reshaping medical tourism through artificial intelligence and robotics. Athens Journal of Tourism, 9(4), 467–486. https://www.athensjournals.gr/tourism/2022-4672-AJT-Hassan-03.pdf

Hassan, V., & Bellos, G. (2022). COVID-19: Reshaping medical tourism through artificial intelligence (AI) and robotics. *Athens Journal of Tourism*, *9*(2), 87–104. DOI: 10.30958/ajt.9-2-2

HAWES, D., SHI, S.-R., DABBS, D. J., TAYLOR, C. R., & COTE, R. J. (2009). Immunohistochemistry. *Modern Surgical Pathology*, 48–70. DOI: 10.1016/B978-1-4160-3966-2.00016-3

Hayat, Y. (2025). Transforming Medical Tourism Through. *Advances in Healthcare Information Systems and Administration*, *425*, 425–458. Advance online publication. DOI: 10.4018/979-8-3693-7888-5.ch017

Haznedar, B. (2010). *Yapay zeka teknikleri kullanarak erkek kısır hastalarda genetik bozukluk varlığının tespiti* [Unpublished master's thesis]. Erciyes University.

Heliades, G., Gkintoni, E., Panas, G., Halkiopoulos, C., & Boutsinas, B. (2024). AI-Enhanced Cognitive Wellness: Integrating NcBT and Human–Computer Interaction in Global Health Tourism. International Conference of the International Association of Cultural and Digital Tourism, Hoagland, A., & Kipping, S. (2024). Challenges in promoting health equity and reducing disparities in access across new and established technologies. *The Canadian Journal of Cardiology*, *40*(6), 1154–1167. PMID: 38417572

Hemrungrojn, S., Saengsai, K., Jakkrawankul, P., Kiattiporn-Opas, C., Chaicha-reenon, K., Amrapala, A., Lapanan, K., Achakulvisut, T., Vateekul, P., Nupairoj, N., Phutrakool, P., Yodlorchai, R., Hiransuthikul, N., & Hengprapom, S. (2024). Accuracy and concordance of DMIND AI application with a renowned depression assessment tool in Thai adults. *Chulalongkorn Medical Journal*, *68*(4), 261–273. DOI: 10.56808/2673-060X.5495

Hendrix, N., Veenstra, D., Cheng, M., Anderson, N., & Verguet, S. (2021). Assessing the economic value of clinical artificial intelligence: Challenges and opportunities. *Value in Health : The Journal of the International Society for Pharmacoeconomics and Outcomes Research*, *25*(3), 331–339. DOI: 10.1016/j.jval.2021.08.015

Hill, M. G., Sim, M., & Mills, B. (2020). The quality of diagnosis and triage advice provided by free online symptom checkers and apps in Australia. *The Medical Journal of Australia*, *212*(11), 514–519. DOI: 10.5694/mja2.50600 PMID: 32391611

Hoivik, E. A., Hodneland, E., Dybvik, J. A., Wagner-Larsen, K. S., Fasmer, K. E., Berg, H. F., Halle, M. K., Haldorsen, I. S., & Krakstad, C. (2021). A radiogenomics application for prognostic profiling of endometrial cancer. *Communications Biology*, *4*(1), 1363. Advance online publication. DOI: 10.1038/s42003-021-02894-5 PMID: 34873276

Ho, K.. (2025). Belief in clinical decision support systems that utilize artificial intelligence: A systematic literature review of healthcare workers' perspectives. *Journal of Medical Internet Research*, *27*, e69678. DOI: 10.2196/69678

Horst, A., Loustalot, P., Yoganathan, S., Li, T., Xu, J., Tong, W., Schneider, D., Löffler-Perez, N., Di Renzo, E., & Renaudin, M. (2025). Federated learning: A privacy-preserving approach to data-centric regulatory cooperation. *Frontiers in Drug Safety and Regulation*, *5*, 1579922. Advance online publication. DOI: 10.3389/fdsfr.2025.1579922 PMID: 40978510

Hosny, A., & Aerts, H. (2019). Artificial intelligence for global health. *Science*, *366*(6468), 955–956. DOI: 10.1126/science.aay5189

Hossain, M. A., Arafat, M. S., Desai, K., Akter, S., & Asha, A. I. (2025). The economic impact of AI-driven remote patient monitoring: A business intelligence perspective on healthcare cost optimization. *International Interdisciplinary Business Economics Advancement Journal, 6*(5), 39–67. Advance online publication. DOI: 10.55640/business/volume06issue05-03

Hryciw, B., Fortin, Z., Ghossein, J., & Kyeremanteng, K. (2023). Doctor-patient interactions in the age of AI: Navigating innovation and expertise. *Frontiers in Medicine, 10*, 1241508. Advance online publication. DOI: 10.3389/fmed.2023.1241508

Hua, D., Petrina, N., Young, N., Cho, J.-G., & Poon, S. (2023). Understanding the factors influencing acceptability of AI in medical imaging domains among healthcare professionals: A scoping review. *Artificial Intelligence in Medicine, 147*, 102698. Advance online publication. DOI: 10.1016/j.artmed.2023.102698

Hussain, K., & Nasir, S. (2026). Regulatory Harmonization in the Digital Age: A Comparative Study of International Legal Frameworks Governing Cyber and Health Data Protection.

İlkılıç, İ. (2021). Tıpta yapay zekâ kullanımının etik açıdan değerlendirilmesi. *SD Sağlık Düşüncesi ve Tıp Kültürü Dergisi, 58(1)*, 18–21. https://sdplatform.com/tipta-yapay-zeka-kullaniminin-etik-acidan-degerlendirilmesi

Inherit, X. (n.d.). *Heva – AI-native healthcare & wellness intelligence platform.* https://www.inheritx.com/portfolio/heva

Işık, C., Islam, H., Ongan, S., Şengöz, A., & Usanmaz, B. (2025). Artificial intelligence (AI) interacted ESG-based sustainable tourism: Economic insights. *Tourism Economics*. Advance online publication. DOI: 10.1177/13548166251346306

Islam, M. M., Bhuiyan, M. R. I., Islam, S. H., Tabassum, M. N., & Billah, M. (2026). Unlocking the mediating and moderating role of information security in information systems: A combined TAM, ISM, and HBM model. *Human Behavior and Emerging Technologies, 2026*(1), 5593002. DOI: 10.1155/hbe2/5593002

Islam, M. T. (2026). AI-ENABLED CUSTOMER-INTERACTION MODELS FOR IMPROVING SERVICE EFFICIENCY IN US HOSPITALITY AND RETAIL OPERATIONS. *American Journal of Interdisciplinary Studies, 7*(01), 94–140. DOI: 10.63125/par85p86

Ismail, M., Khan, S., Khan, F., Noor, S., Sajid, H., Yar, S., & Rasheed, I. (2020). Prevalence and significance of potential drug-drug interactions among cancer patients receiving chemotherapy. *BMC Cancer, 20*(1), 335. Advance online publication. DOI: 10.1186/s12885-020-06855-9 PMID: 32307008

Jacob, B. A. (2024). The lasting effects of the COVID-19 pandemic on K-12 schooling: Evidence from a nationally representative teacher survey (EdWorking-Paper No. 24-1020). Annenberg Institute at Brown University. https://doi.org/DOI: 10.26300/6gh3-vz18

Jain, N., Nagaich, U., Pandey, M., Chellappan, D. K., & Dua, K. (2022). Predictive genomic tools in disease stratification and targeted prevention: A recent update in personalized therapy advancements. *The EPMA Journal, 13*(4), 561–580. DOI: 10.1007/s13167-022-00304-2 PMID: 36505888

Jang, H.-J., & Lee, S. H. (2025). AI-Driven Digital Pathology: Deep Learning and Multimodal Integration for Precision Oncology. *International Journal of Molecular Sciences, 27*(1), 379. DOI: 10.3390/ijms27010379 PMID: 41516254

Jiang, F., Jiang, Y., Zhi, H., Dong, Y., Li, H., Ma, S., Wang, Y., Dong, Q., Shen, H., & Wang, Y. (2017). Artificial intelligence in healthcare: Past, present and future. *Stroke and Vascular Neurology, 2*(4), 230–243. DOI: 10.1136/svn-2017-000101 PMID: 29507784

Jiao, W., Zhang, X., & D'Souza, F. (2023). The economic value and clinical impact of artificial intelligence in healthcare: A scoping literature review. *IEEE Access : Practical Innovations, Open Solutions, 11*, 123445–123457. DOI: 10.1109/ACCESS.2023.3327905

Jiménez, C. (2022). Leading destinations for AI-assisted minimally invasive surgery. *Medical Tourism Magazine*.https://www.magazine.medicaltourism.com/article/leading-destinations-for-ai-assisted-minimally-invasive-surgery

Jobin, A., Ienca, M., & Vayena, E. (2019). The global landscape of AI ethics guidelines. *Nature Machine Intelligence, 1*(9), 389–399. DOI: 10.1038/s42256-019-0088-2

Jorshary, K. M., Sassani, M., Khamoushi, F. S. S., Raoufi, S., & Khamoushi, S. (2025). Ranking of AI-driven strategies for optimizing the health tourism supply chain using stratified BWM. Knowledge and Decision Systems with Applications. https://doi.org/DOI: 10.59543/kadsa.v1i.15051

Kadirov, A., Maksimov, A., & Okhotnikov, I. (2025). Digital technologies as a driver of cross-border trade (on the example of the global telemedicine market). *Russian Journal of Management, 13*(1), 211–232. DOI: 10.29039/2500-1469-2025-13-1-211-232

Kalmenovitz, J., Lowry, M., & Volkova, E. (2025). Regulatory Fragmentation. *The Journal of Finance, 80*(2), 1081–1126. DOI: 10.1111/jofi.13423

Kamassi, A., Abd Manaf, N. H., & Omar, A. (2020). The identity and role of stakeholders in the medical tourism industry: State of the art. *Tourism Review*, *75*(3), 559–574. DOI: 10.1108/TR-01-2019-0031

Karadayi-Usta, S. (2024). Sustainable medical tourism service network with a stakeholder perspective. *Current Issues in Tourism*, *28*(3), 321–340. DOI: 10.1080/13683500.2024.2309148

Karcıoğlu, U. B. (2025). The Impact of Artificial Intelligence on the Patient Journey in Medical Tourism: A Management Framework. *Eurasian Journal of Health Technology Assessment*, *9*(1), 58–67. DOI: 10.52148/ehta.1701664

Karuppan Perumal, M. K., Rajan Renuka, R., Kumar Subbiah, S., & Manickam Natarajan, P. (2025). Artificial intelligence-driven clinical decision support systems for early detection and precision therapy in oral cancer: A mini review. *Frontiers in Oral Health*, *6*, 1592428. Advance online publication. DOI: 10.3389/froh.2025.1592428 PMID: 40356851

Kastrup, N., Holst-Kristensen, A., & Valentin, J. (2024). Landscape and challenges in economic evaluations of artificial intelligence in healthcare: A systematic review of methodology. *BMC Digital Health*, *2*(1), 88. Advance online publication. DOI: 10.1186/s44247-024-00088-7

Kaushik, A., Barcellona, C., Mandyam, N. K., Tan, S. Y., & Tromp, J. (2025). Challenges and Opportunities for Data Sharing Related to Artificial Intelligence Tools in Health Care in Low- and Middle-Income Countries: Systematic Review and Case Study From Thailand. *Journal of Medical Internet Research*, *27*, e58338. Advance online publication. DOI: 10.2196/58338 PMID: 39903508

Keesara, S., Jonas, A., & Schulman, K. (2020). Covid-19 and health care's digital revolution. *The New England Journal of Medicine*, *382*(23), e82. DOI: 10.1056/NEJMp2005835 PMID: 32240581

Khalifa, M., & Albadawy, M. (2024). AI in diagnostic imaging: Revolutionising accuracy and efficiency. *Computer Methods and Programs in Biomedicine Update*, *5*, 100146. Advance online publication. DOI: 10.1016/j.cmpbup.2024.100146

Khanna, A.. (2025). Positions and drawbacks of artificial intelligence in health care: A narrative review. *Interactive Journal of Medical Research*, *14*(1), e53616.

Khanna, N., Maindarkar, M., Fernandes, J., Paul, S., Bhagawati, M., Ahluwalia, P., Ruzsa, Z., Sharma, A., Kolluri, R., Singh, I., Laird, J., Fatemi, M., Alizad, A., Saba, L., Agarwal, V., Sharma, A., Teji, J., Al-Maini, M., Rathore, V., & Suri, J. (2022). Economics of artificial intelligence in healthcare: Diagnosis vs. treatment. *Healthcare (Basel), 10*(12), 2493. Advance online publication. DOI: 10.3390/healthcare10122493

Khan, S. N., Danishuddin, , Khan, M. W. A., Guarnera, L., & Akhtar, S. M. F. (2026). Multi-modal AI in precision medicine: Integrating genomics, imaging, and EHR data for clinical insights. *Frontiers in Artificial Intelligence*, *8*, 1743921. Advance online publication. DOI: 10.3389/frai.2025.1743921 PMID: 41573270

Khan, S., Faruqui, H., Zahid, M., Chaudhry, S., Rehman, Z., Noor, H., & Naushad, M. (2025). Tracking the pandemic through molecular and sequencing tools: A story of SARS-CoV-2 over five years, lessons learned, and further directions. *BMC Infectious Diseases*, *25*(1), 1816. DOI: 10.1186/s12879-025-12200-x PMID: 41291524

Khan, Z., Khan, N., & Zhu, X. (2025). Harnessing artificial intelligence for environmental sustainability via human capital and renewable energy. *Scientific Reports*, *15*(1), 36739. Advance online publication. DOI: 10.1038/s41598-025-20613-6

Khatun, M., Hossain, R., Bhuiyan, M. R. I., Tabassum, M. N., & Riaj, M. A. (2025). *Green entrepreneurship and digital transformation for sustainable development: A systematic review* (In, K., Ed.). [Book title]

Khinvasara, T., Ness, S., & Shankar, A. (2024). Leveraging AI for enhanced quality assurance in medical device manufacturing. *Asian Journal of Research in Computer Science*, *17*(6), 13–35. Advance online publication. DOI: 10.9734/ajrcos/2024/v17i6454

Khizzou, N. B., Aarabe, M., Bouizgar, M., Alla, L., & Benjelloun, A. (2025). The digital transformation of medical tourism: A systematic and bibliometric review of the literature. In Revolutionizing healthcare experience with digital medical tourism (pp. 355–382). DOI: 10.4018/979-8-3693-7888-5.ch015

Kim, S. J., Cho, K. J., & Oh, S. (2017). Development of machine learning models for diagnosis of glaucoma. *PLoS One*, *12*(5), e0177726. DOI: 10.1371/journal.pone.0177726 PMID: 28542342

Kırtıl, İ. G., & Aşkun, V. (2021). Artificial intelligence in tourism: A review and bibliometrics research. *Advances in Hospitality and Tourism Research*, *9*(1), 205–233. DOI: 10.30519/ahtr.801690

Klingelhöfer, D., Braun, M., Dröge, J., Groneberg, D., & Brüggmann, D. (2025). Research on artificial intelligence, machine and deep learning in medicine: Global characteristics, readiness, and equity. *Globalization and Health*, *21*(1), 28. Advance online publication. DOI: 10.1186/s12992-025-01128-1

Koçak, B., Ponsiglione, A., Romeo, V., Ugga, L., Huisman, M., & Cuocolo, R. (2025). Radiology AI and sustainability paradox: Environmental, economic, and social dimensions. *Insights Into Imaging*, *16*(1), 88. Advance online publication. DOI: 10.1186/s13244-025-01962-2

Kocamaz, K. (2007). *Hastane bilgi yönetim sistemlerinde veri madenciliği ve Konya Meram Tıp Fakültesi hastanesindeki hastane bilgi yönetim sistemi uygulamasının incelenmesi* [Unpublished master's thesis]. Selçuk University.

Koprowski, R., Lanza, M., & Irregolare, C. (2016). Corneal power evaluation after myopic corneal refractive surgery using artificial neural networks. *Biomedical Engineering Online*, *15*(1), 121. DOI: 10.1186/s12938-016-0243-5 PMID: 27846894

Kozan, N. (2025, August 9). Sağlık turizminde dijital konsültasyonların yükselişi. *Istanbuldent.* https://www.istanbuldent.com.tr/saglik-turizminde-dijital-konsultasyonlarin-yukselisi/

Krimmer, R., Dedovic, S., Schmidt, C., & Corici, A. A. (2021). Developing Cross-border E-Governance: Exploring Interoperability and Cross-border Integration. *Lecture Notes in Computer Science (Including Subseries Lecture Notes in Artificial Intelligence and Lecture Notes in Bioinformatics), 12849 LNCS*, 107–124. DOI: 10.1007/978-3-030-82824-0_9

Krishnan, G., Singh, S., Pathania, M., Gosavi, S., Abhishek, S., Parchani, A., & Dhar, M. (2023). Artificial intelligence in clinical medicine: Catalyzing a sustainable global healthcare paradigm. *Frontiers in Artificial Intelligence*, *6*, 1227091. Advance online publication. DOI: 10.3389/frai.2023.1227091

Kristyanto, H. (2025, March 3). AI chatbots in travel: Benefits & examples. *Cognigy*. https://www.cognigy.com/blog/ai-chatbots-in-travel-benefits-examples

Krittanawong, C., & Kaplin, S. (2021). Artificial intelligence in global health. *European Heart Journal*, *42*(23), 2322–2324. DOI: 10.1093/eurheartj/ehab036

Kulkarni, P. D. (2025). Competencies for Medical Tourism in India. In *Human Capital Management and Competitive Advantage in Tourism* (pp. 1–40). IGI Global Scientific Publishing., DOI: 10.4018/979-8-3373-0071-9.ch001

Kumar, P., Sharma, S., & Dutot, V. (2023). Artificial intelligence (AI)-enabled CRM capability in healthcare: The impact on service innovation. *International Journal of Information Management*, *69*, 102598. Advance online publication. DOI: 10.1016/j.ijinfomgt.2022.102598

Kupi, M. (2025). The impact of an artificial intelligence-based forecasting model on the development of sustainable tourism. *Geo Journal of Tourism and Geosites*, *61*(3), 1758–1766. Advance online publication. DOI: 10.30892/gtg.61334-1544

Kuwaiti, A. A., Nazer, K., Al-Reedy, A., Al-Shehri, S., Al-Muhanna, A., Subbarayalu, A., Al Muhanna, D., & Al-Muhanna, F. (2023). A review of the role of artificial intelligence in healthcare. *Journal of Personalized Medicine*, *13*(6), 951. Advance online publication. DOI: 10.3390/jpm13060951

Labkoff, S., Oladimeji, B., Kannry, J., Solomonides, A., Leftwich, R., Koski, E., Joseph, A., Lopez-Gonzalez, M., Fleisher, L., Nolen, K., Dutta, S., Levy, D., Price, A., Barr, P., Hron, J., Lin, B., Srivastava, G., Pastor, N., Luque, U. S., & Quintana, Y. (2024). Toward a responsible future: Recommendations for AI-enabled clinical decision support. *Journal of the American Medical Informatics Association : JAMIA*, *31*(12), 2730–2739. DOI: 10.1093/jamia/ocae209

Labonté, R., Runnels, V., Crooks, V. A., Johnston, R., & Snyder, J. (2017). What does the development of medical tourism in Barbados hold for health equity? An exploratory qualitative case study. *Global Health Research and Policy*, *2*(1), 5. Advance online publication. DOI: 10.1186/s41256-017-0025-z PMID: 29202073

Lakhani, P. C., & Sundaram, B. (2017). Deep learning at chest radiography: Automated classification of pulmonary tuberculosis by using convolutional neural networks. *Radiology*, *284*(2), 574–582. DOI: 10.1148/radiol.2017162326 PMID: 28436741

Lam, M. L.-L. (2025). Increasing adoptive capacities of innovative health technologies in the global health care system. *Darnios Aplinkos Vystymas*, *22*(1), 143–151. Advance online publication. DOI: 10.52320/dav.v22i1.381

Larson, D., Bhargavan-Chatfield, M., Tilkin, M., Coombs, L., & Wald, C. (2025). The road map for ACR practice accreditation for radiology artificial intelligence. *Journal of the American College of Radiology : JACR*, *22*(5), 586–592. Advance online publication. DOI: 10.1016/j.jacr.2025.02.008

Lee, J.-W. (2025). Comment on "Japan's Aging Workforce: Determinants and Outlook.". *Asian Economic Policy Review*, *20*(2), 263–264. Advance online publication. DOI: 10.1111/aepr.12507

Leveraging Electronic Health Records and Artificial Intelligence for Automated Health Outcome Analysis. (2026). ISPOR | International Society for Pharmacoeconomics and Outcomes Research. https://www.ispor.org/publications/journals/value-outcomes-spotlight/vos-archives/issue/view/global-threats-from-climate-change/leveraging-electronic-health-records-and-artificial-intelligence-for-automated-health-outcome-analysis

Lewis, A. K., Harding, K. E., Snowdon, D. A., & Taylor, N. F. (2018). Reducing wait time from referral to first visit for community outpatient services may contribute to better health outcomes: A systematic review. *BMC Health Services Research*, *18*(1), 869. DOI: 10.1186/s12913-018-3669-6 PMID: 30458761

Lianos, I. (2025). Access to Health Data, Competition, and Regulatory Alternatives: Three Dimensions of Fairness. *Journal of Competition Law & Economics*, *21*(4), 595–646. DOI: 10.1093/joclec/nhaf016

Li, M., Yin, D., Qiu, H., & Bai, B. (2021). A systematic review of AI technology-based service encounters: Implications for hospitality and tourism operations. *International Journal of Hospitality Management*, *95*, 102930. Advance online publication. DOI: 10.1016/j.ijhm.2021.102930

Lin, R. (2024). AI-Driven Personalized Healthcare: Leveraging Multimodal Data for Precision Medicine. *Proceedings - 2024 IEEE/WIC International Conference on Web Intelligence and Intelligent Agent Technology, WI-IAT 2024*, 693–697. DOI: 10.1109/WI-IAT62293.2024.00112

Liu, J., Mao, S., Lu, L., Jing, Y., Yang, X., Xu, H., & Ren, Y. (2025). The impact of digital economy on the supply chain resilience of cross-border healthcare e-commerce. *Frontiers in Public Health*, *13*, 1570338. Advance online publication. DOI: 10.3389/fpubh.2025.1570338

Liu, R., Rizzo, S., Waliany, S., Garmhausen, M. R., Pal, N., Huang, Z., Chaudhary, N., Wang, L., Harbron, C., Neal, J., Copping, R., & Zou, J. (2022). Systematic pan-cancer analysis of mutation–treatment interactions using large real-world clinicogenomics data. *Nature Medicine*, *28*(8), 1656–1661. DOI: 10.1038/s41591-022-01873-5 PMID: 35773542

Liverani, M., Ir, P., Jacobs, B., Asante, A., Jan, S., Leang, S., Man, N., Hayen, A., & Wiseman, V. (2020). Cross-border medical travels from Cambodia: Pathways to care, associated costs and equity implications. *Health Policy and Planning*, *35*(8), 1011–1020. DOI: 10.1093/heapol/czaa061 PMID: 33049780

Li, Y.-H., Li, Y., Wei, M.-Y., & Li, G. (2024). Innovation and challenges of artificial intelligence technology in personalized healthcare. *Scientific Reports, 14*(1), 14925. Advance online publication. DOI: 10.1038/s41598-024-70073-7

Longoni, C., Bonezzi, A., & Morewedge, C. K. (2019). Resistance to medical artificial intelligence. *The Journal of Consumer Research, 46*(4), 629–650. DOI: 10.1093/jcr/ucz013

Lopes, J. M., Gomes, S., Nogueira, E., Ferreira, J. J., & Dabić, M. (2026). Exploring psychosocial predictors of AI use intention: The moderating role of organisational culture in diverse workplaces. *Behaviour & Information Technology*, •••, 1–19. DOI: 10.1080/0144929X.2026.2626743

López-Naranjo, A. L., Puente-Riofrio, M. I., Carrasco-Salazar, V. A., Erazo-Rodríguez, J. D., & Buñay-Guisñan, P. A. (2025). Artificial intelligence in the tourism business: A systematic review. *Frontiers in Artificial Intelligence, 8*, 1599391. Advance online publication. DOI: 10.3389/frai.2025.1599391

Louati, A., Louati, H., Alharbi, M., Kariri, E., Khawaji, T., Almubaddil, Y., & Aldwsary, S. (2024). Machine learning and artificial intelligence for a sustainable tourism: A case study on Saudi Arabia. *Information (Basel), 15*(9), 516. Advance online publication. DOI: 10.3390/info15090516

Lundström, C., & Lindvall, M. (2023). Mapping the landscape of care providers' quality assurance approaches for AI in diagnostic imaging. *Journal of Digital Imaging, 36*(2), 379–387. DOI: 10.1007/s10278-022-00731-7

Lunt, N., Smith, R., Exworthy, M., Green, S., Horsfall, D., & Mannion, R. (2014). *Medical tourism: Treatments, markets and health system implications*. OECD Publishing., DOI: 10.1787/9789264217406-

Lu, R., Hong, S. H., & Zhang, X. (2018). A dynamic pricing demand response algorithm for smart grid: Reinforcement learning approach. *Applied Energy, 220*, 220–230. DOI: 10.1016/j.apenergy.2018.03.072

Luscii. (2024). *Remote patient monitoring and personalized care pathways*. https://www.luscii.com

Luscii. (n.d.). *Home – Smartest care at home platform for hospitals and GPs*. https://luscii.com/en/home

Macefield, R. C., Blazeby, J. M., Reeves, B. C., King, A., Rees, J., Pullyblank, A., & Avery, K. (2023). Remote assessment of surgical site infection (SSI) using patient-taken wound images: Development and evaluation of a method for research and routine practice. *Journal of Tissue Viability*, *32*(1), 94–101. DOI: 10.1016/j.jtv.2023.01.001 PMID: 36681617

Madappa, D. (2015). Medical tourism and inclusive growth in Karnataka. International Research Journal of Management, IT and Social Sciences, 2(9), 35–42. https://media.neliti.com/media/publications/280787-medical-tourism-and-inclusive-growth-in-fa29387c.pdf

Mahabub Subhani, G., & Sumalakshmi, C. (2025). Case Study on AI-Powered Healthcare: Improving Patient Outcomes with Predictive Analytics. In *Decoding AI: Practical Implementations for Business Operations* (pp. 289–303). Taylor and Francis. DOI: 10.4324/9781003606956-14

Mahmood, U., Shukla-Dave, A., Chan, H.-P., Drukker, K., Samala, R., Chen, Q., Vergara, D., Greenspan, H., Petrick, N., Sahiner, B., Huo, Z., Summers, R., Cha, K., Tourassi, G., Deserno, T., Grizzard, K., Näppi, J., Yoshida, H., Regge, D., & Hadjiiski, L. (2024). Artificial intelligence in medicine: Mitigating risks and maximizing benefits via quality assurance, quality control, and acceptance testing. *BJR Artificial Intelligence*, *1*(1), ubae003. Advance online publication. DOI: 10.1093/bjrai/ubae003

Mahmud, M. S., Rahman, M. M., Lima, R. P., & Annie, E. J. (2021). Outbound medical tourism experience, satisfaction and loyalty: Lesson from a developing country. *Journal of Hospitality and Tourism Insights*, *4*(5), 545–564. DOI: 10.1108/JHTI-06-2020-0094

Majid, G. M., Tussyadiah, I., Kim, Y. R., & Pal, A. (2023). Intelligent automation for sustainable tourism: A systematic review. *Journal of Sustainable Tourism*, *31*(11), 2421–2440. DOI: 10.1080/09669582.2023.2246681

Malhotra, N., & Dave, K. (2022). An Assessment of Competitiveness of Medical Tourism Industry in India: A Case of Delhi NCR. *International Journal of Global Business and Competitiveness*, *17*(2), 215–228. DOI: 10.1007/s42943-022-00060-0

Mamun, A. A., & Alam, M. (2025). Promoting Equity in Public Health: Addressing Inequality and Social Disparities. *Health Science Reports*, *8*(5), e70821. Advance online publication. DOI: 10.1002/hsr2.70821 PMID: 40309625

Manickam, P., Mariappan, S. A., Murugesan, S., Hansda, S., Kaushik, A., Shinde, R., & Thipperudraswamy, S. (2022). Artificial intelligence (AI) and internet of medical things (IoMT) assisted biomedical systems for intelligent healthcare. *Biosensors (Basel), 12*(8), 562. Advance online publication. DOI: 10.3390/bios12080562

Marchionatti, R. (2026). Economics in the MIT-Harvard Network and the New Keynesian Economics. In *Economic Theory in the Twentieth Century, An Intellectual History—Volume IV: Mid-1970s–Early 2000s. Economic Theory in the Age of Globalization* (pp. 65-129). Springer.

Marée, R., Stévens, B., Rollus, L., Rocks, N., Lopez, X. M., Salmon, I., Cataldo, D., & Wehenkel, L. (2013). A rich internet application for remote visualization and collaborative annotation of digital slides in histology and cytology. *Diagnostic Pathology, 8*(S1), S26. Advance online publication. DOI: 10.1186/1746-1596-8-S1-S26

Market.us. (2025). Medical tourism statistics and trends. https://media.market.us/medical-tourism-statistics/

Masjoodi, S., Anbardar, M. H., Shokripour, M., & Omidifar, N. (2025). Whole Slide Imaging (WSI) in Pathology: Emerging Trends and Future Applications in Clinical Diagnostics, Medical Education, and Pathology. *Iranian Journal of Pathology, 20*(3), 257–265. DOI: 10.30699/ijp.2025.2044210.3367 PMID: 40746923

Matias-Guiu, X., Temprana-Salvador, J., Garcia Lopez, P., Kammerer-Jacquet, S.-F., Rioux-Leclercq, N., Clark, D., Schürch, C. M., Fend, F., Mattern, S., Snead, D., Fusco, N., Guerini-Rocco, E., Rojo, F., Brevet, M., Salto Tellez, M., Dei Tos, A., di Maio, T., Ramírez-Peinado, S., Sheppard, E., & Martino, N. (2025). Implementing digital pathology: Qualitative and financial insights from eight leading European laboratories. *Virchows Archiv, 487*(4), 815–826. DOI: 10.1007/s00428-025-04064-y PMID: 40056197

Maurya, S. K. (2026). Justice and Quality of Life: A Philosophical Perspective. In *Exploring Justice as a Social Indicator of Life: Philosophical Foundations and Empirical Approaches* (pp. 1-23). Springer. DOI: 10.1007/978-3-032-10812-8_1

Ma, Y., Shi, N., Li, M., Chen, F., & Niu, H. (2015). Applications of Next-generation Sequencing in Systemic Autoimmune Diseases. *Genomics, Proteomics & Bioinformatics, 13*(4), 242–249. DOI: 10.1016/j.gpb.2015.09.004 PMID: 26432094

Mayo Clinic. (n.d.). *Artificial intelligence*. https://www.mayoclinic.org

Mbanugo, O. J. (2025). *AI-Enhanced Telemedicine: A Common-Sense Approach to Chronic Disease Management and a Tool to Bridging the Gap in Healthcare Disparities*. Department of Healthcare Management & Informatics, Coles College of Business, Kennesaw State University.

McCoy, L., Bihorac, A., Celi, L., Elmore, M., Kewalramani, D., Kwaga, T., Martinez-Martin, N., Prôa, R., Schamroth, J., Shaffer, J., Youssef, A., & Fiske, A. (2025). Building health systems capable of leveraging AI: Applying Paul Farmer's 5S framework for equitable global health. *BMC Global and Public Health*, *3*(1), 58. Advance online publication. DOI: 10.1186/s44263-025-00158-6

McGrath, C. P. (2024). The state and values of AI governance in UK healthcare. In *Research Handbook on Health, AI and the Law: Research Handbooks in Health and Medical Law* (pp. 291–310). Edward Elgar Publishing Ltd. DOI: 10.4337/9781802205657.00026

Medhekar, A., Wong, H. Y., & Hall, J. E. (2020). Health-care providers perspective on value in medical travel to India. *Tourism Review*, *75*(4), 717–731. DOI: 10.1108/TR-06-2019-0276

Meemon, N., Paek, S. C., Pradubmook Sherer, P., Keetawattananon, W., & Marohabutr, T. (2021). Transnational Mobility and Utilization of Health Services in Northern Thailand: Implications and Challenges for Border Public Health Facilities. *Journal of Primary Care & Community Health*, *12*, 21501327211053740. Advance online publication. DOI: 10.1177/21501327211053740 PMID: 34704512

Mengistu, A. K., Getinet, K., Alemayehu, T., Yeneakal, K. A., Gedefaw, A. E., Teym, A., Endalew, B., & Assaye, B. T. (2026). Machine learning predicts prolonged patient length of stay in a resource constrained Ethiopian hospital. *Discover Artificial Intelligence*, *6*(1), 88. DOI: 10.1007/s44163-025-00794-9

Mercolli, L., Rominger, A., & Shi, K. (2024). Towards quality management of artificial intelligence systems for medical applications. *Zeitschrift für Medizinische Physik*, *34*(3), 343–352. DOI: 10.1016/j.zemedi.2024.02.001

Micsik, T., Csellár, L., Patai, Á. V., Jakab, A., Jónás, V., & Molnár, B. (2026). Digitally derived Ki-67 proliferation index for GastroEnteroPancreatic neuroendocrine neoplasms. *Pathology Oncology Research : POR*, *31*, 1612248. Advance online publication. DOI: 10.3389/pore.2025.1612248 PMID: 41574207

Miller, R. A., Pople, H. E.Jr, & Myers, J. D. (1985). Internist-I, an experimental computer-based diagnostic consultant for general internal medicine. In *Computer-assisted medical decision making* (pp. 139–158). Springer New York. DOI: 10.1007/978-1-4612-5108-8_8

Milovanović, B. (2018, May 27). *[DNA Sequencing] Structure of the data analysis pipelines*. Medium. https://medium.com/@bmilovanovic/dna-sequencing-structure-of-the-data-analysis-pipelines-cd7c4de37f35

Ministry of Tourism, Government of India. (2025, August). Foreign tourist arrivals (FTAs) for medical purposes – Jan–Apr 2025. Ministry of Tourism. https://tourism.gov.in/sites/default/files/2025-08/usq.4136%20for%2018.08.2025.pdf

Mishori, R. (2025). Artificial Intelligence Technology in Healthcare and the Digital Divide. In *Digital Health, AI and Generative AI in Healthcare: A Concise, Practical Guide for Clinicians* (pp. 139–147). Springer Science+Business Media. DOI: 10.1007/978-3-031-83526-1_11

Mishra, P., & Kumar, A. (2025). Adoption of AI technologies in hospitals: Effects on consumer behaviour and health outcomes. *Journal of Medicinal and Pharmaceutical Chemistry Research, 7*(5), 1004–1025. DOI: 10.48309/jmpcr.2025.474077.1396

Mitharia, R. K., Mittal, K., & Utami, I. W. (2026). Digital marketing strategies to promote mental health in medical tourism: Opportunities, challenges, and ethical ideas. In Marketing mental wellness in medical tourism (pp. 23–64).

Mittelstadt, B. D., Allo, P., Taddeo, M., Wachter, S., & Floridi, L. (2016). The ethics of algorithms: Mapping the debate. *Big Data & Society, 3*(2), 2053951716679679. DOI: 10.1177/2053951716679679

Mohapatra, A., & Giri, P. A. (2018). Medical tourism gaining grounds in India: Present scenario and way forward. Public Health Review. *International Journal of Public Health Research, 5*(1), 50–52. Advance online publication. DOI: 10.17511/ijphr.2018.i1.07

Molla, C., Bhuiyan, M. R. I., Islam, M. T., & Amin, A. (2026). Mediating role of digital banking adoption on banking performance using the technology–organization–environment model. *Digital Finance, 8*(1), 4. DOI: 10.1007/s42521-025-00168-x

Moyano-Fernández, C., Rueda, J., Delgado, J., & Ausín, T. (2024). May artificial intelligence take health and sustainability on a honeymoon? Towards green technologies for multidimensional health and environmental justice. *Global Bioethics = Problemi di Bioetica, 35*(1), 2322208. Advance online publication. DOI: 10.1080/11287462.2024.2322208

Mubarak, F. (2026). Digital health literacy and the ethics of information access: a systematic review of global trends, equity challenges and policy responses. *Journal of Information, Communication and Ethics in Society*, 1-30.

Mulani, A. O., Godase, V. V., Takale, S. R., & Ghodake, R. G. (2025). Ethical Challenges and Governance of Al in Healthcare, Education, Finance, and Security Sectors. In *Navigating Social Trust in the AI Era* (pp. 123–154). IGI Global., DOI: 10.4018/979-8-3373-7011-8.ch006

Munari, E., Scarpa, A., Cima, L., Pozzi, M., Pagni, F., Vasuri, F., Marletta, S., Dei Tos, A. P., & Eccher, A. (2023). Cutting-edge technology and automation in the pathology laboratory. *Virchows Archiv*, *484*(4), 555–566. DOI: 10.1007/s00428-023-03637-z PMID: 37930477

MYCIN. (2026, February, 8). In Wikipedia. https://en.wikipedia.org/wiki/Mycin

Naaz, F., & Khan, N. (2016). Medical tourism in India: Perspective of Unani medicine. Journal of AYUSH: Ayurveda, Yoga, Unani. *Siddha and Homeopathy*, *5*(3), 52–60.

Nagar, R., Singh, Y., & Jaglan, V. (2021, July). A review on machine learning applications in medical tourism. In *2021 Fourth International Conference on Computational Intelligence and Communication Technologies (CCICT)* (pp. 208–215). IEEE. DOI: 10.1109/CCICT53244.2021.00048

Naili, Y. T., & Mangkunegara, I. S. Purwono, & Baballe, M. A. (2025). Regulatory challenges in ai-based diagnostics: Legal implications of ai use in medical diagnostics. *BIO Web of Conferences, 152*. DOI: 10.1051/bioconf/202515201034

Najar Najafi, N., Hajihassani, H., & Azimzadeh Irani, M. (2025). The Impact of Artificial Intelligence on Cancer Diagnosis and Treatment: A Review. *Cancer Informatics, 24*, 11769351251371273. Advance online publication. DOI: 10.1177/11769351251371273 PMID: 40979169

Nalbant, K. G., & Aydin, S. (2025). A bibliometric approach to the evolution of artificial intelligence in digital marketing. *International Marketing Review*, *42*(2–3), 179–218. DOI: 10.1108/IMR-04-2024-0132

Nardone, V., Marmorino, F., Germani, M. M., Cichowska-Cwalińska, N., Menditti, V. S., Gallo, P., Studiale, V., Taravella, A., Landi, M., Reginelli, A., Cappabianca, S., Girnyi, S., Cwalinski, T., Boccardi, V., Goyal, A., Skokowski, J., Oviedo, R. J., Abou-Mrad, A., & Marano, L. (2024). The Role of Artificial Intelligence on Tumor Boards: Perspectives from Surgeons, Medical Oncologists and Radiation Oncologists. *Current Oncology (Toronto, Ont.)*, *31*(9), 4984–5007. DOI: 10.3390/curroncol31090369 PMID: 39329997

Nasarian, E., Alizadehsani, R., Acharya, U. R., & Tsui, K.-L. (2024). Designing interpretable ML system to enhance trust in healthcare: A systematic review to proposed responsible clinician-AI-collaboration framework. *Information Fusion, 108*, 102412. Advance online publication. DOI: 10.1016/j.inffus.2024.102412

Natarajan, H. P., Chandru, M., & Pushparaj, A. (2026). Advancing Healthcare Diagnostics: A Precision-Driven Approach to Disease Prediction and Personalized Treatment Recommendation. *SN Computer Science*, *7*(3), 220. DOI: 10.1007/s42979-026-04787-y

National University Health System. (2025, February 11). *Alexandra Hospital develops world's novel A.I. algorithm (with international patent) that enhances accuracy and efficiency of robotic total knee replacement.* https://www.nuhs.edu.sg/about-nuhs/news-and-stories/news-and-stories-details/alexandra-hospital-develops-world-s-novel-a.i.-algorithm-%28with-international-patent%29-that-enhances-accuracy-and-efficiency-of-robotic-total-knee-replacement

Nentwig, K., Unterhuber, T., Wolff, K.-D., Ritschl, L. M., & Nieberler, M. (2021). The impact of intraoperative frozen section analysis on final resection margin status, recurrence, and patient outcome with oral squamous cell carcinoma. *Clinical Oral Investigations*, *25*(12), 6769–6777. DOI: 10.1007/s00784-021-03964-y PMID: 33956217

Nesheli, S. I., Rostami, M. R., & Hosseini, S. H. (2026). Developing an Indigenous Model of Customer Experience in Health Tourism in Mazandaran Province Using an Exploratory Mixed-Methods Approach. *Journal of Resource Management and Decision Engineering*, 1-20.

nib Group. (2024, April 29). nib Group launches AI-driven symptom checker [Press release]. https://www.nib.com.au/media/health/nib-launches-ai-symptom-checker

Nikolovski, S., & Petreska, A. (2025). Evaluating GDPR and HIPAA in the Integration of ML/AI for Future-Proofing Healthcare. *Lecture Notes in Networks and Systems, 1446 LNNS*, 289–313. DOI: 10.1007/978-3-031-99201-8_30

Niranjan, S. J., Wallace, A., Williams, B. R., Turkman, Y., Williams, C. P., Bhatia, S., Knight, S., & Rocque, G. B. (2020). Trust but verify: Exploring the role of treatment-related information and patient-physician trust in shared decision making among patients with metastatic breast cancer. *Journal of Cancer Education : The Official Journal of the American Association for Cancer Education*, *35*(5), 885–892. DOI: 10.1007/s13187-019-01538-x PMID: 31062280

Nishant, R., Kennedy, M., & Corbett, J. (2020). Artificial intelligence for sustainability: Challenges, opportunities, and a research agenda. *International Journal of Information Management, 53*, 102104. Advance online publication. DOI: 10.1016/j.ijinfomgt.2020.102104

Nogaroli, R., & Faleiros Júnior, J. L. de M. (2024). Ethical Challenges of Artificial Intelligence in Medicine and the Triple Semantic Dimensions of Algorithmic Opacity with Its Repercussions to Patient Consent and Medical Liability. In *Law, Governance and Technology Series* (Vol. 58, pp. 229–248). Springer Nature. DOI: 10.1007/978-3-031-41264-6_12

Noorbakhsh, J., Farahmand, S., Foroughi pour, A., Namburi, S., Caruana, D., Rimm, D., Soltanieh-ha, M., Zarringhalam, K., & Chuang, J. H. (2020). Deep learning-based cross-classifications reveal conserved spatial behaviors within tumor histological images. *Nature Communications, 11*(1), 6367. Advance online publication. DOI: 10.1038/s41467-020-20030-5 PMID: 33311458

Obermeyer, Z., Powers, B., Vogeli, C., & Mullainathan, S. (2019). Racial bias found in a major health care risk algorithm. *Scientific American*. https://www.scientificamerican.com/article/racial-bias-found-in-a-major-health-care-risk-algorithm

Obermeyer, Z., & Emanuel, E. J. (2016). Predicting the future—Big data, machine learning, and clinical medicine. *The New England Journal of Medicine, 375*(13), 1216–1219. DOI: 10.1056/NEJMp1606181 PMID: 27682033

Obermeyer, Z., Powers, B., Vogeli, C., & Mullainathan, S. (2019). Dissecting racial bias in an algorithm used to manage the health of populations. *Science, 366*(6464), 447–453. DOI: 10.1126/science.aax2342 PMID: 31649194

Olawade, D. B., Clement David-Olawade, A., Aderinto, N., & Wada, O. Z. (2026). Ethical oversight of Artificial Intelligence in Nigerian Healthcare: A qualitative analysis of ethics committee members' perspectives on integration and regulation. *International Journal of Medical Informatics, 206*, 106140. Advance online publication. DOI: 10.1016/j.ijmedinf.2025.106140 PMID: 41092592

Olawade, D. B., Marinze, S., Qureshi, N., Weerasinghe, K., & Teke, J. (2025). The impact of artificial intelligence and machine learning in organ retrieval and transplantation: A comprehensive review. *Current Research in Translational Medicine, 73*(2), 103493. DOI: 10.1016/j.retram.2025.103493 PMID: 39792149

Omoseebi, A., & Samson Anderson, J. L. (2025). *Enhancing Diagnostic Accuracy Through AI-Based Clinical Decision Support Systems*. CDSS.

Omoush, S. A., Alzyoud, J. A. M., El-Omari, N. K. T., & Alzyoud, A. J. A. (2026). The Role of Whole Slide Imaging in AI-Based Digital Pathology: Current Challenges and Future Directions—An Updated Literature Review. *Journal of Molecular Pathology*, *7*(1), 2. DOI: 10.3390/jmp7010002

Onsongo, G., Erdmann, J., Spears, M. D., Chilton, J., Beckman, K. B., Hauge, A., Yohe, S., Schomaker, M., Bower, M., Silverstein, K. A. T., & Thyagarajan, B. (2014). Implementation of Cloud based Next Generation Sequencing data analysis in a clinical laboratory. *BMC Research Notes*, *7*(1), 314. Advance online publication. DOI: 10.1186/1756-0500-7-314 PMID: 24885806

Onyango, M. J. (2025). Effectiveness of digital technology in enhancing blue tourism sustainability in Tanzania. *Journal of Management and Development Research*, *2*(1), 1–10. Advance online publication. DOI: 10.69739/jmdr.v2i1.191

Organization, W. H. (2024). *Evidence and research gaps identified during development of policy guidelines for tuberculosis*. World Health Organization.

Oso, O. B., Alli, O. I., Babarinde, A. O., & Ibeh, A. I. (2025). Navigating cross-border healthcare investments: A risk-opportunity model for emerging markets. *Engineering and Technology Journal*, *10*(2). Advance online publication. DOI: 10.47191/etj/v10i02.10

Ouanes, K., & Farhah, N. (2024). Effectiveness of artificial intelligence (AI) in clinical decision support systems and care delivery. *Journal of Medical Systems*, *48*(1), 98. Advance online publication. DOI: 10.1007/s10916-024-02098-4

Overgaard, S., Graham, M., Brereton, T., Pencina, M., Halamka, J., Vidal, D., & Economou-Zavlanos, N. (2023). Implementing quality management systems to close the AI translation gap and facilitate safe, ethical, and effective health AI solutions. *NPJ Digital Medicine*, *6*(1), 218. Advance online publication. DOI: 10.1038/s41746-023-00968-8

Özçelik Heper, F. (2025). Yapay zeka teknolojilerinden ChatGPT'nin sağlık turizminde potansiyel kullanımı: Güçlü ve zayıf yönleri. *Journal of Silk Road Tourism Research*, *5*(2), 108–122. DOI: 10.5281/zenodo.17671460

Pacci, Z., Atılgan Şengül, Y., Attar, R., Alagöz, O., & Uyar, A. (2021). Yapay zekâ tabanlı klinik karar destek sistemi ile tüp bebek tedavisi gebelik sonucu tahmini. *EMO Bilimsel Dergi, 11(22)*, 27–35. https://search.trdizin.gov.tr/yayin/detay/505635

Packer, C., Labonté, R., & Runnels, V. (2009). Globalization and the cross-border flow of health workers. In *Globalization and health* (pp. 235–256). Routledge.

Pagallo, U., O'Sullivan, S., Nevejans, N., Holzinger, A., Friebe, M., Jeanquartier, F., Jean-Quartier, C., & Miernik, A. (2023). The underuse of AI in the health sector: Opportunity costs, success stories, risks and recommendations. *Health and Technology*, *14*(1), 1–14. DOI: 10.1007/s12553-023-00806-7

Paliwal, M., Chatradhi, N., Singh, A., & Dikkatwar, R. (2024). Smart tourism: Antecedents to Indian traveller's decision. *European Journal of Innovation Management*, *27*(5), 1521–1546. DOI: 10.1108/EJIM-06-2022-0293

Panch, T., Mattie, H., & Atun, R. (2019). Artificial intelligence and algorithmic bias: Implications for health systems. *Journal of Global Health*, *9*(2), 010318. Advance online publication. DOI: 10.7189/jogh.09.020318 PMID: 31788229

Par, S. (2024). Yapay zekânın sağlık alanında kullanımı ve hukuki statüsü. *International Anatolia Academic Online Journal: Social Sciences Journal, 10(2)*, 179–196. https://dergipark.org.tr/tr/pub/iaaoj/issue/85849/1485263

Parate, A. P., Iyer, A. A., Gupta, K., Porwal, H., Kishoreraja, P. C., Sivakumar, R., & Soangra, R. (2024). Review of Data Bias in Healthcare Applications. *International Journal of Online and Biomedical Engineering*, *20*(12), 124–136. DOI: 10.3991/ijoe.v20i12.49997

Passaro, A., Al Bakir, M., Hamilton, E. G., Diehn, M., André, F., Roy-Chowdhuri, S., Mountzios, G., Wistuba, I. I., Swanton, C., & Peters, S. (2024). Cancer biomarkers: Emerging trends and clinical implications for personalized treatment. *Cell*, *187*(7), 1617–1635. DOI: 10.1016/j.cell.2024.02.041 PMID: 38552610

Patel, R., Shukla, S., Patel, N., Sharma, P., Mevada, S., Singh, S., & Prajapati, B. G. (2026). AI-driven patient empowerment and self-care: Implementing AI solutions for enhanced clinical practice. In *Artificial Intelligence in Patient Counselling* (pp. 333–352). Elsevier. DOI: 10.1016/B978-0-443-43823-3.00009-1

Patharia, P., Sethy, P. K., & Nanthaamornphong, A. (2024). Advancements and Challenges in the Image-Based Diagnosis of Lung and Colon Cancer: A Comprehensive Review. *Cancer Informatics*, *23*, 11769351241290608. Advance online publication. DOI: 10.1177/11769351241290608 PMID: 39483315

Patroni, A., Vogka, G., Halkiopoulos, C., & Antonopoulou, H. (2024, September). Emerging trends and digital strategies in medical tourism: Enhancing health and wellness tourism in the modern era. In *International Conference of the International Association of Cultural and Digital Tourism* (pp. 895–922). Springer.

Peet, B. M., Sidoti, A., Allen, R. J.Jr, Nelson, J. A., & Graziano, F. (2025). Artificial Intelligence in Breast Reconstruction: Enhancing Surgical Planning, Aesthetic Outcomes, and Patient-Centered Care. *Journal of Clinical Medicine*, *14*(21), 7821. DOI: 10.3390/jcm14217821 PMID: 41227217

Perna, R., Cruz-Martinez, G., & Fuentes, F. J. M. (2022). Patient mobility within national borders. Drivers and politics of cross-border healthcare agreements in the Spanish decentralized system. *Health Policy (Amsterdam)*, *126*(11), 1187–1193. DOI: 10.1016/j.healthpol.2022.09.009

Pırnar, İ., & Altın, H. (2024). Systematic literature review of health tourism innovation [Revisión sistemática de la literatura sobre innovación en turismo de salud]. *Pasos (El Sauzal)*, *22*(2).

Poalelungi, D. G., Musat, C., Fulga, A., Neagu, M., Neagu, A.-I., Piraianu, A., & Fulga, I. (2023). Advancing patient care: How artificial intelligence is transforming healthcare. *Journal of Personalized Medicine*, *13*(8), 1214. Advance online publication. DOI: 10.3390/jpm13081214

Pocock, N. S., & Phua, K. H. (2011). Medical tourism and policy implications for health systems: A conceptual framework from a comparative study of Thailand, Singapore, and Malaysia. *Global Social Policy*, *11*(1), 64–84. DOI: 10.1177/1468018110393363 PMID: 21539751

Popejoy, A. B., & Fullerton, S. M. (2016). Genomics is failing on diversity. *Nature*, *538*(7624), 161–164. DOI: 10.1038/538161a PMID: 27734877

Porter, M. E. (2010). What is value in health care? *The New England Journal of Medicine*, *363*(26), 2477–2481. DOI: 10.1056/NEJMp1011024 PMID: 21142528

Privitera, G. F., Alaimo, S., Micale, G., Giaimi, L., Mare, M., Lombardo, S. P., Martorana, E., Villa, R., Ferro, A., Forte, S., & Pulvirenti, A. (2026). An open-source clinical bioinformatics pipeline for real-world NGS implementation: Translating genomic variants into actionable treatment strategies in oncology. *Journal of Translational Medicine*, *24*(1), 241. Advance online publication. DOI: 10.1186/s12967-026-07718-w PMID: 41566376

Qiao, Y., Zhao, L., Luo, C., Luo, Y., Wu, Y., Li, S., Bu, D., & Zhao, Y. (2022). Multi-modality artificial intelligence in digital pathology. *Briefings in Bioinformatics*, *23*(6), bbac367. Advance online publication. DOI: 10.1093/bib/bbac367 PMID: 36124675

Quinn, T., Senadeera, M., Jacobs, S., Coghlan, S., & Le, V. (2021). Trust and medical AI: The challenges we face and the expertise needed to overcome them. *Journal of the American Medical Informatics Association : JAMIA, 28*(4), 890–894. DOI: 10.1093/jamia/ocaa268

Quizlet. (n.d.). *HSCI 4100 chapter 8: Clinical decision support.* https://quizlet.com/1086961905/hsci-4100-chapter-8-clinical-decision-support-flash-cards/

Quttainah, M., Singh, P., & Rana, S. (2025). *Assessing the environmental impact of AI-based medical diagnosis using Grey Relational Analysis.* Arab Journal of Administrative Sciences., DOI: 10.34120/ajas.2025.1387

Rad, J. (2025). Health inequities: A persistent global challenge from past to future. *International Journal for Equity in Health, 24*(1), 148. DOI: 10.1186/s12939-025-02526-y PMID: 40410748

Rady, H. A. W. A. (2024). *The role of artificial intelligence to enhance health tourism applications in Egyptian tourist destinations. Minia Journal of Tourism and Hospitality Research.* MJTHR., DOI: 10.21608/mjthr.2024.281385.1150

Rajkomar, A., Dean, J., & Kohane, I. (2019). Machine learning in medicine. *The New England Journal of Medicine, 380*(14), 1347–1358. DOI: 10.1056/NEJMra1814259 PMID: 30943338

Ramteke, P. N., Wankar, T. N., Rao, U., & Arora, S. (2024). Predictive model for medical assistance. International Journal of Advanced Research in Science. *Tongxin Jishu*, 547–551. Advance online publication. DOI: 10.48175/IJARSCT-18282

Ranade, M. (2024). Artificial intelligence in Ayurveda: Current concepts and prospects. *Journal of Indian System of Medicine, 12*(1), 53–59. DOI: 10.4103/jism.jism_60_23

Ranjbar, A., Mork, E., Ravn, J., Brøgger, H., Myrseth, P., Østrem, H. P., & Hallock, H. (2024). Managing risk and quality of AI in healthcare: Are hospitals ready for implementation? *Risk Management and Healthcare Policy, 17*, 877–882. DOI: 10.2147/RMHP.S452337

Rathor, C., Mandloi, V. S., Sachan, I., & Sahu, V. (2025). Artificial intelligence in Ayurveda: A simple overview. *Journal of Ayurveda and Integrated Medical Sciences, 9*(11), 271–275. DOI: 10.21760/jaims.9.11.38

Rawson, B. (2025). Health data justice, epistemological delinking and vernacularisation: Reclaiming knowledge, rights and representation. *International Journal of Law in Context.* Advance online publication. DOI: 10.1017/S1744552325100347

Recuero, M. (2024). Title: Secondary Use of Electronic Health Data: The Future Regulation on the European Health Data Space and its Interplay with Data Protection Law[El uso secundario de datos de salud electrónicos: El futuro Reglamento del Espacio Europeo de Datos de Salu.... *InDret*, (2), 525–551. DOI: 10.31009/InDret.2024.i2.13

Reddy, S. (2024). Generative AI in healthcare: An implementation science informed translational path on application, integration and governance. *Implementation Science : IS*, *19*(1), 57. Advance online publication. DOI: 10.1186/s13012-024-01357-9

Reddy, S., Allan, S., Coghlan, S., & Cooper, P. (2019). A governance model for the application of AI in health care. *Journal of the American Medical Informatics Association : JAMIA*, *27*(3), 491–497. DOI: 10.1093/jamia/ocz192 PMID: 31682262

Regona, M., Yigitcanlar, T., Hon, C., & Teo, M. (2026). Building Trust in Artificial Intelligence: A Systematic Review through the Lens of Trust Theory. *ACM Computing Surveys*, *58*(9), 1–39. DOI: 10.1145/3789256

Reshadi, M. S., & Chehragh, A. M. (2025). A review of medical tourism entrepreneurship and marketing at regional and global levels and a quick glance into the applications of artificial intelligence in medical tourism. *AI & Society*, *40*(5), 4011–4027. DOI: 10.1007/s00146-024-02178-6

Reshma Soman, N., Aswathy Prakash, G., & Azza, H. (2025). Optimizing Hospital Operations with AI-Driven Resource Allocation Tools. In *Synthesis Lectures on Computer Science: Part F698* (pp. 99–110). Springer Nature. DOI: 10.1007/978-3-031-93673-9_10

Reuben, J., Meiri, H., & Arien-Zakay, H. (2024). AI's pivotal impact on redefining stakeholder roles and their interactions in medical education and health care. *Frontiers in Digital Health*, *6*, 1458811. Advance online publication. DOI: 10.3389/fdgth.2024.1458811

Richie, C. (2022). Environmentally sustainable development and use of artificial intelligence in health care. *Bioethics*, *36*(5), 547–555. DOI: 10.1111/bioe.13018

Richie, C., Hinrichs-Krapels, S., Dobbe, R., French, P., Wei, J., Diehl, J., & Kong, R. (2025). Environmental impacts of artificial intelligence in health care: Considerations and recommendations. *Health and Technology*, *15*(6), 1087–1093. DOI: 10.1007/s12553-025-01003-4

Rieke, N., Hancox, J., Li, W., Milletarì, F., Roth, H. R., Albarqouni, S., Bakas, S., Galtier, M. N., Landman, B. A., Maier-Hein, K., Ourselin, S., Sheller, M., Summers, R. M., Trask, A., Xu, D., Baust, M., & Cardoso, M. J. (2020). The future of digital health with federated learning. *NPJ Digital Medicine*, *3*(1), 119. DOI: 10.1038/s41746-020-00323-1 PMID: 33015372

Riva, G., Wiederhold, B. K., & Mantovani, F. (2016). Neuroscience of virtual reality: From virtual exposure to embodied medicine. *Cyberpsychology, Behavior and Social Networking*, *19*(2), 69–76. DOI: 10.1089/cyber.2011.0139 PMID: 26882322

Robbins, C. J., Bates, K. M., & Rimm, D. L. (2025). HER2 testing: Evolution and update for a companion diagnostic assay. *Nature Reviews. Clinical Oncology*, *22*(6), 408–423. DOI: 10.1038/s41571-025-01016-y PMID: 40195456

Rodić, B., Štilić, A., & Marković, L. (2025). Artificial intelligence-driven innovations in health tourism and hospitality: A review of benefits and challenges. Book of Proceedings. https://doi.org/DOI: 10.46793/CASB25.093R

Rodríguez Blanco, A. D., & Gurgel, H. (2026). Cross-border health as a conceptual approach to health mobility beyond borders: A mapping review. *Critical Public Health*, *36*(1), 2598712. DOI: 10.1080/09581596.2025.2598712

Roppelt, J., Kanbach, D., & Kraus, S. (2023). Artificial intelligence in healthcare institutions: A systematic literature review on influencing factors. *Technology in Society*, *75*, 102443. Advance online publication. DOI: 10.1016/j.techsoc.2023.102443

Roski, J., Maier, E., Vigilante, K., Kane, E., & Matheny, M. (2021). Enhancing trust in AI through industry self-governance. *Journal of the American Medical Informatics Association : JAMIA*, *28*(7), 1582–1590. DOI: 10.1093/jamia/ocab065

Rossi, G., Feldberg, B., Krois, J., & Schwendicke, F. (2021). Evaluation of the clinical, technical, and financial aspects of cost-effectiveness analysis of artificial intelligence in medicine: Scoping review and framework of analysis. *JMIR Medical Informatics*, *10*(5), e33703. Advance online publication. DOI: 10.2196/33703

Rudd, J., & Igbrude, C. (2023). A global perspective on data powering responsible AI solutions in health applications. *AI and Ethics*. Advance online publication. DOI: 10.1007/s43681-023-00302-8

Ruggeri, K., Ivanović, N., Razum, J., Kácha, O., Menezes, I. G., Zafari, Z., & Garcia-Garzon, E. (2018). An evidence-based policy for improving choice in global health access through medical travel. *Health Policy (Amsterdam)*, *122*(12), 1372–1376. DOI: 10.1016/j.healthpol.2018.09.017 PMID: 30337161

Russkikh, S. V., Tarasenko, E. A., Grin, S. I., Yugay, M. T., Kryukova, K. K., & Moskvicheva, L. I. (2022). Current opportunities for the export of medical services in Russia [Современные возможности экспорта медицинских услуг в России]. *Farmakoekonomika, 15*(2), 259–266. DOI: 10.17749/2070-4909/farmakoekonomika.2022.119

Sachdeva, C., & Jain, P. (2025). AI-driven innovations in healthcare administration: Streamlining processes for improved operational efficiency. *International Journal of Multidisciplinary Research, 7*(3), 37788. Advance online publication. DOI: 10.36948/ijfmr.2025.v07i03.37788

Sah, A. K. (2025). Prognostic biomarkers: predicting disease outcomes. In *The Potential of Cancer Biomarkers* (pp. 211–238). Elsevier. DOI: 10.1016/B978-0-443-29279-8.00010-7

Sahin, F., Gökalp Özkorkmaz, E., Kaya, S., & Aşır, F. (2024). Yardımcı Üreme Tekniklerinde Yapay Zeka. *Turkish Journal of Clinics and Laboratory, 15*(4), 666–674. DOI: 10.18663/tjcl.1593054

Sainger, G. (2024). Artificial intelligence in healthcare sector in india: Application, challenges and a way. In *Artificial Intelligence Enabled Management: An Emerging Economy Perspective* (pp. 233–247). De Gruyter., DOI: 10.1515/9783111172408-015

Sakhare, N. N., Limkar, S., Mahadik, R. V., Phursule, R., & Godbole, A. (2023). Ethical considerations of AI applications in medicine: A policy framework for responsible deployment. *Journal of Krishna Institute of Medical Sciences University*. https://www.scopus.com/pages/publications/85185456480?origin=scopusAI

Samala, N., Katkam, B. S., Bellamkonda, R., & Rodriguez, R. (2020). Impact of AI and robotics in the tourism sector: A critical insight. *Journal of Tourism Futures, 6*(3). Advance online publication. DOI: 10.1108/JTF-07-2019-0065

Sandberg, D. S. (2017). Medical tourism: An emerging global healthcare industry. *International Journal of Healthcare Management, 10*(4), 281–288. DOI: 10.1080/20479700.2017.1296213

Sangkakorn, K., Traisaeng, A., Intawong, K., & Panyadee, C. (2025). Intelligent Digital Ecosystems for Safe and Sustainable Wellness Tourism. *Wangji Wanglu Jishu Xuekan, 26*(7), 903–912. DOI: 10.70003/160792642025122607006

Sankaye, S. (2011). Telepathology for effective healthcare in developing nations. *The Australasian Medical Journal, 592–595*, 592–595. Advance online publication. DOI: 10.4066/AMJ.2011.855 PMID: 23386872

Saxena, S., Jena, B., Gupta, N., Das, S., Sarmah, D., Bhattacharya, P., Nath, T., Paul, S., Fouda, M. M., Kalra, M., Saba, L., Pareek, G., & Suri, J. S. (2022). Role of Artificial Intelligence in Radiogenomics for Cancers in the Era of Precision Medicine. *Cancers (Basel), 14*(12), 2860. DOI: 10.3390/cancers14122860 PMID: 35740526

Schuitmaker, L., Drogt, J., Benders, M., & Jongsma, K. (2025). Physicians' required competencies in AI-assisted clinical settings: A systematic review. *British Medical Bulletin, 153*(1), ldae025. Advance online publication. DOI: 10.1093/bmb/ldae025

Schwalbe, N., & Wahl, B. (2020). Artificial intelligence and the future of global health. *Lancet, 395*(10236), 1579–1586. DOI: 10.1016/S0140-6736(20)30226-9

Sciberras, M., & Dingli, A. (2023). AI-Readiness. In *Lecture Notes in Networks and Systems* (Vol. 568, pp. 17–21). Springer Science and Business Media Deutschland GmbH., DOI: 10.1007/978-3-031-19900-4_5

Secinaro, S., Calandra, D., Secinaro, A., Muthurangu, V., & Biancone, P. (2021). The role of artificial intelligence in healthcare: A structured literature review. *BMC Medical Informatics and Decision Making, 21*(1), 125. Advance online publication. DOI: 10.1186/s12911-021-01488-9

Selwood, A., Blakely, B., Senthuran, S., Lane, P., North, J., & Clay-Williams, R. (2020). Variability in clinicians' understanding and reported methods of identifying high-risk surgical patients: A qualitative study. *BMC Health Services Research, 20*(1), 427. DOI: 10.1186/s12913-020-05316-0 PMID: 32414412

Semigran, H. L., Linder, J. A., Gidengil, C., & Mehrotra, A. (2015). Evaluation of symptom checkers for self diagnosis and triage: Audit study. *BMJ (Clinical Research Ed.), 351*, h3480. DOI: 10.1136/bmj.h3480 PMID: 26157077

Sensely. (n.d.). *Conversational AI to improve health and drive member engagement.* https://sensely.com

Sensely. (n.d.). *Virtual nurse and AI chatbot solutions.* https://www.sensely.com

Seow, A. N., Choong, Y. O., Moorthy, K., & Choong, C. K. (2021). Predicting medical tourism behavioural intention using social cognition models. *Tourism Review, 76*(2), 374–391. DOI: 10.1108/TR-06-2019-0267

Sezgin, E. (2023). Artificial intelligence in healthcare: Complementing, not replacing, doctors and healthcare providers. *Digital Health, 9*, 20552076231186520. Advance online publication. DOI: 10.1177/20552076231186520

Shaban-Nejad, A., Michalowski, M., & Bianco, S. (2024). Breaking Barriers: The Power of Artificial Intelligence in Advancing Health Equity. *Studies in Computational Intelligence, 1164 SCI*, 1–8. DOI: 10.1007/978-3-031-63592-2_1

Shafik, W. (2025). Artificial Intelligence Integration in Medical Tourism: Medical Breakthroughs-Are We Truly Progressing? In *Navigating Health Information in the Age of Artificial Intelligence* (pp. 1-36). IGI Global Scientific Publishing.

Shafik, W. (2025). Artificial Intelligence Integration in Medical Tourism: Medical Breakthroughs-Are We Truly Progressing? In *Navigating Health Information in the Age of Artificial Intelligence* (pp. 1–36). IGI Global Scientific Publishing. *https://doi.org/*DOI: 10.4018/979-8-3693-5837-5.ch001

Shahmoradi, L., Safdari, R., Ahmadi, H., & Zahmatkeshan, M. (2021). Clinical decision support systems-based interventions to improve medication outcomes: A systematic literature review on features and effects. *Medical Journal of the Islamic Republic of Iran*. Advance online publication. DOI: 10.47176/mjiri.35.27 PMID: 34169039

Shaik, N. (2025). Artificial intelligence in healthcare economics: Transforming cost efficiency, member experience, and preventative care. *European Journal of Computer Science and Information Technology*, *13*(9), 104–114. DOI: 10.37745/ejcsit.2013/vol13n9104114

Shakhawat, H. M., Nakamura, T., Kimura, F., Yagi, Y., & Yamaguchi, M. (2020). [Paper] Automatic Quality Evaluation of Whole Slide Images for the Practical Use of Whole Slide Imaging Scanner. *ITE Transactions on Media Technology and Applications*, *8*(4), 252–268. DOI: 10.3169/mta.8.252

Shalini, N., Sathish, R., Divya Rao, B. J., & Mamatha, H. K. (2024). Impact of Covid-19 on Medical Tourism. In *Medical Tourism in Developing Countries: A contemporary approach* (pp. 117–126). Springer Nature., DOI: 10.1007/978-981-99-8909-6_7

Shamanna, B. R., & Mannava, S. (2023). Introduction to Health Economics. In *Textbook of Community Ophthalmology* (pp. 114–128). CRC Press., DOI: 10.1201/9781003291626-10

Shang, Z., Chauhan, V., Devi, K., & Patil, S. (2024). Artificial intelligence, the digital surgeon: Unravelling its emerging footprint in healthcare – The narrative review. *Journal of Multidisciplinary Healthcare*, *17*, 4011–4022. DOI: 10.2147/JMDH.S482757

Shanmugam, K. R. (2013). *Medical tourism in India: Progress, opportunities and challenges*. Madras School of Economics.

Sharma, P. (2025). Uses and relevance of artificial intelligence in Ayurveda (Review).

Sharma, S., Chauhan, Y., & Tyagi, R. (2023). Artificial intelligence based applications in medical tourism. In 2023 14th International Conference on Computing Communication and Networking Technologies (ICCCNT) (pp. 1–6). IEEE. DOI: 10.1109/ICCCNT56998.2023.10308020

Sharma, A., Shin, H., Santa-Maria, M. J., & Nicolau, J. L. (2022). Hotels and travel industry recovery from COVID-19: The role of digitalization. *International Journal of Hospitality Management*, *101*, 103134. DOI: 10.1016/j.ijhm.2021.103134

Sharma, K., Jain, M., & Dhir, S. (2022). Analysing the impact of artificial intelligence on the competitiveness of tourism firms: A modified total interpretive structural modeling (m-TISM) approach. *International Journal of Emerging Markets*, *17*(4), 1067–1084. DOI: 10.1108/IJOEM-05-2021-0810

Sharma, K., Patel, A., & Ramachandran, A. (2024). Uses and relevance of artificial intelligence in Ayurveda. *Journal of Ayurveda and Integrated Medical Sciences*, *9*(10), 197–200. DOI: 10.21760/jaims.9.10.32

Sharma, V., & Gupta, N. (2025). AI-powered recipe recommendation systems and their role in personalized nutrition. In *AI and the Future of Smart Cooking* (pp. 271–293). IGI Global., DOI: 10.4018/979-8-3373-4042-5.ch010

Shehzad, N., Ramtiyal, B., Jabeen, F., Mangla, S., & Vijayvargy, L. (2024). Metaverse adoption as a cornerstone for sustainable healthcare firms in the industry 5.0 epoch. *Journal of Enterprise Information Management*, *37*(4), 1254–1281. DOI: 10.1108/JEIM-10-2023-0559

Shin, Y., Lee, M., Lee, Y., Kim, K., & Kim, T. (2025). Artificial intelligence-powered quality assurance: Transforming diagnostics, surgery, and patient care—Innovations, limitations, and future directions. *Life (Basel, Switzerland)*, *15*(4), 654. Advance online publication. DOI: 10.3390/life15040654

Shivi, S. (2025). Jurisdictional Challenges In Cross-Border Biomedical Data Privacy: Judicial Approaches And The Impact On Bioanalytical Research Frameworks. *Journal of Applied Bioanalysis, 11*(Special Issue 1), 424–431. DOI: 10.53555/jab.v11si1.432

Shrivastava, U., Song, J., Han, B. T., & Dietzman, D. (2021). Do data security measures, privacy regulations, and communication standards impact the interoperability of patient health information? A cross-country investigation. *International Journal of Medical Informatics, 148*, 104401. Advance online publication. DOI: 10.1016/j.ijmedinf.2021.104401 PMID: 33571743

Siciliani, L., Lafortune, G., Fujisawa, R., Vuik, S., & Hewlett, E. (2023). A review of policies to reduce waiting times for health services across OECD countries: Waiting times for health services. *Nordic Journal of Health Economics, 11*(1), 162–181. DOI: 10.5617/njhe.10214

Siddik, A. B., Forid, M. S., Yong, L., Du, A. M., & Goodell, J. W. (2025). Artificial intelligence as a catalyst for sustainable tourism growth and economic cycles. *Technological Forecasting and Social Change, 210*, 123875. Advance online publication. DOI: 10.1016/j.techfore.2024.123875

Silcox, C., Zimlichmann, E., Huber, K., Rowen, N., Saunders, R., McClellan, M., Kahn, C.III, Salzberg, C., & Bates, D. (2024). The potential for artificial intelligence to transform healthcare: Perspectives from international health leaders. *NPJ Digital Medicine, 7*(1), 97. Advance online publication. DOI: 10.1038/s41746-024-01097-6

Sinsky, C. A., Colligan, L., Li, L., Prgomet, M., Reynolds, S., Goeders, L., Westbrook, J., Tutty, M., & Blike, G. (2016). Allocation of physician time in ambulatory practice: A time and motion study in 4 specialties. *Annals of Internal Medicine, 165*(11), 753–760. DOI: 10.7326/M16-0961 PMID: 27595430

Siyao, P. V. (2024). Enhancing tourists' satisfaction: Leveraging artificial intelligence in the tourism sector. *Pacific International Journal, 7*(3), 89–98. Advance online publication. DOI: 10.55014/pij.v7i3.624

Smith, M., & Puczkó, L. (2014). *Health, tourism and hospitality: Spas, wellness and medical travel* (2nd ed.). Routledge. DOI: 10.4324/9780203083772

Smith, R. D., Chanda, R., & Tangcharoensathien, V. (2009). Trade in health-related services. *Lancet, 373*(9663), 593–601. DOI: 10.1016/S0140-6736(08)61778-X PMID: 19167053

Snyder, J., Crooks, V. A., & Johnston, R. (2012). Perceptions of the ethics of medical tourism: Comparing patient and academic perspectives. *Public Health Ethics, 5*(1), 38–46. DOI: 10.1093/phe/phr034

Snyder, J., Crooks, V. A., & Johnston, R. (2015). Ethical issues in medical tourism: Moving beyond negligence towards a comprehensive framework. *Bioethics, 29*(1), 1–9. DOI: 10.1111/bioe.12106 PMID: 25521968

Snyder, J., Dharamsi, S., & Crooks, V. A. (2011). Fly-By medical care: Conceptualizing the global and local social responsibilities of medical tourists and physician voluntourists. *Globalization and Health*, *7*(1), 6. DOI: 10.1186/1744-8603-7-6 PMID: 21470415

Sobhani, F., Robinson, R., Hamidinekoo, A., Roxanis, I., Somaiah, N., & Yuan, Y. (2021). Artificial intelligence and digital pathology: Opportunities and implications for immuno-oncology. *Biochimica et Biophysica Acta (BBA) -. Revisiones en Cáncer*, *1875*(2), 188520. DOI: 10.1016/j.bbcan.2021.188520 PMID: 33561505

Solaiman, B., Mekki, Y. M., Qadir, J., Ghaly, M., Abdelkareem, M., & Al-Ansari, A. (2025). A "True Lifecycle Approach" towards governing healthcare AI with the GCC as a global governance model. *NPJ Digital Medicine*, *8*(1), 337. Advance online publication. DOI: 10.1038/s41746-025-01614-1 PMID: 40473925

Song, D., & Chen, H. (2025). Artificial intelligence as a catalyst for sustainable tourism: A case study from China. *Systems*, *13*(5), 333. Advance online publication. DOI: 10.3390/systems13050333

Soni, D. C. (2024). An analysis of medical tourism and its role in India's economic development. ShodhKosh. *Journal of Visual and Performing Arts*, *5*(6). Advance online publication. DOI: 10.29121/shodhkosh.v5.i6.2024.5497

Sriram, V., Yilmaz, V., Kaur, S., Andres, C., Cheng, M., & Meessen, B. (2024). The role of private healthcare sector actors in health service delivery and financing policy processes in low-and middle-income countries: A scoping review. *BMJ Global Health*, *8*(Suppl 5), e013408. Advance online publication. DOI: 10.1136/bmjgh-2023-013408 PMID: 38316466

Stackpole, I. (2025, February 13). Emerging AI in medical travel and insurance. *International Travel & Health Insurance Journal (ITIJ)*. https://www.itij.com/latest/long-read/emerging-ai-medical-travel-and-insurance

Stogiannos, N., Malik, R., Kumar, A., Barnes, A., Pogose, M., Harvey, H., McEntee, M., & Malamateniou, C. (2023). Black box no more: A scoping review of AI governance frameworks to guide procurement and adoption of AI in medical imaging and radiotherapy in the UK. *The British Journal of Radiology*, *96*(1152), 20221157. Advance online publication. DOI: 10.1259/bjr.20221157

Strika, Z., Petković, K., Likić, R., & Batenburg, R. (2024). Bridging healthcare gaps: A scoping review on the role of artificial intelligence, deep learning, and large language models in alleviating problems in medical deserts. *Postgraduate Medical Journal*, *101*(1191), 4–16. Advance online publication. DOI: 10.1093/postmj/qgae122

Stroud, A. M., Minteer, S. A., Zhu, X., Ridgeway, J. L., Miller, J. E., & Barry, B. A. (2025). Patient information needs for transparent and trustworthy cardiovascular artificial intelligence: A qualitative study. *PLOS Digital Health*, *4*(4), e0000826. DOI: 10.1371/journal.pdig.0000826 PMID: 40258073

Suanpang, P., & Pothipassa, P. (2024). Integrating generative AI and IoT for sustainable smart tourism destinations. *Sustainability (Basel)*, *16*(17), 7435. Advance online publication. DOI: 10.3390/su16177435

Subasinghe, M., Magalage, D., Amadoru, N., Amarathunga, L., Bhanupriya, N., & Wijekoon, J. L. (2020). Effectiveness of artificial intelligence, decentralized and distributed systems for prediction and secure channelling for Medical Tourism. *2020 11th IEEE Annual Information Technology, Electronics and Mobile Communication Conference (IEMCON)*, 0314–0319. *https://doi.org/*DOI: 10.1109/IEMCON51383.2020.9284898

Sultana, S., Haque, A., Momen, A., & Yasmin, F. (2014). Factors affecting the attractiveness of medical tourism destination: An empirical study on India- Review article. *Iranian Journal of Public Health*, *43*(6), 867–868. https://www.ncbi.nlm.nih.gov/pmc/articles/PMC4401052/

Sumllika, T., Sandya, J. S., Reddy, D. B., Karthik, G., & Rachel, Ch. (2024). AN Advanced Medical Tourism System in India Using Deep Learning Algorithms. In Ragavendiran, S. D. P., Pavaloaia, V. D., Mekala, M. S., & Cabezuelo, A. S. (Eds.), *Innovations and Advances in Cognitive Systems* (Vol. 15, pp. 412–421). Springer Nature Switzerland., DOI: 10.1007/978-3-031-69197-3_32

Sun, J., Zhu, G., Liang, Q., Wen, N., Li, H., & Sun, X. (2025). Machine learning-based predictive model for the perioperative co-occurrence of T-cell-mediated rejection and pneumonia in liver transplantation. *Frontiers in Immunology*, *16*, 1648993. Advance online publication. DOI: 10.3389/fimmu.2025.1648993 PMID: 41041323

Suryawanshi, V., & Bhoyar, V. (2025). The role of AI in enhancing hospital operational efficiency and patient care. *Multidisciplinary Reviews*, *8*(5), 2025153–2025153. DOI: 10.31893/multirev.2025153

Symptomate. (n.d.). *About us & symptom checker*. https://symptomate.com/about

Taherdoost, H., & Ghofrani, A. (2024). AI's role in revolutionizing personalized medicine by reshaping pharmacogenomics and drug therapy. *Intelligent Pharmacy*, *2*(5), 643–650. DOI: 10.1016/j.ipha.2024.08.005

Talukder, M. B., Huda, M. N., Kumar, S., & Hasan, M. M. (2025). Metaverse Future of Digital Medical Tourism. In *Revolutionizing Healthcare Experience With Digital Medical Tourism* (pp. 173–198). IGI Global Scientific Publishing., DOI: 10.4018/979-8-3693-7888-5.ch007

Tarasenko, E. (2025). Technological transformation of medical tourism in Russia as an important segment of the service sector economy. *AlterEconomics*, *22*(2), 320–339. Advance online publication. DOI: 10.31063/AlterEconomics/2025.22-2.8

Tenkorang, P. O., Awuah, W. A., Mannan, K. M., Roy, S., Nkrumah Boateng, P. A., Asiedu, O., Tahiru, M., Ahluwalia, A., Owusu Bediako, N. O., & Darko, K. (2025). The transformative power of telemedicine in delivering effective neurosurgical care in low and middle-income countries: A review. *Brain & Spine*, *5*, 104269. Advance online publication. DOI: 10.1016/j.bas.2025.104269 PMID: 40458419

Terranova, C., Cestonaro, C., Fava, L., & Cinquetti, A. (2024). AI and professional liability assessment in healthcare. A revolution in legal medicine? *Frontiers in Medicine*, *10*, 1337335. Advance online publication. DOI: 10.3389/fmed.2023.1337335

Thangalakshmi, S., Mohankumar, N., Jayanthi, L. N., Blessy, Y. M., Meenakshi, R., & Rajmohan, M. (2025). Telemedicine Platforms with Cloud-Based AI-Driven Diagnostics in Hospitals. *Proceedings of International Conference on Visual Analytics and Data Visualization, ICVADV 2025*, 137–143. DOI: 10.1109/ICVADV63329.2025.10961133

Thapliyal, K., Mukherjee, S. G. A., Sinha, A., & Thapliyal, D. (2025). Revolutionizing healthcare: AI-driven sustainable solutions for a healthier tomorrow. In *2025 International Conference on Biomedical Engineering and Sustainable Healthcare (ICBMESH)* (pp. 1–6). IEEE. https://doi.org/DOI: 10.1109/ICBMESH66209.2025.11182181

The North Solution. (n.d.). *IT consultancy firm | The North Solution*. https://www.thenorthsolution.com/

Times of India. (2025, March 18). Medical tourism on rise post-COVID, govt tells Parliament, launches portal. Times of India. https://timesofindia.indiatimes.com/india/medical-tourism-on-rise-post-covid-govt-tells-parliament-launches-portal/articleshow/119131679.cms

Tiwari, A., Mishra, S., & Kuo, T.-R. (2025). Current AI technologies in cancer diagnostics and treatment. *Molecular Cancer*, *24*(1), 159. Advance online publication. DOI: 10.1186/s12943-025-02369-9 PMID: 40457408

Tokareva, O. (2025). Conceptual model for assessing the economic efficiency of AI solutions in healthcare. *Economics and Management*, *6*(6), 804–815. DOI: 10.35854/1998-1627-2025-6-804-815

Tolkach, Y., Dohmgörgen, T., Toma, M., & Kristiansen, G. (2020). High-accuracy prostate cancer pathology using deep learning. *Nature Machine Intelligence*, *2*(7), 411–418. DOI: 10.1038/s42256-020-0200-7

Topol, E. (2019). *Deep medicine: how artificial intelligence can make healthcare human again*.

Topol, E. (2019). *Deep medicine: How artificial intelligence can make healthcare human again*. Basic Books.

Topol, E. J. (2019). High-performance medicine: The convergence of human and artificial intelligence. *Nature Medicine*, *25*(1), 44–56. DOI: 10.1038/s41591-018-0300-7 PMID: 30617339

Tornimbene, B., Rioja, Z. B. L., Brownstein, J., Dunn, A., Faye, S., Kong, J., Malou, N., Nordon, C., Rader, B., & Morgan, O. (2025). Harnessing the power of artificial intelligence for disease-surveillance purposes. *BMC Proceedings*, *19*(S4, Suppl 3), 20. Advance online publication. DOI: 10.1186/s12919-025-00320-w

Towett, G., Snead, R. S., Grigoryan, K., & Marczika, J. (2023). Geographical and practical challenges in the implementation of digital health passports for cross-border COVID-19 pandemic management: A narrative review and framework for solutions. *Globalization and Health*, *19*(1), 98. DOI: 10.1186/s12992-023-00998-7 PMID: 38066568

Townsend, B. A., Sihlahla, I., Naidoo, M., Naidoo, S., Donnelly, D. L., & Thaldar, D. W. (2023). Mapping the regulatory landscape of AI in healthcare in Africa. *Frontiers in Pharmacology*, *14*, 1214422. DOI: 10.3389/fphar.2023.1214422 PMID: 37693916

Tran, D. (2025, June 18). AI in travel: Top use cases you need to know. *SmartDev*. https://smartdev.com/ai-use-cases-in-travel/

Tripathi, R. P. (2023, November). Harnessing the potential of AI and ML in medical tourism: Challenges, opportunities, and ethical implications. In 2023 3rd International Conference on Technological Advancements in Computational Sciences (ICTACS) (pp. 1068–1072). IEEE.

Tripathi, R. P., & Shalki. (2023). Harnessing the potential of AI and ML in medical tourism: Challenges, opportunities, and ethical implications. In 2023 3rd International Conference on Technological Advancements in Computational Sciences (ICTACS) (pp. 1068–1072). IEEE. https://doi.org/DOI: 10.1109/ICTACS59847.2023.10390358

Tsekouropoulos, G., Vasileiou, A., Hoxha, G., Dimitriadis, A., & Zervas, I. (2023). Sustainable approaches to medical tourism: Strategies for Central Macedonia/Greece. *Sustainability (Basel), 16*(1), 121. Advance online publication. DOI: 10.3390/su16010121

Tuo, Y., Wu, J., Zhao, J., & Si, X. (2025). Artificial intelligence in tourism: Insights and future research agenda. *Tourism Review, 80*(4), 793–812. DOI: 10.1108/TR-03-2024-0180

Turner, L. (2011). Quality in health care and globalization of health services: Accreditation and regulatory oversight of medical tourism companies. *International Journal for Quality in Health Care : Journal of the International Society for Quality in Health Care, 23*(1), 1–7. DOI: 10.1093/intqhc/mzq078

Ueda, D., Walston, S., Fujita, S., Fushimi, Y., Tsuboyama, T., Kamagata, K., Yamada, A., Yanagawa, M., Ito, R., Fujima, N., Kawamura, M., Nakaura, T., Matsui, Y., Tatsugami, F., Fujioka, T., Nozaki, T., Hirata, K., & Naganawa, S. (2024). Climate change and artificial intelligence in healthcare: Review and recommendations towards a sustainable future. *Diagnostic and Interventional Imaging, 105*(11), 453–459. Advance online publication. DOI: 10.1016/j.diii.2024.06.002

UH. (2024, February 18). *Bone Cancer Patients and Others Receiving 3D-Printed Implants at UH*. Uhhospitals.org; University Hospitals. https://www.uhhospitals.org/for-clinicians/articles-and-news/articles/2024/02/bone-cancer-patients-and-others-receiving-3d-printed-implants-at-uh

uHealth. (2024, June 30). Sağlık turizminde yapay zeka (AI) kullanımı. *uHealth*. https://www.uhealth.com.tr/saglik-turizminde-yapay-zeka-ai-kullanimi/

Ullagaddi, P. (2025). Cross-regional analysis of global AI healthcare regulation. *Journal of Computer and Communications, 13*(5), 35–52. DOI: 10.4236/jcc.2025.135005

Unanah, O. V., & Aidoo, E. M.. (2025). The potential of AI technologies to address and reduce disparities within the healthcare system by enabling more personalized and efficient patient engagement and care management. *World Journal of Advanced Research and Reviews, 25*(2), 2643–2664. DOI: 10.30574/wjarr.2025.25.2.0641

United Nations. (2015). *Transforming our world: The 2030 agenda for sustainable development*. United Nations.

UNWTO. (2018). *Medical tourism: Global trends and opportunities*. World Tourism Organization.

Upadhyay, U., Gradisek, A., Iqbal, U., Dhar, E., Li, Y. C., & Syed-Abdul, S. (2023). Call for the responsible artificial intelligence in the healthcare. *BMJ Health & Care Informatics*, *30*(1), e100920. Advance online publication. DOI: 10.1136/bmjhci-2023-100920 PMID: 38135293

Vaidam Health. (n.d.). *Vaidam.com – Top medical tourism company*. https://www.vaidam.com/

Van Delm, K. (2024). EU In-Home Digital Diagnostics – Cross-Border Patient Reimbursement under Threat? In *Digital Health Care outside of Traditional Clinical Settings: Ethical, Legal, and Regulatory Challenges and Opportunities* (pp. 196–210). Cambridge University Press. DOI: 10.1017/9781009373234.019

van Dijk, J. (2020). *The digital divide*. Polity Press.

van Kolfschooten, H., Goosen, S., van Oirschot, J., Schouten, B., Vajda, I., & Willems, L. (2025). Legal, ethical, and policy challenges of artificial intelligence translation tools in healthcare. *Discover Public Health*, *22*(1), 904. Advance online publication. DOI: 10.1186/s12982-025-01277-z PMID: 41487681

Van Wynsberghe, A. (2021). Sustainable AI: AI for sustainability and the sustainability of AI. *AI and Ethics*, *1*(3), 213–218. DOI: 10.1007/s43681-021-00043-6

Varnosfaderani, S. M., & Forouzanfar, M. (2024). The role of AI in hospitals and clinics: Transforming healthcare in the 21st century. *Bioengineering (Basel, Switzerland)*, *11*(4), 337. Advance online publication. DOI: 10.3390/bioengineering11040337

Verma, S., Tiwari, R. K., & Sharma, V. (2025). Travel Health: The Application of Artificial Intelligence and Machine Learning. In *Navigating Innovations and Challenges in Travel Medicine and Digital Health* (pp. 85–102). IGI Global Scientific Publishing. *https://doi.org/*DOI: 10.4018/979-8-3693-8774-0.ch005

Viangteeravat. (2025). AI medical imaging: Artificial Intelligence Provides Added Support for Patient Diagnosis. *Bumrungrad International*. https://www.bumrungrad.com/en/health-blog/march-2020/ai-medical-imaging

Victor, A. (2025). Artificial intelligence in global health: An unfair future for health in Sub-Saharan Africa? *Health Affairs Scholar*, *3*(3), qxaf023. Advance online publication. DOI: 10.1093/haschl/qxaf023

Virani, A., Wellstead, A. M., & Howlett, M. (2020). The north-south policy divide in transnational healthcare: A comparative review of policy research on medical tourism in source and destination countries. *Globalization and Health*, *16*(1), 37. DOI: 10.1186/s12992-020-00566-3 PMID: 32321561

Vishal, M. G. K. A. K. (2023). *Emerging Trends and Economic Impact of Medical Tourism in Punjab: Analysing Growth, Challenges, and Opportunities in Global Healthcare Context.* Wong, B. K. M., & Sa'aid Hazley, S. A. (2021). The future of health tourism in the industrial revolution 4.0 era. *Journal of Tourism Futures, 7*(2), 267–272. DOI: 10.1108/JTF-01-2020-0006

Vishwakarma, L. P., Singh, R., Mishra, R., & Kumari, A. (2023). Application of artificial intelligence for resilient and sustainable healthcare system: Systematic literature review and future research directions. *International Journal of Production Research*. Advance online publication. DOI: 10.1080/00207543.2023.2188101

Vithlani, J., Hawksworth, C., Elvidge, J., Ayiku, L., & Dawoud, D. (2023). Economic evaluations of artificial intelligence-based healthcare interventions: A systematic literature review of best practices in their conduct and reporting. *Frontiers in Pharmacology, 14*, 1220950. Advance online publication. DOI: 10.3389/fphar.2023.1220950

Voets, M., Veltman, J., Slump, C., Siesling, S., & Koffijberg, H. (2021). Systematic review of health economic evaluations focused on artificial intelligence in healthcare: The tortoise and the cheetah. *Value in Health : The Journal of the International Society for Pharmacoeconomics and Outcomes Research, 25*(3), 340–349. DOI: 10.1016/j.jval.2021.11.1362

Von Gerich, H., Helenius, M., Hörhammer, I., Moen, H., & Peltonen, L.-M. (2025). Scoping review on the economic aspects of machine learning applications in healthcare. *International Journal of Medical Informatics, 205*, 106103. Advance online publication. DOI: 10.1016/j.ijmedinf.2025.106103

Vrel, J.-P., Oulmane, S., Boukobza, A., Burgun, A., & Tsopra, R. (2021). A COVID-19 Decision Support System for Phone Call Triage, Designed by and for Medical Students. *Studies in Health Technology and Informatics*. Advance online publication. DOI: 10.3233/SHTI210226 PMID: 34042631

Vural, O., Ozaydin, B., Aram, K. Y., Booth, J., Lindsey, B. F., & Ahmed, A. (2025). An artificial intelligence–based framework for predicting emergency department overcrowding: Development and evaluation study. *JMIR Medical Informatics, 13*, e73960. DOI: 10.2196/73960 PMID: 40961493

Wah, J. N. K. (2025). The rise of robotics and AI-assisted surgery in modern healthcare. *Journal of Robotic Surgery, 19*(1), 311. DOI: 10.1007/s11701-025-02485-0 PMID: 40540146

Wahl, B., Cossy-Gantner, A., Germann, S., & Schwalbe, N. (2018). Artificial intelligence (AI) and global health: How can AI contribute to health in resource-poor settings? *BMJ Global Health, 3*(4), e000798. Advance online publication. DOI: 10.1136/bmjgh-2018-000798

Wang, Q., Li, Y., & Li, R. (2024). Ecological footprints, carbon emissions, and energy transitions: The impact of artificial intelligence (AI). *Humanities & Social Sciences Communications, 11*(1), 1043. Advance online publication. DOI: 10.1057/s41599-024-03520-5

Wang, Q., Su, M., Zhang, M., & Li, R. (2021). Integrating digital technologies and public health to fight COVID-19 pandemic: Key technologies, applications, challenges and outlook of digital healthcare. *International Journal of Environmental Research and Public Health, 18*(11), 6053. DOI: 10.3390/ijerph18116053 PMID: 34199831

Wang, R., & Geng, S. (2024). Achieving sustainable medical tourism: Unpacking privacy concerns through a tripartite game theoretic lens. *Frontiers in Public Health, 12*, 1347231. Advance online publication. DOI: 10.3389/fpubh.2024.1347231

Wang, S., & Zhang, H. (2024). Promoting sustainable development goals through generative artificial intelligence in the digital supply chain: Insights from Chinese tourism SMEs. *Sustainable Development (Bradford)*. Advance online publication. DOI: 10.1002/sd.3152

Wang, Y., Boyd, A. E., Rountree, L., Ren, Y., Nyhan, K., Nagar, R., Higginbottom, J., Ranney, M. L., Parikh, H., & Mukherjee, B. (2026). Ten Core Concepts for Ensuring Data Equity in Public Health. *JAMA Health Forum, 7*(1), 1–11. DOI: 10.1001/jamahealthforum.2025.6031 PMID: 41511794

Wang, Y., Liu, C., Hu, W., Luo, L., Shi, D., Zhang, J., Yin, Q., Zhang, L., Han, X., & He, M. (2024). Economic evaluation for medical artificial intelligence: Accuracy vs. cost-effectiveness in a diabetic retinopathy screening case. *NPJ Digital Medicine, 7*(1), 43. Advance online publication. DOI: 10.1038/s41746-024-01032-9

Wang, Y., Wang, L., Rastegar-Mojarad, M., Moon, S., Shen, F., Afzal, N., Liu, S., Zeng, Y., Mehrabi, S., Sohn, S., & Liu, H. (2018). Clinical information extraction applications: A literature review. *Journal of Biomedical Informatics, 77*, 34–49. DOI: 10.1016/j.jbi.2017.11.011 PMID: 29162496

Weiner, E. B., Dankwa-Mullan, I., Nelson, W. A., & Hassanpour, S. (2025). Ethical challenges and evolving strategies in the integration of artificial intelligence into clinical practice. *PLOS Digital Health, 4*(4), e0000810. Advance online publication. DOI: 10.1371/journal.pdig.0000810 PMID: 40198594

Whig, P., Kasula, B. Y., Yathiraju, N., Ahmed Khan, I., Rai, A., & Mahmood, M. R. (2025). AI/ML-Based Approaches in Healthcare: Transforming Diagnosis, Treatment, and Beyond. In *Convergence of Artificial Intelligence, Machine Learning, and the Internet of Things in Industry 4.0 Applications* (pp. 45-66). Springer.

Williamson, S. M., & Prybutok, V. (2024). Balancing privacy and progress: A review of privacy challenges, systemic oversight, and patient perceptions in AI-driven healthcare. *Applied Sciences (Basel, Switzerland), 14*(2), 675. DOI: 10.3390/app14020675

Winkler, P. W., Zsidai, B., Hamrin Senorski, E., Pruneski, J. A., Hirschmann, M. T., Ley, C., Tischer, T., Herbst, E., Pareek, A., Musahl, V., Oeding, J. F., Oettl, F. C., Longo, U. G., Samuelsson, K., & Feldt, R. (2025). A practical guide to the implementation of AI in orthopaedic research—Part 7: Risks, limitations, safety and verification of medical AI systems. *Journal of Experimental Orthopaedics, 12*(2), e70247. Advance online publication. DOI: 10.1002/jeo2.70247 PMID: 40276496

Wolff, J., Pauling, J., Keck, A., & Baumbach, J. (2020). The economic impact of artificial intelligence in health care: Systematic review. *Journal of Medical Internet Research, 22*(2), e16866. Advance online publication. DOI: 10.2196/16866

Wong, T. Y., & Bressler, N. M. (2016). Artificial intelligence with deep learning technology looks into diabetic retinopathy screening. *Journal of the American Medical Association, 316*(22), 2366–2367. DOI: 10.1001/jama.2016.17563 PMID: 27898977

World Health Organization. (2007). *Everybody's business: Strengthening health systems to improve health outcomes: WHO's framework for action*. WHO Press.

World Health Organization. (2021). *Global strategy on digital health 2020–2025*. World Health Organization.

Wu, C.-J., Raghavendra, R., Gupta, U., Acun, B., Ardalani, N., Maeng, K., Chang, G., Behram, F. A., Huang, J., Bai, C., Gschwind, M., Gupta, A., Ott, M., Melnikov, A., Candido, S., Brooks, D., Chauhan, G., Lee, B., Lee, H.-H., & Hazelwood, K. (2021). Sustainable AI: Environmental implications, challenges and opportunities. arXiv. https://arxiv.org/abs/2111.00364

Wu, H., Jin, K., Yip, C. C., Koh, V., & Ye, J. (2024). A systematic review of economic evaluation of artificial intelligence-based screening for eye diseases: From possibility to reality. *Survey of Ophthalmology, 69*(4), 499–507. Advance online publication. DOI: 10.1016/j.survophthal.2024.03.008

Xia, L., Cao, Z., & Zhao, Y. (2024). Paradigm Transformation of Global Health Data Regulation: Challenges in Governance and Human Rights Protection of Cross-Border Data Flows. *Risk Management and Healthcare Policy*, *17*, 3291–3304. DOI: 10.2147/RMHP.S450082 PMID: 39720184

Xia, L., Li, F., Zhou, Y., & Xue, P. (2024). Mineral policy management perspective: Government effectiveness and digitalization for the Russian economy. *Resources Policy, 91*. *Resources Policy*, *91*, 104845. Advance online publication. DOI: 10.1016/j.resourpol.2024.104845

Xu, T., Wang, W., & Du, J. (2020). An integrative review of patients' experience in the medical tourism. *Inquiry : a Journal of Medical Care Organization, Provision and Financing*, *57*, 0046958020926762. DOI: 10.1177/0046958020926762 PMID: 32513038

Yadav, H., Yadav, P., & Sharma, S. C. (2025). Artificial Intelligence and Machine Learning in Travel Health. In *Navigating Innovations and Challenges in Travel Medicine and Digital Health* (pp. 69–84). IGI Global Scientific Publishing., DOI: 10.4018/979-8-3693-8774-0.ch004

Yan, F., Da, Q., Yi, H., Deng, S., Zhu, L., Zhou, M., Liu, Y., Feng, M., Wang, J., Wang, X., Zhang, Y., Zhang, W., Zhang, X., Lin, J., Zhang, S., & Wang, C. (2024). Artificial intelligence-based assessment of PD-L1 expression in diffuse large B cell lymphoma. *NPJ Precision Oncology*, *8*(1), 76. Advance online publication. DOI: 10.1038/s41698-024-00577-y PMID: 38538739

Yang, P., Lv, Y., Chen, X., & Lv, J. (2024). Digital finance, natural resource constraints and firms' low-carbon behavior: Evidence from listed companies. *Resources Policy, 89*. *Resources Policy*, *89*, 104637. Advance online publication. DOI: 10.1016/j.resourpol.2024.104637

Yan, R., Zhang, S., Zhang, H., & Qiu, H. (2026). To engage or not to engage? A qualitative investigation into educators' and learners' perspectives on AI in tourism higher education. *Journal of Hospitality and Tourism Technology*, •••, 1–23. DOI: 10.1108/JHTT-06-2025-0498

Yan, X., Han, Z., Ye, P., Yeh, A. G. O., Xu, X., Lee, A. W., Cheung, K. M., Gong, P., & He, S. (2024). Governing cross-border healthcare in mainland China: A scoping review of national policies from 2002 to 2022. *The Lancet Regional Health. Western Pacific*, *45*, 101032. DOI: 10.1016/j.lanwpc.2024.101046 PMID: 38516291

Yelli, Ö. F., & Karaman, A. (2024). Sağlık turizmi yönetiminde yapay zekânın rolü. In *8th Hodja Akhmet Yassawi International Congress on Scientific Research*. Konya, Türkiye.

YesilScience. (2022, October 24). 72 sağlıkta yapay zeka uygulaması. *YesilScience*. https://yesilscience.com/tr/yapay-zeka-ve-saglik/

Yıldırım, B. F. (2021). *Bilgi sistemi olarak e-Nabız uygulamalarının sağlık turizmi hastaları için geliştirilmesi: Bir model önerisi* [Doctoral dissertation]. Ankara University.

Yılmaz, F., Mete, A. H., Fidan Türkön, B., & İnce, Ö. (2022). Sağlık hizmetlerinin geleceğinde metaverse ekosistemi ve teknolojileri: Uygulamalar, fırsatlar ve zorluklar. *Eurasian Journal of Health Technology Assessment*, *6*(1), 12–34. DOI: 10.52148/ehta.1082705

Yogeshappa, V., Hallur, J., & Parameshwara, P. K. (2024). Elevating patient care: The integration of artificial intelligence in quality assurance practices. *International Journal of Health Sciences.*, *7*(7), 67–87. Advance online publication. DOI: 10.47941/ijhs.2340

Yorgancioglu Tarcan, G., Yalçın Balçık, P., & Sebik, N. B. (2024). Türkiye ve dünyada sağlık hizmetlerinde yapay zekâ. *Lokman Hekim Dergisi*, *14*(1), 50–60. DOI: 10.31020/mutftd.1278529

Yousefi, F., Gholami, M., &Biabanikhankahdani, R. (2025). The Role of Artificial Intelligence in the Development of Health Tourism. *International Healthcare Review (Online)*. .DOI: 10.56226/132

Yun, T., & Zhang, L. (2025). International partnerships in AI-driven healthcare: Opportunities and challenges for advancing the UN sustainable development goals—A perspective. *Healthcare (Basel)*, *13*(16), 2053. Advance online publication. DOI: 10.3390/healthcare13162053

Yu, S., Liang, Y., Zhu, Z., Olaniyi, O. N., & Khan, N. (2024). Dutch disease perspective of energy sector: Natural resources and energy sector nexus with the role of renewable energy consumption. *Resources Policy, 90. Resources Policy*, *90*, 104740. Advance online publication. DOI: 10.1016/j.resourpol.2024.104740

Zaim Gökbay, İ. (2021). Tıpta yapay zeka uygulamaları: Antik çağdan yapay zekaya teşhis ve tedavi yöntemlerinin gelişim sürecinde klinik karar destek sistemlerinin evrimine genel bakış. In Bozbuğa, N., & Gülseçen, S. (Eds.), *Tıp bilişimi* (pp. 673–691). İstanbul Üniversitesi Yayınevi., DOI: 10.26650/B/ET07.2021.003.33

Zhang, J., Wang, Y., Ruan, Q., & Yang, Y. (2024). Digital tourism interpretation content quality: A comparison between AI-generated content and professional-generated content. *Tourism Management Perspectives*, *53*, 101279. Advance online publication. DOI: 10.1016/j.tmp.2024.101279

Zhang, J., Xiang, S., & Li, L. (2025). Economic implications of artificial intelligence-driven recommended systems in healthcare: A focus on neurological disorders. *Frontiers in Public Health, 13*, 1588270. Advance online publication. DOI: 10.3389/fpubh.2025.1588270

Zhang, J., & Zhang, Z.-M. (2023). Ethics and governance of trustworthy medical artificial intelligence. *BMC Medical Informatics and Decision Making, 23*(1), 269. Advance online publication. DOI: 10.1186/s12911-023-02103-9

Zhang, Y., Peng, D., & Zhang, A. (2025). Artificial intelligence in cancer diagnostics: Governance for equity in low- and middle-income countries. *African Journal of Reproductive Health, 29*(12), 93–103. DOI: 10.29063/ajrh2025/v29i12s.10 PMID: 41489265

Zheng, S., Cui, X., & Ye, Z. (2025). Integrating artificial intelligence into radiological cancer imaging: From diagnosis and treatment response to prognosis. *Cancer Biology & Medicine, 22*(1), 6–13. DOI: 10.20892/j.issn.2095-3941.2024.0422 PMID: 39907115

Zorn, K. K., Simonson, M. E., Faulkner, J. L., Carr, C. L., Acuna, J., Hall, T. L., Jenkins, J. F., Drummond, K. L., & Curran, G. M. (2022). Can Automated Alerts in the Electronic Health Record Encourage Referrals for Genetic Counseling and Testing Among Patients at High Risk for Hereditary Cancer Syndromes? *JCO Oncology Practice, 18*(7), e1219–e1224. DOI: 10.1200/OP.21.00641 PMID: 35316088

Zuhair, V., Babar, A., Ali, R., Oduoye, M., Noor, Z., Chris, K., Okon, I., & Rehman, L. U. (2024). Exploring the impact of artificial intelligence on global health and enhancing healthcare in developing nations. *Journal of Primary Care & Community Health, 15*, 21501319241245847. Advance online publication. DOI: 10.1177/21501319241245847

About the Contributors

Viana Hassan is actively involved in academic and research work in Tourism & Cultural Management in Lebanon and Malta. She is the Founder and CEO of European Tourism and Events training Academy, She got her Ph.D. in Tourism Management and Cultural from Saint Joseph University, Beirut. Her Thesis was entitled "Medical Tourism in Lebanon". She has more than 19 years of tourism experience in many related Travel and Tourism Fields, varying from airline sales experience (MEA), to Co-management several Lebanese Travel agencies. She is an Experienced Lecturer with more than 16 years' experience at several universities in Lebanon (Lebanese University, A.U. L, Lebanese International University, Islamic University), the Institute of Tourism Studies, STC higher education partner of Wolverhmapton University UK and University of Malta (Malta), GBS Malta, Scholars School system (UK) with a demonstrated history of working in the Higher education industry, Skilled in Tourism Management, Customer service, Branding, Event Management, Airline Business Management, Niche Tourism, Business operations management, Customer acquisition and Medical Tourism. Dr. Viana has participated in international conferences (Expo Dubai 2020, 7th Medical Tourism World Summit..) including Athens, Paris, Vienna, Dubai, Valencia, India, Turkey, Indoneisa, Saudi Arabia, Tanzania, Poland, Cyprus, Thailans etc.

Vikas Sharma is an Assistant Professor in the field of Hotel Management with experience spanning academia and the hospitality industry. He currently serves as an Assistant Professor at Subharti College of Hotel Management, Swami Vivekanand Subharti University, Meerut, where he has been employed since June 2022. His previous academic roles include positions at Om Sterling Global University, Hisar, and HRIT University, Ghaziabad. Before his academic career, Dr. Sharma worked as a Demi Chef de Partie at ITC Grand Bharat, Gurugram, further solidifying his industry expertise. Dr. Sharma holds a Ph.D. in Hotel Management, focusing on the regional cuisine of Braj and its application in tourism promotion, from Swami

Vivekanand Subharti University. He also has a Master of Tourism and Travel Management and a Bachelor's degree in Hospitality and Hotel Administration. Additionally, he has gained various certifications, including an Advanced Diploma in Computer Applications. Dr. Sharma has contributed to several research papers, many of which have been published in peer-reviewed journals, including studies on tourism, digital marketing, work-life balance, and sustainable practices in hospitality. His work has appeared in indexed journals like Journal of Tourism Insights and International Journal of Scientific Research in Multidisciplinary Studies. In addition to his academic work, Dr. Sharma has been actively involved in research and development, including the publication of several chapters in books related to sustainability, AI in tourism, and food tourism. He has also presented at numerous national and international conferences. His research interests and contributions include AI-driven customer engagement strategies, sustainable tourism practices, and the intersection of food tourism with local culinary traditions. Dr. Sharma has also been awarded for his excellence in teaching and service in the hospitality industry.

***

Lawal Abdulwahab Olamilekan is a dedicated academic with a PhD in Economics from the Universiti Brunei Darussalam, School of Business and Economics, highlighting his advanced expertise. His research interests include natural resource economics, health economics, development, and macroeconomics, with a focus on Africa and emerging economies. He holds a Master's degree in Health Economics and a Bachelor's in Economics Education from Taraba State University, Nigeria. With over six years of experience, he has taught and supervised students across Nigeria, Somalia, Somaliland, and Brunei. His teaching expertise covers economics, management, and public health, while his research contributions include conference papers, journal articles, and book chapters. Lawal's proficiency in quantitative and qualitative methodologies, coupled with his skills in econometric modeling and software such as Stata, SPSS, Python, and EViews, demonstrates his technical proficiency. He is a member of the World Economics Association and the Institute of Chartered Economists of Nigeria, actively involved in research that bridges health policy, governance, and economic development for sustainable growth.

Shilpi Bose is an accomplished academician with over three years of teaching experience. She has published multiple research papers in nationally and internationally reputed journals. She holds one patent and has also qualified the IBPS examination. Her academic interests lie in Human Resource Management, with a focus on employee well-being and work-life balance.

Constantinos Challoumis is a Visiting Professor at the National and Kapodistrian University of Athens (NKUA), at AUEB, and at CNAM University (France) via Descartes College, and an Assistant Professor in IT, Law, and Management at Philips University. He holds a PhD in Economics (NKUA), is a Postdoc cand. (NKUA), and has 7 BScs (1 of which is a cand.) and 8 MScs (1 of which is a cand.). His research spans economics, accounting, law, technology, and quantitative modeling.

Sharjeel Chaudhry is a molecular pathologist affiliated with Dow University of Health Sciences (DUHS), Karachi, Pakistan. His primary research interests lie in the molecular mechanisms of disease, with a particular focus on head and neck pathology, including infectious and inflammatory conditions, genetic disorders, degenerative diseases, and oral cancer. He is actively involved in translational research aimed at enhancing diagnostic accuracy and personalizing therapeutic strategies in oral health and systemic diseases. Dr. Chaudhry has authored and co-authored several peer-reviewed publications in reputed journals. He is a member of the European Society of Pathology. Dr. Chaudhry has also presented his research at various national and international scientific forums. Committed to bridging the gap between clinical practice and molecular research, Dr. Chaudhry aims to contribute significantly to the early diagnosis, prevention, and treatment of complex oral and systemic pathologies through molecular-based approaches.

Somnath Roy Choudhury is the Associate Professor of Management and Commerce at YBN University, Ranchi. He has published over 45 research papers, holds four patents, and has authored two books and two book chapters indexed in Scopus. He upholds the principles of Discipline, Determination, and Dedication in academic and administrative leadership.

Nercü Durmuş Aydın is a faculty member at Tokat Gaziosmanpaşa University. Specializing in tourism, Dr. Aydın currently serves in the Health Tourism Management Program. Her academic interests include health tourism, sustainable tourism development, artificial intelligence in tourism, digitalization in tourism, and marketing in tourism. Dr. Aydın actively participates in research and academic activities aimed at strengthening both the theoretical and practical aspects of tourism and health tourism management.

Zarmina Ehtesham is a dental surgeon and oral oncology researcher based in Karachi, Pakistan. She earned her Bachelor of Dental Surgery (BDS) from Hamdard University. Currently, she is pursuing an MPhil in Molecular Pathology at the Dow Diagnostic Research & Reference Laboratory (DDRRL), Dow University of Health Sciences. Her research interests span oral medicine, oral mucosal diseases, and oncology, with a particular focus on the molecular basis of head and neck cancers and their clinical manifestations

Kabara Halabi is an experienced educator and PhD candidate in Educational Psychology with a focus on cross-cultural studies of personal values, social support, and academic performance. He holds a Master of Education from Universiti Sultan Zainal Abidin, Malaysia, and a Bachelor's degree in Education Economics from Bayero University, Nigeria. With over nine years of teaching experience at a college of education, Auwal has developed strong expertise in teacher training and curriculum development. His research integrates both qualitative and quantitative methods to explore the psychological and socio-cultural factors influencing student well-being and behavior. Auwal has presented at international conferences, contributed to academic publications, and remains committed to advancing inclusive, value-based education through teaching, research, and policy engagement.

Harendra is a seasoned Hospitality personal with 18 years of experience both in industry and Acedemics. Working as a Head of Department at Dewan Ihm Meerut. Also a Research scholar at swami vivekanand subharti university meerut (UttarPradesh).

Siddhartha Juyal is Assistant Professor at Graphic Era Deemed to be University, a seasoned professional in the field of hospitality management with over 14 years of experience.

Baljit Singh Kalsi is a highly qualified professional with over two decades of experience in industry and academia. He has authored numerous research papers published in reputed national and international journals. Dr. Kalsi holds two patents and has organized several conferences and seminars under his guidance. He is a firm believer in imparting quality education as the foundation for the development of a skilled and empowered India.

Adarsh Kumar is an Assistant Professor in the Department of Management at ITM, Gwalior, (M.P) India. He holds a Ph.D. in Management and has over eight years of experience in teaching, research, and academic administration. He currently serves as the Criteria Coordinator for NAAC and NBA, contributing to quality assurance, accreditation processes, and institutional development initiatives. Previously, he worked with the Ministry of Tourism, Government of India, where he was involved in project-based assignments related to tourism development and policy implementation. His academic and research interests include marketing management, consumer behavior, digital marketing, tourism marketing, and the application of emerging technologies in management education. Dr. Kumar has published research in peer-reviewed journals and contributed to edited volumes. His current research focuses on AI-driven personalization, consumer engagement, trust, and privacy in digital platforms. He is actively engaged in mentoring postgraduate students and integrating research with managerial practice.

Ajay Kumar is an accomplished academician and tourism professional with over nine years of experience in teaching, research, and industry practice. He is currently serving as an Assistant Professor at Chandigarh College of Hospitality, CGC Landran, Mohali, where he is also contributes to institutional quality insurance. He holds a Master's degree in Tourism Administration from Himachal Pradesh University and is pursuing a Ph.D. in Tourism Management from CT University, Ludhiana, Punjab. His academic interests include sustainable tourism, adventure tourism, food tourism, and the application of technology in hospitality. He is the author of books, book chapters, and numerous research papers published in national and international journals, and holds copyrights and patents related to smart tourism innovations. He is a dedicated mentor and researcher, actively engages in conferences, editorial work, and capacity-building programs to advance tourism education and research.

Alok Kumar is an Assistant Professor specializing in Food Production (Bakery) at RKDF University, Ranchi. He emphasizes practical and hands-on learning in baking, confectionery, and dessert production. With a strong background in modern and traditional bakery arts, he is actively involved in curriculum design, workshops, culinary competitions, and industry-standard teaching practices. His dedication to innovation and student mentorship sets him apart in the field of culinary education.

Sanjeev Kumar is a Professor in Lovely Professional University, India.

Yatendra Kumar is currently working as Assistant Professor, SRM Institite of Science and Technology, Delhi NCR Campus, Modinagar, Ghaziabad.

Pawan Mehra is currently working in Graphic Era Hill University.

Aditya Narayan Mishra is an Assistant Professor in the Department of Law at Prestige Institute of Management and Research, Gwalior, with over six years of teaching experience. He holds a B.A.LL.B. from National Law Institute University (NLIU), Bhopal, and an LL.M. (Criminal Law). He has completed his Ph.D. in Law from Vikram University, Ujjain, and is a two-time UGC-NET qualified scholar. His academic interests include Criminal Law, Company Law, and Constitutional Law. He is actively engaged in teaching, research, and academic writing, and is known for his clear and practical approach to legal education.

Mragendra Mishra is an Assistant Professor II of History at Amity University, Gwalior(M.P.) with over six years of academic experience. He qualified the UGC-NET exam in history subject. He earned his Ph.D. from Jiwaji University, Gwalior, with specialization in princely state administration and policing systems. His research interests include modern Indian history, sociology, and socio-legal studies. He is actively involved in teaching, research writing, and academic administration, and contributes to interdisciplinary scholarship through publications and edited works.

Ankit Prakash is a seasoned academician associated with RKDF University, Ranchi. He has published extensively in both national and international journals and holds five patents. In addition to his research work, he has successfully organized numerous conferences and seminars. His expertise spans across innovation, research methodologies, and academic leadership. He has Published many research paper in national and international Journal.

Vinay Punia has 14 Years of rich experience in the Hospitality industry with a blend of Industry and Academia, during the industry Mr. Punia worked with The Park, Westin and Millenium Hotels and in Academia with Subharti University-Meerut, Graphic Era Hill University- Haldwani Campus.

Sachin Sharma is currently working as Assistant Professor, ITS College of Pharmacy, Muradnagar, Ghaziabad, India.

Kuldeep Singh currently serves as an Assistant Professor in Amity School of Hospitality, Amity University, Haryana, India. He completed his Ph.D. in tourism from Maharshi Dayanand University (Rohtak) India in 2021. He is also a UGC (Net- JRF qualified). Dr. Singh has also served the tourism industry for a couple of years and more than three years in academics. Dr. Singh has so far published more than 40 research articles in both international and national referred journals as well as in edited books in the field of Tourism. Currently, He is serving as an editor of book series in various reputed publications (Emerald, IIP series). Dr. Singh is passionate about the academic areas of Service Quality Management, Rural tourism, Ecotourism, and Sustainable tourism. He also won an aspiring researchers welcome award from Indian Hospitality Congress. His credentials may be verified on various research platforms like Google Scholar, SSRN, LinkedIn, Academia, and Research Gate.

Sangeeta Kumari Sinha holds a Ph.D. in Zoology from Savitribai Phule Pune University and has completed postdoctoral research at National Centre for Cell Science. She has also pursued Data Science training from IBM, strengthening her interdisciplinary expertise. With 12 years of teaching experience, she is currently teaching at Nowrosjee Wadia College, where she is actively involved in teaching Zoology and Biotechnology students. She is passionate about making learning engaging and effective, with a strong interest in AI-based educational tools that enhance teaching and learning outcomes. She remains committed to continuous growth and meaningful contributions to the field of education.

Pankaj Kumar Tyagi is a dedicated academician, researcher, and consultant. He is currently serving as Professor of Tourism and Management at the University Institute of Tourism and Hospitality Management, Chandigarh University, and also works as a Research Fellow at INTI International University, Malaysia. Dr Tyagi holds a Master's in Tourism and Management, an M.Phil. in Tourism, and a Ph.D. in Tourism. With more than 22 years of experience, He has worked across teaching, research, training, and consultancy. His key areas of interest include destination management, sustainable and regenerative tourism, management operations, and emerging technologies. Dr. Tyagi has authored or edited 25 books and published over 50 research papers in reputed international journals. His work focuses on innovation, sustainability, and technology in tourism and hospitality. He also serves as a reviewer for international journals, helping to maintain high academic standards in research.

Neeraj Verma has 4 years of industrial experience with Royal Caribbean Cruise, ITC and Raddison Group and 1-year academic experience.

Index

A

C

D

E

G

H

M

www.ingramcontent.com/pod-product-compliance
Lightning Source LLC
LaVergne TN
LVHW061525290926
849162LV00004B/671